RESEARCH HANDBOOK ON THE ECONOMICS OF INSURANCE LAW

RESEARCH HANDBOOKS IN LAW AND ECONOMICS

Series Editors: Richard A. Posner, *Judge, United States Court of Appeals for the Seventh Circuit and Senior Lecturer, University of Chicago Law School, USA* and Francesco Parisi, *Oppenheimer Wolff and Donnelly Professor of Law, University of Minnesota, USA and Professor of Economics, University of Bologna, Italy*

Edited by highly distinguished scholars, the landmark reference works in this series offer advanced treatments of specific topics that reflect the state-of-the-art of research in law and economics, while also expanding the law and economics debate. Each volume's accessible yet sophisticated contributions from top international researchers make it an indispensable resource for students and scholars alike.

Titles in this series include:

Research Handbook on Public Choice and Public Law
Edited by Daniel A. Farber and Anne Joseph O'Connell

Research Handbook on the Economics of Property Law
Edited by Kenneth Ayotte and Henry E. Smith

Research Handbook on the Economics of Family Law
Edited by Lloyd R. Cohen and Joshua D. Wright

Research Handbook on the Economics of Antitrust Law
Edited by Einer R. Elhauge

Research Handbook on the Economics of Corporate Law
Edited by Brett McDonnell and Claire A. Hill

Research Handbook on the Economics of European Union Law
Edited by Thomas Eger and Hans-Bernd Schäfer

Research Handbook on the Economics of Criminal Law
Edited by Alon Harel and Keith N. Hylton

Research Handbook on the Economics of Labor and Employment Law
Edited by Michael L. Wachter and Cynthia L. Estlund

Research Handbook on the Economics of Insurance Law
Edited by Daniel Schwarcz and Peter Siegelman

Research Handbook on the Economics of Insurance Law

Edited by

Daniel Schwarcz

Professor, University of Minnesota Law School, USA

Peter Siegelman

Professor, University of Connecticut Law School, USA

RESEARCH HANDBOOKS IN LAW AND ECONOMICS

Edward Elgar PUBLISHING

Cheltenham, UK • Northampton, MA, USA

Published by
Edward Elgar Publishing Limited
The Lypiatts
15 Lansdown Road
Cheltenham
Glos GL50 2JA
UK

Edward Elgar Publishing, Inc.
William Pratt House
9 Dewey Court
Northampton
Massachusetts 01060
USA

A catalogue record for this book
is available from the British Library

Library of Congress Control Number: 2015933448

This book is available electronically in the Elgaronline
Law subject collection
DOI 10.4337/9781782547143

MIX
Paper from responsible sources
FSC® C013056

ISBN 978 1 78254 713 6 (cased)
ISBN 978 1 78254 714 3 (eBook)

Typeset by Servis Filmsetting Ltd, Stockport, Cheshire
Printed and bound in Great Britain by T.J. International Ltd, Padstow

Contents

Contributors

Kenneth S. Abraham, David and Mary Harrison Distinguished Professor of Law, University of Virginia School of Law

Danial Asmat, Economist, U.S. Department of Justice, Antitrust Division

Ronen Avraham, University of Texas Law School & Tel Aviv University Faculty of Law

Tom Baker, William Maul Measey Professor of Law and Health Sciences, University of Pennsylvania Law School

Elizabeth F. Brown, Associate Professor, University of Wisconsin-La Crosse

Pierre-André Chiappori, E. Rowan and Barbara Steinschneider Professor of Economics, Columbia University

Martin F. Grace, Regents' Professor and James S. Kemper Professor, Department of Risk Management and Insurance, Georgia State University

Scott E. Harrington, Alan B. Miller Professor, Wharton School, University of Pennsylvania

Dwight Jaffee, Willis Booth Professor of Banking, Finance, and Real Estate, Haas School of Business, University of California, Berkeley

Robert W. Klein, Associate Professor, Department of Risk Management and Insurance, Georgia State University

Howard C. Kunreuther, James G. Dinan Professor, The Wharton School, University of Pennsylvania

James Kwak, Associate Professor and William T. Golden Scholar, University of Connecticut School of Law

Kyle D. Logue, Wade H. and Dores M. McCree Collegiate Professor of Law, University of Michigan Law School

John A. Nyman, Professor, School of Public Health, University of Minnesota

Mark V. Pauly, Bendheim Professor, The Wharton School, University of Pennsylvania

Daniel Schwarcz, Professor of Law, University of Minnesota Law School

Peter Siegelman, Roger Sherman Professor of Law, University of Connecticut School of Law

Charles Silver, McDonald Endowed Chair in Federal Civil Procedure, School of Law, University of Texas at Austin

Richard Squire, Professor of Law, Fordham University School of Law

Sharon Tennyson, Professor of Policy Analysis and Management and Director of Cornell Institute for Public Affairs, Cornell University

Introduction

Daniel Schwarcz and Peter Siegelman

Insurance law and insurance economics each have long and distinguished scholarly histories, but participants in the two disciplines have not always communicated well across academic silos. As a result, legal analysis of insurance tends to ignore or simplify the economic implications of doctrinal rules and regulatory approaches. For example, the use of behavioral economics to understand anomalies in insurance demand has generated important insights that legal scholars and regulators are only beginning to assimilate. Meanwhile, economic models of insurance are often too divorced from legal realities and institutional details to offer clear policy guidance. Thus, careful study of different companies' homeowner's insurance policies reveal significant variations that present challenges for economic models of competition in insurance markets.

This *Research Handbook on the Economics of Insurance Law* seeks to bridge the historical divide between insurance economists and insurance law scholars. By bringing together original and accessible contributions by many of the top thinkers in each domain, the *Handbook* provides a uniquely robust perspective on the many ways in which insurance law, regulation, and policy are impacted by insurance economics, as well as the many ways in which the economics of insurance is structured by law, regulation, and policy. In doing so, the *Handbook*'s broader goal is to encourage more policy-relevant insurance economics scholarship and more economically sophisticated legal scholarship by promoting conversation across the two disciplines.

The contributions to this volume are divided into four parts. The first set of chapters focuses on issues surrounding how and why individuals purchase insurance. Topics examined in this part include the legal and regulatory relevance of pervasive behavioral anomalies in insurance supply and demand, and individuals' motivations for purchasing health insurance. The second group of contributions examines the role of the state in insurance markets, asking when government insurance programs or extensive insurance regulation are sensible and how they should be structured. Specific chapters examine topics ranging from the definition of social insurance to the role of the state in facilitating the provision of catastrophe insurance. In Part III, several chapters focus on insurance regulatory topics, including the regulation of risk classification, and the long-standing debate between state and federal regulation in insurance. The final cluster of chapters addresses insurance law in the courts, tackling subjects such as the distinction between mandatory and default terms in insurance law and liability insurers' duties to defend and settle. Collectively, the *Handbook* will help scholars across disciplinary categories integrate the new insights of insurance economics with the flourishing body of research in insurance law, so that each discipline can recognize and build on the contributions of the other.

PART I: WHY AND HOW DO INDIVIDUALS PURCHASE INSURANCE?

Much insurance law and regulation is deeply impacted by questions regarding how and why individuals purchase insurance. Howard Kunreuther and Mark Pauly have been pioneers in this arena, focusing on the impact of behavioral anomalies in insurance markets. In 'Behavioral Economics and Insurance: Principles and Solutions', they contrast the empirical evidence about how consumers (and, importantly, insurance companies) actually behave with the predictions of standard rational actor theories. The match between theory and practice can charitably be characterized as poor. Consumers routinely fail to purchase insurance for low-probability/high-cost events for which theory predicts robust demand. And insurers respond to new risks (such as terrorism) with 'intuitive' or 'rule-of-thumb' behavior, often over-reacting by eliminating coverage altogether. In keeping with their assessment of the weakness of individual and firm decision-making on insurance matters, the authors propose four key principles that should govern the regulation of insurance markets: (1) insurance against rare but catastrophic risks should be required for all individuals; (2) premiums should be set so as to reflect risk, thereby providing incentives for mitigation; (3) access and affordability issues should be paid for with lump-sum transfers, rather than by artificially lowering premiums; and (4) longer-term/multi-period coverage should be used to the greatest extent feasible, so as to avoid classification risk and mitigate irrational non-renewal of policies by consumers when risks fail to materialize.

Regardless of why individuals purchase insurance, they often do so through an intermediary. Such intermediaries may supply policyholders with valuable information, advice, and services. But insurance intermediaries' commission-based compensation arrangements also create the risk that they will provide customers with biased advice. Daniel Schwarcz and Peter Siegelman's chapter ('Insurance Agents in the Twenty-first Century:

The Problem of Biased Advice') assesses this risk, in the context of insurance markets for consumers and small businesses. They conclude that available evidence about the pervasiveness of biased advice is less robust than might be expected, but generally suggests that the risk is indeed substantial. Schwarcz and Siegelman also argue that the legal and regulatory tools directed at limiting biased advice are themselves limited in their effectiveness. Ultimately, they suggest that institutional-cum-technological developments present new opportunities for limiting the frequency and harm of biased advice, but also pose new risks of potential consumer harm.

John Nyman's contribution to this volume, 'Moral and Other Hazards of Economic Analysis of Health Insurance', also examines issues surrounding individuals' motivations for purchasing coverage, focusing on the specific context of health insurance. Building on his earlier work that developed a new theory of the demand for health insurance, Nyman emphasizes that health insurance allows individuals to demand more medical services when they become ill. Economists have long characterized insurance-induced demand for health care as moral hazard, and have concluded that it is unambiguously welfare reducing. Nyman questions this conclusion, however. In his model, insurance is actually a way to provide additional income to those who are sick, which in turn enables them to purchase expensive medical care that would be beyond their reach in its absence. For instance, few if any kidney transplants would be demanded by uninsured consumers whose kidneys have failed (given that the cost is so high and few private financing options are available); and few if any kidney transplants would be demanded by insured consumers whose kidneys are healthy, even if the price of such a procedure had dropped to zero. As a result, even though all who are insured face a low price for such a procedure, the low price would only be effective in increasing demand by those who are actually ill. Therefore, the increase in demand that has typically been seen as moral hazard is really due to a transfer of income from those who purchase insurance and remain healthy to those who purchase insurance and become ill. Nyman's analysis has various significant and counter-intuitive policy implications, such as suggesting that cost-sharing should be reduced for many types of health care services, and that the general strategy of controlling health care costs by reducing the amount of care consumed is seriously misguided.

Ronen Avraham's chapter also focuses on the nature of consumers' demand for insurance, asking: 'Does the Theory of Insurance Support Awarding Pain and Suffering Damages in Torts?' The answer, according to Avraham, is an unequivocal 'Yes'. Many commentators have argued that individuals do not (and should not) demand insurance for non-monetary losses that do not lower their marginal utility of wealth.

From this perspective, tort laws that provide victims with compensation for pain and suffering effectively force them to purchase insurance that they don't value. Avraham disputes this logic on several levels. First, he suggests that so-called 'pure non-monetary losses' are exceedingly rare in practice, and are difficult to define even in theory. Moreover, non-monetary losses are likely to be correlated with monetary losses, and this correlation generates a demand for insurance covering both types of losses even under the traditional model used by law and economics scholars. Coverage of non-monetary losses can also be demanded under many plausible alternatives to expected utility theory. Avraham also takes issue with the empirical evidence that some have interpreted as suggesting a lack of demand for coverage of non-monetary losses. Finally, and most provocatively, he suggests that future advances in neuroscience may make it possible to accurately measure mental states associated with pain and suffering, obviating the need for the subjective testimony that introduces so much noise into the assessment of these damages.

PART II: THE ROLE OF THE STATE IN INSURANCE MARKETS

Whether through direct government programs or through an extensive regulatory regime, the state plays a vital role in most insurance markets. This is perhaps most obvious in the context of the robust social insurance programs that exist in most Western countries: in the US, for example, Social Security and Medicare alone comprise almost 9 percent of Gross Domestic Product (GDP). In '"Social Insurance", Risk Spreading, and Redistribution', James Kwak asks a fundamental question about such programs: Are they really insurance, or are they simply covert tax-and-transfer schemes that redistribute income? The question is of enormous political importance, since framing these programs as insurance makes them substantially more popular than if they are described as transfers from rich to poor. Kwak proposes a novel answer to the ontological question: The balance between risk spreading and redistribution varies with the information that participants have and the time frame under consideration. This year's Medicare payments are transfers from the currently young and healthy to those who are already old and sick. But over a longer horizon – say 50 years – we do not know who will ultimately be (old and) sick, so that the risk of future illness is real, albeit not yet realized. Since there is no single 'correct' time frame, there is no 'essence' of social insurance, which means that there is always room for policy disagreements about how to define the category.

Catastrophe insurance is another arena in which the state almost invariably plays an important role. Any line of insurance in which large numbers of claims are likely to be highly correlated across individual policies can be labeled 'catastrophe insurance'. As Dwight Jaffee explains in 'Catastrophe Insurance', private insurers are often unwilling or unable to supply robust insurance of this type to the public. Doing so requires the insurer to maintain large amounts of readily-available capital, a practice which is difficult due to various tax and investment issues. Even with appropriate capital, catastrophe insurance inevitably poses magnified insolvency risk to an offering company. Moreover, mechanisms such as private reinsurance, catastrophe-linked securities, and monoline coverage are each limited in their ability to facilitate the private provision of catastrophe insurance. For these reasons, many catastrophe insurance markets have become government-dominated in recent decades, with the government either directly providing coverage or reinsuring coverage initiated by private insurers. Reviewing each of the major US catastrophe insurance programs, Jaffee observes that most of them have difficulty setting risk-based premiums in practice, which also tends to undermine their ability to induce policyholders to adopt efficient risk-mitigation strategies. Moreover, these programs tend to crowd out private market alternatives. Echoing some of Kunreuther and Pauly's suggestions, Jaffee suggests that government involvement in catastrophe insurance markets should be reformed to encourage risk-based premiums and avoid subsidies.

Scott Harrington's chapter ('US Health Care Reform') on the Affordable Care Act (the 'ACA' or 'Obamacare') focuses on the unique difficulties arising from the interaction of public and private forces in the provision of health insurance. Harrington begins by noting many of the criticisms of health insurance and health care markets prior to reform, including the high number of uninsured, the persistently large increases in the cost of public and private health insurance, and private insurers' discrimination against less healthy potential policyholders. In response, the ACA fundamentally reformed health insurance markets by (among other things) expanding the availability of public insurance through Medicaid, creating a host of new regulations and requirements for private insurers, and establishing both new subsidies and penalties designed to encourage the purchase of private coverage. After thoroughly reviewing many of the details of these changes, Harrington urges caution and patience in assessing their effects. While the evidence is generally favorable regarding Massachusetts' parallel reforms in 2006, distinctive features of Massachusetts' pre-reform environment make it hard to know to what extent the ACA's national impact will be similar. Meanwhile, trends in potential adverse selection, rate changes, subsidy levels, and participation rates in the insurance exchanges are still unclear, as are the various direct and indirect effects that the Act might have on employer-sponsored insurance.

PART III: INSURANCE REGULATION

As suggested above, regulation plays a dominant role in the contexts of health insurance and catastrophe insurance. But regulation is fundamental to all insurance markets. The central goal of such regulation is to ensure that insurers have the financial capacity to pay policyholders' claims. This is the subject of Elizabeth Brown and Robert Klein's chapter, 'Insurance Solvency Regulation: A New World Order?' Brown and Klein begin by briefly laying out the economic rationales for solvency regulation, which include information asymmetries, principal agent problems, and negative externalities. They also provide an overview of the political economy of solvency regulation, which is deeply influenced by its lack of salience to the general public and the clear compliance costs such regulation creates for the industry. From this base, they focus their attention on competing models of solvency regulation across the globe. Such analysis is vital, they suggest, given the increasing globalization of insurance and financial services markets. Their broad-ranging analysis describes regulatory initiatives in the National Association of Insurance Commissioners' Solvency Modernization Initiative, the European Union's Solvency II project, and the International Association of Insurance Supervisors' 'soft law' projects. With respect to each initiative, Brown and Klein provide an in-depth look at proposed and adopted changes to three core tools of solvency regulation: capital requirements, group supervision, and corporate governance.

In 'Classification Risk and Its Regulation', Kenneth Abraham and Pierre-André Chiappori address another fundamental, albeit oft-neglected, element of insurance regulation: The regulation of insurers' risk classification practices. Much has been written on the degree to which insurers should be allowed to charge higher premiums to certain groups or individuals who are at higher risk of loss than others. Abraham and Chiappori usefully decompose policyholder risk into two components – the risk of suffering a loss, and the risk of being classified by an insurer as high risk. In a world where everyone pays the same premium for coverage, there is no classification risk, only 'occurrence' risk (e.g., the risk that you develop a given illness). But where policyholders are classified into groups and charged different premiums (that reflect group average risks of developing that illness), things look different. The overall risk of loss now has two components: the risk of winding up in a high-risk group (and paying a higher premium as a result) and the risk of actually experiencing a loss, *given* that one is in the high-risk group. Abraham and Chiappori explain why classification risk is likely to be significant for many kinds of risk we face, and demonstrate that – unlike pure 'loss' risk – it is essentially impossible to insure against in an unregulated competitive insurance market, which will thus fail to spread risk optimally. Viewed in this light, the authors point out, the ACA's combination of mandated coverage and severe restriction on the variables that can be used to price insurance essentially eliminates classification risk for health insurance. But it does so at the potential cost of unleashing significant adverse selection problems. The severity of these problems depends on a variety of theoretical and empirical unknowns (such as the covariance of riskiness and risk-aversion in the population, and the nature of the equilibrium in competitive insurance markets).

Instead of tackling specific regulatory topics such as solvency or risk classification regulation, Martin Grace's chapter, 'Economics of State versus Federal Regulation', examines what level of government should actually conduct insurance regulation. The chapter's central premise is that the unit of government best able to internalize the costs and benefits of insurance regulation should be charged with conducting that regulation. Applying this principle to a range of insurance regulatory functions, Grace suggests that some types of insurance regulation (such as market conduct regulation) may be best conducted at the state level, because they are substantially impacted by local tastes and preferences. For other types of insurance regulation (such as solvency regulation), the federal government may be the optimal regulator because the quality of that regulation has a nation-wide impact or because regulation itself enjoys large economies of scale. Throughout, Grace emphasizes that these issues turn on empirical data regarding the costs and benefits of regulation, which are not always clear or comprehensive enough to definitively resolve the question of what level of government is best suited to conduct insurance regulation.

PART IV: COURTS AND INSURANCE

Courts play a vital role in regulating insurance markets. Tom Baker and Kyle Logue's chapter, 'Mandatory Rules and Default Rules in Insurance Contracts', examines a fundamental, though surprisingly under-addressed, question regarding such regulation: When should insurers be able to alter judicially constructed insurance rules through policy language? As a descriptive matter, the answer is often unclear, as courts are frequently silent about whether a given insurance contract rule such as *contra proferentem* is actually a default (which parties can change as they see fit), or a mandatory rule (which cannot be varied, even if the parties would prefer to do so). From a normative perspective, Baker and Logue conclude that the answer depends on at least two factors. The first is whether we can trust the contracting parties to fully incorporate all of the socially relevant effects of the rule they choose to adopt. For instance, a rule that generates negative externalities for third parties – as is rarely the case in ordinary contracts, but is often true in insurance – should not be within the powers of the parties to alter. Second, we also might not trust the parties – in particular, unsophisticated consumers – to fully take account of the consequences of rules choices for *themselves*. This is particularly the case given that behavioral frailties in insurance demand (see Kunreuther and Pauly, Chapter 1 in this volume) have long been recognized as particularly acute. But where parties are sophisticated enough to avoid such frailties, and where their behavior generates no significant externalities, they should be free to design their insurance contracts precisely as they wish. The authors conclude by discussing the crucial role played by administrative regulation of insurance contracts, explaining why courts should give deference to regulators' choices of which rules are defaults and which are mandatory.

Another central question regarding the role of courts in regulating insurance markets is what damages should be available when insurers are deemed to have violated their contractual obligations. In many states, a policyholder who believes her insurer has failed to pay a claim in full and on time may seek emotional distress and/or punitive damages based on a theory of insurer bad faith. In 'The Law and Economics of Insurance Bad Faith Liability', Danial Asmat and Sharon Tennyson examine the economic justification for this kind of liability. Imperfectly competitive insurance markets permit insurers to behave opportunistically by taking longer to settle claims and by paying less than the full amount due, without significant harm to their reputations. Liability for bad faith may be justifiable to prevent this kind of behavior. Whether bad faith liability is in fact justified, however, depends on a series of further conditions, especially the way that courts and legislatures craft the legal rules governing such liability. The authors consider the growing empirical literature on bad faith liability to determine the effect of these rules on the volume of insurance claims, settlements, and formal disputes. Their conclusion is that the presence of bad faith liability has increased settlement amounts and reduced the underpayment of claims, but it has failed to reduce the volume or cost of litigation for disputed claims in court.

Charles Silver's chapter ('Basic Economics of the Defense of Covered Claims') focuses on another knotty problem in insurance law: a liability insurer's duty to defend policyholders when they are sued. Silver notes that all policies containing a duty to defend raise efficiency issues because the common law and policy language generally provide the insurer with exclusive control of the defense, but policyholders are impacted in numerous monetary and non-monetary ways by decisions regarding how much to invest in that defense. In some cases – such as when policyholders have a self-insured retention or substantial reputational concerns relating to liability – this problem can be addressed by granting policyholders more explicit control over the defense. But this solution raises its own difficulties, given the obvious consequences of an inadequate or excessively costly defense to insurers providing indemnity coverage. As Silver explores, liability insurers normally use a number of mechanisms to efficiently limit the costs of providing a defense to their policyholders. These include elevating the defending insurer to the status of a co-client, operating in-house staff counsel, maintaining specialized panel counsel, using litigation management guidelines and audits, and employing value-based fee arrangements.

Closely related to the duty to defend is liability insurers' duty to settle, which is the topic of Richard Squire's chapter ('The Artificial Collective-action Problem in Lawsuits against Insured Defendants'). As with the duty to defend, the law governing the duty to settle is principally motivated by the fact that liability insurance splits the consequences of liability between the insurer and the policyholder. In the duty to settle context, courts have historically focused on how limits on coverage create inadequate incentives for insurers to settle claims that might produce a judgment in excess of the underlying policy limit. The common law response to this risk is to permit insurers to maintain authority over settlement, but to penalize insurers who unreasonably refuse to settle. However, this solution generates both litigation costs and uncertainty. Scholarly proposals to hold insurers strictly liable for excess judgments have their own faults, Squire argues. In particular, they are problematic when policyholders have some say in settlement decisions, as when the policyholder is asked to contribute personally to a settlement or settles directly with the plaintiff and then seeks reimbursement from the carrier. In such cases, strict liability fails to respond to the fact that policyholders have excessive incentives to settle. Squire argues that all of these problems could be solved simply by allowing the defendant and each liability insurer to enter into separate settlements with the plaintiff, which cover only that party's segment of potential responsibility for damages. Unlike the common law or strict liability proposals, this solution, Squire demonstrates, would eliminate the source of the underlying conflict of interest. In advancing this novel argument, Squire convincingly addresses important criticisms of his proposal, including the fact that it would result in more frequent contributions from policyholders and would raise questions of who would pay for the costs of continuing litigation expenses when the insurer has settled out of the case but the policyholder has not.

Instead of focusing on particular insurance law doctrines, Tom Baker and Peter Siegelman show how liability insurance itself profoundly impacts tort law. 'The Law and Economics of Liability Insurance: A Theoretical and Empirical Review'[1] examines how liability insurance shapes who gets sued, for what, who wins, and how much (if any) is awarded in damages. Baker and Siegelman summarize and critique the extensive theoretical and empirical literature on the effects of liability insurance. Liability insurance will be welfare-enhancing if insurers can curtail the moral hazard problems it creates, and the authors suggest that this is probably true in most cases. Nevertheless, they point to some situations (in particular, *ex post* moral hazard, which describes the effects of insurance on claiming rates) that are not encompassed by the standard model and that may weaken or even overturn its conclusions.

CONCLUSION

The chapters in this *Handbook* cover a wide range of topics. But every single chapter demonstrates the fundamental relationship between insurance law and regulation, on the one hand, and insurance economics, on the other. Just as insurance law and regulation must be informed by economics, so too must insurance economics appreciate the ways in which law and regulation structure and define insurance markets. Unfortunately, institutional and historical factors have created a substantial wall between insurance economists and scholars of insurance law and regulation. This *Handbook* seeks to help break down this wall by providing those interested in insurance across academic silos with accessible and integrative contributions from many of the top insurance economists and legal scholars.

We are delighted to thank the people and institutions who made this volume possible. In particular, we received generous support from the University of Connecticut Law School's Insurance Law Center, which contributed funds for a symposium at which many of the chapters were presented and discussed. The Center's former director, Professor

---

[1] This chapter is reprinted, with permission of the authors, publisher and editor, from Jennifer Arlen (ed.), *Research Handbook on the Economics of Torts* (Cheltenham, UK and Northampton, MA, USA: Edward Elgar 2013).

Patricia McCoy, was an enthusiastic supporter of this project from the start, and we thank her for her advice, encouragement, and assistance with the planning. Patricia Carbray made sure that everything ran smoothly, with help from students at the *Connecticut Insurance Law Journal*. We were also fortunate to have research assistance from Lokys Gust at the University of Minnesota.

PART I

WHY AND HOW DO INDIVIDUALS PURCHASE INSURANCE?

1. Behavioral economics and insurance: Principles and solutions

Howard C. Kunreuther and Mark V. Pauly

INTRODUCTION

It is easy for consumers to make mistakes in insurance markets, especially when deciding whether to purchase insurance against low-probability, high-consequence (LP-HC) events. Consumers have a hard time collecting and processing information to determine the likelihood and consequences of these risks, with which (by definition) they have had limited or no experience. Hence, people often rely on feelings and intuition rather than careful thought when it comes time to decide what coverage to purchase.

On the supply side, insurance companies face the risk of experiencing large claims payments, only part of which can be spread or diversified away through the law of large numbers if losses are highly correlated. Decision makers in the insurance industry and those who regulate, litigate, and legislate about insurance are also likely to make mistakes for the same reasons that consumers do. They often rely on their intuition rather than undertaking deliberative thinking because they have limited information from past experience on which to base their decisions.

In this chapter we take a realistic but optimistic view of the prospects for improving the functioning of insurance markets. Our primary goal is to specify, explain, and justify principles for structuring and governing insurance markets to account for buyers and sellers who make mistakes, both cognitive and systematic, that lead to their failure to maximize expected utility or expected profits. A secondary goal is to propose market and regulatory structures in accordance with these principles.

We use two recent examples of legislation – the Biggert-Waters Act and the Affordable Care Act (ACA) – to illustrate how insurance could be redesigned to adhere to these principles much of the time, but not all the time. These public policies are intended to encourage consumers to purchase insurance that they ought to have, but often do not. We also consider other possible policies designed to correct systematic examples of people buying insurance at high premiums when deliberative decision making suggests that it would be more appropriate to go without coverage. We conclude by building on these examples to suggest future strategies involving the public and/or private sector.

BEHAVIORAL ECONOMICS AND INSURANCE: CORE FINDINGS AND POLITICAL PROSPECTS

According to insurance theory, those at risk benefit from incurring a small cost in the form of a premium to obtain protection against an event that could produce significant financial losses but that has a low probability of occurrence. If insurance can be offered with relatively small administrative costs, so it is reasonably priced, a risk-averse individual should prefer a smaller certain premium to taking the chance of experiencing a large loss (Arrow 1971). If properly designed and priced, insurance also offers incentives in the form of premium reductions for people who mitigate their risk in a cost-effective way, if the insurer can accurately incorporate the impact these mitigation measures will have on reducing the likelihood and/or consequences of events for which they offer financial protection (Shavell 1979).

There is considerable empirical evidence that many consumers fail to take advantage of insurance protection against losses of property and health, and do not invest in efficient loss reduction measures in the LP-HC setting. In both cases they fail to behave in ways that would not only benefit them personally *ex ante*, but might also enhance social welfare if there are societal concerns about people's *ex post* wellbeing. Behavioral economics offers some explanations for these decisions and suggests remedies. However, designing these solutions may require interventions by public and private institutions beyond just structuring information and options to take advantage of individuals' decision processes.

To illustrate this point, field and controlled experiments in behavioral economics reveal that consumers are sometimes more likely to select a default option rather than going to the trouble of opting out in favor of some other alternative. These findings have been used to encourage consumers to choose options that are in their best interests, such as better (dominant) 401(k) plans (Madrian and Shea 2001) and to adopt the 'Save More Tomorrow' plans that encourage consumers to earmark a portion of their increased earnings into these plans (Thaler and Benartzi 2004). Default options have also been used to increase the number of organ donations (Johnson and Goldstein 2003) and in other programs detailed in the important book, *Nudge: Improving Decisions about Health, Wealth, and Happiness* (Thaler and Sunstein 2008). To date, this framing technique has been applied to situations where the outcome is either known with certainty, or when the chosen option (such as a recommended 401(k) plan), has a higher expected return than the other options.

For decisions under uncertainty that involve insurance, the economic benefits of having coverage are reaped when the (low-probability) loss-producing event occurs and the claims payments are greater than the premiums paid by the buyer. If no loss occurs, the person would have been better off financially, after the fact, by not having purchased insurance. It is unlikely that people who failed to purchase insurance would reverse course if a loss did not occur, or purchase coverage without having suffered a loss even if insurance purchase was the default option.

In this regard, there is considerable empirical evidence that insurance behavior is guided by misperception of risk, and the use of simple but inappropriate heuristic decision rules. Many who do not purchase property and health insurance perceive the likelihood of a serious event to be below their threshold level of concern. Individuals are often unwilling to voluntarily buy insurance coverage against a particular risk until after experiencing a loss. Many who purchased a policy are likely to cancel it if they have not made a claim after several years because they consider their insurance purchase to be a poor investment decision (Kunreuther, Pauly, and McMorrow 2013).

Policymakers who value economic efficiency as a policy goal may choose to utilize more stringent policy tools, such as premium subsidies or mandatory coverage, to induce individuals to protect themselves when they should, according to insurance theory, have invested in protection. Mandating insurance against losses from LP-HC events, such as natural disasters or serious illnesses, can also be justified from the vantage point of social welfare if the majority of taxpaying citizens feel that those at risk should protect themselves financially before losses occur, rather than relying afterwards on federal disaster relief covered by taxpayers' money.

As noted above, two significant pieces of legislation in the last two years have recognized the biases and heuristics utilized by individuals at risk, and have taken steps to address them. The Biggert-Waters Act in July 2012 (112th Congress 2012) passed major reforms to the National Flood Insurance Program (NFIP) by recognizing that insurance premiums should reflect risk. It also authorized the Federal Emergency Management Agency (FEMA) to fund a study on the affordability of flood insurance, focusing on the role that means-tested vouchers (in the same spirit as food stamps) and other forms of subsidy could play.[1] The ACA passed in 2010 (111th Congress 2010), initiated numerous reforms in health insurance to expand coverage. It imposes penalties if consumers do not buy coverage, while recognizing the need to make the purchase of insurance more feasible for low- and medium-income individuals. The ACA offers insurance to individuals and small groups through exchanges to be subsidized with means-tested tax credits. Both Acts encourage the adoption of risk reducing measures in ways that consumers might not voluntarily choose to do.

Other countries have also incentivized individuals to undertake protective measures and mandated the purchase of insurance against natural disasters and health risks. In the case of natural hazards, in France, New Zealand, and Spain, the government plays a key role by providing insurance coverage against all disasters and requiring those at risk to protect themselves with insurance (OECD 2008). With respect to health insurance, all developed countries other than the United States have achieved virtually universal coverage of catastrophic medically related expenses with a combination of subsidies and mandated penalties, financing premiums primarily through tax or tax-like instruments.

Even so, challenges to such universal requirements persist in all countries. Mandates usually permit exceptions (for higher income people, for non-citizens, for certain classes of risk or types of medical care). Inadequate subsidies lead some consumers to complain that their premiums are unaffordable. Public support for mandates in the US is still rather weak, and other countries are having second thoughts about some aspects of their programs. So it is clear that in a democracy, any normative theory will have to be modified so that the proposed programs are politically acceptable.

---

[1] As higher premiums began to be phased in for some properties around the United States based on Biggert-Waters, many homeowners claimed that they would not be able to afford coverage and/or that they were being treated unfairly. In response, the Homeowner Flood Insurance Affordability Act of 2014 passed Congress with substantial support from both the House and Senate and was signed by the President in March 2014. The legislation eliminates or delays the implementation of many of the rate changes made in Biggert-Waters and highlights the importance of dealing with affordability issues by providing additional funding for a study by the National Research Council now underway on this topic and the first of two reports from the NRC Committee was published in the spring of 2015 (National Research Council 2015).

INTUITIVE THINKING BY CONSUMERS, INSURERS AND REGULATORS

For LP-HC events such as natural disasters, terrorism or catastrophic health-related expenses, neither consumers, nor insurers or regulators, behave in accordance with the dominant normative theory of insurance. Instead, people seem to follow their intuitions. After a severe loss, insurers may withdraw from covering this risk because they focus on the losses from a worst-case scenario without adequately reflecting on the likelihood of this event occurring in the future. For example, following 9/11 most insurers refused to offer coverage against terrorism without considering the chances of a future terrorist attack (Kunreuther, Pauly and McMorrow 2013). State insurance commissioners sometimes restrict insurers from setting very high premiums that reflect risk, for example, for coastal property, in part to address equity and fairness issues, sacrificing efficiency in the process. Following the severe hurricanes of 2004 and 2005 in Florida, regulators resisted proposed rate increases, and the state-funded company, Citizens Property Insurance Corporation, filled the gap by providing relatively inexpensive insurance (Kunreuther and Michel-Kerjan 2011).

With all these challenges to decision making, consideration of some ways to improve the choice process may be helpful while recognizing the obstacles to changing behavior. If decision makers were to be more systematic and deliberative in their thinking when making choices under uncertainty, they would likely compare alternatives by estimating the likelihoods of different events occurring and their consequences, and make trade-offs between the expected costs and benefits of each alternative.

BOX 1.1 INTUITIVE AND DELIBERATIVE DECISION MAKING

INTUITIVE THINKING, SYSTEM 1

Operates automatically and quickly, with little or no effort and no voluntary control.

Uses simple and concrete associations, including emotional reactions or simple rules of conduct that have been acquired by personal experience with events and their consequences.

DELIBERATIVE THINKING, SYSTEM 2

Initiates and executes effortful and intentional abstract cognitive operations when needed.

Cognitive operations include complex computations and formal logic.

The characterization of judgment and choice that distinguishes intuitive thinking from deliberative thinking builds on a large body of cognitive psychology and behavioral decision research. A recent summary has been provided by Daniel Kahneman in his stimulating book *Thinking, Fast and Slow* (Kahneman 2011) as detailed in Box 1.1.

Intuitive thinking often draws upon the experiences, expectations, goals and beliefs of the parties involved in the decision. Such sources and heuristics typically require far less effort than more detailed analysis of the trade-offs among the options. Even when decision makers make an effort to think carefully, the intuitive appeal of some heuristics implies that they still make mistakes. While intuitive processes often lead to reasonably good decisions, they do *not* work well for LP-HC events, either because of a decision maker's undue focus on a recent event or because individuals perceive the likelihood of an extreme event to be below their threshold level of concern.

Deliberative thinking with respect to assessing risks requires considerable time and attention and the use of decision tools such as probability estimation, Bayesian updating, and the use of formal logic. Consumers at risk would ideally decide whether to purchase insurance – and if so, how much coverage – by comparing the expected costs and benefits of a set of different alternatives available to them using models of choice such as expected utility theory (von Neumann and Morgenstern 1944) or decision analysis (Raiffa 1968). If insurance premiums reflected risk, and risk-averse households used these models (i.e., acted rationally), those facing a LP-HC event would purchase coverage as long as there were no budget constraints. If all consumers at risk (rather than just a fraction of them) undertook deliberative (System 2) thinking, then risk-based flood insurance and catastrophic health insurance coverage would be viewed as highly valuable and would be purchased by almost everyone.

Consumer Behavior

While intuitive perceptions of risk are relatively accurate over a broad range of situations where one has considerable experience, individuals are likely to deviate from expert assessments of unfamiliar risks that involve small probabilities and high degrees of uncertainty (Cutler and Zeckhauser 2004; Kunreuther, Pauly, and McMorrow 2013). These events are subject to the *availability bias* where the judged likelihood of an event depends on its salience (Tversky and Kahneman 1973). There is thus a tendency to ignore rare risks until after a disaster occurs.

This is a principal reason why individuals tend to purchase insurance only after a disaster and cancel their policies several years later when they have not suffered a loss and perceive the likelihood of a disaster as so low that they do not pay attention to its potential consequences. An in-depth analysis of the entire portfolio of the NFIP revealed that the median tenure of flood insurance was between two and four years while the average length of time in a residence was seven years (Michel-Kerjan, Lemoyne de Forges, and Kunreuther 2012). This behavior occurs even when homeowners are required to purchase flood insurance as a condition for a federally insured mortgage because financial institutions are not enforcing this regulation.

Rational risk-averse consumers should attach high value to insurance that protects them against losses which are large relative to their wealth. The relatively thin market for catastrophic health coverage is due to the unwillingness of a majority of buyers to pay a relatively small additional premium for essentially unlimited coverage. This may be the reason that 55 to 60 percent of private group insurance (which covers more than 90 percent of those with private insurance) contained some kind of lifetime cap on benefits before health reform, which prohibited such limits (Musco and Somers 2012). The choices to limit coverage of catastrophic health-related events for employment-based groups were generally made by employers or unions, not individual workers. These agents for the employees should have strong incentives to avoid such mistakes, but they still make them. This same mistake in insurance design has been made by the government for the public Medicare Part A plan, where there are limits for coverage of inpatient care in any one year.

Such coverage limits seem irrational given the low costs and high benefits of protection. In a large insurance plan, very few beneficiaries would reach the typical upper limit, usually in the millions of dollars. Those groups who self-insure could buy reinsurance at relatively low prices to cover the costs of these events. The incremental premium to remove such limits is very low – less than 1 percent of what the insurer is currently charging (PricewaterhouseCoopers 2009). For example, if health insurance costs $2,000 a year, then removing the upper limit would add less than $20 to the premium. And yet many consumers ended up with coverage that did not include this low cost of added protection. The recent reform legislation requires all new private health insurance contracts to eliminate such limits (Musco and Somers 2012).

Insurer Behavior

It is easy to understand how consumers make mistakes about insurance. Surprisingly, insurance managers, despite high levels of expertise and strong incentives to make logical decisions, also make errors with respect to situations where there is uncertainty or ambiguous information regarding the low probability risks they face. When insurers have limited data and limited past experience with extreme events, there is a tendency for them to engage in intuitive thinking when determining what coverage to offer against specific risks and how much to charge.

To illustrate, prior to the terrorist attacks of September 11, 2001, actuaries and underwriters, despite their mathematical expertise and experience, did not specify a price for protection against terrorism coverage nor did they exclude this coverage from their standard commercial policies. This implied that they were essentially covering this risk for the very modest add-on for unspecified events included in typical property insurance premiums. The failure to examine the financial risks associated with terrorism was surprising given the attempted bombing of the World Trade Center in 1993, the 1995 Oklahoma City bombing and other terrorist attacks throughout the world. This behavior by insurers is in the spirit of a 'safety-first' model originally proposed by Roy (1952) and applied to insurance by Commissioner James Stone of Massachusetts. He suggested that an underwriter who wants to determine the conditions for a specific risk to be insurable will focus on keeping the probability of insolvency below some threshold level of concern rather than trying to maximize expected profits (Stone 1973). From discussions with insurance underwriters today, this safety-first model still characterizes their behavior.

Following 9/11, most insurance companies completely changed course and refused to offer any coverage against terrorism, considering it to be an uninsurable risk despite increased buyer demand. The few who did provide insurance charged extremely high premiums (Wharton Risk Center 2005). Prior to these terrorist attacks, Chicago's O'Hare Airport had $750 million of terrorism insurance coverage at an annual premium of $125,000. After 9/11, insurers offered the airport only $150 million of coverage at an annual premium of $6.9 million. The airport was forced to purchase this policy since it could not operate without coverage (Jaffee and Russell 2003). Golden Gate Park in San Francisco was simply unable to obtain terrorism coverage at any price (Smetters 2004).

If actuaries and underwriters had used the more formal models of choice that characterize deliberative (System 2) thinking for determining protection against these extreme events, they would have more accurately estimated the change in likelihood of future terrorist attacks in different parts of the country and their potential consequences. Insurers could then have determined what types and amounts of coverage they would want to offer and the prices they would have to charge so as to maximize their expected future profits based on their current portfolio of policies. It seems implausible to us that they would have concluded that the likelihood of terrorist attacks took such a large jump as to call for the kinds of premiums just described.

In contrast, private insurers have been willing to offer catastrophic coverage for health insurance; its absence usually reflects inadequate demand by consumers as discussed above. Because illnesses that are financially catastrophic for patients are uncorrelated, even health insurers of moderate size are not concerned about a large loss relative to their portfolio from a single person's high medical expense. In this case, a person's very expensive medical treatment is potentially catastrophic for the person, but one such event will not sink any health insurer of reasonable size – and these events rarely happen to more than a tiny fraction of any health insurer's portfolio of risks.

Regulator Behavior

Insurance regulators have aided Florida homeowners in hurricane-prone areas by keeping property insurance costs lower than they would be if private insurers were free to charge premiums that reflected risk. Following Hurricane Andrew in 1992, insurers were only allowed to raise rates gradually over the next decade and were restricted from canceling existing homeowners' policies. Moreover, political pressure from residents in hurricane-prone areas to reduce homeowners' premiums led the state legislature in 2007 to form a residual market mechanism, Citizens Property Insurance Corporation, which offers premiums at highly subsidized rates, thus undercutting the private market. Today, Citizens is the largest provider of wind coverage in Florida. There have been no severe hurricanes in the state since 2005, but if Citizens suffers a severe loss from a large hurricane in the coming years, it would likely become insolvent. In this case, Florida would have to levy a tax on its residents and potentially request disaster assistance from the federal government (Jaffee, Chapter 6 in this volume).

This example illustrates behavior triggered by apparent short-term intuitive thinking by regulators and legislators. (We cannot distinguish between cognitive flaws in regulators' minds and the political pressures to go along with cognitive flaws in voters' minds.) The strategy yields positive returns if there is no hurricane damage in Florida in the near future, but the current premium structure will lead to aggregate claims payments that exceed premiums in the long run. If regulators had undertaken a more systematic analysis of the long-term impacts of their behavior, they would not have formed Citizens in this manner by allowing it to charge highly subsidized premiums. They should have permitted insurers to charge premiums reflecting risk and found other ways to aid those residing in hurricane-prone areas needing special treatment. Just as low-income families are provided with food stamps to buy groceries, low-income residents could be given means-tested insurance vouchers so they can afford the higher risk-based premiums.

CHALLENGES FOR MAKING POSITIVE CHANGES

A key challenge in utilizing economic incentives to improve insurance choices is that these incentives may be viewed by some citizens as being unfair or inequitable. Suppose, for example, the house that a homeowner purchased years ago is now categorized as being in a floodplain, or a family's vacation cottage on the coast now faces a greater risk of hurricane damage due to climate change. At the time the property was bought, damage from hurricanes and floods was not considered a problem. Or suppose some people's current health status is adversely affected by past behavior or genetic disease propensities. Premiums that reflect their current property or health-related risk are likely to be viewed as unfair by the affected individuals because they feel the premiums are too high. But for insurance to operate efficiently, it is necessary for insurers to raise premiums for those now facing a higher likelihood of a property loss or illness. Insurers would then be in a position to charge lower premiums to those who have low expected claims, so that purchasing coverage is viewed as an attractive option for this group.

If premiums do *not* reflect the hazardous location of property or adverse genetic conditions, insurance will be *ipso facto* subsidized for these high-risk individuals. They will have less reason to undertake actions to reduce their risk if they are able to do so because they will not be rewarded with lower premiums. Failure to risk-rate premiums creates moral hazard. Another result will be that lower-risk consumers who undertake deliberative thinking will tend to purchase less insurance. In fact, they may avoid purchasing insurance altogether if premiums are set higher than they should be, perceiving insurance to be a bad buy. On the other hand, the high risks will insure even small losses because they consider coverage to be a bargain. This behavior will lead to problems of adverse selection. There is either inefficient exposure to risk or inefficient costs of processing small claims. The moral hazard distortion in incentives occurs when individuals can change behavior in ways that alter risk; the adverse selection distortion in insurance purchasing occurs regardless of whether risk variation is endogenous or exogenous.

In summary, insurance is a policy tool that has two principal purposes –

encouraging cost-effective investment in loss reduction measures via premium reductions, and providing financial protection should those at risk suffer severe losses. A system of insurance where premiums are not risk based fails to address these two objectives effectively. Under such a system, insurers will have limited or no financial incentive to offer reductions in premiums to individuals who undertake loss reduction measures. In fact, insurers are losing money on these individuals in the long run and would prefer that they bought coverage elsewhere. Individuals who are not highly risk averse are unlikely to purchase coverage if they are charged a premium somewhat greater than their expected loss.

With respect to state regulation, insurance commissioners may feel compelled to restrict prices on those facing high risks because they rely on vocal consumers' support; their desire for re-election may override their concern for the common good (Pauly, Kunreuther, and Vaupel 1984).

To address these challenges we propose the following guiding principles for making insurance more transparent, understandable, and equitable, with the dual objectives of improving individual and social welfare.

> *Principle 1: Require insurance against rare catastrophic risks.* Given the reluctance of individuals to voluntarily purchase insurance against losses that are large relative to their wealth or income, catastrophic coverage should be required for all individuals who face this risk, no matter how small its probability.

> *Principle 2: Premiums must reflect risk.* Insurance premiums should accurately reflect risk to signal to individuals how safe and healthy they are, and to encourage individuals to undertake measures to reduce their vulnerability to illness and/or property losses that would reduce their premiums.

> *Principle 3: Dealing with equity and affordability issues.* Any special treatment given to consumers at risk (e.g., low-income uninsured, high-risk moderate income groups, or inadequately insured individuals) should come from means-tested insurance vouchers financed by the federal government or at a state level through general taxes and *not* through subsidies generated by higher insurance premiums on lower-risk buyers.

> *Principle 4: Multi-year insurance.* A multi-year policy provides stability of premiums since it prevents individuals from being reclassified into higher risk strata during the term of the contract. Such policies currently exist for life insurance and long-term care coverage (Abraham and Chiappori, Chapter 9 in this volume).

In the case of property insurance, where only annual policies are currently marketed, a multi-year policy could be coupled with long-term loans for cost-effective hazard reduction measures. The homeowner would be rewarded for undertaking these investments, inasmuch as the yearly cost of the loan is likely to be less than the annual premium reduction. State insurance regulators would have to allow insurers to charge premiums that reflect the reduced risk for those who take the loans and higher premiums for those who do not.

Even before the ACA was passed, health insurance policies achieved multi-year premium stability by including guaranteed renewability at class average premiums as a policy feature. Under this arrangement, insurers promise not to single out those whose risk rises for selective premium increases. This gives the insurer an incentive to keep the insureds healthy, since the insurer is at risk for higher expenses that might be preventable. Guaranteed renewability also protects consumers from premium increases due to deterioration in their health.

Given that the federal government is the principal provider of flood coverage to homeowners, it should be feasible to require multi-year policies tied to the property, thus satisfying *Principles 1* and *4*. Given that many people cancel their policies if they have not suffered a loss, this requirement needs to be well enforced in the future. For premiums to reflect risk, FEMA needs to improve the accuracy of its flood maps as recommended by the Government Accountability Office (2004). FEMA's Map Modernization Program will result in maps prepared in digital format for 92 percent of the continental US population. Land development and natural changes to the landscape and/or to hydrologic systems require continuous map maintenance and updates. The National Research Council (2009) and the National Academy of Sciences are now undertaking a study of means-tested insurance vouchers to deal with equity and affordability issues (*Principle 3*).

The ACA for health insurance, passed only after a major legislative and legal battle, embodies *Principles 1* and *3*. Insurance offered to individuals and small groups through exchanges is to be subsidized with means-tested tax credits (*Principle 3*). The ACA mandates penalties on those who do not purchase insurance to encourage the purchase of catastrophic protection (*Principle 1*). However, the penalties are weak and may not be enough to induce low-risk people to purchase coverage. The generous subsidies in the ACA should be enough to motivate the purchase of coverage by lower income people who undertake deliberative thinking, but the 'outreach' (marketing) activities of the Health Insurance Marketplaces run by states or the federal government may also need to use insights from behavioral economics to address the problem of take-up of coverage; they need to frame the information they provide in a way that convinces people of the true loss probability and deters them from using the heuristics and biases discussed above. Specifically, it would be important to have a better understanding of why low-risk people who could have afforded insurance did not purchase it, and how they might be expected to change behavior as regulation increases their premiums but also imposes a mandate and markets coverage more aggressively.

The ACA does *not* adhere to *Principle 2*, as it permits only very limited risk rating of premiums (restricted primarily to location, age, and smoking behavior). Healthy younger people who are not eligible for generous subsidies will correctly regard the premiums they will be required to pay in the new regulated exchanges as high relative to the benefits they can expect to collect, and no amount of truthful outreach may convince them to buy. Even if the prospective buyers are healthy through good luck, not because of behavioral factors, they will not find insurance to be a rational purchase unless there were substantial penalties or subsidies. They may purchase the minimum coverage required, when they might have been eager to buy considerably more insurance if premiums were tailored to their risk. There is also some modest public subsidy of reinsurance to offset the cost to those with high lifetime risks. *Principle 4* (multi-year pricing) is, as noted, already required for individual health insurance but the additional limits on risk-based pricing in the new legislation noted above may attenuate the value of the feature, since protection against premium increases has no value if people can pay low premiums even if they become higher risks.

Both laws exemplify much of what is needed to improve individual and insurer behavior. They are designed to move people's behavior from intuitive processes to more deliberative thinking with respect to LP-HC events. The contentious and continuing debate over both pieces of legislation, shows that the policy process does not automatically or easily generate such corrections; there needs to be persistent and dedicated political leadership based on skilled use of correct principles.

To be sure, both legislative proposals were directed at more than rectifying the mistakes by insurers, consumers, and state regulatory officials that arise from behavioral biases and simplified heuristics. They were also designed to reduce losses and alleviate the fiscal burden on governments. Unfortunately, some of the attempts to improve equity end up distorting insurance premiums and, in doing so, frustrate other features in the legislation that were designed to improve the decision making process. We feel that the guiding principles outlined above are linchpins for improving the choices of both insurers and insureds.

TOWARD A TAXONOMY OF GOVERNMENT INTERVENTIONS TO DEAL WITH INSURANCE ANOMALIES

Property and health insurance are instructive cases for examining the rationale and design of effective government interventions, whether through insurance regulation, laws that provide mandates and/or subsidies, or nudges through reframing options that lead people to make better choices. The flood and health insurance legislation are at the aggressive end of the spectrum as they involve heavy regulation of offerings and required coverage. Is this kind of heavy weaponry appropriate for other insurance anomalies that arise from intuitive thinking?

We hypothesize that there are three features that suggest public intervention on this scale is appropriate.

> *Feature 1*: Anomalous behavior that involves under-purchase rather than over-purchase of insurance or protection.
>
> *Feature 2*: Anomalous behavior that causes large harm to a population's wellbeing that is of concern to others for any reason – altruistic, social welfare, or ethical.
>
> *Feature 3*: Settings where individuals have difficulty taking steps to reduce their risk.

Health insurance for lower income people fits all three of these characteristics. Many low-income people do not have insurance, and the absence of coverage can cause serious harm to health if it inhibits the use of effective care. These families' health levels and (perhaps) their financial status are of concern to their fellow citizens. Individuals are sometimes reluctant to undertake preventive health measures, such as their failure to take statin drugs after a heart attack, even when insurance fully covers the cost (Choudhry, Avorn, and Glynn 2011) or not having their children vaccinated against contagious disease.

Lower income homeowners present a similar case. Many of these families are uninsured because they cannot afford coverage. Few individuals in high-risk areas voluntarily invest in measures to reduce their losses from future disasters (Kunreuther, Meyer, and Michel-Kerjan 2013). If they suffer serious damage from a severe disaster, the public is concerned with their plights and there is sympathy (if not funding) so these disaster victims can remain in their current location rather than moving to a safer spot.

When one or more of these three features is absent, the case for public intervention of the type embodied in the ACA or Biggert-Waters is weaker.

We are usually most concerned about people whose use or consumption of some key good falls below some ideal level, and less concerned when it rises above the desirable amount (*Feature 1*). Purchasing overpriced warranties illustrates the case where there is an absence of all of the above features, since the impact on the person buying the warranty and others is likely to be minimal. In cases such as these, intervention usually involves warning consumers, providing them with better information and offering them a chance to get their money back after second thoughts. We conclude that in situations where the consequence of excessive insurance is just wasted money rather than physical impairment or significant reduction in assets or wealth, it may not be worth the effort for governments to try to correct such modest mistakes. Indeed, the maximum loss from mistakenly buying insurance that is overpriced or unneeded is simply the cost of the insurance. In contrast, the loss in welfare from not buying needed insurance could be very high indeed.

Risks (of any type) that primarily affect people in higher income brackets, or risks that affect people across the income spectrum but that can be avoided are also less appropriate candidates for aggressive intervention, even if the consequences of under-purchasing insurance are large. In these cases, concern by others (*Feature 2*) is lacking. For example, if Warren Buffett, famously frugal, had decided not to buy health insurance before he was 65, there would not be a strong public policy interest in getting him to do so. There are no health insurance subsidies for the not-very-poor (households with incomes over 400 percent of poverty), though there is a mild penalty associated with not purchasing coverage for the purpose of maintaining the risk pool so as to subsidize high risks as a matter of social concern (*Feature 2*).

Another example commonly cited as an insurance anomaly is the under-purchase of annuities. People with accumulated assets should be interested in converting their wealth to annuities so they can maintain their standard of living for as long as they live. There were proposals in the early days of the Obama administration from a Treasury official to reframe choices people make when they retire so taking an annuity was the default option for 401(k) accounts (Gale et al. 2008). And there is a great deal of academic literature on the subject that also points to framing as the cause of the problem – without explaining why the correct framing does not prevail in a competitive market (Kunreuther, Pauly, and McMorrow 2013).

The primary reasons for the lack of interest or enthusiasm for encouraging the purchase of annuities is that this is a problem facing the upper middle class elderly, who are not a population of major social concern. Almost everyone has a compulsory annuity in the form of Social Security, and its benefits are usually enough to keep people in all income classes above the poverty line (even if just barely). Utilizing some of the limited stock of political capital to mobilize government to solve a problem that affects primarily people with six-figure incomes does not have any traction.

The other example of under-protection is in the area of life insurance. Although most people do have some life insurance protection, they may buy too little and often make the mistake of dropping their coverage soon after purchasing it because they feel the premiums are too high given budget constraints (Gottlieb and Smetters 2012). Here again, life insurance is largely a concern of the middle class and above, and largely protects the bequests they leave to their heirs so there is little concern by others (that is, *Feature 2* is lacking) and hence no public intervention. The availability of Social Security death and survivors' benefits further attenuates the public policy motivation to deal with this problem beyond applying band-aids in the form of mandatory disclosure of information.

Over-purchasing insurance is another story. Sometimes people do so for good reason. For example, the partial payment of group medical and dental insurance by employers due to the tax advantages on group health insurance suggests that one should have more insurance than one would otherwise purchase.

On the other hand, many people purchase more coverage than would be implied by System 2 thinking. The most prevalent case is *deductible aversion*: the desire for low deductibles (Sydnor 2010; Kunreuther, Pauly, and McMorrow 2013). By undertaking deliberative thinking, one should realize that the savings (premium reduction) associated with a high deductible (on automobile, homeowners', or individual health insurance) more than compensate for the additional payments should one suffer a loss.

There are many hypotheses about why people make this mistake: They overestimate the chances of collecting on the lower deductible, they want to increase the chances of collecting on their policy so they can view insurance as a positive investment, or they just want peace of mind and freedom from regret. There are some serious puzzles in the literature regarding this anomaly. For example, many individuals do not make a claim on their policy when their losses exceed the deductible, which suggests they should have taken a higher one (Braun et al. 2006). If insurance markets are competitive, how can overpriced low deductible plans survive? Here again, there are few rules and few advocates for public policy to deal with this problem because purchasing a low deductible does not satisfy any of the three features listed above.

Then there are some cases where insurance or insurance-like arrangements can be bundled with other products. Individuals often go for the bundle even when portions of the package are overpriced. Insurance for rental cars, appliance warranties, or the purchase of flight insurance all exhibit this characteristic. We could not find a single public policy initiative actually undertaken in the United States intended to discourage this behavior when these examples show that individuals clearly misunderstand the purposes of insurance (Liebman and Zeckhauser 2008). (This is not to deny that such interventions are sometimes advocated for some countries (Competition Commission 2003).) These mistakes in consumer purchasing so far do not seem to rise to the level of social concern because they normally do not relate to behaviors that are of a concern to others (*Feature 2*). They also do not satisfy the characteristics of *Features 1* and *3*.

More specifically, there are almost no regulations beyond standard consumer protection rules that are intended to affect the usual cases of anomalous over-purchase. However, there are some exceptions. For example, the state of California does require disclosure that the driver's own automobile insurance normally applies to a rental car so that purchase of additional insurance to cover the collision damage waiver may not be needed.[2]

There is usually no requirement that sellers of automobiles or appliances that provide warranties hold reserves to assure payment of liabilities under those warranties should a manufacturer go bankrupt, although there are reserves and other insurance-type regulations for firms that sell 'freestanding' warranties. (The United Kingdom does require a 'cooling off' period after a warranty is purchased during which the purchase can be canceled (*Warranty Week* 2004).) And there are no rules to forbid the purchase or warn consumers of the rationale for not purchasing low deductible insurance if it carries a very high incremental premium relative to the actuarial value of the additional coverage.

There have been some attempts by the US Treasury to encourage the purchase of private annuities by workers with 401(k) accounts (Lieber 2010), as noted above. In February 2012 the rules for 401(k)s were changed to make it easier for employers to offer their own annuity option to employees who might wish to convert their 401(k), and to exempt payments for the 'longevity insurance' form of an annuity (one in which annuity payments do not start until an older age) from the minimum distribution rules for IRA balances (Ellis 2012). For life insurance, there are no regulations regarding how premiums can be set for multi-year term insurance.

---

2 See www.ehow.com/facts_5753168_california-regulations-rental-car-insurance.html.

To summarize, in a world where the intrinsic imperfection of government intervention is both more in evidence and more frequently acknowledged than in the past, there is little call for policies designed to deal with insurance against events that mostly affect moderate risks for people in the higher income brackets.

INSURANCE WHEN BAD THINGS CAN HAPPEN, BUT NOT OFTEN

As already noted, insurers have had a difficult time maintaining a steady and reliable supply of reasonably priced coverage against losses that are rare but correlated, with terrorism and natural disasters as two examples. Even if insurers examine past data in a systematic manner, there can still be a problem caused by imprecision in estimating future periods' loss probabilities when events are rare and the world is changing over time.

Consider the easy case where science and past information are sufficient to convince buyers of insurance, managers of insurance firms and insurance regulators of the true probability of a loss-producing event. To illustrate, suppose one estimates that the likelihood of a flood next year is 1 in 100 and that this probability will remain constant for the foreseeable future. Then there will be no disagreement by the relevant parties as to how to estimate the likelihood of a future flood occurring. There are some cases that satisfy this condition where our mathematical models are so well validated and so unambiguous and convincing that experts are in agreement, like the return of Halley's Comet.

But what if it has been 50 years since the last Big Flood, and we know that the world is changing? For example, there are data on global warming and its potential impact on sea level rise, but with considerable uncertainty surrounding these estimates. In cases such as this, we cannot rely on either recent data and/or theoretical models to provide an assured, defensible, and unambiguous estimate of the loss probability.

If insurers charge premiums for windstorm or flood insurance based on a low but positive probability of a damaging event, it is likely that there will be no disaster for years, in which case the insurer will accumulate enormous underwriting profits. These reserves will be needed to pay claims when a serious disaster does occur. But the general public and regulators may become uncomfortable upon learning that the insurer's surplus has increased significantly from a series of disaster-free years, claiming that the premiums being charged are too high.

As discussed earlier, Florida addressed this issue by forming a state-backed insurer (Citizens Corporation) that charges subsidized premiums.

Critics have rightly noted that this arrangement potentially puts all Florida taxpayers at risk should there be a severe hurricane and Citizens does not have enough surplus to pay all the claims. In other words, an intense minority of (often high-wealth) property owners residing in hurricane-prone areas are being highly subsidized by all the residents in Florida.

There is another alternative: mutual insurance. Under this arrangement, if one subsidizes the premiums, everyone who purchases the insurance will be assessed if reserves and premiums are inadequate when a disaster occurs. Collecting this assessment *ex post* may be difficult, so an alternative (in effect) is to charge higher than actuarially fair premiums but tell purchasers that a portion of their payment is being held in a fund that they personally own. Dividends can be declared if the event does turn out to be rarer than originally anticipated. In this arrangement, policyholders bear the full cost of their coverage if an event occurs, but get money back if it does not. In effect, they are protected, with insurance sold at a moderate net price whether the probability turns out to be high or low (Pauly, Kunreuther, and Vaupel 1984).

SUPPLEMENTING THE GUIDING PRINCIPLES IN ADDRESSING THESE CHALLENGES

The four guiding principles can be supplemented by utilizing approaches that alleviate some of the biases that constitute intuitive (System 1) thinking.

In the case of buyers, we recommend that when presenting information on the likelihood of an LP-HC event occurring, one stretches the time horizon. Rather than saying that there is a 1 in 100 chance next year of damage from a severe hurricane, reframe the same probability by saying that the chance that one's property will be damaged from a hurricane in the next 25 years is greater than 1 in 5. Empirical studies have shown that data presented in this fashion raises the probability that individuals will take protective measures (Slovic, Fischhoff, and Lichtenstein 1978; Weinstein, Kolb, and Goldstein 1996).

One of the biggest challenges is to convince consumers that if they do not suffer losses from a disaster or incur health-related expenditures next year, the purchase of insurance was not a waste of money. It is extremely difficult to get the message across that those at risk should celebrate not having collected on their insurance policy. One way to do this is to remind people that something serious could happen to them next year, so they should not cancel their insurance policy without good reason.

Finally, providing transparent information related to the rationale for insurance should go a long way to helping the general public better understand this policy tool. Insurance can then fulfill the roles it is designed to play: reducing future losses and financially protecting those at risk.

REFERENCES

111th Congress. 2010. H.R. 3590 (111th): Patient Protection and Affordable Care Act. Text as of August 25, 2010. Washington, DC: United States Government Printing Office (GOP). www.govtrack.us/congress/bills/111/hr3590/text (accessed September 27, 2013).

112th Congress. 2012. H.R. 4348 (112th): MAP-21. Title II – Flood Insurance. Text as of September 29, 2012. Washington, DC: United States Government Printing Office (GOP). www.govtrack.us/congress/bills/112/hr4348/text (accessed September 27, 2013).

Arrow, K. 1971. *Essays in the Theory of Risk Bearing*. Chicago, IL: Markham.

Braun, M., P. Fader, E. Bradlow, and H. Kunreuther. 2006. Modeling the 'Pseudodeductible' in Homeowners Insurance. *Management Science* 52: 1258–72.

Choudhry, N., J. Avorn, and R. Glynn. 2011. Eliminating Copayments for Patients After Myocardial Infarction Improves Adherence and Some Outcomes. *New England Journal of Medicine* 365: 2088–97.

Competition Commission. 2003. Extended Warranties on Domestic Electrical Goods: A Report on the Supply of Extended Warranties on Domestic Electrical Goods within the UK – Volumes 1, 2 and 3. Available at http://webarchive.nationalarchives.gov.uk/+/http://www.competition-commission.org.uk/rep_pub/reports/2003/485xwars.htm#summary (accessed July 25, 2014).

Cutler, D. M., and R. Zeckhauser. 2004. Extending the Theory to Meet the Practice of Insurance. In R. Herring and R. E. Litan, eds., *Brookings-Wharton Papers on Financial Services*. Washington, DC: Brookings Institution Press, pp. 1–53.

Ellis, B. 2012. Obama's Latest Retirement Rescue Plan: Annuities. Available at http://money.cnn.com/2012/02/02/pf/rules_retirement_annuities/ (accessed March 2, 2015).

Gale, W. G., J. M. Iwry, D. C. John, and L. Walker. 2008. Increasing Annuitization in 401(k) Plans With Automatic Trial Income. *The Hamilton Project, Discussion Paper 2008-02*. Washington, DC: The Brookings Institution.

Gottlieb, D., and K. Smetters. 2012. Narrow Framing and Life Insurance. *NBER Working Paper No. 18601*. Cambridge, MA: National Bureau of Economic Research.

Government Accountability Office (GAO). 2004. *Flood Map Modernization Program Shows Promise, but Challenges Remain*. Washington, DC: GAO04-417.

Jaffee, D., and T. Russell. 2003. Market Under Stress: The Case of Extreme Event Insurance. In R. Arnott, B. Greenwald, R. Kanbur and B. Nalebuff, eds., *Economics for an Imperfect World: Essays in Honor of Joseph E. Stiglitz*. Cambridge, MA: MIT Press.

Johnson, E., and D. Goldstein. 2003. Do Defaults Save Lives? *Science* 302: 1338–9.

Kahneman, D. 2011. *Thinking, Fast and Slow*. New York, NY: Farrar, Straus and Giroux.

Kunreuther, H., R. J. Meyer, and E. Michel-Kerjan. 2013. Overcoming Decision Biases to Reduce Losses from Natural Catastrophes. In E. Shafir, ed., *Behavioral Foundations of Policy*. Princeton, NJ: Princeton University Press, chapter 23, pp. 398–413.

Kunreuther, H., and E. Michel-Kerjan. 2011. *At War with the Weather*. Cambridge, MA: MIT Press.

Kunreuther, H., M. V. Pauly, and S. McMorrow. 2013. *Insurance and Behavioral Economics: Improving Decisions in the Most Misunderstood Industry*. New York, NY: Cambridge University Press.

Lieber, R. 2010. The Unloved Annuity Gets a Hug from Obama. *New York Times*, January 28.

Liebman, J., and R. Zeckhauser. 2008. Simple Humans, Complex Insurance, Subtle Subsidies. In H. Aaron and L. Burman, eds., *Using Taxes to Reform Health Insurance: Pitfalls and Promises*. Washington, DC: Brookings Institution, pp. 230–62.

Madrian, B., and D. Shea. 2001. The Power of Suggestion: Inertia in 401(k) Participation and Savings Behavior. *Quarterly Journal of Economics* 116: 1149–225.
Michel-Kerjan, E., S. Lemoyne de Forges, and H. Kunreuther. 2012. Policy Tenure Under the U.S. National Flood Insurance Program. *Risk Analysis* 32(4): 644–58.
Musco, T., and B. Somers. 2012. Under the Affordable Care Act, 105 million Americans No Longer Face Lifetime Limits on Benefits. ASPE Issue Brief. US Department of Health and Human Services. Available at http://aspe.hhs.gov/health/reports/2012/lifetimelimits/ib.shtml (accessed February 13, 2015).
National Research Council. 2009. *Mapping the Zone: Improving Flood Map Accuracy*. Washington, DC: The National Academies Press.
National Research Council. 2015. Affordability of National Flood Insurance Program Premiums—Report 1. Washington, DC: The National Academies Press.
Organisation for Economic Co-Operation and Development (OECD). 2008. Financial Management of Large-Scale Catastrophes. Policy Issues in Insurance, No. 12. Paris: OECD Publishing. DOI:10.1787/9789264041516-en (accessed September 27, 2013).
Pauly, M. V., H. Kunreuther, and J. Vaupel. 1984. Public Protection Against Misperceived Risks: Insights from Positive Political Economy. *Public Choice* 43(1): 45–64.
PricewaterhouseCoopers. 2009. The Impact of Lifetime Limits. A Study Prepared for the National Hemophilia Foundation on Behalf of the Raise The Caps Coalition. Available at www.amcp.org/WorkArea/DownloadAsset.aspx?id=12211 (accessed March 2, 2015).
Raiffa, H. 1968. *Decision Analysis: Introductory Lectures on Choices Under Uncertainty*. Reading, MA: Addison-Wesley.
Roy, A. D. 1952. Safety First and the Holding of Assets. *Econometrica: Journal of the Econometric Society*, 431–49.
Shavell, S. 1979. On Moral Hazard and Insurance. *Quarterly Journal of Economics* 93(4): 541–62.
Slovic, P., B. Fischhoff, and S. Lichtenstein. 1978. Accident Probabilities and Seat Belt Usage: A Psychological Perspective. *Accident Analysis and Prevention* 10: 281–5.
Smetters, K. 2004. Insuring Against Terrorism: The Policy Challenge. In R. Litan and R. Herring, eds., *Brookings-Wharton Papers on Financial Services*, Washington, DC: Brookings Institution Press, pp. 139–82.
Stone, J. 1973. A Theory of Capacity and the Insurance of Catastrophic Risks: Part I and Part II. *Journal of Risk and Insurance* 40: 231–43, 339–55.
Sydnor, J. 2010. (Over)Insuring Modest Risks. *American Economic Journal: Applied Economics* 2: 177–99.
Thaler, R. H., and S. Benartzi. 2004. Save More Tomorrow: Using Behavioral Economics to Increase Employee Savings. *Journal of Political Economy* 112: S164–87.
Thaler, R. H., and C. R. Sunstein. 2008. *Nudge: Improving Decisions about Health, Wealth, and Happiness*. New Haven, CT: Yale University Press.
Tversky, A., and D. Kahneman. 1973. Availability: A Heuristic for Judging Frequency and Probability. *Cognitive Psychology* 5(1): 207–33.
von Neumann, J. and O. Morgenstern. 1944. *Theory of Games and Economic Behavior*. Princeton, NJ: Princeton University Press.
Warranty Week. 2004. 'Extended Warranties in the UK' January 20. Available at www.warrantyweek.com/archive/ww20040120.html (accessed February 13, 2015).
Weinstein, N., K. Kolb, and B. Goldstein. 1996. Using Time Intervals Between Expected Events to Communicate Risk Magnitudes. *Risk Analysis* 16: 305–8.
Wharton Risk Center. 2005. TRIA and Beyond: Terrorism Risk Financing in the U.S. Philadelphia: The Wharton School, University of Pennsylvania.

2. Insurance agents in the twenty-first century: The problem of biased advice

Daniel Schwarcz and Peter Siegelman

Insurance intermediaries who focus their efforts on individuals and small businesses face an ever-shifting landscape. As with the travel agents of the 1990s, their value in facilitating insurance transactions is increasingly being challenged by technological advances (McKinsey & Co. 2013). Websites and mobile 'apps' already offer consumers the opportunity to bypass traditional insurance intermediaries by providing automated underwriting and policy-selection guidance. And the continuing implementation of health insurance exchanges may well accelerate these technological shifts as consumers become increasingly comfortable with making their insurance purchases online.

This chapter suggests that these technological innovations in insurance distribution systems hold significant promise not only to decrease insurance costs, but also to improve consumer matching with appropriate and affordable coverage. This conclusion arises out of the chapter's assessment that insurance consumers currently face a meaningful risk that traditional insurance agents will subvert their clients' interests to maximize commissions. At root, this risk stems from various market failures, including massive information asymmetries between consumers and insurance intermediaries, the credence–good nature of insurance and the magnitude of consumers' behavioral biases in making insurance decisions. But it also emerges out of important legal and regulatory failures that leave consumers with few, and generally ineffective, safeguards against misconduct by insurance agents.

Technological developments in insurance distribution can limit these risks by providing consumers with tailored information and advice, and by providing regulators with an accurate and accessible record of the insurance sales process. However, technological development creates risks as well; for instance, it may increase the ability of self-interested parties to locate and take advantage of particularly vulnerable consumers. For these reasons, insurance regulation should proactively adapt to technological developments in insurance distribution. Such adaptation should include making consumer-relevant information more broadly available and proactively monitoring online insurance distribution systems to ensure that they provide consumers with accurate and unbiased information.

This chapter begins by examining the economic value that insurance agents can provide to individuals and small businesses. It then explores how intermediaries' interests diverge from those of consumers in ways that can undermine the quality and objectivity of the advice they provide. It reviews the surprisingly small theoretical and empirical literature on these questions, concluding that there is good reason to believe that insurance agents can – and, for a meaningful subset, probably often do – fail to effectively serve consumers' interests. The chapter then argues that existing legal and regulatory responses to these problems are limited and crucially depend on their level of enforcement by state regulatory authorities, which available information suggests is highly variable. The chapter concludes by suggesting that the continuing evolution of online insurance markets and related technological advances may improve insurance advice for consumers by supplanting the role of traditional agents, and that regulatory adaptation can help maximize the potential of this transformation while limiting its risks to insurance consumers.

PART I: THE POTENTIAL VALUE-CREATING ROLE OF INSURANCE AGENTS

Insurance intermediaries – who are typically labeled 'agents' in markets catering to individuals and small businesses – are a small subset of a much larger class of individuals and institutions that facilitate trade between buyers and sellers. These market intermediaries constitute an essential structure through which a great deal of trade takes place. Indeed, one estimate suggests that the market value of all intermediation is approximately 25 percent of US gross national product (GNP) (Spulber 1996).

As with many market intermediaries, insurance agents' primary role is to inform and advise consumers about available product options, either from a single insurer (in the case of captive agents) or from multiple carriers (in the case of 'independent' agents). Such guidance can be helpful because insurance products are extremely complicated and, at least in certain product lines, quite variable (Schwarcz 2011). Yet consumers generally do not read their insurance contracts and would not understand them even if they did (Boardman 2010). As a result, comparison shopping can be quite difficult in non-commoditized insurance lines, such as homeowners or cash value life insurance. Just as important, consumers' wealth, attitudes towards risk, and riskiness are extremely heterogeneous, which means that optimal policy features – such as limits, deductibles and endorsements – are correspondingly variable. Collectively, these facts create opportunities for intermediaries to play a useful role in matching consumers with appropriate insurance products and carriers (Cummins and Doherty 2006; Karaca-Mandic et al. 2013).

Insurance agents can also play an important role in de-biasing consumers. Individuals are subject to various well-established heuristics and biases when it comes to making insurance decisions (Johnson et al. 1993; Baker and Siegelman 2014; Kunreuther and Pauly, Chapter 1 in this volume). Framing effects, loss-aversion, availability bias, affective clouding and a large and growing catalog of other behavioral frailties have been demonstrated in both simulated and real-world insurance purchases. For instance, consumers routinely buy insurance they should rationally avoid, such as bicycle theft coverage (Browne et al. 2012), homeowner policies with low deductibles (Sydnor 2010) and extended warranties on relatively inexpensive consumer durables (Baker and Siegelman 2013). Simultaneously, consumers avoid or under-consume insurance they should rationally want, such as flood or life insurance (Kunreuther et al. 2013; Browne et al. 2012; Cutler and Zeckhauser 2004; Logue 2001). Insurance agents could help reverse these tendencies, particularly when consumer biases would otherwise lead to insufficient insurance demand, as in the case of disaster insurance and term life insurance.

Insurance agents may also provide various additional services to consumers. For instance, they can assist consumers by delivering proof of insurance, changing or updating coverage or answering specific questions about coverage. In some cases, agents can also help prepare a claim and perhaps even advocate for its prompt payment. Finally, insurance agents can provide policyholders with various risk management and mitigation tips, such as suggesting cost-efficient precautions like alarm systems or fire extinguishers.

Insurance agents may also theoretically play a role in promoting the interests of insurers, rather than purchasers, by contributing to carriers' underwriting and rating of policyholders, though this is becoming increasingly uncommon. In contrast to most products, the profitability of insurance depends on purchaser characteristics, about which policyholders may know more than insurers.[1] Insurers attempt to limit, and oftentimes reverse,[2] this information asymmetry through various tools, such as

---

[1] Insurance is not the only type of financial product with this characteristic: The profitability of credit also depends on the characteristics of purchasers.

[2] Even though the standard assumption in economic theory is that consumers know more about their own riskiness than insurers do (Akerlof 1970; Rothschild and Stiglitz 1976), in many consumer markets the reverse may well be true; insurers often have better information than consumers about their risk levels, as they have access not only to information about policyholders' credit scores, magazine

statistical modeling and coverage applications. To the extent that agents have access to additional information about policyholder characteristics relevant to risk, they can contribute to these insurer efforts to underwrite and rate coverage. There is some indirect evidence suggesting that insurance intermediaries have played this role in some commercial markets.[3] However, in recent years, it has become increasingly uncommon for agents serving consumers and small businesses to play a meaningful role in front-line rating and underwriting. Improvements in insurers' risk-assessment tools and their accelerating access to 'big data' have limited the capacity of market intermediaries to provide helpful information to insurers in most consumer-oriented markets (Schwarcz 2010; McKinsey & Co. 2013). 'As a sign of how much has changed, many carriers now actively restrict the ability of even their own field staff to deviate from modeled prices' (McKinsey & Co. 2013).

PART II: INSURANCE AGENTS AND THE RISK OF CONSUMER MANIPULATION

Traditionally, the central question for the economics of insurance intermediaries has been the relative advantages of different distribution and compensation systems for insurers (Kim et al. 1996; Venezia et al. 1999; Regan and Tennyson 2000). For example, researchers have often investigated how firms should design a distribution system to acquire necessary information and provide proper incentives for marketing staff (Ma et al. 2014). Even research examining whether independent agents provide better customer service than exclusive agents focuses on understanding the competitive or regulatory forces that promote one type of distribution system over another (Barrese et al. 1995; Kang 2011). By contrast, the degree to which insurance distribution systems harm or ultimately benefit consumers has received notably less attention. For instance, an excellent

subscriptions, and internet browsing habits, but also to the function that turns all this information into an optimal prediction of policyholder riskiness. Moreover, as Cohen and Siegelman (2010: 63–7) point out, even when policyholders know something about themselves that insurers do not (e.g. driving style), insurers may nevertheless be able to make relevant predictions about risk (probability of an accident) better than policyholders can.

[3] For example, Regan and Tennyson (1996) find that markets with heterogeneous populations are more likely to be served by independent intermediaries. This is consistent with intermediaries playing a front line underwriting role because independent intermediaries' compensation is more heavily weighted towards commissions, which provide better incentives for agents to screen customers.

survey of the literature on insurance distribution systems (Regan and Tennyson 2000) devoted only four pages (of 55) to this question.

But whether or not insurance agents provide competent and trustworthy advice to consumers is a central question for insurance law and regulation. Assuring a minimum bar of competence and trustworthiness among agents is the primary motivation for a host of regulatory requirements and liability rules, including licensing requirements, suitability laws and doctrines such as waiver, estoppel and the duty to procure coverage. In recent years, regulatory actions in the US (Fitzpatrick 2006; New York State Insurance Department 2011) and abroad (Kochenburger et al. 2010) have placed renewed emphasis on these concerns in light of the fact that insurance intermediaries are typically compensated exclusively by insurers on the basis of commissions, which can be calculated either as a percentage of policyholders' premiums ('ordinary premiums') or on the volume, persistence, and/or profitability of their book of business ('contingent commissions').[4] These compensation arrangements can create potential conflicts of interest for insurance intermediaries, as illustrated by various scandals involving insurance distribution, including 'bid-rigging' by the largest commercial insurance broker, Marsh & McClennan, and the widespread sale of 'vanishing premiums' policies whose premiums failed to vanish as promised by the agents who sold them (Fischel and Stillman 1997).

This Part begins by considering the somewhat broader context of financial advice-giving by potentially conflicted market intermediaries.[5] It then reviews insurance-specific theory on the prevalence of biased advice by insurance intermediaries, concluding (unsurprisingly) that much depends on initial assumptions about market conditions. Finally, it examines existing empirical evidence on biased advice by insurance intermediaries and similarly-situated financial advisers. Although insurance-specific evidence is ultimately quite limited, we conclude that the extant empirical literature, considered as a whole, suggests that the problem of biased advice by insurance agents is likely to be significant.

---

[4] In retail trade, intermediaries not only receive payment from customers, but are sometimes also paid by sellers for shelf space (Anderson 1979). This dual compensation occurs on occasion in the commercial sphere, where brokers may receive both fees from their customers and commissions from insurers.

[5] We focus on the advice-giving or matching role of insurance intermediaries, and ignore the possibility that the front-line underwriting functions of agents may undermine consumer interests by driving a wedge between buyers and sellers. As described above, the underwriting role of agents in markets serving individuals and small businesses seems to be largely evaporating due to technological change.

1. A Simple Model of Potential Bias by Advice-Giving Intermediaries

A recent survey article (Inderst and Ottaviani 2012b: 497) presents a useful model that illustrates how financial advice in general can 'be instrumental for overcoming consumers' informational deficiencies or [can] . . . be leveraged to exploit these deficiencies'.[6] In the model, consumers can choose one of two alternatives, A or B. These could represent two different financial products, or one might be thought of as not buying the financial product at all. Consumers are heterogeneous, so that choice A is better for some consumers and choice B is better for others. Each consumer is ignorant about which is the better product for him or her, and we assume for simplicity that the consumer assigns a probability ½ that either of {A, B} is the better choice.

Consumers' ignorance about which option is better motivates the need for advice. The intermediary reaches a determination (subject to some residual uncertainty) about which is the more desirable financial product after gathering information about the consumer and the available choices. This determination can be summarized as the adviser's subjective probability, q, that choice A is better for the consumer than B. Of course, this implies a complimentary probability $(1 - q)$ that B is superior to A. An ideal adviser would recommend the choice that has the largest probability of being correct, based on the evidence she has accumulated. Intuitively, then, the intermediary makes a biased recommendation if she recommends B (or A) even though q is actually larger (or smaller) than ½. In this extremely spare model, the consumer simply accepts whatever choice the adviser recommends.

The seller pays the adviser a commission f_A when the adviser recommends A and f_B when the adviser recommends B. Commissions are the adviser's sole source of compensation. Apart from the commission she receives, the adviser also has some additional interest in recommending that the consumer purchase the superior product for that consumer. This interest might be based on the adviser's conscience or altruistic motives, on fear of legal or regulatory repercussions, or on a desire to build a reputation for high-quality service. All of these motives can be conveniently summarized by a 'disutility' parameter ρ that represents the adviser's cost of making the wrong recommendation.

The adviser's recommendation is determined by the commissions she receives and her disutility from making an incorrect recommendation.

---

6 The authors complicate the model along a variety of dimensions that are not necessary for our purposes.

Consider recommending product A. This yields a commission of f_A. If the recommendation is ill-advised, however – and this occurs with probability $(1 - q)$ – the adviser incurs a cost of ρ. Thus, the adviser's expected net gain from recommending product A is:

$$EV(A) = f_A - (1 - q)\rho. \qquad (2.1)$$

Symmetrically, the expected net gain from recommending product B is:

$$EV(B) = f_B - q\rho, \qquad (2.2)$$

since B is the incorrect choice with probability q. We can solve for the threshold value of q – call it q^* – such that the adviser has the same expected payoff whether she recommends A or B, and hence is indifferent about which to recommend. That value is:

$$q^* = \frac{1}{2} - \frac{f_A - f_B}{2\rho}. \qquad (2.3)$$ [7]

It follows that for values of q greater than q^*, the adviser will recommend product A, while for values below q^*, B will be recommended.

Several conclusions follow from this extremely simple setup. First, only when the commissions for A and B are equal, so that $q^* = ½$, will the adviser always makes an unbiased recommendation for every consumer. Any difference in the commissions will cause q^* to diverge from ½, and will therefore lead to biased recommendations in favor of one or the other choice for some consumers. Second, when A's commission (f_A) is larger than B's (f_B), q^* will be smaller than ½ and the adviser's recommendations will be biased towards A, implying that A will sometimes be recommended even when the adviser believes that B is more likely to be the preferable choice. (Of course, the reverse is true when $f_A < f_B$.) Third, larger values of the mismatch disutility parameter (ρ) reduce the extent of bias. When ρ is very large, the difference in commissions ($f_A - f_B$) does not matter much, because the penalty for being wrong dominates any potential monetary gain from recommending the wrong policy. Thus, large values of ρ promote unbiased recommendations. Finally, if option B is understood as buying no financial product at all, a pure commission-based compensation

[7] Inderst and Ottaviani (2012b: 499) have $q^* = ½ - (f_A - f_B)/\rho$, but this appears to be an algebraic mistake. Regardless, since q is a probability, it must lie between 0 and 1, which in turn means that $f_A - f_B$ must not be too large in absolute value, nor ρ too small.

system offers the adviser no reward for recommending this option (since f_B must be zero when B is the no-purchase option). Thus, unless ρ is also 0 (in which case the expression is undefined), an adviser compensated purely by commission will always be biased towards recommending purchase over non-purchase.

This model can also be expanded to consider how bias might influence the effort of intermediaries. Suppose that intermediaries' subjective probability that A is the correct policy is $\tilde{q}$, and is a function of effort, *e*. That is, by expending effort, agents can learn more about the individual and/or the menu of options {A, B} from which the consumer will choose. Under reasonable assumptions, biased agents will sometimes expend less effort than unbiased agents and will never expend more to determine consumers' preferred products. The basic intuition for this result is that effort is always worth at least as much to an unbiased (and risk-neutral) agent as a biased one, because an unbiased agent always gains from any cost-effective effort that improves on $q^* = ½$ (maximal uncertainty), whereas a biased agent does not.[8] Biased agents thus will always make at least as many wrong recommendations as unbiased agents, and sometimes more.

While the model described above is a useful way to fix ideas about how differential rewards could lead to biased recommendations, it has many obvious shortcomings. The most important is that it does not offer an equilibrium account in which agents have to consider the behavior of consumers or rival recommenders, instead simply folding this into the disutility parameter. The actual dimensions of the disutility parameter depend on various considerations that are specific to insurance markets. We discuss these below.

---

8 Suppose that the agent who makes no effort will estimate $q = ½$. A biased agent does not gain from effort that pushes against the direction of bias, and also gains nothing from effort that moves the subjective probability $\tilde{q}$ without exceeding the threshold for a changed decision, q^*. For example, suppose an agent's initial subjective evaluation of $\tilde{q}$ (given no effort) is ½. Let that agent's threshold value for q^* be 0.75, and suppose that as a result of his effort, the agent is led to revise his estimate of $\tilde{q}$ to 0.6. This increment in q is useless, because the agent will recommend policy B for both the initial and final values of $\tilde{q}$. The same logic applies *a fortiori* to effort that ends up lowering $\tilde{q}$, say to 0.4. Since the agent will recommend policy B for both $\tilde{q} = 0.5$ and $\tilde{q} = 0.4$ (both values are lower than the threshold), the effort has no payoff. The case in which bias does *not* influence effort occurs when the optimal amount of effort without bias is sufficient to move the agent's estimate of q beyond the threshold created by the presence of bias.

2. The Effects of Insurance Intermediary Compensation: Theory

In recent years, some scholars have begun to explore how the themes described in the general model above play out in the specific context of insurance. In some cases they have developed their own formal models, and in others they have explored how key factors related to the disutility parameter are likely to play out in insurance markets. Unfortunately, the bottom line is that few robust conclusions emerge, with much depending on the initial model assumptions or the particulars of the insurance markets examined.

Gravelle (1994) was the first to examine the relationship between compensation and the quality of advice in a rigorous model. Focusing on life insurance, he finds that intermediaries who are compensated by insurer-paid commissions reduce consumer costs but that intermediaries who are compensated by fees paid by policyholders provide better advice. This result is driven by a crucial assumption in the model: that the *only* way a consumer can gain information about life insurance is via an agent. Thus, while agents compete with each other for customers, they as a group have a monopoly on the relevant information. As a result, when consumers pay separately for advice, the equilibrium fee will be at the monopoly level, since there is no longer competition between agents for customers. Given a downward-sloping demand curve, fewer consumers enter the market.

Hofmann and Nell (2011) reach a different conclusion, suggesting that a fee-for-advice (consumer pays) system *is* socially optimal, even though commission-based compensation (insurer pays) may be better for insurers (in part because it facilitates collusion between insurers and brokers). Unlike Gravelle's model, consumers in Hofmann and Nell's model can either access heterogeneous insurance policies directly or can utilize the services of an agent to access coverage. In their model, agent-assisted search increases product differentiation (which is endogenous – insurers choose their location in product space in a monopolistic competition framework), and hence paradoxically *reduces* competition among insurers.

Focht et al. (2013) come to yet a different conclusion, suggesting that in some situations commission-based compensation may ironically *prevent* biased advice by insurance intermediaries. In their model, both pay-for-advice and commission systems generally result in unbiased advice due to competitive forces. However, when brokers are paid by consumers, they can strategically threaten insurers to divert customers to another insurer so as to extract a side-payment not to do so. If insurers do not make the side-payment, then the intermediary provides the customer with biased advice in order to follow through on the threat to the insurer. These dynamics are avoided by a commission structure.

Perhaps the most complete and careful theoretical modeling of insurance intermediation is Eckardt's (2007), which uses search-theoretic models that allow for heterogeneity in insurance policies, consumer search costs, consumer valuations of insurance and intermediaries' costs. Although the implications of her model are numerous,[9] the most relevant here is that in a competitive market place, the presence of consumer search costs allows low-quality intermediaries to survive in equilibrium; competition does not lead to uniformly higher quality. And when consumers know more about their riskiness than insurers do:

> [I]nsurance intermediaries have incentives to provide incorrect, false or misleading information about insurance products to consumers because they can earn information rents. Due to the experience and credence goods characteristics of information services, [there are no good ways to] signal[ ] . . . high quality services. Because insurance companies have an interest in strong sales efforts by insurance intermediaries, they set incentives [that] . . . induce intermediaries to provide low information quality . . . All in all, market forces set only weak incentives for insurance intermediaries to provide high quality services. (Eckardt 2007: 151–3)

Several papers also present arguments that are not formally modeled about the likelihood that intermediaries will compromise the interests of policyholders in order to increase their compensation. Focusing on insurance brokers operating in commercial property/casualty markets, Cummins and Doherty (2006) argue that competition among brokers tends to limit the risk that brokers will steer policyholders to inappropriate coverage in order to maximize their short-term commission payments. They attribute the prevalence of contingent commissions, in particular, to the capacity of these payments to incentivize agents to perform useful front-line underwriting. They argue that these commissions can benefit both insurer and insured by limiting the risk of adverse selection.[10]

---

[9] She also finds that a monopolistic intermediary is beneficial for consumers with medium willingness to pay. The main reason is economies of scale. The intermediary is assumed to have a fixed cost of acquiring knowledge about the various insurance products available, but a very low marginal cost to communicate it to consumers. If each individual searches independently, however, then each has to pay the costs of acquiring the relevant information, and total costs are higher (Eckardt 2007: 94–6). Eckardt's model also suggests that consumers with very low value of information are priced out of intermediation in equilibrium – they do no search at all. Those with very high value of information find that the quality of information provided by the intermediary is too low, given the equilibrium fee charged, and so choose to search themselves (Eckardt 2007: 94–6).

[10] Similarly, Maas (2010) focuses on intermediaries who serve commercial (rather than consumer) purchasers. Based on interviews with risk managers at

Subsequent research by Regan and Kleffner (2010) and Ju and Tu (2011) finds that the payment of contingent commissions does lead to better and more consistent underwriting in commercial markets.

Schwarcz (2007; 2008) argues that these principles have limited application in consumer-driven insurance markets, where commissions are more likely to cause agents to offer biased advice.[11] Insurance in general, and insurance intermediation in particular, are classic credence goods, whose true value is difficult for consumers to ascertain even after purchase (Darby and Karni 1973).[12] This is for several reasons: many policyholders never submit large claims or only do so many years after purchase; the complexity of insurance products means that consumers are generally ill-equipped to assess how their coverage would have differed if they made an alternative purchase; and the biases and heuristics that pervasively impact consumers' insurance decisions limit their capacity to assess what kinds of intermediation services are in their best interest. For these reasons, agents are unlikely to be penalized by reputational sanctions or loss of repeat business when they offer self-serving advice. Schwarcz takes particular aim at contingent commissions, which can entrench large commission differentials ($f_A - f_B$ in the model above) even when carriers compete on the basis of commission rates. Additionally, he notes that in life insurance markets, agents' receipt of a single commission at the time of purchase creates an incentive for intermediaries to encourage excessive switching ('churn') of policies.

In sum, the theoretical literature on insurance intermediaries offers various competing arguments and hypotheses. Much depends on specific features of the markets being evaluated. Unsurprisingly, commentators seem more optimistic that biased advice can be limited in commercial insurance markets with relatively savvy policyholders than in markets serving individuals and small businesses. But equilibrium is also highly sensitive to various institutional and behavioral details, such as whether purchasers can search on their own, whether the content of policies is

---

firms who purchase insurance, he concludes that brokers do 'create value' for the customers through the provision of ancillary services. However, most of these services would not be relevant for ordinary consumers.

[11] Schwarcz (2007) also argues that contingent commissions may have ambiguous effects in commercial markets because they may undermine the capacity of high-risk policyholders to be truthful with their brokers, since they fear doing so will cause them to be steered to higher-cost carriers or coverage.

[12] Carlin (2009) points out that complexity in retail financial markets may in part be driven by strategic considerations. In his model, firms benefit from consumer confusion caused when firms add complexity to their pricing structures.

endogenous, whether intermediaries can negotiate commissions with insurers, and the nature and extent of consumers' deviations from rationality. In many plausible models, competition between intermediaries does not guarantee optimal (or even appropriate) behavior towards consumers.[13] At a minimum, most models suggest that there is scope for insurance intermediaries to expropriate rents at the expense of insurance purchasers.

3. Empirical Evidence on Insurance Agents in Consumer Markets

Given the many countervailing influences on agents' behavior, the extent to which agents actually provide welfare gains to consumers is ultimately an empirical question. Although relevant evidence is scant – especially for the US – the data that are available suggest that insurance intermediaries operating in consumer-driven marketplaces may not be serving consumer interests in an effective manner. We consider both empirical evidence on financial advice generally and on the performance of insurance agents in particular. Of necessity, we draw on studies undertaken in other countries, acknowledging that these data are not necessarily applicable to the US market, where competitive and regulatory structures may be quite different.

(a) Evidence from other kinds of consumer-oriented financial intermediaries

Recent years have seen the emergence of an empirical literature assessing the performance of financial intermediaries in contexts *outside* of insurance, such as mutual fund advisers. While not exactly on point, this literature is comparatively well developed and involves many of the same basic considerations as are at play in insurance markets.

Collectively, this literature suggests that financial intermediaries serving ordinary consumers often offer poor advice, presumably because doing so increases their own compensation. The underlying studies – many of which are not yet published – are summarized in Table 2.1. To be sure, most of the studies suffer from several problems. For example, as many of the studies note, comparing outcomes between advised and unadvised consumers using observational data confounds possible selection effects with adviser effects: those who choose to consult an adviser may

---

[13] Gabaix and Laibson's (2006) shrouded pricing model, to give just one example, demonstrates how relatively modest behavioral flaws may forestall competition between sellers, allowing them to earn significant rents in equilibrium, at the expense of consumers.

Table 2.1 Recent empirical studies of financial advisers

Study	Context	Method	Conclusion
Bergstresser et al. (2009)	Performance of mutual funds held by consumers	Comparison of returns and risk by direct vs. brokered mutual funds, across large sample of funds	Adjusting for risk, funds sold by brokers underperform funds sold through direct channels (even before subtracting distribution charges)*
Bhattacharya et al. (2012)	German retail brokerage/ financial adviser	Random offer of (unbiased) financial advice to 8,000 consumers	Few customers accepted offer, and among those who did, advice was rarely followed, even though it would have improved financial performance; acceptance rate was highest among the best-educated and richest
Bluethgen et al. (2008)	4,363 clients of German bank that provides financial advice to customers	Comparison of advised vs. unadvised accounts	Advised accounts are more diversified, but pay higher fees and have the same portfolio volatility as unadvised accounts
Bluethgen, Meyer and Hackethal (2008)	Survey of 260 German independent financial advisers	Survey/analysis of adviser quality	Advisers vary substantially in quality; advisers charging fixed fees (vs. commissions) and those with more skill provide better advice
Hackethal et al. (2012)	32,000 randomly selected customers of online brokerage and German bank	Comparison of performance in advised and unadvised accounts	Presence of financial adviser lowers net returns, worsens risk-return tradeoff, and increase account turnover, consistent with commission-maximization
Kramer (2012)	16,000 clients of Dutch bank that also provides investment advice	Comparison of advised and unadvised large accounts, as well as those that switch categories	No difference in risk-adjusted performance across account types (but only weak controls for selection effects)
Mullainathan et al. (2012)	284 visits to advisers by 'testers' in the Boston area	Field experiment using randomized audit study in which testers ask for advice, starting with four different artificial portfolios	Advisers favored actively managed portfolios with high fees; 'the market for financial advice does not serve to de-bias clients but in fact exaggerates biases that are in the adviser's financial interest, while leaning against those that do not generate fees'

Study	Context	Method	Conclusion
Chalmers and Reuter (2012)	Roughly 5,000 participants in Oregon University system's defined contribution plan	Comparison of customer characteristics and portfolio performance of those who choose between a 'high-touch' and 'low-touch' adviser	On a risk-adjusted basis, the typical investor choosing the lower-advice provider outperforms the typical investor choosing the higher-advice provider
Levitt and Syverson (2008)	100,000 home sales in Cook County, IL	Comparison of time to sell for homes owned by agent vs. homes represented by agent	Agents leave their own homes on the market for 9.5 days longer, and sell them for 3.7% more, than they do for otherwise identical homes in which they represent the actual owner

Note: * Unless 'brokers deliver substantial intangible benefits that we do not observe[,] . . . there [appear to be] material conflicts of interest between brokers and their client'.

be systematically different from those who do not, in ways that influence their financial performance apart from any effects attributable to their adviser (Mullainathan et al. 2012; Hsieh et al. 2013). Additionally, many of the studies use European data and look at relationships (e.g. between consumers and their bank, which may also provide investment advice) for which there are no direct parallels in US insurance markets. On the other hand, some of the studies are able to clearly identify sub-optimal advice because the advice given is so conspicuously at odds with basic finance theory. For example, it is easy to show that some portfolios of assets are dominated by (have both lower returns and more risk than) others; an adviser who recommends a dominated portfolio has unequivocally failed to serve the interests of his client. By contrast, it is often more difficult to assess whether an intermediary has recommended an unsuitable insurance policy to a client.

As Table 2.1 suggests, only two (Kramer 2012; Bluethgen et al. 2008) of the nine studies find that consumers are arguably well served by their financial advisers. To varying degrees, the others conclude that advisers steer at least some clients towards assets or portfolios with poor risk-return tradeoffs and large brokerage commissions. The most compelling (and relevant) is Mullainathan et al. (2012), who used a field experiment technique that sent trained auditors (with a variety of experimenter-assigned portfolios) to ask for advice from financial advisers in the Boston area. The authors conclude that 'advisers fail to de-bias their clients and often reinforce biases that are in their [advisers'] interests. Advisers encourage returns-chasing behavior and push for actively managed funds that have higher fees, even if the client starts with a well-diversified, low-fee portfolio.' Other convincing studies echo these results in different contexts. For instance, Chalmers and Reuter (2012) find that the portfolios of participants in the Oregon state pension plan who choose a more expensive and 'sophisticated' adviser perform worse than those chosen under the advice of an adviser who provided only minimal services. Similarly, Levitt and Syverson (2008) demonstrate that real estate agents tend to advance their interests at the expense of clients by encouraging them to sell too quickly. This is true even though realtors' commissions are paid directly by their clients, rather than their clients' counter-parties as in the insurance context.

The bottom line conclusion from the studies in Table 2.1 is that intermediaries in a variety of financial settings often fall short of providing consumers with optimal or even appropriate advice. To be sure, the regulatory and competitive environments faced by these intermediaries are not the same as those confronting insurance intermediaries, so it is possible that these problems are much less prevalent in insurance markets in the US. But we do not think this is likely, given that neither regulation nor competition is stronger for insurance agents than other types of financial intermediaries.

(b) Direct evidence on the performance of insurance intermediaries

Table 2.2 summarizes four empirical approaches to studying how insurance intermediaries influence consumer welfare.

(i) Audit studies or field experiments Potentially the most powerful evidence of how insurance consumers fare comes from so-called 'field experiments' (Levitt and List 2007) that use trained auditors who pose as actual consumers and are sent to randomly selected intermediaries to observe their behavior in a natural setting. While imperfect (Heckman and Siegelman 1993), experimental data are nevertheless a powerful lens through which to evaluate how well insurance intermediaries promote consumer welfare. Most importantly, audit studies can track specific measure(s) of consumer welfare with great precision. Auditors' fictionalized biographies can be designed so that there is a clear 'right' choice for someone in their situation, and researchers can then observe whether intermediaries recommend that choice. And since researchers have complete control of background variables such as the 'consumer's' apparent

Table 2.2 Techniques for empirical study of insurance intermediaries (after Eckardt 2007)

Type of data	Technique	Example	Comments
Audit, 'mystery shopper' or field experiment	Dummy customers sent to agents to observe their recommendations	Anagol et al. (2012)	Allows for control of more dependent variables and eliminates selection effects; no US studies, however
Consumer complaints	Analysis of customer complaints to regulators, others	Brown and Minor (2012)	Unclear how well consumer complaints capture agent misbehavior, which may go undetected or unreported
Ethics studies*	Interviews with intermediaries to evaluate their responses to ethical issues	Román and Munuera (2005)	Unclear whether answers track actual practice; limited ability to evaluate frequency of ethical problems; adopts sellers' point of view
Statistical comparisons	Comparison of costs, outcomes, etc. across different distribution methods or compensation schemes	Browne et al. (2012)	Most designed to test theories of industrial organization. No direct evaluation of consumer welfare

Note: * Given the many methodological problems inherent in such studies, not least of which is their focus on ethical aspirations rather than actual behavior, we will not discuss them further. Most of these studies also suffer from very low response rates and questionable sampling frames. Readers interested in pursuing this literature further may consult Garnick et al. (1998); Cupach and Carson (2002); Román and Munuera (2005); Cooper and Frank (2002); or Haron et al. (2011).

wealth, sophistication and behavioral biases, audits allow for precise measurement of how intermediaries respond to such variables. Finally, because auditors can be randomly assigned to intermediaries, concern for selection effects, which are always a problem in observational data, is minimized.

Although there are apparently no field experiments involving insurance intermediaries in the US, international experiments suggest that agents may not substantially advance consumer welfare. German researchers conducted a few small audits in the early 2000s: as summarized by Eckardt (2007: 152), these investigations yielded 'consistent . . . results. Most intermediaries fall short of attaining the benchmark; information quality [presented to test consumers] is usually quite low.' These results are consistent with a recent high-quality field experiment studying the performance of intermediaries in the Indian life insurance market. Anagol et al. (2012) conclude that intermediaries do not provide much useful information, or direct consumers to suitable products. Instead, intermediaries 'recommend and sell products that maximize . . . [their own] well-being, with little or no regard for the customer' (Anagol et al. 2012: 1). In particular, the authors find that:

> [D]espite the fact that term [insurance] is an objectively better policy, between 60 and 80 percent of . . . visits [by auditors] end with a recommendation that the customer purchase whole life insurance. . . . [E]ven when customers [expressly] signal that they are most interested in term insurance and need risk coverage, more than 60 percent of audits result in whole insurance being recommended. (Anagol et al. 2012: 17)

The amounts at stake are not trivial, since the appropriate policy yields benefits that are as much as seven times greater than the inappropriate one (Anagol et al. 2012: 8). Moreover, even when the more-suitable policy has a higher commission (and is thus more profitable for the agent, conditional on its being sold):

> [A]gents have a strong incentive to cater to the initial preferences of customers in order to close the sale; contradicting the initial preference of customers, even when they are wrong, may not be a good sales strategy. Thus, salesmen are unlikely to de-bias customers if they have strong initial preferences to products that may be unsuitable for them. (Anagol et al. 2012: 4)

We do not know whether agents in the US behave similarly, but there appear to be ample opportunities to engage in such behavior.

(ii) Complaints Another approach to studying the relationship between intermediaries and consumer welfare focuses on consumer complaints to regulatory authorities. These data can illuminate the extent of practices that consumers find objectionable enough to complain about, but they do not reveal anything about the prevalence of problems consumers do not notice or deem to be serious. Moreover, complaint data are difficult to interpret because they embody the behavior of both intermediaries (who choose how to treat the consumer) and consumers (who choose whether to complain about their treatment). Econometric identification – isolating the behavior of the intermediary from that of the consumer – poses a

Table 2.3 Numbers of consumer complaints against agents/agencies, by reason × line (Texas Department of Insurance: 2009: 1–2013: 2)

Reason for complaint	Line of coverage						
	Home	Life	Auto	Health	Credit	Total	
Agent handling	961	640	734	265	96	2,696	42.9%
Conversion	731	149	343	156	52	1,431	22.8%
Misrepresentation	253	832	95	167	10	1,357	21.6%
Unauthorized acts	109	56	41	68	58	332	5.3%
Misleading advertising	21	90	7	30	0	148	2.4%
Commissions	35	35	1	41	4	116	1.8%
Improper inducements	4	9	7	0	94	114	1.8%
Twisting	2	28	0	12	0	42	0.7%
Non-disclosure of coverage	0	36	0	0	0	36	0.6%
Churning	0	12	0	0	0	12	0.2%
Tie-in sales	1	0	0	0	0	1	0.0%
Total	2,117	1,887	1,228	739	314	6,285	100%
	33.7%	30.0%	19.5%	11.8%	5.0%	100%	

Source: Authors' computations from TDI data, available at www.tdi.texas.gov/consumer/icis/index.html.

significant challenge, and especially so if consumers are understood as less-than-perfectly rational actors.

Table 2.3 provides the volume of complaints to the Texas Department of Insurance ('TDI') by Texas consumers against agents and insurance agencies from the first quarter of 2009 through the second quarter of 2013. Texas is the only state that publicly reports consumer complaints against agents and agencies. Since there are roughly 150,000 insurance agents in Texas, the probability of a complaint is obviously very low – on the order of 1 percent per year. This result is equally compatible with a low incidence of violations or a high incidence coupled with a low detection rate, so the data do not reveal anything about how often insurance agents misbehave.[14] Most complaints allege misfeasance in 'Agent Handling' (a broad term that covers any improper practice), Conversion (misappropriation of

[14] There is a substantial body of empirical scholarship in socio-legal studies on the 'Dispute Pyramid,' which tends to suggest that both detection of wrongdoing and formal complaints (conditional on detection) are rare (Pandya and Siegelman 2013; Kolodinsky 1995; Venezian 2002).

premiums paid) or Misrepresentation. Home and Life together account for almost two-thirds of the complaints received.

Several studies use this type of data to compare the prevalence of complaints against captive agents who work exclusively for a single insurer and independent agents who represent multiple insurers. Focusing on data from 5,406 complaints about life insurance agents filed with TDI, Brown and Minor (2012: 2) find that consumers are more likely to complain about captive agents than independent agents. In an initial draft, they attribute this result to the fact that '[better] salespeople cannot set their own prices to extract surplus from the larger expected consumer benefits [they provide]; instead, they extract surplus through greater misconduct' (Brown and Minor 2012: 2). But this interpretation seems questionable, for reasons related to the larger problem with complaint data described above; in particular, it is hard to eliminate the possibility that the result is driven more by variations in the different intermediaries' customer bases than in actual behavior of intermediaries themselves.[15] Barrese et al. (1995) also find a relationship between distribution mechanisms and complaints: Automobile policies sold by independent agents generate fewer complaints than those sold by captive agents, other things equal. Importantly, complaints in this study cover the entire relationship between the insurer and the insured, and are not limited to those about the selling agent. Based on this result, the authors conclude that independent agents provide better customer service than captive agents.

Other studies focusing on insurance complaint data are not specific to intermediaries, but nonetheless may have implications for understanding the quality of advice offered by agents. For instance, Chan (1999) uses the volume of complaints against a company (per dollar of insurance written, by zip code) as a measure of insurance quality. He finds that zip codes with a higher proportion of racial or ethnic minorities experience higher complaints per dollar of insurance written. To the extent that biased or incompetent advice from intermediaries drives any part of Chan's findings, the results are broadly consistent with the theoretical work of Fong (2005), who suggests that expert sellers will disproportionately take advantage of less-informed buyers, which would likely include racial/ethnic minorities.

(iii) Statistical comparisons Finally, there are a diverse group of statistical studies that examine questions such as whether there is a relationship

---

[15] For instance, it may be that policyholders who purchase from captive agents rightly associate their agents with their insurer, and so are more likely to blame their agent when they are upset with their carrier.

between customer satisfaction and the type of distribution system (direct vs. independent agents) or the method of compensating intermediaries (contingent vs. straight commissions). Such studies can shed light on which distribution system is best for the insurer, but since they do not contain a measure of consumer welfare or suitability, they shed less light on how consumers fare.

Browne et al. (2012) use statistical analysis of a single company's sales patterns to conclude that insurance agents can play an important role in de-biasing consumers. They focus on a German insurer that sells both directly to consumers and via agents. Overall, the company's customers are almost twice as likely to purchase bicycle theft insurance as they are to purchase flood insurance (Browne et al. 2012: Table 3). This pattern probably reflects irrational behavior; insurance against low-value/high frequency losses such as bicycle theft is generally not rational, whereas insurance against high-value/low frequency losses (such as flooding) typically is. But Browne et al. (2012) find that consumers who purchase their insurance through an agent, rather than directly, were less likely to adopt a seemingly irrational insurance purchasing strategy; such consumers were more likely to buy flood insurance than those who bought directly, although they were no less likely to purchase bicycle theft insurance. While plausible, the authors' conclusion that agents play an important role in de-biasing consumers might be overstated. In particular, the causal attribution might be faulted for failing to control for selection effects. Consumers buying their insurance through an agent might be more risk-averse or otherwise inclined to buy flood insurance, even if there were no agent available. If such selection (on variables unobservable to the researchers) is important,[16] the attribution of a causal role to insurance agents would be misplaced. Even granting the authors' causal interpretation of the role of agents, moreover, such de-biasing is not uniform across products. Agents seemed to de-bias consumers when doing so produced more commissions (buying more flood insurance) but not when it produced fewer commissions (buying less bicycle insurance). These results are consistent with commission-maximization by agents.

Eckardt (2007) conducted a survey of independent German insurance

[16] Browne et al. (2012: 16) do point out that there does not appear to be selection based on any policyholder characteristics that they can observe. But Hsieh et al. (2013: 1) provide empirical evidence from Taiwan that 'high-risk policyholders prefer to purchase insurance from an independent agent, whereas those with lower risks tend to buy insurance from direct writer channels'. And it is always appropriate to worry about selection on variables that are not directly observable.

intermediaries in 2001. (Eckardt and Räthke-Döppner (2010) use the same data and reach essentially the same conclusions.) Her dependent variable, allegedly a measure of the quality of information provided by each intermediary, was the 'information index' (168). This was constructed as the unweighted sum of responses to 27 Likert-scaled questions about the importance of various aspects of customer needs. The information index was then regressed on numerous explanatory variables to assess how 'information quality' responded to measures of the level of local market competition, an intermediary's educational background, and so on. Intermediaries operating in more-competitive markets did not have higher 'information indexes'; this led Eckardt (2007: 216) to conclude that 'competition works poorly in inducing intermediaries to provide high quality information services when consumers have only incomplete and asymmetric information'. However, the response rate in Eckardt (2007) was quite low (only 20 percent of those approached completed a survey). More significantly, it is not at all clear that the survey responses measured 'information quality' in any meaningful way, since the questions merely asked respondents to evaluate the importance (on a 1–5 point Likert scale) they believed a particular factor had for consumers.

Using data from a large broker, Wilder (2004) concludes that contingent commissions do influence agents' decisions about where to place insurance. Agents who have an equity stake in the brokerage benefit directly from contingent commissions, which are paid to the firm as a whole, not individual agents. These equity-owners are more likely to write policies with insurers offering contingent fees than are agents without any equity stake. Although Wilder (2004) does not provide a welfare analysis of the distortions caused by contingent commissions, he notes that 'agents with an interest in maximizing the agency's profits consider contingency fees as they place insurance'.

PART III: LEGAL AND REGULATORY CONSTRAINTS ON BIASED ADVICE

One important goal of insurance law and regulation is to ensure the competence and trustworthiness of insurance agents and to punish misconduct by specific agents. To the extent that these mechanisms work well, they may limit the risks associated with biased advice by increasing the magnitude of the disutility parameter (ρ) for intermediaries. And if current law or regulations do not do a good job, there may be alternatives that could more effectively reduce the risk of misbehavior by insurance agents. For these reasons, this Part reviews some of the most important tools of insurance law and regulation that may constrain the behavior of agents. Although empirical evidence on the point is limited, it concludes that many of these tools, as they are currently constructed and enforced, do little to limit the risk of self-serving behavior by agents. It also suggests that, while certain legal and regulatory reforms could better police agent misconduct, the potential effectiveness and efficiency of such reforms are hard to quantify.

1. Insurance Agents' Duties to Policyholders

Although aggrieved policyholders can sue insurance agents for breaching their duty of care as professionals, most states narrowly limit the scope of this duty so that liability generally has little deterrent effect. Under the law of most states, agents only have legal duties to procure the coverage that a policyholder has requested and to notify policyholders if this proves impossible. Agents generally do not have a legal obligation to affirmatively explain coverage, advise policyholders about coverage options or provide disinterested advice (Jerry and Richmond 2007: 680). In most states, these principles are subject to one or more exceptions. Perhaps the most common such exception is that an insurance intermediary who has a 'special relationship' with a policyholder may also have heightened obligations to that policyholder, such as a duty to advise about the appropriateness of available coverage options (Richmond 2012; Jerry and Richmond 2007; Swift 1998; Sakall 2000). The definition of a 'special relationship' varies substantially by state, but it is usually limited to situations where intermediaries take on a broad advisory role on behalf of policyholders, such as when insurance is provided as part of a broader package of financial advice provided by the agent. It is also often linked, explicitly or implicitly, to whether the intermediary is principally acting as the legal agent for the insurer (i.e. an insurance agent) or the policyholder (i.e. an insurance broker). This distinction itself can turn on several factors, such as the intermediary's authority to act for the carrier and the intermediary's description of his or her role and responsibilities to clients.

These liability rules likely do little to constrain most forms of self-serving behavior by insurance agents. In large part, this is because the exceptions to the normally limited duties of agents are quite narrow, particularly for intermediaries operating in consumer-driven markets, who by convention are usually denominated 'agents' rather than 'brokers'. Additionally, these exceptions are notoriously blurry and overlapping, meaning that litigation seeking to enforce duties against agents is 'fact-driven and unpredictable' (Beh and Willis 2009). This uncertainty limits the capacity of risk-averse policyholders to pursue their grievances in court. A further limitation of these rules in constraining biased advice from insurance agents is that policyholders generally only sue when they have been denied coverage. In these cases, however, any agent wrongdoing that contributed to the lack of coverage is likely to be attributable to incompetence or ignorance rather than active consumer manipulation, as self-interested agents will generally have an incentive to sell more, rather than less, insurance.

To be sure, enhancing agents' duty to advise policyholders might well improve matters. Moreover, there are reasonably good arguments for such reforms. First, even assuming that individuals know more about their personal assets and risk preferences than agents – a claim which is hardly obvious (Cohen and Siegelman 2010) – agents are much better situated than consumers to appreciate the insurance implications of these facts. Such insurance know-how cannot be easily transmitted to consumers; it requires training and experience. Insurance agents, on the other hand, can easily solicit information from policyholders about their assets, property, risks and risk tolerances in the course of recommending coverage options. Because agents are better able than individuals to avoid the risk of inappropriate selection of insurance coverage, placing this risk on them would help to reduce it more effectively than leaving it with individual consumers, as most jurisdictions do. Second, while increasing the legal obligations of agents would likely increase the costs of coverage, it would also provide policyholders with a form of insurance against the risk that they purchased inappropriate coverage. Given that purchasers of insurance are generally risk-averse, it seems likely that many would be willing to pay for this legally mandated protection, particularly because they cannot otherwise insure against this risk (Baker 2008).[17] By contrast, intermediaries can and do purchase E&O (errors and omissions) insurance, which spreads the risks they are legally obligated to bear. Thus, enhancing the ability of policyholders to sue agents for improper or inadequate advice would facilitate spreading of this risk via E&O insurance.

However, expanding the legal duties of agents is hardly a panacea. Most importantly, it is likely that courts would have difficulty reliably identifying improper or biased advice from agents. The quality of different insurance options is often subjective, depending on numerous factors such as price, claims service, coverage scope, financial security and risk-mitigation services. Moreover, the factual record concerning the communications between agents and customers at the time of sale may frequently be

---

[17] One company attempted to market a product that would fund coverage dispute litigation. But this product faces problems – most notably adverse selection and moral hazard – that seem to have limited its popularity.

unclear. Courts that were over-eager to find violations of agents' obligations to policyholders could well undermine efficient coverage exclusions and inefficiently raise the cost of coverage. Meanwhile, under-enforcement would do little to advance the policy goals discussed above, while increasing the costs and uncertainty of coverage litigation.

2. Disclosure of Conflicts of Interest to Policyholders

Most states do not require agents to affirmatively disclose to policyholders any conflicts of interest they may have stemming from differential commission rates. This is true in all states other than New York, although some states do require insurance *brokers* (defined as intermediaries who represent the policyholder in the placement of coverage or receive direct payment from them) to disclose potential conflicts of interest to policyholders (Fitzpatrick 2006). These rules mean that consumers often have little appreciation of how agents are compensated and the ways in which this compensation might generate conflicts of interest. Even when disclosures inform policyholders about the potential conflicts of interest facing insurance intermediaries, it is not clear that this limits the risk of biased advice. Disclosure-oriented approaches to similar regulatory problems have routinely failed in the past, for reasons that are linked to the nature of the underlying market failure; informing consumers that intermediaries may have a conflict of interest does little to empower consumers to respond to this risk (Schwarcz 2007). Moreover, empirical research suggests that disclosures of conflicts of interest can backfire, enhancing consumer trust of market intermediaries and increasing the willingness of intermediaries to act on their conflicts of interest (Lacko and Pappalardo 2004; Ben-Shahar and Schneider 2011; Cain et al. 2005).[18]

3. Suitability Requirements

For a variety of insurance products, regulatory rules require insurers and agents to have 'reasonable grounds' to believe that a product is 'suitable' for a consumer after having made a reasonable inquiry into the consumer's particular needs and circumstances. In the case of insurance products that

---

[18] Inderst and Ottaviani (2012a: 782) suggest that disclosure of commissions may undermine efficiency because it could have a disparate impact on the 'more cost-efficient firm and, thus, result[ ] in a reduction in this firm's market share'. At the same time, some recent research suggests that disclosures of conflicts of interest may be more effective when they clearly state that they are legally required (Taha and Petrocelli 2013).

are also regulated as securities – including variable annuities and variable life – these suitability rules are a matter of federal law, subject to newly revised Financial Industry Regulatory Authority (FINRA) rules.[19] States also frequently impose suitability requirements for these hybrid products. In recent years, some states have extended suitability rules to a number of non-security insurance products, including fixed annuities and long-term care insurance (NAIC 2010; NAIC 2008).

If enforced well, suitability rules can help to meaningfully mitigate the risk of incompetent and self-interested advice. Indeed, suitability rules are targeted at the risk that agents will undermine their clients' interests in order to generate commissions. They operate, moreover, not only on the level of individual agents – who face personal risks of fines and license suspension or revocation for selling unsuitable products – but also at the firm level. Insurers who sell products subject to suitability rules have developed extensive systems to review sales and ensure that they are suitable.

Despite their capacity to limit the risk of biased advice, suitability rules have three important limitations. First, and most obviously, they currently apply only to a narrow range of insurance products: no property/casualty insurance products are subject to suitability rules, nor are many life and annuity insurance products (unless they are simultaneously treated as securities). This limitation, of course, could easily be addressed by regulatory reform that expanded suitability rules to a broader set of insurance products. A second, and more intractable, limitation of suitability rules is that they only target the most egregious forms of misconduct. There is obviously a big gap between a product being 'suitable' and optimal. As such, suitability rules do nothing to ensure that agents will not steer policyholders to less desirable, albeit 'suitable' products, when doing so results in higher commission payments. Third, it is not clear that suitability rules are well enforced. State laws requiring insurance sales to be suitable cannot be enforced through a private cause of action in most states.[20] As a result, state regulators are the only enforcers of suitability regulations governing non-securities insurance policies. Whether such enforcement is effective is an unanswered question.

---

[19] FINRA Rule 211.

[20] While suitability violations can support a private cause of action under federal securities rules, these are generally resolved through arbitration by FINRA. Although Section 921 of Dodd–Frank allows the Securities Exchange Commission (SEC) to prohibit these mandatory arbitration provisions, the SEC has not yet acted on this authority.

4. Estoppel

Another potential legal constraint on agent misbehavior is the doctrine of estoppel. Estoppel applies when an agent makes a misrepresentation on which a policyholder relies to his or her detriment. In limited circumstances, courts will enforce the agent's coverage representation against the insurer. However, this rule is likely to do little to deter biased advice by agents. First, many states significantly limit the scope of estoppel by holding that it can only be used to negate coverage defenses (such as a claim that the policyholder intentionally caused the loss) or the failure of a condition (such as the condition that the policyholder report coverage promptly). The doctrine, on this view, cannot create additional coverage beyond that which is provided in the policy (Jerry and Richmond 2007). This restriction on the doctrine obviously limits the extent to which it targets agent misrepresentations of coverage. Second, even in states that allow for estoppel claims to increase the scope of coverage, the doctrine is subject to important limitations. Most importantly, it does not apply to material *omissions*, which are often much more important in mis-selling cases than misrepresentations. Finally, evidentiary problems are substantial in estoppel cases, which often turn on conflicting accounts of oral statements that were made many years before any dispute arose.

5. Licensing Requirements and Unfair Trade Practices

Every state requires individuals who sell insurance to acquire a license, though the types of licenses available as well as the requirements for obtaining a license vary by state (GAO 2009).[21] In general, individuals must pass an exam and background check to acquire a license.[22] The background check assesses whether the aspiring agent has, among other things, violated any insurance laws or regulations, intentionally misrepresented the content of an insurance policy or application, committed an insurance unfair trade practice or engaged in fraudulent, coercive or dishonest practices.[23] Agents can be fined or have their licenses suspended or revoked if they are found to have engaged in any of these practices.

---

[21] For the last decade, the NAIC has attempted to streamline and harmonize different states' producer licensing rules. At present, these rules continue to vary, but most states grant reciprocity to agents that have received a license under another state's process.

[22] Some states also require pre-licensing education, but this is not true of all states (NAIC 2008).

[23] Producer Licensing Model Act, adopted by substantial majority of states.

Recent evidence provides reason to be skeptical that licensing standards are an effective means for ensuring agent quality. Lex et al. (2014) examine whether new licensing rules for German insurance agents improved the matching of consumers with insurance policies. To measure the quality of agent advice, they focus on how likely an individual who purchased coverage through the agent is to cancel coverage, on the assumption that individuals who are poorly matched with coverage will be more likely to switch to a different policy in the next policy year. They find that, while the new rules substantially reduced the number of agents by causing part-time agents to drop out of the market, there was no meaningful difference in rates of policy cancellation between the customers of agents who dropped out of the market and those who did not.

Of course, agent licensing in Germany and the European Union operates differently than it does in the US, and it is certainly possible that it limits poor agent advice in the US more effectively than it does in Germany. But whether this is so depends crucially on how well these licensing rules are enforced, particularly with respect to the rules linked to unfair sales and trade practices. Available evidence suggests that state policing of insurance agents is highly variable by state. Several Government Accountability Office (GAO) reports have found that only some states conduct nationwide criminal background checks, and states vary significantly in their capacity to determine whether an applicant has been the subject of a regulatory action or complaint in another state (GAO 2009). Data regarding the frequency of actions against producers[24] similarly suggest substantial variability in state oversight of insurance agents.[25] On average, each year states take regulatory action against one out of approximately every 200 resident producers licensed in their state, with the majority of these actions being fines, followed by license revocations and denials. But as illustrated in Figure 2.1, these rates vary dramatically across states, with some states taking action against one out of every 100 or so agents each year, and others only taking action against approximately one out of every 1,000 agents each year.

[24] This includes suspensions, revocations, cease and desist orders, denial orders, fines, and restitutions.

[25] The figure is calculated from data in the 2011 NAIC Resources Report, which reports both the number of licensed resident producers per state and the number of actions against producers per state.

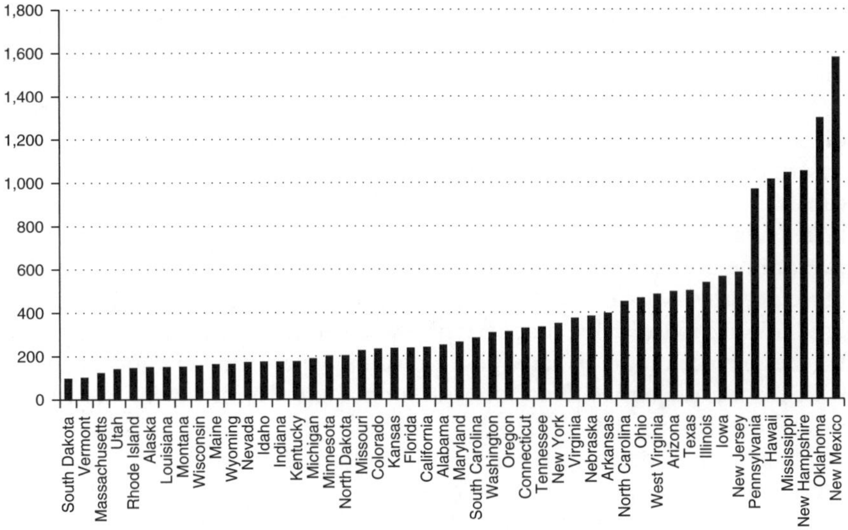

Note: Georgia and Delaware are omitted because of anomalies in their reported data. American Samoa, Guam, the Virgin Islands, Puerto Rico, DC and the Northern Mariana Islands are omitted for non-comparability.

Figure 2.1 Insurance agents per regulatory action, by state (2010)

PART IV: TOWARDS THE FUTURE: FACILITATING THE TECHNOLOGICAL REVOLUTION

Although legal and regulatory reforms designed to hold insurance agents more accountable might help limit the real – if hard to quantify – risk of biased advice, both the effectiveness and the efficiency of any such reforms are unclear. Meanwhile, insurance distribution platforms are rapidly evolving to embrace technology in ways that may increasingly threaten the viability of traditional insurance agents. Consider, for instance, that millions of individuals are now purchasing their health insurance online through state and federal health insurance exchanges. In the property/casualty insurance domain, insurance decision engines already provide policyholders with personalized advice about coverage limits and policy options based on consumers' answers to simple questions.[26] And in the life

[26] See, for example, www.esurance.com/coverage-counselor, which promises to 'find the car insurance that's right for you' after the user 'just answer[s] a

insurance sphere, search engines designed to facilitate comparison shopping of term life insurance have already revolutionized the market (Brown and Goolsbee 2002).

Indications are that these forces will only continue to limit the role of traditional insurance agents in distributing insurance products. As described above, carriers are increasingly finding that insurance agents can no longer provide useful front-line underwriting services, given the increasing data and technology that are at carriers' disposal. Meanwhile, fast online access via computers and smartphones is becoming more and more pervasive. As a recent McKinsey report explained: 'there has been a gradual shift in the value that carriers and customers (both retail and small business) place on many activities traditionally performed by local agents, which is increasingly calling into question what role they will play in the future' (McKinsey & Co. 2013).

These technological advances hold substantial promise to improve the insurance advice that individuals receive. Artificial intelligence can leverage data about consumer preferences to offer personalized advice to individuals that is more objective and consistent than the advice offered by individual agents. (Surprisingly, even simple algorithms often do better than 'experts' at making predictions across a wide variety of fields (Grove and Meehl 1996).) It can also be designed to facilitate consumer choice by setting intelligent defaults, limiting consideration sets, and providing calculation aids (Johnson et al. 2013). The continuing evolution of state and federal health insurance exchanges should provide a variety of real-world settings that will yield new insights into how best to present insurance information to consumers and facilitate consumer decision-making.

Additionally, the developers of technology-driven insurance intermediation may have relatively good incentives to design these systems to provide consumers with objective advice. The advice provided by technology-driven intermediation is much more transparent than the advice provided by individual insurance agents; it can be accessed by anyone, anywhere, at any time. This should improve the capacity of regulators to identify problematic advice and enforce existing laws when necessary. It may also allow analysts, consumers and watchdog groups to identify and publicize problems with specific intermediation systems and push consumers to competitors with superior intermediation services. Another significant

---

few simple questions'. For another example, see Picwell (http://picwell.net/), an application that optimally matches a consumer's prescription drug requirements with coverage provided by Medicare Part D insurers, saving an average of $365 per year.

difference between human and computer intermediation lies in the cost structure of each. Human intermediation entails some up-front costs in the form of investment in human capital (such as knowledge of various insurance products) by agents. But the majority of the costs are the time and effort incurred in serving each consumer. By contrast, a computerized intermediary has high sunk costs, but virtually no marginal costs of providing service; once the software is written, it can be made available at essentially no cost[27] to as many customers as want it (Shapiro and Varian 1999). This creates significant economies of scale – cost per user falls with the number of users – which in turn places a huge premium on the reputation and reliability of the intermediary.

Of course, technological innovation in insurance intermediation also creates new risks as well. For instance, technology may increase the ability of firms or individuals to target particularly vulnerable segments of the population for the sale of low-value or inappropriate insurance coverage. Moreover, new insurance distribution platforms can exploit individuals' personal data in ways that are difficult or impossible for conventional insurance intermediaries. For instance, many websites that purport to provide consumers with multiple premium quotations in fact operate as 'lead generators' for agents, who then use user's contact information to repeatedly attempt to sell them coverage.

Due both to its promise and its potential pitfalls, we believe that law and regulation can and should actively encourage the evolution of technology-driven insurance intermediation. First, insurance lawmakers and regulators should embrace 'smart disclosure' by making publicly available and accessible machine-readable data sets on insurance market information (Schwarcz 2014). This might include not only information about different carriers' products and prices, but also information relevant to assessing product quality – such as claims payment rates, rates of policy cancellation and non-renewal, and lapse rates. These types of data are the fuel that feeds technological innovation in market intermediation, allowing small start-ups with limited capital to develop tools for individuals to assess competing products and carriers based on more fine-tuned analysis of their insurance needs and preferences (Thaler and Tucker 2013; Forman and Gron 2011).

Second, insurance regulators should proactively monitor technology-driven insurance intermediation to ensure the accuracy of information provided to consumers and the appropriate use of consumer information.

---

27 The software would, of course, need to be updated as new products become available or new laws and regulations are passed.

Traditionally, insurance regulators have been largely reactive in identifying misconduct in the sale of insurance products, relying principally on consumer complaints to identify problems with particular agents. But technological innovation creates a variety of new opportunities for regulators to identify inaccurate or misleading sales tactics, including simple Google searches, experimentation with insurance apps and websites, and direct requests to the operators of these platforms to explain the algorithms and data that undergird these systems. Insurance regulators might even be able to monitor technology-driven insurance intermediation tools using social media.

Finally, law and regulation could facilitate the development of more effective technology-driven market intermediation by developing better information about the risks associated with the status quo. As described above, the available evidence about the extent of insurance agent misbehavior is remarkably under-developed, with the best evidence coming from analogous financial contexts and/or studies in other countries. Insurance regulators could develop much better information on this front by funding, or conducting on their own, the types of audit experiments that we described earlier. Regulators of health and safety routinely inspect restaurants for health and safety violations. It is not at all clear why such proactive regulatory scrutiny is not similarly appropriate in the insurance domain.

REFERENCES

Akerlof, George A. 1970. 'The Market for "Lemons": Quality Uncertainty and the Market Mechanism.' 84 *The Quarterly Journal of Economics* 488–500.

Anagol, Santosh, Shawn Cole and Shayak Sarkar. 2012. 'Understanding the Incentives of Commissions Motivated Agents: Theory and Evidence from the Indian Life Insurance Market.' Available at http://ssrn.com/abstract=1978876.

Anderson, Evan E. 1979. 'An Analysis of Retail Display Space: Theory and Methods.' 52 *The Journal of Business* 103–18.

Baker, Tom. 2008. *Insurance Law and Policy*. New York: Aspen Publishers.

Baker, Tom, and Peter Siegelman. 2013. 'You Want Insurance With That? Using Behavioral Economics to Protect Consumers from Add-On Insurance Products.' 20 *Connecticut Insurance Law Journal* 1–60.

Baker, Tom, and Peter Siegelman. 2014. 'Behavioral Economics and Insurance Law: The Importance of Equilibrium Analysis.' In Doron Teichman and Eyal Zamir, eds., *Oxford Handbook of Behavioral Economics and the Law*. Oxford: Oxford University Press.

Barrese, James, Helen I. Doerpinghaus and Jack M. Nelson. 1995. 'Do Independent Agent Insurers Provide Superior Service? The Insurance Marketing Puzzle.' 62 *Journal of Risk and Insurance* 297–308.

Beh, Hazel, and Amanda M. Willis. 2009. 'Insurance Intermediaries.' 15 *Connecticut Insurance Law Journal* 571–98.

Ben-Shahar, Omri, and Carl E. Schneider. 2011. 'The Failure of Mandated Disclosure.' 159 *University of Pennsylvania Law Review* 647–749.

Bergstresser, Daniel, John M. R. Chalmers and Peter Tufano. 2009. 'Assessing the Costs and Benefits of Brokers: A Preliminary Analysis of the Mutual Fund Industry.' 22 *Review of Financial Studies* 4129–56.

Bhattacharya, Utpal, Andreas Hackethal, Simon Kaesler, Benjamin Loos and Steffen Meyer. 2012. 'Is Unbiased Financial Advice to Retail Investors Sufficient? Answers from a Large Field Study.' 25 *Review of Financial Studies* 975–1032.

Bluethgen, Ralph, Steffen Meyer and Andreas Hackethal. 2008. 'High Quality Financial Advice Wanted!' Available at www.researchgate.net/publication/242076326_High-Quality_Financial_Advice_Wanted.

Bluethgen, Ralph, Andreas Gintschel, Andreas Hackethal and Armin Müller. 2008. 'Financial Advice and Individual Investors' Portfolios.' Available at http://papers.ssrn.com/sol3/papers.cfm?abstract_id=968197.

Boardman, Michelle. 2010. 'Insuring Understanding: The Tested Language Defense.' 95 *Iowa Law Review* 1075–124.

Brown, Jeffrey R., and Austan Goolsbee. 2002. 'Does the Internet Make Markets More Competitive: Evidence from the Life Insurance Industry.' 110 *Journal of Political Economy* 481–507.

Brown, Jennifer, and Dylan B. Minor. 2012. 'Misconduct in Credence Goods Markets.' NBER Working Paper 18608.

Browne, Mark J., Christian Knoller and Andreas Richter. 2012. 'Behavioral Bias, Market Intermediaries and the Demand for Bicycle and Flood Insurance.' Munich Risk and Insurance Center Working Paper.

Cain, Daylian M., George Loewenstein, and Don A. Moore. 2005. 'The Dirt on Coming Clean: Perverse Effects of Disclosing Conflicts of Interest.' 34 *The Journal of Legal Studies* 1–25.

Carlin, Bruce I. 2009. 'Strategic Price Complexity in Retail Financial Markets.' 91 *Journal of Financial Economics* 278–87.

Chalmers, John, and Jonathan Reuter. 2012. 'What is the Impact of Financial Advice on Retirement Portfolio Choice and Outcomes?' NEBR Working Paper 18158.

Chan, Thomas S. F. 1999. 'Service Quality and Unfair Racial Discrimination in Homeowners Insurance.' 66 *Journal of Risk and Insurance* 83–97.

Cohen, Alma, and Peter Siegelman. 2010. 'Testing for Adverse Selection in Insurance Markets.' 77 *Journal of Risk and Insurance* 39–84.

Cooper, Robert W., and Garry L. Frank. 2002. 'Ethical Challenges in the Two Main Segments of the Insurance Industry: Key Considerations in the Evolving Financial Services Marketplace.' 36 *Journal of Business Ethics* 5–20.

Cummins, J. David, and Neal A. Doherty. 2006. 'The Economics of Insurance Intermediaries.' 73 *Journal of Risk and Insurance* 359–96.

Cupach, William R., and James M. Carson. 2002. 'The Influence of Compensation on Product Recommendations Made by Insurance Agents.' 40 *Journal of Business Ethics* 167–76.

Cutler, David M., and Richard A. Zeckhauser. 2004. 'Extending the Theory to Meet the Practice of Insurance.' In Robert Litan and Richard Herring, eds., *Brookings-Wharton Papers on Financial Services*.

Darby, Michael R., and Edi Karni, 1973. 'Free Competition and the Optimal Amount of Fraud.' 16 *Journal of Law and Economics* 67–88.

Eckardt, Martina. 2007. *Insurance Intermediation: An Economic Analysis of the Information Services Market*. Heidelberg: Physica Verlag.

Eckardt, Martina, and Solvig Räthke-Döppner. 2010. 'The Quality of Insurance Intermediary Services – Empirical Evidence For Germany.' 77 *Journal of Risk and Insurance* 667–701.

Fischel, Daniel R., and Robert S. Stillman. 1997. 'The Law and Economics of Vanishing Premiums Life Insurance.' 22 *Delaware Journal of Corporate Law* 1–36.

Fitzpatrick, Sean M. 2006. 'The Small Laws: Eliot Spitzer and the Way to Insurance Market Reform.' 74 *Fordham Law Review* 3041–71.

Focht, Uwe, Andreas Richter and Jörg Schiller. 2013. 'Intermediation and (Mis-) Matching in Insurance Markets: Who Should Pay the Insurance Broker?' 80 *Journal of Risk and Insurance* 329–50.

Fong, Yuk-fai. 2005. 'When Do Experts Cheat and Whom Do They Target?' 36 *The RAND Journal of Economics* 113–30.

Forman, Chris, and Anne Gron. 2011. 'Vertical Integration and Information Technology Investment in the Insurance Industry.' 27 *Journal of Law, Economics and Organization* 180–218.

Gabaix, Xavier, and David Laibson. 2006. 'Shrouded Attributes, Consumer Myopia, and Information Suppression in Competitive Markets.' 121 *Quarterly Journal of Economics* 505–40.

Garnick, Deborah W., Katherine Swartz and Kathleen Carley Skwara. 1998. 'Insurance Agents: Ignored Players in Health Insurance Reform.' 17(2) *Health Affairs* 137–43.

Government Accountability Office (GAO). 2009. 'NAIC and State Regulators Have Made Progress in Producer Licensing, Product Approval, and Market Conduct Regulation, but Challenges Remain.'

Gravelle, Hugh. 1994. 'Remunerating Information Providers: Commissions Versus Fees in Life Insurance.' 61 *Journal of Risk and Insurance* 425–57.

Grove, William M., and Paul E. Meehl. 1996. 'Comparative Efficiency of Informal (Subjective, Impressionistic) and Formal (Mechanical, Algorithmic) Prediction Procedures: The Clinical–Statistical Controversy.' 2 *Psychology, Public Policy and Law* 293–323.

Hackethal, Andreas, Michael Haliassos and Tullio Jappelli. 2012. 'Financial Advisors: A Case of Babysitters?' 36 *Journal of Banking and Finance* 509–24.

Haron, Hasnah, Ishak Ismail and Shaikh Hamzah Abdul Razak. 2011. 'Factors Influencing Unethical Behaviour of Insurance Agents.' 2(1) *International Journal of Business and Social Science* 84–100.

Heckman, James J., and Peter Siegelman. 1993. 'The Urban Institute Audit Studies: Their Methods and Findings.' In Michael Fix and Raymond Struyk, eds., *Clear and Convincing Evidence: Measurement of Discrimination in America*. Washington: Urban Institute Press.

Hofmann, Annette, and Martin Nell. 2011. 'Information Cost, Broker Compensation and Collusion in Insurance Markets.' 63 *Schmalenbach Business Review* 287–307.

Hsieh, Shu-Hui, Chun-Ting Liu, and Larry Y. Tzeng. 2013. 'Insurance Marketing Channel as a Screening Mechanism: Empirical Evidences from Taiwan Automobile Insurance Market.' 39 *Geneva Papers on Risk and Insurance Issues and Practice* 90–103.

Inderst, Roman, and Marco Ottaviani. 2012a. 'Competition through Commissions and Kickbacks.' 102 *American Economic Review* 780–809.

Inderst, Roman, and Marco Ottaviani. 2012b. 'Financial Advice.' 50 *Journal of Economic Literature* 494–512.

Jerry, Robert H. II, and Douglas S. Richmond. 2007. *Understanding Insurance Law*. New Providence: LexisNexis.

Johnson, Eric, John C. Hershey, Jacqueline Meszaros and Howard C. Kunreuther. 1993. 'Framing, Probability Distortions and Insurance Decisions.' 7 *Journal of Risk and Uncertainty* 35–51.

Johnson, Eric J., Ran Hassin, Tom Baker, Allison T. Bajger and Galen Treuer. 2013. 'Can Consumers Make Affordable Care Affordable? The Value of Choice Architecture.' University of Pennyslvania Institute for Law and Economics Research Paper 13-28. Available at www.russellsage.org/sites/all/files/Johnson_CanConsumers.pdf.

Ju, Lan, and Zhiyong Tu. 2011. '"Buffering" Effect of Insurance Intermediaries: Does the Use of Contingent Commissions Dampen the Insurance Underwriting Cycle?' Mimeo.

Kang, Han B. 2011. 'An Empirical Analysis of the Service Quality in the Automobile Insurance: A Log-Linear Model.' 1(7) *Journal of Business and Economic Research* 47–51.

Karaca-Mandic, Pinar, Roger Feldman and Peter Graven. 2013. 'The Role of Agents and Brokers in the Market for Health Insurance.' NBER Working Paper 19342.

Kim, Won-Joong, David Mayers and Clifford W. Smith, Jr. 1996. 'On the Choice of Insurance Distribution Systems.' 63 *Journal of Risk and Insurance* 207–27.
Kochenburger, Peter, Richean Zhiyan Li and Pierpaolo Marano. 2010. 'Conflict of Interest of Insurance Brokers.' 1 *European Insurance Law Review* 21–32.
Kolodinsky, Jane. 1995. 'Usefulness of Economics in Explaining Consumer Complaints.' 29 *Journal of Consumer Affairs* 29–54.
Kramer, Marc M. 2012. 'Financial Advice and Individual Investor Portfolio Performance.' *The Free Library*. Available at www.thefreelibrary.com/Financial advice and individual investor portfolio performance.-a0295777024.
Kunreuther, Howard C., Mark V. Pauly and Stacey McMorrow. 2013. *Insurance and Behavioral Economics: Improving Decisions in the Most Misunderstood Industry*. New York: Cambridge University Press.
Lacko, James M., and Janis K. Pappalardo. 2004. 'The Effect of Mortgage Broker Compensation Disclosures on Consumers and Competition: A Controlled Experiment.' Federal Trade Commission. Available at www.ftc.gov/reports/effect-mortgage-broker-compensation-disclosures-consumers-competition-controlled-experiment.
Levitt, Steven D., and John A. List. 2007. 'What Do Laboratory Experiments Measuring Social Preferences Reveal about the Real World?' 21(2) *Journal of Economic Perspectives* 153–74.
Levitt, Steven, and Chad Syverson. 2008. 'Market Distortions When Agents are Better Informed: The Value of Information in Real Estate Transactions.' 90 *Review of Economics and Statistics* 599–611.
Lex, Christoph, Andreas Richter and Sharon Tennyson. 2014. EU Intermediary Regulation and its Impact on Agent Quality. Available at http://publicchoicesociety.org/content/papers/sharontennyson-1013-2014-1014.pdf.
Logue, Kyle. 2001. 'The Current Life Insurance Crisis: How the Law Should Respond.' 32 *Cumberland Law Review* 1–67.
Ma, Yu-Luen, Nat Pope and Xiaoying Xie. 2014. 'Contingent Commissions, Insurance Intermediaries, and Insurer Performance.' 17 *Risk Management and Insurance Review* 61–81.
Maas, Peter. 2010. 'How Insurance Brokers Create Value – A Functional Approach.' 13 *Risk Management and Insurance Review* 1–20.
McKinsey & Co. 2013. 'Agents of the Future: The Evolution of the Property Casualty Distribution System.' 1–21. Available at www.mckinsey.com/~/media/mckinsey/dotcom/client_service/financial%20services/latest%20thinking/insurance/agents_of_the_future_the_evolution_of_property_and_casualty_insurance_distribution.ashx.
Mullainathan, Sendhil, Markus Noeth and Antoinette Schoar. 2012. 'The Market for Financial Advice: An Audit Study.' NBER working paper 17929.
National Association of Insurance Commissioners (NAIC). 2008. 'Revisions and Clarifications to the Uniform Licensing Standards.' Available at www.naic.org/documents/committees_ex_pltf_producer_licensing_ul_standards_revised.pdf.
National Association of Insurance Commissioners (NAIC). 2010. 'Suitability in Annuity Transactions Model Regulation.' Available at www.naic.org/store/free/MDL-275.pdf.
New York State Insurance Department. 2011. Part 30 to Title 11 of the Official Compilation of Codes, Rules, and Regulations of the State of New York (Regulation No. 194).
Pandya, Sachin S., and Peter Siegelman. 2013. 'Underclaiming and Overclaiming.' 38 *Law & Social Inquiry* 836–62.
Regan, Laureen, and Anne Kleffner. 2010. 'The Role of Contingent Commissions in Property-Liability Insurer Underwriting Performance.' Available at www.aria.org/rts/proceedings/2010/Compensation_Regan.pdf.
Regan, Laureen, and Sharon Tennyson. 1996. 'Agent Discretion and the Choice of Insurance Marketing System.' 39 *Journal of Law and Economics* 637–66.
Regan, Laureen, and Sharon Tennyson. 2000. 'Insurance Distribution Systems.' In Georges Dionne, ed., *The Handbook of Insurance*. Norwell: Kluwer Academic.

Richmond, Douglas R. 2012. *New Appleman on Insurance Law Library Edition*. New Providence: LexisNexis, Volume 1, Chapter 2: Agents and Brokers.
Román, Sergio, and José Luis Munuera. 2005. 'Determinants and Consequences of Ethical Behaviour: An Empirical Study of Salespeople.' 39 *European Journal of Marketing* 473–95.
Rothschild, Michael, and Joseph Stiglitz. 1976. 'Competitive Insurance Markets: An Essay on the Economics of Imperfect Information.' 90 *Quarterly Journal of Economics* 629–49.
Sakall, Daniel G. 2000. 'Can the Public Really Count on Insurance Agents to Advise Them? A Critique of the "Special Circumstances" Test.' 42 *Arizona Law Review* 991–1015.
Schwarcz, Daniel. 2007. 'Beyond Disclosure: The Case for Banning Contingent Commissions.' 25 *Yale Law and Policy Review* 289–336.
Schwarcz, Daniel. 2008. 'Redesigning Consumer Dispute Resolution: A Case Study of the British and American Approaches to Insurance Claims Conflict.' 83 *Tulane Law Review* 735–812.
Schwarcz, Daniel. 2010. 'Regulating Insurance Sales or Selling Insurance Regulation?: Against Regulatory Competition in Insurance.' 94 *Minnesota Law Review* 1707–88.
Schwarcz, Daniel. 2011. 'Reevaluating Standardized Insurance Policies.' 77 *University of Chicago Law Review* 1263–348.
Schwarcz, Daniel. 2014. 'Transparently Opaque: Understanding the Lack of Transparency in Insurance Consumer Protection.' 61 *UCLA Law Review* 394–462.
Shapiro, Carl, and Hal R. Varian. 1999. *Information Rules: A Strategic Guide to the Network Economy*. Cambridge: Harvard Business Review Press.
Spulber, Daniel F. 1996. 'Market Microstructure and Intermediation.' 10(3) *Journal of Economic Perspectives* 135–52.
Swift, Ken. 1998. 'How Special Is Special? An Insurance Agent's Duty to Advise.' 21 *Hamline Law Review* 323–35.
Sydnor, Justin. 2010. '(Over)insuring Modest Risks.' 2 *American Economic Journal: Applied Economics* 177–99.
Taha, Ahmed, and John V. Petrocelli. 2013. 'Disclosures about Disclosures: Can Conflict of Interest Warnings Be Made More Effective?' Available at http://ssrn.com/abstract=2284212.
Texas Department of Insurance. 2010–14. 'Internet Complaints Information System.' Available at www.tdi.texas.gov/consumer/icis/index.html.
Thaler, Richard H., and Will Tucker. 2013. 'Smarter Information, Smarter Consumers.' *Harvard Business Review*, Jan–Feb. 3–11.
Venezia, Itzhak, Dan Galai, and Zur Shapira. 1999. 'Exclusive vs. Independent Agents: A Separating Equilibrium Approach.' 40 *Journal of Economic Behavior and Organization* 443–56.
Venezian, Emilio. 2002. 'Complaints Ratios: What (or Where) is the Beef?' 20(4) *Journal of Insurance Regulation* 19–46.
Wilder, Jeffrey M. 2004. 'Competing for the Effort of a Common Agent: Contingency Fees in Commercial Insurance.' U.S. Department of Justice, Antitrust Division Working Paper No. EAG03-4. Available at http://ssrn.com/abstract=418061.

3. Moral and other hazards of economic analysis of health insurance

John A. Nyman

CONVENTIONAL THEORY OF MORAL HAZARD

Perhaps no single concept has influenced economists' perspective on the desirability of health insurance in the United States as much as 'moral hazard.' Moral hazard was a term coined by insurers to represent the increase in losses that occurred once something or someone (a cargo ship, an automobile, a house, a life, health, and so on) became insured. As its name suggests, moral hazard was viewed originally as an ethical issue by insurers, but economists transformed it into a scientific term that simply described a type of human behavior that was derived from self-interest. For economists, moral hazard has traditionally referred to any increase in the loss or payout from the insurer that is caused by becoming insured. If the increased loss is manifested as an increase in the probability of a loss occurring, then it is referred to as *ex ante* moral hazard. If the increased loss is manifested by an increase in the amount of the loss once the event has occurred, then it is referred to as *ex post* moral hazard. In the United States, it is the concept of *ex post* moral hazard that has dominated policy related to health insurance. Thus, the fear associated with moral hazard is not whether the presence of insurance will cause people to take less care to prevent illness, but that it will lead to more use of healthcare for a given level of illness – more frequent doctor visits, an additional hospitalization, and so on.

As a health policy issue, the concept of moral hazard debuted in 1968 with a famous 'Comment' by Mark Pauly that appeared in the *American Economic Review* (Pauly 1968). Pauly's paper was in response to an earlier, and even more famous, article in the same journal on the benefits of health insurance by subsequent Nobel laureate Kenneth Arrow (Arrow 1963). Arrow had taken the conventional model of the demand for insurance presented in 1948 by Milton Friedman and L. J. Savage and applied it to evaluate the desirability of *health* insurance (Friedman and Savage 1948). Arrow concluded that if consumers (1) maximize their expected utility ('utility' is a measure of the consumer's satisfaction, a concept that, in the conventional model, is derived solely from income that is spent on goods and services other than healthcare); (2) are averse to risk (that is, they prefer certainty to uncertainty, and this preference is manifested by utility, as a function of income, increasing with income at a decreasing rate); and (3) face an actuarially fair insurance premium (with actuarially fair insurance, the premium consists only of the amount that the insurer is expected to pay out to cover the expenses of the insured, and not any additional amounts to cover administrative costs, such as agent fees or claims processing, or profits), then the case in favor of insurance is 'overwhelming' (Arrow 1963). While it can never be known whether a connection to Arrow's article existed, only two years after the publication of Arrow's paper, the major health insurance programs of the twentieth century in America, Medicare and Medicaid, were enacted.

In his 1968 response, however, Pauly took issue with the view that health insurance always increased welfare, suggesting that Arrow had not taken into account the fact that insurance acts to distort the market by artificially lowering the insurance price of medical care – the coinsurance rate – to the consumer. As a result, insured consumers purchase more healthcare and cause the insurer to pay out more for healthcare. Indeed, as consumers purchase more complete coverage – that is, coverage with increasingly lower coinsurance rates – the size of the payout increases. This is the moral hazard 'problem' that has become the central issue of health insurance. According to Pauly's model, the increases in spending due to lower coinsurance rates are inefficient because the cost of producing the care has not changed, even though its price to the 'consumer' has fallen. The insurer is still paying for the entire cost of producing that care. It is inefficient, according to Pauly, because if the insured consumer actually had to pay the full cost of care, he or she would never have purchased this additional healthcare. It is simply not worth it. Thus, moral hazard has created an inefficiency or loss of welfare because the value of the additional healthcare consumed with insurance is worth less than the cost of producing it.

Pauly's argument can best be summarized by reference to what may be the most famous diagram in health economics. In Figure 3.1, the vertical axis represents the price, P, of healthcare – the price has the dimensions of a number of dollars per unit of healthcare – and the horizontal axis represents the number of units, M, of healthcare that are consumed. (A unit of healthcare is a concept that does not really exist in real life, but it is useful for economists to think of it as if it does.) The demand curve for healthcare is the downward sloping curve, D, showing the various units of healthcare consumed as the price to the consumer changes.

Pauly assumed that each unit of healthcare costs the same amount, C, to produce. As a result, the costs of the units of healthcare can be represented

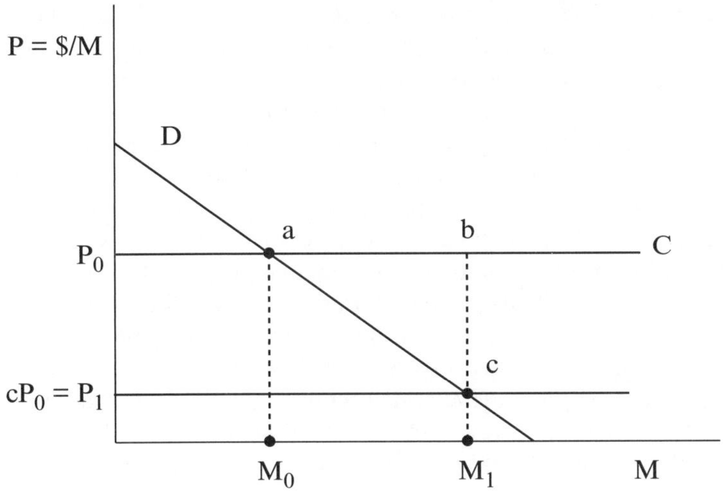

Figure 3.1 *Pauly's moral hazard welfare loss*

as a horizontal curve across all levels of M. If the price were originally set at the cost of producing the care, that is, if $P_0 = C$, then M_0 units of healthcare would be purchased by the uninsured consumer. If instead the consumer were insured and faced a lower price of care because he or she only had to pay the coinsurance rate, c, for a unit of healthcare, then the *effective* price faced by the consumer is $cP_0 = P_1$ and the consumer consumes M_1 units of healthcare. Moral hazard is represented by the difference between these two amounts, $M_1 - M_0$. Thus, as Pauly noted, moral hazard has nothing to do with ethics or morality; it is simply a response to a price change, something that consumers do all the time.

The inefficiency with moral hazard, according to Pauly, was that people were consuming additional healthcare, and this healthcare was worth less to them than it cost to produce. To see this, it is first necessary to find the value of the healthcare to the consumer. The demand curve is usually 'read' from left to right, but it can also be read right to left to show value. That is, instead of picking a price and finding how many units of healthcare would be demanded, one can instead pick a unit of healthcare (on the horizontal axis) and read off of the demand curve what is the most that the consumer is willing to pay (on the vertical axis), a measure of the value of that unit. Thus, the value of the M_0 unit is P_0. The next unit after M_0 would be worth a little less, as represented by the demand curve, and the last additional unit consumed by the insured person, M_1, would be worth exactly P_1. The value of all the additional units of healthcare could be represented by the area under the demand curve, area acM_1M_0. The cost of producing the additional care is found by recognizing that each unit costs C to produce so the total cost of the additional healthcare is represented by the area under the cost curve, or abM_1M_0. The cost of producing the moral hazard exceeds the value of moral hazard to the consumer by area abc, which is a measure in dollars of the inefficiency or the welfare loss from moral hazard. Pauly thought that, if this moral hazard welfare loss were great enough, it might mean that, contrary to Arrow's conclusion, the value of insurance 'could well be negative' (Pauly 1968: 534).

So, according to Pauly, when insurers determine their premiums, they must take into account these additional costs of this low-value care that people consume only when insured – the moral hazard. For consumers, this means that the actuarially fair premium – reflecting what the insurer expects to pay for the care – exceeds the value of what they expect to purchase if they were to become ill. And, were it not for the fact that health insurance premiums are purchased with pre-income-tax income in the United States, and as a result are subsidized by the federal government, insurance would be so overpriced because of the moral hazard premium that people would find it not worth buying. According to the conventional view, it is only because of this subsidy that the premiums are reduced sufficiently to make health insurance worthwhile to purchase.

Pauly's model was accepted by almost all American economists as reflecting one component of the welfare effect of insurance (Feldman and Morrisey 1990). Thus, the conventional theory taught in health economics classes held that people desired insurance in order to obtain a welfare gain from the avoidance of the risk of a large healthcare expenditure (according to Friedman and Savage's classic model), but that the moral hazard from health insurance generated a welfare loss that must be subtracted from the risk avoidance gain. A number of economists used this theory to calculate the net gain from health insurance at the prevailing coverage levels and to determine the coinsurance rate that would be necessary for health insurance to increase welfare, rather than decrease it. In one particularly influential study, Martin Feldstein found that health insurance at its current coverage levels in the late 1960s produced a 'very substantial welfare loss' and that raising the coinsurance rate from its present level to at least 67 percent – that is, for every $100 of spending, only $33 should be covered by the insurer and the rest, $67, by the consumer who becomes ill, regardless of the amount of spending – would increase net welfare (Feldstein 1973). The conventional model held that the problem with health insurance was to find the right trade-off between the avoidance of risk and having coinsurance rates that do not distort behavior too much (Zeckhauser 1970).

In the 1970s, a group of researchers from RAND Corporation led by

Joseph Newhouse convinced the federal government to fund a social experiment in order to understand better the effect of cost-sharing on consumption of healthcare, and on health. The resulting RAND Health Insurance Experiment was the largest and most expensive social experiment ever conducted in the United States (Newhouse et al. 1993). The scientific impetus for the experiment was that no one really knew how consumers would respond to changes in cost-sharing – applying coinsurance rates and deductibles of different amounts (Manning et al. 1987). Studies had been conducted using data derived from simply recording the amount of healthcare that was consumed by consumers facing different coinsurance rates. For example, uninsured consumers face high coinsurance rates, since they pay 100 percent of the cost of care, and consume a certain amount of care. Insured consumers face lower coinsurance rates, and consume more care. Simply comparing the amount of healthcare purchased by consumers facing various coinsurance rates was a standard way in early studies to determine how the coinsurance rate influences the quantity of healthcare consumers choose to purchase. But the early studies based on this observational data were biased by self-selection. That is, economists would have liked to know how much more healthcare consumers would purchase if they were assigned a lower coinsurance rate at random; but the observational data generated information on the expenditures of consumers *who chose to purchase health insurance with a lower coinsurance rate*. Consumers desire to purchase insurance when they are ill, especially insurance with low cost-sharing provisions, and the ill are more likely to consume additional healthcare. So, if observational data were used, the analysis would show a stronger relationship than is warranted between low coinsurance rates and spending merely because the ill are more likely to be both insured and consume more healthcare.

The RAND Health Insurance Experiment avoided this issue by assigning participants to different cost-sharing and deductible groups at random. The findings of the RAND Experiment confirmed what the earlier studies had shown, but put a finer point on the estimates. Those who were provided care free of any charges consumed more care than those who had to pay a coinsurance rate. Comparing free care to those who faced a coinsurance rate of 95 percent (until $1,000 in out-of-pocket expenses were incurred and then any additional care was free), those with free care had 67 percent more face-to-face visits, 45 percent more total expenditures, and 29 percent more hospital admissions (Newhouse et al. 1993). But, even more important, the additional healthcare consumed by those with free care generated no important increases in actual *health* compared to those with cost-sharing. Of the battery of tests given to RAND participants, only corrected vision and blood pressure improved for those with free care, and the blood pressure improvement was of questionable statistical significance. While the RAND evidence also suggested that the poor and ill seemed to be hurt disproportionately by cost-sharing, the message that received most of the attention in health policy circles was the overall lack of a health effect (Hoffman 2006).

The empirical results from the RAND Experiment fit the conventional theory like a hand in a glove. Spending increased dramatically for those who were randomized into the free care arm, but there were no important increases in health as a result. This matched exactly the theoretical view that the additional healthcare consumed by those who were insured was not worth the cost of producing that care, and provided a confirmatory check on the theory.

It would be difficult to overstate the influence of the RAND Health Insurance Experiment on the thinking of economists and other policy-makers. Because it was a randomized experimental trial, it provided what was generally regarded as the gold standard estimates of the effect of coinsurance rates on healthcare consumption. The findings dominated the field of health economics during the remaining years of the twentieth century and into the early years of the twenty-first. Many dissertations were written using the data from the Experiment and the editor of the flagship journal in the field, the *Journal of Health Economics*, had been the lead economist on the project. It is not surprising that US health policy during this period reflected the influence of Pauly and Feldstein, and the findings of the RAND Health Insurance Experiment, as is discussed in the next section.

POLICY FROM CONVENTIONAL THEORY

A number of policy positions flowed from conventional theory of moral hazard. Here are some of the most important ones.

As mentioned above, one of the major policy implications of the conventional theory of moral hazard is that consumers are purchasing too much coverage because health insurance has been subsidized by permitting premiums for health insurance obtained through an employer to be paid for with pre-income-tax income. For example, if the employee's marginal tax rate were 15 percent, health insurance premiums would be cheaper by 15 percent than anything else the person would purchase with after-tax income. A number of economists called for the elimination of this tax subsidy using the moral-hazard-related argument that too much coverage was being purchased (e.g. Feldstein and Friedman 1977). In addition, there was also an equity argument against the subsidy. The income tax was (intended to be) progressive. But a progressive tax necessarily generates a regressive tax *subsidy* because those earning the most derive the greatest tax reduction from the exemption.

A second important implication of the conventional view of moral hazard was that health insurance was no longer regarded as a solution, but as more of a problem in its own right (Gladwell 2005). The empirical work by health economists during this period pointed to the inefficiency and welfare losses caused by health insurance, rather than the welfare gains. Indeed, during this period, no papers were written by health economists documenting the gains from insuring the uninsured, nor were there any calls to do so based on a rigorous economic analysis. Whether this lack of scientific support had an effect on actual policy, however, is not known.

A third policy implication was that cost-sharing could be imposed with no important effects on health. While insurers and employers were well aware of the issue of moral hazard and were already in the process of replacing the limited, but first dollar, coverage of Blue Cross and Blue Shield contracts with the unlimited coverage with cost-sharing of the 'major medical' policies sold by private insurance companies, the theory provided additional impetus to increase coinsurance rates and apply deductibles (Hoffman 2006). In the 1990s, health savings accounts coupled with high deductible insurance policies – what has become known as 'consumer-driven healthcare' – were promoted by some economists as a policy solution to the moral hazard problem because large deductibles put more of the patient's 'skin in the game' (Bloche 2006), thereby reducing consumers' incentives to 'over-use' healthcare.

Finally, increases in cost-sharing were seen not only as a solution to the inefficiency of moral hazard, but also as a solution to the general increase in healthcare costs occurring in the United States over time. As the healthcare sector of the economy claimed an increasingly greater portion of national economic output, health economists' preoccupation with moral hazard meant that their policy recommendations focused on reducing the quantity of healthcare consumed. With a few exceptions, there was little recognition that national health expenditures were determined by both healthcare price levels and the quantities purchased, and that prices were being set at inefficiently high levels in the healthcare sector by providers who possessed a substantial degree of monopoly pricing power. Indeed, the preoccupation with moral hazard as a source of welfare loss led to a perception that high prices were beneficial because they made cost-sharing more effective: a 20 percent coinsurance rate would reduce more office visits when the price of an office visit is set at \$200 than at \$100 (Crew 1969; Pauly 1995).

As a result, most cost-reducing policy recommendations during the latter part of the twentieth century were directed at reducing the quantity of healthcare consumed. The major health policy initiative of the 1980s, managed care, represented essentially a supply-side attempt to reduce quantity by utilization review, selection of low-prescribing providers for insurance networks, and capitated payments to providers. Indeed, one of the most revealing studies in this regard showed the obvious surprise that the authors felt when they discovered that managed care actually worked (lowered costs) by reducing the prices paid to providers, rather than reducing the quantity of care provided to patients, as was the original intent of managed care (and health maintenance) organizations (Cutler et al. 2000).

ISSUES WITH CONVENTIONAL THEORY

A number of 'anomalies' (Kuhn 1962) to the conventional theory have been recognized (Nyman 2003). The importance of these anomalies is that, viewed altogether, they suggest that the conventional theory is fundamentally flawed, and that a different theory of both the demand for health insurance and moral hazard is needed in order to explain why consumers benefit from purchasing health insurance.

First, the gain from health insurance in conventional theory was based on the assumption that, because of the concave shape of utility as a function of income, consumers prefer a certain loss (paying a premium every year) to an uncertain one of the same expected magnitude (paying a larger but actuarially equivalent medical bill in the event of illness) (Friedman and Savage 1948). In the 1970s, however, Daniel Kahneman and Amos Tversky began a series of experiments that showed, time after time, just the opposite: consumers preferred an uncertain financial loss to a certain one of the same expected magnitude (Kahneman and Tversky 1979; Tversky and Kahneman 1988). Thus, the fundamental nature of the gain from insurance (that had been the basis of Feldstein's study and other studies calculating the gain from insurance) was called into question.

Second, the conventional theory focused entirely on the financial loss associated with contracting a disease. According to this theory, the payment of a large medical bill was viewed in the same way as the financial loss associated with a house burning to the ground. There was no recognition that, in contrast to the loss of a house to fire, the payment of a medical bill was one side of a quid pro quo transaction. In return for the payment, the individual would receive medical care, and the medical care received could be very valuable to the ill consumer. Thus, an important welfare gain and source of value appeared to be missing from the conventional theory.

Third, the presumption that consumers preferred a certain loss to an uncertain loss of the same expected magnitude implied that consumers could always afford to pay for the required healthcare (the uncertain loss) in the event of illness. However, many types of procedures (as well as the routine healthcare required to care for those with chronic diseases) have costs that far exceed the incomes and assets of many of those who become ill. For example, most consumers could not afford to purchase a $300,000 liver transplant out of their own resources if their liver failed. But, if the chance of a liver failure was only 1 in 75,000 annually, actuarially fair insurance coverage could be obtained for only $4 annually, a more affordable amount. Thus, for many consumers, the needed healthcare would be accessible only through insurance, and not otherwise. This meant that, not only did Friedman and Savage's standard model simply not apply to some expensive care because it was unaffordable without insurance, but also a portion of Pauly's moral hazard was represented by care – the expensive, but standard care for those with severe diseases – that would otherwise be beyond the resources of many of the ill.

Fourth, a number of post-RAND empirical studies showed that the additional healthcare from health insurance generates health gains that appear to be substantial, and some even well worth the cost of producing them (this literature is reviewed by Hadley 2003). For example, researchers found patients who suffered from myocardial infarctions and who had insurance received more care and were less likely to die than those without insurance (Young and Cohen 1991). In a review of those studies that adequately dealt with selection issues, Joseph Freeman and his colleagues found that all of the studies showed substantial health effects generated by health insurance, especially those that studied the effect of insurance on the poor and the ill (Freeman et al. 2008). Therefore, in contrast to the RAND Experiment's conclusions that insurance generated no important health effects, these studies showed that insurance did improve the health of those who had it. Moreover, there were at least some cases where the additional medical treatment made possible by insurance coverage generated increases in health that were worth more than the cost of producing the care. This is in contrast to the conventional theory, which simply assumed that *all additional healthcare* generated by insurance was not worth the cost.

These anomalies in the conventional theory were not generally recognized as such at the time. And in fact, in 1983, Pauly provided a little-noticed refinement of his theory, suggesting that the moral hazard welfare loss applied only to a much more limited set of healthcare interventions (he suggested routine physician care, prescriptions, dental care, and the like) than most economists had assumed. Furthermore, Pauly wrote:

> [T]he relevant theory, empirical evidence, and policy analysis for moral hazard in the case of serious illness has not been developed. This is one of the most serious omissions in the current literature . . . (Pauly 1983: 83)

Despite these cautionary comments from an influential economist, researchers continued to use the conventional model and to press for increases in cost-sharing provisions in order to reduce moral hazard of any clinical type. For example, in 1996 and using RAND data, Willard Manning and Susan Marquis concluded that the coinsurance rate should be raised to about 45 percent for all types of care, across the board and with no maximum on the level of out-of-payment payments, in order to reduce moral hazard and maximize net welfare from health insurance (Manning and Marquis 1996).

In addition, a flaw in the RAND Health Insurance Experiment received late recognition (Nyman 2007; 2008). Specifically, those in the cost-sharing arms dropped out of the Experiment at a rate that was 16 times greater than those in the free-fee-for-service arm. Even though this represented the most dramatic behavioral change caused by cost-sharing in the entire experiment, it was not acknowledged as a potential source of bias nor was it ever explained by the RAND researchers. The best explanation for this behavior was that those in the cost-sharing arms left the experiment when they became ill, in order to revert back to their pre-RAND insurance policies and avoid incurring the RAND cost-sharing payments (Nyman 2007). Thus, the RAND Experiment eliminated a bias due to the selection of the ill into better coverage when choosing a health insurance policy, but substituted instead a bias due to selection of the ill away from worse coverage at the time of attrition from the experiment. If the ill exited the experiment, only to be treated outside the experiment where the amount of care received was not observed, then it would appear that healthcare had declined for those in the cost-sharing arms, and also that there was little difference in health effects. But this would have been because participants in both arms were receiving the care that they required, given the health statuses of those who remained in the experiment (Nyman 2007; 2008).

Interestingly, the RAND researchers sent mixed signals regarding whether this attrition had actually biased the RAND findings. In the retrospective summary of all the conclusions from the Experiment written in 1993, Newhouse and his RAND colleagues wrote that '[w]e concluded that neither refusal of the enrollment offer nor withdrawal from the Experiment subsequent to enrollment caused any appreciable bias' (Newhouse et al. 1993: 26). This position was reiterated in a response (Newhouse et al. 2008) to a paper raising the attrition bias issue (Nyman 2007). Yet, in a paper that Newhouse first made public in 2008 by posting it on his website, but that had apparently been written in 1988 (as evidenced by the references in Newhouse et al. 1993), RAND researchers Willard Manning, Naihua Duan and Emmett Keeler had found that there were 34 percent too few hospitalizations among those who dropped out of the cost-sharing arms than would be expected (Manning et al. 1988/1993). The authors of this paper concluded that:

> The data from the Health Insurance Experiment indicate that individuals who dropped out behaved differently (in ways that measured characteristics and time on the study could not explain) than those who stayed to the end of the study. Thus, past inferences based largely on stayers are biased. For outpatient care, the bias was quite small. But for inpatient care, there was a moderate bias which understated the effect of family pay plans with catastrophic coverage. (Manning et al. 1988/1993: 16)

In other words, those who left the experiment in the cost-sharing plans should have exhibited a greater amount of healthcare use than was observed. Regardless of the apparent dissembling, this admitted bias raises questions about the RAND Experiment's ability to claim 'gold standard' status and, more importantly, its ability to conclude that cost-sharing can reduce healthcare, and especially hospitalizations, with no important effect on health.

INCOME EFFECTS

One of the provinces of economic analysis is the evaluation of the desirability of certain economic behaviors, that is, the determination of whether or not certain economic behaviors are efficient in the sense that they improve society's welfare. Economists have a number of tools with which to accomplish this, but one of the most important is the income effect. The income effect essentially determines, if a person has an additional $100 of income, how it would be spent. The importance of income effects derives from the fact that additional income can be spent on any marketable good or service. If we assume that the consumer is making the best possible choices (given her own preferences), then knowing how the additional income would be spent identifies the choices that generate the greatest utility for the consumer.

Income effects are used to determine the efficiency of many types of behaviors. For example, we all know that an exogenous reduction in the market price will cause consumers to purchase more of a good. Economists recognize, however, that part of this behavior is due to the fact that, when the price of a good that a consumer has been buying drops, consumers have more disposable income and this additional income can be spent on anything of their choosing, including more of the good in question. The other part of the increase is the opportunistic substitution of a bargain good for others whose prices remain unchanged. Thus, when the price of gasoline falls, consumers may decide to take a vacation by car (buy more gasoline) in part because the cost of commuting to their jobs has fallen and they have more disposable income – the income effect. But the decision to vacation by car also stems from the fact that a car vacation is now cheaper relative to traveling by plane or train. The welfare implications of a demand increase resulting from higher real income are fundamentally different from the welfare implications of a demand increase that results from consumers taking advantage of a bargain.

The original theory of the demand for health insurance developed by Friedman and Savage did not recognize any income effects at all (Friedman and Savage 1948). It was not until John Marshall and David de Meza published their respective models of the demand for health insurance that it was recognized that, if an individual received a payout of additional income from the insurer upon becoming ill, the payout would likely cause an increase in the amount of medical care purchased (Marshall 1976; de Meza 1983). Similarly, Pauly's original theory of moral hazard generated by a reduction in the coinsurance price did not recognize an income effect. Typical of the thinking was Newhouse's summary of the mechanism by which health insurance impacts the quantity of healthcare demanded. He wrote:

> For the purpose of studying the relationship between health insurance and demand . . . insurance is like a subsidy to purchase medical care; that is, it lowers the per-unit price of care. Although there is an income effect caused by premiums or taxes paid to finance the insurance benefits, these income effects can be shown to be empirically negligible in their effect on the demand for care . . . (Newhouse 1978: 9)

So, although Newhouse recognized one type of income effect associated with insurance – the effect that derived from the fact that a consumer must pay a premium in order to obtain a lower coinsurance price and that that payment reduces the amount of income that remains to pay for healthcare at the coinsurance rate – he thought that this income effect was too small to worry about. According to this view, becoming insured means only that one faces a lower cost per unit of healthcare purchased, and this effect is captured solely by a price reduction and a movement along the observed demand curve, as in Figure 3.1.

The coinsurance price reduction in insurance, however, contains a second and more important income effect (Nyman 1999a; 1999b; 2003).

Specifically, the coinsurance price reduction is the vehicle by which income is transferred from those who purchase insurance and remain healthy, to those who purchase insurance and become ill. For example, assume that a consumer has $50,000 in income and faces an annual 10 percent chance of contracting breast cancer. Without insurance, if the consumer became ill with breast cancer, she would pay $20,000 out of pocket for a mastectomy. With an insurance contract that would pay 80 percent of costs (a coinsurance rate of 20 percent), the consumer who contracts cancer would purchase the mastectomy costing $20,000, plus a breast reconstruction for another $20,000 and two extra days in the hospital for $4,000. Total spending with insurance is $44,000, with moral hazard spending representing $24,000 of that amount. (This moral hazard is the additional demand for healthcare generated by the presence of insurance: in this example, it is the difference between the $44,000 spent by the insured consumer and the $20,000 spent by the uninsured consumer.) The insurer pays 80 percent of the total bill, so the insurer's expense is $35,200, and the rest, $8,800, is paid out-of-pocket by the insured consumer who becomes ill. Given the 10 percent annual chance of contracting breast cancer, the actuarially fair premium for this insurance is $3,520, which all consumers who purchase this contract pay, whether they become ill or not. So, $35,200 came out of the insurance pool to pay for the ill consumer's care, and $3,520 of this amount represented the premium paid by that same consumer. Thus, compared to being uninsured, the consumer with this coinsurance contract benefitted from $31,680 that was transferred out of the insurance pool to physicians, hospitals and other providers, and used to pay for her care.

Paying off with a coinsurance price reduction produced an additional $24,000 in moral hazard spending. What part of that $24,000 was due to an income effect, that is, to the $31,680 transfer of income out of the insurance pool? To find that, we would need to know how much healthcare the consumer who becomes ill would purchase if she instead had purchased a policy (that cost the same $3,520 in premiums) that paid off with a direct income payment to her of $35,200 upon becoming ill (and with healthcare priced at its original levels). If such an insurance policy existed, it would be a type of 'contingent claims' insurance policy: the payoff being a claim on a specific part of the insurance pool, payable contingent upon becoming ill.[1] Again, compared to being uninsured, this scenario represents an

[1] This arrangement is similar to that found in many auto insurance policies. When a car is damaged, the insurer decides how much it would cost to repair the vehicle, and then gives the owner a check for this amount. Whether the owner chooses to use that sum to fix the car or for something else is up to the consumer.

income transfer of $31,680 out of the insurance pool from those who purchase insurance and remain healthy. Suppose that, if she were paid off with $35,200 directly, she would purchase the $20,000 mastectomy (that she would have purchased without insurance), plus the $20,000 breast reconstruction procedure, but not the additional two days in the hospital for $4,000. If so, then $20,000 of the $24,000 in moral hazard spending is efficient because it is an income effect: the additional income could be spent on anything of her choosing, and she chose to purchase the breast reconstruction, implying that this purchase maximizes her utility. Indeed, we can assume that she would have been willing to pay *at least* $20,000 for this breast reconstruction *and likely more than that* because her income had increased by $31,680, compared to being uninsured. The amount over and above $20,000 that she is willing to pay represents the *consumer surplus*, a measure of the welfare gain from obtaining that procedure. She would not have purchased the two extra days in the hospital because, even though she had more income, the two extra days were not worth the $4,000 she would have to pay for them.

This income effect analysis shows that part of what appeared to be a totally inefficient purchase of additional care because it is generated by the coinsurance rate is, in fact, efficient. The $20,000 in moral hazard spending for the breast reconstruction is efficient because the same breast reconstruction would have been purchased with the income that could have been transferred directly to the consumer with a contingent claims policy with the same premium and same payment from the insurer. It also shows that some of the additional care – the $4,000 in moral hazard spending for the two extra days in the hospital – is inefficient because it would not have been purchased with the additional income. Indeed, this portion of moral hazard is a result of using the price reduction – from full price to a coinsurance price of 20 percent – to transfer the income in the insurance contract. This analysis implies that moral hazard can be decomposed into efficient and inefficient portions, and that the welfare implications of moral hazard are much more subtle than were recognized by conventional theory.

MORAL HAZARD UNDER THE NEW THEORY

The anomalies and the decomposition of moral hazard have led to the formulation of a new theory of why consumers purchase health insurance (Nyman 2003). The new theory holds that consumers purchase health insurance in order to gain additional income when ill. That is, consumers purchase health insurance because the gain in utility from this additional income when ill is greater than the loss of utility from paying the premium and remaining healthy, assuming that the premium is actuarially fair. Consumers derive more utility from additional income when ill in large part because they can use that income to purchase additional healthcare, compared to the amount they would purchase if uninsured.

Indeed, one of the major functions of health insurance is to gain access to healthcare that would be unaffordable if uninsured and relying on one's own resources. According to the Medical Expenditure Panel Survey, the distribution of healthcare spending is highly skewed, with the top-spending 5 percent of the population incurring about half of the total annual expenditures, and the lowest-spending 50 percent of the population incurring only about 3 percent of the expenditures (Stanton and Rutherford 2005). The skew in the expenditure distribution reflects the fact that most healthcare expenditures are consumed by those who become ill (Schoenman and Chockley 2012). Because of the high cost of healthcare and the unequal distribution of income and financial assets, many Americans who become ill would not be able to afford the cost of standard care without insurance. Moreover, consumers may not be able to obtain a loan for a risky procedure when ill, and they may not have the time or ability to save enough to cover the cost of the procedure themselves. In such a healthcare environment, moral hazard is best exemplified by standard care – resections for those with cancer or coronary bypass graft procedures for those with coronary heart disease – rather than the frivolous designer sunglasses or prescriptions for erectile dysfunction drugs that are often used to characterize its inefficiency. That is, at least a part – and probably a very substantial part – of moral hazard in healthcare is represented by standard care that would not be affordable or accessible without insurance and that provides significant health benefits to those who receive it.

The new analysis also recognizes that there still may be a moral hazard welfare loss from insurance policies that use a coinsurance price reduction to transfer income to the ill, but it also suggests that this welfare loss might not be nearly as important as conventional theory originally held it to be. This is because there is often a cost of transacting business that is independent of the benefits from the actual quid pro quo purchase. For example, the purchase of real estate often involves legal fees that have little to do with the utility gained from a new house or the cost of building one.

Such transactions costs are common and occur in many contexts. They are part of purchasing a health insurance contract. Indeed, they provide the explanation for why we do not observe health insurance structured as a contingent claims insurance contract that transfers income directly to the ill: the transactions costs associated with such a contract would be too great. In such an insurance contract, there would be sizable up-front legal and research costs from drafting a document that specified the various amounts of income that would be paid out for each health and treatment contingency. Additional ongoing costs would be incurred from employing the medical personnel to verify that a person actually had the illness that was claimed and what illness it was, in order to trigger the transfer of income to the consumer. (Such verification would be essential, because having an insurance policy that paid off in cash would tempt consumers (and some doctors) to gin-up imaginary illnesses for which the insurer could be billed.) Seen in this light, an insurance policy that pays off by providing free (or low coinsurance rate) care directly, rather than by providing the amount of money needed to purchase that care, represents a substantial savings in transactions costs. And if transactions costs are minimized when the standard coinsurance insurance contract is used (compared with all the possible ways to transfer income to the ill), then they can essentially be ignored in the welfare analysis.

Although Newhouse (1978) suggested that the income that is paid for health insurance premiums would have little effect on healthcare spending, and therefore would be ignorable in the analysis of moral hazard from health insurance, this is unlikely to be true today (if it ever was). Health insurance premiums for a family averaged almost $16,000 in 2012 (Kaiser Family Foundation/Health Research & Educational Trust 2012) and median incomes were around $51,000 for a household in the same year (Noss 2013). As a result, premiums represent somewhere between a fifth and a quarter of median income, depending on whether the household received health insurance from an employer. It is unlikely that such a large percentage reduction of income would not affect healthcare spending. This may be especially true for those at the lower end of the income distribution. As a result, it is necessary to incorporate two income effects into the analysis of moral hazard. The first income effect captures the consequences of paying an increasingly larger premium in order to obtain an insurance contract with an increasingly smaller coinsurance rate. And, at a given coinsurance rate, the second income effect captures the fact that within a coinsurance price reduction is a transfer of income from policyholders who remain healthy to policyholders who become ill.

Figure 3.2 shows the analysis of moral hazard under the new theory. Again, the demand curve for healthcare is the downward sloping curve, D, showing the units of healthcare consumed as the price to the ill consumer changes exogenously. Also, the cost of producing each unit of healthcare is again represented by the constant amount, C. If the market price were originally set at the cost of producing the care, that is, if $P_0 = C$, then M_0 units of healthcare would be purchased by the uninsured consumer. If instead the consumer purchased an insurance contract, she would no

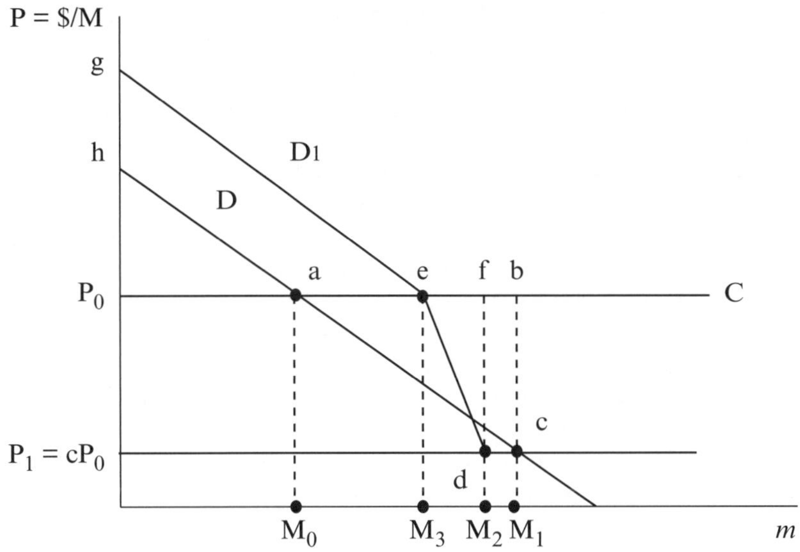

Figure 3.2 Decomposition of moral hazard

longer directly pay the full cost of the healthcare she used. Instead, she would pay for her care via a 'flat' up-front premium and a copay amount, c, that represents a fixed percentage of the cost of each unit of care she consumes. Crucially, the premium reduces the amount of income the consumer has left over to pay for healthcare at the coinsurance price. Thus, for any coinsurance rate, such as for the rate purchased in this diagram, c, the amount of healthcare actually purchased with insurance, M_2, would be less than the amount, M_1, that would have been purchased if the price of healthcare simply had fallen exogenously to P_1 (with no premium charge and thus no income effect). In general, this first income effect would be captured by D_1, a demand curve that is steeper than D (for any coinsurance rate lower than 1), and would describe the change in the quantity of healthcare demanded as an increasingly lower coinsurance price is purchased through an insurance contract.

The second income effect is due to the fact that the coinsurance rate is used to transfer income from those who purchase insurance and remain healthy, to those who purchase insurance and become ill. This income effect is captured by the shifting of the demand curve to the right. This shift to the right reflects the notion that, with an *increase* in income generated by the income transfer in insurance, more healthcare would be demanded at every price by an ill person. The effect is straightforward for those prices above P_0, but for the prices below P_0, it is necessary also to take into account the first income effect and greater premium paid in order to obtain the lower coinsurance price. As a result, Figure 3.2 shows that the new insurance demand curve, D_1, has a kink in it at the original price, P_0.

In Figure 3.2, moral hazard is represented by the quantity $M_2 - M_0$, rather than $M_1 - M_0$, in order to account for effect on quantity of healthcare demanded of the premium payments necessary to purchase the coinsurance price, c. Moral hazard can be decomposed into a portion that is due to the income transfer, $M_3 - M_0$, and a portion that is due to using a coinsurance price reduction to transfer income, $M_2 - M_3$.

A key observation is that these two types of moral hazard have completely opposite welfare implications. The income-transfer-generated moral hazard ($M_3 - M_0$) represents an increase in welfare: consumers buy more healthcare because the income transferred to them via insurance enables them to obtain care that they value at more than its cost, but would not be able to purchase absent an increase in income (via insurance). The moral hazard generated by using a price reduction to transfer income to the ill, ($M_3 - M_2$), represents a reduction in welfare, because these units of care are valued by the consumer at less than what it costs to produce them, and are purchased only because the coinsurance has made them appear artificially cheap.

Under the conventional theory of moral hazard in health insurance, all insurance-induced spending is wasteful, and the moral hazard welfare loss is thus represented by area abc in Figure 3.1. But taking full account of income effects dramatically changes the welfare calculus. Instead of the large welfare loss represented by triangle abc, the loss is reduced to area efd in Figure 3.2,[2] and we now see a welfare *gain* represented by area geah. This gain represents an increase in the consumer surplus – what the consumer with additional income would be willing to pay over and above what she would have to pay if she were charged a price equal to P_0, reflecting the true cost, C, of producing the healthcare (Willig 1976). In sum, the new analysis of moral hazard holds that the use of a price reduction (via a coinsurance fee) to transfer income has both a positive and a negative

[2] As with the original Pauly analysis, ($M_2 - M_3$) in Figure 3.2 is the (portion of) moral hazard generated by using a price reduction to transfer income. Its value is represented by the area edM_2M_3 under the insurance demand curve D_1. It costs efM_2M_3 to produce, so the difference is triangle efd. This amount represents in dollars the difference between the cost of producing this additional healthcare and its value to consumers, taking into account the fact that in order to obtain a lower price, the consumer must purchase it as part of an insurance contract.

effect on welfare, and the net of those effects represents the overall welfare effect of moral hazard.

It is important to recognize the larger theoretical context into which this analysis of moral hazard must be placed. The new theory of the demand for health insurance holds that consumers purchase insurance because the gain from an income transfer if ill exceeds the loss from paying a premium (and therefore having less income) if healthy. This difference in relative effects of income on utility in these two states of health is due in large part to the fact that most people regard improving health as being exceedingly precious. Thus, having more income to pay for healthcare when ill will almost certainly produce greater utility gains than having more income when healthy (that is, not paying the insurance premium). For example, an extra $50,000 to spend on cancer treatment if ill with cancer generates a larger (expected) utility gain than the (expected) utility lost from paying a $10,000 premium payment if healthy and forgoing a vacation to Florida (or whatever consumer goods and services would have been purchased with the $10,000).

This analysis of the welfare implications of moral hazard assumes that the consumer has become ill and that the healthcare that is represented by the horizontal axis of Figure 3.2 is of the type – coronary bypass grafts, chemotherapy, bowel resections, and the like – that only those who are acutely ill would purchase. It would also include the similarly constrained healthcare for the management of chronic diseases like diabetes and asthma. Although the expenditures on such healthcare represents the vast majority of healthcare spending in the United States (Schoenman and Chockley 2012), not all moral hazard spending depends on becoming ill first. As a result, one limitation of this new analysis is that it applies best to those procedures and other healthcare services that a healthy person would never choose to purchase. For the types of healthcare for which being ill is *not* a prerequisite, the original Pauly model may be more applicable.

POLICY IMPLICATIONS OF THE NEW THEORY

This new theory of moral hazard generates several policy recommendations that differ substantially from those that follow from the conventional theory.

First, the conventional theory of moral hazard suggests that consumers are purchasing too much coverage – coinsurance rates are too low – because health insurance has been subsidized by permitting premiums for health insurance obtained through an employer to be paid for with pre-income-tax income. Under the new theory, it can no longer be assumed that all moral hazard is inefficient. Instead, because some of the additional spending is efficient and some is inefficient, cost-sharing should be applied only to those services for which the additional spending is inefficient.[3] For those healthcare services that are efficient, no copayment should be applied or, indeed, they should possibly even be subsidized to encourage this type of moral hazard. This theory anticipated the work by Michael Chernew, William Encinosa and Richard Hirth to tailor coinsurance rates to different procedures and the subsequent identification and promotion of what has become known as 'value-based insurance design' (Chernew et al. 2000; Chernew et al. 2007). Thus, the coinsurance rates suggested by Feldstein (67 percent or higher) and Manning and Marquis (45 percent with no maximum out-of-pocket payment) were not only too high because they were based on Pauly's demand analysis, but also inappropriate because they were to be applied across the board to all healthcare.

Second, instead of a problem, health insurance is once again a solution. Because of the gains from the portion of moral hazard caused by the income transfer when ill, health insurance can generate gains. These gains are, however, more difficult to assess empirically because they are based on a consumer deriving more utility from income in the ill state (used, in large part, to pay for additional healthcare) than in the healthy state (used to pay for additional consumer goods and services), and this difference in state-dependent utility from income has not been researched. (Some researchers have investigated the difference in utility derived from income spent on non-healthcare consumption goods and services in the ill and healthy states (for example, Viscusi and Evans 1990), but no one has investigated the difference in utility from income spent on any types of goods and services – healthcare or other – in the ill and healthy states.) However, it is clear that the welfare loss calculations from previous estimates of the welfare implications understate the value of health insurance.

Regarding the tax subsidization of health insurance, while the focus in the past has been on the additional coverage (lower coinsurance rates) caused by the subsidy, with the new theory, the focus shifts to the additional newly insured consumers caused by the subsidy. It is still

---

[3] It should be noted that once the distinction between efficient and inefficient moral hazard was made (Nyman 1999a; 1999b), some economists adopted the view that only the additional spending that was inefficient actually constituted moral hazard (Cutler and Zeckhauser 2000). The efficient type of moral hazard was referred to as a liquidity effect (Chetty 2008). Because this distinction was not made originally, this chapter adopts the original definition of moral hazard as encompassing both types.

true that paying for employer-sponsored health insurance with pre-tax income favors high income earners, but the new subsidies under the Patient Protection and Affordable Care Act of 2010 have been more progressive.

Third, it can no longer be assumed that cost-sharing can be imposed with no important effects on health. The many studies showing a health gain from the (moral hazard) healthcare purchases caused by becoming insured, and the attrition bias discovered in the RAND Health Insurance Experiment suggest that health insurance improves health, especially among those who are low income or already ill. While some questions have recently arisen from whether the analysis of the Oregon Medicaid lottery will ultimately be consistent with these studies or a troubling exception (Baicker et al. 2013), the preponderance of data suggest that health insurance improves health.

Finally, the policy emphasis on reducing the quantity of healthcare consumed in order to reduce national health expenditures runs counter to the beneficial effect of moral hazard on health. Quantity could be reduced by policies that failed to insure the uninsured or by the policies implemented to reduce quantity among the insured – cost-sharing, managed care and 'consumer-driven healthcare'. Interestingly, these policies appear to have worked to reduce the amount of healthcare consumed in the United States. Compared with the average of our peers in the G7 countries in 2010, Americans went to the doctor half as frequently and spent about half as many days in the hospital, yet still spent over twice as much per person on healthcare (Organization for Economic Cooperation and Development 2013). The preoccupation with the welfare loss from moral hazard in the United States appears to have distracted policymakers from those policies designed to reduce prices by reducing the market power of providers and health plans. Of the policies associated with the Affordable Care Act of 2010, the ones establishing health insurance exchanges and the Independent Payment Advisory Board have the most potential to reduce premiums and per unit payments to providers, and the most potential to reduce healthcare costs.

REFERENCES

Arrow, K. J. 1963. Uncertainty and the Welfare Economics of Medical Care. *American Economic Review* 53, 941–73.

Baicker, K., S. Taubman, B. Wright, H. L. Allen, M. Bernstein, J. H. Gruber, J. P. Newhouse, E. C. Schneider, B. J. Wright, A. M. Zaslavsky, and A. Finkelstein. 2013. The Oregon Health Insurance Experiment: Effect of Medicaid on Clinical Outcomes. *New England Journal of Medicine* 368, 1713–22.

Bloche, M. G. 2006. Consumer-Directed Health Care. *New England Journal of Medicine* 355, 1756–9.

Chernew, M. E., W. E. Encinosa, and R. A. Hirth. 2000. Optimal Health Insurance: The Case of Observable, Severe Illness. *Journal of Health Economics* 19, 585–609.

Chernew, M. E., A. B. Rosen, and A. M. Fendrick. 2007. Value-Based Insurance Design. Health Affairs Web Exclusive. Available at http://content.healthaffairs.org/content/26/2/w195.long (accessed August 5, 2014).

Chetty, R. 2008. Moral Hazard versus Liquidity and Optimal Unemployment Insurance. *Journal of Political Economy* 116, 173–234.

Crew, M. 1969. Coinsurance and the Welfare Economics of Medical Care. *American Economic Review* 5, 906–8.

Cutler, D. M., and R. J. Zeckhauser. 2000. The Anatomy of Health Insurance. In A. J. Culyer and J. P. Newhouse, eds., *Handbook of Health Economics Volume 1A*. Amsterdam: Elsevier.

Cutler, D. M., M. McClellan, and J. P. Newhouse. 2000. How Does Managed Care Do It? *RAND Journal of Economics* 31, 526–548.

de Meza, D. 1983. Health Insurance and the Demand for Medical Care. *Journal of Health Economics* 2, 47–54.

Feldman, R., and M. A. Morrisey. 1990. Health Economics: A Report on the Field. *Journal of Health Politics, Policy and Law* 15, 627–45.

Feldstein, M. S. 1973. The Welfare Loss of Excess Health Insurance. *Journal of Political Economy* 81, 251–80.

Feldstein, M., and B. Friedman. 1977. Tax Subsidies, the Rational Demand for Insurance, and the Health Care Crisis. *Journal of Public Economics* 7, 155–78.

Freeman, J. D., S. Kadiyala, J. F. Bell, and D. P. Martin. 2008. The Causal Effect of Health Insurance on Utilization and Outcomes in Adults: A Systematic Review of US Studies. *Medical Care* 46, 1023–32.

Friedman, M., and L. J. Savage. 1948. The Utility Analysis of Choices Involving Risk. *Journal of Political Economy* 56, 279–304.

Gladwell, M. 2005. The Moral Hazard Myth. *The New Yorker*. August 29.

Hadley, J. 2003. Sicker and Poorer – The Consequences of Being Uninsured: A Review of the Research on the Relationship between Health Insurance, Medical Care Use, Health, Work, and Income. *Medical Care Research and Review* 60, 3S–75S.

Hoffman, B. 2006. Restraining the Health Care Consumer: The History of Deductibles and Co-payments in U.S. Health Insurance. *Social Science History* 30, 501–28.

Kahneman, D., and A. Tversky. 1979. Prospect Theory: An Analysis of Decision under Risk. *Econometrica* 47, 263–91.

Kaiser Family Foundation/Health Research & Educational Trust. 2012. 2012 Employer Health Benefits Survey. Available at http://kff.org/private-insurance/press-release/family-health-premiums-rise-4-percent-to/ (accessed August 5, 2014).

Kuhn, T. S. 1962. *The Structure of Scientific Revolutions*. Chicago, IL: University of Chicago Press.

Manning, W. G., and M. S. Marquis. 1996. Health insurance: Tradeoffs revisited. *Journal of Health Economics* 20, 289–94.

Manning, W. G., N. Duan, and E. B. Keeler. 1988/1993. *Attrition Bias in a Randomized Trial of Health Insurance*. Santa Monica, CA: RAND Corporation.

Manning, W. G., J. P. Newhouse, N. Duan, E. Keeler, A. Leibowitz, and M. S. Marquis. 1987. Health Insurance and the Demand for Medical Care: Evidence from a Randomized Experiment. *American Economic Review* 77, 251–77.

Marshall, J. M. 1976. Moral Hazard. *American Economic Review* 66, 880–90.

Newhouse, J. P. 1978. *The Economics of Medical Care*. Reading, MA: Addison-Wesley.

Newhouse, J. P. and the Insurance Experiment Group. 1993. *Free for All? Lessons from the RAND Health Insurance Experiment*. Cambridge, MA: Harvard University Press.

Newhouse, J. P., R. H. Brook, N. Duan, E. B. Keeler, A. Leibowitz, W. G. Manning, M. S. Marquis, C. N. Morris, C. E. Phelps, and J. E. Rolph. 2008. RAND Attrition in the

RAND Health Insurance Experiment: A Response to Nyman. *Journal of Health Politics, Policy and Law* 33, 295–308.
Noss, A. 2013. *Household Income: 2012, American Community Survey Briefs*. Washington, DC: U.S. Department of Commerce, U.S. Census Bureau.
Nyman, J. A. 1999a. The Value of Health Insurance: The Access Motive. *Journal of Health Economics* 18, 141–52.
Nyman, J. A. 1999b. The Economics of Moral Hazard Revisited. *Journal of Health Economics* 18, 811–24.
Nyman, J. A. 2003. *The Theory of Demand for Health Insurance*. Stanford, CA: Stanford University Press.
Nyman, J. A. 2007. American Health Policy: Cracks in the Foundation. *Journal of Health Politics, Policy and Law* 32, 759–83.
Nyman, J. A. 2008. Health Plan Switching and Attrition Bias in the RAND Health Insurance Experiment. *Journal of Health Politics, Policy and Law* 33, 309–17.
Organisation for Economic Cooperation and Development. 2013. StatExtracts. Available at http://stats.oecd.org/index.aspx.
Pauly, M. V. 1968. The Economics of Moral Hazard: Comment. *American Economic Review* 58, 531–7.
Pauly, M. V. 1983. More on Moral Hazard. *Journal of Health Economics* 2, 81–5.
Pauly, M. V. 1995. When Does Curbing Health Care Costs Really Help the Economy? *Health Affairs* 14, 68–82.
Schoenman, J. A., and N. Chockley. 2012. *The Concentration of Health Care Spending*. Washington, DC: National Institute for Health Care Management Foundation.
Stanton M. W., and M. K. Rutherford 2005. The High Concentration of U.S. Health Care Expenditures. Rockville (MD): Agency for Healthcare Research and Quality. Research in Action Issue 19. AHRQ Pub. No. 06-0060.
Tversky, A., and D. Kahneman. 1988. Rational Choice and the Framing of Decisions. In A. Tversky, ed., *Decision Making*. Cambridge: Cambridge University Press.
Viscusi, W. K., and W. N. Evans. 1990. Utility Functions That Depend on Health Status: Estimates and Economic Implications. *American Economic Review* 80, 353–74.
Willig, R. D. 1976. Consumer Surplus Without Apology. *American Economics Review* 66, 589–97.
Young, G. J., and B. B. Cohen. 1991. Inequities in Hospital Care, the Massachusetts Experience. *Inquiry* 28, 255–62.
Zeckhauser, R. 1970. Medical Insurance: A Case Study of the Tradeoff between Risk Spreading and Appropriate Incentives. *Journal of Economic Theory* 2, 10–26.

4. Does the theory of insurance support awarding pain and suffering damages in torts?

Ronen Avraham

INTRODUCTION

The short answer to the question in the title is 'Yes'.

Here is the long answer. When medical malpractice causes a man to lose his prostate, a woman to lose her womb, or a child to lose her kidney, the victim's economic loss (actual medical costs and diminished earning capacity) is often relatively small. Yet, few would dispute that the victim has suffered a huge and real loss beyond the economic one. But what kind of a loss? Tort law would identify it as non-economic loss, which serves as a catch-all for many losses such as pain and suffering, mental anguish, emotional distress, and loss of enjoyment of life.

Despite the undisputable loss associated with pain and suffering harms, the dominant view in the economic analysis of tort law is that damages for pain and suffering should either be significantly reduced or even entirely eliminated. Indeed, the most prevalent tort reform of the last thirty years has been imposing a cap on pain and suffering recovery.

But what makes pain and suffering harm, as opposed to all other kinds of harms, the dominant target of tort reformers?

To answer this question, this chapter adopts an economic perspective, exploiting the deep connection between pain and suffering harms and the economic theory of insurance. In fact, based on the premise that tort law is most efficient when it is compared to and inspired by a hypothetical insurance contract between plaintiffs and defendants, many law and economic scholars have argued that plaintiffs should not be compensated for non-economic loss. The reason is that the theory of insurance predicts that plaintiffs would not be willing to pay a fair premium for such coverage in a hypothetical insurance contract with the defendants. Moreover, advocates of this view argue that as an empirical matter, there is no pain and suffering coverage in private insurance markets, a fact which supports the theoretical claim. Finally, some law and economics scholars argue that even if consumers demanded coverage for pain and suffering harm, the potential benefits of pain and suffering damages are largely negated by their haphazardness, which introduces considerable risk into the entire US tort system (Garber 1998; Viscusi 1991), as well as by the high cost of administering them via tort law, which stems, among other things, from the difficulty to verify them objectively which in turn might lead to exaggerations and malingering.

In this chapter I expose the weaknesses in the dominant view and argue that even from a law and economics perspective, and even adopting the insurance paradigm to analyze pain and suffering damages in tort law, pain and suffering damages *should* be awarded. I start by laying out the assumptions underlying the economic model and question their validity. I show how the model generates the opposite outcome when paired with different, not less realistic, assumptions. I then show that a careful reading of the empirical evidence would suggest that, when it makes sense, people do demand coverage for pain and suffering losses. Lastly, I argue that because there is no convincing theoretical argument or valid empirical evidence that administering pain and suffering damages is objectively high, or even more expensive, than administering any other component of a tort lawsuit, it is incoherent to argue that the high administrative costs endemic to tort litigation should only preclude compensation for pain and suffering. As to their ease of manipulation, I argue that tort law has found ways to combat this risk and that technological progress in brain science will soon reduce and eventually eliminate this problem.

At the end of the day, I argue, there is nothing unique about pain and suffering damages which justifies their elimination or even capping. From an insurance industry-wide perspective, pain and suffering damages are uncorrelated losses and therefore do not really impose special hardships on defendants' insurance companies, or at least not hardships that insurance companies or their reinsurers cannot handle. Indeed, third-party liability insurance for pain and suffering losses has been provided for over a century, including during periods of 'tort crisis'. It is true that compensating for pain and suffering losses increases defendants' liability insurance premium compared to a regime where defendants do not have to pay such damages, but such an increase in premium brings with it some benefits as well. First, it provides compensation for the victims for a loss they would, from an *ex ante* perspective, want to be compensated for. And second, as has been shown multiple times, this increase is efficient because it guarantees optimal levels of safety (for a recent account of this claim see Choi and Spier 2014).

SHOULD THERE BE PAIN AND SUFFERING DAMAGES IN TORTS AT ALL?

Tort law has several functions: compensating victims, providing signals about optimal behavior, deterring tortfeasors-to-be, and more (Shavell 2003).[1] The focus in this chapter is indeed on optimal deterrence and optimal compensation, both from an insurance theory perspective. An optimal insurance contract (hypothetically signed between potential plaintiffs and potential defendants) should be designed to minimize the costs of: (a) risk-bearing; (b) accidents; (c) accident-avoidance by all parties; and (d) (perhaps) administrative costs. Does the optimal insurance contract require awarding pain and suffering damages?

An optimal insurance contract, reflecting an efficient tort system, seems to be one which creates the expectation in potential tortfeasors that they will be liable for the full amount of damages that they cause. By and large, only full internalization of harm by defendants provides them with proper incentives to take care. And, because non-economic harm is real (think about the prostate, the womb or the kidney) full internalization requires compensating for such harm, without even allowing the victim to prospectively waive such liability in private contracts (Wickelgren 2006; Arlen and MacLeod 2003).

The discussion could end here, but law and economics scholars have found three efficiency-based reasons to object to awarding pain and suffering damages. First, that the tort system over-deters and that to offset that effect pain and suffering damages should be reduced and perhaps abolished altogether. Second, that pain and suffering losses are not demanded by insureds in real or hypothetical insurance markets and therefore should not be compensated in tort. And third, that tort law is an inefficient system for transferring damages (especially pain and suffering damages) to the injured relative to a first-party insurance system, and therefore should be abolished. I discuss these three critiques in order.

A. Pain and Suffering Should be Reduced to Offset the Tort System's Over-Deterrence

There are several arguments for why awarding pain and suffering damages will create over-deterrence. The first argument goes something like this:

---

1 Chamallas and Wriggins (2010) note that 'public policy' is also a goal of torts. See also, Bovbjerg et al. 1989: 925.

Pain and suffering is highly subjective and manipulable, and plaintiffs can easily inflate their real loss so as to collect higher-than-optimal damages. However, proponents of this claim ignore the fact that this difficulty is more likely to cause pain and suffering damages to be too low rather than too high. Why? Because courts have responded to the threat of exaggerated damages by disallowing evidence (such as 'day in the life' videos) and arguments (such as per diem arguments) that might help plaintiffs recover more. If damages for pain and suffering are therefore hard to prove, and the burden is on the plaintiff to prove them, might we not think they could be too small rather than too large?

The second over-deterrence argument is that tort law does not operate in a vacuum. Government agencies and the public are two other entities sending defendants signals about desired deterrence. Indeed, one study of automobile safety improvements found that product liability law is just one of several forces that induces car manufacturers to consider making pro-safety decisions (Graham 1991). Given that defendants are deterred by forces other than tort plaintiffs, might the elimination of pain and suffering damages not be useful to prevent over-deterrence?

Market reputation, regulatory action, and the tort system complement each other, because the filing of litigation is often the impetus for news coverage of product dangers, which can influence both market reputation and regulatory changes (Goldberg and Zipursky 2010). Law and economics scholars have recognized the importance of this complementarity (Shavell 1984). However, even if one accepts that there might be good reasons to reduce tort damages, so that defendants will not be over-deterred, (a claim I will reject in the next paragraph) eliminating pain and suffering damages requires an *additional* claim about why we should eliminate them and not, say, damages for future loss of income. Alas, such an argument has never been provided.

But does the tort system really over-deter? In great contrast to loud voices who claim that tort law over-deters, most tort scholars have argued that tort law *under*-deters and therefore that pain and suffering damages have an instrumental role in providing optimal deterrence after all. Why does it under-deter? Because in the real world, there are many barriers to filing suit, including difficulties in finding a lawyer (due to various tort reform statutes which made tort suits unprofitable for lawyers), difficulties in identifying the tortfeasor, as well as various other types of litigation costs. Thus, tortfeasors will often escape suit, and their expected payouts will be less than the losses they generate. To create the proper incentive to avoid damages, a premium must be added to the monetary damages recovered by plaintiffs. While most legal economists support *punitive damages* for that purpose, some pure-tort scholars have argued that pain and suffering damages do and should serve that goal.[2] Indeed, under the common law conceptualization of these types of damages, both punitive damages (which are supposed to punish defendants for their egregious behavior, not for the fact that plaintiffs don't sue) and pain and suffering damages (which are supposed to compensate plaintiffs for their non-economic harm) are equally distant from the goal of offsetting under-suit. Therefore, it is not theoretically obvious, even if typically assumed by law and economics scholars, that punitive damages should serve as the hook to correct for under-deterrence.

To sum up this point, because pain and suffering damages *are* arguably genuine harms (a point on which I will elaborate below), the default position should be that the tort system should act to deter potential tortfeasors from causing these harms (Avraham 2006; Geistfeld 1995; Shavell 1987). Whether defendants are over- or under-deterred is an empirical question, although in all likelihood they are under-deterred. Those who believe that defendants are under-deterred should definitely support awarding these damages if only to offset under-suit (even if they happen to dispute that pain and suffering harm is completely genuine). Those who believe that defendants are over-deterred might have a prima facie argument for reducing tort damages, yet singling out pain and suffering damages requires additional justification, which they fail to convincingly provide.

B. Pain and Suffering Losses are Not Demanded by Insureds and therefore Should Not Be Compensated in Tort

This critique was developed by law and economics scholars who analyzed tort law as a kind of mandatory third-party insurance system. An alternative to third-party insurance is first-party insurance; and since a rational tort victim would not demand pain and suffering coverage in her first-party insurance contract, tort law should not award victims pain and suffering damages. Or at least so goes the argument.

The analogy between tort law and insurance has long been familiar to courts and scholars. In the products liability arena, the insurance paradigm holds that manufacturers are in a better position than consumers to obtain insurance, spread losses, and more efficiently curtail accident costs (Rahdert 1995). Justice Traynor's concurrence in *Escola v. Coca Cola Bottling Co.*, was one of the first judicial recognitions of the insurance

---

2 Compare Polinsky and Shavell (2010) (punitive damages should be used to offset undersuit) with Goldberg and Zipursky (2010) (pain and suffering should be used to offset undersuit).

paradigm as a basis for changing tort law (150 P.2d 436, 461 (Cal. 1944) (Traynor, J, concurring)). Decades ago, Guido Calabresi (1970) was the first modern scholar to conclude that tort law functions as a kind of third-party insurance system and to develop the insights to be drawn from viewing tort as an alternative to first-party insurance as a means of allocating accident costs. Since then, many other law and economics scholars have looked at the desirability of pain and suffering damages by applying the concept that the tort system is an alternative to first-party insurance markets. Accordingly, they believe that the proper way to evaluate the desirability of pain and suffering damages in tort law is to ask how much, if any, people would be willing to pay for first-party insurance coverage that compensates for pain and suffering loss (Rubin 1993; Danzon 1984; Polinsky and Shavell 2010).[3]

And the answer? Apparently not much. Law and economics scholars who have studied consumer demand for pain and suffering insurance have found evidence that consumers do not purchase first-party insurance for pain and suffering losses on the free market (Priest 1987; Cooter 1989; Calfee and Rubin 1992; Schwartz 1988).[4] They therefore conclude that mandatory insurance for pain and suffering provided by the tort system is not desired by consumers, and is thus presumptively inefficient.

Figure 4.1 shows the neo-classical way to present the theoretical argument for why people demand insurance.

Curve V(1) presents an individual's utility as function of his wealth. The curve is concave because people's utility increases with greater wealth, although at a diminishing rate. That is, the amount of utility people get from an additional dollar of wealth when they are poor is larger than from an additional dollar when they are rich. The slope of the utility function is the individual's marginal utility of wealth. At low wealth levels, the curve is steep, because marginal utility is high: a small increase in wealth generates a large rise in the person's utility. At the other extreme, where wealth is high, its marginal utility is small: the curve is almost flat, indicating that a one dollar increase in wealth will not generate a large increase in utility.

The concavity of the graph has been interpreted as also representing

---

3 For the alternative view that deterrence is the dominant function of tort law see Landes and Posner 1987.

4 Additionally, Croley and Hanson (1995) survey the literature and find widespread agreement with the absence of a demand for non-pecuniary insurance; however, they also provide a theoretical basis for a rational consumer to purchase pain and suffering insurance.

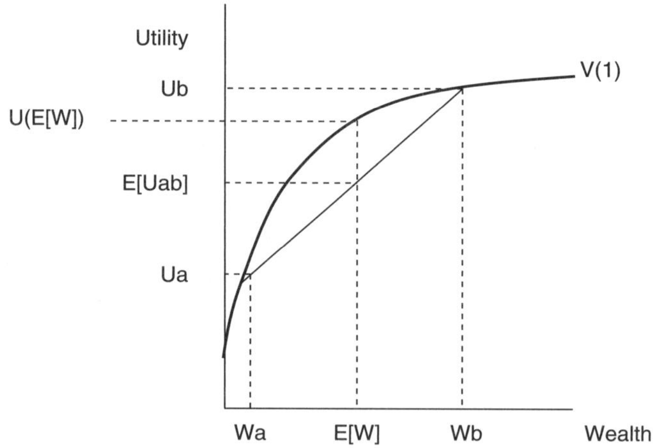

Figure 4.1 Utility as a function of wealth

risk aversion.[5] To see this, suppose that a person starts with some wealth *before* experiencing any loss. This starting point is represented by Wb. Assume that there is a 50 percent chance the individual will be involved in an accident which will cause him to lose wealth and wind up at wealth level Wa. (There is also a 50 percent chance he will experience no loss at all and remain at Wb.) If the accident occurs, his utility falls from Ub to Ua.

Without insurance, because there is a 50 percent chance he would have either utility Ua or Ub, his average, or expected utility will be the average of these two points, represented in the graph by point E[Uab]. If the person did decide to purchase insurance, he would lose for sure the premium, which due to the high risk involved will be very high. After paying the fair premium (the premium which represents the expected risk without any profits to the insurance company) the person would have a wealth of E[W] and a utility of U(E[W]). But then he would no longer face a risk of loss; he is insured. As the graph shows, the person has more utility from U(E[W]) than from E[Uab]. He prefers to pay a premium (and forsake some amount of money for sure) than to face the relevant gamble. In other words, the person would prefer to shift money from the 'before the accident' state of the world, where his marginal utility of money is relatively low, to the 'after the accident' state

[5] As I showed elsewhere, this representation confuses expected utility theory and Bernoulli's utility function. I proceed with this representation as it is the convention.

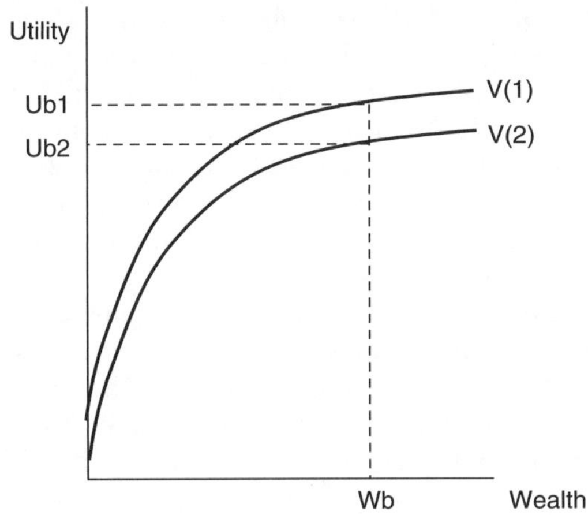

Figure 4.2 Utility as a function of wealth – adding non-monetary losses

of the world, where his marginal utility is relatively high. This shift of wealth makes sense because the person loses less utility from paying a premium than he expects to gain from having insurance coverage. This is how the demand for insurance for monetary loss is usually explained and rationalized.

Figure 4.2 shows what happens when non-monetary losses are introduced.

Curve V(2) represents the person's utility function after a non-monetary loss. As one can see the only change is a shift downwards of Curve V(1) representing the fact that the person lost no wealth but only utility. His 'after the accident' utility is Ub2 which is lower than the utility before it – Ub1. The loss is, after all, just non-monetary. Here, the argument goes, people will not shift money to the 'after the accident' state of the world because the marginal utility is exactly the same. No gain in utility is experienced from such a shift. And, if one takes into account that insurers profit from these transactions, so the premium is not actuarially fair, then the conclusion is that insureds lose from buying insurance against non-monetary losses, and hence will not demand any such coverage. This is how the lack of demand for insurance for non-monetary losses is usually explained and rationalized (Cook and Graham 1977).

To sum up, under the dominant law and economics view, the reason consumers don't purchase pain and suffering insurance is that suffering a non-pecuniary loss frequently will not alter an individual's need for money. That is, a purely non-pecuniary loss will – by definition – not change the utility of an additional dollar of wealth (Shavell 1987).[6] Only in cases where a non-pecuniary loss raises someone's marginal utility of wealth (for example, if the victim values a post-loss dollar highly because it is needed to pay for daily care), will the rational consumer be willing to pay for insurance against this kind of loss (Shavell 1987; Shavell 2003). Because purchasing insurance is giving up money today for the receipt of money in a contingency, consumers will only purchase insurance if money is more valuable in that contingency.

Evidence from the market seems to support this conclusion. Shavell (2003), for example, concludes that because actual insurance policies tend to cover only pecuniary losses, this suggests that, on the whole, non-pecuniary losses do not raise the value of money to consumers, or that their effect on people's marginal utility is usually small. Shavell further contends that there is good evidence that policyholders tend to insure property only for its market value, and do not purchase coverage for sentimental value, suggesting that they deem non-pecuniary losses unworthy of insuring against. Under this view, payments in tort for pain and suffering damages are almost universally too high because consumers would be willing to pay almost nothing for insurance that provided equivalent coverage for such losses (Shavell 2003). Awarding pain and suffering damages forces consumer to pay for something they do not value, which is inefficient.

As one would expect, some tort theorists have rejected the comparison between first-party insurance markets and the tort system. Goldberg and Zipursky (2010) argue that people have many reasons for being uninsured or underinsured. Thus the assumption that private insurance markets precisely illustrate the value assigned to injury compensation is flawed, and therefore any first-party insurance scheme will systematically undercompensate (Goldberg and Zipursky 2010).[7]

But here I am not interested in rejecting the insurance paradigm. Rather, I argue that even if one grants its assumptions, there are several problems with the conclusion that pain and suffering damages should be rejected.

---

[6] George Priest (1987) notes: 'Non-pecuniary losses do not affect the marginal value of wealth across states of the world . . . Losses representing pain and suffering or other emotional effects of an injury, therefore, are never insured in first party markets because it is not worthwhile for consumers to pay the premiums necessary to support coverage of them.'

[7] They also note that many people lack first-party insurance altogether, and for these people the tort system represents their only form of insurance. People may place great value on accident insurance and still not purchase it because they lack the resources.

a. Monetary and non-monetary losses are not easily distinguishable in practice

Shavell's (2003) conclusion that a rational consumer will only insure against monetary damages is based on the assumption that the value of money for compensating non-monetary harm is not higher in the 'after the accident' state of the world. Shavell uses an example of a person who loses an irreplaceable family portrait with immense sentimental value as evidence for this assertion. He notes that even if the portrait is destroyed, there is no reason to believe that the owner's need for money will increase. However much he may regret the loss, the utility he would obtain from having more money to spend would be unchanged from its pre-accident level (Shavell 2003). Thus, no net utility will be gained from shifting money from the pre-accident level to the post-accident level; they will exactly offset each other. And, given that shifting money is costly, it is better not to do so.

However, often it is hard to tell whether the victim's marginal utility of money will increase or decrease after the accident. Consider someone who lost her leg. Does that *increase* her marginal utility of money (because she needs more emotional support)? Or does it *decrease* her marginal utility of money because she now cannot go skiing? Either is possible on net, and for many injuries it may be quite hard to say what the effect on marginal utility from money is (Cook and Graham 1977).

Moreover, our legal system does not (and should not) actually allow offsetting costs in the way described above. That is, the defendant cannot tell the plaintiff: my negligent behavior which caused your leg loss saved you money on ski trips, and therefore this saving should be deducted from the damages owed to you. Nor will it hear a plaintiff's response: sure, but you also deprived me of my hedonic satisfaction from taking these ski trips so you should add back to the calculus damages for that as well. This is just not how our legal system can or should work.

Thus, when we constrain the analysis to types of losses the legal system actually takes into account, it seems as if in most cases where tort law awards pain and suffering damages, people's need for money *is* actually higher after the accident. Economic analysis demonstrates that when victims are risk-averse, *all* reductions in wealth due to pecuniary losses increase their post-accident marginal utility of money. As we saw, according to the standard analysis a reduction of wealth is represented as a movement to the left along the utility curve. In contrast, a non-pecuniary loss represents a downward shift in the entire utility function, without any reduction in the victim's monetary wealth. While not *necessarily* true, in reality, most of what courts consider *non*-pecuniary losses do in all likelihood increase the victim's marginal utility of wealth, just as monetary losses do. Indeed, the typical case involving pain and suffering damages is not about a lost family portrait, but rather about a severe physical injury accompanied by an emotional distress. Shavell (2003) himself notes this in an example of a person who needs continuous medical care after an accident, which increases her need for money to pay for the continuous care. Shavell would consider these medical expenses a pecuniary loss and therefore worthy of compensation in tort law. But what if the person who needs continuous care after an accident also needs counseling for depression? Would treatment for such suffering also be a pecuniary loss? If the cost of a psychiatrist to help cope with the limitations of disability and continuous pain can be considered pecuniary loss, what about the loss of income from her spouse who divorces her because she is now disabled, depressed, and a much greater drain on the household's resources than before the accident? Would compensation for the loss of the spouse's income be pecuniary loss?

This inquiry serves to illustrate the confusion between the way that economists and lawyers regard the definitions of pecuniary and non-pecuniary losses. If opponents of pain and suffering damages in tort law only object to damages for the loss of family portraits (because almost everything else should be considered monetary), then despite the rhetorical gap between them and proponents of pain and suffering damages, there is no such gap at all between the camps in practice.

b. Monetary and non-monetary losses are not easily distinguishable even in theory

The previous section argued that in practice it is hard to distinguish between monetary and 'non-monetary' harms. In this section I advance a more radical claim: the distinction may not even be valid in theory. Indeed, confusion about the line between monetary and non-monetary damages is something that both scholars and courts have struggled with. Prosser (1941), one of the leading tort scholars of all time, has said that there is no normative distinction to be drawn between physical injury, illness, or psychic distress. Harm is harm. The Restatement (Third) also recognized the problems that courts experienced defining physical harm under §436A of the Second Restatement Comment c, where the 'loose' boundary between physical and emotional harm led to court confusion as to whether emotional harm was permitted under the Second Restatement (American Law Institute 2012). Feldman (2005) argues that the legal distinction between economic and non-economic damages did not originate in the discipline of economics and is not justified by economic principles. Indeed, any economist will agree that wealth is not the equivalent of well-being. Insurance that provides '[f]ull coverage in a monetary sense is not the same as [insurance that offers] full coverage in a sense of total well-being' (Schlesinger and Doherty 1985). Modern economics values welfare, and while welfare may be a function of wealth, many things that are considered 'non-economic' by modern tort law are also included in the modern economist definition of welfare. Feelings such as fear, anxiety, shock, and humiliation are considered non-economic harms by modern tort law, but these are properly understood as components or determinants of welfare (Adler and Posner 2008). Indeed, even within the law and economics movement proponents of the dominant view against awards of pain and suffering damages acknowledge this difference between wealth and well-being (Kaplow and Shavell 2001).

To better see the argument, one only needs to replace the horizontal axis in Figure 4.1 with something like 'resources' (a term suggested by the philosopher Ronald Dworkin) or 'capabilities' (a term suggested by Nobel Laureate in Economics Amartya Sen) or any other such term which encompasses the basic intuition that people care about stuff other than just money. Then, any reduction in 'resources' or 'capabilities' or such, for monetary or non-monetary reasons, can generate a demand for insurance. Only two assumptions are needed. First, that money can improve one's utility, even if the source of the loss did not originate in loss of wealth. For example, that people who became disabled (without any associated wealth loss because, for example, they are fully insured against such losses) will get a boost in their utility if they receive money they can spend on things that matter to them, like donating to the Chicago Symphony Orchestra or the Gates Foundation. This assumption seems quite intuitive and does not require further justifications. The second assumption is that people experience diminishing marginal utility from 'resources' or 'capabilities', that is, their utility from having more (more money, less anxiety, less pain, etc.) is smaller the larger their welfare is. This assumption also seems intuitive. Given these two assumptions, one can easily replicate the argument used by neo-classical economists to justify the demand for insurance for monetary coverage and apply it to any 'resources' or 'capabilities' loss, including non-monetary losses.

Thus, it is not obvious that even for law and economics scholars (who are guided by the principle that an increase in the post-accident marginal utility of money justifies compensation) there is a valid theoretical basis for the separation of monetary and non-monetary damages. If correct, this undermines the law and economics contention that non-pecuniary losses can be singled out as inefficient.

c. The theoretical lack of demand argument assumes independence of monetary and non-monetary losses

In this section I return to the theoretical framework used to analyze the problem of pain and suffering damages (which as we saw above, uses the insurance paradigm) and accept the notion which I rejected above that monetary and non-monetary damages can be theoretically and practically distinguished. I surrender to the conventional wisdom on its own terms. And yet, I argue that a critical problem with the conventional wisdom is that it assumes that pecuniary and non-pecuniary damages are *independent* of each other. However, the mathematics of the conventional economic model for the demand for pain and suffering insurance by rational insureds changes once we drop the independence assumption. And when the math changes, the implications change as well.

The model on which law and economics scholars relied to develop their claim for the undesirability of pain and suffering damages was introduced by economists Cook and Graham in the late 1970s (Shavell 1987; Cook and Graham 1977). Assuming pecuniary and non-pecuniary losses are independent, Cook and Graham used Expected Utility Theory (the leading theoretical framework for rational choice under uncertainty) to show that rational people will not insure against pure non-pecuniary losses, what they called 'irreplaceable commodities'. But, as economists Doherty and Schlesinger demonstrated in two papers in the mid-1980s, dropping the independence assumption changes the math and the ultimate conclusion (Doherty and Schlesinger 1983; Schlesinger and Doherty 1985). Unfortunately, the insight presented by Doherty and Schlesinger has not attracted as much attention as the original Cook and Graham model did. Redoing the math but without assuming monetary and non-monetary losses are independent of each other, Doherty and Schlesinger conclude that where insurance is available for the monetary loss, but not available for a separate and positively correlated non-monetary loss, it would be optimal for the rational consumer to purchase more than full coverage on the monetary insurable event. Citing Cook and Graham (1977) they write: '[I]nsurance is only an indemnification for a loss, [and] even with full coverage of monetary values, the world is a risky place. Insuring so-called "Irreplaceable commodities" is an example' (Schlesinger and Doherty 1985: 404).

Indeed, in the real world, pain and suffering damages are more likely to arise from the same incident as an insured monetary loss than from an incident which does not involve such loss, and thus pain and suffering damages are *not* independent of monetary loss in a variety of cases. For example, in a case of a lightning strike,[8] a person may suffer immediate physical impacts such as cardiac arrest, but may also suffer from chronic pain, depression, dizziness, sleep disorders and other long term neurological conditions (Cherington 2003). While these injuries have an economic component – the cost of treatment and potentially lost wages – they may also have a non-pecuniary aspect that is not independent of the pecuniary loss, such as permanent neurological damage. In fact, it seems that dependence between pecuniary and non-pecuniary harms is the norm rather than the exception, and the assumption of independence is not well grounded in reality. In our example, a rational lightning-victim-to-be *will* purchase more than full coverage on health expenses and lost wages to help compensate for the additional non-pecuniary loss related to chronic pain or sleep deprivation.

In sum, once we allow for interdependency between monetary and non-monetary losses, then even Expected Utility Theory predicts that rational insureds may demand such coverage.[9]

d. The theoretical lack of demand argument relies on expected utility theory

Another way to reach the same conclusion is to abandon the expected utility framework altogether. For example, Croley and Hanson (1995) propose an alternative theoretical basis that *can* support a consumer's purchase of first-party pain and suffering insurance. They use a Rawlsian veil of ignorance approach, where the consumer decides where to distribute money across undecided possible future states of being. In an accident state of being, an accident will happen and the insurance will pay benefits; and in a non-accident state, no accident will happen and the consumer will not receive any return on the premiums paid (Croley and Hanson 1995).

---

[8] Despite their reputation for being rare, lightning strikes are the second leading cause of storm-related death, accounting for more than 80 deaths a year on average (Holle et al. 1995).

[9] Law and economic scholars might respond that lightning simply changes the marginal utility of money 'on the ground' not only via insurable monetary losses but also via non-insurable non-pecuniary losses. Because under this claim the non-pecuniary losses are assumed to increase the marginal utility of wealth, they will lead the policyholder to over-insure the monetary losses. The answer to this argument is similar to the one made above in the context of the family portrait. While scholars' response may save the model presented by Cook and Graham (1977) from the modification presented by Schlesinger and Doherty (1985), a claim I need not discuss here, what is obviously clear is that rational insureds, under both versions of the model, will want to purchase coverage for substantial non-pecuniary losses.

According to Rawls' (1971) maximin criterion, individuals behind the accident veil will distribute goods equally to different states of existence, except to the extent that more will be given to the worst-off individual or group.

Under this framework, Croley and Hanson (1995) consider what the consumer should do if the consumer wishes to buy insurance for an accident which harms her in both monetary and non-monetary ways (recall the lightning example above). Insuring only against monetary losses will leave that consumer worse off in the accident state of the world because the consumer will also suffer non-monetary losses. Even if the consumer enjoys money less in the accident state, she may still want to transfer money from the non-accident state because of the desire to avoid an exceedingly low baseline in any state of the world. Under this analysis it is perfectly sensible for a consumer to wish to transfer money to a future accident state in excess of the monetary losses suffered in the accident, even if the money will confer less enjoyment in that accident state (Croley and Hanson 1995).

Rawls' (1971) maximin principle requires assuming either infinite risk aversion (Harsanyi 1975) or some level of uncertainty aversion (Ellsberg 1961; Schroeder 2007). The first assumption is a highly unrealistic assumption whereas the second is not.

I am obviously not advocating here to abandon Expected Utility Theory, nor that it should be updated to encompass valid observations about human behavior. Others, including Nobel Laureate in Economics Daniel Kahneman, are much better positioned than I am to do that. Indeed, I will come back to this point in the next sub-section. My claim here is more modest: no single theoretical framework is perfect – each has its own problematic assumptions. But when different sensible theoretical frameworks point to the same direction (people will demand coverage for pain-and-suffering damages), one has stronger reasons to believe the direction is the correct one.

e. The theoretical lack of demand argument relies too heavily on the apparent lack of empirical evidence for demand

Another problem with the conventional wisdom is that it relies too heavily on what it perceives to be the empirical evidence that shows people do not demand pain and suffering coverage. Indeed, whether people would demand pain and suffering coverage could and should be assessed empirically. That is, policymakers could use Expected Utility Theory as a starting point, but then inquire whether in the real world, people do in fact demand coverage for pain and suffering losses. If they do not, that would serve as a support for the theory. If they do, law and economics scholars might have to revise their theoretical model of the demand for insurance.

So what do the empirics suggest? Granted, when one looks at private insurance markets, one finds little evidence of demand for pain and suffering coverage, suggesting law and economics scholars may be correct after all. Nevertheless, there are several reasons to believe that people would demand pain and suffering coverage, despite the apparent lack of empirical evidence. The first reason comes from behavioral economics. Theorists such as Nobel Laureate in economics Daniel Kahneman (2011) offer an alternative explanation for why people do not buy insurance for pain and suffering: people often make decisions relying on intuitive 'fast thinking', rather than on careful, deliberative 'slow thinking.' The target of behavioral economists is Expected Utility Theory, which serves to determine the value of people's prospects (Kahneman 2003). Specifically, economists expect people to choose actions yielding the highest expected utility. Kahneman's (2011) experiments identify systematic differences between the expected utility formula and the decisions people make in the real world, particularly when calculating probability and appraising utility. As Tversky and Kahneman (1986) concluded, 'deviations of actual behavior from the normative model are too widespread to be ignored, too systematic to be dismissed as random error, and too fundamental to be accommodated by relaxing the normative system'.

Psychologists and behavioral economists offer a variety of explanations for why people underestimate risks, and might irrationally fail to purchase insurance, especially for pain and suffering losses. (See Kunreuther and Pauly, Chapter 1 in this volume.) One stream focuses on the cognitive processes. People allow familiar scenarios to override statistical information, underestimate the probability of unfamiliar events, and treat gains and losses differently even though Expected Utility Theory predicts they should be treated the same (Kahneman 2011). In relation to purchasing insurance, many people discount the probability that dangerous events will occur when the probability is low, treating the risk as zero (Kunreuther 1976). Consumers also tend to view themselves as less vulnerable to a particular risk than others, and often overestimate their control over risks, believing that they can prevent harms from happening to them (Prentice and Roszkowski 1991–92; Langer and Roth 1975).

Non-pecuniary damages are particularly susceptible to these misperceptions because consumers apparently believe that non-pecuniary damages can be overcome through willpower, in a way that monetary damages cannot. Not only do people tend to overestimate their ability to avoid risks, they also tend to ignore information that contradicts their irrational confidence (Latin 1994). Lay people also find non-pecuniary damages harder to predict because they are more abstract and difficult to conceptualize, and are thus discounted when purchasing insurance. Moreover, a variety of other factors prevent the risk calculation presumed by Expected Utility Theory.[10] The net result is that consumers tend to underestimate rather than overestimate risks, particularly non-pecuniary risks (Latin 1994). Systematic discounting of risk may therefore explain why people do not purchase insurance in general and insurance for pain and suffering coverage in particular.

A second reason why one might not find any empirical evidence of market demand for pain and suffering damages is that the decision to buy first-party insurance is not made in a vacuum. Rather, it is made in the shadow of the existing legal system and the benefits it provides to the injured. That tort law already provides damages for pain and suffering losses provides a reason in and of itself for why people do not demand insurance for such loss in the private market. Moreover, the existing Social Security, health insurance and Workers' Compensation markets reduce the need to purchase first-party insurance under the current system (Avraham 2005). In other words, because the same injury may give rise to several claims in tort, Workers' Compensation and Social Security (and be covered by the victim's health insurance), the demand for pain and suffering coverage in the private market is weakened: many people are already substantially insured by alternatives to first-party coverage.

A third reason why it is difficult to find empirical support for the demand for pain and suffering coverage is a lack of supply. There are a number of supply-side limitations on the availability of pain and suffering insurance. Take adverse selection. If information is either unverifiable or unobservable, the information is considered non-contractable, and insurance companies will not attempt to write an enforceable contract that turns on that information (Croley and Hanson 1995). Pain and suffering might be uniquely susceptible to adverse selection problems because of the inherent privacy of the experience of pain (Kolber 2011). The privacy of subjective experience has enormous consequences for insurers, because only the insureds have true access to the private experience of pain. Adverse selection may occur in the case of pain and suffering insurance because (insurers may believe) consumers may know in advance that they are more prone to non-pecuniary losses than the average person. Those high non-pecuniary loss consumers might be willing to purchase

---

[10] These irrational factors include illiteracy (inability to understand warnings), inattention and incompetence by children or others, reliance on intermediaries, and information overload. All reasons why people would not take the time or understand the information necessary to make a rational choice on risk (Latin 1994). See also Hanson and Kysar 1999.

more insurance, and this behavior will drive up the price of the insurance. This would drive some consumers out of the market, even if they would have purchased the insurance at a lower cost (Croley and Hanson 1995). Because insurers will have difficulty predicting which consumers will have more non-pecuniary losses and are unable to segregate insureds into different risk pools, adverse selection concerns might prevent insurers from providing non-pecuniary loss insurance (Croley and Hanson 1995; Schwartz 1988). As was forcefully argued by Croley and Hanson (1995), the tort system, with its mandatory coverage of all persons and its meticulous adversarial inquiry into plaintiff's harm, might be a better institution to solve this problem.

Lastly, social norms may also limit the extent to which people are willing to purchase insurance against pain and suffering, because valuing emotional intangibles such as relationships in terms of money is widely viewed as repugnant (Croley and Hanson 1995; Roth 2007; Zelizer 1997). In sum, learning from the markets about people's preferences might be a problem when preferences revealed on the market are constrained by cognitive biases, available information, social or economic pressures, and contractual rules (Sunstein 1986; 1993).

And yet, a careful look at the market suggests that people might well demand insurance coverage for pain and suffering loss, despite the numerous problems just discussed (Avraham 2005). Patricia Danzon (1984) finds that there is a demand for pain and suffering coverage despite a multitude of market impediments.[11] A key example of consumers demanding pain and suffering insurance is uninsured motorist bodily injury insurance, which reimburses injured motorists when they are injured by a motorist without insurance or in a hit-and-run accident. Uninsured motorist bodily injury insurance is widely demanded by consumers – between 90 and 99 percent of consumers purchase uninsured motorist coverage when given a choice – and primarily compensates for pain and suffering (O'Connell and Joost 1986; Schwartz 1987).

There is also recent experimental work which has found direct evidence that consumers demand pain and suffering coverage in the absence of other recovery mechanisms such as tort law (Avraham 2005). The experiments were designed to directly investigate individuals' insurance preferences. Those findings provide direct evidence that consumers are willing to purchase insurance for pain and suffering losses at roughly the same amount as the insurance they are willing to purchase for monetary losses

---

[11] She also concludes that pain and suffering awards in tort law exceed the demand seen in the first party insurance market. See also, Avraham 2006.

(Avraham 2005).[12] Comparing the amount spent on the two types of insurance by each individual revealed that the vast majority of study participants treated the two types of insurance identically, either buying both types of insurance or buying neither (Avraham 2005).

f. Summary

There are various reasons why there could not be market demand for pain and suffering insurance, and yet there is direct evidence in the market for willingness to purchase first-party insurance for pain and suffering. Thus, a foundational pillar underlying the dominant viewpoint crumbles. When paired with the more realistic assumption that pecuniary losses and non-pecuniary losses are correlated; that most non-economic losses are substantial and do change people's marginal utility of money; and that people would be willing to buy first-party insurance for pain and suffering if other market impediments did not exist, then even the economic model would lead to the conclusion that pain and suffering damages are efficient and welfare maximizing. Hence, efficiency-minded tort law *should* compensate for such losses. Similar conclusions would almost certainly follow if one takes into account the myriad cognitive biases or abandons the Expected Utility Theory altogether.

The next section discusses a different critique: that tort law, and in particular the law's procedures for pain and suffering damages, is too haphazard and too expensive to administer, relative to the benefits.

C. Pain and Suffering Damages are Too Haphazard and Costly

The claim above has several implications. Let's take them one by one.

a. The entire tort system is too costly

A major line of arguments against pain and suffering damages is that awarding these damages creates a huge burden on the entire tort system. Some argue that this provides a reason to eliminate 'only' pain and suffering damages, while others have argued that the entire tort system should be eliminated (Rubin 1993; O'Connell 1975). Indeed, the cost of the tort system is quite high compared to other administrative and insurance mechanisms, such as Workers' Compensation and Social Security. What might seem like the conventional wisdom asserts that using the courts

---

[12] The difference between the demand for pain and suffering insurance and the demand for monetary damage insurance was not found to be statistically significant (Avraham 2005).

to compensate victims imposes costs that are higher than administrative costs in either the first-party insurance system or government regulatory agencies. In the case of product liability, economic studies have found that victims receive somewhere between $0.46 and $0.57 of every dollar paid by defendants to compensate them for their injuries (Tillinghast-Towers Perrin 2003; Kakalik and Pace 1986; Hersch and Viscusi 2007; Danzon 2000). The litigation system therefore imposes a tax of approximately one dollar for every dollar compensated.

Indeed, critics of the tort system have labeled pain and suffering damages a 'tort tax', which costs every American, under some estimates, about $2,400 per year (*Investor's Business Daily* 2008). Another critic estimates the cost of torts in America at over $865 billion per year (McQuillan and Abramyan 2007). Business consultants at McKinsey & Co. indicate that tort risks rank highly among the factors businesses consider when deciding where to establish operations (McQuillan and Kriss 2009). The Chamber of Commerce reports that the vast majority of businesses consider the legal climate when considering business location decisions (US Chamber of Commerce 2005). Some even contend that the cost of the tort system undermines American competitiveness in the global economy (Shen 2007; Shuchman 1997; Cross 2011).

Moreover, because victims ultimately keep only some of what they receive (some goes to lawyers and some is turned-over to first-party insurers under subrogation arrangements), victims end up with less than half of what defendants pay under the tort system (Polinsky and Shavell 2010). This has led Polinsky and Shavell (2010) to argue that the value of the compensation received through the tort system is even lower than the numbers suggest, since first-party insurance payouts cover the most important needs, while the tort system meets only the remaining and less important needs. In short, the tort system provides only a residual and very 'leaky' means of compensating victims.

The main problem with the numbers cited above is that they are wrong, as they often count the cost of the tort system as including the size of the awards, when those are not costs but legitimate transfers. If I run over your foot with my car and cause $1,000 in damage, the critics count the entire $1,000 payment as 'cost' of the *tort system* when it is nothing of the kind. The $1,000 harm to your foot is indeed a social cost, but not of the tort system. Rather, it is a cost of my negligence towards you. The real cost of the tort system – those associated with administering liability and processing the award – are usually *much* smaller than the amount awarded.

b. Awarding pain and suffering damages is too costly

The claim that gets more traction is not that tort law should be eliminated altogether, but only that *pain and suffering damages* should be done away with. Why? Because administering these damages is so costly that it causes an increase to defendants' liability insurance premium, which is then rolled over to consumers.

Opponents of pain and suffering damages explain that while pecuniary damages lend themselves to accurate estimates, pain and suffering are hard to quantify (King 2004). As a result, victims can inflate or otherwise manipulate their losses in order to receive higher damage awards (Kolber 2007).

And yet, even that more modest claim is probably wrong. Courts have long justifiably recognized that individualized pain and suffering recovery is a foundational principle of tort damages (Rabin 2011). Under any of the foundational principles of tort law: making a victim whole, the deterrence rationale, or (as argued above) under an insurance rationale, it is clear that all damages suffered should be compensated, not just those that lend themselves easily to a back-of-the-envelope calculation. Even if pain and suffering damages are hard to estimate, setting them at zero, which is what denying these damages implies, cannot plausibly be optimal even if it saves costs, given all the other benefits these damages have and which we have discussed above.[13]

But just as arguing that pain and suffering damages are never justified due to their high administrative costs is wrong, so is the opposite argument that pain and suffering damages are *always* justified. Indeed, some tort theorists have argued that the costs, while high, are nevertheless worth paying. Because tort law's function is to provide standards of optimal behavior, right and wrong, to the citizenry, the delays and expense of the tort system are intrinsic parts of it, and therefore are justified even if they are caused by awarding pain and suffering damages (Goldberg and Zipursky 2010). The difficulty with this approach is that it does not really explain what its limits are. Does it not matter at all how costly the administrative costs of the tort system are? Does it not matter that if these costs are too high it might prevent plaintiffs from being able to bring law suits and get their day in court? Thus, it is hard to see how the high costs of awarding pain

[13] While it is true that sometimes, a biased estimate with a lower variance is better than an unbiased estimate with a higher variance, the point in the text is that those who call for abolishing pain and suffering damages are calling in effect for not even trying to estimate the magnitude of damages, which is problematic given their significance.

and suffering damages, assuming these costs are exceptionally high, are a priori always justified.

I therefore continue with the assumption that pain and suffering damages might be unjustified, if their costs are too high compared to their benefits.

But are the costs of administrating pain and suffering damages really high? Opponents of pain and suffering argue that these damages are easily manipulable. Are they? Some research has indeed concluded that pain responses are largely uncorrelated with the degree of verifiable harm, such as the extent of tissue damage (Main 2003). Rather, it is the individual's psychosocial context, cultural background, beliefs, coping mechanisms, and emotional states that dramatically influence the perception of pain (Eich et al. 1999). Most studies, however, suggest that seriousness of injury is an important predictor of awards (Sloan and Hsieh 1990; Vidmar et al. 1998; Diamond et al. 1998). More recent studies even suggest that seriousness of injury is an important predictor of *pain and suffering* awards (Chang 2015). Since courts observe the seriousness of the injury there is a limit to the extent plaintiffs can inflate their pain and suffering loss.

Moreover, even if plaintiffs strategically inflate their reported non-monetary losses, courts have developed ways of dealing with such problems: prohibitions on day-in-life videos, prohibitions on golden-rule arguments (where the jury is asked to put themselves in the shoes of the plaintiffs), prohibitions on the per diem rule, etc. are a few examples for rules which limit plaintiffs' plea strategies. Indeed, courts have been estimating pain and suffering losses in negligence cases as well as in the context of intentional torts for centuries.

Lastly, and perhaps most importantly, though we are still years away from a complete understanding, psychiatry and neuroimaging are making progress on understanding and verifying pain as well as a host of other emotional conditions (Kolber 2007).[14]

Let's start with psychiatry, and specifically with progress in defining and quantifying a verifiable form of pain and suffering called post-traumatic stress disorder (PTSD). Under the guidelines established by the American Psychiatric Association, PTSD requires direct experience of a traumatic event that causes intrusion symptoms such as dreams or memories, avoidance symptoms such as avoiding situations which remind the victim of the traumatic event, mood and cognition changes, and irritable behavior or

[14] Aside from pain fMRI is also being used to explore happiness, sadness, anger, fear, and disgust. It is also changing our understanding of deception, responsibility, and behavior prediction (citations omitted).

startle responses (American Psychiatric Association 2013). PTSD symptoms must persist for more than a month and cause significant difficulties in personal life (American Psychiatric Association 2013). It is not impossible that plaintiffs will fake PTSD symptoms especially when they know their recovery is dependent upon it, yet all in all, PTSD represents a more verifiable and commonly encountered form of pain and suffering harm than ever before.

To the more skeptical, an exciting progress can be found in the field of neuroimaging. Functional magnetic resonance imaging (fMRI) has shown great promise in identifying objective measures of pain, and a recent study was able to use fMRI processes to identify specific neurologic signatures that identified subjects' sensing of pain with an extremely high level of accuracy (Wager et al. 2013). This may indicate that science is very close to being able to verify the existence and extent of pain being felt by an accident victim. In other words, the subjectivity and the ability to exaggerate pain and perhaps suffering may soon be a thing of the past. No longer will juries and triers of fact have reason to doubt the existence of pain. Science may provide a way for us to quantify damages for pain with certainty equal to or even greater than the quantification already available for physical damages. Just as X-ray imaging can verify a claim about a bone fracture, so will fMRI be able to verify a claim about emotional distress. Indeed, neurobiology has uncovered data which provide objective criteria for determining the existence and degree of depression. A summary of key literature in the area of Major Depressive Disorder (MDD) found that MDD is an 'illness with significant neurobiological consequences involving structural, functional and molecular alterations in several areas of the brain' (Maletic et al. 2007).[15] This is another key step towards bringing pain and suffering damages into the realm of the objectively verifiable.

Scientific progress of this kind is important because one serious issue that has plagued pain and suffering awards is the issue of malingering, or continuing to report pain symptoms after the pain has ceased, often for the purpose of continuing to receive disability benefits or inflating pain and suffering awards (Cunnien 1997). Though malingering is difficult to estimate, some have argued that between 34 and 40 percent of chronic pain patients might malinger (Mittenberg et al. 2002; Gervais et al. 2001; Kolber 2007). While it may or may not be the result of malingering, studies have indicated that those involved in personal injury litigation tend to have worse treatment outcomes than similarly injured people who are not

---

[15] This review of the literature also suggests that pharmacotherapy can restore underlying physiology and provide suggestions for clinical treatment.

seeking compensation (Mendelson 1997). (Of course, causality might run both ways: stress and delays from the tort system may actually cause worse treatment outcomes, or those with worse treatment outcomes might file more tort suits.) Malingering presents a very pressing need for a verifiable mechanism through which to confirm the existence and extent of pain. But with recent scientific progress, this might not be an issue for long.

Despite this progress, it is important to remember that medical science is still years away from removing the doubt surrounding the very personal experience of pain. Nevertheless, the progress made by medical science towards verifying pain and suffering undercuts or will soon undercut the argument that defendants' liability insurance premiums are unnecessarily high due to pain and suffering non-verifiability.

c. Pain and suffering damages are too haphazard

Critics' next argument against pain and suffering damages is that they give rise to a lack of horizontal equity or consistency among awards for outwardly-similar injuries (Bovbjerg et al. 1989). The claim here is related to the claim made in the previous sub-section. The difficulty in measuring pain and suffering objectively leaves considerable scope for individual judges or juries to determine the amount awarded based on their own idiosyncratic assessments (Diamond et al. 1998). But the observed lack of horizontal equity in the tort system does not necessarily indicate flawed damage calculations. On the one hand, heterogeneity in awards for what appears objectively to be 'the same' injury might arise because factfinders treat like cases differently. On the other hand, it could also arise because factfinders correctly understand that individuals who appear to suffer a similar injury do not experience the same degree of pain and suffering (Chamallas and Wriggins 2010). Heterogeneity in awards may be a feature, not a bug.

The haphazardness argument often appears with the claim about run-a-way juries. And yet, run-a-way juries might also be just a myth. There is some evidence that the damage range awarded by juries is comparable, if not a smaller range, to those awarded by judges or arbitrators (Vidmar and Rice 1993; Eisenberg et al. 2002). Moreover, a comparison study of US and European pain and suffering awards found similar levels of horizontal inequity among European cases, despite the fact that most European countries have implemented rules intended to minimize horizontal inequity (Sugarman 2005). This suggests that differences between cases that are not observable to the researcher, but that are observable to the factfinder, may indeed be a primary driver of the apparent lack of horizontal consistency.

In sum, observed horizontal inequity might not reflect a real problem. But even if there is lack of horizontal equity on the ground, refusing to award pain and suffering damages is still not necessarily justified. If anything, horizontal inequity simply indicates a need for an efficient process that provides more guidance for whoever is making the damage determination. I will say something about it in my concluding remarks.

d. Summary

I have argued that awarding pain and suffering damages has not been proven to be too costly or haphazard, and that the future will likely bring with it cheaper and more consistent ways to estimate such losses. However, even if one believes the high costs of the tort system and its haphazardness are not justified, it is still puzzling that these costs have motivated calls for limiting or eliminating pain and suffering damages, but not pecuniary damages. Why? Because in fact, the tort system's high administrative costs are probably equally caused by both pecuniary and non-pecuniary awards.

Indeed, economic damages are all too often also very difficult to quantify (Rabin 2011). Who knows what a child's career would look like when she grows up? And yet no one argues damages for loss of future income should be abolished from tort law for being too speculative. Even future medical costs are not that easy to determine because technological progress can make the future treatment of current injuries more expensive or less expensive, without anyone able to tell. Take for example, the famous *Seffert v. Los Angeles Transit Lines*, known for Judge Traynor's strong dissent about the lower court's award of pain and suffering damages. As Rabin has observed, the cost of a lifetime of drug and medical expenses were dramatically underestimated (the plaintiffs received $1,000 in total for drugs for an expected life time of thirty-four years). While best known for illustrating the difficulty of estimating pain and suffering damages, the case actually demonstrates the difficulty of quantifying pecuniary losses (364 P.2d 337 (Cal. 1961)). Robert Rabin, one of the leading tort scholars in the country, concludes that while pain and suffering certainly present monetization difficulties, pecuniary damages such as lost wages, and future expenses are subject to similar difficulties (Rabin 2011).

Moreover, no study has convincingly linked the tort system's high administrative costs to provision of pain and suffering damages. Perhaps counterintuitively, awarding pain and suffering might be the cheaper part of the process. Why? Precisely because monetary harm is more subject to objective proof than is pain and suffering harm, proving monetary harm is probably *more* expensive. To prove monetary harm in an objective fashion requires competing experts to assess a plaintiff's future medical costs, future loss of income, etc. when the future of both the job markets and health care markets are highly uncertain. In contrast, to recover pain and suffering damages, plaintiffs' lawyers often need do little more than just ask for them.

CONCLUDING REMARKS

This chapter demonstrated that in contrast to the conventional wisdom among law and economic scholars, the theory of insurance supports the claim that pain and suffering damages are desirable in tort law and therefore worthy of being covered by liability insurance. When Expected Utility Theory incorporates the reasonable assumptions that non-pecuniary and pecuniary damages are not independent, or when we take into account barriers to the supply of (in contrast to the demand for) pain and suffering insurance in the market, or that no reasonable economic basis justifies devaluing non-pecuniary damages in relation to their pecuniary counterparts, or any of the other arguments made above, then law and economics scholars will actually justify pain and suffering awards. The criticisms of the tort system for incommensurability, delays, and inefficiency should not be used to justify eliminating or limiting pain and suffering damages because these criticisms are overstated and because the same arguments can largely be leveled against pecuniary recoveries.

All in all, any difficulties in estimating pain and suffering damages can be resolved by employing various estimation mechanisms such as ones depending on medical costs (Avraham 2006), loss of pleasure of life scales (Berla et al. 1990), Quality Adjusted Life Years (Karapanou 2014; Adler 2006), and even legislated or court-mandated schedules, as is routinely done in various countries in Europe.

Indeed, examples from other countries and proposals put forward by scholars all show the feasibility of preserving non-pecuniary damages while addressing the efficiency and monetization concerns that plague the current system.

REFERENCES

Adler, Matthew. 2006. 'QALYs And Policy Evaluation: A New Perspective' *Yale J. Health Pol'y, L. & Ethics* 1.

Adler, Matthew, and Eric Posner. 2008. 'Happiness Research and Cost-Benefit Analysis' 37 *Journal of Legal Studies* S253.

American Law Institute. 2012. *Restatement (Third) of Torts: Physical & Emotional Harm*. 8 Scope Note. American Law Institute.

American Psychiatric Association. 2013. *Diagnostic and Statistical Manual of Mental Disorders* (fifth edition) 271–4.
Arlen, Jennifer, and W. Bentley MacLeod. 2003. 'Malpractice Liability for Physicians and Managed Care Organizations' 78 *New York University Law Review* 1929.
Avraham, Ronen. 2005. 'Should Pain-and-Suffering Damages Be Abolished from Tort Law?: More Experimental Evidence' 55 *University of Toronto Law Journal* 941.
Avraham, Ronen. 2006. 'Putting a Price on Pain-and-Suffering Damages: A Critique of the Current Approaches and a Preliminary Proposal for Change' 100 *Northwestern Law Review* 87, 96.
Berla, Edward P., Michael L. Brookshire, and Stan V. Smith. 1990. 'Hedonic Damages and Personal Injury: A Conceptual Approach' 3(1) *Journal of Forensic Economics* 1–8.
Bovbjerg, Randall R., Frank A. Sloan, and James F. Blumstein. 1989. 'Valuing Life and Limb in Tort: Scheduling Pain and Suffering' 83 *Northwestern University Law Review* 908, 924.
Calabresi, Guido. 1970. *The Costs of Accidents: A Legal and Economic Analysis*. New Haven, CT: Yale University Press.
Calfee, John, and Paul Rubin. 1992. 'Some Implications of Damages Payments for Nonpecuniary Losses' 21 *Journal of Legal Studies* 371.
Chamallas, M., and J. Wriggins. 2010. *The Measure of Injury: Race, Gender, and Tort Law*. New York, NY: New York University Press 179, 370.
Chang, Yun-chien. 2015. 'Pain and Suffering Damages in Personal Injury Cases: An Empirical Study' (forthcoming).
Cherington, M. 2003. 'Neurologic Manifestations of Lightning Strikes' 60(2) *Neurology* 182, 185.
Choi, Albert H., and Kathryn E. Spier. 2014. 'Should Consumers be Permitted to Waive Products Liability? Product Safety, Private Contracts, and Adverse Selection' *Journal of Law, Economics, and Organization*: ewt019.
Cohen, A., and R. Dehijia. 2004. 'The Effect of Automobile Insurance and Accident Liability Laws on Traffic Fatalities' 47(2) *Journal of Law and Economics* 357, 393.
Cook, Philip J., and Daniel A. Graham. 1977. 'The Demand for Insurance and Protection: The Case of Irreplaceable Commodities' *The Quarterly Journal of Economics* 143–56.
Cooter, Robert. 1989. 'Towards a Market in Unmatured Tort Claims' 75 *Virginia Law Review* 383, 392.
Croley, Steven P., and Jon D. Hanson. 1995. 'The Non-Pecuniary Costs of Accidents: Pain-and-Suffering Damages in Tort Law' 108 *Harvard Law Review* 1785, 1798, 1822, 1850, 1853.
Cross, Frank B. 2011. 'Tort Law and the American Economy' 96 *Minnesota Law Review* 28, 44.
Cunnien, Alan J. 1997. 'Psychiatric and Medical Syndromes Associated with Deception' in Richard Rogers, ed., *Clinical Assessment of Malingering and Deception* (second edition). New York, NY: Guilford Press.
Danzon, Patricia. 1984. 'Tort Reform and the Role of Government in Private Insurance Markets' 13 *Journal of Legal Studies* 517, 520.
Danzon, Patricia. 2000. 'Liability for Medical Malpractice' in A. J. Culyer and J.P. Newhouse, eds., *Handbook of Health Economics*, Amsterdam: Elsevier. Vol. 1, Chapter 26.
Diamond, Shari Seidman, Michael J. Saks, and Stephen Landsman. 1998. 'Juror Judgments About Liability and Damages: Sources of Variability and Ways to Increase Consistency' 48 *DePaul Law Review* 301, 302, 317.
Doherty, Neil A., and Harris Schlesinger. 1983. 'Optimal Insurance in Incomplete Markets' 91(6) *Journal of Political Economy* 1049.
Eich, Eric, Ian A. Brodkin, John L. Reeves, and Anuradha F. Chawla. 1999. 'Questions Concerning Pain' in Daniel Kahneman, Edward Diener, and Norbert Schwarz, eds., *Well-Being: The Foundations of Hedonic Psychology*. New York, NY: Russell Sage Foundation. 155, 160.

Eisenberg, T., N. LaFountain, B. Ostrom, D. Rottman, and M. T. Wells. 2002. 'Juries, Judges, and Punitive Damages: An Empirical Study' 87 *Cornell Law Review* 743, 744.
Ellsberg, Daniel. 1961. 'Risk, Ambiguity, and the Savage Axioms' 75(4) *Quarterly Journal of Economics* 643–69.
Feldman, Heidi, Li. 2005. 'Loss,' Georgetown Law Faculty Publications and Other Works Paper 919. 4. Available at: http://scholarship.law.georgetown.edu/facpub/919.
Garber, Steven. 1998. 'Product Liability, Punitive Damages, Business Decisions and Economic Outcomes' *Wisconsin Law Review* 237, 290–1.
Geistfeld, Mark. 1995. 'Placing a Price on Pain and Suffering: A Method for Helping Juries Determine Tort Damages for Nonmonetary Injuries' 83 *California Law Review* 773, 782.
Gervais, Roger O., Paul Green, Lyle M. Allen III, and Grant L. Everson, 2001. 'Effects of Coaching on Symptom Validity Testing in Chronic Pain Patients Presenting for Disability Assessments' 2 *Journal of Forensic Neuropsychology* 13, 14.
Goldberg, John C. P., and Benjamin C. Zipursky. 2010. 'The Easy Case for Products Liability Law: A Response to Professors Polinsky and Shavell' 123 *Harvard Law Review* 1919, 1930–1, 1938–9.
Graham, John D. 1991. 'Product Liability and Motor Vehicle Safety' in Peter W. Huber and Robert E. Litan, eds., *The Liability Maze: The Impact of Liability Law on Safety and Innovation*. Washington, DC: Brookings Institution. 183–4.
Hanson, Jon. D., and Douglas A. Kysar. 1999. 'Taking Behavioralism Seriously: The Problem of Market Manipulation' 74 *N. Y. U. Law Review* 630, 699.
Harsanyi, John. 1975. 'Can the Maximin Principle Serve as a Basis for Morality? A Critique of John Rawls's Theory' 69 (2) *The American Political Science Review* 594–606.
Hersch, Joni, and W. Kip. Viscusi. 2007. 'Tort Liability Litigation Costs for Commercial Claims' 9 *American Law & Economics Review* 330, 359, table 5.
Holle, Ronald L., Raúl E. López, K. Howard, J. Vavrek, and J. Allsopp. 1995. 'Safety in the Presence of Lightning' December 15(4) *Seminars Neurology* 375–80.
Investor's Bus. Daily. 2008. 'A Barrister's Baloney' *Investor's Bus. Daily* (L.A.) December 5, 2008. A10.
Kahneman, Daniel. 2003. 'Maps of Bounded Rationality: Psychology for Behavioral Economics' 93 *American Economic Review* 1449.
Kahneman, Daniel. 2011. *Thinking, Fast and Slow*. New York, NY: Farrar, Straus, and Giroux. 21–2.
Kakalik, James S., and Nicholas M. Pace. 1986. *Costs and Compensation Paid in Tort Litigation*. Santa Monica, CA: Rand Publishing Co. ix tbl. S.3. Available at: http://www.rand.org/content/dam/rand/pubs/reports/2006/R3391.pdf.
Kaplow, Louis, and Steven Shavell. 2001. 'Fairness Versus Welfare' 114 *Harvard Law Review* 961, 997.
Karapanou, V. 2014. *Towards a Better Assessment of Pain and Suffering Damages for Personal Injuries. A Proposal Based on Quality Adjusted Life Years*. Cambridge, MA: Intersentia. 1–250.
King, Joseph H. Jr. 2004. 'Pain and Suffering, Noneconomic Damages, and the Goals of Tort Law' 57 *S. M. U. Law Review* 163.
Kolber, Adam J. 2007. 'Pain Detection and the Privacy of Subjective Experience' 33 *American Journal of Law & Medicine* 433, 435, 437.
Kolber, Adam J. 2011. 'The Experiential Future of the Law' 60 *Emory Law Journal* 585, 596.
Kunreuther, Howard. 1976. 'Limited Knowledge and Insurance Protection' 24 *Public Policy* 227, 250.
Landes, William, and Richard Posner. 1987. *The Economic Structure of Tort Law*. Cambridge, MA: Harvard University Press. 186–7.
Langer, Ellen J., and Jane Roth. 1975. 'Heads I Win, Tails It's Chance: The Illusion of Control as a Function of the Sequence of Outcomes in a Purely Chance Task' 32 *Journal of Personality & Social Psychology* 951, 954.
Latin, Howard A. 1994. '"Good" Warnings, Bad Products, and Cognitive Limitations' 41 *UCLA Law Review* 1193.
Main, Chris J. 2003. 'The Nature of Chronic Pain' in Peter W. Halligan, Christopher Bass,

and David A. Oakley, eds., *Malingering and Illness Deception*. Oxford: Oxford University Press. 171, 172.
Maletic, V., M. Robinson, T. Oakes, S. Lyengar, S. G. Ball, and J. Russell. 2007. 'Neurobiology of Depression: An Integrated View of Key Findings' 61(2) *International Journal of Clinical Practice* 2030–40.
McQuillan, Lawrence J., and Hovannes Abramyan. 2007. Op-Ed., 'The Tort Tax' *Wall Street Journal* March 27. A18.
McQuillan, Lawrence J., and Mark Kriss. 2009. Op-Ed., 'To Revive New York's Economy, Attack Lawsuit Abuse' *New York Daily News*. November 18. Available at: www.nydaily-news.com/opinion/revive-new-york-economy-attack-lawsuit-abuse-article-1.417910.
Mendelson, George. 1997. 'Outcome-Related Compensation: In Search of a New Paradigm' in Richard Rogers, ed., *Clinical Assessment of Malingering and Deception* (second edition). New York, NY: Guilford Press. 220, 222.
Mittenberg, W., C. Patton, E. M. Canyock, and D. C. Condit. 2002. 'Base Rates of Malingering and Symptom Exaggeration' 24 *Journal of Clinical and Experimental Neuropsychology* 1094, 1096.
O'Connell, Jeffrey. 1975. *Ending Insult to Injury? No Fault Insurance for Products and Services*. Urbana, IL: University of Illinois Press.
O'Connell, Jeffrey, and Robert H. Joost. 1986. 'Giving Motorists a Choice Between Fault and No-Fault Insurance' 72 *Virginia Law Review* 61, 79, n. 52.
Polinsky, Mitchell A., and Steven Shavell. 2010. 'The Uneasy Case for Product Liability' 123 *Harvard Law Review* 1437, 1459.
Prentice, Robert A., and Mark E. Roszkowski. 1991–92. '"Tort Reform" and the Liability "Revolution": Defending Strict Liability in Tort for Defective Products' 27 *Gonzaga Law Review* 251, 291.
Priest, George L. 1987. 'The Current Insurance Crisis and Modern Tort Law' 96 *Yale Law Journal* 1521, 1546–7, 1553.
Prosser, William L. 1941. *Handbook of the Law of Torts* §34. St Paul, MN: West Publishing Co. 211–12.
Rabin, Robert L. 2011. 'The Pervasive Role of Uncertainty in Tort Law: Rights and Remedies' 60 *DePaul Law Review* 431, 444.
Rahdert, Mark. 1995. *Covering Accident Costs: Insurance, Liability, and Tort Reform*. Philadelphia, PA: Temple University Press.
Rawls, John. 1971. *A Theory of Justice*. Cambridge, MA: Harvard University Press. 75–8.
Roth, Alvin E. 2007. 'Repugnance as a Constraint on Markets' 21(3) *Journal of Economic Perspectives* 37–58.
Rubin, Paul. 1993. *Tort Reform by Contract*. Washington, DC: AEI Press.
Schlesinger, Harris, and Neil A. Doherty. 1985. 'Incomplete Markets for Insurance: An Overview' 52(3) *Journal of Risk and Insurance* 402–23.
Schroeder, Drew. 2007. 'Rawls and Risk Aversion'. Available at: www.cmc.edu/pages/faculty/ASchroeder/docs/RawlsMaximin.pdf.
Schwartz, Alan. 1988. 'Proposals for Product Liability Reform: A Theoretical Synthesis' 97 *Yale Law Journal* 353, 362–7.
Schwartz, Gary T. 1987. 'A Proposal for Tort Reform: Reformulating Uninsured Motorist Plans' 48 *Ohio State Law Journal* 419, 428.
Shavell, Steven. 1984. 'A Model of the Optional Use of Liability and Safety Regulation' 15(2) *Rand Journal of Economics* 271.
Shavell, Steven. 1987. 'Economic Analysis of Accident Law' Cambridge, MA: Harvard University Press. 245–7.
Shavell, Steven. 2003. 'Economic Analysis of Accident Law,' working paper 9694. 9-10. Available at: www.nber.org/papers/w9694.pdf.
Shen, Ji Yao, Derek Dunn, and Yun Shen. 2007. 'Challenges Facing U.S. Manufacturing and Strategies' 23 *Journal of Industrial Technology* April 1 – October 5.
Shuchman, Philip. 1997. 'It Isn't that the Tort Lawyers are so Right, It's Just that the Tort Reformers are so Wrong' 49 *Rutgers Law Journal* 485, 504.

Sloan, Frank, and Chee Ruey Hsieh. 1990. 'Variability in Medical Malpractice Payments: Is the Compensation Fair?' 24 *Law & Society Review* 997.

Sugarman, Stephen D. 2005. 'A Comparative Law Look at Pain and Suffering Awards' 55 *DePaul Law Review* 399, 413.

Sunstein, Cass R. 1986. 'Legal Interface with Private Preferences' 53 *University of Chicago Law Review* 1129, 1146.

Sunstein, Cass R. 1993. *After the Rights Revolution: Reconceiving the Regulatory State*. Cambridge, MA: Harvard University Press. 40, 44.

Tillinghast-Towers Perrin. 2003. U.S. Tort Costs: Update 17. Available at: www.towersperrin.com/tillinghast/publications/reports/2003_Tort_Costs_Update/Tort_Costs_Trends_2003_Update.pdf.

Tversky, Amos, and Daniel Kahneman. 1986. 'Rational Choice and the Framing of Decisions' 59 *Journal of Business* S251.

US Chamber of Commerce. 2005. Harris Interactive U.S. Chamber of Commerce State Liability Systems Ranking Study 13. Available at: http://courts.delaware.gov/superior/pdf/harris_2005.pdf.

Vidmar, Neil, and Jeffrey Rice. 1993. 'Assessments of Noneconomic Damages Awards in Medical Negligence: A Comparison of Jurors with Legal Professionals' 78 *Iowa Law Review* 883, 898.

Vidmar, Neil, Felicia Gross, and Mary Rose. 1998. 'Jury Awards for Medical Malpractice and Post-Verdict Adjustments of Those Awards' 48 *DePaul Law Review* 265, 268–9.

Viscusi, W. Kip. 1991. *Reforming Products Liability*, Cambridge, MA: Harvard University Press. 50.

Wager, Tor D., Lauren Y. Atlas, Martin A. Lindquist, Mathieu Roy, Choong-Wan Woo, and Ethan Kross. 2013. 'An fMRI-Based Neurologic Signature of Physical Pain' 368, no. 15. *New England Journal of Medicine* 1388–97.

Wickelgren, Abraham L. 2006. 'The Inefficiency of Contractually-Based Liability with Rational Consumers' 22 *Journal of Law, Economics, and Organization* 168.

Zelizer, Viviana. 1997. *The Social Meaning of Money*. Princeton, NJ: Princeton University Press.

PART II

THE ROLE OF THE STATE IN INSURANCE MARKETS

5. 'Social insurance', risk spreading, and redistribution

James Kwak[1]

Record peacetime federal budget deficits, ominous projections for the growth of the national debt, and the rise of Tea Party conservatism have stimulated a national debate over the size of government, the role of government, and fiscal policy in the United States. In that debate, major domestic spending programs, beginning with Social Security[2] and Medicare, play a starring role. The common perception, at least within the Beltway, is that these programs must be brought under control: spending on Social Security and Medicare together is projected to grow from 7.9 percent of gross domestic product (GDP) in 2013 to 11.3 percent of GDP over the next 25 years, or from 41 percent to 47 percent of total federal spending excluding interest payments on debt (CBO 2013b).[3] Beyond the numbers, however, lies the more fundamental question of whether the federal government should be using these programs to shift resources among different segments of the population on such a vast scale.

The most common defense of Social Security, Medicare, unemployment insurance, and similar government policies is that they constitute 'social insurance', commonly thought of as government-orchestrated protection against specific risks faced by most if not all people. This protection arguably increases social welfare for the same reasons that insurance is beneficial – that is, it increases the expected utility of risk-averse individuals. Critics, however, argue that these programs are not insurance (or not very good insurance), but instead are tax-and-transfer schemes. These attacks come mostly from conservatives, for whom one-size-fits-all

[1] I thank Laura Femino for editing assistance, Dan Schwarcz and Peter Siegelman for their extensive suggestions, and the participants in a University of Connecticut Insurance Law Center symposium on The Law and Economics of Insurance for comments.

[2] When used on its own, the term 'Social Security' here refers to the Social Security Old Age, Survivors, and Disability Insurance (OASDI) program.

[3] The figures in the text are from the Extended Alternative Fiscal Scenario and are net of offsetting program receipts, primarily Medicare premium payments. The Congressional Budget Office estimates gross program spending at 8.4 percent of GDP in 2013 and 12.3 percent of GDP in 2038 (CBO 2013b).

government services funded by compulsory levies are usually inferior to leaving those services up to a free market. But some progressives also object to the insurance features of these programs, which sometimes mandate that high-income participants receive benefits that they seem not to need. These critics prefer means-tested public assistance to social insurance because it more efficiently transfers resources to those who need them most.

This chapter addresses the question of what role social insurance programs perform: insurance, redistribution via taxes and transfers, or something else. In the first part of this chapter, I pragmatically use the term 'social insurance' to mean 'those programs that are generally considered social insurance',[4] drawing examples primarily from Social Security (including old age, survivors, and disability insurance), Medicare (including Parts A, B, and D), and unemployment insurance. I take this approach for two reasons. First, academic specialists acknowledge the slippery nature of social insurance and struggle to define it precisely. Atkinson (1991: 113) observes: 'There is indeed a lot of the proverbial elephant about social insurance: we may not be able to define an elephant, but we recognise one when we see it'; according to Graetz and Mashaw (1999: 25) 'Social insurance has no "essence"'. Second, my goal is to describe and analyze a major component of government social policy as it exists today – not to begin with a logically precise definition that settles every question in advance.

In this chapter, I argue that social insurance programs do play the risk-spreading role of private insurance, but they also serve an *ex ante* redistributive function more typical of tax-and-transfer schemes. I show that the balance between risk spreading and redistribution varies depending on the information that participants have about their current and future circumstances, which depends in turn on the time frame under consideration. In other words, a given program will look more or less like private insurance or public assistance depending on the time horizon chosen. Programs like Social Security appear to be simply redistributive when viewed over a short time frame, such as one year, because we know who will be net beneficiaries and who will be net payers. Over a lifetime, however, outcomes are much harder to foresee, and so these programs spread risk over the entire pool of participants – the core function of insurance. This fundamental ambiguity is one reason why social insurance programs are always

4 Even people who argue that social insurance is not insurance, or is not a meaningful concept generally, still use examples from the same list of programs in making their points.

subject to debates over framing, particularly given the political interests involved.

As background, part I of this chapter compares various government programs to private insurance before summarizing some of the prominent ways of conceptualizing social insurance. Part II proposes a new way to think about social insurance programs: as risk-spreading arrangements that are more rational or less rational for participants depending on the time frame that they consider and the amount of information that they possess about their personal circumstances. Even under this approach, however, it remains impossible to pin down exactly where social insurance begins and ends, as shown in part III. Part IV discusses alternative framings of social insurance programs to serve competing political ends – implying that we cannot ever settle the debate over what social insurance *is*.

I. PRIVATE INSURANCE AND SOCIAL INSURANCE

The concept of social insurance is ambiguous because it is the product of historical contingency. Government intervention to protect the old, the young, the out-of-work, the disabled, and the sick has taken many forms, beginning, according to the conventional narrative, with the programs introduced by German Chancellor Otto von Bismarck in the late nineteenth century. Since then, observers have been struggling to bring conceptual order to this complicated history.

A. Risk Spreading and Redistribution

The core function of any insurance program is spreading risk among a pool of participants. In theory, insurance works because human beings are risk averse. If premiums are set equal to expected losses, risk-averse purchasers benefit (in utility terms) and sellers break even; even if premiums include transaction costs and a return on the capital invested in insurers, purchasers will often be made better off because of risk aversion. A private product or a government program provides insurance to the extent that it spreads the risk of uncertain future events across the people who face that risk. It is also insurance to the extent that it allows a participant to shift her resources among different future states of the world (that is, from states in which a loss does not occur to states in which it does occur).

Insurance necessarily involves redistribution in the relatively trivial sense that, seen retrospectively, cash is transferred from people who do not suffer losses to those who do. At the time people purchase insurance, however, this is not redistribution, assuming that each individual pays for her expected losses in the form of premiums.[5] In practice, insurance also redistributes resources in another, more substantive sense. Among any group of insureds, even those whom the insurer identifies as equivalent risks, some will have a higher than average risk of loss and others will have a lower than average risk. The fact that they pay the same premiums[6] means that, *ex ante*, there is redistribution from low-risk participants to high-risk participants (see Abraham 1986: chapter 4). One objective of insurance underwriting is to identify and price degrees of risk accurately in order to avoid undercharging high-risk people and overcharging low-risk people. When this is difficult or costly – for example, health insurers may lack the information necessary to identify individual health risks – the problem of adverse selection can arise: if insurers charge a single price to both low- and high-risk people, the former may choose not to buy insurance (since its costs outweigh its expected benefits), leaving only the latter in the pool of insureds and forcing insurers to increase their prices commensurately. The inability of insurers to identify and account for differing levels of riskiness in individual behavior can also contribute to moral hazard: the (theoretically) increased propensity of people to take on risk if they are insured against it.

In unregulated private markets, some people will buy insurance and others will not. People decline to buy insurance for several reasons. The best reason is that they simply do not need it: even risk-averse people are effectively risk-neutral with respect to small changes in wealth and thus should not insure themselves against small losses (Rabin and Thaler 2001). But there are many other, more worrisome reasons for underinsurance. Insurers may not offer needed insurance because of some market failure. Individuals may underestimate their own risk of loss. They may recognize the risk they face, but may not be aware that insurance exists. They may not be able to find insurance at a fair price – one that only moderately exceeds their expected losses. Or, even given a fair price, they may not be able to afford it. As a result, people face significant risks against which they have no protection. The programs generally thought of as social insurance attempt to make insurance available to these people for one or more reasons of public policy. For example, Social Security Disability Insurance is motivated in part by the belief that people should have some

5 For brevity, I do not mention transaction costs and capital costs here.

6 By 'the same premiums,' I mean the same premium per dollar of insured value.

protection from being physiologically or mentally unable to work, even if they are unable to buy that protection in the private market; Social Security Old Age and Survivors Insurance is motivated in part by the need to protect people from outliving their savings, a risk that is otherwise difficult to insure.

B. What the Government Does

This section discusses Social Security, Medicare, and unemployment insurance, which in the United States are typically thought of as canonical examples of social insurance.[7] These programs typically use one or more mechanisms to provide insurance that is considered socially beneficial but that, in the opinion of policymakers, would not be sufficiently provided or purchased in a purely private market. The principal program features include compulsory participation, underwriting constraints, and explicit subsidies. The insurance is often provided by a public entity, but may be delivered by private companies under a statutory mandate.

First, compulsory participation is a requirement that a program cover all people in a certain class. In the United States, Medicare Part A (hospital insurance) and unemployment insurance are mandatory for virtually all workers, as is Social Security with a few narrow exceptions. This means that contributions must be paid by or on behalf of workers,[8] who thereby gain a right to benefits. Compulsory participation overcomes potential adverse selection problems because low-risk individuals cannot opt out of insurance, which would drive up premiums for everyone else. Not all programs commonly thought of as social insurance are mandatory, however; Medicare Parts B (medical insurance) and D (prescription drugs) are not paid for by or on behalf of workers until they become beneficiaries, and participation is voluntary.[9]

Second, government insurance programs often place constraints on underwriting, which limit the ability of insurers to decide whom they want to insure and at what price. In a theoretical free market, insurers can use

---

[7] See, for example, National Academy of Social Insurance, 'Learn'. Available at www.nasi.org/learn.

[8] Contributions can be paid by employees, employers, or both. Even if they are paid by employers, at least some of the burden probably falls on employees in the form of lower wages.

[9] Medicare Part A is financed by a payroll tax levied on current workers. Parts B and D are financed by premiums paid by current beneficiaries and by general tax revenues.

any factors to differentiate between high-risk and low-risk insureds.[10] With social insurance – especially if it is compulsory – some limits on risk underwriting may be necessary either to make insurance affordable to everyone or because of fairness concerns. Medicare does not differentiate among participants according to their health status, either during their working years or when collecting benefits; if it did charge premiums based on existing medical conditions, many people would probably not be able to afford Parts B and D. Unemployment insurance is experience rated (premiums are based in part on losses incurred in prior periods), so businesses that incur higher losses pay higher premiums. The rating system does not consider the riskiness of individual workers, however, so an employer does not pay higher premiums for an employee with a history of involuntary job losses.[11] Social Security does not treat people differently based on their expected longevity or their risk of disability. These constraints redistribute wealth *ex ante* from people with low risks to people with high risks on the dimensions along which underwriting does not occur.

Third, government programs often incorporate explicit subsidies either from 'outside' or from within the pool of insureds. These subsidies are in addition to the implicit subsidy created by underwriting constraints. For example, the lack of medical underwriting in Medicare Part B is an implicit subsidy from healthy people to people with chronic illnesses that helps reduce the cost of insurance for the latter. That is not enough to make Medicare Part B affordable, however: if every beneficiary were charged the average expected losses for the entire pool, Part B would likely be too expensive for most, largely because the elderly incur high health care costs on average. Therefore, approximately 75 percent of the costs of Part B are an explicit subsidy paid out of general revenues collected from income and other taxes. Primary unemployment insurance is provided by state funds financed by employer contributions, but extended benefits during periods of high unemployment are paid for by the federal government out of general revenues. In these cases, the subsidies come from outside the insured pool in the sense that they are not funded directly by insureds. To the extent that those who pay into general revenues (which are largely comprised of individual income taxes) overlap with those in the insured pool, however, subsidies also represent redistribution among participants.

Social Security, too, provides explicit subsidies from within the pool

---

[10] In actual private insurance markets, anti-discrimination rules place constraints on underwriting.

[11] That prior history might make an employer less willing to hire a given employee, however, because of the prospect of higher premiums in the future.

of participants. The program's founders recognized that some degree of redistribution was necessary to provide meaningful insurance to all (Hacker 2002: 107). Social Security accomplishes this goal by using a progressive benefit formula: low earners receive a higher percentage of their contributions as benefits than do high earners. This formula compensates for the fact that high earners make higher contributions while working. On balance, the program transfers income from high earners to low earners, at least on an expected basis (CBO 2006).

These are the main features that allow government programs to offer insurance where the unregulated private market would fail.[12] Compulsory participation overcomes adverse selection as well as behavioral frailties that might limit demand for insurance; limits on underwriting reduce price differences across participants and (from one perspective) make the system more fair; and subsidies attempt to close any remaining affordability gap. In addition, government programs are backed by a sovereign state with the power to tax, whether benefit payments are made directly by the government or by entities implicitly backstopped by it. This ability to raise money when necessary makes it possible to protect against losses that are difficult to estimate far in the future.

The examples described in this section are all government policies that intend to make insurance more available. That insurance, however, does not have to be directly provided by a government entity. Medicare Part D prescription drug plans are sold by private companies within a federal regulatory scheme that includes a risk adjustment mechanism to compensate insurers for their high-risk enrollees. In part III I discuss additional insurance markets – including workers' compensation, auto liability insurance, and individual health insurance under the Affordable Care Act of 2010 – which bear several of the hallmarks of social insurance but are primarily sold by private companies, with considerable government regulation. In all of these cases, a regulated private market can plausibly achieve the public policy goal: universal availability at moderate cost.

C. Conceptions of Social Insurance

In practice, as described above, the programs usually thought of as social insurance are a messy, inconsistent combination of general insurance

[12] There are also ways in which social insurance programs are similar to private market products. For example, Medicare uses deductibles and copayments, and unemployment insurance imposes benefit limits, both to control costs and to mitigate moral hazard concerns.

principles with statutory mandates, regulations, and subsidies. This confusion makes it possible to conceptualize social insurance in several different ways. In addition, how people think about these programs has always been influenced by political debate. In the United States, the classic, once-conventional understanding of Social Security – as an insurance policy in which payroll tax 'premiums' buy a right to future benefits – was manufactured by politicians and bureaucrats eager to distinguish the program from non-contributory 'welfare' alternatives and to invoke contract law in its defense (Campbell and Morgan 2005: 179; Simon 1986: 1450–1).[13] More recently, critics of Social Security have framed it as a personal retirement savings vehicle rather than a risk-spreading mechanism – because, for many relatively affluent workers, Social Security provides lower expected returns than, say, a personal account invested in the stock market (Campbell and Morgan 2005: 188).[14] In this subsection I briefly outline three influential descriptions of social insurance.

First, it is common in the United States to define social insurance by listing the idiosyncratic features of Social Security, the federal government's flagship domestic program: mandatory participation for (most) workers, self-financing through earmarked participant contributions, benefits linked to contributions, and no means testing (that is, no restricting benefits to the poor).[15] Graetz and Mashaw (1999: 57) describe the

---

[13] Social Security Old Age Insurance (OAI) – the core of what we now consider 'Social Security' – was created alongside a non-contributory, means-tested Old Age Assistance (OAA) program, which was then more visible and popular because more people qualified for OAA than for OAI at the time (Campbell and Morgan 2005: 176–7).

[14] The relatively lower returns for Social Security are a product of its somewhat progressive benefit formula and its much lower investment risk relative to the stock market; adjusted for risk, it's less clear that Social Security underperforms the stock market.

[15] For example, Wikipedia defines social insurance as any 'government-sponsored program' with: benefits defined by statute; an explicit financing mechanism; funding by payments by or on behalf of participants; and compulsory or near-universal participation. Wikipedia, 'Social Insurance'. Available at http://en.wikipedia.org/wiki/Social_insurance. The Merriam-Webster Concise Encyclopedia defines social insurance as a '[c]ompulsory public-insurance program that protects against various economic risks', and continues, 'Social-insurance contributions are normally compulsory and may be made by the insured person's employer and the state as well as by the individual. Social insurance is usually self-financing, with contributions being placed in specific funds for that purpose.' Merriam-Webster, 'Social Insurance'. Available at www.merriam-webster.com/dictionary/social insurance. The basic principles of universal participation, required contributions, and a dedicated insurance fund were also established in the

'conventional conception' of social insurance (which they challenge) as 'mandatory, earnings-related, near-universal protection against loss of wage income and fringe benefits, provided to contributing workers and their families through a publicly administered system financed by dedicated taxes.' Ball (1947: 338–40), who later served as commissioner of the Social Security Administration, defined social insurance as an 'earned right' available to all workers, based on contributions to a dedicated fund, whose payments 'are made to individuals on the basis of a work record and are part of the reward for services rendered'. When Brown (1956) attempted to describe the distinctly American 'philosophy of social insurance', he essentially repeated the features of Social Security: contract-like benefits, universal coverage, benefits linked to contributions, protection for dependents, and joint contributions by employees and employers. Early advocates for Medicare consciously adopted this model because they saw the concept of earned benefits as crucial to garnering political support (Oberlander 2003: 24–5). Some central 'social insurance' programs, however, only loosely fit this common model. Medicare, for example, provides equal coverage to all beneficiaries, regardless of past contributions. Medicare Parts B and D are voluntary, and are funded by individual beneficiary premiums and general tax revenues, not dedicated contributions from employees or employers. As noted above, Part D is provided by private companies under a public regulatory scheme.

Second, economists have defined a more abstract model of social insurance as a rational government response to failures in private insurance markets, most notably adverse selection (Atkinson 1991: 115–16; Barr 1992: 749–55; Zweifel 2000: 937–9). Another problem is that if the magnitude and frequency of losses are hard to estimate over the long term, worries about insurer solvency can make private insurance untenable, necessitating government regulation or provision of insurance. Arrow (1963: 961–4) identifies several problems with the market for health insurance that undermine the private insurance model. Diamond (1977: 279–81) justifies Social Security (or something close to it) on various grounds, including market failures that jeopardize secure retirement. In addition to the failure of markets to supply certain types of insurance, behavioral constraints may limit demand for valuable insurance products in that people do not rationally evaluate either risk or insurance benefits. Decisions to purchase annuities, for example, can be significantly influenced by the framing of the options presented (Brown et al. 2013).

Beveridge Report (1942), which outlined the principles of the postwar welfare state in the United Kingdom.

Since risk-averse individuals are usually made better off by insurance at a price that reflects their expected losses (with reasonable transaction costs and insurer profits), there is a strong case that the government should make such insurance available when the private market fails to do so. Insurance against unemployment, longevity, and illness in old age were effectively unavailable to many people prior to government intervention, and so social insurance can be thought of as a response to these market failures.[16] This purely economic conception of social insurance, however, only loosely conforms to existing programs. The idea that government should limit intervention to solving market failures – therefore providing only the insurance policies that would be available under perfect market conditions and with perfectly rational consumers – inadequately describes actual policy. In the health care sector, for example, this constraint would defeat one of the core purposes of government-provided insurance, since many high-risk individuals (such as the disabled or the elderly, who are covered by Medicare) could not afford private insurance, even if fairly priced (Arrow 1963: 963). Indeed, Nyman (2004) argues that explicit health insurance subsidies (or a national health insurance program) increase social welfare.

A third conception of social insurance describes it as the set of programs dedicated to a specific policy objective: 'to moderate the risks of current income loss or inadequacy by providing secure cash or near-cash entitlements on the occurrence of defined risks' (Graetz and Mashaw 1999: 65; see also Marmor et al. 2014: 10). Social insurance sets out to solve a coherent problem: 'Families live almost exclusively by labor income; they therefore demand protection against circumstances and events that take them out of the workforce and cut off labor income' (Graetz and Mashaw 1999: 47). This problem only arose in its current form with the development of an urban, industrial economy based on wage labor, in which unemployment and retirement became discrete events; this explains why social insurance first appeared in late nineteenth century Europe (Atkinson 1991: 120–2). On this view, social insurance includes all government policies designed to protect people from lack of access to labor income, encompassing not only government insurance programs, but also means-tested, non-contributory programs (sometimes known as 'welfare'), and tax subsidies such as the exclusion for employer-provided fringe benefits (Graetz and Mashaw

[16] It is possible that the efficiency costs of government insurance, as opposed to free market provisioning, might outweigh the welfare gains of the individuals benefiting from the insurance (Priest 2003). Much economic research focuses on the question of the optimal level of such insurance (e.g. Chetty 2006; Chetty and Finkelstein 2013).

1999: 62–3). To the extent that other workplace policies mitigate employee risk – thus reducing the need for government involvement – they might be thought of as part of an overall public-private social insurance system.[17]

None of these common conceptions of social insurance is necessarily wrong, as each describes different phenomena or implies different policy recommendations. Under each view, social insurance is not quite the same thing as private insurance, but nor is it simply a form of tax-funded public assistance. Instead, social insurance represents some hybrid of private insurance principles and government coercion. In the remainder of this chapter, I propose a new model of social insurance that focuses on this hybrid nature.

The question, here and in the broader political debate, is to what extent these government programs still constitute insurance – as opposed to tax-and-transfer schemes that redistribute resources from the affluent to the needy. From one perspective, for example, Social Security Disability Insurance is in fact insurance: all workers pay premiums, and those who suffer disability-related unemployment (the insurable event) receive payouts. From another perspective, however, it looks a lot like a public assistance program: a more or less flat tax on wage income is used to pay benefits to people with disabilities – a set of specific conditions that merit assistance. The only thing that seems out of place in a tax-and-transfer system is the fact that benefits are linked to prior contributions. Even then, however, the progressive benefit formula (under which high earners receive relatively little credit for their higher contributions) shrinks the variance in benefit payments, reducing the importance of prior payments. Social Security retirement benefits exhibit a similar duality. On the one hand, all participants make contributions while working, and those who live the longest (one of the conditions they are buying insurance against) receive the largest payouts; on the other hand, a tax on current wage income is used to fund annuities for elderly people with work histories. Again, the unusual feature is that those benefits are calculated on the basis of earlier contributions, but the benefit formula, coupled with the fact that Social Security payments are taxable only for higher-income households, smooth out the distribution of benefits considerably.

---

17 According to Charny (1986: 1601), in the United States, 'when these two forms of social insurance [private and government] are taken together, employers appear to be the entities that have been primarily responsible for workers' social welfare'. In the United States, protection against the risks of old age and ill health has largely been outsourced to the private sector, especially when compared to many European countries (Hacker 2002: 276).

In short, many government insurance programs can be seen either as insurance products comparable to those available from the private market or as tax-and-transfer schemes akin to public assistance (Zweifel 2000: 954–5). They combine both the risk-spreading function of insurance and a redistributive function significantly greater than that inherent in private insurance products.[18] For decades, Social Security and Medicare were conventionally regarded as contributory insurance programs that conferred on participants a right to benefits, spreading unavoidable risks across all of society. More recently, however, their fundamental ambiguity has helped fuel political and ideological debates over what these programs are and how, if at all, they should be modified (Campbell and Morgan 2005).

II. RISK, INFORMATION, AND TIME

The government can affect the provision of insurance in many different ways. At one end of the spectrum is competitive private insurance with no government intervention (except general-purpose rules such as anti-fraud statutes or constitutional barriers against discrimination). At the other end are public assistance programs, which provide blanket protection from risk at no explicit cost. All of the programs that are cited as examples of social insurance exist somewhere in between these two extremes. (Other regulated insurance markets that are *not* usually thought of as social insurance, such as automobile liability insurance, also sit on this spectrum, and will be discussed later.)

Fundamentally, any product or program along this spectrum effects both risk spreading and redistribution. It is not simply the case that social insurance programs spread risk 'less' and redistribute 'more' than private insurance, while spreading risk 'more' and redistributing 'less' than public assistance. Risk necessarily involves some probability distribution over potential outcomes. For any insurance product or government program, as we shorten the time frame under consideration, we gain more information about what outcomes are likely to occur: risk decreases, the likely outcomes become clearer, and as a result the program looks more like redistribution. Conversely, as our time horizon lengthens, risk increases; with less certainty about who will end up with which outcome, *ex ante* redistribution diminishes. Social insurance programs may appear to be

---

[18] Indeed, this may be a political strength of social insurance: the risk-spreading features partially obscure the *ex ante* redistribution, defusing potential opposition (Zweifel 2000: 944).

primarily redistributive when assessed over a short time frame, for which we have relatively good information, but function more like insurance over many decades or a lifetime (see Sinn 1996).

Private insurance policies typically have a term of one year. Even insurance that both seller and purchaser intend to remain in force for decades, such as life insurance or long-term care insurance, is priced on an annual basis and can be canceled at the end of the policy-year or with shorter notice (by the purchaser, if not the seller).[19] For a product such as personal automobile insurance, the insurer uses its underwriting model to estimate the expected losses for each applicant and then charges an appropriate price. Ideally, from the insurer's perspective, insureds pay their expected losses (plus transaction costs and profits), so there is little or no *ex ante* redistribution, and the product simply spreads the risk of accidents among all drivers. In practice, since insureds often have private information about their riskiness and since efficient underwriting systems don't perfectly assess risk, there is typically some redistribution from people who have higher risk than predicted by the insurer's underwriting model to those who have lower risk (Abraham 1986: 78).

Applying a short-term perspective to government insurance programs often makes them appear to be simple tax-and-transfer schemes. At the limit, consider the current cash flows of the principal social insurance programs. At this moment, workers are transferring money to the elderly and the disabled via payroll taxes and to the unemployed via unemployment insurance contributions paid by their employers. All taxpayers are transferring money to the elderly via the general revenues that subsidize Medicare Parts B and D. Given a short enough time horizon, the insurable events (disability, injury, etc.) have already occurred, and we know for whom. All that is left is to transfer the cash. In this respect, there is no difference between insurance and public assistance. This very short term perspective is not particularly informative, however, because the same observation can be made of private insurance. Although I pay for automobile insurance with the expectation of coverage for future losses, my monthly premiums are being used, in part, to compensate other people for accidents they suffered last month.

More significant differences appear when we widen the time frame to one year. In general, my risk of an auto accident in the coming year is

---

[19] The insurer may guarantee an annual premium for a certain number of years, as in level term life insurance. Alternatively, the insurer may state an annual premium for the life of the policy but reserve the right to apply for changes to its overall pricing model, as in some long-term care insurance.

largely independent of whether or not I suffered an accident in the previous year.[20] With many government-sponsored programs, by contrast, the insurable event triggers compensation for a period of years or even the rest of the insured's lifetime. At the beginning of any year, many people face a very low risk of disability, while some face a risk that approximates 100 percent.[21] In some cases, the insurable event is also highly predictable over the short term. This is true of Social Security's old age insurance, for example: most participants have no chance of receiving benefits over the next year, while some are certain to.

From the one-year perspective, then, there is a very clear difference between personal automobile insurance and Social Security or Medicare: if the market functions effectively, the former is a plausible bargain for any risk-averse driver, while the latter is either a very good deal (for current beneficiaries) or a very bad deal (for other workers). Put another way, if Social Security were only going to operate for one more year, most current workers would opt out if they could. Social Security and Medicare do little to spread risk over a short time period, since the predictability of outcomes means that there is little risk to spread. This is the perspective taken by the many commentators who assert that Social Security and Medicare transfer resources from working-age people to the elderly (e.g. Cogan 2011). A similar, though weaker argument can be made about unemployment insurance. Although firms pay contributions based on their past losses (claims paid to their former employees), most workers know that they do not face the average risk of unemployment, even within their company. People with more secure jobs at the beginning of the year, perhaps because of seniority or specific skills, get a bad deal from unemployment insurance, while those with less secure jobs get a good deal.

This is clearly an incomplete perspective, however. Social Security and Medicare would probably not be as popular as they are if they simply transferred wealth from a majority of the population to a minority. While automobile insurance makes sense as a risk-spreading device over a one-year policy period, many social insurance programs only make economic sense over a longer time frame – and do indeed operate over one. From a lifetime perspective, Social Security looks like this: an individual

---

20 People who were involved in accidents in the previous year, on average, are probably more likely to be in accidents in the coming year, but this is generally the result of some underlying factors (eyesight, miles driven, etc.), *not* the fact of having been in an accident.

21 From the insurer's perspective, the risk is never 100 percent because there is some chance that the insured (and any dependents qualifying for benefits) will die during the next year.

entering the workforce in her early twenties expects that she will pay a percentage of her wage income throughout her career; in exchange, she expects to receive an annuity beginning around age sixty-seven that insures her against longevity risk, as well as coverage in case of disability and protection for her dependents should she die prematurely. Considering her cohort, we know that some members will earn high average incomes, some will earn low average incomes, some will become disabled, some will die young, and some will live long past the time they retire. The risks they face include low earnings, disability, dying young with dependents, and outliving their savings. Social Security protects all participants by paying more in benefits to those who suffer these insurable events, thereby spreading these risks across the entire group.

From a lifetime perspective, Social Security does spread risk across individuals, and is attractive to a much larger proportion of participants than from a one-year perspective. At age twenty-two, most people have only a vague notion of how much they will earn over the next half-century, how healthy they will be, how many dependents they will have, and how long they will live.[22] At that point, it is highly plausible that many would choose to participate in Social Security (or vote in its favor), precisely because they lack information about their futures. Some might regret that choice four decades later – corporate executives and law firm partners, for example – but that is because of information that was not available to them when entering the workforce. The same principle holds true for unemployment insurance. In their early twenties, people do not know if they are likely to hold secure or insecure jobs for most of their careers, and therefore should be more supportive of the existence of an unemployment insurance program that, on an expected basis, transfers wealth from the secure to the insecure.

As discussed previously, insurance can also be thought of as a way for a person to shift resources between future states of the world. Again, whether a given insurance product performs this function depends on the time frame chosen. Private automobile insurance shifts money between the states of the world in which you do not cause an accident to those in which you do; this is meaningful over a one-year time frame because you generally face some risk of an accident over the next twelve months. Considering Social Security Old Age Insurance and Medicare Part A, most working-age people face only one possible state of the world over

[22] While it is possible that people might be able to use private information to estimate their future income, there is little evidence that they actually do so effectively (Krueger and Bowen 1993; Siegelman 2004).

the next year – the state in which they pay contributions but do not receive benefits.[23] For a person in her early twenties, however, these programs do shift resources between future states: from futures in which she has high earnings, is healthy, and dies shortly after retirement, to futures in which she has low earnings, has poor health in retirement, and outlives her savings.

This is not to say that a lifetime perspective is necessarily correct for all purposes. For a program like Social Security or Medicare, there is always the risk that the rules will change. For example, Congress could legislate higher Social Security payroll taxes or lower benefits, making the bargain worse than it initially seems. If a young person believes that Social Security is unlikely to be around when she retires, then she should evaluate the program using a shorter time horizon, in which case she might prefer not to participate. If she is confident that the political coalition sustaining Social Security will survive, then she should apply a longer time horizon.

In any case, unconsciously conflating different time horizons is a common error. The idea that the individual health insurance mandate of the Affordable Care Act is bad for young, healthy people (e.g. Hederman and Winfree 2010) overlooks the fact that people age and health deteriorates. (It also overlooks the possibility that the individual mandate, by bringing everyone into the market, causes insurers to lower prices to a point where most people want to buy insurance (Boleslavsky and Campos 2013).) The idea that Social Security is a money-losing proposition for high-income, middle-aged people is based on information that has become available over the course of their working careers; while they might have been able to estimate their future income when entering the workforce (based on their education, parents' income, test scores, etc.), that estimate would still have carried risk – precisely the risk that Social Security provides insurance against. In both of these examples, the program in question looks like a bad deal only because there is little risk over the chosen time frame or because enough time has passed that the need for insurance has greatly diminished.

Many analyses that purport to measure the 'returns' on payroll tax contributions to government insurance programs suffer a similar flaw: ignoring the existence of risk, which is tantamount to assuming unavailable information. For example, one argument for Social Security privatization is based on comparing a hypothetical worker's eventual retirement

---

23 This is a slight simplification: a worker could stop working and therefore stop paying payroll taxes, but in that case there is still no shifting of resources from the state of the world in which she continues working.

benefits with the amount she would accumulate by investing her payroll taxes in the securities markets (e.g. Shipman 1995). This comparison ignores the very significant risk that any person's actual income will vary significantly from the hypothetical level, as will her risk of disability.[24] In short, this approach assumes away risk and in doing so ignores the risk-spreading function of Social Security. The same no-risk assumption, of course, also makes private market insurance a money-losing proposition: if people were sure to experience average outcomes, there would be no reason to buy insurance. A compulsory government program may have a negative expected value for a given participant – just like private insurance has a negative expected value if premiums are priced accurately. To conclude that the program is a bad deal for that participant is to assume that she will actually experience her expected outcome – information that we never have in advance.

Distributional studies that measure the relative fortunes of income groups often take a similar approach, comparing the experience of hypothetical average people in each category (e.g. CBO 2006). This analysis is useful in showing the *ex post* redistribution accomplished by a given program, but it does not reveal whether that program is good *ex ante* for any given person in any income group, because that person cannot assume that her position in the income distribution will remain fixed for the rest of her life.

These examples show the importance of information about likely outcomes in assessing the government income and health insurance programs that are often described as social insurance. These programs, like private insurance, spread risk to the extent that we do not know who will suffer losses over the relevant time frame. With common forms of private insurance, such as automobile insurance, we cannot predict who will file claims and receive payouts over the one-year policy period. The difference with social insurance is that for the next year, we often *do* know who will receive benefits, or at least who is more likely to, which makes these programs seem redistributive over a short time frame. Because we know the short-term winners and losers, many programs like Social Security

---

[24] It also ignores the risk that stock market returns will deviate from whatever benchmark is selected, the risk that an annuity comparable to Social Security retirement benefits will not be available when the worker retires, and the risk that the annuity provider will go bankrupt. For a fuller analysis, see, e.g. Geanakoplos et al. (1999); Furman (2005). On the other hand, the calculation of Social Security's future benefits ignores the risks that Congress may change the terms of those benefits and that future payroll taxes may not be sufficient to cover currently scheduled benefits.

and Medicare could not be sustained on a purely voluntary basis, at least not in anything close to their current form. As our time horizon expands, however, we have less information about who will suffer losses, and these programs perform more of a risk-spreading role and less of a redistributive role.

What Social Security, Medicare, unemployment insurance, and similar programs share is that, although many people are clearly made worse off by them in the short term, they offer insurance that most people should rationally buy if the policy period were each person's entire lifetime (and the administrative costs were not unreasonably high). I consider this time frame dependence a central feature of social insurance – more central than how a given program is financed, or whether it is solely administered by a government agency. Social insurance is valuable when we have little information about our lives; once we accumulate the relevant information, its risk-spreading function is diminished, and individuals become either the sources or the beneficiaries of redistribution.

Government provision of social insurance then makes sense for more fundamental political reasons than the simple fact that some degree of administrative coordination is required to make a program work. After all, a group of private individuals could theoretically choose to enter into a social insurance scheme and hire an insurance company to administer it. First, a sovereign government with the power to tax (and, more importantly, to borrow) has a considerable advantage over private companies when it comes to insuring risks that may not materialize for several decades, especially when the magnitudes of those risks are difficult to estimate far in advance (as with health care costs, for example).[25] Second, a government can enforce continued participation, including payment of premiums or contributions, past the point where an individual would rationally want to cancel her insurance 'policy'.[26] Third, and most important, a democratic government at least theoretically has the power

[25] The federal government's minimal solvency risk is a major reason why private catastrophe insurance markets tend to be replaced or backstopped by government insurance programs (Jaffee, Chapter 6 in this volume). Government catastrophe insurance shares some features of social insurance. One major difference is that, in general, catastrophe insurance spreads risk even over a relatively short time frame, since the incidence of catastrophes is difficult to predict even in the short term.

[26] A private insurer can achieve a similar result by charging premiums that exceed expected losses for several years and premiums that are less than expected losses for successive years, so that it becomes increasingly irrational for the insured to cancel the policy. In effect, the insured will only buy the policy if she evaluates it over a long time horizon.

to enact an insurance scheme that benefits a majority of citizens and then compel participation by the remaining minority. This is crucial because, even if we make the strong assumption that everyone would opt into a given program at age 22, at any given moment there are many older people who have more information about their lives and, on that basis, would prefer to opt out. Social insurance can be seen as a mechanism by which a society composed of multiple generations commits itself to a bargain that is beneficial to most people, but only over the very long term.[27]

III. BLURRY LINES

The previous part argued that social insurance is redistributive when viewed over a short time frame but spreads risk over a longer time frame, and that therefore it can make sense for people to collectively commit themselves to a social insurance scheme via democratic mechanisms. Even if this is true in principle, however, it is not entirely clear where social insurance begins and ends, for three reasons discussed in this section. First, government intervention imports redistributive principles into seemingly private insurance markets. Second, means-tested public assistance programs might be thought of as risk-spreading schemes given sufficient uncertainty about the future. Finally, at the limit posed by the Rawlsian veil of ignorance, almost any government program funded by a progressive tax system could be seen as a form of risk sharing.

A. Private Insurance

As discussed above, private insurance spreads risk among participants over a one-year time horizon, while social insurance generally requires a longer time frame to make sense as a risk-spreading mechanism. On closer inspection, however, it can be difficult to differentiate clearly between the two. It is true that there are some insurance markets that operate more or less independently of government intervention – say, kidnap and ransom

[27] Government provision or price regulation of insurance also suffers from several problems, notably the difficulty of pricing risk on an actuarially fair basis in a political environment (Jaffee, Chapter 6 in this volume; Brown 2010: chapters 1–2, 5–6). The welfare benefits of social insurance should be evaluated against these costs. The efficiency costs of inaccurate pricing, however, may be less relevant depending on the policy motivation for a specific program. For example, if the goal of Medicare is to ensure equal access to affordable health care for the elderly, then the incentive effects of underpricing are less of a policy concern.

insurance for companies doing business overseas. But the government does play a role in several of the largest and most important insurance markets in ways that reflect some basic principles of social insurance.

Workers' compensation insurance, which is often considered a type of social insurance (e.g. Graetz and Mashaw 1999; Moss 2002), illustrates the difficulty of determining where the private market ends and where government intervention begins. In most states, workers' compensation insurance is provided by private companies that behave in a more or less competitive manner: insurers segment the universe of possible customers, target the customer groups they want to serve, market to them (often via insurance brokers), and use underwriting to filter out risks they do not want to take.[28] Alternatively, companies can choose to self-insure. Workers' compensation is similar to social insurance, however, in that it is mandatory for all employers. Because some companies might not be able to find insurance in a completely free market – for example, because their operations present new types of risk that no insurer has experience with – most states operate a state insurance fund that will sell insurance to any company. In addition, because insurance companies can fail, states administer guaranty associations that will pay claims on behalf of insolvent insurers. Many states also closely regulate the rates that insurers are allowed to charge their customers, essentially as a matter of public policy.

In summary, although most workers' compensation policies are sold by private parties, the net effect is that all employees are guaranteed the same state-mandated benefits at prices overseen by the state. From the employer's perspective, the difference between a required insurance premium and a tax is relatively small.[29] Experience rating imperfectly limits the degree of cross-subsidization within the pool of insured firms, but rate regulation can effectively subsidize the entire employer sector by suppressing insurance premiums. The resulting system is broadly similar to unemployment insurance, although the latter is administered by the state rather than by private insurers. As with other social insurance programs, there are certainly people who are made worse off by workers' compensation insurance and would rationally opt out: wealthy executives with good health plans, for example, who do not need insurance and would prefer to get their workers' compensation premiums (that is, the premiums their employers pay to insure them) in cash. For many people entering the workforce,

---

[28] In North Dakota, Ohio, Washington, and Wyoming, workers' compensation insurance is provided solely by state insurance funds, although companies can self-insure in some cases.

[29] The major difference is that the employer has some ability to look for a lower premium in the market.

however, the workers' compensation requirement is a good thing because they may value the insurance now or in the future, but might not be able to negotiate for it in the labor market or buy it in the private insurance market.[30]

These similarities should be no surprise, since universal workers' compensation insurance was established as a result of political pressure and for reasons of public policy, not by market forces (Moss 2002: 162–9). The historical difference between workers' compensation and unemployment insurance is that the former was enacted in the 1910s, when government-run insurance was an anomaly, and the latter in the 1930s, when the Great Depression and the New Deal made the idea of government administration politically acceptable.

Even automobile liability insurance, however, bears several of the traits of social insurance. Although most people purchase personal auto insurance from private companies in a competitive market, they are required to carry minimum liability coverage by state law. Liability insurance protects drivers from having to pay for the losses they cause to third parties. If those losses exceed the driver's assets, any insurance benefits the injured party and not the driver; therefore, people will tend to undervalue liability insurance, buying too little of it or even none at all (Smith and Wright 1992). Mandatory liability insurance ensures that victims of automobile accidents are not forced to absorb all of the losses caused by uninsured drivers.[31] This spreads the risk of accidents more widely than would be the case in a purely free market, as does typical social insurance: drivers with few assets, who face little financial risk and might prefer not to buy insurance, cannot escape sharing at least some of the aggregate risk. Because they are forced to buy insurance that does not benefit them, there is some redistribution from them to everyone else (the prospective victims of the accidents that they cause). In addition, with mandatory insurance, there must be some mechanism to provide coverage to people who would otherwise be uninsurable, such as a young driver with a record of multiple

---

[30] In theory, one could imagine a world in which some firms carry workers' compensation insurance, others do not and pay slightly higher wages, and employees sort themselves between the two. Historically, however, workers' compensation insurance did not become widely available until after state laws made it mandatory. Workers' only remedy in case of injury on the job lay in tort claims against employers, which were rarely successful. Reliance on tort liability also posed the risk of large judgments for employers and arguably did not create the appropriate incentives to prevent accidents (Moss 2002: 162–9).

[31] This protection can be secured by buying uninsured motorist coverage, but this essentially forces the insured to pay *ex ante* for accidents caused both by her and by uninsured drivers.

serious accidents. Some states place uninsurable drivers in an assigned risk pool and essentially force insurers to sell them policies at regulated rates. To the extent that these policies are priced below their actuarially fair value, drivers in the assigned risk pool are subsidized by other drivers.[32]

Minimum liability insurance requirements cause risk to be spread more broadly than it would be in a purely private market; people who would rationally prefer not to have insurance are forced to bear some of the collective risk. In addition, states regulate auto insurance rates both because of perceptions that certain rating factors are unfair or inappropriate (credit score, for example) and because of voters' desire for lower premiums (Jaffee and Russell 1998). In addition to their efficiency costs, underwriting restrictions and price constraints have redistributive effects that are justified either on fairness or affordability grounds. The net effect of these government interventions in the auto insurance market is to cause some drivers to pay more than their expected losses for insurance while others pay less. From a longer-term perspective, however, those who do not know to which category they will belong several years in the future could plausibly support the existence of such a system.

The health insurance regime established by the Affordable Care Act is another hybrid of private insurance and social insurance principles. Private companies compete by offering health plans to individuals and small businesses on exchanges run by states or by the federal government, but are subject to underwriting constraints to ensure that poor risks are not priced out of the market. Individual and employer mandates require most people to purchase insurance or pay a penalty, which is meant to ensure near-universal coverage. Like workers' compensation, this health insurance system seems like social insurance administered through private companies. In the short term, many people can estimate whether the Affordable Care Act makes them better or worse off; but in the long term, the Act's mandates and underwriting restrictions provide valuable insurance against the possibility of developing expensive, chronic illnesses.[33]

---

32 No-fault insurance goes further by limiting the extent to which people who cause accidents suffer the consequences of liability, since one driver ordinarily cannot hold another liable for damages (although there are frequent exceptions). While mandatory liability insurance is based on the premise that automobile accidents are an inherent risk of modern living against which everyone should be protected, no-fault insurance is based on the additional premise that accidents are somewhat random events and the people who cause them (according to common law tort rules) should not bear a disproportionate share of their costs.

33 Even before the Affordable Care Act, however, health insurance for the non-elderly was not a simple free market. Most notably, the tax exclusion for employer-provided health plans represents a major subsidy to employees with such

I do not claim that there are no real differences between private insurance and social insurance. There are, however, many different forms of government intervention in insurance markets that increase the population over which risk is spread, redistribute resources among groups in the short term (typically by forcing people to buy insurance they may not want), and arguably provide legitimate insurance benefits to most people over the long term. These interventions make private insurance function more like what we typically call social insurance.

B. Public Assistance

Earlier I described Social Security, Medicare, and unemployment insurance as programs that do little to shift risk in the short term but make sense as insurance when viewed over a longer time frame. These observations can also apply to other programs such as Medicaid that are generally considered public assistance rather than social insurance. With unemployment insurance, the bargain is that contributions today are exchanged for benefits in case of involuntary job loss in the future. With Medicaid, the bargain is that individual income taxes (and relatively small amounts of other taxes) today are exchanged for health benefits in case of poverty in the future. The same distributional characteristics apply: rich people who pay high taxes and have little chance of becoming poor are likely to be net losers, while young people with uncertain prospects are more likely to benefit from the insurance.

In these respects, there is no clear difference of kind between Medicaid and unemployment insurance or any other social insurance program. Medicaid does depart from the textbook social insurance paradigm in that it is not financed directly by contributions paid by or on behalf of employees. But this is arguably a difference more of framing than of substance. On the front end, Social Security contributions are 12.4 percent of wage income up to a cap ($117,000 in 2014). There is no dedicated Medicaid tax. Congress, however, could create a Medicaid payroll tax equal to 4.4 percent of wage income up to the same cap and simultaneously create a refundable income tax credit of exactly the same amount.[34]

plans – paid for by taxpayers, whether or not they benefit from the subsidy. This constitutes a perverse kind of risk spreading: people with employer-based health coverage can offload some of their health risk onto the population at large.

[34] In 2012, total Social Security payroll tax receipts were $589.5 billion, at a rate of 10.4 percent (reduced from 12.4 percent for two years only by the December 2010 tax cut) (*The 2013 Annual Report of the Board of Trustees of the Federal Old-Age and Survivors Insurance and Federal Disability Insurance Trust Funds.*

This would have no economic effect on anyone, yet it would give Medicaid the dedicated financing mechanism supposedly typical of social insurance. On the back end, a dedicated trust fund is only distinguishable from general revenues if the trust fund imposes a hard constraint on program spending. In the past, however, Congress increased funding for the Social Security trust funds when their solvency was threatened;[35] it remains politically likely that Congress will take corrective action before letting the trust funds run dry.[36] In effect, the trust fund mechanism is simply a means of documenting a preference for a certain relationship between taxes and benefits – a preference that can and almost certainly will be revisited when necessary.

The final way in which Medicaid does not conform to more traditional social insurance programs is that there is no explicit work requirement to qualify for benefits. Again, this is less of a difference than it may seem. For example, Medicare actually does not have a work requirement. Any US citizen or permanent resident over the age of 65 can buy Part A by paying a monthly premium (which is waived for people who have sufficient work credits), and can buy Part B simply by paying the same monthly premium as people with work records.[37]

There are some Medicaid recipients who have neither worked nor are the spouse or dependent of someone who has worked. These individuals arguably have never paid into the system at all (outside of the state sales taxes that partly fund Medicaid) – something that could never happen with Medicare. But for most people, Medicaid is functionally similar to Social Security, Medicare, or unemployment insurance: you pay taxes in one period and collect benefits in another in certain states of the world. Most

Available at www.ssa.gov/oact/tr/2013/tr2013.pdf, p. 6). Total federal Medicaid spending was $251 billion, or 4.4 percent of the Social Security payroll tax base (CBO 2013a). This analysis ignores a couple of loose ends, such as state Medicaid spending and the fact that the level of the Medicaid payroll tax would have to be set every year, but the basic principle is the same.

35 Social Security Amendments of 1983, Pub. L. 98-21, 97 Stat. 65.

36 Federal backstop entities with 'dedicated' funding mechanisms have often been bailed out by general revenues when faced with the prospect of insolvency, including the Federal Savings and Loan Insurance Corporation during the savings and loan crisis of the 1980s and the National Flood Insurance Program after Hurricane Katrina. The federal government even bailed out non-governmental backstop entities Fannie Mae and Freddie Mac in 2008 during the financial crisis.

37 Centers for Medicare & Medicaid Services, 'Original Medicare (Part A and B) Eligibility and Enrollment'. Available at www.cms.gov/Medicare/Eligibility-and-Enrollment/OrigMedicarePartABEligEnrol/.

importantly, Medicaid shares with typical social insurance programs the feature that it looks like a tax-and-transfer scheme from a one-year perspective but spreads risk among participants (all residents) over a longer time horizon. In the short term, there are clear winners and losers; in the long term, as the risk-spreading function becomes more significant and the value of the insurance increases, more people are made better off by the program's existence. It is plausible that fewer people would choose to participate in Medicaid than in Social Security or unemployment insurance, if given the option, because Medicaid's stringent eligibility thresholds make it less likely that a given person will benefit from it in the future – but this is a difference of degree, not of kind. Medicaid still has insurance value for people who are not current beneficiaries, which may help explain the program's enduring popularity.[38]

This is one reason why it is difficult to draw clear lines that distinguish social insurance from other public policies that spread risk. Whether a program spreads risk and among whom depends on the time horizon chosen. Over a long enough time frame, programs like Medicaid, Supplemental Nutrition Assistance Program (food stamps), and Temporary Assistance for Needy Families provide valuable insurance even to people who do not currently receive benefits and are unlikely to receive benefits in the next several years. Of course, there are many people who are unlikely ever to qualify for benefits and for whom the marginal tax burden is large enough that any insurance they receive is vastly overpriced. But this is equally true of classic social insurance programs like Social Security and unemployment insurance.

C. Government Programs and Progressive Taxation

There will always be some groups of people who do not currently benefit from social insurance programs. The extremely wealthy, for example, are probably not risk-averse over the range of losses against which social insurance protects; in addition, under most plausible financing schemes, the very wealthy are sure to be net contributors *ex ante*. Earlier I discussed the perspective of a young person entering the workforce with limited information about her future. But even among people whose working lives have not yet unfolded, some should still rationally oppose Social Security

---

[38] For example, a 2011 survey found 69 percent of respondents opposed to reducing spending on Medicaid, even in the context of reducing the national debt. *Washington Post-ABC News Poll*, 14–17 April 2011. Available at www.washingtonpost.com/wp-srv/politics/polls/postpoll_04172011.html.

and Medicare based on the information they already possess about themselves and the risks they face. In particular, the very rich know that they are unlikely to need insurance at any point in their lifetimes.

But what if people had to consider public policy choices with no information about themselves? This is the situation behind the veil of ignorance posited by philosopher John Rawls (1971). If people did not know their positions in the income distribution, would they support Social Security, Medicare, and even Medicaid? Rawls seems to have thought so: he argued that one principle that would emerge behind the veil of ignorance is that any inequalities of treatment should be 'to the greatest benefit of the least advantaged' (p. 302). That is, to the extent that government policy benefits some people at the expense of others, it should benefit the less-advantaged at the expense of the more-advantaged, which is precisely what both social insurance and public assistance aim to do. People who are alive today need insurance against risks that may materialize during the rest of their lives; people behind a veil of ignorance need insurance against discovering that they have few assets and low incomes, lack valuable job skills, have poor health, and so on. Medicaid and food stamps are examples of that kind of insurance. They generally tend to benefit the least advantaged because they are largely paid for by taxpayers with moderate or high incomes while supporting people with low incomes.[39]

The veil of ignorance can be thought of as the outer limit as we extend our time frame outward from the typical one-year policy. As the time horizon expands, people have less information about their personal circumstances and therefore face more risk. This decreased information and increased risk make social insurance programs, which may seem like simple transfers in the short term, appear more and more like valuable insurance. At the limit, behind the veil of ignorance, any such program has no *ex ante* redistributive component because everyone faces the same risks equally (see Sinn 1996: 261–2; Barr 1992: 795). From this perspective, public assistance or tax-and-transfer programs can be thought of as a kind of insurance because they effectively spread risk (the risk of poverty) across the entire population. Varian (1980) argues that redistributive taxation can be justified as a form of social insurance because it protects people against variance in their future income streams. Although the veil of ignorance is a purely theoretical construct, it is perhaps most closely approached in the real world by the perspective of parents considering the future welfare of their children. As Sinn (1996: 259) argues: 'The risk of not having a successful career is substantial for young, and even more

---

39 On Rawls and insurance, see also Abraham (1986: 26–9).

so for unborn, children. Knowing these risks, parents may well opt for a program of income redistribution to insure their children against bad luck in terms of missed opportunities, illness, injuries and an unfavourable endowment of innate abilities.'

The programs we think of as social insurance share certain key features: they behave like redistributive tax-and-transfer schemes given short time frames and full information, and like risk-spreading insurance policies given longer time frames and less information. This dual nature is characteristic of a broad spectrum of government policies, ranging from tax subsidies for purchasing insurance on the one hand to public assistance programs on the other. At the extremes, free market insurance has (in theory) no *ex ante* redistributive component, and a pure tax-and-transfer program (e.g. a wealth tax combined with a flat cash grant to all citizens) has no risk-spreading component except behind the veil of ignorance. Between those endpoints, however, there are no clear boundaries where social insurance begins or ends. The crucial function of social insurance, on this view, is using government power to spread risk in ways that very well might fail in the free market (because too many people might rationally decline to participate), but that most people would choose when evaluated over a long time frame. A wide range of public policies serve this function, to varying degrees.

IV. LABELS AND POLITICS

Large federal budget deficits in the wake of the recent financial crisis, coupled with projections of increasing government outlays due to an aging population and increasing health care costs, have made controlling the growth of the national debt a major political issue (see Johnson and Kwak 2012). As the most expensive domestic spending programs other than national defense, Social Security, Medicare, and Medicaid sit at the center of this discussion, and framing plays a crucial role.

The most common label for these programs (as well as temporary assistance for needy families (TANF), food stamps, and so on) in contemporary discourse is 'entitlements'. On the one hand, this seems like a reasonable word to use: most of these programs pay benefits to anyone who meets prescribed eligibility criteria and is therefore entitled to them.[40] The idea that participants are entitled to benefits is also consistent with

[40] Technically speaking, recipients have a legal right to benefits even in the absence of annual appropriations by Congress (Schick 2007: 209–12).

the analogy between social insurance and private insurance contracts (Simon 1986) and may help protect those benefits as inviolate. In the context of federal government programs, however, 'entitlement' has had a decidedly negative connotation at least since the 1970s, when it became shorthand for government benefits (Liberman 2012; see also M. Bernstein 2012). That pejorative tone is related to the usage of the term in popular psychology, as in a 'sense of entitlement'. Today, 'entitlement' is the term of choice among many conservatives to denote government benefits that people expect but do not deserve in some usually unspecified moralistic sense. For example, in his notorious '47 percent' remarks, Republican presidential candidate Mitt Romney said (Corn 2012):

> there are 47 percent who are with [Obama], who are dependent upon government, who believe that they are victims, who believe that government has a responsibility to care for them, who believe that they are entitled to health care, to food, to housing, to you-name-it. That that's an entitlement. And the government should give it to them.

In this context, 'entitlements' seem not like insurance benefits earned by prior premium payments, but instead like transfers paid for by someone else. (A few sentences later, Romney added: 'These are people who pay no income tax.')

Having recognized the importance of framing, some progressives prefer to use 'social insurance' as the umbrella term at least for Social Security and Medicare (e.g. Hertzberg 2013). 'Insurance' implies a contractual system in which benefits are earned by paying premiums in a prior period; 'social' evokes the notion of social solidarity, while also serving as a vague explanation for all the differences between social insurance and private insurance. I have argued in this chapter that 'social insurance' is a plausible label not only for Social Security and Medicare, but also for public assistance programs such as Medicaid; while they differ from private insurance and have clear winners and losers in the short term, they all spread risk when viewed over a sufficiently long time frame. At the same time, any government program that possesses the key features of social insurance can also be described as a tax-and-transfer scheme, since in the short term certain people are almost certain to pay higher taxes and other people are almost certain to receive benefits. This latter characterization of social insurance as a form of tax-funded welfare program (Wilkinson 2005; Samuelson 2011) is implied by the conservative rhetoric of entitlements, which contrasts one group of contributors with another group of recipients. At the other end of the political spectrum, proposals to make Social Security more progressive are rooted in a discomfort with the 'insurance' aspect of social insurance. If we are willing to jettison the idea of actuarial fairness (that is, the idea that there should be some relationship between contributions and benefits), we could explicitly make the system more redistributive by reducing or eliminating benefits for high earners and raising benefits for low earners.

This debate over labels can never be definitively settled, and not just because of the political stakes involved. It is not clear what evaluative time frame is appropriate for programs that redistribute wealth in the short term but spread risk over the long term. We might make better policy choices behind the veil of ignorance, but of course it does not exist. Since Social Security is a program that most people pay into for decades before receiving benefits, it makes conceptual sense to think of it as a compact among people entering the workforce at different times with little information about their futures. In a practical sense, however, any working democracy has to take into account the preferences of the entire population, which includes people of all ages. Asking people to vote as if they were entering the workforce (or behind the veil of ignorance) is a thought experiment, not a practical option in a democracy. Social insurance programs will only succeed politically if they can muster the support of a majority of the electorate at a single moment.

As programs that transfer resources primarily to the elderly, Social Security and Medicare enjoy a structural advantage, and not just because people tend to think fondly of their grandparents. As people age, they gain information about their life circumstances. Those who earn high incomes and amass personal savings may, by middle age, wish they had never had to pay payroll taxes for Social Security and Medicare Part A as well as higher-income taxes to subsidize Medicare Parts B and D. But by that point, with much of their contributions in the past and all of their benefits in the future, these programs may be a good deal for them on a prospective basis. In other words, by the time people realize that they *would have* been better off without Social Security and Medicare, they will in fact be better off if these programs continue to exist. Politically, these programs can be sustained by a coalition of young people who value the insurance they provide and old people who are currently receiving benefits. (The same could be true of Medicaid because a large proportion of benefits are paid to the elderly, primarily in the form of long-term care coverage (N. Bernstein 2012).) Cash assistance is in the opposite political situation. The former Aid to Families with Dependent Children program, for example, was portrayed as welfare for young, single mothers, so it had little perceived insurance value for much of the population.

It is also important to remember that major American social insurance programs do not provide a true contractual commitment to pay benefits in the future in exchange for contributions made today, since the government has the power to change those benefits in the interim – as Congress has done periodically with both Social Security and Medicare. As discussed in part II, the discretionary nature of benefits weakens the case for applying a long time horizon to such programs because there is no certainty that those programs will exist decades in the future. If we discount future benefits at a high enough rate to account for political risk, then we are left with little more than the short term – and in the short term, social insurance looks a lot like redistribution through taxes and transfers. This is a central reason why opponents of social insurance programs often highlight their long-term solvency risks. If young people can be made to believe that Social Security will collapse, they will evaluate the program over a short time horizon and may rationally oppose it – making that belief self-fulfilling. Conversely, social insurance supporters tend to argue that these programs can be made sustainable with relatively modest modifications (Johnson and Kwak 2012: chapter 7), which should make young people value them more highly and support their continued existence.

Another factor that affects political support for social insurance is rising inequality. Social insurance provides protection against certain risks – most notably the financial risks due to low lifetime earnings, disability, unemployment, or living for a long time after retirement. The greater the perceived risk, the more people value insurance, even if it has a negative expected value for them. Increasing wealth inequality, however, means that there are more very rich people who are unlikely ever to need social insurance benefits and are therefore almost certain to lose money through participation. Perhaps more importantly, low levels of social mobility in the United States (compared to other advanced industrialized countries) mean that people born into the top echelons of the income distribution are relatively likely to stay there (DeParle 2012); lower risk of becoming poor should rationally translate into a lower valuation of social insurance. Together, high inequality and low social mobility could help explain the fact that US social insurance programs tend to be weaker than those of most societies with similar economic characteristics.

Fundamentally, the hybrid nature of social insurance means that any program can always be framed either as risk spreading or as redistribution. Because there is no single correct time frame over which to evaluate these programs, the debate over whether, say, Social Security is a zero-sum transfer from young to old or a positive-sum insurance scheme can never be definitively resolved. In a democracy, individuals have the right to apply their personal time horizons when making political choices. For example, senior executives with golden parachutes and for-cause termination clauses are perfectly justified in evaluating unemployment insurance from their current situations – and forming a Super PAC (Political Action

Committee) to campaign against it. The fact that social insurance is itself subject to the political process – for all the rhetoric of contractual commitments, there is no actual enforceable contract – only highlights these basic ambiguities.

In this context, social insurance programs could indeed benefit most people over the course of their lives, but still fail to gain or maintain majority support because people cannot be required to adopt a lifetime perspective in making voting decisions today. It is comparatively easier to explain to someone how a given program is costing her money today than to explain how its insurance features increase her long-term expected utility. It is harder still to convince someone who no longer needs insurance that she should adopt the perspective of unborn strangers when evaluating current programs. The 'makers versus takers' rhetoric recently adopted by some conservatives is designed, among other things, to highlight the immediate-term redistributive impact of social insurance as well as other government programs. Defending social insurance programs requires a coalition between people who, at this point, are likely to benefit from redistribution (current Social Security and Medicare recipients, for example[41]) and other people who value the insurance that the programs provide. This, in turn, requires a clear understanding of the long-term risk-spreading function of social insurance programs. This contest between alternative labels may have a significant impact on the evolution of these programs and the degree to which risk is actually shared within advanced industrial societies.

REFERENCES

Abraham, Kenneth S. 1986. *Distributing Risk: Insurance, Legal Theory, and Public Policy.* New Haven, CT: Yale University Press.

Arrow, Kenneth J. 1963. 'Uncertainty and the Welfare Economics of Medical Care' 53 *American Economic Review* 941–73.

Atkinson, Anthony B. 1991. 'Social Insurance: The Fifteenth Annual Lecture of the Geneva Association' 16 *Geneva Papers on Risk and Insurance Theory* 113–31.

Ball, Robert M. 1947. 'Social Insurance and the Right to Assistance' 21 *Social Service Review* 331–44.

Barr, Nicholas. 1992. 'Economic Theory and the Welfare State: A Survey and Interpretation' 30 *Journal of Economic Literature* 741–803.

Bernstein, Michael A. 2012. 'The War over "Entitlements"' Reuters, November 2. Available at http://blogs.reuters.com/great-debate/2012/11/02/the-war-over-entitlements/.

---

[41] Proponents of restructuring Medicare (for example, converting it to a voucher system) routinely promise to exempt anyone age 55 or higher in order to split this coalition.

Bernstein, Nina. 2012. 'With Medicaid, Long-Term Care of Elderly Looms as a Rising Cost' *The New York Times*, September 6.
Beveridge, Sir William. 1942. *Report of the Inter-Departmental Committee on Social Insurance and Allied Services*. London: His Majesty's Stationery Office.
Boleslavsky, Raphael, and Sergio J. Campos. 2013. 'Does the Individual Mandate Coerce?' 68 *University of Miami Law Review* 1–18.
Brown, J. Douglas. 1956. 'The American Philosophy of Social Insurance' 30 *Social Service Review* 1–8.
Brown, Jeffrey R., ed., 2010. *Public Insurance and Private Markets*. Washington, DC: American Enterprise Institute.
Brown, Jeffrey R., Jeffrey R. Kling, Sendhil Mullainathan, and Marian V. Wrobel. 2013. 'Framing Lifetime Income' 1 *Journal of Retirement* 27–37.
Campbell, Andrea Louise, and Kimberly J. Morgan. 2005. 'Financing the Welfare State: Elite Politics and the Decline of the Social Insurance Model in America' 19 *Studies in American Political Development* 173–95.
Charny, David. 1986. 'The Employee Welfare State in Transition' 74 *Texas Law Review* 1601–43.
Chetty, Raj. 2006. 'A General Formula for the Optimal Level of Social Insurance' 90 *Journal of Public Economics* 1879–901.
Chetty, Raj, and Amy Finkelstein. 2013. 'Social Insurance: Connecting Theory to Data' in Alan J. Auerbach, Raj Chetty, Martin Feldstein, and Emmanuel Saez, eds., *Handbook of Public Economics*, Vol. 5. Amsterdam: North Holland.
Cogan, John. 2011. 'The Millionaire Retirees Next Door' *Wall Street Journal*, May 12.
Congressional Budget Office (CBO). 2006. *Is Social Security Progressive?* Economic and Budget Issue Brief, December 15. Available at www.cbo.gov/publication/18266.
Congressional Budget Office (CBO). 2013a. *Medicaid Spending and Enrollment Detail for CBO's May 2013 Baseline*. Available at www.cbo.gov/sites/default/files/cbofiles/attachments/44204-2013-05-Medicaid.pdf.
Congressional Budget Office (CBO). 2013b. *The 2013 Long-Term Budget Outlook*, Long-Term Budget Projections, September 2013 Release. Available at www.cbo.gov/publication/45308.
Corn, David. 2012. 'Secret Video: Romney Tells Millionaire Donors What He Really Thinks of Obama Voters' *Mother Jones*, September 17. Available at www.motherjones.com/politics/2012/09/secret-video-romney-private-fundraiser.
DeParle, Jason. 2012. 'Harder for Americans to Rise from Lower Rungs' *The New York Times*, January 5.
Diamond, P. A. 1977. 'A Framework for Social Security Analysis' 8 *Journal of Public Economics* 275–98.
Furman, Jason. 2005. 'Would Private Accounts Provide a Higher Rate of Return Than Social Security?' Center on Budget and Policy Priorities. Available at www.cbpp.org/files/6-2-05socsec.pdf.
Geanakoplos, John, Olivia S. Mitchell, and Stephen P. Zeldes. 1999. 'Social Security Money's Worth' in Olivia S. Mitchell, Robert J. Myers, and Howard Young, eds., *Prospects for Social Security Reform*. Philadelphia, PA: University of Pennsylvania Press.
Graetz, Michael J., and Jerry L. Mashaw. 1999. *True Security: Rethinking American Social Insurance*. New Haven, CT: Yale University Press.
Hacker, Jacob S. 2002. *The Divided Welfare State: The Battle over Public and Private Social Benefits in the United States*. Cambridge: Cambridge University Press.
Hederman, Rea S., Jr., and Paul L. Winfree. 2010. 'How Health Care Reform Will Affect Young Adults' Heritage Center for Data Analysis. Available at www.heritage.org/research/reports/2010/01/how-health-care-reform-will-affect-young-adults.
Hertzberg, Hendrik. 2013. 'Sense of Entitlement' *New Yorker*, April 8.
Jaffee, Dwight M., and Thomas Russell. 1998. 'The Causes and Consequences of Rate Regulation in the Auto Insurance Industry,' in David F. Bradford, ed., *The Economics of Property-Casualty Insurance*. Chicago, IL: University of Chicago Press.

Johnson, Simon, and James Kwak. 2012. *White House Burning: The Founding Fathers, Our National Debt, and Why It Matters to You.* New York, NY: Pantheon.
Krueger, Alan B., and William G. Bowen. 1993. 'Policy Watch: Income-Contingent College Loans' 7 *Journal of Economic Perspectives* 193–201.
Liberman, Mark. 2012. 'Entitlement' Language Log, October 6. Available at http://languagelog.ldc.upenn.edu/nll/?p=4240.
Marmor, Theodore R., Jerry L. Mashaw, and John Pakutka. 2014. *Social Insurance: America's Neglected Heritage and Contested Future.* Los Angeles, CA: CQ Press.
Moss, David A. 2002. *When All Else Fails: Government as the Ultimate Risk Manager.* Cambridge, MA: Harvard University Press.
Nyman, John A. 2004. 'Is "Moral Hazard" Inefficient? The Policy Implications of a New Theory' 23 *Health Affairs* 194–99.
Oberlander, Jonathan. 2003. *The Political Life of Medicare.* Chicago, IL: University of Chicago Press.
Priest, George L. 2003. 'Government Insurance Versus Market Insurance' 28 *Geneva Papers on Risk and Insurance* 71–80.
Rabin, Matthew, and Richard H. Thaler. 2001. 'Anomalies: Risk Aversion' 15 *Journal of Economic Perspectives* 219–32.
Rawls, John. 1971. *A Theory of Justice.* Cambridge, MA: Belknap Press.
Samuelson, Robert J. 2011. 'Why Social Security Is Welfare' *Washington Post*, March 7.
Schick, Allen. 2007. *The Federal Budget: Politics, Policy, Process*, 3rd edition. Washington, DC: Brookings Institution.
Shipman, William G. 1995. 'Retiring with Dignity: Social Security vs. Private Markets' Cato Institute Social Security Choice Paper No. 2.
Siegelman, Peter. 2004. 'Adverse Selection in Insurance Markets: An Exaggerated Threat' 113 *Yale Law Journal* 1223–81.
Simon, William H. 1986. 'Rights and Redistribution in the Welfare System' 38 *Stanford Law Review* 1431–516.
Sinn, Hans-Werner. 1996. 'Social Insurance, Incentives and Risk Taking' 3 *International Tax and Public Finance* 259–80.
Smith, Eric, and Randall Wright. 1992. 'Why Is Automobile Insurance in Philadelphia So Damn Expensive?' 82 *American Economic Review* 756–72.
Varian, Hal R. 1980. 'Redistributive Taxation as Social Insurance' 14 *Journal of Public Economics* 49.
Wilkinson, Will. 2005. 'Social Security and the Insurance Illusion' *Freeman*, September 1.
Zweifel, Peter. 2000. 'The Division of Labor Between Private and Social Insurance' in Georges Dionne, ed., *Handbook of Insurance.* Boston, MA: Kluwer Academic Publishers.

6. Catastrophe insurance

Dwight Jaffee

1. INTRODUCTION

Catastrophe insurance is a generic term applied to a range of insurance lines with the common feature that claims are likely to be highly correlated across individual policies. The most common examples are natural disasters (earthquakes, floods, wind damage), terrorism, and financial guarantees (against losses on mortgage loans, municipal bonds, and credit default swaps). The term is also sometimes applied to coverage for large industrial accidents where the underlying risks are also low probability, but high consequence, events.

Figure 6.1 shows the aggregate losses annually from natural catastrophes world-wide from 1980 to 2012. The dollar amounts are large and an upward trend in the overall losses is apparent. Table 6.1 provides details in terms of the ten costliest natural catastrophes since 1980. Neither data set, however, includes losses from either financial catastrophes or terrorist attacks. With regard to financial catastrophes, Jaffee (2011) places an upward bound of $1 trillion on the loss in market value on subprime mortgages that defaulted during the US subprime crisis.[1] For terrorism losses, Hartwig (2011) estimates the total economic losses from the 9/11 attacks to be as high as $200 billion.

Losses created by catastrophic events are borne by one of three sources: (1) the individuals and firms directly suffering the losses; (2) insurance companies; or (3) governments. While no datasets dependably aggregate values over time for the share of losses among the three sectors, some data are available for individual events. Jaffee and Russell (2013), for example, review data showing the rising government share for a number of large recent events. Equally importantly, as shown in

[1] A significant part of these losses were covered by credit default swaps issued by such insurance firms as AIG, MBIA, and Ambac. Private mortgage insurers, such as Genworth, MGIC, and Radian, also provided subprime mortgage coverage. The US government insured another set of mortgage losses directly through the Federal Housing Administration (FHA) and indirectly through its bailout of Fannie Mae and Freddie Mac.

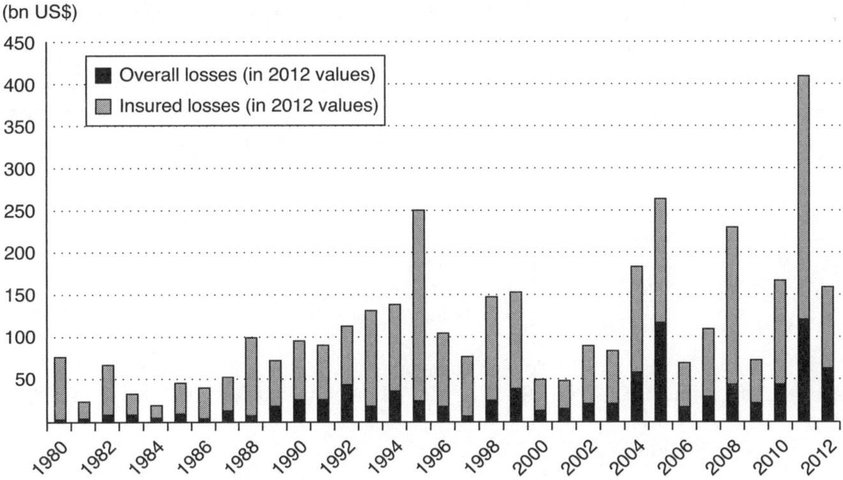

Source: Geo Risks Research, NatCat SERVICE – as at January 2013, © 2013 Munich Re.

Figure 6.1 Natural catastrophes worldwide, 1980 to 2012, insured and total losses

Figure 6.1, the share of losses backed by insurance remains remarkably low.[2]

Overall, insurance serves three separable economic roles: risk transfer, price discovery, and incentive to mitigate. Risk transfer, moving risks from individuals and firms to insurance entities, is the most evident of these functions. Price discovery is a second insurance function, whereby the premiums quoted by insurance firms provide information concerning the likelihood of possible future events. Finally, mitigation involves taking direct action to reduce or eliminate the risks.

Given the large financial losses that occur when catastrophes strike, we expect risk transfer for catastrophic losses to be close to complete, and/or for substantial mitigation to occur. In practice, however, as we see in Figure 6.1, the take-up rate for catastrophe insurance is remarkably low. Mitigation activity is also generally limited, even when risk-based insurance premiums provide an incentive for individuals and firms to mitigate the risks they face. We take up both these issues later in this chapter.

Insuring catastrophe risks raises unique issues because the law of large

---

2 As shown in Table 6.2, Hurricane Katrina created $62 billion in insured losses, the largest amount on record.

Table 6.1 Loss events worldwide 1980–2014 – ten costliest events ordered by overall losses

Date	Event	Affected area	Overall losses in US$ m original values	Insured losses in US$ m original values	Fatalities
11.3.2011	Earthquake, tsunami	Japan: Aomori. Chiba. Fukushima. Ibaraki. Iwate. Miyagi. Tochigi. Tokyo. Yamagata	210,000	40,000	15,880
25–30.8.2005	Hurricane Katrina, storm surge	USA: LA, MS, AL, FL	125,000	62,200	1,322
17.1.1995	Earthquake	Japan: Hyogo, Kobe, Osaka, Kyoto	100,000	3,000	6,430
12.5.2008	Earthquake	China: Sichuan, Mianyang, Beichuan, Wenchuan, Shifang, Chengdu, Guangyuan, Ngawa, Ya'an	85,000	300	84,000
23–31.10.2012	Hurricane Sandy, storm surge	Bahamas, Cuba, Dominican Republic, Haiti, Jamaica, Puerto Rico, USA, Canada	68,500	29,500	210
17.1.1994	Earthquake	USA: CA, Northridge, Los Angeles, San Fernando Valley, Ventura, Orange	44,000	15,300	61
1.8–15.11.2011	Floods	Thailand: Phichit, Nakhon Sawan, Phra Nakhon Si Ayuttaya, Pathumthani, Nonthaburi, Bangkok	43,000	16,000	813
6–14.9.2008	Hurricane Ike	USA, Cuba, Haiti, Dominican Republic, Turks and Caicos Islands, Bahamas	38,000	18,500	170

Date	Event	Affected area	Overall losses in US$ m original values	Insured losses in US$ m original values	Fatalities
27.2.2010	Earthquake, tsunami	Chile: Concepción, Metropolitana, Rancagua, Talca, Temuco, Valparaiso	30,000	8,000	520
23.10.2014	Earthquake	Japan: Honshu, Niigata, Ojiya, Tokyo, Nagaoka, Yamakoshi	28,000	760	46

Source: Munich Re, NatCatSERVICE, 2015 © Münchener Rückversicherungs-Gesellschaft, Geo Risks Research, NatCatSERVICE.

numbers is generally not applicable, in contrast to standard lines such as auto insurance. The key implication is that insurers must hold substantially more capital to back catastrophe lines than they hold for standard lines where diversification is effective across individual policies. And catastrophe insurers generally do not hold sufficient capital to ensure they can pay all possible claims on catastrophe lines.[3] As a result, policyholders for catastrophe lines inevitably face at least some counterparty risk, meaning that the policyholders may not receive full payment for all of their valid claims.[4]

Insolvency risk raises serious concerns for the insurers of catastrophic

[3] The original Lloyd's of London provided a successful exception over several centuries. The key was the contingent capital provided by a number of very wealthy families – called the 'Names' – who pledged all of their wealth if and when their funds were required to pay claims. However, this feature of Lloyd's failed in the 1990s as the result of extremely large US asbestos claims. Following that, Lloyd's was reorganized in the form of a standard capital-on-the-balance-sheet insurer.

[4] There is, of course, a small chance that a standard line insurer such as an auto insurer could have inadequate capital in the event that an unexpectedly larger number of claims arose in the same year. However, most US states have created mutual guarantee plans for standard consumer insurance lines, whereby if one insurer were to fail, all the other insurers chartered in that state for that line must cover valid policyholder claims up to certain amounts. States have not created mutual guarantee plans to cover insurer defaults on the various catastrophe lines, presumably because if the 'big one' occurs, all of the catastrophe insurers will be facing severe financial distress at the same time.

risks as well as for their policyholders. For insurers, the main concern relates to deadweight costs – such as legal and accounting costs – that uniquely arise if the insurer becomes bankrupt. These costs take on special relevance because most insurers are conglomerates, offering insurance across many lines. If such a conglomerate insurer were to become bankrupt, the firm might lose franchise value associated with its standard insurance businesses.

An obvious solution to the bankruptcy risk facing conglomerate insurers is simply to exit the relevant catastrophe insurance lines. However, in order to reach an exit decision, the insurer's management must recognize that the firm's exposure to the catastrophe line is creating a substantial risk for the overall conglomerate. In practice, recognition of the need to exit catastrophe lines has been the result of large events that far exceeded what the insurer had previously considered its maximum probable loss. Table 6.2 provides a list of the major lines facing significant catastrophe risk and the dates at which a significant part of the US industry chose to exit the line as the result of a major event where the losses significantly exceeded the industry's prior estimates.

Given the fundamental economic importance of providing individuals and firms with access to catastrophe insurance, the exit of the private insurance industry from each line has inevitably created a government response (as shown in Table 6.2). For the flood, terrorism, and mortgage guarantee risks, a substantial part of the response has been provided by federal government insurance. For the wind damage and earthquake risks, which were perceived as primarily affecting only specific states, state entities were created. In all cases, governments accepted their role as the backstop when the private market for catastrophe insurance disappeared.

Table 6.2 The failure of private catastrophe insurance following major events

Catastrophe risk	Event date(s)	Event name	Primary replacement
Floods	1950s/1960s	Major US floods	US National Flood Insurance Program
Wind damage	1992	Hurricane Andrew	Florida Hurricane Catastrophe Fund
Earthquakes	1994	Northridge earthquake	California Earthquake Authority
Terrorism	2001	9/11 attack	US Terrorism Risk Insurance Act
Mortgage guarantee	2008	Subprime mortgage collapse	Mortgage market reforms in process

The agenda for the remainder of this chapter is as follows. Section 2 discusses in more detail the unique capital and bankruptcy risks associated with private carriers' provision of catastrophe insurance. Section 3 discusses the issues that arise in government provision of catastrophe insurance for those lines where there is no longer a sufficient private market supply. Section 4 provides a summary and conclusions.

2. THE UNIQUE ISSUES OF OFFERING AND REGULATING PRIVATE CATASTROPHE INSURANCE

A unique problem arises for catastrophe insurance because the annual premiums received by the insurer necessarily represent only a small fraction of the indemnification payment that will become due if and when the dire event occurs. For example, when insuring a 1 in 100 year event, the annual actuarially fair premium would equal, by definition, just one percent of the total loss. However, in principle, catastrophe insurance companies could hold capital reserves to cover even the worst outcomes. Furthermore, under ideal conditions, there are no costs associated with holding this capital for two reasons:

1) The premiums charged policyholders should equal the expected losses due to claims. So while the capital suppliers may face exceptionally good or bad outcomes depending on the actual claims, the additional capital they provide should face an 'even bet' in terms of exceptionally good or bad outcomes.
2) The capital suppliers will receive the investment returns earned on their capital. In principle, these returns will be at par with the returns the capital suppliers could have earned on alternative investments outside of the insurance firm.

In practice, however, tax and investment issues create high costs of capital for catastrophe insurance firms; see Jaffee and Russell (1997). At least four major factors can be identified:

1) US tax rules do not allow an insurer to create tax deductible reserve accounts against future losses.[5] That is, an event must occur before an

[5] This restriction has little relevance for standard insurance lines where the events and settlements primarily occur within the policy year, in

insurer can create tax deductible reserve accounts for that event. The result is that the returns earned on capital invested in an insurer generally face the corporate income tax, resulting in double taxation.
2) Catastrophe insurers would have to hold very large amounts of capital relative to the annual premium income they earn. This could place them at risk of an unfriendly takeover, since the acquirer could let the policies expire after a year and then have free use of the capital.
3) The management of a catastrophe insurer with a large capital trove could become lax in running the firm since the large capital position provides a safety net.
4) Rating agencies may provide lower ratings for the debt issued by insurers that hold catastrophe risks, since in practice the probability that losses will exceed capital resources is substantially higher on catastrophe lines. This raises the cost of capital for such firms.

These factors create major impediments to operating a catastrophe insurer with a large capital base. The result is that once an insurer recognizes the potentially huge losses it faces on a line subject to substantial catastrophe risk, it generally takes action to limit the exposure. The most direct, and most common, action is simply to exit the catastrophe line altogether, and I evaluate the ramifications of this strategy in section 3. First, however, it is useful to consider three devices that can potentially resolve the problem, thus allowing private insurers to continue to offer coverage against catastrophe risks. The three devices are reinsurance, catastrophe bonds, and monoline structures, which are considered in turn.

2.1 Reinsurance

With reinsurance, the insurer – that is, the primary insurer who writes the policies – cedes some risk to a reinsurance firm for a fee. Reinsurance firms have the benefit that they can aggregate catastrophe risks over geographic regions and catastrophe lines, thus achieving benefits of diversification that are often not available to primary insurers. Nevertheless, if reinsurers are chartered in the US, they face the same tax, accounting, and incentive issues that confront primary insurers. The result is that US reinsurers accept only modest exposures on catastrophe risks, which in turn leads primary insurers to provide only limited catastrophe coverage for US consumers and firms.

---

comparison with the catastrophe lines where events may occur only once a decade.

In practice, the largest reinsurers are actually in Europe (where the insurance tax laws do allow tax deductible reserves against future losses) or in the Caribbean (where a number of countries have created special tax havens). But here too, reinsurance coverage is insufficient to allow the primary US insurers to be the primary providers of catastrophe coverage for US consumers and firms. One issue is that, given the size of the US catastrophe risk, these reinsurers cannot obtain sufficient diversification to allow them to take on the required amounts of US catastrophe risk. A second issue is that US insurance regulators institute 'haircuts' when judging the degree to which foreign reinsurance provides regulatory credit as a hedge against the catastrophe risk held by US insurers. The regulators argue that they cannot verify the counterparty risk of foreign reinsurers, and therefore a discount must be applied in evaluating the hedging value of such reinsurance.

The upshot is that reinsurance plays a limited role in creating a viable supply of private insurance against catastrophe risks in the US.

2.2 Catastrophe Bonds

In principle, financial markets have the potential to provide a direct and dependable source of capital for both primary insurers and reinsurers in support of private markets for catastrophe insurance. In particular, the financial markets could prove to be a deep source of capital, since catastrophic losses of even $100 billion should be manageable when compared to a stock market in which daily losses of a trillion dollars are not uncommon. As a result, a direct link to the capital markets has developed in the form of insurance linked securities, with catastrophe bonds the most active example for catastrophe risks.

Catastrophe bonds are debt securities issued by insurance and reinsurance firms with the unique feature that the issuer's responsibility for paying back the principal amount is forgiven if the prescribed catastrophe event occurs during the life of the bond. The result is that the exposure to the catastrophe risk is transferred from the insurer to the capital investors that purchase the bonds. Figure 6.2 shows the dollar volume of catastrophe bonds issued and outstanding from 1997 to 2013. With only $18 billion in bonds outstanding as of 2013, it is apparent that catastrophe bonds currently cover only a small share of world-wide catastrophe risks. Nevertheless, there is hope that the market will expand significantly in the future.

A key advantage of catastrophe bonds for investors, especially on those bonds that reference natural disasters, is that the risk of loss could have a low correlation with the losses that occur on stock and

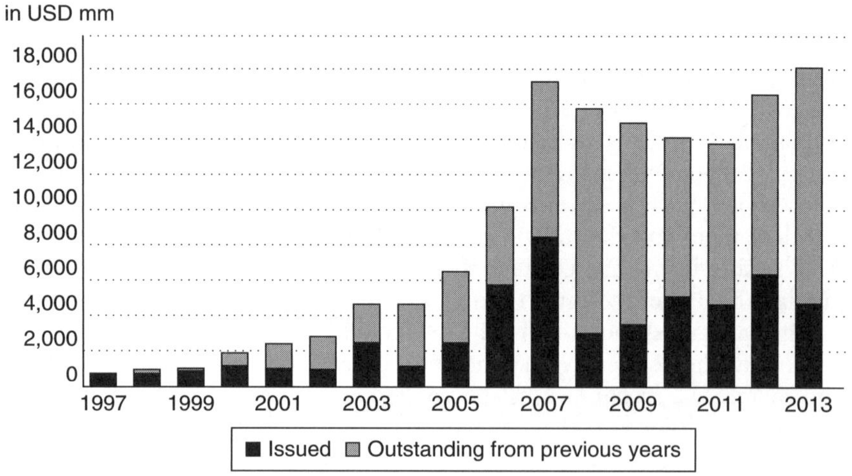

Source: Swiss Re (2014).

Figure 6.2 Catastrophe bonds issued and outstanding, 1997 to 2013

bond portfolios as a result of changing economic conditions. Thus, in principle, the interest rate required on catastrophe bonds could reflect only the expected loss due to the catastrophic event, with no additional risk premium that would derive from a correlation with macroeconomic conditions. Unfortunately, in practice, catastrophe bond investors have required interest rates that far exceed the expected loss that can be reasonably attributed to the referenced catastrophe. It is not unusual, for example, that a bond covering a catastrophe risk with an expected annual loss of 1 percent will yield as much as 5 percentage points above the risk-free rate.[6]

At least three explanations have been offered to explain the high risk premiums that are now invariably associated with the cost of issuing catastrophe bonds:

> Risk Aversion: The distribution of returns to catastrophe bond investors has the unique structure that when the insured event occurs, the investors lose their entire investment.[7] It appears that capital market

[6] See Bantwal and Kunreuther (2000) and Froot (2001) for discussions of the apparent price anomaly with respect to catastrophe bonds.

[7] Catastrophe bonds can be compared in this regard with junk bonds, sometimes called high-yield corporate bonds, where the market yields do not appear

investors have a special risk aversion with respect to this return distribution, and this is one factor contributing to the observed risk premia on catastrophe bonds.

Ambiguity Aversion: Estimating the expected loss of a catastrophe risk is a particularly difficult statistical problem because, by their very nature, catastrophes occur infrequently, and therefore data are limited. Thus, while an unbiased estimate of the expected loss may be available, investors will recognize that there may be a broad band of uncertainty around this point estimate. There is evidence that investors may require additional compensation to carry out investments that feature such ambiguity.[8]

Asymmetric Information: Investors may be concerned that the insurance firm issuing the catastrophe bond has special information that the expected loss for the insured event is greater than generally recognized.[9]

The actual experience of investors with catastrophe bonds over the last fifteen years has generally been extremely positive, since the existing bonds have had only very limited exposure to the catastrophes that actually occurred. Nevertheless, as is evident in Figure 6.2, the volume of risk transfer achieved through catastrophe bonds remains extremely small relative to the world-wide exposure to catastrophe risks as shown in Figure 6.1. As with reinsurance, catastrophe bonds are thus likely to play only a limited role in creating a viable supply of private insurance against catastrophe risks in the US for the foreseeable future.

---

to include such high risk premiums. The key here is that when the issuer of a junk bond defaults, the investors are still likely to receive a significant recovery based on the remaining liquidation value of the firm.

[8] Kunreuther et al. (1995), Hogart (2002), and Kunreuther and Pauly (2004), provide discussions of the behavioral aspects of risk-taking with respect to catastrophe. The difficulty of estimating the effects of global warming on catastrophe risks may also contribute to ambiguity aversion.

[9] Concerns of asymmetric information were particularly relevant for earlier catastrophe indemnity bonds where the payoff to the issuing insurer was determined by the losses sustained on the insurer's actual portfolio of policies. More recent catastrophe bonds have resolved this issue by stipulating payoffs that depend on industry-wide losses or, in an even more extreme form, on fixed payoffs that depend only on the occurrence of a precisely specified physical event.

2.3 Monoline Insurers[10]

Monoline insurance structures provide a third solution to the unwillingness of US conglomerate insurers to offer coverage against catastrophe risks. A monoline insurer is a US chartered insurance firm that offers coverage on only a single line. Therefore, there is no concern that losses suffered on a catastrophe line could reduce or eliminate the franchise value of other insurance lines operated by the insurer.[11] On the other hand, monoline insurers also lose the diversification benefit available to multiline insurers who can apply their capital to whichever lines happen to have exceptional losses at any given time.[12] Ibragimov et al. (2008) show that it can be optimal for monoline structures to be a component of insurance markets, especially when the number of separate insurance lines is limited, the losses on the lines are correlated, or the losses on the lines have fat tails (as do catastrophe lines).

Most monoline insurers in the US provide financial insurance against the risk of default by either residential mortgage or state and local government borrowers.[13] We now consider the two primary forms of monoline insurance, private mortgage insurance and financial guarantee insurance.

---

[10] See Jaffee (2006) for a general introduction to monoline insurers and a specific discussion of private mortgage insurance monolines and how they developed from the interaction of market and regulatory forces.

[11] Insurance holding companies – what we have been calling conglomerates – can own both monoline and multiline insurance subsidiaries. The monoline subsidiaries, however, have no claim on the capital held by any other subsidiary or by the holding company. In this sense, the monoline status can provide protection against contagion even within a holding company structure. In contrast, with a multiline insurer, which could be a subsidiary of a holding company, the capital of the multiline insurer is available to pay losses on any and all of the lines insured by the multiline entity.

[12] For example, assume there are N independent insurance lines in an economy that can be organized under either a single conglomerate or under N monoline insurers. Also assume the goal is to restrict the likelihood of an insurer default to no more than a given value α. The capital necessary for the conglomerate to reach the safety goal of α will necessarily be less than the aggregate capital required by the N monolines to reach the safety goal of α individually.

[13] There are a very limited number of insurers that provide monoline protection against either earthquake or wind damage hazards. These insurers have had limited market penetration, probably in good part because potential policyholders recognize there would be a high likelihood of insurer default if the 'big one' were actually to occur.

2.3.1 Private mortgage insurance

Private mortgage insurance became active in the US during the real estate boom of the 1920s, but these insurers all failed in the real estate collapse of the Great Depression. Understandably, no states were prepared to charter new private mortgage insurers for several decades.

In 1956, however, the State of Wisconsin adopted legislation to charter new monoline insurers for private mortgage insurance. The National Association of Insurance Commissioners (NAIC) then created a task force to develop 'model' legislation, based on the Wisconsin law, which could be readily adopted by all states. By the 1960s, most states had adopted a version of the NAIC model code for private mortgage insurance. Based on the experience of the Great Depression, this code recognized the catastrophic risk facing private mortgage insurers, and thus made special capital and investment requirements:[14]

1) A 4 percent capital ratio applies to risk in force. Risk in force is the insurer's actual risk, not the full mortgage value. For example, if the firm insures the first 20 percent of losses on a $100,000 mortgage, the risk is $20,000. The insurer would then need to hold $800 of capital for this risk.
2) A contingency reserve, equal to one-half of all premiums received, must be maintained for ten years (unless released to pay claims). This reserve structure is unique to mortgage insurers, and recognizes that the relevant time frequency for catastrophic mortgage losses is better measured by a decade than by the annual basis applied to standard insurance lines.
3) Monoline mortgage insurers are prohibited from originating mortgages or investing in either mortgages or real estate. This regulation makes it impossible for a mortgage insurer to expand its exposure to mortgage default risk by making mortgage loans or by holding real estate or mortgage-related securities in its investment portfolio.

The standard mortgage insurance policy indemnifies the policy beneficiary (the mortgage investor) against losses created by a covered borrower default, in an amount equal to the first 20 or 30 percent of the lost mortgage principal. Mortgage insurance indemnification applies only to losses created by the credit risk of the borrower. That is, the standard policy explicitly excludes all other factors that may also trigger mortgage

---

[14] The revised version of the current private mortgage insurance model code is available at: www.naic.org/store/free/MDL-630.pdf.

defaults, such as losses created by fire, earthquakes, floods, hurricanes, and defective titles. To obtain protection against these excluded factors, mortgage lenders often require borrowers to maintain separate insurance policies against the respective risks.[15]

The private mortgage insurance industry has faced enormous claims in the aftermath of the subprime mortgage crisis. Some monoline insurers were bankrupted, but a larger part of the industry still exists because they have rescinded a large number of their policies, claiming that the insured mortgages were made fraudulently or that their risk characteristics were not properly disclosed. Many legal cases are pending on these actions, and the future of these firms will depend on how the cases are decided.[16]

2.3.2 Financial guarantee insurance

The second common monoline insurance line is financial guarantee coverage. Modern financial guarantee insurance in the US dates to 1971, when Ambac first insured municipal bonds. As the industry grew, the NAIC recognized this catastrophe line also required a model monoline code. The NAIC financial guarantee model code was first published in 1986 and paralleled the already existing private mortgage insurance monoline code.[17] The NAIC financial guarantee model code was soon adopted by many states, most importantly New York state in 1989.

The first financial guarantee monolines focused on municipal bond insurance. However, starting in the late 1990s, some financial guarantee monolines began to insure residential mortgage-backed-securities (RMBS) – securities backed by pools of residential mortgages. Starting in the early 2000s, the financial guarantee monolines began to insure more complex securities backed by residential mortgages, particularly collateralized debt obligations (CDOs) and credit default swaps (CDS). As the subprime mortgage expanded from 2004 through 2007, the financial guarantee monolines were increasingly insuring securities backed by subprime mortgages.

Ultimately, the subprime mortgage market crashed, creating enormous claims on the financial guarantee monoline insurers. Some failed outright,

---

[15] Mortgage lenders face the economic decision between imposing the insurance cost on the borrower or charging a higher interest rate and then accepting the increased risk of a loan default created by the catastrophic event.

[16] It appears that the private mortgage insurance operated successfully for as long as it had primarily because the US housing markets had a remarkable run of stable or rising house prices until the US subprime mortgage crisis.

[17] The revised version of the current financial guarantee code is available at: www.naic.org/store/free/GDL-1626.pdf.

whereas others remained in business by separating the still solvent and profitable municipal bond insurance business from the huge losses arising in the divisions insuring securities backed by subprime mortgages. These insurers have also rescinded many of the mortgage-related policies, claiming that the underlying mortgages were made fraudulently. As with the private mortgage insurers discussed earlier, the ultimate fate of these policies will be determined by pending litigation regarding these actions.

2.3.3 Next steps for the monoline insurers

We have seen that the monoline insurers providing private mortgage and financial guarantee insurance are currently operating under great financial distress. Indeed, the ability of the remaining firms to survive depends critically on the outcome of the current lawsuits challenging the ability of these insurers to rescind policy coverage due to claims that the risk characteristics of the insured instruments had not been properly disclosed. Only the municipal bond monolines will clearly survive the current crisis.

Whatever the resolution of the current law suits, the future of the monoline mortgage insurers – providing either direct private mortgage insurance or indirect mortgage insurance through CDO and CDS default coverage – will depend critically on how the US mortgage market is reformed. Two developments are particularly relevant:

1) It seems likely that financial guarantee insurance covering mortgage borrower default risks within CDO and CDS contracts will not be reinstated for the foreseeable future. It is worth remembering that approximately 25 years passed before private mortgage insurance became viable following the collapse of that industry at the start of the Great Depression.
2) The future of the private mortgage insurance monolines is closely tied to the future of the government sponsored enterprises (GSEs), Fannie Mae and Freddie Mac. The GSEs have been the largest purchasers of private mortgage insurance by a large margin, and this has continued unabated under their government conservatorship that began in September 2008.[18]

However, a major reform of the US mortgage market is clearly underway, and it seems highly likely the GSEs will not return to their

18 The GSE charters require that they obtain 'credit enhancements' if they guarantee mortgages with a down payment ratio of less than 20 percent. Private mortgage insurance is by far the most common credit enhancement used by the GSEs.

previous private market status; see US Treasury (2011) and Jaffee and Quigley (2013). Instead, the mortgage functions previously carried out by the GSEs are likely to be transferred in part to explicitly private market entities and in part to explicitly government entities. On the government side, the likely effect will be to expand government mortgage insurance to middle-income borrowers based on the existing FHA model for lower income borrowers. In this case, a significant part of the private mortgage insurance business would be replaced by explicit government insurance.

3. GOVERNMENT PROVISION OF CATASTROPHE INSURANCE

As shown in Table 6.2, private markets for insurance covering natural disasters and terrorism have systematically been transformed into government-dominated insurance programs. And as discussed in the previous section, it is likely the government will also replace some part, and perhaps a large part, of the existing monoline insurers that provide coverage against default by mortgage borrowers. It thus appears that the greater part of catastrophe insurance will continue to be provided by government entities in the US. This section considers how these government entities operate and what changes might be desirable for the future.

3.1 The Political Economy of Government Catastrophe Insurance

The risk-sharing benefits of insurance intrinsically require a social undertaking – 'self-insurance' is another name for no insurance. Thus, when private insurance markets fail, individuals and firms are quick to petition the government to fix the failure, even if this means that the government becomes the insurer. There is also the recognition that if the government will provide post-disaster aid, it could be more efficient to provide insurance to cover the losses.[19] But there are also long-standing objections to government insurance based on the proposition that government insurance is likely to be less efficiently provided than comparable coverage by a private industry.

---

[19] For further discussions of post-disaster government aid, see Cummins et al. (2010) and Jaffee and Russell (2013). For a historical analysis of the role of government in disaster aid, see Moss (2002).

As a result, government interventions into catastrophe insurance have always been politically and economically contentious. On the one hand, consumer advocates, economists, and the insurance industry itself frequently cheer the advent of government catastrophe insurance. For example, Edward Liddy, president of Allstate Insurance in the *Wall Street Journal* of 6 September 2005, stated:

> The insurance industry is designed for those things that happen with great frequency and don't cost that much money when they do. It's the infrequent thing that costs a large amount of money to the country when it occurs – I think that's the role of the federal government.

The Noble prize-winning economist, Kenneth Arrow (1963: 945 and 961) has also been a proponent for government insurance when the private markets are unable to provide coverage:

> The non-existence of markets for the bearing of some risks in the first instance reduces welfare for those who wish to transfer those risks to others for a certain price, as well as for those who would find it profitable to take on the risk at such prices.
>
> The welfare case for insurance policies of all sorts is overwhelming. It follows that the government should undertake insurance in those cases where the market, for whatever reason, has failed to emerge.

On the other hand, Priest (2003) firmly rejects government insurance, questioning its effectiveness in two key regards:

1) The ability of government to enforce risk-based pricing of insurance – meaning that higher risks are charged higher premiums by the government sponsor. If government insurers instead adopt a single-premium level for all-risks, then the high risks are subsidized. The subsidy has the disturbing element that the government may actually encourage some of its citizens to place themselves in harm's way.
2) The ability of government insurers to control moral hazard, which is to say behavior by the insured parties that expands their exposure to the underlying risk. An example here would be the failure of government insurers to require that policyholders take actions to mitigate the losses that could result from an event. The continuing subsidies provided for flood insurance for homes on the flood plains of major rivers is a clear example.

In the end, the effectiveness of government insurance should be determined by the facts on the ground – how does government insurance actually operate. With this goal in mind, we now outline the experience with the major government programs for catastrophe insurance.[20]

3.2 The Experience with Government Catastrophe Insurance Plans[21]

I begin with a brief summary of the major catastrophe insurance programs run by government entities in the US. These programs cover risks from floods, earthquakes, wind damage, and terrorism. The discussion here is keyed to the catastrophe events and government insurance programs summarized earlier in Table 6.2. As will be immediately apparent, the government programs come in two forms. In one form, the government is the insurer and directly holds the risk. In the second form, the government is a reinsurer, providing a hedge to the private insurer that directly holds the risk. In all cases, however, the insurance is actually sold by private market entities.

3.2.1 National Flood Insurance Program (NFIP)[22]

Flood insurance is the longest-standing of the government interventions in the catastrophe insurance markets in the US, dating from 1968. It is a federal program, initiated, expanded, and revised by Congress. Congress required that the government set the premiums on an actuarial basis, but at the same time it has allowed deep subsidies for homes that existed at the time each community entered the program. The effect is that expected losses on grandfathered properties are five times those on newly built homes, with an average annual grandfather subsidy of $610, compared with a total premium of $310 on newly constructed homes; see Government Accountability Office (2010). It has reached the point that the NFIP is willing to purchase the grandfathered homes to save the high cost of future claims! As a result of the NFIP losses from Hurricane Katrina, the program required a bailout from the US Treasury of close to $20 billion.

---

[20] See also Hirshleifer (1953; 1955) for a discussion of the World War II insurance provided by the US federal government. These papers also provide valuable general insights into the pros and cons of government insurance.

[21] The discussion in this section is an updated and expanded version of Jaffee (2006). See Insurance Information Institute (2005) and Government Accountability Office (2010) for excellent overall descriptions of the major government catastrophe insurance plans. The GAO study, in particular, covers state programs not discussed in the current chapter.

[22] See Michel-Kerjan (2010) for an excellent introduction to the National Flood Insurance Program.

The US Congress recently passed the Flood Insurance Reform Act of 2012 which calls on the Federal Emergency Management Agency (FEMA), and other agencies, to make a number of changes to the way the NFIP is run. Key provisions of the legislation will require the NFIP to raise rates to reflect true flood risk, make the program more financially stable, and change how Flood Insurance Rate Map (FIRM) updates impact policyholders. The changes will mean premium rate increases for some – but not all – policyholders over time. However, it remains unclear how and when these changes will be implemented.

In contrast to the US, the United Kingdom (UK) has maintained a well-functioning private market for flood risks. The UK system long operated as a private/public partnership, in which the government 'guaranteed' levees and required good upstream practices, but the insurance rates and risks were all handled entirely within the private markets. However, rising claim rates from recent events have forced a change that will now involve a specialized flood reinsurance entity; see Association of British Insurers (2013).

3.2.2 Florida Hurricane Catastrophe Fund (FHCF)[23]

Hurricane Andrew hit Florida in 1992, creating huge property damage and bankrupting ten Florida insurers. The state's mutual guarantee plan paid covered claims against these firms, but the entire Florida hurricane insurance industry was revealed to be at risk to a future event. Since most mortgage lenders in Florida require borrowers to maintain a hurricane risk policy, a functioning hurricane insurance industry was considered essential in Florida. Furthermore, private reinsurance coverage for Florida's hurricane risk was considered insufficient and highly undependable.

As a result, in 1993, the FHCF was created. The FHCF operates as a public–private partnership, with the private sector still holding the first-loss position, but with the FHCF providing a dependable source of reinsurance.[24] Of course, as with any catastrophe insurer, the FHCF faces the task of maintaining sufficient capital resource to pay catastrophic claims. The FHCF includes several unique factors that help it to maintain sufficient capital resources:

---

[23] See Grace and Klein (2009) for an introduction to hurricane insurance and the FHCF. The legal and regulatory rulings for the Florida Hurricane Catastrophe Fund are available at: www.sbafla.com/fhcf/Home/LegislativeIssues/LegislationIssues/tabid/338/Default.aspx.

[24] It should be noted that the largest primary hurricane insurer in Florida, Citizens Property Insurance Corporation, is also a state run insurer for homeowners who cannot obtain cover elsewhere.

1) The Internal Revenue Service provided the FHCF with a tax-exempt status, meaning that it could accumulate capital against future events on a tax-free basis.
2) If hurricane claims exceed the FHCF's resources, the FHCF must borrow funds by issuing bonds. The bonds are repaid with mandatory assessments on a wide range of property and casualty insurance policies, and that may continue for as long as 30 years. The assessments, however, have limits with regard both to each year's event and to the aggregate outstanding. It is thus quite possible that the FHCF could reach its limit on bond issues.[25] The implication is that government entities, showing behavior similar to that of the private insurers, may impose limits on the amount of catastrophic coverage they are willing to provide.
3) If the FHCF resources, including bond issue powers, are exceeded, the primary insurers are at risk of receiving prorated payments on their reinsurance contracts. One alternative is that the State of Florida would bailout the FHCF or its bond investors.
4) The cost of FHCF coverage has remained lower than the cost of private reinsurance due to the FHCF's tax-exempt status and lack of any profit-motivated risk premium. However, these benefits are achieved in part due to the implicit guarantee of the State of Florida.

Even with these features, the 2004 and 2005 storm seasons deeply stressed the ability of the FHCF to make payments to insurers, and forced a significant volume of bond issues. Since the bonds are repaid from *ex post* assessments that are passed onto Florida policyholders, ultimately the policyholders will pay the cost of the past events. Furthermore, since Florida mortgage lenders normally require wind damage coverage, the homeowners have little choice but to continue to buy the hurricane insurance, whatever the cost. However, there is good news. Florida has avoided any serious hurricanes in recent years, allowing the FHCF to replenish its capital resources to a significant degree; see Florida Catastrophic Storm Risk Management Center (2013).

---

[25] In view of this possibility, in 2008, the Florida State Board of Administration (the administrator of the FHCF) purchased put options from Berkshire Hathaway, Inc., that required Berkshire Hathaway to purchase $4 billion of FHCF bonds paying 6.5 percent interest in the event a hurricane causes losses exceeding $16 billion.

3.2.3 California Earthquake Authority (CEA)[26]

The CEA is a program created by the California legislature in the aftermath of the Northridge earthquake of 1994. Although state funds are not committed to the CEA, it operates under rules set by the legislature and it is possible that state funds would be made available to support the program if that became necessary. The enabling legislation required that the premiums be 'actuarially based,' but scientists disagree substantially over what the correct numbers are. In fact, there was political intervention to 'temper' the differences in premiums initially proposed across the different major fault lines in California.

With 800,000 policies in force, $600 million in annual premium revenue, and almost $10 billion in claim-paying capacity, the CEA now writes about 70 percent of all residential earthquake policies sold in California.[27] The strategy of the CEA is primarily to use the premiums received to purchase reinsurance or catastrophe bond protection. The high costs to obtain reinsurance or catastrophe bond coverage are necessarily reflected in the premiums charged the customers. Indeed, less than 12 percent of applicable homeowners are currently purchasing CEA coverage, presumably indicating they prefer to 'self-insure' rather than pay the CEA premium rates. There is also consternation over the standard 15 percent deductible, although few consumers opted for a new 10 percent deductible (presumably because the premium is still higher). It is also enlightening that mortgage lenders in California do not require earthquake coverage as the basis for a home loan, no doubt because earthquakes rarely create serious damage to properly secured, wood-framed, detached homes.[28]

3.2.4 Terrorism Risk Insurance Act (TRIA)

The TRIA was created in the aftermath of the 11 September 2001 attack on the US. A significant part of the building damage created by the attack was insured, leading the insurers immediately to indicate they would not renew any terrorism policies in the absence of a government reinsurance program. This threatened the real estate construction industry, since mortgage lenders generally required commercial properties to maintain

---

[26] For a very useful introduction to the California Earthquake Authority, see Zanjani (2008).

[27] See Pomeroy (2010) for the testimony of Glenn Pomeroy, the current CEO of the CEA, before the US House Committee on Financial Services.

[28] Earthquake insurance is not a component of standard homeowner insurance policies. Prior to the Northridge Earthquake of 1994, it was generally available as a rider to the standard homeowner policy. Today, most insurers direct their policyholders to the CEA if they wish to purchase coverage.

'all-risks' coverage, which includes terrorism coverage. In November 2002, the first TRIA legislation was passed. This legislation had a 2005 sunset provision, but was renewed in 2005, again in 2007, and most recently in January 2015, confirming Milton Friedman's adage that 'there is nothing so permanent as a temporary government program'. It is noteworthy that the renewals have all retained the basic structure and principles of the original legislation, but have steadily reduced the government's (and hence the taxpayer's) exposure. The basic structural elements of TRIA are:

1) Premium setting is left fully in the hands of the insurance firms, who are also in the first-loss position with respect to any claims.
2) The government reinsurance is offered without charge, but is subject to substantial deductibles and coinsurance requirements.[29] It is these deductibles and coinsurance terms that have been raised with the successive renewals, thus limiting the government's ongoing exposure.
3) Any government payments on claims are also subject to a recovery through future assessments on the insurers and their policyholders. Since there have been no TRIA claims to date, it remains unclear whether the government would actually enforce its right of assessment following a terrorist attack.[30]
4) The coverage is provided only against terrorist attacks. Thus losses created by other like nuclear, chemical, or biological disasters would not be covered under TRIA.

3.2.5 Summary features of the government catastrophe insurance plans

In closing this section, we highlight the three key features of the government plans:

1) *Premium Setting*. We have seen that the government insurance plans for floods and California earthquakes are required to set 'actuarially determined' premiums, with the intent that the premiums should be

---

[29] Most European countries have enacted similar government-based terrorism insurance programs. However, unlike the US, the European programs all charge a fee for the reinsurance. This is actually a European Union (EU) requirement, since the EU rules prohibit individual countries from providing this form of subsidy. Nevertheless, the markets for European terrorism insurance appear to be functioning acceptably well.

[30] A similar issue arises under the bank deposit coverage provided by the Federal Deposit Insurance Corporation (FDIC). While in principle the FDIC could recover losses by raising premiums on the surviving banks, it is unclear if this would be enforced if the additional costs threatened the failure of even more banks.

risk-based. However, in practice this has not occurred, and both plans appear to include a degree of cross subsidization. At least for the flood program, this has created significant losses for the plan. Similarly, for the two government reinsurance programs – for terrorism and Florida hurricanes – the reinsurance is subsidized, although both plans have the right to recover losses from the insurers and their customers.

2) *Policy Sales and Marketing*. The government insurance plans considered here all outsource the function of policy sales to private market agents. Private market policy sales are necessarily the case for the TRIA and Florida Hurricane reinsurance plans, since these government plans are providing only reinsurance, with the primary coverage remaining with the private market insurers. The incentives to write these policies appears to work well. The CEA and the NFIP policies are also sold by authorized private market agents, who then transfer the risk to the government plan. It appears that the fee income provides sufficient incentive for these agents to market the policies.
3) *Claims Adjustment*. The situation here is the same as policy sales, namely that the government plans all outsource this function to private market insurers.

3.3 Further Effects of Government Catastrophe Insurance

Beyond the specific features of the government catastrophe programs just described, there are two other important effects of government insurance: crowding out of private market activity and a failure to provide incentives for mitigation. We discuss these in turn.

3.3.1 Crowding out of private market activity

Given the subsidies that are a systematic aspect of government catastrophe insurance programs, most private competitors are crowded out of the marketplace.[31] This is most evident for terrorism reinsurance, where the reinsurance coverage is offered at no cost, and for the Florida hurricane reinsurance, where the cost is well below what private market reinsurers would likely charge.[32] Not surprisingly, no private market competitors

---

[31] To be clear, reference here is primarily to the consumer lines for earthquake, flood, and hurricane insurance. Commercial property is typically not covered by the government programs, and that coverage is provided by the private markets. However, see Dixon et al. (2007) for the issues that arose in the market for commercial hurricane insurance following the costly events of 2004 and 2005.

[32] In addition, participation in the FHCF is mandatory for all Florida hurricane insurers.

exist for either of these government reinsurance programs. The same is true for the NFIP based on the relatively deep subsidies that are provided. The situation is more complex for the CEA, since its policies are attractive to only a small proportion of California homeowners. Indeed, some private insurers chose not to join the CEA, and under California law must offer their own earthquake policies to their homeowner insurance customers.

Perhaps the most important ramification of the crowding out of private market activity is that there is no objective standard against which to judge the efficiency of the government programs. Indeed, a common argument for continuing the government programs is that no private market alternative exists. But this argument loses its force if the absence of primary market alternatives is primarily the result of subsidies built into the government programs.

3.3.2 Mitigation activity

Mitigation activity is the most desirable risk management mechanism since it can reduce or even eliminate the losses created by catastrophes. In situations where mitigation eliminates both the risk and the need for insurance, a sufficient condition for optimal mitigation is clear: carry out all mitigation activities where the present value of mitigation costs is less than the present value of the insurance premiums that are saved. In fact, the incentives for mitigation should be even greater than the savings in insurance premiums, since it is surely better to have one's home standing after a catastrophe than to receive insurance indemnification in order to rebuild a home in ruins.

For insurance to provide the correct incentives for mitigation activity, however, risk-based premiums must accurately reflect the true expected loss of the event.[33] In the opposite case, if insurance premiums are constant across risk, or are subsidized, then the incentive to mitigate is muted. Indeed, when insurance premiums are below the true expected loss, there is actually a disincentive for mitigation. That is, property owners may prefer to pay the lower insurance premiums than the higher costs required to mitigate the risk.

The importance of risk-based insurance premiums in promoting efficient mitigation activity becomes even clearer in terms of the observed behavioral tendencies of individuals to underestimate the expected costs of catastrophes. Howard Kunreuther, for example, has documented a variety of behavioral situations in which individuals improperly evaluate

---

[33] I include here under risk-based premiums features of the insurance policy such as deductibles or coinsurance which have raised the effective premium.

the expected loss from low probability, high cost, events, and therefore carry out insufficient mitigation; see Kunreuther (1996; 2006).

Even in the absence of risk-based premiums, government insurance programs can still expand mitigation activity by providing information about the benefits of mitigation to their customers. Indeed, the legislation for both the FHCF and the CEA required the entities to promote mitigation activities among their clienteles. Unfortunately, it seems that neither agency has been very successful in this regard.

3.4 Alternative Proposals for Government Catastrophe Insurance[34]

Given the imperfect results with government insurance, in this section we consider three proposals that hold some promise for improving the situation. The 'traditional insurance' proposal would have the federal government act as a reinsurer. The 'insurer of last resort' proposal would make a fundamental change in the way the government intervenes in the catastrophe insurance market. The 'comprehensive disaster insurance' proposal would change the format of the catastrophe insurance policy itself. We consider these in turn.[35]

3.4.1 The federal government as a traditional reinsurer

A traditional insurance solution to the issue of funding and recapitalizing catastrophe risks was originally proposed by Lewis and Murdock (1996; 1999), and Cummins et al. (1999). In their programs, the government would provide standard excess of loss (XOL) reinsurance for all catastrophic losses up to specified limits. The reinsurance reimbursements would be based on industry losses, not indemnity contracts for each insurer's book of business. This would limit the need for the government to evaluate the underwriting standards of each of the individual insurers. However, it would also create substantial 'basis risk' for the individual insurers, since the government's reinsurance would provide a poor hedge against the insurer's actual book of business.

As discussed above, the federal government did create the TRIA reinsurance plan for terrorism risks following the 9/11 attack and this did

---

[34] Government Accountability Office (2010) provides an overview of current proposals for increased federal involvement in catastrophe insurance. See also Cummins (2006) and Jaffee and Russell (2008; 2010).

[35] Another proposal would allow US insurers to receive tax deductions for additions to their reserve accounts even when the actual event had not occurred. However, the evidence from Europe, where such tax deductions are already allowed, is that private insurers still remain reluctant to take on catastrophic risks.

incorporate standard XOL features. However, as also noted, TRIA reinsurance is provided without charge to all insurers that cover US terrorism risk. Although TRIA has been twice renewed, no serious consideration has been given to creating a further federal government reinsurance program for hurricane or earthquake risks.[36] For this reason, we next consider two alternative solutions that may also place the taxpayer at less risk.

3.4.2 An insurer of last resort[37]

Like private market catastrophe insurers, government plans incur high costs to maintain large capital resources. In the case of the CEA, these costs are passed on to policyholders, leading to a low take-up rate among California homeowners. In the cases of the NFIP, the FHCF, and the TRIA, the capital costs are subsidized in various ways.

One possible solution to this dilemma is to allow government insurers to hold less capital but to recover any resulting losses with assessment surcharges on future insurance premiums. This feature is already embedded to some degree in the Florida hurricane and federal terrorism reinsurance plans. More recently, an explicit proposal has been made by the CEA; see Pomeroy (2010) and the proposed Catastrophe Obligation Guarantee Act (a part of HR 2555). The key idea is that the CEA, and other state insurance programs, could operate with lower capital resources based on an option to issue bonds guaranteed by the US Treasury if claims from a major event exceeded the available resources of the state insurance entity. The bonds would provide the state plan with the cash to pay its claims and would be repaid by premium surcharges on future policies.

This role for the federal government has been described as the 'insurer of last resort', in parallel with the acknowledged role of the Federal Reserve as the 'lender of last resort'. In both cases, the principle is that the government can usefully provide resources to a financial institution that is facing a temporary liquidity imbalance. However, in the case of banks, the Federal Reserve loans are provided only to banks that are currently solvent, whereas in the case of insurers, solvency would be achieved only through the receipt of future premiums.

A number of fundamental policy issues are raised by such a proposal:

---

36 The willingness of the federal government to insure terrorist risks may also reflect the notion these are attacks on the country as a whole, and that it is a government responsibility to stop such events.

37 See Jaffee and Russell (2008) for a more detailed discussion of insurer of last report proposals.

1) Are the national benefits of well-functioning catastrophe insurance markets of sufficient importance that the federal government should provide an insurer of last resort facility?
2) Is it a proper role for the federal government to backstop state insurance plans?
3) If the federal backstop is interpreted as a subsidy, is such a subsidy warranted?[38]

At the time of writing, no federal backstop to state insurance plans has been enacted. And given the country's current fiscal situation, it would seem unlikely any plan will be enacted in the foreseeable future.

3.4.3 Comprehensive disaster insurance[39]

An alternative solution to the catastrophe insurance dilemma is to change the catastrophe insurance policy to one that covers 'all-risks' – that is, all the major natural catastrophes, floods, hurricanes, and earthquakes – in a single policy.[40] There would be at least two key benefits from such a change:

1) Insurers offering the all-catastrophe-risks policy would achieve a greater degree of diversification than an equivalent set of insurers each offering coverage against only one of the natural disasters. Indeed, it is possible that the benefit of diversification would cause private insurers voluntarily to reenter the natural disaster catastrophe lines.
2) The settlement of claims on existing catastrophe policies is often made more complex due to the difficulty of determining exactly which catastrophe policy should pay the claim. For example, the problem of separating wind damage from flood damage was particularly challenging following Hurricane Katrina, resulting in extensive litigation.

There is precedent for comprehensive disaster insurance. Going back to 1954, a Spanish government agency – the Consorcio de Compensation

---

[38] See Lucas (2010) for a collection of papers that discuss the conceptual issues in determining the level of a government subsidy and then evaluate a wide range of government insurance programs.

[39] See Kunreuther (2008) for a more detailed discussion of comprehensive disaster insurance plans.

[40] Terrorism is generally not included in such proposals because it is a risk primarily facing trophy commercial buildings, and which the federal government already covers through the TRIA. It should also be noted that the proposal here is to create a new all-catastrophes policy. This would be in addition to the standard homeowners policy that generally does not cover the various natural disasters.

de Seguros (CCS) – has provided catastrophe insurance covering natural disasters and various political and social events including terrorism. The coverage is a mandatory add-on to property insurance policies that are marketed by the private sector. France also has a similar 'all-risks' policy.

A comprehensive disaster insurance program for the US would have to be configured to deal with a variety of issues including:

1) Should the new all-catastrophes cover be a mandatory component of all homeowner policies, or should homeowners have the option to exclude the catastrophe coverage?
2) How would the program encourage homeowners to mitigate the risks they face?
3) Could a comprehensive disaster insurance policy be designed to provide coverage and guaranteed premium rates for longer than a year?[41]

As developed in both National Association of Insurance Commissioners (2009) and Government Accountability Office (2010), the major disadvantage of a comprehensive disaster insurance program arises if the federal government provides some dimension of the coverage at a subsidized rate. As discussed above, this would incentivize citizens to continue to build homes and live in the most dangerous areas. It would also put federal taxpayers at risk of paying claims in excess of premiums received, which raises fundamental issues of fairness given that the risk of natural disasters is not evenly distributed across the country. Finally, as a result of crowding out, subsidized government insurance would further reduce the likelihood of a private catastrophe insurance industry.

Given the above issues and the country's current fiscal situation, it would seem unlikely any plan will be enacted in the foreseeable future.

4. CONCLUSIONS

The large amount of capital required to maintain a private market for catastrophe insurance poses unique difficulties. As the private markets for catastrophe insurance have ceased to work, one by one, government – at both the state and federal levels – has been called on to help or replace the private market. But with the possible exception of the federal terrorism

---

[41] See Jaffee et al. (2010) for a discussion of long-term catastrophe insurance policies.

insurance program, the government programs for earthquake, flood, and hurricane insurance have all exhibited significant failings of their own.

In view of the rather dire experience with the existing government interventions in catastrophe insurance markets in the US, Jaffee and Russell (2008) and Wharton Risk Management and Decision Center (2008) have advocated a simple proposition:

> *When intervening in catastrophe risk insurance markets, government plans should mimic as closely as possible what operating private markets would have been expected to do.*

Following this rule, government plans would generally incorporate two key principles:

1) Use risk-based premiums in setting the price charged for each individual risk. Risk-based premiums create the proper incentives for policyholders to take actions to mitigate the underlying risks. In the case of location-based real estate risks, property owners would have incentive not to build in particularly risky locations.
2) Do not offer subsidies in setting the premiums on individual risks and certainly do not subsidize the riskiest locations. Not only do subsidies violate principle (1), but they also crowd out any potential private market initiatives.

Of course, to follow these principles, the government must have the will to reject requests to provide special help to affected individuals, regions, or industries.

REFERENCES

Arrow, Kenneth (1963), 'Uncertainty and the Welfare Economics of Medical Care', 53 *American Economic Review*, 941–73.

Association of British Insurers (2013), Government and Insurance Industry Flood Agreement (Statement of Principles), available at: www.abi.org.uk/Insurance-and-savings/Topics-and-issues/Flooding/Government-and-insurance-industry-flood-agreement.

Bantwal, V., and Howard Kunreuther (2000), 'A Cat Bond Premium Puzzle?', 1 *The Journal of Psychology and Financial Markets*, 76–91.

Cummins, David (2006), 'Should the Government Provide Insurance for Catastrophes', 88 (4) *Federal Reserve Bank of St. Louis Review*, July/August, 337–79.

Cummins, David, Christopher M. Lewis, and Richard D. Phillips (1999), 'Pricing Excess-of-Loss Reinsurance Contracts against Catastrophic Loss', in Kenneth A. Froot (ed.), *The Financing of Catastrophe Risk*, Chicago, IL: University of Chicago Press.

Cummins, D., M. Suher, and G. Zanjani (2010), 'Federal Financial Exposure to Natural Catastrophe Risk', in D. Lucas (ed.), *Measuring and Managing Federal Financial Risk*, Chicago, IL: University of Chicago Press, pp. 61–92.

Dixon, Lloyd, James W. Macdonald, and Julie Zissimopoulos (2007), 'Commercial Wind Insurance in the Gulf States', Occasional Paper, Rand Institute for Civil Justice, available at: www.rand.org/content/dam/rand/pubs/occasional_papers/2007/RAND_OP190.pdf.
Florida Catastrophic Storm Risk Management Center (2013), 'The State of Florida's Property Insurance Market', 2nd Annual Report, College of Business, the Florida State University; available at: www.stormrisk.org/sites/default/files/2nd%20Annual%20Insurance%20Market%20Rpt-FSU%20Storm%20Risk%20Center.pdf.
Froot, K.A. (2001), 'The Market for Catastrophe Risk: A Clinical Examination', 60(2–3), *Journal of Financial Economics*, 529–71.
Government Accountability Office (2010), 'Natural Catastrophe Insurance Coverage Remains a Challenge for State Programs', GAO-10-568R.
Grace, Martin, and Robert Klein (2009), 'The Perfect Storm: Hurricanes, Insurance, and Regulation', 12(1) *Risk Management and Insurance Review*, 81–124.
Hartwig, Robert (2011), '9/11 and Insurance: The Five Year Anniversary', Insurance Information Institute, available at: www.iii.org/sites/default/files/docs/pdf/September%2011%20Anniversary.pdf.
Hirshleifer, J. (1953), 'War Damage Insurance', 35(2) *The Review of Economics and Statistics*, 144–53.
Hirshleifer, J. (1955), 'Compensation for War Damage: An Economic View', 55(2) *Columbia Law Review*, 180–94.
Hogart, Robin (2002), 'Become a "Riskier" Place?', from the Social Science Research Council web page, 'Insurance and Safety: Has the World Become a Riskier Place After September 11?', Perspectives from the Social Sciences, Recovery; available at: www.ssrc.org/sept11/essays/hogarth.htm.
Ibragimov, Rustam, Dwight Jaffee, and Johan Walden (2008), 'Insurance Equilibrium with Monoline and Multiline Insurers', available at: www.escholarship.org/uc/item/4qj300xb.
Insurance Information Institute (2005), 'Public/Private Mechanisms for Handling Catastrophic Risks in the United States', available at: http://archives.tci1.org/publications/disasterpaper.pdf.
Jaffee, Dwight (2006), 'Monoline Restrictions, with Applications to Mortgage Insurance and Title Insurance', 28 *Review of Industrial Organization*, 83–108.
Jaffee, Dwight (2011), 'Bank Regulation and Mortgage Markets', 8(2) *Berkeley Business Law Journal*, 8–28.
Jaffee, Dwight, and John Quigley (2013), 'The Future of the Government Sponsored Enterprises: The Role of Government in the US Mortgage Market', in Edward Glaeser and Todd Sinai (eds.), *Housing and the Financial Crisis*, Cambridge, MA: NBER.
Jaffee, Dwight, and Thomas Russell (1997), 'Catastrophe Insurance, Capital Markets, and Uninsurable Risks', 64(2) *Journal of Risk and Insurance*, 205–30.
Jaffee, Dwight, and Thomas Russell (2008), 'Financing Catastrophe Insurance: A New Proposal', in John Quigley and Larry Rosenthal (eds.), *Risking House and Home*, Berkeley, CA: Berkeley Public Policy Press.
Jaffee, Dwight, and Thomas Russell (2010), 'Does the Terrorism Insurance Market Still Need Government Support', in Jeffrey R. Brown (ed.), *Public Insurance and Private Markets*, American Enterprise Institute.
Jaffee, Dwight, and Thomas Russell (2013), 'The Welfare Economics of Catastrophic Losses and Insurance', 38 *The Geneva Papers on Risk and Insurance*, 469–94.
Jaffee, Dwight, Howard Kunreuther, and Erwann Michel-Kerjan (2010), 'Long-Term Property Insurance', 29 *Journal of Insurance Regulation*, 167–88.
Kunreuther, H. (1996), 'Mitigating Disaster Losses through Insurance', 12(2–3) *Journal of Risk and Uncertainty*, 171–87.
Kunreuther, H. (2006), 'Disaster Mitigation and Insurance: Learning from Katrina', 604(1) *The Annals of the American Academy of Political and Social Science*, 208–27.
Kunreuther, H. (2008), 'Reflections on US Disaster Insurance Policy for the 21st Century', in John Quigley and Larry Rosenthal (eds.), *Risking House and Home*, Berkeley, CA: Berkeley Public Policy Press.

Kunreuther, H., and M. Pauly (2004), 'Neglecting Disaster: Why Don't People Insure against Large Losses', 28(1) *Journal of Risk and Uncertainty*, 5–21.
Kunreuther, H., J. Meszaros, R. Hogarth, and M. Spranca (1995), 'Ambiguity and Underwriter Decision Processes', 26 *The Journal of Economic Behavior and Organization*, 337–52.
Lewis, Christopher M., and Kevin C. Murdock (1996), 'The Role of Government Contracts in Discretionary Reinsurance Markets for Natural Disasters', 63(4) *Journal of Risk and Insurance*, 567–97.
Lewis, Christopher M., and Kevin C. Murdock (1999), 'Alternative Means of Redistributing Catastrophic Risk in a National Risk Management System', in Kenneth A. Froot (ed.), *The Financing of Catastrophe Risk*, Chicago, IL: University of Chicago Press.
Lucas, Deborah (2010), *Measuring and Managing Federal Financial Risk*, Chicago, IL: University of Chicago Press.
Michel-Kerjan, Erwann (2010), 'Catastrophe Economics: The National Flood Insurance Program', 24(4) *Journal of Economic Perspectives*, 165–86.
Moss, David A. (2002), *When All Else Fails: Government as the Ultimate Risk Manager*, Cambridge, MA: Harvard University Press.
National Association of Insurance Commissioners (NAIC) (2009), 'Natural Catastrophe Risk: Creating a Comprehensive National Plan', available at: www.naic.org/documents/committees_c_natural_catastrophe_plan_final.pdf.
Pomeroy, Glenn (2010), 'Testimony Before the House Committee on Financial Services, Hearing on Approaches to Mitigating and Managing Natural Catastrophe Risk', 10 March 2010.
Priest, George (2003), 'Government Insurance Versus Market Insurance', 28(1) *The Geneva Papers on Risk and Insurance*, 71–80.
Swiss Re (2014), *Insurance Linked Securities Market Update*, available at: http://media.swissre.com/documents/2015_jan_ils_market_update.pdf.
US Treasury (2011), 'Reforming America's House Finance Market: A Report to Congress', available at: www.treasury.gov/initiatives/documents/reforming%20america's%20housing%20finance%20market.pdf.
Wharton Risk Management and Decision Center (2008), 'Managing Large-Scale Risks in a New Era of Catastrophes', available at: http://opim.wharton.upenn.edu/risk/library/Wharton_LargeScaleRisks_FullReport_2008.pdf.
Zanjani, George (2008), 'Public versus Private Underwriting of Catastrophe Risk: Lessons from the California Earthquake Authority', in John M. Quigley and Larry A. Rosenthal (eds.), *Risking House and Home: Disasters, Cities, Public Policy*, Berkeley, CA: Berkeley Public Policy Press.

7. US health care reform

Scott E. Harrington

I. INTRODUCTION

The US Congress passed and President Obama signed the Patient Protection and Affordable Care Act ('Affordable Care Act' or 'ACA') in March 2010, completing what is arguably the most significant social legislation in the United States since the enactment of Medicare and Medicaid in 1965. Broadly similar in key respects to the Massachusetts health care reform law enacted in 2006, the ACA expands health insurance coverage beginning in 2014 by: (1) mandating that individuals obtain qualified health insurance or pay a financial penalty (the 'individual mandate'); (2) subsidizing the cost of coverage for low-to-moderate income persons and for some small, low-wage employers; (3) requiring employers with 50 or more employees to offer health coverage or pay fines (later delayed until 2015); and (4) expanding eligibility for publicly funded Medicaid programs in participating states. The US Supreme Court ruled 5-4 in June 2012 that the individual mandate was constitutional under the federal government's taxing power and upheld the statute, with the important exception that the states could not be compelled to expand Medicaid under threat of the federal government withholding all federal Medicaid funding.

The ACA required the establishment of health insurance exchanges (later named 'Marketplaces') for individual and small group health insurance markets in each state for coverage effective January 1, 2014, with premium subsidies available only for coverage purchased through an exchange. With certain exceptions, insurers within or outside of the exchanges are restricted to offering coverage in specified coverage tiers, with guaranteed issue of coverage at rates that do not reflect health status or pre-existing conditions. As of March 31, 2014, 8 million people had selected a health plan through the exchanges, and several million had likely enrolled in Medicaid under the ACA's expanded eligibility criteria in states that expanded Medicaid.

The ACA received no Republican votes and has been heavily politicized from its inception. The highly publicized cancellation of non-complying health plans and technical failures accompanying the rollout of the ACA exchanges in 2013, along with delays in fully implementing some of the law's provisions, have further fueled the already partisan debate about the efficacy of the law, which shows no signs of abatement.

This chapter provides an overview of economic research and analysis related to the ACA's key provisions for expanding the number of US residents with health insurance. The focus is on the economics of those provisions and their expected effects, as opposed to debates over the law's fundamental fairness, constitutionality, or comparison to more sweeping interventions to expand health insurance, or to reforms that would rely more heavily on voluntary contracting and private markets.[1] The chapter begins with background on the broad context of health care reform, including high and growing costs of health care, health insurance, and federal health care spending, the large numbers of uninsured, and health insurance market performance. It next outlines the ACA's key provisions for expanding coverage, discusses the economics of those provisions, and reviews the law's projected costs and impact on federal budget deficits. Evidence, issues, and uncertainties concerning the law's likely effects are then considered, including evidence and potential lessons from studies of the Massachusetts' reforms; premium rates, coverage take-up, adverse selection, cost sharing, and narrow provider networks; and potential effects on employer decisions to offer health insurance and labor markets. The conclusion further highlights the substantial economic and political uncertainties that remain concerning the magnitude, cost, and stability of the ACA's coverage expansion, which preclude strong predictions about its effects and future.

II. THE CONTEXT OF REFORM

Three broad issues set the stage for enactment of the ACA: (1) high and growing medical costs, health insurance premiums, and federal health care spending; (2) high and growing numbers of uninsured; and (3) perceived failures in private health insurance markets.

---

[1] Parts of this chapter draw from, update, or expand upon my earlier work, especially Harrington (2010a; 2011). The economics literature on the economics of health insurance and expanding US coverage is extensive, spanning many decades, including broad treatments of the economics of reform and earlier reform proposals (e.g., Pauly 1986; Weisbrod 1991; Cutler 1994; Gruber 2008b; CBO 2008). Other reviews of research on health insurance and health insurance markets include Gruber (2000) and Cutler and Zeckhauser (2000).

1. Medical Costs, Premiums, and Federal Spending

While the ACA focuses on expanding coverage, the high and rapidly growing cost of health care and insurance and the projected growth in government spending on Medicare and Medicaid played major roles in the policy debate, and its passage depended heavily on the Congressional Budget Office's (CBO) projection that it would not increase federal budget deficits over a 10 year time-frame. Figure 7.1 shows US national health expenditures (NHE) as a percentage of Gross Domestic Product (GDP) overall and by major source of spending during 1990–2011. Figure 7.2 shows for the same period nominal annual percentage growth in per capita NHE as well as the amounts by which these figures differed from percentage changes in the consumer price index (CPI) and per capita GDP. The share of GDP devoted to health care grew from 12.5 percent in 1990 to 17.9 percent during 2009–2011, percentages far above other countries.[2] For 2011, projected spending for Medicare/Medicaid (including the Children's Health Insurance Program (CHIP)) represented 6.4 percent of GDP, and private health insurance spending (including employer-sponsored self-funded plans) represented 5.9 percent of GDP. In contrast to growing expenditures by public and private insurers, out-of-pocket spending represented a relatively constant 2 percent of GDP throughout 1990–2011, and the percentage of total health care spending paid out of pocket declined. High and growing per capita health expenditures and more prevalent third-party payments were accompanied by high and growing average health insurance premiums.[3]

A central question in the health care reform debate is the extent to which much higher US spending compared with other developed countries is associated with higher quality of health care and, if so, whether higher quality is worth the cost. Explanations of higher US health care spending generally point to significantly higher compensation of health care providers and historically greater rates of technology adoption and diffusion, along with the lesser role played by government and correspondingly

---

[2] Projected NHE as a percent of GDP for 2012 and 2013 are 17.9 percent and 18.0 percent, respectively (Cuckler et al. 2013).

[3] During the ACA debate in 2009, the Kaiser/HRET survey of employer-sponsored health benefits reported an average premium (employer and employee combined) for family coverage of $13,375 (growing to $16,351 in 2013, Kaiser Family Foundation 2009; 2013a). Average health insurance premiums are much lower in individual markets, largely because of greater average cost-sharing, less generous benefits, and insurer risk selection and rating in these markets. According to a survey of 2.5 million individual market policies, the average premium for family coverage in 2009 was $6,328 (AHIP 2009).

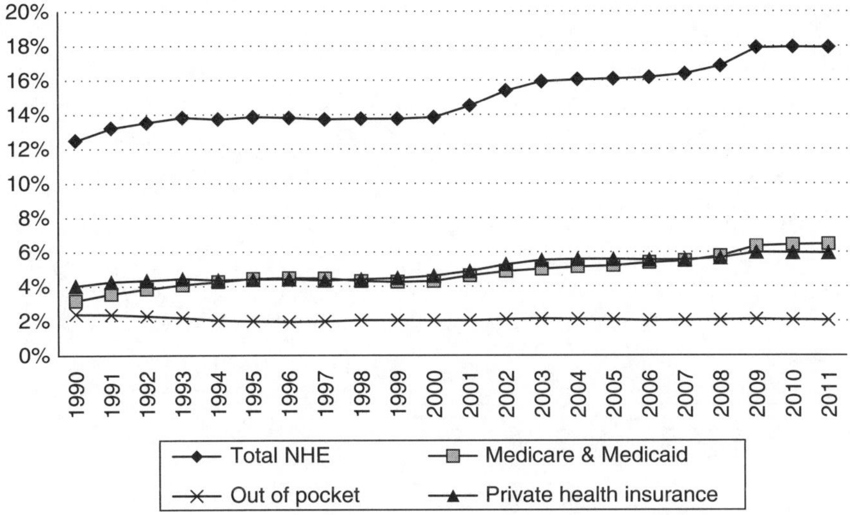

Note: Author's calculations with national health expenditure data: NHE by type of service and source of funds: calendar years 1960–2011.

Figure 7.1 US health care spending as percent of GDP, 1990–2011

greater private sector role in financing US medical care (see, e.g., CBO 2008 for an overview). Additionally, economists generally agree that a primary driver of cost growth is incentive misalignment in US health care payment and delivery, including: (1) relatively generous insurance coverage for most people with insurance; (2) generally modest restrictions on choice of providers and access to specialists; (3) prevalent fee-for-service payment to providers; and (4) no overt government limits on total spending. These characteristics have encouraged cost growth generally and are commonly believed to produce excessive utilization of low-valued health care. Many economists have devoted considerable attention to the individual income tax exclusion for the costs of employer-provided coverage in promoting generous coverage and discouraging tighter managed care arrangements to limit moral hazard and control costs (Feldstein 1973; Pauly 1986).

Moral hazard plays an important role in the incentive misalignment story, and most of the literature on moral hazard in health insurance has focused on how generous insurance can lead to excessive utilization of medical care. On the other hand, debate exists about the relative importance of coverage-induced excessive utilization versus 'efficient moral hazard', whereby health insurance facilitates the consumption of medical care that is highly valued by consumers but which would not be possible without

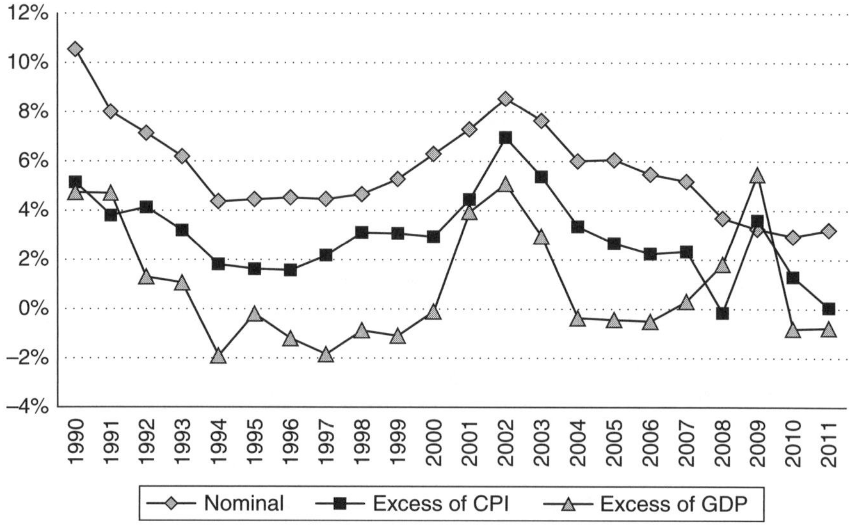

Note: Author's calculations with national health expenditure data: NHE by type of service and source of funds: calendar years 1990–2011.

Figure 7.2 Annual growth in NHE per capita 1990–2011

insurance (see Nyman, Chapter 3 in this volume). My own view is that much of the economic literature has paid too little attention to the role of health insurance in financing the consumption of expensive but high-valued care.

A number of studies have explored the causes of the recent slowdown in aggregate health care and Medicare spending and whether slower growth will likely continue (Ryu et al. 2013; Cutler and Sahni 2013; Levine and Buntin 2013; Chandra, Holmes, and Skinner 2013). They generally suggest that the economic recession, increased cost sharing by patients, and health care reform all contributed, but that considerable uncertainty exists as to the magnitude of different influences and whether the slowdown will persist. The CBO and the Center for Medicare and Medicaid Services (CMS) continue to project large and unsustainable increases in federal spending on health care, in significant part due to aging of the population (CBO 2013b and 2014; CMS 2013).

2. The Uninsured

The ACA's dominant focus is on expanding health insurance to the previously uninsured. Figure 7.3 shows estimated proportions of the US

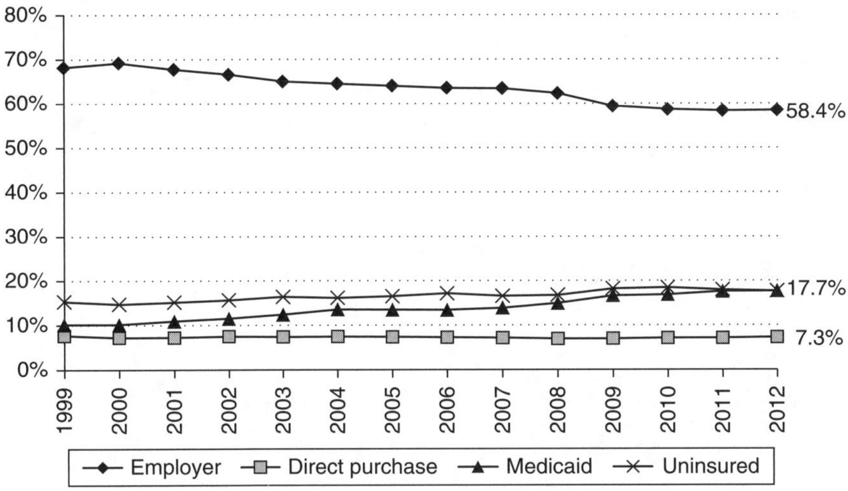

Source: US Census Bureau. Table HIB-2. Health Insurance Coverage Status and Type of Coverage All Persons by Age and Sex: 1999 to 2012. People as of March of the following year. www.census.gov/hhes/www/hlthins/data/historical/HIB_tables.html.

Figure 7.3 Estimated percentages of US under age 65 population by health insurance status

population under age 65 without health insurance and with employer-sponsored, directly purchased (individual), and Medicaid coverage during 1999–2012 based on the Current Population Survey (CPS).[4] An estimated 49 million US residents under age 65 did not have health insurance when the ACA was enacted in 2010, representing 18.4 percent of the under age 65 population.[5] As shown in Figure 7.4, the likelihood of adults being uninsured generally declines significantly with age. Approximately 28 percent of people age 18–34 were estimated as uninsured in 2010 compared with approximately 15 percent of people aged 55–64. Estimated uninsured rates for each age group increased after 2007, with the exception of the age 18–24 category, where the estimated uninsured rate dropped

[4] Other insured people under age 65 had Medicare or military coverage. Some people had more than one source of coverage. Gruber (2008b) comprehensively reviews the causes and consequences of uninsurance and potential reforms to expand coverage.

[5] An estimated 50 million of uninsured for all ages represented 16.3 percent of the total population.

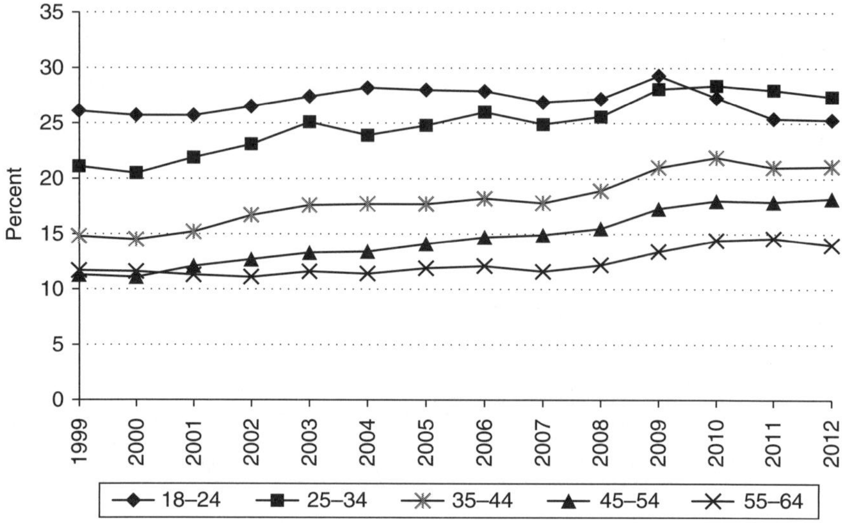

Source: US Census Bureau. Table HIB-2. Health Insurance Coverage Status and Type of Coverage All Persons by Age and Sex: 1999 to 2012. People as of March of the following year. www.census.gov/hhes/www/hlthins/data/historical/HIB_tables.html.

Figure 7.4 Estimated percentages uninsured by age group

since 2010 following the ACA's requirement that carriers who offer coverage for dependents make the coverage available to policyholders' children under the age of 26.

Compared with the non-elderly insured, the uninsured on average have significantly lower income and educational attainment, are less likely to be employed full time, are more likely to be African American and/or of Hispanic origin, and are less likely to report being in very good or excellent health. It has been estimated in recent years that roughly a quarter of the uninsured were eligible for Medicaid but had not enrolled, roughly 10 million lived in households that included an individual who had declined employer-sponsored coverage, 4–5 million or more had incomes above 400 percent of the federal poverty level (FPL), and at least several million were undocumented residents (Kaiser Family Foundation 2009; NIHCM 2008; also see Bundorf and Pauly 2006; Gruber 2008b).[6]

[6] Bundorf and Pauly (2006) develop several measures of the affordability of coverage and estimate that from one-quarter to three-quarters of the uninsured in 2000 could 'afford' coverage.

Why people fail to insure

As reviewed by Gruber (2008b) and others, a variety of factors may explain the large numbers of uninsured. These include: (1) actuarially unfair premiums due to administrative expense and profit loadings in insurance premiums that outweigh the effects of any available tax subsidies; (2) asymmetric information, adverse selection, and regulatory rating restrictions that make coverage unattractive for uninsured individuals who are relatively healthy; (3) legal mandates for health insurance to cover services that may not be valued by some individuals; (4) behavioral factors that reduce willingness to pay for coverage; and (5) implicit insurance protection provided by bankruptcy protection and safety-net programs, which crowd out the purchase of coverage.

My own view is that while each of these factors matters, the dulling effects of implicit insurance protection on the demand for coverage play a central role, especially for the uninsured with incomes well above the poverty level. Federal law effectively compels hospitals to provide emergency/acute care to stabilize patients without regard to ability to pay, thus implicitly insuring some of the costs of acute care for the uninsured. Other safety-net programs allow some uninsured persons with low incomes to obtain free care from community health centers, or to spend down following adverse events to qualify for public Medicaid coverage.

Sinn (1982) provides an early and insightful theoretical treatment of the demand for insurance against loss of wealth in the presence of a socially guaranteed minimum wealth level, showing that risk averse expected utility maximizers might fail to insure potential claims even at actuarially fair premiums. The intuition is that the minimum wealth guaranty provides a form of catastrophic protection that substitutes for market insurance. The implication for health insurance demand is that rational, risk averse agents may be unwilling to pay the premiums needed to insure against the risk of medical expenses that are large in relation to their assets and minimum wealth protected by bankruptcy law. Consistent with the theory, Bernard, Banthin, and Encinosa (2009) show that, controlling for income, the probability of obtaining health insurance declines with assets. More directly, Mahoney (2012) shows that the probability that an individual has health coverage is positively related to his or her net assets at risk after considering the effects of bankruptcy protection.[7] Another implication of the research on implicit insurance protection is that low income persons could

---

7 Koch (2013) develops and estimates a structural economic model suggesting that repealing the requirement of emergency room care without regard to ability to pay would increase the fraction of the population that obtains health insurance.

prefer coverage of low-to-moderate expenses with relatively low total coverage limits (such as so-called 'Mini-Med' plans, which provide some coverage of routine medical costs but not large expenditures) and rely on the safety-net for severe episodes.

Altruism as a rationale for expanding coverage

Broad economic rationales for government intervention to expand health insurance emphasize altruism and/or negative externalities from the uninsured. With respect to altruism, Pauly (1971; 2000) and others emphasize that many (relatively well-off) insured people derive utility from enhanced access to health care and reduced financial risk for low income people, and that they are willing to pay higher taxes or otherwise support interventions to promote universal coverage.[8]

Numerous studies have examined whether the enhanced access to medical care from health insurance significantly improves health outcomes.[9] As discussed in a review by Levy and Meltzer (2008), however, causal interpretation in such studies is often problematic given the possible omission of control variables that affect both health insurance purchases and health outcomes. The original RAND Health Insurance Experiment provided evidence that, with certain exceptions and some disagreement as to interpretation, increased patient cost sharing (less complete health insurance coverage) had little if any effect on health outcomes.[10] More recently, evidence from a randomized assignment of eligibility for Medicaid coverage in Oregon provided little evidence of a positive impact of coverage on most physical health measures over a two-year horizon, but the results suggested a positive effect on mental health (Baicker et al. 2013). Earlier results within the first year had suggested a positive impact of coverage on self-reported physical and mental health (Finkelstein et al. 2012). In a recent example of a study employing non-randomized design, Sommers, Long, and Baicker (2014) provide evidence of significant reductions in all-cause mortality and in deaths from causes amenable to health care in Massachusetts following the enactment of its health care reform law in 2006 versus a propensity-score matched control group of counties from other states.

When considering altruistic motives and the relationship between insurance and health, the possibility that health insurance with risk insensitive

---

8 The altruistic motive is also consistent with the notion that health insurance allows people to finance and consume high-valued care (see Nyman, Chapter 3 in this volume).

9 Courtemanche and Zapata (2012) provide a recent summary.

10 See Aron-Dine, Einav, and Finkelstein (2013) for discussion and update.

premiums could generate '*ex ante*' moral hazard by discouraging investment in healthy behavior is also relevant. Bhattacharya et al. (2011), for example, provide evidence that being insured increases obesity.[11] Whether insurance affects healthy behavior has been debated in the context of workplace wellness and related programs that link employees' premiums and/or cost sharing to behavior (such as smoking), or to sustaining achievable health metrics (such as cholesterol levels), including ACA expansion of the extent to which employer-sponsored group health plans can tie premiums and/or cost sharing to these factors (see Horwitz, Kelly, and DiNardo 2013).

Reducing negative externalities from the uninsured

Reducing negative externalities provides another motivation for expanding health insurance. Expanding coverage may reduce the spread of communicable disease or, more broadly, promote societal stability. In addition and more relevant in the policy debate, the provision of unpaid medical services to the uninsured, including the legal mandate for hospitals to provide emergency care, imposes costs on providers, some of which are shifted to taxpayers and/or insured plans. The income transfer from such uncompensated care, while progressive, may produce deadweight costs, including from the substitution of more costly emergency care for primary care.[12]

Hadley et al. (2008) estimated that the uninsured paid about a third of the cost of their medical care and estimated $56 billion in uncompensated care for all providers in 2008, with government funding covering about 75 percent of the costs. The American Hospital Association (2013) reports that uncompensated hospital care costs have consistently averaged about 6 percent of total hospital costs since 1980, amounting to $41 billion in 2011. While the magnitude and incidence of uncompensated care are subject to debate, the general issue has played a meaningful role in the policy debate over coverage expansion.[13]

---

[11] Also see Klick and Stratmann (2007). Cole, Kim, and Krueger (2012) develop and calibrate a structural model of the effects on health of regulations on health-related wage discrimination and prohibitions on health plans charging premiums related to health status.

[12] See Kolstad and Kowalski (2012a). Using regression discontinuity analysis of young people aging out of parents' health insurance, however, Anderson, Dobkin, and Gross (2012) found that losing insurance led to a large reduction in emergency care use, suggesting that expanding coverage could increase such use.

[13] Hospital organizations generally have been strong supporters of coverage expansion through the ACA. See Al-Ississ and Miller (2013) for discussion and evidence of negative hospital stock price reactions to the election of Scott

3. Insurance Market Performance

Perceived failures in health insurance markets played a significant role in the debate leading to the ACA's enactment, especially for the individual and small group markets. The ACA's minimum medical loss ratio and health insurance rate review provisions (discussed below) reflect views that health insurance competition and pre-ACA state regulation did not adequately discipline insurers' expenses and profits. The most salient pre-ACA criticism of insurance markets, however, was private insurers' risk rating and underwriting.

Premium loadings and competition

According to NHE data, the projected 'net cost' of private health insurance (premiums less benefits, including for self-funded plans using estimated premium equivalents) for 2010 was just over $100 billion, representing 12 percent of projected expenditures for private health insurance and 4 percent of projected NHE.[14] Consistent with that result for 2010, the estimated 'medical loss ratio' for all private health insurance (the ratio of medical benefits to total premiums, including premium equivalents for self-funded plans) averaged 87.7 percent during 1965–2010, with little or no trend (see Figure 7.5). Put differently, the margin in premiums for insurers' administrative expenses and profits (ignoring investment income from pre-payment of premiums, which on average equals a very small percentage of premiums) averaged 12.3 percent.[15]

Health insurers' profit margins have typically averaged about 3–5 percent of revenues (less for nonprofit insurers (Harrington 2010a; 2010b)). Data reported to state insurance regulators during 2006–09 indicate that aggregate medical loss ratios ranged from 85 to 88 percent for all insured coverage (including Medicare supplement and Medicare Advantage plans) and from 83 to 87 percent for comprehensive major medical coverage (Donahue 2010). Table 7.1 shows aggregate ratios of

---

Brown as US Senator for Massachusetts in 2010, which at the time reduced the likelihood of ACA passage. In contrast to the evidence for hospitals, Gruber and Rodriguez (2007) estimated that a sample of 4,000 physicians on average had negative uncompensated care costs. The fact that many uninsured patients paid more for comparable treatments than fees paid by insurers more than offset losses from non-paying patients.

[14] The data are from NHE tabulations by type of expenditure and source of funds, calendar years 1965–20, with projections for 2010–2020 (www.cms.gov/). The projections are based on the 2009 version of the NHE accounts released in January 2011.

[15] The ratios in Figure 7.5 equal one minus the ratio of net cost to premiums.

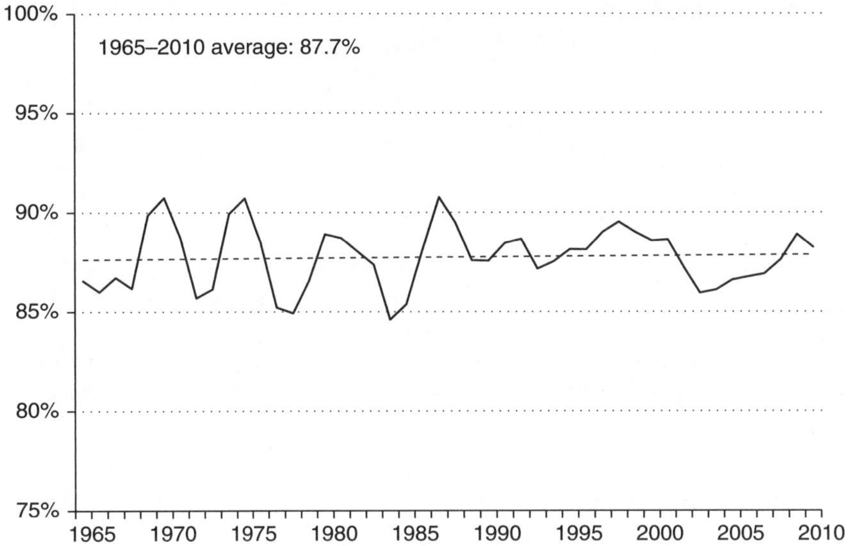

Note: Author's calculations with national health expenditure data: NHE amounts by type of expenditure and source of funds – calendar years 1965–2010 in PROJECTIONS format. Projections for 2010 (based on the 2009 version of the NHE released in January 2011).

Figure 7.5 Estimated US medical loss ratio for private health insurance, 1965–2010 (including premium equivalents for self-funded plans)

medical costs and various categories of administrative expenses to premiums for 2010, using data reported by insurers in response to ACA reporting requirements, before the ACA's rules on medical loss ratios and premium rebates took effect.

Administrative expense ratios for individual and small group health insurance have long been regarded by many people as too high, including claims of ratios of 25–30 percent of premiums or more, especially when compared with low administrative expenses for Medicare (less than 2 percent of medical costs).[16] These views and assertions of excessive health insurer profits played a significant role in the acrimonious ACA debate

[16] Sherlock (2009) notes that assertions that administrative expenses in the individual and small group markets are often 30 percent higher are based on estimates by Hay Huggins for the Congressional Research Service (1988), which in significant part were based on underwriters' projections, and that such assertions often are based on ratios of expenses to medical claim costs rather than premiums.

Table 7.1 Insured plan medical costs, administrative expenses, and pre-tax underwriting profits (percentage of total premiums in 2010)

	Individual	Small group	Large group
Medical costs	77.8%	80.0%	86.5%
Quality improvement and fraud prevention	0.7%	0.7%	0.7%
Claims adjustment	3.9%	2.6%	2.3%
Distribution	6.9%	5.2%	2.3%
General and administrative	7.8%	4.6%	4.0%
Premium taxes and fees	3.0%	3.6%	2.3%
Pre-tax underwriting profit	−0.1%	3.2%	1.9%
TOTAL	100%	100%	100%
ACA Medical Loss Ratio	80.9%	83.8%	89.3%

Note: Author's calculations from supplemental health exhibit.

over a proposed public plan option, which would have established a government health insurer to compete with private plans on the exchanges. The aggregate data discussed above and illustrated in Table 7.1 and Figure 7.5 imply a much lower potential reduction in premiums, however, if profits could be substantially eliminated and administrative expenses could be cut significantly.

Analyses of private health insurance markets have provided relatively limited evidence of specific market failures that would generate excessive administrative costs, if not profits. On the one hand, health insurance market concentration is often high at the state and metropolitan levels, especially for individual insurance (e.g., Robinson 2004; American Medical Association 2007; GAO 2009; Austin and Hungerford 2009; also see Scanlon et al. 2006), raising concerns about market power.[17] It is not clear, however, why market power would inflate administrative costs. In

[17] The limited federal antitrust exemption for the 'business of insurance' has little effect on health insurers. Insurers' relationships with medical care providers, such as the inclusion of 'most favored customer' clauses in hospital contracts, are not exempted from antitrust scrutiny. In contrast to property/casualty insurance, health insurance has no history of joint rate making that is protected by the exemption. Health insurer mergers have been subject to federal antitrust scrutiny since at least the early 1970s, and mergers and acquisitions of health insurers are subject to approval by state regulators.

addition, concentration varies widely across states and market segments (individual, small group, and large group). The causes of such variation, and the nature and scope of possible barriers to entry, are not fully understood, and research has provided only mixed evidence of adverse effects from increased concentration (see, e.g., Dafny 2010; Dafny, Duggan, and Ramanarayanan 2012; Moriya, Vogt, and Gaynor 2010; also see Conover and Miller 2010; Gaynor and Town 2011).

Cebul et al. (2011) posit a model in which consumer search frictions can lead to high marketing expenses and prices in health insurance markets by allowing some inefficient insurers to survive and contribute to higher administrative expenses and premiums by other insurers. Based on comparison of premium distributions for insured and self-insured employer plans, they conclude that frictions significantly increase premiums and that a public health insurance option could improve efficiency by reducing distortions in pricing and marketing expenses. Their theoretical model, however, does not consider the potential role of brokers in reducing search frictions, which I regard as a significant flaw. Their empirical conclusions depend on having adequately controlled for risk and other factors that could produce premium differences between insured and self-insured plans, which also strikes me as problematic.

Risk rating, adverse selection, and guaranteed renewability

Health insurers' risk rating and underwriting were widely condemned during the ACA debate. When permitted by law, insurers generally consider the applicant's health and characteristics that may correlate with health when deciding what prices and terms to offer new applicants and whether to offer coverage at all.[18] Applicants with pre-existing health conditions face higher than average premiums, more limited coverage, or are not offered any coverage. People who are born with or develop costly conditions before seeking coverage could consequently face high premiums and/or limited coverage in the individual market (Abraham and Chiappori, Chapter 9 in this volume; Hendren 2013). Additionally, individuals who lost employer-sponsored coverage and exhausted their ability to continue coverage under federal and state law could face high individual market premiums and/or exclusion of coverage for one or more pre-existing conditions.[19] This is because, while pre-ACA state and federal

18 Abraham and Chiappori, Chapter 9 in this volume, focus on the resulting classification risk and its regulation.

19 According to AHIP (2009) survey data, the overall denial rate for the individual insurance market was 12.7 percent in 2009, ranging from about 10 percent for applicants under age 35 to roughly 30 percent for applicants aged 60–64. The

laws (e.g., the Health Insurance Portability and Accountability Act) generally required insurers to offer coverage to persons previously insured for minimum periods of time, they did not require insurers to offer coverage at rates that do not reflect health status.

As is well known, insurers have strong incentives to classify prospective customers based on observable characteristics that are correlated with the frequency and severity of claims in order to mitigate or avoid adverse selection. When classification is costly, the costs produce deadweight welfare losses if classification only redistributes income across risk types. Theoretical work on general insurance in the presence of asymmetric information by Crocker and Snow (1986) demonstrates that risk rating can be efficient when the risk of loss depends on behavior and classification costs are low, as would be true if classification is based on readily observable characteristics.

Studies of whether asymmetric information results in adverse selection in health insurance have been inconclusive. Some evidence is consistent instead with 'advantageous selection', where consumers with lower risk of loss are more likely to buy coverage (Fang, Keane, and Silverman 2008; also see Finkelstein and McGarry 2006). In a study with possible implications for medical coverage, Hendren (2013) develops and tests a model in which asymmetric information about future expenditures associated with observable health conditions could cause insurers to reject applicants, and he provides evidence consistent with that hypothesis for long-term care, disability, and life insurance.

A number of theoretical and empirical studies (see Abraham and Chiappori, Chapter 9 in this volume) have considered the more complicated case of health insurance in a multi-period framework where agents face two risks: (1) the risk of requiring costly care in a given period; and (2) the risk of developing a condition during the period that will require costly care in future periods (i.e., the risk of becoming high risk or 'reclassification risk'). Employer-sponsored health insurance provides protection against reclassification risk while the person is employed. Pre-ACA federal and state laws dealing with continuation of coverage (as well as labor market competition among employers) provided some protection against reclassification risk when changing jobs, thus reducing the potential for 'job lock' associated with risk rating of coverage for people who could lose

---

extent to which applicants denied coverage were able to obtain coverage from another insurer or source is not known. The AHIP survey reported that 34 percent of offers were at higher than standard premium rates (29 percent of the offers were at standard rates and 36 percent were below standard rates) and that six percent of offers included a waiver of coverage for one or more health conditions.

health coverage as a result of changing employment. Consistent with some degree of job lock, however, Gruber and Madrian (2004; also see Gruber 2000) provided evidence that continuation of coverage mandates by some states and the federal government increased job mobility.

Even before the ACA, most individual market policies were guaranteed to be renewable at rates that change with the experience of a given risk pool rather than the health status of an individual policyholder, and laws in most states and federal law included regulations that require guaranteed renewable coverage with a given insurer. If, however, policyholders who remain healthy tend to seek out new coverage and leave a given risk pool, the rates for those who remain will increase accordingly, undermining the stability of guaranteed renewability in individual (and small group) health insurance markets.

From a theoretical perspective, unregulated private insurance markets may be able to solve some of the problems associated with rating non-group policyholders on the basis of health-related factors, although Abraham and Chiappori (Chapter 9 in this volume) are pessimistic about this possibility. Cochrane (1995) develops a theoretical model of time-consistent health insurance that involves severance payments to policyholders who become high risk in amounts sufficient to fund the cost of future higher premiums. Pauly, Kunreuther, and Hirth (1995; also see Pauly et al. 2011) develop a model where front-loading of premium schedules is sufficient to fund lifetime claims and provide incentives for policyholders who remain low risk to maintain coverage. Herring and Pauly (2006) estimate a competitive premium schedule that provides such incentives and increases with age. Consistent with some degree of pooling of the risk of becoming high risk, Pauly and Herring (2007) provide evidence that premiums paid for individual health insurance increase less than proportionately with health risk and that health risk has only small effects on the likelihood of obtaining coverage. Pauly and Lieberthal (2008) provide evidence that the likelihood of losing health insurance is greater for small group plans than for individual coverage, attributing that finding to high loadings and guaranteed renewability in the individual market.

In addition to issues of pre-existing conditions and reclassification risk, health insurers' pre-ACA risk rating practices also resulted in policy rescissions in the individual market, generating substantial controversy, litigation, and in some states new regulation prior to the ACA. This issue played an important role in the ACA debate, figuring prominently in Congressional hearings and President Obama's speeches. Traditional practice, governed by common law, statute, and regulation, was for insurers to rely on accurate disclosure of health-related information by applicants without conducting a detailed investigation of medical history, but instead conducting more detailed and costly reviews of a subset of applications following policy issue – sometimes when expensive treatment was sought (and sometimes referred to as 'post-claims underwriting').

State laws generally permitted rescission of coverage (declaring the policy void) on the basis of material misrepresentation, i.e., providing incorrect information that affected the insurer's decision to offer coverage or the premium charged. Although some states required an intent to deceive or that the misrepresentation was related to the actual claim, coverage often could be rescinded if information provided by the applicant was false and affected the insurer's decision, even if the errors were unintentional and unrelated to the illness for which the individual sought treatment. Along with controversy over risk rating and pre-existing condition exclusions, health insurers' rescission practices contributed to an impression that such practices were insufficiently and ineffectively regulated and that health insurance markets were fraught with opportunistic behavior by insurers. I have argued elsewhere (Harrington 2010a) that the scope of any problems regarding rescissions was exaggerated in the debate surrounding passage of the ACA, implying that the ACA's prohibition on rescissions without fraud that took effect in 2010 would not have major consequences.[20]

III. THE ACA

Consistent with earlier reform debates, the dialog preceding and following the ACA's enactment manifested deep differences in underlying philosophical attitudes towards the ends and means of US health care reform.[21] The ACA reflects a specific set of policy choices from a broad menu of approaches to expanding health insurance coverage within the existing framework of public and private coverage, including expanded public coverage, taxpayer subsidization of the purchase of private market coverage, restrictions on private insurance risk rating, and mandatory coverage requirements. This section summarizes and provides additional context for the ACA's key provisions expanding coverage and regulating health insurance. It also reviews government projections of the ACA's effects on the numbers of insured persons, sources of coverage, federal deficits, and health care spending.

---

[20] Harrington (2010a) provides additional discussion of rescission practices and implications of prohibiting rescissions unless fraud can be proved.

[21] Pauly (2004) considers how such differences contributed to health reform gridlock over many years.

1. Coverage Expansion

The ACA has numerous, complex provisions affecting patients, providers, employers, health insurers, and taxpayers.[22] Numerous options existed for subsidizing coverage expansion through either enhancing taxpayer funded public coverage or providing tax subsidies/credits for purchasing private coverage (Gruber 2008b; CBO 2008: Ch. 2; Furman 2008).[23] Like the 2006 Massachusetts reforms, its central provisions for expanding coverage are Medicaid expansion, subsidies for the purchase of private coverage, and individual and employer mandates. The ACA also established an insurance program for previously uninsured persons with pre-existing conditions pending the onset of its central provisions in 2014.

Medicaid expansion

Given the Supreme Court's holding that the ACA provision requiring states to expand Medicaid or lose existing federal funding was unconstitutional, states have the option to expand Medicaid coverage to all non-Medicare eligible people with incomes up to 138 percent of the FPL, including non-disabled, non-elderly adults without dependent children. The federal government will finance 100 percent of the cost of expansion through 2016, gradually declining to 90 percent in 2020 and later. As of March 2014, 27 jurisdictions were expanding Medicaid, 19 were not, and five were debating (Kaiser Family Foundation 2014). Several of those expanding had received approval to expand coverage using federal dollars for the newly eligible to purchase private coverage through the state's exchange.

Premium tax credits and cost-sharing subsidies

Beginning in 2014, premium tax credits are provided to individuals/families with income between 138–400 percent of the FPL and without an offer of employer-sponsored coverage for the purchase of a Qualified

---

[22] Kaiser Family Foundation (2011) provides a detailed summary of the law.

[23] One criterion for assessing those options is how much additional coverage can be achieved for a given amount of additional government cost (direct spending and tax expenditures). Jonathan Gruber, a leading economist who played a significant consultancy role in the design of the ACA and the earlier reforms in Massachusetts, conducted a number of studies using a microsimulation model suggesting that expanded public coverage was advantageous on this 'bang for the buck' dimension (Gruber 2003; 2005; 2008b). Gruber (2011b) considers the effects of modifying the tax exclusion for employer-sponsored coverage post ACA.

Health Plan in an ACA exchange.[24] The law also reduces cost sharing for persons with incomes up to 250 percent of the FPL who purchase silver plans (see below), with greater reductions for lower income individuals/families.

The premium credits will limit premium contributions to specified percentages of income (e.g., 3–4 percent for incomes between 138 and 150 percent of FPL, increasing to 9.5 percent for incomes between 350 and 400 percent of FPL). (For states that choose not to expand Medicaid (see below), persons/families with income from 100–138 percent of FPL will be heavily subsidized if they purchase coverage on the exchange, but people with incomes below 100 percent of the FPL will not be eligible for subsidies.) The restriction of subsidies to persons not offered a qualified employer-sponsored plan is designed to encourage employees to take up employer offers and discourage them from dropping such coverage and moving to the exchanges, which would drive up the cost of subsidies.

Individual mandate

Beginning in 2014, most legal residents who meet income tax filing thresholds are mandated to have health insurance that meets minimum requirements or pay a tax (penalty), unless the cost of minimum qualified coverage exceeds 8 percent of their income. The tax penalty for non-compliance with the 'individual mandate' is the greater of $95 (up to three times that amount for families) or 1 percent of taxable income in 2014, increasing to the greater $695 or 2.5 percent of taxable income in 2016, and indexed to inflation in later years.

In principle, an individual mandate with meaningful penalties for non-compliance can significantly increase the number of people with coverage, improve their access to medical care, reduce uncompensated care costs, and, as suggested by Gruber (2008b) and others, reduce the net cost of coverage expansion. An individual mandate can play an important role in facilitating guaranteed issue of coverage and restrictions on rate classification. Such restrictions reduce premiums for high risks while increasing premiums for low risks, thus discouraging low risks from purchasing coverage. A meaningful mandate limits this effect and adverse selection by requiring younger/healthier people to buy coverage, thus helping to subsidize the purchase of coverage by older/less healthy people, and reducing the amount of government subsidy needed to achieve a given level of coverage expansion.

On the other hand, a mandate imposes costs on people who are required

---

[24] Monahan (2011) provides detailed analysis of the ACA's subsidy provisions.

either to buy coverage against their will (and above the value of the coverage to them) or pay the 'tax' for non-compliance. Significant subsidies and/or exemptions from the mandate are required to avoid a disproportionate burden on low income people. The cost of premium subsidies that accompany a mandate, including from crowd-out of non-subsidized care, will be borne largely by unsubsidized parties and taxpayers, plausibly swamping aggregate savings to those groups from reductions in the burden of uncompensated care.

Employer mandate, penalties, and tax credits

With implementation delayed until at least 2015, businesses with 50 or more employees that do not offer health coverage and have one or more full-time employees receiving a premium credit on an insurance exchange will pay a penalty of $2,000 per full-time employee, excluding the first 30 employees. Businesses with 50 or more employees that offer coverage to employees that either fails to meet a 60 percent actuarial value standard or requires an employee to contribute more than 9.5 percent of income towards coverage will pay a penalty equal to the lessor of $3,000 per employee who receives a premium tax credit for coverage through an exchange (see below), or $2,000 per employee, again excluding the first 30 employees. Beginning with the 2010 tax year, employers with 25 or fewer employees and with annual wages averaging less than $50,000 became eligible for tax credits for offering coverage if they pay at least 50 percent of the cost of coverage. The credit varies over time and phases out as a function of the number of employees and average wages.

Given that many of the traditionally uninsured have been employed at firms that do not offer health insurance, mandating that employers either offer coverage or pay fines provides a direct mechanism for encouraging coverage expansion. Theoretical and empirical work, however, indicates that the cost of employer-mandated coverage would fall largely on employment in the form of reduced wages, and, if minimum wage constraints are binding, reduced employment of low-productivity workers (Summers 1989; Gruber 1994; 2000). Numerous studies have emphasized these limitations of employer mandates as a means for expanding coverage (e.g., Lee and Warren 1999; Burkhauser and Simon 2008; Baicker and Levy 2008; also see Herring and Pauly 2010). The ACA's exemption of small employers from the mandate, many of which do not offer coverage and pay relatively low wages, is broadly consistent with the goal of reducing such adverse effects. Rather than coverage expansion, the principal function of the law's employer mandate may be to discourage some larger employers that would offer coverage absent the ACA from dropping coverage.

Pre-existing condition insurance plans

The ACA created a temporary program with $5 billion budgetary authority to provide state or federally administered subsidized coverage at the state level to individuals with pre-existing medical conditions who had been uninsured for at least six months. Twenty-seven states opted to operate their own plan; ten subsequently converted to federal operation. While total enrollment was initially projected to reach 300,000 or more, take-up in the plans was initially slow and much lower than anticipated. Enrollment increased over time in conjunction with premium reductions and changes to broaden coverage. The average cost per enrollee then turned out to be much higher than expected. New enrollment was suspended in early 2013 to keep costs within the budget, with total enrollment of just over 100,000 in July 2013 (CCIIO 2013). The federal plans are being phased out in conjunction with the opening of the exchanges in 2014; state plans have the option of terminating or maintaining their plans.

2. Insurance Market Regulation

Health insurance exchanges

The ACA required the establishment in each state of health insurance exchanges for the individual and small group markets (or for both markets combined).[25] The exchanges began enrollment in October 2013. Subsidies for individual coverage are only available within an exchange. States had the option of establishing and operating their own exchanges, partnering with the federal government, or having the federal government establish and run the exchange on its own. Seventeen jurisdictions chose to establish their own exchanges, subject to detailed federal rules. Seven chose to partner with the federal government, taking on a subset of administrative functions. The remaining 27 jurisdictions opted to have the federal government run their exchanges (Kaiser Family Foundation 2013b). The basic features of these exchanges varied in important ways. Some states opted for a certification model, where all insurers meeting specified criteria could participate in the exchange; others chose an active purchase model, actively negotiating and selecting insurers. The US Department of Health and Human Services (HHS) originally indicated that it would take the former approach for federal exchanges but later switched to active negotiation. Data released by HHS in September 2013 indicated that an average of eight insurance carriers would participate in the individual

[25] In 2013 the HHS retitled the 'exchanges' to 'Marketplaces'. I use the former term throughout.

market exchanges for the 36 states with available data, ranging from a low of two carriers to a high of 13 (ASPE 2013).[26]

While enrollment quickened early in 2014, the botched rollout of the federal exchanges and many state-run exchanges beginning October 1, 2013 deterred early enrollment and heightened debate about the law's efficacy. The widespread scope and causes of the technical problems are difficult to fathom. The question arose as to whether the early failures could have a permanent negative impact on enrollment and aggravate adverse selection, and some theoretical research has explored the possibility that a death spiral ('bad equilibrium') could ensue (Scheuer and Smetters 2014). If severe adverse selection were to occur, however, I believe it would more likely be attributable to the basic design of the reforms than a dysfunctional launch of the exchanges.

For small employer groups, states had the option of including businesses with 100 or fewer or 50 or fewer employees until 2016, when all businesses with 100 or fewer employees must be eligible to purchase coverage in an exchange. States are permitted to expand eligibility to larger employers beginning in 2017. For 2014, small employer exchanges run by the federal government and in some states will not allow employees to choose among insurers as had originally been planned, but instead all employees of a business choosing exchange coverage will be enrolled in a single plan.

Required benefits and benefit tiers

The ACA required a number of changes in insurance plan design prior to 2014, including mandatory coverage of preventive services without patient cost sharing, extension of coverage to adult children up to age 26 for all individual and group plans, and restrictions/elimination of lifetime and annual benefit limits. With the exception of grandfathered plans and certain plans that were later allowed to be renewed temporarily (see below), individual and small group plans were required to offer 'minimum essential benefits' starting in 2014. HHS regulations allow states flexibility in specifying these minimum benefits, which typically are patterned after a popular plan for the small group market in a state. Plans must cover at least 60 percent of the actuarial value of eligible benefits using an HHS minimum value calculator for an assumed population, with maximum cost sharing equal to health savings account maximums.

All insurers, irrespective of whether they are offering coverage in an exchange, are restricted to offering plans in four coverage tiers, along

---

[26] The extent to which the carriers in a state are under common ownership was not reported.

with a catastrophic plan for young adults up to age 30. Bronze, silver, gold, and platinum plans will cover approximately 60 percent, 70 percent, 80 percent, and 90 percent, respectively, of eligible medical costs, based on an HHS actuarial value calculator assuming standardized populations and tier-specific claim distributions.[27]

Mandatory offers at adjusted community rates

Going beyond pre-ACA restrictions in most states, all health insurers in the individual and small group markets must (since 2014) accept all applicants regardless of health status, without basing premiums on health status or excluding coverage for pre-existing conditions.[28] Enrollment is permitted during annual open enrollment periods; penalties for having previously failed to enroll are not permitted. An insurer has to price ACA-compliant policies using a single-risk pool, excluding catastrophic policies, grandfathered plans, and non-compliant policies that are permitted to be renewed through October 2016 (see below). Unless that state combines the individual and small group markets, a separate (but single) risk pool is required for each market. Premium rates are allowed to vary only by coverage tier, number of dependents, geographic region, age (within a 3–1 ratio for ages 21–64), and tobacco use (1.5–1 ratio). Detailed HHS regulations specify how the factors can be incorporated, including a specific baseline schedule for age-based rating. With respect to geography, most states have multiple rating areas, with the larger states commonly having 10–15 or more separate rating areas.

The 3-to-1 restriction on age rating has been controversial for requiring younger people to pay higher premiums to help subsidize older people. It has contributed to concern that many younger enrollees will be discouraged from purchasing coverage despite the mandate and premium subsidies and to significant attention being paid to the age mix of enrollees for 2014. The rationale for an age rating restriction to cap premiums for older enrollees in addition to providing income-based subsidies has not been transparent. The main goal, however, may be to reduce the scope of rate increases for healthy, older people, who will no longer be able to purchase individual coverage that reflects their good health, but must instead be rated as part of a single-risk pool that includes the healthy and sick.

---

[27] States are permitted to establish Basic Health Plans for people with incomes between 138 and 200 percent of the FPL and receive 95 percent of the subsidy that would have been paid through the exchange. There has been little state activity in this regard.

[28] The ACA prohibited inclusion of pre-existing condition exclusions and rating for children effective 2010.

Grandfathered and transitional plans

Health plans in existence as of the ACA's enactment in 2010 were not required to meet the law's rating rules and benefit requirements, with a number of important exceptions. Such plans could not exclude coverage of pre-existing conditions for children six months after enactment and for adults as of 2014. They also were required to extend dependent coverage to children up to age 26 and eliminate/restrict annual and lifetime benefit limits (subject to a possible waiver by HHS). Grandfathered status would be lost if a health plan made certain changes, such as increasing the deductible or employee premium contribution above specified thresholds, and many individual and employer-sponsored plans lost grandfathered status.

During the transition to ACA's rating and benefit requirements for 2014, some millions of individual market policyholders received notices that their existing, non-grandfathered policies would terminate and that they could enroll in ACA-compliant plans, often with different premiums, coverage terms, and provider networks. This led to substantial uproar over the perceived violation of President Obama's repeated promises during the ACA debate that 'if you like your plan, you can keep it'. HHS subsequently authorized states to allow existing, non-compliant plans to be renewed another year, and later authorized renewals through October 2016 (allowing some coverage to continue until October 2017). Although some states did not permit the extension, allowing insurers in other states to continue plans that do not conform to the ACA's 2014 requirements is expected to lead to some amount of adverse selection for the ACA risk pools, as people who continue their existing plans are likely to be healthier on average than those who instead enroll in ACA-compliant plans.

Risk adjustment, reinsurance, and risk corridors

The ACA and attendant HHS regulations established three programs designed to help stabilize health insurance markets and disincentivize insurer risk selection in the new environment of guaranteed issue and adjusted community rating for ACA-compliant plans (US HHS 2012b): (1) a permanent risk adjustment program; (2) a three-year transitional reinsurance program; and (3) a three-year transitional risk corridor program for plans offered through the exchanges.

The risk adjustment program applies to ACA-compliant individual and small group plans sold through or outside of the exchanges. It will adjust insurers' revenues to reflect differences in the average health status of their enrollees. Insurers with healthier than average enrollees will essentially make payments to insurers with less healthy enrollees. Risk adjustment is designed to facilitate guaranteed issue and pricing of coverage without regard to enrollees' health status and the law's restriction on varying rates in relation to age. It will help protect a health plan from large losses that could arise if they attract sicker than average enrollees and reduce incentives for insurer risk selection.

The temporary reinsurance program applies to ACA-compliant individual plans sold through and outside of the exchanges. Subject to an overall cap, it will reimburse insurers for 80 percent of medical costs for individual enrollees with medical costs above $45,000 in 2014. (The threshold was originally set at $60,000, but it was lowered by HHS in response to concerns over the exchange rollout and permitted continuance of non-complying plans.) For 2015, the program is scheduled to provide payment of 50 percent of the amount of medical costs for an enrollee above $70,000. The reinsurance program is financed by fees assessed against all enrollees in insured and self-funded health plans. The program is designed to reduce volatility in insurers' claim costs attributable to very high cost enrollees beyond that contemplated in the risk adjustment program, and, by assessing fees against enrollees in large insured group and self-funded employer plans, to lower average premiums in the individual market.

In contrast to the risk adjustment and reinsurance programs, the risk corridor program only applies to individual coverage sold through the exchanges. It is designed to address aggregate pricing uncertainty for three years commencing January 1, 2014. Given the magnitude of rating and coverage changes required by the law, and the fact that many enrollees in plans will have previously been uninsured, health insurers had to confront enormous uncertainties when pricing plans, including the percentage of people who will enroll, their health status, their likely utilization of medical services, and competitors' pricing. The risk corridor program reduces insurers' risk, thus encouraging their participation in the new exchanges and helping to promote market stability. While the details are complex, the program essentially will reimburse insurers for part of the excess if their costs exceed target amounts in relation to the premiums charged. An insurer will be reimbursed for 50 percent of any costs from 103 to 108 percent of the target and 80 percent of any costs above 108 percent of the target. If costs instead turn out to be lower than the targets, insurers will have to pay fees equal to a portion of the gains. Specifically, an insurer will pay a fee equal to 50 percent of the shortfall if costs fall within 92 to 97 percent of the target and 80 percent of any additional shortfall if costs are less than 92 percent of the target. HHS has announced several changes to the details of the program to enhance payments in response to potentially higher claim costs from the permitted continuation of non-compliant plans.

Controversy has arisen over funding of the risk corridor program.

Consistent with program's goal, there is no statutory requirement that payments to insurers be limited to collections from insurers. Some critics have argued that the program could therefore provide a means for the federal government to 'bail out' health insurers if claims experience in the exchanges turns out to be bad, that HHS does not have budgetary authority to pay out more than it receives from that program, and that Congress should require that the program be budget neutral. CBO projections of the ACA's revenues and costs assume that the risk corridor program will be budget neutral. A requirement of budget neutrality, however, would substantially undermine the program's ability to reduce the risk to insurers that costs could be much higher than predicted, thus discouraging their participation in the exchanges and putting upward pressure on pricing.

Minimum medical loss ratios and rate review

The ACA established minimum medical loss ratio (MLR) requirements of 80 percent for the individual and small group health insurance markets and 85 percent for the large group market. Beginning with 2011 experience, insurers whose medical claims and expenditures on specified activities to improve health care quality total less than the required percentages of premiums (less certain taxes and fees) in a given state are required to rebate the shortfalls to customers. Rebates totaled $1.1 billion for 2011 experience and $504 million for 2012 experience (US HHS 2012a; CCIIO 2013).[29]

The ACA also authorized HHS, in conjunction with the states, to establish a process for annual review of 'unreasonable' health insurance rate increases. Insurers must justify such rate increases to HHS and relevant state regulators prior to implementation, and to 'prominently post such information on their Internet websites', with public disclosure otherwise ensured by HHS. The ACA, however, did not require regulatory approval of rate changes by the states or permit HHS to deny rate increases. (About two-thirds of the states require regulatory approval of health insurance rates.)

HHS set 10 percent as the threshold for 'unreasonable' rate increases beginning September 1, 2011, and has maintained it at that level. (Although the statute permitted adoption of state-specific thresholds, HHS denied requests by Alaska and Wisconsin for higher thresholds in 2012.) Insurers that propose increases of 10 percent or more must file a preliminary justification with HHS and the state, which is posted on

---

29 Harrington (2013) contains detailed description of the rules, their potential consequences, and related literature. Also see McCue, Hall, and Liu (2013).

an HHS website and the insurers' websites. If the state or HHS deems the increase unreasonable and the insurer nonetheless implements the increase (in those states that do not require regulatory approval of rates), the insurer must submit a final justification to regulators and post it on the insurer's website.

The ACA authorized the HHS to assume responsibility for review of proposed rate increases at or above the 10 percent threshold if it deems that a state does not have an effective rate review process. HHS regulations subsequently established detailed criteria for effective rate review. As of April 2014, HHS was responsible for the reviews of rates for the individual market in five states (Alabama, Missouri, Oklahoma, Texas, and Wyoming). The ACA also authorized $250 million for Health Insurance Rate Review Grants for states to improve their rate review. The funds, which have been authorized to specific states in several cycles, have been used to expand the scope of rate review and rate filing requirements, improve information technology, improve consumer interfaces (such as rate review websites), and hire staff.

The ACA's MLR and rate review provisions have required extensive rulemaking and compliance efforts by insurers. As I have explained in great detail elsewhere (Harrington 2010b; 2013), the potential benefits from these provisions in promoting coverage expansion at affordable rates are at best arguable, and they entail considerable risks of unintended consequences and politicization of health insurance rating.

3. Coverage and Cost Projections

Coverage expansion

The CBO projected in March 2011 (CBO 2011), before the Supreme Court's decision, that the ACA would result in 34 million more people with health insurance in 2021 than if the law had not been passed.[30] Half of this population would be covered by Medicaid and half by private health insurance. The projected proportion of the population without health insurance would be 8 percent (5 percent of legal residents), or 23 million people, compared with a projected 20 percent (17 percent of legal residents), or 58 million people, who would be uninsured without the law.

Figure 7.6 shows CBO May 2013 coverage projections for the year 2023, which reflect changes due to the Supreme Court's decision on

---

[30] CBO projections are based on an elaborate microsimulation model (CBO 2007; also see CBO 2008 and Gruber 2011a).

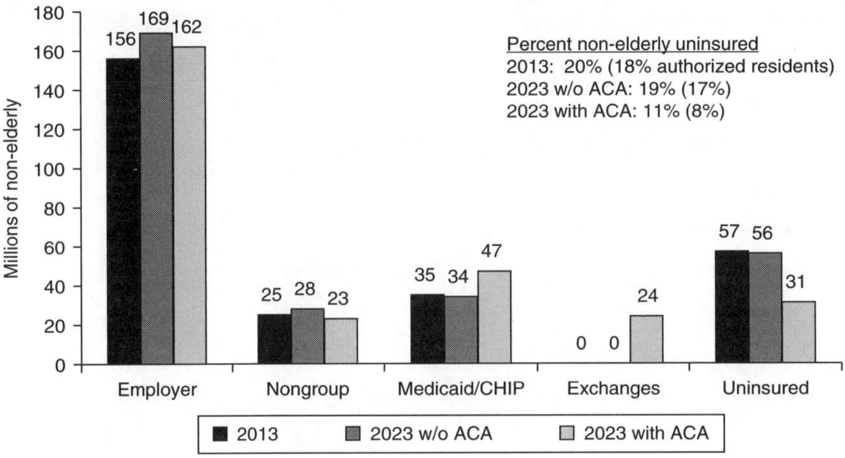

Source: CBO (2013a).

Figure 7.6 Congressional Budget Office projections of insured population by type of coverage

Medicaid expansion.[31] The CBO then projected that the ACA will result in 25 million more people being insured, with 13 million more people in Medicaid, exchange enrollment of 24 million, and 31 million uninsured (8 percent of legal residents).[32] It also projected that 7 million fewer people will have employer-sponsored coverage in 2023 than without the law but that employer coverage will remain dominant. This issue and other projections are discussed further below.

Projected costs, financing, and effects on federal deficits

Figure 7.7 shows CBO projections as of July 2012 (the latest comprehensive projections) of the ACA's impact on federal spending, revenues, and deficit for the 10-year period 2013–22 (from the CBO's score of House Republican legislation to repeal the law, CBO 2012). The CBO projected a gross cost (before offsets for individual and employer penalties) of coverage expansion during that period of approximately $1.7 trillion,

[31] Updated coverage projections in April 2014 changed little, while the projected direct costs of premium subsidies were somewhat lower.

[32] The CBO did not model state-specific Medicaid expansion. Holahan et al. (2013) model state specific enrollment changes; also see Parente and Feldman (2013).

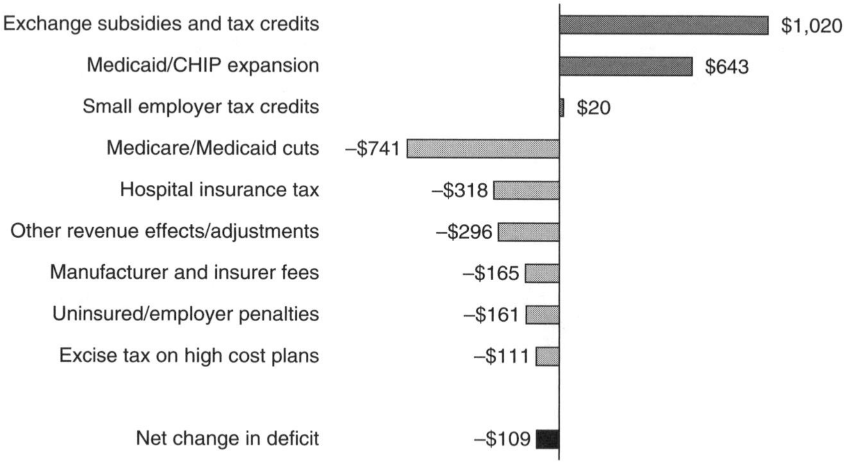

Source: Author's compilation from CBO (2012).

Figure 7.7 Congressional Budget Office cost projections for the ACA, 2013–22

with exchange subsidies representing about three-fifths of the cost and Medicaid expansion representing most of the remainder.

The coverage expansion costs are financed by Medicare and Medicaid spending cuts, a variety of new taxes, and penalties on non-complying employers and individuals. Cuts to Medicare principally are driven by projected Medicare reimbursement reductions to non-physician providers and decreased funding of Medicare Advantage. New taxes include a Medicare (hospital insurance) tax equal to 3.8 percent of unearned income for taxpayers with adjusted gross incomes above $200,000 for individuals and $250,000 for joint filers. That tax and an additional 0.9 percent Medicare hospital insurance tax on earned income for those filers are projected to generate $318 billion during 2013–22, with another $165 billion coming from levies on health insurance, pharmaceutical, and medical device companies.

CBO projections also anticipate $111 billion in direct tax revenues from the ACA's excise tax on high cost health plans. This tax will come into force in 2018 and amount to 40 percent of health plan costs (aggregate values) in excess of $10,200 for individual coverage and $27,500 for family coverage (subject to certain exceptions, with thresholds indexed for general inflation beginning in 2020). In order to reduce or avoid the excise tax, employers with high cost plans will likely decrease plan costs by increasing cost sharing and/or adopting more effective care management programs. Many firms are already taking such steps. The CBO projects other tax revenues and adjustments of close to $300 billion, which in significant part reflect expected increases in taxes from slower growth in tax expenditures associated with the exclusion of the cost of employer-sponsored coverage from employees' taxable income.

Overall, the CBO's 2012 projections suggest that the law will reduce federal deficits by $109 billion during 2013–22, and that these deficit reductions will continue in later years.[33] Whether the ACA will reduce federal deficits as the CBO anticipates has been heavily debated, with a particular focus on whether projected cuts in Medicare spending are likely to be achievable (e.g., Holtz-Eakin and Ramlet 2010; CMS 2011; also see Gruber 2011a; Holtz-Eakin 2011). My guess is that the savings, if any, will be lower than projected.

Medicare and total spending

Figure 7.8 shows projected Medicare spending as a proportion of GDP during 2010–40 from the 2009 Medicare Trustees' report (pre-ACA), and the Trustees' post-ACA reports in 2011 and 2013. The Trustees' projections assume a roughly 30 percent reduction in Medicare physician reimbursement under prior legislation to control spending growth, which Congress has repeatedly overridden with stopgap measures. They also assume significant cuts in non-physician provider reimbursement and Medicare Advantage under the ACA. Figure 7.8 also shows alternative projections as of 2011 and 2013 from the CMS (2011; 2013), which, according to CMS, assume more realistic spending for physician and hospital reimbursement. The ACA's effects notwithstanding, projected longer-term Medicare spending remains problematic (also see CBO 2013b; 2014).

To be sure, the ACA establishes a number of additional cost-saving mechanisms, which, while uncertain in their effects and projected to save relatively little over ten years, could eventually help reduce Medicare spending growth below projected rates. These mechanisms include the law's authorization and subsequent growth of Medicare Accountable Care

33 These projected deficit reductions are less than the $143 billion of deficit reduction anticipated in the CBO's projections for 2010–19 at the time of enactment, which included $70 billion due to inclusion in the legislation of the CLASS (Community Living Assistance Services and Supports) program. This program was a federal long-term care insurance program that the CBO projected would generate significant revenue and little cost in its early years, but which was later determined by HHS to be financially unviable.

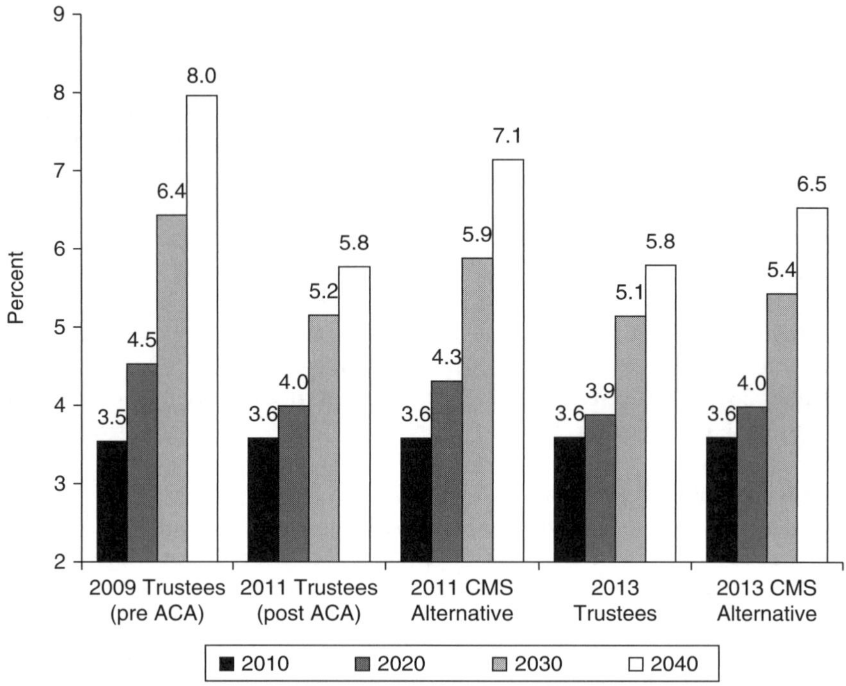

Source: Boards of Trustees of the Federal Hospital Insurance and Federal Supplementary Medical Insurance Trust Funds (2009; 2011; 2013) and CMS (2011; 2013).

Figure 7.8 Projected Medicare spending as percent of GDP, 2010–40

Organizations, which allow provider groups to share in potential savings from lowering Medicare spending, and establishment of episode-based payment under the ACA's Center for Medicare and Medicaid Innovation. The law also created the Patient Centered Outcomes Research Institute to fund comparative effectiveness research of different medical treatments, which might help identify some types of care that are ineffective yet costly compared with alternatives. Additionally, the ACA authorized the creation of a 15-member Independent Payment Advisory Board (IPAB) that would be required to submit proposed cuts in Medicare spending to Congress if spending growth exceeds specified targets.[34]

---

[34] The Board has yet to be appointed. Its recommendations would be implemented by HHS unless Congress approved measures to produce equivalent savings or waived this requirement by a super-majority. The law limits significantly

Regarding total health care spending, CMS projected in 2010 that the ACA would increase NHEs by $311 billion during 2010–19 (CMS 2010), and it later projected that the law will increase total spending by $621 billion through 2022 (Cuckler et al. 2013). Regardless of the uncertainty surrounding specific projections, a significant increase in total health care spending would hardly be surprising given the law's emphasis on expanding health insurance.

IV. EVIDENCE AND ISSUES

This section first summarizes some evidence and implications of the effects of the Massachusetts reforms, which included Medicaid expansion, premium subsidies, and an individual and employer mandate. It then briefly considers two additional important issues: (1) potential premium rates, take-up, adverse selection, cost sharing, and provider networks in the exchanges; and (2) potential impacts on employers' decisions to offer coverage and on employment.

1. Evidence from Massachusetts

Evidence suggests that the Massachusetts reforms to expand Medicaid, subsidize coverage for lower income persons, mandate that individuals obtain coverage, and mandate that other than small employers offer coverage substantially increased rates of insurance coverage. Long, Yemane, and Stockley (2009) use a difference-in-difference (D-D) framework to provide evidence of significant reductions in the uninsurance rate in Massachusetts versus other states. Similarly, Long, Yemane, and Stockley (2010) provide evidence of a significant reduction in the number of uninsured young adults. The reform's impact on small group markets is less clear. Cogan, Hubbard, and Kessler (2010) present evidence that the Massachusetts reforms were associated with an increase in small group market premiums; Graves and Gruber (2012) challenge those findings, concluding in part that the changes estimated are not statistically reliable. Kolstad and Kowalski (2012b) estimate that because newly insured employees valued coverage, the deadweight costs of the Massachusetts

the types of actions the IPAB can recommend. It cannot, for example, propose reductions in benefits, increases in beneficiary premiums or co-payments, or cuts in reimbursements to hospitals and certain other providers that were otherwise subject to cuts under the law through 2018–19.

employer mandate were minimal and much lower than if the government had expanded health insurance with a tax on wages.

Evidence also suggests that, prior to its 2006 reforms, Massachusetts health insurance markets experienced substantial adverse selection from its community rating rules, which was partially alleviated by the individual mandate. Hackmann, Kolstad, and Kowalski (2012) show that Massachusetts counties with larger increases in insurance coverage from the reforms had the smallest increase in average hospital costs for the insured population post reform. This result suggests that on average people who became insured were relatively healthy, which in turn is consistent with adverse selection into insurance prior to the 2006 mandate. They note that mandated community rating in Massachusetts prior to 2006 (with a 2-1 age band) could have led to adverse selection and higher premiums pre-reform. Hackmann, Kolstad, and Kowalski (2013) provide evidence that individual market premiums and costs decreased significantly in response to the mandate, 'consistent with an initially adversely selected insurance market', and they estimate significant welfare gains from the mandate.

Did the Massachusetts reforms improve access to health care and health? As summarized by Courtemanche and Zapata (2012); Long and Stockley (2011) report evidence of a decrease in unmet medical needs among low income adults, albeit with some delays in individuals being able to locate providers. Kolstad and Kowalski (2012a) find some evidence of favorable effects on emergency room use, preventive care, and quality of hospital care. Miller (2012) finds evidence of reduced emergency room use for non-urgent care. Extending an analysis by Yelowitz and Cannon (2010), Courtemanche and Zapata (2012) analyze data from the Behavioral Risk Factor Surveillance System, and provide evidence that the Massachusetts reforms were associated with better self-assessed health and improved behavioral determinants of overall health, concluding that health insurance 'had a sizable impact' on health. As noted earlier, Sommers, Long, and Baicker (2014) provide evidence of significant reductions in all-cause mortality and in deaths from causes amenable to health care in Massachusetts following the enactment of its reforms.

How informative are the Massachusetts results for the ACA? Gruber (2008a; 2011a) reviews Massachusetts' experience and why it could be informative nationally. He describes how the Massachusetts law was associated with a large reduction in the number of uninsured, an increase in employer coverage offers, premium reductions in the individual market, and costs in line with projections at the time of enactment. Commenting on Gruber (2008a), Pauly (2008) expresses concern with the potentially large deadweight costs of taxes and redistribution if the Massachusetts model were applied nationally.

The Massachusetts experiment is distinctive from the ACA in a number of respects.[35] Over 90 percent of Massachusetts residents had health insurance before 2006, compared with 82.6 percent nationally when the ACA was passed. It is likely to be much more challenging and costly to achieve low uninsured rates in states with much larger uninsured populations. Moreover, the details of the Massachusetts insurance market reforms differ from the ACA, including tougher penalties for non-compliance with its mandate and its merger of the individual and small group markets for rating purposes.[36] Importantly, Massachusetts laws requiring guaranteed issue and adjusted community rating, which substantially predated the 2006 individual mandate and other reforms, very likely contributed to adverse selection. There is a qualitative distinction between mandating insurance *after* having mandated community rating, as opposed to simultaneously mandating both, with potentially significant implications for premiums and insurance take-up.

2. Premiums, Take-Up, Adverse Selection, Cost Sharing, and Narrow Networks

According to the HHS exchange enrollment report (ASPE 2014), over 8 million people had selected a plan in the individual market exchanges by the end of open enrollment on March 31, 2014, including 2.2 million people aged 18–34, with nearly half of those selecting plans during March. Close to 7 million people had been determined to be eligible for Medicaid/CHIP through the exchange portals.[37] Data were not available on how many of those selecting exchange plans had paid premiums. Eighty-five percent of those selecting plans were eligible for premium subsidies. At least half of those selecting plans likely had coverage prior to the opening of the exchanges. The HHS report notes as well that at least several million

[35] From a political perspective, because Massachusetts had an uncompensated care fund and special funding through a federal government Medicaid waiver, it did not have to raise taxes or cut other expenditures to finance coverage expansion, at least initially.

[36] The ACA allows states the option of merging the individual and small group markets, and several states are considering that option.

[37] The Medicaid/CHIP figure does not include people who obtained coverage directly from state agencies. Estimates were not available on how many of those deemed eligible for Medicaid/CHIP were due to the ACA Medicaid expansion provisions.

people had purchased ACA-compliant plans outside of the exchanges, and that several surveys and related analyses suggested a several point drop in the percentage of people aged 18–64 without health insurance from September 30, 2013 through March 31, 2014 (see ASPE 2014).

The ultimate magnitude of coverage expansion from the ACA will depend on the number and population of states that expand Medicaid, on the take up of subsidized coverage in the exchanges, on the purchase of unsubsidized coverage in and outside of the exchanges, and on employer and employee decisions regarding group coverage. The take up of subsidized coverage in the exchanges in turn will be determined by perceptions of the value of coverage and by required premiums net of subsidies. Given that ACA premium subsidies for subsidy-eligible exchange enrollees are designed to cap the percentage of income that must be paid towards premiums, for a given level of take-up, higher premiums will increase aggregate subsidies and costs to taxpayers.

Considerable speculation, analysis, and rhetoric have been devoted to the magnitude of premiums for exchange coverage and the potential that high premiums could result in reduced enrollment, adverse selection, and a potential death spiral. The issues are far more nuanced than much of the debate. What matters from the perspective of prospective enrollees is the premium net of available subsidies and, along with the effects of potential penalties for violating the mandate, premium subsidies will mitigate adverse selection.[38] While premiums net of subsidies are key for demand, the level and growth of premiums are nonetheless important because of the effects on potential purchasers who do not qualify for subsidies, the effects on the total cost of subsidies, and the important role that the cost of health insurance played in the ACA debate.

Average premiums will depend in significant part on the extent to which previously uninsured young and/or healthy people purchase coverage. Additionally, the ACA's impact on premiums will vary across states due to differences in demographics, prior restrictions on risk rating, and other market-specific factors. The ACA's minimum coverage requirements mandate more generous benefits than purchased by many persons previously insured in individual markets, which will tend to increase

---

[38] Studies of states with significant rating restrictions but without a coverage mandate or premium subsidies have produced mixed results. Some early work suggested relatively small effects on the overall number of persons with insurance, with increased coverage for higher risk persons offset by reductions in coverage for lower risk persons (e.g., Buchmueller and DiNardo 2002). Later work has provided more evidence of higher premiums, adverse selection, and market instability (e.g., Lo Sasso and Lurie 2009).

average insured medical costs and premiums.[39] As discussed earlier, increases in coverage generosity might have beneficial effects on access to medical care and health, but they could also lead to cost-increasing utilization of low-valued care. Costs and premiums also could increase if prices rise for certain medical services as a result of significant increases in demand for care due to coverage expansion, with a relatively fixed supply of providers.

The CBO's analysis of the US Senate bill that essentially became the ACA estimated that broader required coverage and an attendant increase in utilization of medical care would cause average premiums (before subsidies) to increase in individual markets by 10 to 13 percent by 2016 compared with projected premiums had the ACA not been enacted (CBO 2009). The CBO noted that the estimated increase would be 27 to 30 percent if not for its assumptions of significant savings in administrative costs from the new exchanges, guaranteed issue, and rating rules and of some shift in the insured population towards younger and healthier buyers.

The CBO speculated that adverse selection from the law's low penalties for violating the mandate was 'likely to be limited'. The ACA's modest 'taxes' for violating the mandate generated substantial pushback by health insurers, however, who had previously agreed to support most of the proposed insurance underwriting and rating restrictions provided they were coupled with a strong mandate. Two industry-sponsored studies predicted substantially higher medical costs and premium increases for individual coverage than what would be projected under prior law, in significant part due to increased utilization of services and adverse selection from the weak mandate combined with underwriting and rating restrictions (PricewaterhouseCoopers 2009; Oliver Wyman 2009).

More recently, the CBO (2014) estimated that average premiums for the lowest premium silver plan on exchanges in 2014 would be 15 percent lower than it had projected in 2009, based on updated estimates of the age, sex, health status, and geographic distribution of those who would be obtaining coverage through the exchanges, attributing the reduction in

---

39 Early evidence indicated that the impact of immediate changes in insurance coverage under the ACA (elimination of pre-existing condition exclusions for children, extension of coverage for dependents to age 26, 100 percent coverage of preventive care, and removal/limitation of lifetime/annual benefit limits) contributed modestly to health insurance premium increases, with larger effects for the individual market than for group coverage. For example, a late 2010 survey of health insurers suggested these changes could increase average premiums in 2011 by 1–2 percent for group plans and 3–5 percent for individual plans (Aon Hewitt 2011).

part to the use of narrow networks by insurers, and lower provider fees.[40] In contrast, Parente and Ramlet (2014) used a microsimulation model to predict large premium increases over five years and attendant lower enrollment in the exchanges.[41]

Several studies have compared exchange premiums for 2014 to insurers' premium quotes in 2013. The Manhattan Institute (2013), for example, used data available from the finder.healthcare.gov website to calculate for six age-gender cohorts average pre-ACA premiums for the five lowest premium plans in the most populous zip code in each county and state. Using information on coverage denials and premium surcharges for poor health from that website, a weighted average rate was calculated for each cohort assuming a 75 percent premium increase for those surcharged and that those denied found coverage at three times the original rate. The statewide average of the adjusted rates for each cohort was then compared to the average exchange premium across counties for the five cheapest plans in each state. Based on this comparison, the average rates for the exchanges were 41 percent higher than the pre-ACA adjusted rates, with substantial variation across states (Roy 2013).

Measurement issues and political salience aside, premium changes from the law will represent only part of the story. To the extent that the ACA mandates more complete coverage of expenses than previously obtained by many people, premiums will increase but expected out-of-pocket expenses will decline. Pauly, Harrington, and Leive (2014) provide estimates of the changes in premiums, average out-of-pocket payments, and the sum of premiums and out-of-pocket payments (denoted 'total expected price') for a sample of consumers from the CPS who bought individual, self-only coverage in 2010–12. They compare total expected prices in California and in 23 states with federally managed exchanges and with minimal prior state premium regulation before the ACA with estimates of total expected prices if those persons were to purchase silver or bronze coverage after reform, before the effects of any premium subsidies. They find that the average prices increased by 14 to 28 percent, with similar changes in California and the federal exchange states, which they attribute primarily to higher premiums in exchanges associated with insurer expectations of a higher risk population being enrolled.

Apart from premium rates and potential 'sticker shock', some previously

---

[40] HHS indicated that average exchange premiums for 36 states were lower than it had projected earlier using the CBO's projection methodology (ASPE 2013).

[41] Other simulation studies to forecast spending and premiums include Gabel et al. (2012), Parente and Feldman (2013), and Nowak et al. (2013).

uninsured persons might experience 'coverage shock' when they discover the amount of cost sharing required by their coverage (at least persons with incomes above 250 percent of poverty who do not qualify for cost sharing subsidies). While helping to make premiums more affordable, significant cost sharing has generated concerns that some newly insured persons will forgo valuable care. In addition, many plans offered on the exchanges have relatively narrow provider networks, which, while tending to lower premiums, provide less choice of providers than many plans available pre-ACA (or outside of the exchanges post-ACA). This could reduce the attractiveness of coverage for a given premium net of any subsidy and produce some degree of 'network shock' and complaints of a two-tiered system. Concern also has been expressed about the availability of medical services if millions of newly insured people seek additional care. At this point, it is anyone's guess as to how such concerns will play out.

3. Effects on Employer-Sponsored Coverage and Labor Markets

The literature on expansion of public health insurance programs documents significant crowd-out of private insurance by public coverage (Cutler and Gruber 1996). Considerable uncertainty exists concerning the ACA's potential effects on employers' decisions to offer health insurance and whether those that do will self-insure or purchase commercial coverage.[42] Uncertainty also exists with respect to the law's effects on employment. In particular, some employers may attempt to circumvent the employer mandate by avoiding expansion to 50 or more workers and substituting more part-time employment.

Theoretical and empirical work on employer-sponsored health insurance stresses that on average employees bear the cost of non-cash compensation, including employers' contributions to health insurance (see Gruber 2000 for a review). Employee benefits in general and employer-sponsored health insurance in particular are provided when their value to employees exceeds the reduction in cash compensation needed to fund them. Employees will prefer to obtain health insurance through work if the cost and package of services are superior to what could be obtained by receiving higher cash compensation, which could be used to purchase individual coverage.

[42] Regarding the latter issue, several studies suggest concern that some small employers with relatively healthy employees could decide to self-insure to avoid paying higher premiums that do not reflect health status, retaining the option to purchase coverage if the health status for their employees deteriorates (see, e.g., Hall, 2012; Monahan and Schwarcz 2013).

As a result, the extent to which the ACA could allow many employees (or self-employed persons) to get coverage through the individual market with comparable benefits to employer-sponsored coverage at a lower net cost than through employment is important. This will depend broadly on: (1) the magnitude of premium subsidies available in the exchanges; (2) the magnitude of the forfeiture of the tax exclusion from employer-sponsored coverage; (3) the size of employer penalties for not offering coverage; (4) differences in loadings for administrative costs and profits for exchange versus employer coverage; (5) possible differences in network size and choice of physicians for exchange versus employer plans; and (6) possibly reduced job lock given guaranteed issue and adjusted community rating for all individual and small group plans.

In general, the balance will be most likely to shift towards exchange coverage for lower wage workers who qualify for significant exchange subsidies and receive relatively low value from the tax exclusion for employer-sponsored coverage. As discussed earlier, the CBO projects that the ACA will reduce employer-sponsored coverage by 7 million people relative to coverage projections in the absence of the ACA (from 169 million to 162 million; see Figure 7.6). As summarized by Buchmueller, Carey, and Levy (2013), alternative microsimulation model projections by RAND, the Urban Institute, the Lewin Group, and CMS also suggest relatively modest changes in employer-sponsored coverage, and employer surveys generally indicate that most employers would continue to offer coverage in 2014 and at least through the first few years following enactment.[43]

Apart from any crowd-out of unsubsidized private coverage overall or of employer-sponsored coverage specifically, an inherent drawback of public insurance and subsidized private non-group coverage is the potential negative effect on labor supply, with attendant deadweight welfare losses. The eligibility for public coverage or premium subsidies is conditional on having low income. The ACA's Medicaid and premium subsidies decline significantly with increases in income and can produce a significant jump in health insurance costs for persons who move from just below to just above the 400 percent of FPL threshold for eliminating subsidies, resulting in significant implicit taxes on additional earnings.

---

[43] Holtz-Eakin and Smith (2010) projected large reductions in employer-sponsored coverage based on an analysis of subsidy levels, penalties, and wage increases that employers could provide by dropping health plans (also see Austin et al. 2013). Buchmueller, Carey, and Levy (2013) note that the Holtz-Eakin and Smith analysis assumed that employers could selectively drop coverage for low income workers and did not consider possible increased demand for employer coverage as a result of the individual mandate.

The potential effects of the ACA on labor markets, however, are complex and highly uncertain. A February 2014 CBO report (CBO 2014) describes in detail the factors that could influence the supply and demand for labor and thus effects on employment and hours worked, including expansion of Medicaid eligibility, income-based premium subsidies for insurance purchased through the exchanges, penalties for employers that do not offer coverage, and the ACA's new taxes imposed on labor income for higher-income workers. The CBO's 2014 projections of the ACA's impact on the number of hours implied a reduction in the number of full-time equivalent workers of about 2.5 million by 2024, reflecting fewer workers employed and more people working fewer hours. Other research suggests the possibility of significantly greater effects, especially in the form of increased part-time employment to keep weekly hours below the ACA's 30 hour threshold, which will allow those workers to seek subsidized coverage on the exchanges and avoid employer penalties (e.g., Mulligan 2014).[44]

V. CONCLUSION

While the ACA has begun to increase significantly the number of US residents with health insurance, substantial economic and political uncertainties clearly remain concerning the ultimate magnitude, cost, and stability of the ACA's coverage expansion. Major economic uncertainties exist with respect to: (1) the magnitude of take-up of health coverage by the previously uninsured; (2) the scope of adverse selection and the effects on premium rates, take-up, and the cost of premium subsidies; (3) whether additional states will expand Medicaid and, if so, the details of expansion; and (4) whether the law's statutory reductions in Medicare spending will be sustainable without significant disruptions to hospitals and/or Medicare Advantage carriers. The law's ultimate success or failure will hinge on how these and other influences evolve over time.

Regarding political uncertainty, partisan gridlock will make near-term legislative action to 'fix' any problems with the law that become apparent during implementation highly unlikely. Significant changes to the law,

---

44 Garthwaite, Gross, and Notowidigdo (2013) provide evidence of a large increase in labor supply in Tennessee following the state's disenrollment of 170,000 residents from public health insurance in 2005. The authors conclude: 'The results suggest that the Affordable Care Act – which similarly affects adults not traditionally eligible for public health insurance – may cause large reductions in the labor supply of low income adults.'

or perhaps even a successful 'repeal and replace' effort by opponents, will depend on unpredictable federal election results in 2014 and 2016, if not later. If Republicans were to capture the Presidency and hold governing majorities in both the House and Senate in 2017, significant changes would be more likely. Even then, however, proponents of major modifications or of repeal and replacement of the ACA, for example with universal, refundable tax credits for the purchase of health insurance, would likely face substantial hurdles to reducing the ACA's income-based premium subsidies and Medicaid expansion. A more likely outcome under that scenario could be the enactment of lesser, market-oriented reforms to reduce regulatory burdens and increase consumer choice within the broad framework established by the ACA.

REFERENCES

Al-Ississ, Mohamad, and Nolan H. Miller. 2013. 'What Does Health Reform Mean for the Health Care Industry? Evidence from the Massachusetts Special Senate Election', 5 *American Economic Journal: Economic Policy* 1–29.

American Hospital Association (AHA). 2013. 'Uncompensated Hospital Care Cost Fact Sheet', January.

American Medical Association (AMA). 2007. 'Competition in Health Insurance – A Comprehensive Study of US Markets, 2007 Update', The American Medical Association.

America's Health Insurance Plans (AHIP). 2009. 'Individual Health Insurance 2009 – A Comprehensive Survey of Premiums, Availability, and Benefits', Washington, DC: AHIP Center for Policy Research, October 1.

Anderson, Michael, Carlos Dobkin, and Tal Gross. 2012. 'The Effect of Health Insurance Coverage on the Use of Medical Services', 4 *American Economic Journal: Economic Policy, American Economic Association* 1–27.

Aon Hewitt. 2011. '2011 Health Insurance Trend Driver Survey', Aon Corporation.

Aron-Dine, Aviva, Liran Einav, and Amy Finkelstein. 2013. 'The Rand Health Insurance Experiment, Three Decades Later', 27 *Journal of Economic Perspectives* 197–222.

ASPE Office of Health Policy. 2013. 'Health Insurance Marketplace Premiums for 2014', *ASPE Issue Brief*, September 25. Available at http://aspe.hhs.gov/health/reports/2013/MarketplacePremiums/ib_marketplace_premiums.cfm (accessed November 27, 2013).

ASPE Office of Health Policy. 2014. 'Health Insurance Marketplace: Summary Enrollment Report for the Initial Annual Open Enrollment Period', *ASPE Issue Brief*, May 1. Available at http://aspe.hhs.gov/health/reports/2014/MarketPlaceEnrollment/Apr2014/ib_2014Apr_enrollment.pdf (accessed June 15, 2014).

Austin, D. Andrew, and Thomas L. Hungerford. 2009. 'The Market Structure of the Health Insurance Industry', Congressional Research Service Report for Congress, November 17. Available at www.fas.org/sgp/crs/misc/R40834.pdf (accessed November 20, 2013).

Austin, Daniel R., Anna Luan, Louise L. Wang, and Jay Bhattacharya. 2013. 'Small Increases to Employer Premiums Could Shift Millions of People to the Exchanges and Add Billions to Federal Outlays', 32 *Health Affairs* 1531–7.

Baicker, Katherine, and Helen Levy. 2008. 'Employer Health Insurance Mandates and the Risk of Unemployment', 11 *Risk Management and Insurance Review* 109–32.

Baicker, Katherine et al. 2013. 'The Oregon Experiment – Effects of Medicaid on Clinical Outcomes', 368 *New England Journal of Medicine* 1713–22.

Bernard, Didem M., Jessica S. Banthin, and William E. Encinosa. 2009. 'Wealth, Income, and the Affordability of Health Insurance', 28 *Health Affairs* 887–96.
Bhattacharya, Jay, M. Kate Bundorf, Noemi Pace, and Neeraj Sood. 2011. 'Does Health Insurance Make You Fat?' In Michael Grossman and Naci Mocan, eds., *Economic Aspects of Obesity*. Chicago, IL: University of Chicago Press, 35–64.
Boards of Trustees, Federal Hospital Insurance and Federal Supplementary Medical Insurance Trust Funds. 2009. 2009 Annual Report. Washington, DC, May 12.
Boards of Trustees, Federal Hospital Insurance and Federal Supplementary Medical Insurance Trust Funds. 2011. 2011 Annual Report. Washington DC, May 13.
Boards of Trustees, Federal Hospital Insurance and Federal Supplementary Medical Insurance Trust Funds. 2013. 2013 Annual Report. Washington, DC, May 31.
Buchmueller, Thomas, and John DiNardo. 2002. 'Did Community Rating Induce an Adverse Selection Death Spiral? Evidence from New York, Pennsylvania, and Connecticut', 92 *American Economic Review* 280–94.
Buchmueller, Thomas, Colleen Carey, and Helen G. Levy. 2013. 'Will Employers Drop Health Insurance Coverage because of the Affordable Care Act?', 32 *Health Affairs* 1522–30.
Bundorf, M. Kate, and Mark V. Pauly. 2006. 'Is Health Insurance Affordable for the Uninsured?', 25 *Journal of Health Economics* 650–763.
Burkhauser, Richard V., and Kosali I. Simon. 2008. 'Who Gets What from Employer Pay or Play Mandates?', 11 *Risk Management and Insurance Review* 75–102.
Cebul, Randall D., James B. Rebitzer, Lowell J. Taylor, and Mark E. Votruba. 2011. 'Unhealthy Insurance Markets: Search Frictions and the Cost and Quality of Health Insurance', 101 *American Economic Review* 1842–71.
Center for Consumer Information and Insurance Oversight (CCIIO). 2013. 'State by State Enrollment in the Pre-Existing Condition Insurance Plan.' Available at www.cms.gov/CCIIO/Resources/Fact-Sheets-and-FAQs/pcip-enrollment.htm (accessed November 22, 2013).
Centers for Medicare & Medicaid Services (CMS). 2010. 'Estimated Financial Effects of the Patient Protection and Affordable Care Act', memorandum from Richard Foster, Chief Actuary, April 22.
Centers for Medicare and Medicaid Services (CMS). 2011. 'Projected Medicare Expenditures under an Illustrative Alternative Scenario with Alternative Payment Updates to Medicare Providers', memorandum from John Shatto and M. Clemens, May 13.
Centers for Medicare & Medicaid Services (CMS). 2013. 'Projected Medicare Expenditures under an Illustrative Alternative Scenario with Alternative Payment Updates to Medicare Providers', memorandum from John Shatto and M. Clemens, May 31.
Chandra, Amitabh, Jonathan Holmes, and Jonathan Skinner. 2013. 'Is this Time Different? The Slowdown in Healthcare Spending', presented at the Fall 2013 Brookings Panel on Economic Activity, Washington, DC, September 19–20.
Cochrane, John. H. 1995. 'Time-Consistent Health Insurance', 103 *Journal of Political Economy* 446–73
Cogan, John F., R. Glenn Hubbard, and Daniel Kessler. 2010. 'The Effect of Massachusetts' Health Reform on Employer-Sponsored Insurance Premiums', 13 *Forum for Health Economics and Policy* 1–8 [Article 5].
Cole, Harold L., Soojin Kim, and Dirk Krueger. 2012. 'Analyzing the Effects of Insuring Health Risks: On the Trade-off between Short Run Insurance Benefits vs. Long Run Incentive Costs', NBER Working Paper No. 18572. Cambridge, MA: National Bureau of Economic Research.
Congressional Budget Office (CBO). 2007. 'CBO's Health Insurance Simulation Model: A Technical Description', October 31. Available at www.cbo.gov/publication/19224 (accessed November 22, 2013).
Congressional Budget Office (CBO). 2008. 'Key Issues in Analyzing Major Health Insurance Proposals', December 18. Available at www.cbo.gov/publication/41746 (accessed November 22, 2013).

Congressional Budget Office (CBO). 2009. 'An Analysis of Health Insurance Premiums under the Patient Protection and Affordable Care Act', November 30. Available at www.cbo.gov/publication/25004 (accessed November 22, 2013).
Congressional Budget Office (CBO). 2011. Letter from Douglas Elmendorf, Director, to Speaker of the House, John Boehner, on revenue effects of H.R. 2, Repealing the Job-Killing Health Care Law Act, February 18.
Congressional Budget Office (CBO). 2012. Letter from Douglas Elmendorf, Director, to Speaker of the House, John Boehner, on spending and revenue effects of H.R. 6079, the Repeal of Obamacare Act, July 24.
Congressional Budget Office (CBO). 2013a. 'CBO's May 2013 Estimate of the Effects of the Affordable Care Act on Health Insurance Coverage', May. Available at www.cbo.gov/publication/43900 (accessed November 22, 2013).
Congressional Budget Office (CBO). 2013b. 'The 2013 Long-Term Budget Outlook', September 17. Available at www.cbo.gov/publication/44521 (accessed November 22, 2013).
Congressional Budget Office (CBO). 2014. 'The Budget and Economic Outlook: 2014 to 2024' February.
Congressional Research Service. 1988. 'Costs and Effects of Extending Health Insurance Coverage', Library of Congress, Washington, D.C., October
Conover, Christopher J., and Thomas P. Miller. 2010. 'Why a Public Plan is Unnecessary to Stimulate Competition', AEI Working Paper No. 162. Washington, DC: American Enterprise Institute for Public Policy Research.
Courtemanche, Charles J., and Daniela Zapata. 2012. 'Does Universal Coverage Improve Health? The Massachusetts Experience', NBER Working Paper 17893. Cambridge, MA: National Bureau of Economic Research.
Crocker, Keith and Arthur Snow. 1986. 'The Efficiency Effect of Categorical Discrimination in the Insurance Industry', 94 *Journal of Political Economy* 321–44.
Cuckler, Gigi A., Andrea M. Sisko, Sean P. Keehan, Sheila D. Smith, Andrew J. Madison, John A. Poisal, Christian J. Wolfe, Joseph M. Lizonitz, and Devin A. Stone. 2013. 'National Health Expenditure Projections, 2012–22: Slow Growth until Coverage Expands and Economy Improves', 32 *Health Affairs* 1–12.
Cutler, David M. 1994. 'A Guide to Health Care Reform', 8 *Journal of Economic Perspectives* 13–29.
Cutler, David M., and Jonathan Gruber. 1996. 'Does Public Insurance Crowd Out Private Insurance?', 111 *Quarterly Journal of Economics* 391–430.
Cutler, David M., and Nikhil R. Sahni. 2013. 'If Slow Rate Of Health Care Spending Growth Persists, Projections May Be Off by $770 Billion', 32 *Health Affairs* 841–50.
Cutler, David M., and Richard J. Zeckhauser. 2000. 'The Anatomy of Health Insurance.' In Anthony J. Culyer and Joseph P. Newhouse, eds., *Handbook of Health Economics*, Volume 1A. Amsterdam: Elsevier Science, 563–643.
Dafny, Leemore S. 2010. 'Are Health Insurance Markets Competitive?', 100 *American Economic Review* 1399–431.
Dafny, Leemore, Mark Duggan, and Subramaniam Ramanarayanan. 2012. 'Paying a Premium on Your Premium? Consolidation in the US Health Insurance Industry', 102 *American Economic Review* 1161–85.
Donahue, Debra A. 2010. 'Health Plans See Revenue Shift Away from Commercial', *Healthcare Business Strategy*, Mark Farrah Associates, May 10. Available at www.markfarrah.com/healthcare-business-strategy/Health-Plans-See-Revenue-Shift-Away-from-Commercial.aspx (accessed November 22, 2013).
Fang, Hangming, Michael P. Keane, and Daniel Silverman. 2008. 'Sources of Advantageous Selection: Evidence from the Medigap Insurance Market', 116 *Journal of Political Economy* 303–50.
Feldstein, Martin S. 1973. 'The Welfare Loss of Excess Health Insurance', 81 *Journal of Political Economy* 251–80.
Finkelstein, Amy, and Kathleen McGarry. 2006. 'Multiple Dimensions of Private

Information: Evidence from the Long-Term Care Insurance Market', 96 *American Economic Review* 938–58.

Finkelstein, Amy, Sarah Taubman, Bill Wright, Mira Bernstein, Jonathan Gruber, Joseph P. Newhouse, Heidi Allen, Katherine Baicker, and The Oregon Health Study Group. 2012. 'The Oregon Health Insurance Experiment: Evidence from the First Year', 127 *Quarterly Journal of Economics* 1057–106.

Furman, Jason. 2008. 'Health Reform through Tax Reform: A Primer', 27 *Health Affairs* 622–32.

Gabel, J. R., R. Lore, R. D. McDevitt, J. D. Pickreign, H. Whitmore, M. Slover, and E. Levy-Forsythe. 2012. 'More Than Half of Individual Health Plans Offer Coverage that Falls Short of What Can Be Sold Through Exchanges as of 2014', 31 *Health Affairs* 1339–48.

Garthwaite, Craig, Tal Gross, and Matthew J. Notowidigdo. 2013. 'Public Health Insurance, Labor Supply, and Employment Lock', NBER Working Paper 19220. Cambridge, MA: National Bureau of Economic Research.

Gaynor, Martin, and Robert J. Town. 2011. 'Competition in Health Care Markets', NBER Working Paper 17208. Cambridge, MA: National Bureau of Economic Research.

Government Accountability Office, US (GAO). 2009. 'Private Health Insurance: 2008 Survey Results on Number and Market Share of Carriers in the Small Group Health Insurance Market', GAO-09-363R, February 27. Available at http://gao.gov/assets/100/95991.pdf (accessed November 26, 2013).

Graves, John A., and Jonathan Gruber. 2012. 'How Did Health Care Reform in Massachusetts Impact Insurance Premiums?', 102 *American Economic Review: Papers and Proceedings* 508–13.

Gruber, Jonathan. 1994. 'The Incidence of Mandated Maternity Benefits', 84 *American Economic Review* 622–41.

Gruber, Jonathan. 2000. 'Health Insurance and the Labor Market.' In Anthony J. Culyer and Joseph P. Newhouse, eds., *Handbook of Health Economics*, Volume 1A. Amsterdam: Elsevier Science, 645–706.

Gruber, Jonathan. 2003. 'Evaluating Alternative Approaches to Incremental Health-Insurance Expansion', 93 *American Economic Review: Papers and Proceedings* 271–6.

Gruber, Jonathan. 2005. 'Tax Policy for Health Insurance.' In James M. Poterba, ed., *Tax Policy and the Economy*, Volume 19. Cambridge and London: MIT Press, 39–63.

Gruber, Jonathan. 2008a. 'Massachusetts Health Care Reform: The View from One Year Out', 11 *Risk Management and Insurance Review* 51–63.

Gruber, Jonathan. 2008b. 'Covering the Uninsured in the United States', 46 *Journal of Economic Literature* 571–606.

Gruber, Jonathan. 2011a. 'The Impacts of the Affordable Care Act: How Reasonable Are the Projections?', 64 *National Tax Journal* 893–908.

Gruber, Jonathan. 2011b. 'The Tax Exclusion for Employer-Sponsored Health Insurance', 64 *National Tax Journal* 511–30.

Gruber, Jonathan, and Brigitte C. Madrian. 2004. 'Health Insurance, Labor Supply, and Job Mobility: A Critical Review of the Literature.' In Catherine G. McLaughlin, ed., *Health Policy and the Uninsured*. Washington, DC: Urban Institute Press, 97–178.

Gruber, Jonathan, and David Rodriguez. 2007. 'How Much Uncompensated Care Do Doctors Provide?', 26 *Journal of Health Economics* 1151–69.

Hackmann, Martin B., Jonathan T. Kolstad, and Amanda E. Kowalski. 2012. 'Health Reform, Health Insurance, and Selection: Estimating Selection into Health Insurance Using the Massachusetts Health Reform', 102 *American Economic Review: Papers and Proceedings* 498–501.

Hackmann, Martin B., Jonathan T. Kolstad, and Amanda E. Kowalski. 2013. 'Adverse Selection and an Individual Mandate: When Theory Meets Practice', NBER Working Paper No. 19149. Cambridge, MA: National Bureau of Economic Research.

Hadley, Jack, John Holahan, Theresa Coughlin, and Dawn Miller. 2008. 'Covering the Uninsured in 2008: Current Costs, Sources of Payment, and Incremental Costs', 27

Health Affairs w399-w425 [published online before print: August 2008]. doi: 10.1377/hlthaff.27.5.w399.

Hall, Mark A. 2012. 'Regulating Stop-Loss Coverage May Be Needed to Deter Self-Insuring Small Employers from Undermining Market Reforms', 31 *Health Affairs* 316–23.

Harrington, Scott E. 2010a. 'The Health Insurance Reform Debate', 77 *Journal of Risk and Insurance* 5–38 [earlier version distributed as American Enterprise Institute Working Paper No. 161, December 2009].

Harrington, Scott E. 2010b. 'Regime Change for Health Insurance Regulation: Rethinking Rate Review, Medical Loss Ratios, and Informed Competition', December 8 issue of *Beyond Repeal and Replace: Ideas for Real Health Reform*, Washington, DC: American Enterprise Institute.

Harrington, Scott E. 2011. 'The Continuing Debate on Health Insurance Reform', Networks Financial Institute Policy Brief, 2011-PB-09.

Harrington, Scott E. 2013. 'Medical Loss Ratio Regulation under the Affordable Care Act', 50 *Inquiry* 9–26.

Hendren, Nathaniel. 2013. 'Private Information and Insurance Rejections', 81 *Econometrica* 1713–62.

Herring, Bradley, and Mark Pauly. 2006. 'Incentive-Compatible Guaranteed Renewable Health Insurance Premiums', 25 *Journal of Health Economics* 395–417.

Herring, Bradley, and Mark Pauly. 2010. '"Play-or-Pay" Insurance Reforms for Employers – Confusion and Inequity', 362 *New England Journal of Medicine* 93–5.

Holahan, John, Matthew Buettgens, Caitlin Carroll, and Stan Dorn. 2013. 'The Cost and Coverage Implications of the ACA Medicaid Expansion: National and State-by-State Analysis', The Urban Institute, September 23. Available at www.urban.org/UploadedPDF/412707-The-Cost-and-Coverage-Implications-of-the-ACA-Medicaid-Expansion.pdf (accessed November 27, 2013).

Holtz-Eakin, Douglas. 2011. 'Does Massachusetts Health Reform Point the Way to Success with National Reform?', 30 *Journal of Policy Analysis and Management* 178–91.

Holtz-Eakin, Douglas, and Michael J. Ramlet. 2010. 'Health Care Reform is Likely to Widen Federal Budget Deficits, Not Reduce Them', 29 *Health Affairs* 1136–41.

Holtz-Eakin, Douglas, and Cameron Smith. 2010. 'Labor Markets and Health Care Reform: New Results', American Action Forum, May 27. Available at http://americanactionforum.org/sites/default/files/OHC_LabMktsHCR.pdf (accessed November 27, 2013).

Horwitz, Jill R., Brenda D. Kelly, and John E. DiNardo. 2013. 'Wellness Incentives in The Workplace: Cost Savings through Cost Shifting to Unhealthy Workers', 32 *Health Affairs* 468–76.

Kaiser Family Foundation and Health Research and Educational Trust (HRET). 2009. 'Employer Health Benefits 2009 Annual Survey.' Available at http://kaiserfamilyfoundation.files.wordpress.com/2013/04/7936.pdf (accessed November 27, 2013).

Kaiser Family Foundation and Health Research and Educational Trust (HRET). 2011. 'Summary of New Health Reform Law', [updated April 23, 2013]. Available at http://kaiserfamilyfoundation.files.wordpress.com/2011/04/8061-021.pdf (accessed November 27, 2013).

Kaiser Family Foundation and Health Research and Educational Trust (HRET). 2013a. 'Employer Health Benefits 2013 Annual Survey', August 20. Available at http://kff.org/private-insurance/report/2013-employer-health-benefits/ (accessed November 27, 2013).

Kaiser Family Foundation and Health Research and Educational Trust (HRET). 2013b. 'State Decisions For Creating Health Insurance Marketplaces.' Available at http://kff.org/health-reform/state-indicator/health-insurance-exchanges/ (accessed November 22, 2013).

Kaiser Family Foundation and Health Research and Educational Trust (HRET). 2014. 'Current Status of Medicaid Expansion Decisions.' March 26, 2014. Available at http://kff.org/health-reform/current-status-of-the-medicaid-expansion-decision/ (accessed June 9, 2014).

Klick, J. and T. Stratmann. 2007. 'Diabetes Treatments and Moral Hazard', 50 *Journal of Law and Economics* 519–38.

Koch, Thomas G. 2013. 'Bankruptcy, Medical Insurance, and a Law with Unintended Consequences. Health Economics', *Health Economics* [Article first published online: September 4]. DOI: 10.1002/hec.2985 (accessed November 26, 2013).
Kolstad, Jonathan T., and Amanda E. Kowalski. 2012a. 'The Impact of Health Care Reform on Hospital and Preventive Care: Evidence from Massachusetts', 96 *Journal of Public Economics* 909–29.
Kolstad, Jonathan T., and Amanda E. Kowalski A. 2012b. 'Mandate-Based Health Reform and the Labor Market: Evidence from the Massachusetts Reform', NBER Working Paper 17933. Cambridge, MA: National Bureau of Economic Research.
Lee, Dwight, and Ronald Warren. 1999. 'Mandated Health Insurance and the Low-Wage Labor Market', 20 *Journal of Labor Research* 505–15.
Levine, Michael, and Melinda Buntin. 2013. 'Why Has Growth in Spending for Fee-for-Service Medicare Slowed?', CBO Working Paper 2013-06. Washington, DC: Congressional Budget Office.
Levy, Helen, and David Meltzer. 2008. 'The Impact of Health Insurance on Health', 29 *Annual Review of Public Health* 399–409.
Lo Sasso, Anthony T., and Ithai Z. Lurie. 2009. 'Community Rating and the Market for Private Non-Group Health Insurance', 93 *Journal of Public Economics* 264–79.
Long, Sharon K., and Karen Stockley. 2011. 'The Impacts of State Health Reform Initiatives on Adults in New York and Massachusetts', 46 *Health Services Research* 365–428.
Long, Sharon K., Alshadye Yemane, and Karen Stockley. 2009. 'Another Look at the Impacts of Health Reform in Massachusetts: Evidence Using New Data and a Stronger Model', 99 *American Economic Review Papers and Proceedings* 508–11.
Long, Sharon K., Alshadye Yemane, and Karen Stockley. 2010. 'Disentangling the Effects of Health Reform in Massachusetts: How Important are the Special Provisions for Young Adults?', 100 *American Economic Review: Papers and Proceedings* 297–302.
Mahoney, Neale. 2012. 'Bankruptcy as Implicit Health Insurance', NBER Working Paper 18105. Cambridge, MA: National Bureau of Economic Research.
Manhattan Institute. 2013. 'Obamacare: Know Your Rates – Rate Changes, Subsidy Beneficiaries, and More'. Available at www.manhattan-institute.org/knowyourrates (accessed December 19, 2013).
McCue, Michael, Mark A. Hall, and Xinliang Liu. 2013. 'Impact of Medical Loss Regulation on the Financial Performance of Health Insurers', 23 *Health Affairs* 1546–51.
Miller, Sarah. 2012. 'The Effect of Insurance on Outpatient Emergency Room Visits: An Analysis of the 2006 Massachusetts Health Reform', 96 *Journal of Public Economics* 893–908.
Monahan, Amy. 2011. 'On Subsidies and Mandates: A Regulatory Critique of ACA', 36 *Journal of Corporation Law* 781.
Monahan, Amy and Daniel Schwarcz. 2013. 'Limiting the ACA's Threats to Small Group Health Insurance Markets', 16 *Risk Management and Insurance Review*.
Moriya, Asako S., William B. Vogt, and Martin Gaynor. 2010. 'Hospital Prices and Market Structure in the Hospital and Insurance Industries', 5 *Health Economics, Policy, and Law* 459–79.
Mulligan, Casey B. 2014. 'The Economics of Work Schedules under the New Hours and Employment Taxes', NBER Working Paper No. 19936, February.
National Institutes for Health Care Management (NIHCM). 2008. 'Understanding the Uninsured: Tailoring Policy Solutions for Different Subpopulations', NIHCM Policy Issue Brief, April. Available at www.nihcm.org/pdf/NIHCM-Uninsured-Final.pdf (accessed November 27, 2013).
Nowak, S. A., C. Eibner, D. M. Adamson, and E. Saltzman. 2013. 'Effects of the Affordable Care Act on Consumer Health Care Spending and Risk of Catastrophic Health Costs', Rand Corporation, Research Report RR-383-CMF.
Oliver Wyman. 2009. 'Insurance Reforms Must Include a Strong Individual Mandate and Other Key Provisions to Ensure Affordability', October 14. Available at www.oliver wyman.com/media/Importance_of_Strong_Individual_Mandates_-_Public_Memo.pdf (accessed November 26, 2013).

Parente, Stephen T., and Roger Feldman. 2013. 'Microsimulation of Private Health Insurance Take-Up Following the US Supreme Court Decision Upholding the Affordable Care Act', 48 *Health Services Research* 826–49.
Parente, Stephen T., and Michael Ramlet. 2014. 'National and State Impact Analyses of the ACA on Insurance Prices and Enrollment Beyond 2014', Medical Industry Leadership Institute Working Paper, May 20.
Pauly, Mark V. 1971. *Medical Care at Public Expense*. New York, NY: Praeger Publishers.
Pauly, Mark V. 1986. 'Taxation, Health Insurance, and Market Failure in the Medical Economy', 24 *Journal of Economic Literature* 629–75.
Pauly, Mark V. 2000. 'Optimal Health Insurance', 25 *The Geneva Papers on Risk and Insurance* 116–27.
Pauly, Mark V. 2004. 'Conflict and Compromise in Universal Health Insurance Plans', 32(3) *The Journal of Law, Medicine and Ethics* 465–73.
Pauly, Mark V. 2008. 'Massachusetts Evades Employer Mandates: Lessons for other States?', 11 *Risk Management and Insurance Review* 65–73.
Pauly, Mark V., and Bradley Herring. 2007. 'Risk Pooling and Regulation: Policy and Reality in Today's Individual Health Insurance Market', 26 *Health Affairs* 770–9.
Pauly, Mark V., and Robert Lieberthal. 2008. 'How Risky is Individual Health Insurance?', 27 *Health Affairs* 242–9.
Pauly, Mark V., Scott Harrington, and Adam Leive. 2014. '"Sticker Shock" in Individual Insurance under Health Reform', NBER Working Paper w20223, June.
Pauly, Mark V., Howard Kunreuther, and Richard A. Hirth. 1995. 'Guaranteed Renewability in Insurance', 10 *Journal of Risk and Uncertainty* 143–56.
Pauly, Mark V., Kai Menzel, Howard Kunreuther, and Richard A. Hirth. 2011. 'Guaranteed Renewability Uniquely Prevents Adverse Selection in Individual Health Insurance', 43 *Journal of Risk and Uncertainty* 127–39.
PricewaterhouseCoopers Staff. 2009. 'Potential Impact of Health Reform on the Cost of Private Health Insurance Coverage', PricewaterhouseCoopers LLP, October 1.
Robinson, James C. 2004. 'Consolidation and the Transformation of Competition in Health Insurance', 23 *Health Affairs* 11–24.
Roy, A. 2013. '49-State Analysis: Obamacare to Increase Individual-Market Premiums by Average of 41%.', *The Apothecary* [Forbes Blog], November 4.
Ryu, Alexander J., Theresa B. Gibson, M. Richard McKellar, and Michael E. Chernew. 2013. 'The Slowdown in Healthcare Spending in 2009–11', 32 *Health Affairs* 835–40.
Scanlon, Daniel P., Michael E. Chernew, S. Swaminathan, and William Lee. 2006. 'Competition in Health Insurance: Limitations of Current Measures for Policy Analysis', 63 *Medical Care Research and Review* 37S–55S.
Scheuer, Florian and Kent Smetters. 2014. 'Could a Website Really Have Doomed the Health Exchanges? Multiple Equilibria, Initial Conditions and the Construction of the Fine', NBER Working Paper No. 19835, February.
Sherlock, Douglas B. 2009. 'Administrative Expenses of Health Plans', Sherlock Company, Prepared for Blue Cross and Blue Shield Association.
Sinn, Hans-Werner. 1982. 'Kinked Utility and the Demand for Human Wealth and Liability Insurance', 17 *European Economic Review* 149–62.
Sommers, Benjamin D., Sharon K. Long, and Katherine Baicker. 2014. 'Changes in Mortality After Massachusetts Health Care Reform: A Quasi-experimental Study', 160 *Annals of Internal Medicine* 585–93.
Summers, Lawrence H. 1989. 'Some Simple Economics of Mandated Benefits', 79 *American Economic Review: Papers and Proceedings* 177–83.
US Department of Health and Human Services (US HHS). 2012a. 'The 80/20 Rule: Providing Value and Rebates to Millions of Consumers', June 21. Available at www.cms.gov/CCIIO/Resources/Forms-Reports-and-Other-Resources/mlr-rebates06212012a.html (accessed November 22, 2013).
US Department of Health and Human Services (US HHS). 2012b. 'Patient Protection

and Affordable Care Act; Standards Related to Reinsurance, Risk Corridors and Risk Adjustment', 77 *Federal Register* 17220-52, March 23.

Weisbrod, Burton A. 1991. 'The Health Care Quadrilemma: An Essay on Technological Change, Quality of Care, and Cost Containment', 29 *Journal of Economic Literature* 523–52.

Yelowitz, Aaron, and Michael F. Cannon. 2010. 'The Massachusetts Health Plan: Much Pain, Little Gain', 657 *Policy Analysis*, Washington, DC: Cato Institute, January 20.

PART III

INSURANCE REGULATION

8. Insurance solvency regulation: A new world order?

Elizabeth F. Brown and Robert W. Klein

I. INTRODUCTION

> I give myself very good advice, but I very seldom follow it.
> Alice in *Alice in Wonderland* by Lewis Carroll

Insurance solvency regulation seeks to reduce the risk that an insurer will be unable to meet its financial obligations due to financial distress or bankruptcy and to promote confidence in the financial stability of the insurance sector. It is based on a societal judgment of the optimal risk-return trade-off involved with insurance transactions, in which solvency regulations that allow for greater flexibility for insurers lead to a wider range of possible product/price options but expose consumers to greater risk in return for these benefits. Solvency standards for insurance companies vary around the globe in accordance with different assessments of the optimal risk-return trade-off as well as different regulatory philosophies.

This chapter assesses the ongoing efforts to reform the insurance regulatory systems in the major insurance markets, primarily the United States (US) and the European Union (EU), in the wake of the recent financial crisis and other economic developments. It examines the economic theories underpinning these systems and why different countries have come to different conclusions regarding the best way to regulate the solvency of insurance companies. In addition, we discuss how the globalization of the insurance industry has led to efforts for greater coordination and harmonization of solvency standards nationally through the Solvency Modernization Initiative (SMI) of the National Association of Insurance Commissioners (NAIC), regionally through efforts like the EU's Solvency II, and internationally through projects, like the Common Framework for the Supervision of Internationally Active Insurance Groups (ComFrame) of the International Association of Insurance Supervisors (IAIS). Further, we undertake a critical assessment of the most significant areas of solvency reforms in the US and EU; specifically capital requirements, corporate governance, and group supervision. As we delve into these substantive aspects of regulation we offer observations on how practical and political realities, as well as other factors, often influence the policies that are adopted. Our chapter concludes with observations on the likely direction for the evolution of insurance solvency regulation in the future.

II. THE ECONOMICS OF INSURANCE SOLVENCY REGULATION

A good place to start a discussion of insurance solvency regulation is a review of the basic economic principles that should guide its design from a normative perspective, as well as an examination of how political-economic factors influence its actual structure and implementation. We believe that these principles should generally guide the design of insurance insolvency regulation in various countries, i.e., they are not specific to any particular country. That said, we also understand that the application of these principles to any given country must consider that jurisdiction's particular circumstances, e.g., its level of economic development, the sophistication of its consumers, etc. In contrast, the intersection of politics and economics can yield much different results from country to country based on a variety of factors. Ultimately, one can articulate a vision of a solvency regulation scheme that adheres to a set of commonly accepted principles but the interplay of politics and economics can lead to results that depart significantly from that vision.

A. Principles for Solvency Regulation

The economic foundation for regulation is based on the presence of market failures (see, e.g., Spulber 1989; Viscusi, Harrington, and Vernon 2000). These market failures are judged against the social welfare maximizing conditions for perfect competition. Perfect competition requires numerous buyers and sellers in a market, the lack of barriers to entry and exit, perfect information, and a homogenous product. Under these conditions, the joint surplus or gains from trade of producers and consumers is maximized. Of course, few if any markets satisfy the conditions for perfect competition in the real world. Hence, in assessing the need for and benefits of regulation in an imperfect world, markets are often judged against a standard of 'workable competition' which reasonably approximates the conditions for perfect competition to the degree that government intervention cannot improve social welfare (Scherer and Ross 1990).

In the presence of market failures, optimal regulation will attempt to replicate the conditions of a competitive market and maximize social welfare (Skipper and Klein 2000; Klein 2012). Such replication is only possible if regulators have perfect information and can determine and implement the correct market solutions; an assumption that may not be valid under some circumstances. In practice, not all market failures can necessarily be remedied by regulation and the desirability of any particular regulatory intervention must be assessed in terms of regulators' ability to 'correct' a specified market failure and any deadweight costs associated with regulatory intervention that may exceed the benefits from intervention. Further, the proposition that regulators can remedy market failures and achieve the highest possible net gain in social welfare presumes that they will employ 'best practices' and the most efficient measures to address market failures.

These general principles suggest the possible efficiency of insurance solvency regulation. Insurance markets are subject to several potential market failures, including severe asymmetric information and principal-agent problems, both of which could lead some insurance companies to incur excessive financial risk, engage in abusive market practices that harm consumers, or both (Munch and Smallwood 1980). Insurance consumers, particularly individuals and households, face significant challenges in judging the financial risk of insurers and properly understanding the terms of insurance contracts. It is therefore costly for consumers to properly assess an insurer's financial strength in relation to its prices and quality of service.[1] Meanwhile, owners of insurance companies have diminished incentives to maintain a high level of safety to the extent that their personal assets are not at risk for unfunded obligations to policyholders that would arise from insolvency. Insurers also can increase their risk after policyholders have purchased a policy and paid premiums – a 'principal-agent' problem that may be very costly and difficult for policyholders to control. While the customers of non-financial firms also face severe information problems, the significant fiduciary role of banks and insurance companies, coupled with these information problems, have prompted virtually every country to subject these institutions to substantial financial regulation.

Solvency regulation may also attempt to address the prospect of negative externalities that may be associated with an insurer's failure (Saunders and Cornett 2003). Financial regulators are concerned about 'contagion'

---

[1] The costs of determining financial soundness are much lower today than they were in the past as anyone with knowledge and access to the Internet can check an insurer's claims paying ability – provided by rating agencies – on the Internet. However, rating agencies cannot engage in enforcement actions (although they may pressure insurers to correct problems) and most countries do not accept the notion that they are an adequate substitute for government regulation.

and the possibility that a spike in insurer insolvencies could induce a 'crisis of confidence' that may have negative effects on the industry.[2] Further, there may be negative externalities associated with excessive insurer insolvency risk as the costs of unpaid claims may be shifted beyond policyholders to their creditors (Saunders and Cornett 2003). Hence, it is common for the regulation of financial institutions to be coupled with some form of insolvency guarantees (e.g., deposit insurance, insurance guaranty associations, etc.) that cover at least a portion of the obligations of bankrupt firms.

Arguably, the goal of optimal insurance solvency regulation should not be to minimize insolvencies, as the costs of achieving such a goal would likely exceed the perceived benefits (Grace, Klein, and Phillips 2003). A more reasonable goal would be to minimize or limit the social cost of insurer insolvency. This social cost is more than the lost equity of the insurer, as it includes the effects on policyholders and third parties who are creditors of insurance policyholders. Regulators can potentially limit insolvency risk by requiring insurers to meet a set of financial standards and taking appropriate actions if an insurer assumes excessive default risk or experiences financial distress (see, e.g., Cummins, Harrington, and Klein 1995).

B. The Political Economy of Solvency Regulation

The term 'political economy' has different interpretations but here we use it to refer to how the intersection of politics and economic interests affect the solvency regulation of insurance companies. Most countries regulate financial services, including insurance, primarily at the national level.[3] The US, however, has left insurance regulation primarily in the hands of state regulators.

While the 2008 financial crisis led to the creation of the Federal Insurance Office (FIO) in 2010, it has no independent regulatory authority. Its powers are limited mainly to advising other federal agencies and

---

[2] This is analogous to the concern that the failure of one bank could cause depositors to withdraw their funds from other banks. While such an event has not actually occurred in the insurance industry, a spike in the number of life insurance company insolvencies in the late 1980s and early 1990s led to a decline in consumers' confidence in the financial stability of the life insurance industry (Klein 1995).

[3] About three dozen nations in the world maintain a federal system of government or a central system of government that allows for the delegation of authority to regional entities under certain circumstances. The vast majority of these nations also regulate insurance primarily at the national level.

Congress on insurance issues. In order to obtain the information it needs to fulfill its advisory duties, the FIO may subpoena information from insurers and their affiliates but only after it has attempted to obtain the required information from existing federal and state regulatory agencies or from publically available sources. The Dodd-Frank Wall Street Reform and Consumer Protection Act of 2010 (the 'Dodd-Frank Act') did give the US Treasury Secretary and the US Trade Representative the power to negotiate bilateral or multilateral agreements covering prudential standards for insurance or reinsurance. The Dodd-Frank Act refers to such agreements as 'covered agreements'. The FIO may advise the US Treasury Secretary and the US Trade Representative during such negotiations but it is not authorized to carry on such negotiations. Following the entry into force of such an agreement, the FIO may determine if existing state laws conflict with the provisions in the covered agreement and therefore are preempted as a result.

As this book goes to press, the US Treasury Secretary and the US Trade Representative have not negotiated any covered agreements. While the FIO recommended that the US Treasury Secretary and the US Trade Representative should negotiate a covered agreement on reinsurance collateral requirements, neither the US Treasury Secretary nor the US Trade Representative have shown much interest in beginning negotiations for a covered agreement on reinsurance collateral requirements (FIO 2013).[4]

Even in the area of group supervision, the US traditionally has not regulated insurance groups on a consolidated basis at the federal level unless one of the group's subsidiaries was a bank or a savings and loan.[5] Prior to the financial crisis of 2008, an insurance group could effectively pick its federal regulator by which depository institution it chose to own. If it owned a bank, the Federal Reserve regulated the group on a consolidated

---

[4] Reinsurers provide insurance to other insurance companies who buy it as a means of risk management. If the reinsurer is providing insurance to an insurance company that is domiciled in a state that has not licensed or accredited the reinsurer, then the reinsurer must post collateral to provide some assurance that they will meet their obligations under the insurance contracts. The obligation to post collateral is referred to as a reinsurance collateral requirement.

[5] It should be noted that most insurance groups regulated at the federal level are financial conglomerates that offer a wide range of financial products (banking, securities, derivatives, etc.) and not just insurance. As a result, it is not necessarily helpful to label these firms as 'insurers' because the risks that they pose are far larger than the risks posed by a traditional insurance company given the breadth of the products that they offer. As a result, the prudential supervision of such financial conglomerates needs to take into account the full mix of products that they offer.

basis but if it owned a savings and loan, the Office of Thrift Supervision (OTS) regulated the group on a consolidated basis. If it did not own a bank or savings and loan, then no federal regulator had the authority to subject the insurance group to mandatory supervision on a consolidated basis. Allowing financial conglomerates to pick the agency that would regulate them on a consolidated basis proved disastrous, as the case of the American International Group (AIG) dramatically illustrated. AIG was regulated by the OTS, an agency with approximately 1,000 employees who had little experience evaluating the risks posed by insurance much less the derivative products that ultimately led to the US government bailout of AIG.

Even after the Dodd-Frank Act, most insurance groups still will not have a federal regulator unless they own a bank or a savings and loan. The Dodd-Frank Act merged the OTS's group supervisory functions into the Federal Reserve so that the Federal Reserve now regulates on a consolidated basis any insurance group that includes a bank or savings and loan. In addition, the Federal Reserve regulates any insurance group that was classified as a bank holding company with $50 million in assets that received bailout funds from the US government during the 2008 financial crisis. Finally, the Dodd-Frank Act established a new interagency body – the Financial Stability Oversight Council (FSOC) – that can place any insurance group under the supervision of the Federal Reserve if two-thirds of the FSOC's members determine that the insurance group poses a risk to the financial stability of the US. As of March 31, 2015, the FSOC has only designated three insurance groups, AIG, Prudential Financial, Inc., and MetLife Inc. to be subject to Federal Reserve supervision on a consolidated basis because they were deemed to pose a risk to the financial stability of the US. AIG, however, was already regulated by the Federal Reserve as a thrift holding company. Given the small number of insurance groups directly affected by the changes in the Dodd-Frank Act, it is not clear that the federal government is supervising significantly more insurance groups on a consolidated basis now than it was supervising before the 2008 financial crisis.

Thus, part of the explanation for the differences in insurance solvency standards among nations can be attributed to the differences between national and state-level politics and their interactions with economic concerns. For example, US state governments tend to be less concerned with the international implications of insurance solvency regulation than the national governments of other countries because, unlike national governments, the states are not responsible for conducting foreign affairs or engaging in international economic cooperation.

A long strain of scholarship on regulatory behavior is also pertinent to the political economy of insurance solvency regulation. A seminal work in this strain was written by Stigler (1971) who postulated a *theory of economic regulation* in which the concentrated interests of firms tend to prevail over the diffused interests of consumers in the transfer of wealth through regulation. Peltzman (1976) subsequently generalized Stigler's model to allow for the regulatory bias between consumers and firms to vary depending upon cost and demand conditions and the relative political sensitivities of consumers to prices and firms to profits.

Political scientists, such as Meier (1985; 1988), have criticized Stigler's economic theory of regulatory behavior for being too simplistic and one-dimensional, citing many cases in which consumer influence and regulatory costs have been imposed on industries despite consumers' lack of organization. He postulated an alternative multi-dimensional model in which regulatory policy is influenced by various actors – industry groups, consumer groups, regulatory agencies, and political elites – and applied this construct to insurance regulation (Meier 1988). The saliency and complexity of regulatory issues also affect the ability of these different actors to affect public policy, according to Meier. Greater complexity tends to increase the influence of those with expertise (industry and regulators) while greater saliency attracts consumer attention and the intervention of political elites.[6]

It should be noted that this body of work has primarily focused on traditional consumer protection rules but it is possible to draw out its implications for solvency regulation. First, solvency regulatory policies do not appear to be salient among insurance buyers, whereas they are of great interest to insurance companies and of some interest to insurance agents and brokers. Second, solvency regulation tends to be highly technical in nature. This has two effects: 1) specific policies and their implications are difficult to understand for most insurance buyers; and 2) insurance companies sometimes have an edge over regulators when it comes to policy negotiations, depending upon the sophistication and expertise of regulators and the complexity of the issue. Third, regulators are typically placed in the position of balancing political considerations with their own sense of what is in the best interest of consumers in effectuating a reasonable solvency regulatory scheme. The political considerations regulators must contend with include the insurance industry's lobbying efforts with legislators and regulators and the fact that more stringent solvency regulations

---

[6] See Roe (1993) for a discussion of the relatively greater political influence of insurance companies in the early 1900s.

can result in higher insurance prices and decreased coverage availability; things that insurance buyers are aware of and do care about (Jaffee and Russell 1998; Klein 1995).[7]

Although these factors suggest that the industry will have a strong influence on the ultimate scope and character of solvency regulation, it is not obvious how the industry might attempt to utilize this influence. From one perspective, one might expect that insurers will typically favor less regulation and oppose efforts to strengthen regulatory standards. On the other hand, one could argue that financially-strong insurers would have an interest in favoring stringent regulation because: 1) compliance with strengthened standards would be less costly for them than it would be for other insurers; 2) less stringent regulation allows financially weak insurers to operate and take business away from strong insurers; and 3) insurance company failures enabled by inadequate regulation can have adverse effects on the entire industry, tarnishing its reputation and potentially triggering guarantee association assessments on solvent carriers (Bohn and Hall 1999; Grace, Klein and Phillips 2003).[8]

What we observe is that most insurers tend to understand and accept the notion that there must be an effective and efficient solvency regulatory system. At the same time, they seem to be wary of new regulations and toughened standards. When new standards and requirements are proposed, many insurers and their trade associations seek modifications that make any proposed changes less onerous in their view. In essence, they seem to place greater weight on how such changes will affect their compliance costs than any 'benefits' they might obtain from 'raising the bar' for high-risk and financially weak insurers. Hence, as regulators seek to revise and modernize their standards and policies, they must engage in intense bargaining with the industry in reaching compromises that both sides can live with. Regulators are often at a disadvantage in such negotiations as the industry typically has considerably more technical resources that it can bring to bear than regulators (Meier 1991). Further, regulators must give

[7] As discussed earlier, regulators are generally cognizant of the need to balance solvency requirements with the supply of insurance. The problem they face, however, is that consumers tend to react negatively to higher insurance prices without an appreciation of the need to ensure that insurers' default risk remains within reasonable bounds.

[8] Meier (1988) observes that the extent to which insurance companies advocate the same position on a particular regulatory issue affects their influence, i.e., the more unified they are the more likely they are to prevail on that issue, all other things equal. It is our observation, based on reading through numerous industry comment letters and position papers, that insurers tend to express very similar views on most proposed changes to insurance solvency regulations.

due consideration to the market effects of proposed regulatory reforms that insurers allege will occur as a result of these reforms.[9]

III. IMPORTANT DEVELOPMENTS AND INITIATIVES

We now turn to important developments and initiatives that are affecting insurance solvency regulation in the US and around the world. Insurance regulation has continued to evolve over time in response to changes in the industry and other developments that have prompted regulators to modify their policies and methods. In this evolution, regulators have employed new technologies and advanced their ideas about what constitutes best practices. Over the history of insurance regulation there have been episodes of relatively dramatic reforms that have been motivated by crises or changes in the economic and political environment surrounding insurance regulation. Arguably, we are currently seeing one of these episodes reflected in the SMI in the US, Solvency II in the EU, and the advancement of international regulatory standards and programs. Below we discuss significant economic trends that are spurring changes in insurance solvency regulation and review the most important of the associated regulatory initiatives.

A. Economic Trends

Insurance and its regulation are strongly affected by significant economic trends. Insurance companies continue to change and innovate to serve the risk management needs of growing and evolving economies as well as respond to important developments in financial markets. One way of tracking the growth of the insurance industry is to look at changes in the gross domestic product (GDP) attributed to insurance companies and their related activities relative to changes in the GDP for an entire country's economy. Figure 8.1 shows insurance GDP (life and non-life) in the US in 2012 dollars and as a percentage of total GDP over the period 1980–2012. As can be seen from this figure, insurance GDP has increased

[9] As noted above, insurers tend to advocate very similar positions on proposed solvency regulatory reforms. In other words, with few exceptions (e.g., changes to reinsurance collateral requirements), regulators are unable to pit one segment of the industry against another. Hence, Meier's (1991) argument that considerable fragmentation in the insurance industry undermines its political influence does not appear to be applicable to solvency regulation as a general rule.

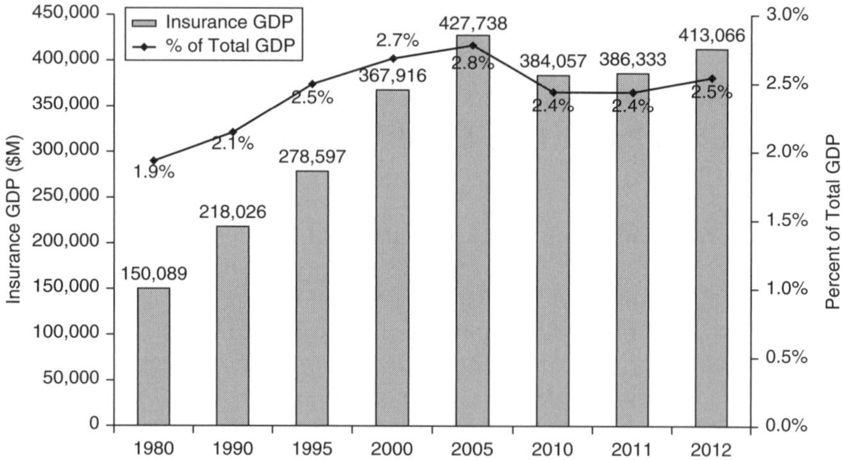

Source: Bureau of Economic Analysis and authors' calculations.

Figure 8.1 Gross domestic product in insurance (in 2012 dollars) 1980–2012

almost three-fold over this period. More importantly, the share of total GDP attributable to insurers has risen from 1.9 percent to 2.5 percent. This suggests that insurance has played an increasingly important role in the US economy over time and underscores the significance of its regulation.[10]

Figure 8.2 shows total insurance premiums (life and non-life) as a percentage of GDP for the years 2003 and 2012 for major regions in the world.[11] Interestingly, with the exception of Latin America, insurance premiums as a percentage of GDP fell from 2003 to 2012. The reasons for this decline are not obvious, but the fallout from the recent financial crisis as well as the maturation of insurance markets in developed economies could be contributing factors. The most recent report by Swiss Re on world insurance trends indicates that global insurance premiums began to increase again in 2012 fueled by growth in emerging markets and Asia (Swiss Re 2013).

---

[10] Readers should note there is a significant difference between insurance premiums and insurance GDP. More specifically, insurance GDP is a measure of the value added by the insurance industry which is calculated by subtracting input costs from industry revenues (premiums plus investment income).

[11] It should be noted that Figure 8.1 uses a 'value added' approach to calculating the insurance sector's share of national GDP whereas Figure 8.2 simply divides insurance premiums by each region's GDP.

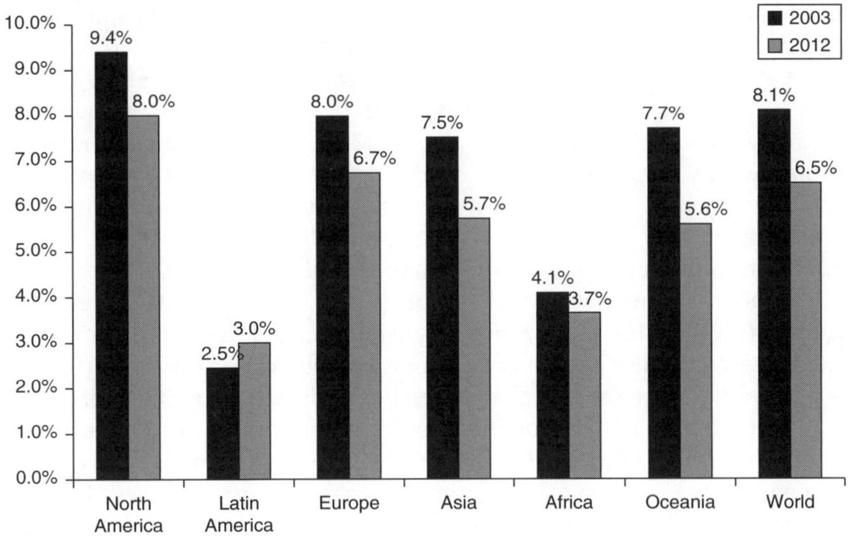

Source: Swiss Re 2013.

Figure 8.2 Insurance premiums as a percentage of GDP: 2003 and 2012

A second important economic trend is the growing integration and interdependence of financial markets. Insurance companies operated in relative isolation from other financial services firms for many years, but that is no longer the case. Today, insurers vie with other financial institutions in the sale of certain products that compete with life insurance and annuities as well as other instruments used to manage risk. Further, a number of holding companies predominantly engaged in the business of insurance also have banking and investment subsidiaries and many financial holding companies have insurance subsidiaries. Because of these developments, the linkage between insurance companies and other financial institutions has strengthened and insurers are more susceptible to problems in financial markets, such as systemic risk.[12] This makes insurance regulators' jobs

[12] There are different views as to whether insurance companies contribute to systemic risk in the economy. (See Grace 2010; Cummins and Weiss 2014; and Schwarcz and Schwarcz 2014.) That said, there appears to be little disagreement that insurance companies are susceptible to systemic risk in the sense that they can suffer significant adverse effects from broader problems in the financial sector that decrease the value of their assets (Wang et al. 2009).

much more complicated and also requires greater coordination among the principal regulators of the different types of financial services firms.

The recent financial crisis has influenced and added greater impetus to solvency modernization initiatives in the US, EU and other countries. While Solvency II and the SMI preceded the financial crisis, the crisis prompted insurance regulators to rethink and refocus certain aspects of solvency reforms, particularly in the areas of corporate governance, risk management and group supervision. It has also brought greater federal attention to the supervision of insurance companies in the US as reflected in the Dodd-Frank Act and several of its provisions, including the establishment of the FIO and a process by which certain insurance companies can be designated as systemically important financial institutions (SIFIs), which would make them subject to regulation by the Federal Reserve.

A third significant development is the globalization of insurance and financial services markets. Over time, an increasing number of insurance companies have expanded their business into other countries. Foreign companies have increased their penetration of US insurance markets while US companies have sought to extend their business in foreign markets. Figure 8.3 compares the amount of insurance sold by US companies in foreign countries with the amount of insurance sold by foreign companies in the US in 2009. Insurance premiums written abroad by subsidiaries of

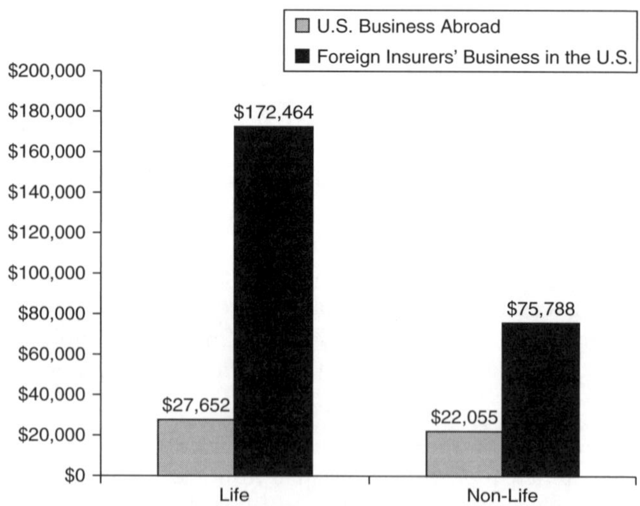

Source: Insurance Information Institute.

Figure 8.3 Insurance industry cross-border sales ($M): 2009

US companies totaled $49.7 billion while their foreign counterparts had sales of $248.3 billion in the US. These statistics indicate the cross-border trade in insurance is significant. Unfortunately, comparable historical data on cross-border sales of insurance are unavailable, but it is reasonable to surmise that over the long term there has been a significant increase in such sales.

This development also has important implications for insurance solvency regulation. Understandably, most regulators are concerned about the quality of the supervision of foreign companies operating in their jurisdiction. This is one of the principal motivations behind the development of regional and international regulatory standards and reform programs such as the SMI in the US. It has also led to discussions between countries regarding 'regulatory equivalence'; i.e., will the regulators in Country A accept the regulatory policies enforced in Country B as 'equivalent' to their own and vice-versa. US and EU regulators are currently engaged in such a discussion, although the recent enactment by the EU of the Omnibus II Directive has reduced the urgency of resolving the differences in approaches by allowing the EU to deem certain nations as 'provisionally equivalent' for a ten-year period under certain circumstances (European Union 2014). Finally, greater cross-border trade in insurance has compelled insurance regulators in various countries to work more closely together in coordinating their solvency oversight of internationally active insurance companies.

B. Significant Initiatives

These economic trends have prompted the US, EU, and the IAIS to undertake several significant initiatives aimed at addressing the solvency issues that such trends have raised. These initiatives include the NAIC's SMI, the EU's Solvency II, and the IAIS's ComFrame and related programs.

The US, EU, and the IAIS represent the three most important entities for developing insurance regulatory norms. The US and the EU are important because over two-thirds of the world's insurance premiums are written by insurance firms from these two areas. The IAIS is the most important international body for the development of insurance regulatory norms. The IAIS's membership is broader than comparable international bodies for banking or securities. It has almost 140 nations who are members while the Basel Committee on Banking Supervision, which establishes international guidelines for banking, has fewer than 30 nations who are members. While the US and the EU establish legally binding requirements for insurers operating within their borders, the IAIS influences insurance standards globally by promulgating non-binding principles and norms that attempt to influence and shape the content of the domestic insurance laws of its member nations over time.[13]

1. Solvency modernization initiative

The NAIC's SMI constitutes a fairly ambitious effort by US state regulators to examine and reform several key elements of their system for insurance solvency regulation. As described by the NAIC, 'The SMI is a critical self-examination of the United States' insurance solvency regulatory framework and includes a review of international developments regarding insurance supervision, banking supervision, and international accounting standards and their potential use in US insurance regulation' (NAIC 2012). The SMI, which began in 2008, has six major components: 1) capital requirements; 2) risk management; 3) corporate governance; 4) group supervision; 5) reinsurance; and 6) statutory accounting and financial reporting. A significant number of NAIC committees, task forces, and working groups have been involved in developing specific recommendations in each of these areas, which can take various forms including model laws, model regulations, and guidelines, among others.

The individual states, however, must ultimately support any NAIC recommendations in order for them to become law and be enforced.[14] In the past, the states generally have adopted the NAIC recommendations regarding solvency regulations, although they have not applied them uniformly to all insurers nor have they enforced them uniformly (FIO 2013).

We leave the discussion of significant elements of the SMI to section V but it is helpful here to briefly comment on the political-economic forces affecting the SMI and the NAIC's quasi-legislative process in determining the specific reforms that have or will be adopted.[15] Unlike the slate

---

[13] These non-binding principles and norms are referred to as 'soft law' because they are not enforceable through sanctions or other penalties, unlike some bilateral or multilateral treaties or agreements, like the General Agreement on Trade in Services, which are considered 'hard law' because their provisions are enforceable through sanctions or other penalties.

[14] Specific laws or changes to laws must be enacted by each state in order to become effective in each state. Other NAIC documents, guidelines, etc. that are incorporated by reference in existing state laws and/or regulations (e.g., annual statement blanks, changes to RBC formulas, etc.) become automatically effective unless a state chooses to remove or modify such reference in its laws and/or regulations. Most of the significant changes that have been adopted or are being considered by adoption by the NAIC under the SMI will require changes to state laws and/or regulations.

[15] We characterize the process by which the NAIC develops and adopts regulatory reforms as 'quasi-legislative' in the sense that any proposed reform proceeds

of solvency regulatory reforms that the NAIC adopted in the late 1980s and early 1990s, the SMI is not motivated by a dramatic rise in insurer insolvencies or some other crisis, although the recent financial crisis has added a new wrinkle to the NAIC's reform agenda. Arguably, at least two of the principal motivators behind the SMI are Solvency II and the development of international regulatory standards in the context of the growing globalization of the insurance business. Gone are the days when US regulators could operate in relative isolation without concern to how their policies conformed to those employed in other countries. Now US regulators must bring their policies up to a level consistent with international standards and generally accepted notions of what constitutes best practices in insurance solvency regulation.

This observation is not meant to imply that US regulators would not want to employ best practices for their own reasons. The issue is whether the policies US regulators believe make the most sense in an American context are acceptable to regulators in other countries. Their hope is that the US version of solvency regulatory reform will be deemed sufficient by other regulators so that there will be no conflicts over regulatory equivalency. It would be surprising if international acceptance of the policy reforms being developed under the SMI did not weigh on the minds of the NAIC's leadership; how this may be affecting the decisions being made is a matter of speculation for outsiders. US regulators also must deal with federal officials' assessment of the adequacy of SMI reforms as well as lobbying by the insurance industry. Hence, there are several forces pulling on US insurance regulators as they proceed down the path of reform through the SMI.

2. Solvency II

The EU began considering replacing Solvency I over ten years ago because it only set minimum prudential standards, while several national regulators within the EU imposed more stringent capital standards. As a result, insurers operating within the EU were subject to different solvency standards depending on which national regulator supervised them, creating an uneven playing field.

Solvency II aims to establish a harmonized regime for solvency regulation organized around three pillars.[16] Pillar I defines quantitative

---

through a series of working groups and committees and ultimately must be approved by a majority of the NAICS 56 members in order for it to be adopted. This is a much different process than what would occur in a federal regulatory agency.

[16] Financial regulators in the EU began discussing further insurance solvency regulatory reforms beyond Solvency I in the early 2000s, which eventually culminated in the adoption of the Solvency II Directive in 2009.

financial requirements, including capital adequacy rules, for insurance firms (European Union 2009). Pillar II defines the supervisory activities of each national authority (European Union 2009). Pillar III defines the reporting and public disclosure requirements for insurance firms and supervisory authorities (European Union 2009). The European Insurance and Occupational Pensions Authority (EIOPA) has set January 1, 2016 as the deadline for the delivery of the regulatory and supervisory framework for the technical implementation and application of Solvency II.

In addition, Solvency II would require that non-EU insurance companies be regulated both at the entity and group levels by a supervisory authority equivalent to the national authorities within the EU in order for their capital held outside of the EU to count towards their capital requirements (European Commission 2008). It is unclear at this time if US state regulation would be deemed equivalent under this standard, or to what extent the states would have to change their laws and regulations to be deemed equivalent. In the long run, Solvency II *may* pressure US regulators to adopt the same or similar standards for regulating insurance so that US insurance companies with international operations are not handicapped when they try to compete in the EU. It remains to be seen how this interplay between the US and the EU over regulatory equivalency will ultimately influence US regulatory standards.

For now, the EU has unilaterally resolved the matter by allowing the European Commission and EIOPA jointly to classify a non-EU country, like the US, as having solvency standards that are 'provisionally equivalent' to those required under Solvency II as long as they meet certain standards. The Omnibus II Directive that contains the requirements for provisional equivalence entered into force on April 16, 2014. The requirements for being deemed provisionally equivalent include, among other things: 1) a finding that the non-EU nation has a solvency regime in place that meets the requirements for Solvency II or that such a regime may be adopted by the non-EU nation in the future; 2) the non-EU nation has a risk-based regime that employs both quantitative and qualitative solvency requirements; 3) the non-EU nation has legislation in place that would allow it to exchange confidential supervisory information with EIOPA and other authorities; and 4) the non-EU nation has an independent system of supervision (European Union 2014). The non-EU nation does not need to apply to the European Commission and EIOPA in order to be deemed by them as provisionally equivalent. Provisional equivalence may be granted for an initial ten-year period and may be renewed for an unlimited number of additional ten-year periods when that initial period expires. Under the Omnibus II Directive, the European Commission and EIOPA could classify the US state insurance regulatory regimes as provisionally equivalent without the states having to apply or make any commitments to change their solvency standards (European Union 2014).

The EU felt pressured to enact this compromise after lobbying from many large EU insurers with US operations. Prudential, one of the UK's largest insurance companies, even warned that it was considering relocating its operations out of London because of the Solvency II equivalence requirements and the questions raised about whether the US would meet them (Grey 2013).

3. International standards and programs

For over a decade the IAIS has promoted the convergence of market conduct and prudential requirements around the world by encouraging nations to adopt regulations that conform to its Insurance Core Principles (ICPs), which are non-binding principles and norms (IAIS 2011). IAIS members consider the ICPs as roughly equivalent to the standards set for banks under the Basel Accords. Unlike the Basel Accords for banks, however, the ICPs do not establish clear, uniform capital standards for insurers.

The IAIS's ICPs seek to develop a framework for insurance supervision, under which the insurance supervisor should concentrate on financial requirements, governance requirements, and market conduct requirements.[17] The IAIS promotes a common regulatory structure that uses a risk-based methodology including both quantitative elements for capital adequacy, as well as qualitative elements for governance, market conduct, and disclosure (IAIS 2007). The ICPs apply to insurers at both the legal entity level and the group level. The common structure also outlines preconditions for effective supervision and supervisory actions. The IAIS does not mandate that insurance supervisors use one method for creating solvency regulations that account for all relevant risks.

The IAIS envisions the insurer's responsibility as managing risk and the insurance regulator's responsibility as guaranteeing that the insurer meets this obligation. Thus, the IAIS encourages supervisors to require that an insurer 'translate its risk exposure as far as practicable into quantitative measures which provide a sound and consistent basis for the setting of premium levels, determining technical provisions and deciding on the economic capital it finds optimal from its risk management perspective'

---

[17] Financial requirements concern the 'financial aspects of an insurer's operations' including its capital adequacy and solvency; governance requirements concern 'how an insurer is governed'; and market conduct requirements concern 'how an insurer conducts its business and presents itself to the market' (IAIS 2005).

(IAIS 2007). IAIS standards would allow supervisors to give individual insurers a great deal of latitude in terms of assessing and reserving for the risks they face. In fact, the IAIS believes that such risk-sensitive regulatory requirements are preferable to fixed ratios or limits because they provide insurers with better incentives for managing risk, discourage regulatory arbitrage, and enable the better use of resources.

IV. THE CAUSES OF INSURANCE COMPANY FAILURES

As we delve more deeply into the most important elements of insurance solvency regulation it is helpful to have some understanding of the significance and the causes of insurance company failures. Unfortunately, international statistics on insurer insolvencies are not available. However, data compiled by A.M. Best on insurer insolvencies in the US can provide some insights that may have a broader application. Figure 8.4 shows insurance company impairment trends in the US for the period 1980–2012. As can be seen from this figure, the number of insurer impairments is somewhat cyclical, especially in the property-casualty sector.[18] The frequency of property-casualty impairments is driven primarily by the underwriting cycle and secondarily by catastrophes (e.g., Hurricanes Andrew and Iniki in 1992). Life-health impairments tend to be affected more by macroeconomic factors such as changes in interest rates and declines in asset values. This suggests that regulators need to be attentive to these factors that can cause spikes in insurance company failures.

A.M. Best also assigns a primary cause to each of these insurer impairments.[19] Figures 8.5 and 8.6 show the results of this analysis for property-casualty and life-health insurer impairments respectively.[20] As

---

[18] A.M. Best designates an insurer as a Financially Impaired Insurance Company (FIC) as of the first regulatory action taken by an insurance department, whereby the insurer's: 1) ability to conduct normal business operations is adversely affected; 2) its capital and surplus have been deemed to be inadequate to meet legal requirements; and/or 3) its general financial condition has triggered regulatory concern. Hence, an insurance company need not be insolvent to be considered financially impaired.

[19] The assignment of the primary cause of the financial impairment of an insurance company is based on a determination of A.M. Best financial analysts. It is understood that the assignment of a primary cause of an impairment does not rule out other causes which also could contribute to that impairment, which, in fact, may be related to the primary cause.

[20] These figures show the breakdown of insurer impairments by the primary cause assigned to each impairment by A.M. Best.

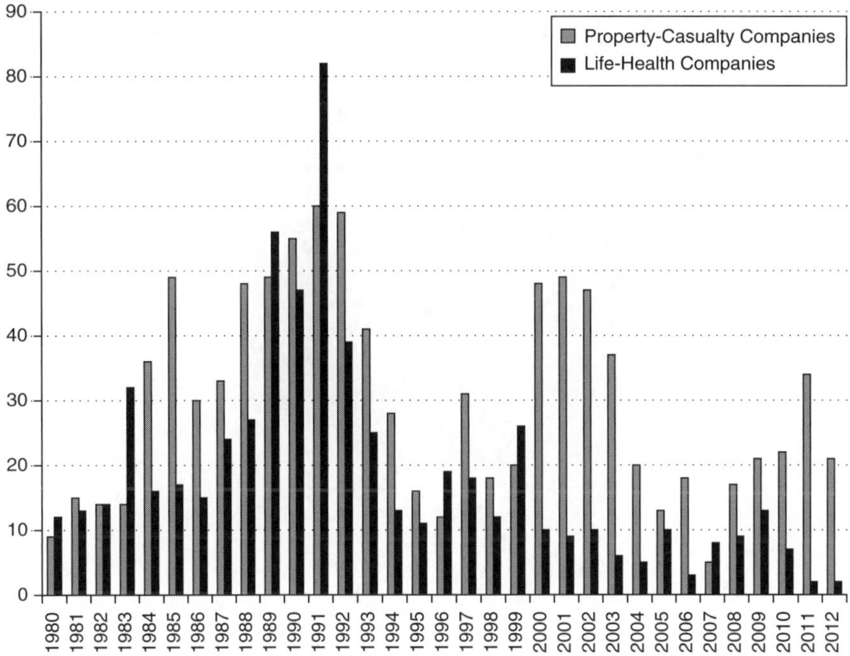

Source: A.M. Best.

Figure 8.4 Insurance company impairments in the US 1980–2012

can be seen from these charts, deficient loss reserves/inadequate pricing is by far the leading cause of property-casualty insurer impairments (42 percent) followed by rapid growth (13 percent). Reserve deficiencies and inadequate prices go hand in hand as property-casualty insurers rely heavily on estimates of historical losses to determine their prices going forward. This is a problem that becomes chronic in 'soft markets' but also can be an issue for certain insurers in 'normal markets'. Deficient loss reserves and inadequate pricing have also been the leading causes of life-health insurer impairments (29 percent) although less significant than for property-casualty insurers, followed by affiliate problems (18 percent) and investment problems (15 percent). Identifying the primary causes of insurance company failures should help to guide regulators as to the areas that warrant the greatest attention in solvency supervision.

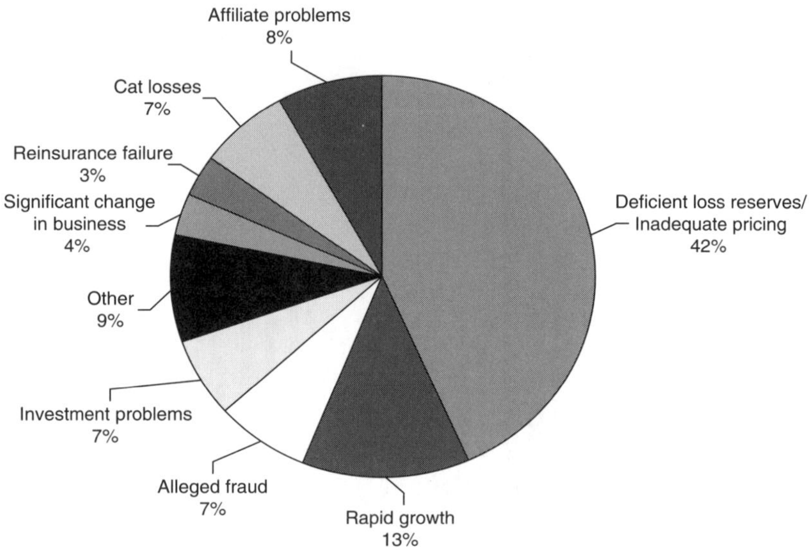

Source: A.M. Best.

Figure 8.5 Primary causes of property-casualty insurer impairments in the US (1969–2012)

V. PRINCIPAL AREAS OF REGULATORY ATTENTION

Although the various solvency initiatives cover a range of important aspects of regulation, of particular interest here are how they address capital standards, corporate governance, and group supervision. In our opinion, the reforms being developed in these areas are likely to have the most significant effects on insurance companies and, potentially, on insolvency costs. These areas of regulatory reform also have been especially contentious. It is to these specific areas of solvency regulation that we now turn.

A. Capital Regulation

Capital requirements receive prominent attention in the SMI, Solvency II, and the ICPs, consistent with the view that they are a critical element of both insurance and banking supervision. The amount of capital that an insurance company holds is important as it provides a cushion to absorb adverse financial developments such as unexpected increases in its claims

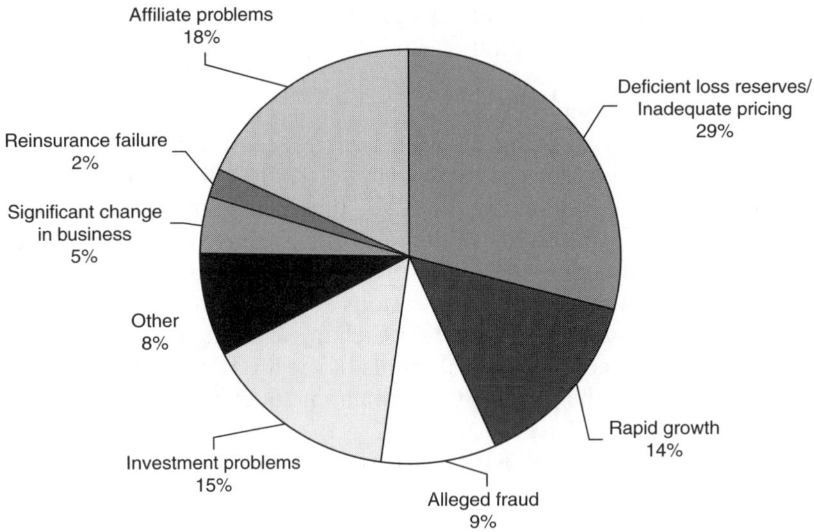

Source: A.M. Best.

Figure 8.6 *Primary causes of life health insurer impairments in the US (1969–2012)*

or a decline in the value of its assets.[21] All other things equal, the more capital an insurer holds relative to the risks it is exposed to, the less likely it is to become financially impaired or insolvent. It is for this reason that regulators in every jurisdiction impose minimum capital requirements for insurance companies and why changes to capital requirements under the various solvency initiatives are garnering considerable attention.

Insurer capital requirements can be determined in several different ways. Fixed capital requirements were common for insurance companies prior to the 1990s. Since then, most of the major countries have moved towards some form of volume-based or risk-based approach to determining insurance company capital standards (ChandraShekar and Warrier 2007; Eling, Klein and Schmit 2009).[22] These approaches typically utilize

[21] The term 'capital' is shorthand for 'capital and surplus' which is essentially the same thing as the net worth of an insurance company (i.e., the value of its assets minus the value of its liabilities). Specific accounting rules applied to insurance companies determine how their capital and surplus is calculated.

[22] Also see Holzmuller (2009) for a comparison and critique of capital standards in the US, the EU (Solvency II), and Switzerland.

formulas or internal or standard models to determine the amount of capital an insurer should hold for regulatory purposes.

1. Capital standards in the US

In the US, insurers are subject to fixed capital requirements set by each state as well as uniform risk-based capital (RBC) standards based on complex formulas developed by the NAIC that have been adopted by every state.[23] Different formulas are required for property-casualty, health, and life insurance companies. In each of these RBC formulas, selected factors (e.g., 10 percent) are multiplied by various accounting values (e.g., assets, reserves, or premiums) to produce RBC charges for each item. Stochastic modeling is only used in certain elements of the life RBC formula.[24]

Components of the life RBC formula include: C0 – Asset Risk – Affiliates; C1 –Asset Risk – Other; C2 – Insurance Risk; C3 – Interest Rate Risk, Health Credit Risk, and Market Risk; and C4 – Business Risk. The property-casualty and health formulas take a slightly different approach to each of these components to reflect the differences in the risks associated with the different insurance types. Components of the property-casualty RBC formula include: R0 – Asset Risk – Subsidiary Insurance Companies; R1 – Asset Risk – Fixed Income; R2 – Asset Risk – Equity; R3 – Asset Risk – Credit; R4 – Underwriting Risk – Reserves; and R5 – Underwriting Risk – Net Written Premium. Components of the health RBC formula include: H0 – Asset Risk – Affiliates; H1 – Asset Risk – Other; H2 – Underwriting Risk; H3 – Credit Risk; and H4 – Business Risk.

The calculated risk charges are then summed into the categories identified above and a covariance adjustment is performed to reflect the assumed independence of certain risks. The covariance adjustment is shown in the formula below which is used to determine a property-casualty insurer's Authorized Control Level (ACL) RBC.[25]

---

[23] An insurer is required to have capital that meets or exceeds the higher of the two standards.

[24] Model-based components are used to assess the interest rate risk associated with fixed annuities and the market risk, interest rate risk, and expense-recovery risk of variable annuities.

[25] To illustrate how the covariance adjustment works, assume the following. The respective unadjusted RBC amounts for a hypothetical property-casualty insurer are: R0 = \$20M; R1 = \$30M; R2 = \$60M; R3 = \$10M; R4 = \$75M; and R5 = \$100M. Without the application of the 0.5 factor and the square root part of the formula, the insurer's total RBC would be \$20,245 million. With the application of the square root adjustment this amount is reduced \$162.2 million and the application of the 0.5 factor reduces this further to \$81.1 million. It

$$ACLRBC = 0.5[R0 + \sqrt{R1^2 + R2^2 + R3^2 + R4^2 + R5^2}]$$

The covariance adjustment presumes that most risks in the RBC formula are fully independent. This approach was likely adopted due to its simplicity, even though in reality one would expect that correlations among different risk categories would vary (Butsic 1993). The NAIC recognizes this issue and is revising its approach to more accurately represent the degree of correlation among risks and to allow for correlations between 0 and 1. This is important because if the correlation between two risk categories exceeds 0 then the current formula will result in lower RBC amounts for insurers than a more accurate reflection of the interdependence of these risks would warrant.

An insurer's RBC is compared to its actual total adjusted capital (TAC) to determine whether any company or regulatory action is required.[26] Certain company and regulatory actions are prescribed if a company's TAC falls below its RBC. Four RBC levels for company and regulatory action have been established, with more strict action required for companies as they reach lower ratios of RBC to TAC (see Table 8.1).

When the NAIC developed and adopted its RBC formulas in the early 1990s, there was a great deal of concern that setting insurers' RBC levels too high could force unwarranted company and regulatory actions. The primary objective at the time was to institute a new and better approach to determine insurers' regulatory capital even if it was imperfect. Indeed, for most insurers the capital required under the RBC formulas was significantly higher than the fixed capital requirements that they had previously been required to maintain. That said, as revealed in Figure 8.7, the vast majority of insurers have capital that greatly exceeds their company action RBC levels (Klein 2013). Klein and Wang (2007) also revealed that the Best Capital Adequacy Ratios (BCARs) for US property-casualty insurance companies are considerably lower for most insurers than their RBC

should be noted that 0.5 factor is used to calculate an insurer's ACL RBC (also known as the '100 percent level') which is the amount that is reported in the insurer's annual financial statement. However, company action is required at 200 percent of the ACL, which is known as the Company Action Level (CAL) RBC (see Table 8.1).

[26] In calculating an insurer's TAC, certain adjustments are made to an insurer's reported capital and surplus. For example, for a life company, its Asset Valuation Reserve (AVR) and 50 percent of its dividend liability is added to its capital and surplus to calculate its TAC.

Table 8.1 RBC action levels

Action level	Percent of ACL	Requirements
Company action	200	Company must file plan
Regulatory action	150	Commissioner must examine insurer
Authorized control	100	Commissioner authorized to seize insurer
Mandatory control	70	Commissioner required to seize insurer

ratios.[27] Whether US regulators have set the bar too low for insurers' regulatory capital requirements is debatable. So too is the accuracy of the RBC formulas in measuring insurers' financial risk. Less accurate formulas will lead to more 'false positives' (i.e., adequately capitalized companies deemed to be deficient) the higher RBC levels are set.

Several empirical studies have tested the accuracy of US RBC ratios in 'predicting' which insurers will fail or become insolvent. These studies have generally concluded that RBC has minimal predictive power when compared or combined with other measures of insurers' financial risk.[28] While these studies raise questions about the accuracy of US RBC in terms of measuring the risk profile of an insurer, they do not constitute an explicit test of RBC's effectiveness in achieving its regulatory objectives. Further empirical analysis of the effectiveness of the US RBC system would be helpful in evaluating its stringency as well as its accuracy in identifying insurers that warrant some form of regulatory intervention, ideally before they become insolvent and impose bankruptcy costs on guaranty associations and policyholders and claimants who are unprotected or not fully protected by guaranty associations. Ultimately, the effectiveness of the current US approach to capital standards and any proposed changes should be evaluated in terms of a set of clear objectives for these standards, such as holding down insolvency costs below some established parameter.

Arguably, the US approach to determining RBC requirements reflects

---

27 Best's Capital Adequacy Ratios (BCARs) are used by A.M. Best in its financial analysis of insurance companies and assignment of financial strength ratings to these companies. The BCARs were first used after the NAIC adopted its RBC requirements and while they appear to employ some similar elements to RBC, it is reasonable to presume that there are some substantial differences between RBC and BCAR as indicated by the differences between insurers' RBC ratios and their BCARs. More detailed information on the BCAR system can be obtained from A.M. Best's website at http://www.ambest.com/.

28 See Cummins, Harrington and Klein (1995), Grace, Harrington and Klein (1998a), Cummins, Grace, and Phillips (1999), and Pottier and Sommer (2002).

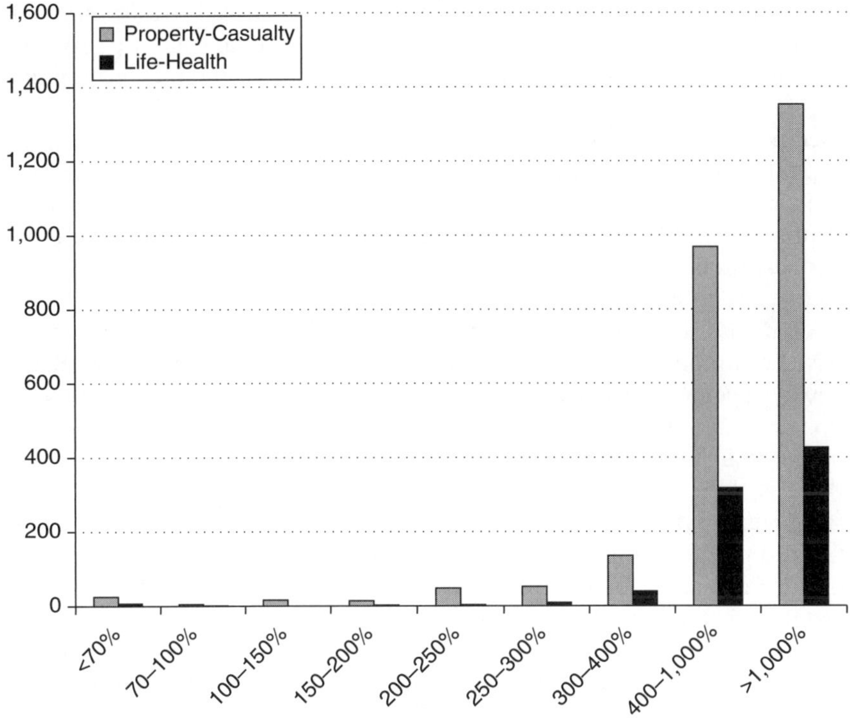

Source: NAIC database, authors' calculations.

Figure 8.7 Distribution of insurers by TAC/RBC: 2010

both the heights and the limits to what can be achieved with a formula-based method. When first adopted, the US system was considered relatively advanced compared with regulatory capital requirements in other countries, and was seen as a significant improvement over fixed capital requirements. However, over time, regulators' use of static formulas to determine insurers' capital requirements has come to be seen by many academics as increasingly outmoded in view of the improvements that have occurred in dynamic financial analysis (DFA) and the use of models to assess and manage insurers' financial risk. For example, Holzmuller (2009) and Cummins and Phillips (2009) have criticized the US system's reliance on static formulas and its failure to make more extensive use of stochastic modeling and scenario testing.

If properly structured, a model-based approach to determining regulatory capital requirements for insurance companies has the potential for being superior to a formula-based approach. A model-based approach has the desirable attributes of compelling insurers to take a more forward-looking and comprehensive view of their financial risk and determining a regulatory capital amount that is better tailored to fit a particular insurer's specific needs and circumstances. Many insurers are already performing capital modeling and incorporating enterprise risk management (ERM) practices in their risk management activities. Hence, a model-based approach would seem most consistent with the regulatory goal of employing best practices to ensure that regulatory policies and standards are effective and efficient.[29]

That said, others have expressed concerns about relying on a model-based approach to determining insurers' capital requirements (Vaughan 2009). Specifically there are issues with respect to errors in input assumptions, over-reliance on model results, and deliberate manipulation of internal capital models to achieve favorable regulatory treatment. Further, there is the concern that regulators lack the resources and expertise to adequately evaluate the internal models used by insurance companies. Cummins and Phillips (2009) respond to these concerns by recommending that US insurers should be allowed to use internal models but that a standard model should also be run for every insurer and that an insurer should be permitted to hold capital less than that indicated by the standard model only if thoroughly justified by the insurer. This approach would be complemented by a 'model evaluation office' to assist regulators in reviewing and vetting internal models.

Under the SMI, the Capital Adequacy (E) Task Force is re-evaluating the RBC formulas, factors, and methodology, concentrating first on material existing or emerging risks and the method to combine risk charges (i.e., the covariance adjustment) and making other adjustments to reflect other SMI changes, such as statutory accounting (principles-based reserving) or reinsurance modifications. The Task Force has identified four priority areas for implementation:

- introduction of an explicit property-casualty catastrophe risk charge;
- identifying and applying defined statistical safety levels to relevant historical data where appropriate when considering new risk types or reviewing existing risk factors;

[29] Enterprise risk management refers to an integrated approach to risk management that considers all relevant risks that a firm faces and involves the development of a coordinated approach to managing these risks using various management tools including, but not limited to, insurance (Lam 2003).

- refinement to the invested asset risk charges in all three formulas and review of the impact of the asset valuation reserve on the calculation of the RBC ratios; and
- development of an explicit risk charge for operational risk.[30]

The NAIC has generally rejected the idea of using a model-based approach in favor of a formula-based approach in determining insurers' capital requirements as well as an economic capital requirement akin to the solvency capital requirement (SCR) under Solvency II (Vaughan 2009).[31] At present, the NAIC is only considering adding modeling to its formulas where it believes a formula-based approach is ineffective. The only specific area where this has been identified outside of existing modeling required for the life RBC formula is a catastrophe component for the property-casualty RBC formula. While some have suggested that the NAIC could develop and test a standard model as an alternative or adjunct to the current RBC formulas, it does not appear that US regulators are taking any steps in that direction (Cummins and Phillips 2009).

The NAIC rationale for adhering to a formula-based approach appears to be the potential problems with internal capital modeling discussed above. There may also be a certain amount of inertia involved in that US regulators have become comfortable with the basic framework of RBC and see no compelling reason to consider a paradigm shift to the kind of system that the EU is developing. Further, in working with state insurance departments, we observe that very few US state regulators are trained in the disciplines of economics, finance and quantitative methods in contrast with federal and European regulatory agencies, which could help explain US regulators' discomfort with DFA. It is also interesting to note that when US regulators are queried about the limitations of RBC they respond that it is only intended to set minimum regulatory capital levels for insurers and that they rely heavily on other regulatory tools to

---

30 Operational risk, as defined by the Basel Committee, is 'the risk of a change in value caused by the fact that actual losses, incurred for inadequate or failed internal processes, people and systems, or from external events (including legal risk), differ from expected losses' (Basel Committee 2001).

31 As explained further below, under Solvency II, insurers will be subject to both a minimum capital requirement (MCR) and a solvency capital requirement (SCR). The SCR is intended to represent the amount of economic or target capital that insurance needs to continue its operations. An insurer that falls below its SCR but exceeds its MCR *may* be subject to regulatory intervention. Regulatory action is required for insurers that fail to meet their MCR.

trigger timely action against high-risk or financially distressed insurers that exceed their RBC requirements.

The FIO has also criticized the formula-based approach employed by the states. In its 2013 report on how to modernize insurance regulation in the US, the FIO urged the state regulators to incorporate international best practices, standards and principles when revising their RBC methodology (FIO 2013). In addition, the FIO criticized the states for not applying the RBC standards uniformly. In its conclusion, the FIO noted that the lack of uniformity in prudential matters was 'felt acutely' and that 'federal involvement will be necessary' to address this lack of uniformity (FIO 2013).

Thus, the threat of increased federal involvement hangs over the heads of the state regulators if they fail adequately to address the problems with the current RBC standards and their application. The FIO, however, lacks the power to make good on this threat. Federally imposed entity level prudential standards for individual insurance companies can only come into existence by an act of Congress or by an international agreement negotiated by the US Treasury and the US Trade Representative's Office (USTR) and approved by Congress.[32]

2. Capital standards in the EU

The capital standards being developed under Solvency II in the EU under the oversight of the EIOPA have also received considerable attention. When the EU began working on a common set of capital standards, it was able to take advantage of the advances in risk analysis and modeling that have occurred since the NAIC initially developed its RBC standards

---

[32] The Federal Reserve may impose prudential standards on financial conglomerates that own insurance subsidiaries and for which the Federal Reserve provides supervision on a consolidated basis. These financial conglomerates include bank holding companies (BHCs), thrift holding companies (THCs), and financial holding companies (FHCs), certain BHCs that received TARP funds, and any nonbank financial company classified as a SIFI by FSOC. The vast majority of these entities supervised by the Federal Reserve are conglomerates that own a bank or a thrift and so are classified as BHCs, THCs, or FHCs. Thus, they would not be classified as nonbank financial companies under the Dodd-Frank Act. The Federal Reserve has supervised such banking conglomerates for years.

What is new under the Dodd-Frank Act is the Federal Reserve's ability to impose prudential standards on nonbank financial companies that do not own a bank or savings and loan. The Federal Reserve's ability to have a significant impact on prudential standards for companies that are predominantly involved in insurance will depend heavily on how many insurance conglomerates are classified as SIFIs by the FSOC. To date, the FSOC has taken a conservative approach regarding which nonbank financial companies that it will classify as SIFIs.

in the early 1990s. A primary goal of Solvency II is to develop and implement harmonized RBC standards across the EU. The intent is to take an ERM approach towards capital standards that will provide an integrated solvency framework that covers all significant risk categories and their interdependencies (Eling, Klein and Schmit 2009).

Based on the Solvency II directives that have been adopted to date, there will be two levels of regulatory capital requirements. The first level is the SCR, also known as 'target capital', that is intended to represent the economic capital an insurer needs to hold that will allow it meet its claims obligations within a prescribed safety level. The economic capital for a given insurer will be derived by using a value at risk (VaR) calibration at a 99.5 percent confidence level over a one-year time horizon.[33] The SCR will encompass all risk categories that are viewed as significant by regulators, including underwriting, market, credit, and operational risk as well as risk mitigation techniques employed by insurers (e.g., reinsurance and securitization).

The second level is the minimum capital requirement (MCR) which is the minimum amount of capital that an insurer would be required to hold and below which policyholders would be subject to an 'unacceptable' level of risk (in the view of regulators). The MCR would be calibrated at an 85 percent VaR confidence level and bounded between 25 and 45 percent of an insurer's SCR. An insurer that fails to meet its MCR would be subject to immediate regulatory intervention. An insurer that falls between its MCR and SCR may be subject to regulatory action based on regulators' determination of whether corrective steps are warranted.

EU regulators are considering the use of both standard and internal models, or some combination of both, to calculate the MCR and the SCR. In the standard model, the risk charges for each risk at the target safety level would be determined by one of two methods: the 'factor method' or the 'scenario method'. Under the factor method, the risk charge is calculated by applying a factor to an accounting value. Under the scenario method, the risk charge is determined by taking the difference between the insurer's net asset value, or 'NAV' (which is equivalent to capital and

---

[33] As explained by the European Commission, Value at Risk (VaR) is a commonly used measure in financial services to assess the risk associated with a portfolio of assets and liabilities. VaR answers the following question: how much money would be lost, if events develop in an adverse and unexpected way? More precisely, VaR measures the worst expected loss under normal conditions over a specific time interval at a given confidence level. For example, if VaR is measured over a one-year period at a confidence level of 99.5 percent then this corresponds to the worst loss one would expect to occur in a single year over the next two hundred years.

surplus in US statutory accounting terminology), as of the statement date and the insurer's NAV restated, as of the same statement date, based on a scenario affecting one or more risk elements. As delineated above in relation to determining the SCR, the standard model includes underwriting risk, market risk, credit default risk, and operational risk, based on aggregations of sub-risks, such as market interest rate risk and non-life underwriting catastrophe risk. With the exception of operational risk and non-life catastrophe risk, these are the same risk categories encompassed by RBC. Capital charges are determined using a bottom-up approach, where the capital required to meet the 99.5 percent VaR target is first calculated for each sub-risk, then aggregated to compute a total company SCR using a prescribed correlation matrix. The same approach would be used to calculate the MCR to meet the 85 percent VaR target bounded between 25 and 45 percent of the SCR.

The EU has been subjecting both standard models and internal models to a series of quantitative tests to assess their performance and potential impact on insurers (EIOPA 2011). These tests have revealed potential issues and flaws in these models as well as generated critical regulatory and industry comments. Also, as we noted earlier, capital models are subject to various problems, including but not limited to errors in input assumptions, design flaws, misuse and misinterpretation of model outcomes and deliberate manipulation of models to produce lower required capital levels. As a consequence, there have been adjustments to the technical specifications for determining insurers' capital requirements – a process which is taking longer to conclude than originally contemplated. The issues encountered in fleshing out the details of the EU's capital standards have contributed to the delay in the full implementation of Solvency II which has been extended to 2016. That said, we need to point out that the adjustments to the technical specifications for determining insurers' capital requirements will not address all the potential problems of internal capital models noted above.

At present, the EU approach in Solvency II reflects a fundamental philosophical difference to the US regarding the appropriate level of insurer insolvencies to permit. By using a 99.5 percent VaR confidence level for SCR, the EU is attempting to reduce the frequency of insurer insolvencies to a very low level. The safety levels embodied in US RBC are implicit and not explicit. Experts who have attempted to estimate these implicit safety levels have concluded that they vary by risk element and are lower than the SCR VaR confidence level.[34] Hence, it appears that the current US

[34] For example, an analysis by a working group of the Casualty Actuarial Society estimated that the risk charges for reserve and premium risk in the R4

RBC approach reflects a greater willingness to allow insurers to fail and to protect policyholders through payouts from the state guaranty funds. This could change, as the NAIC has sought the assistance of outside technical groups in calibrating US RBC which could result in higher uniform safety levels for each risk element in the RBC formulas.

These differences cannot be completely explained by differences in the concentration levels of the insurance markets within the US and Europe. On average, the five largest general insurance groups captured over 60 percent of the market share in the 15 largest European countries in 2006, an increase in concentration of almost 25 percent from 1993 (Association of British Insurers Research Department 2007). However, the US market is also relatively concentrated, albeit less so than in Europe. For example, the top 25 property-casualty insurers in the US tend to capture over 60 percent of the market share (Barrese, Lai, and Scordis 2007).

3. IAIS capital standards

IAIS capital standards are based not only on ICPs but on structure elements that illustrate the concepts on which the solvency regime is based. The structure elements provide that the capital requirements for an insurer must take into account not only the level of liabilities, including the risk margin for those liabilities, but also asset-liability mismatch risk, and volatility risks. For some countries, adopting the IAIS standards would result in substantial changes in their solvency regulations for insurance companies. Figure 8.8 gives an example of how the valuing of assets and liabilities under a traditional formula-based solvency approach, such as the US RBC system, would differ significantly from the market-consistent approach advocated by the IAIS, which is closer to Solvency II.

The IAIS's ComFrame initiative for internationally active insurance groups (IAIGs) began in 2010 and builds and expands on the solvency requirements developed in the ICPs (IAIS 2013a).[35] ComFrame attempts to address the unique problems posed by IAIGs. The complexity of the IAIG's operations and the cross-border nature of their activities require

---

and R5 components of the property-casualty RBC formula have been effectively calibrated to 87.5 percent VaR over the claim run-off period (reserves) and a 87.5 percent VaR for one year of new business (premium) (Casualty Actuarial Society 2012).

[35] ComFrame defines an IAIG as being comprised of at least one insurance legal entity that writes premiums in at least three jurisdictions with at least 10 percent of its gross premiums written outside its home jurisdiction and that has total assets of at least $50 billion or has gross written premiums of not less than $10 billion (IAIS 2012).

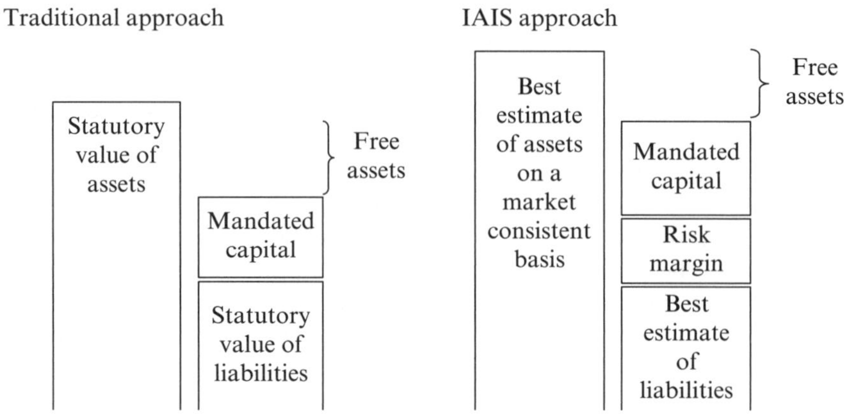

Figure 8.8 Traditional versus IAIS approach

insurance supervisors to engage in coordinated supervision. ComFrame has three main goals: 1) develop effective methods for group-wide supervision of IAIGs; 2) create a comprehensive framework to allow supervisors to address group-wide activities and risks; and 3) encourage global convergence of regulatory and supervisory standards and procedures (IAIS 2012).

In 2013, the IAIS decided to incorporate a risk-based global insurance capital standard (ICS) as part of ComFrame at the urging of the G-20's Financial Stability Board (FSB),[36] which wanted a 'quantitative capital standard' established for IAIGs (IAIS 2013b; FSB 2013a). The IAIS began to develop the ICS in early 2014 and is using field testing through 2018 to refine it. The IAIS has not yet disclosed exactly how it will determine the ICS, although it has indicated that it will be based on a risk-based total balance sheet approach. During field testing, the IAIS will examine three methods for the valuation basis for the balance sheet – two of which rely on the IAIG's own economic capital models and one of which relies on generally accepted accounting principles. IAIS members are not expected to begin implementing ComFrame, including the ICS, until 2019.

[36] The FSB is an international body comprised of the national financial supervisory authorities of 24 nations, six international organizations, and six international standard-setting bodies. According to its website, the FSB was designed to promote financial stability by developing and supporting 'effective regulatory, supervisory and other financial sector policies'. It was created on April 2, 2009 out of the Financial Stability Forum when both its membership and its mandate were expanded because of the perceived need in the wake of the financial crisis for a stronger international body to promote financial stability.

Some US insurance regulators and industry officials have questioned whether that time table is still feasible given the number of issues that need to be resolved. These issues regarding the ICS include, among others, whether it will be risk-based or outcome-based, whether it will allow for the use of internal models, how to calibrate the different regulatory standards imposed on IAIGs by different jurisdictions, whether the ICS will provide a regulatory floor or will add a new layer of regulation on top of the existing domestic regulations, how to ensure that the ICS is consistently applied especially given the differences in accounting standards worldwide, and what the costs for supervisors and firms will be to implement the ICS.

The IAIS is separately working with the FSB to develop additional capital requirements for global systemically important insurers (G-SIIs). G-SIIs are a subset of the IAIGs that would be classified as SIFIs because of the systemic risks that they may pose to the international financial system. On July 18, 2013, the FSB announced that nine insurers would be designated as G-SIIs: Allianz SE, AIG Inc. (AIG), Assicurazioni Generali S.p.A., Aviva plc, Axa S.A., MetLife Inc., Ping An Insurance (Group) Company of China Ltd., Prudential Financial Inc., and Prudential plc (FSB 2013a). In November 2014, the FSB decided to identify for 2014 the nine G-SIIs identified in 2013 and to postpone a decision on the G-SII status of reinsurers, pending further development of its methodology. The IAIS agreed to begin developing straightforward, basic capital requirements (BCRs) for G-SIIs in 2014 (IAIS 2013b).[37] The BCRs will form the basis for the higher loss absorbency (HLA) requirements that the G-SIIs will be required to meet.[38] These global efforts to deal with the solvency issues posed by IAIGs and the systemic issues posed by G-SIIs will transform national standards for prudential regulation and may force nations to converge towards an agreed upon set of best practices.

4. Optimal capital standards?

There are a range of opinions among insurance scholars as to the optimal approach to determining regulatory standards for insurance companies. At one end of this spectrum, there is the view that simple 'solvency ratios' (e.g., premiums to surplus, surplus to assets, etc.) are preferable and that more complex methods do not yield sufficiently greater benefits in terms

---

37 Basic capital requirements or BCRs are designed to provide a minimum, uniform group-wide standard for the capital adequacy of G-SIIs.

38 Higher loss absorbency or HLA requirements build on the BCRs and set the additional capital needs of G-SIIs in light of the risks that they pose to the financial system.

of achieving regulatory objectives that would justify the higher costs of such methods.[39] At the other end of this spectrum, researchers such as Cummins and Phillips (2009) and Holzmuller (2009) seem to favor the model-based approaches being developed or employed in the EU (Solvency II). In the middle of this spectrum, there is the view that simple capital models may be preferable to complex models for regulatory purposes (Grace, Leverty, Phillips and Shimpi 2015).

Given this lack of consensus among insurance scholars and the fact that no researcher has yet conducted a definitive cost-benefit analysis of alternative approaches to setting regulatory capital standards, we are not in a position to assert that any jurisdiction has adopted an approach that is clearly optimal. That said, we reiterate our opinion that a properly designed, model-based approach has the potential of being superior to a formula-based approach. Further, if insurers will be allowed to use internal models to determine their capital requirements, regulators must be able and willing to establish and enforce appropriate standards for their design and use if they are to achieve their regulatory objectives. Hence, in our view, the issue lies with how best to craft model-based regulatory capital standards that appropriately balance their benefits and costs. Further research to that end would have significant value in terms of the advice that insurance scholars might offer to regulators.

B. Corporate Governance

The recent financial crisis drove home the point that models and other quantitative techniques for evaluating risks have their limitations. As a result, both domestic and international regulators of insurance have sought to incorporate more qualitative assessments of risk. One area that they have targeted in this quest is corporate governance, an area that insurance regulators have traditionally viewed as reserved for corporate law, and that did not require additional regulations designed specifically for insurers.

1. Corporate governance under the SMI

The NAIC, as part of its SMI, views corporate governance as playing a part in maintaining the solvency of insurers. The NAIC developed the

---

[39] The benefits of any regulatory measure, including capital standards, would include (but not be limited to) reduced insolvency costs and increased confidence in the financial solidity of the industry. The costs of a given regulatory measure would include enforcement costs, compliance costs, and higher insurance premiums, among others.

US Insurance Financial Solvency Framework and its Core Principles. Principle #3 requires on-site risk-focused examinations, which include an evaluation of an insurer's corporate governance, with an emphasis on practices and procedures used by the insurer to identify and mitigate all significant risks. In the event of inadequate corporate governance safeguards, the regulator may take corrective measures.

As with most US solvency regulation, state regulators of insurers operating in multiple states are encouraged to defer to the regulator in the NAIC accredited domiciliary state who is referred to as the lead regulator. In addition, for insurance financial conglomerates, state regulators are advised to conduct one coordinated examination of the holding company and its subsidiaries.

The NAIC has also proposed a Corporate Governance Annual Filing Model Act that would require insurers to provide detailed reports on their corporate governance procedures to the relevant state regulator. The utility of this additional filing seems minimal, as the filings seem to be merely informational and do not appear to give the regulator the authority to take corrective actions if it deems the insurer's procedures to be inadequate.

The most important corporate governance initiative in the US, however, is the NAIC's recent adoption of an Own Risk and Solvency Assessment (ORSA). Originally conceived by EU regulators as a critical element of the qualitative measures envisioned under Pillar II of Solvency II, the ORSA is a document prepared and filed by an insurer that aims to provide regulators with a wealth of information about company risk profiles and risk management. The two primary goals of the ORSA are to 'foster an effective level of enterprise risk management at all insurers' and to 'provide a group-level perspective on risk and capital, as a supplement to the existing legal entity view' (NAIC 2011). If properly designed and prepared, ORSA reports will provide regulators with a valuable new tool in assessing the risks undertaken by insurers and how well they are managing those risks.

After extensive negotiations with the insurance industry, the NAIC developed an ORSA manual in November 2011 that provides guidelines to insurance companies on how their ORSA reports should be prepared (NAIC 2011). An insurer's ORSA report must assess the adequacy of its risk management and current, and likely, future solvency position, internally document the process and results, and provide a high-level summary report annually to its domiciliary regulator, if requested. The ORSA would contain three major sections: 1) a description of its risk management policy; 2) quantitative measurements of its risk exposure in normal and stressed environments; and 3) a prospective solvency assessment. The ORSA manual goes on to outline detailed requirements for each section. It will now be up to each state to enact implementing legislation to establish and enforce an ORSA requirement. What will be achieved with the ORSA will depend greatly on the quality of the information that will be provided by insurers and how regulators will use that information. The FIO has expressed reservations as to 'whether the state regulators possess sufficient resources with the prerequisite technical skills and experience' to properly review and evaluate the ORSA reports (FIO 2013).

2. Solvency II and corporate governance

As in the US, the Solvency II corporate governance principles are layered on top the existing national laws governing business associations and the duties of their shareholders, management, and employees. Most insurers were already following similar corporate governance principles and procedures before the enactment of Solvency II. Some, however, may have undergone some internal reorganization in order to get their structures to track the format required by Solvency II.

Solvency II envisions regulators taking a larger role in monitoring an insurer's corporate governance. Pillar II of Solvency II deals with Systems of Governance and focuses on four areas: 1) ORSAs and capital management; 2) risk management system; 3) policy processes and procedures; and 4) key functions (European Union 2009).[40] As in the US, of these, ORSAs are the most important.

Pillar II will require every insurer to conduct its ORSA. This includes a regular assessment of an insurer's solvency needs and how it is addressing those needs going forward. In such an assessment, an insurer would be expected to highlight areas where its assessment deviates significantly from its SCR assumptions. ORSA also requires insurers to implement an appropriate process for identifying and quantifying their risks. Insurers will further need to demonstrate that their assessments are integrated into their strategic decision-making process. As a result of this process, a regulator might require an insurer to hold more capital than its SCR.

Interestingly, it appears that the ORSA requirement that has been adopted by the NAIC will be less prescriptive than the ORSA requirement

---

[40] The risk management system is intended to detail a firm's objectives, risk management principles, risk appetite, and assignments for managing risk. The policy processes and procedures set forth the internal controls for the firm that focus on compliance with existing laws, evaluating the effectiveness of meeting the firm's objectives, and the availability and accuracy of financial and non-financial information. The key functions focus on the firm's operations in the areas of risk management, compliance, internal audits, actuarial functions, and outsourcing any services or processes to an outside provider.

that is being developed by the EU. Whether this will be an issue with the EU or the FIO is unclear. It is clear that US insurers were strongly opposed to the more prescriptive ORSA requirement that was initially proposed by the NAIC. US regulators may argue that the ORSA requirement that was adopted will have sufficient specificity to achieve its intended objectives. Ultimately, the adequacy of any ORSA requirement either in the US or the EU will need to be judged by its effectiveness in encouraging insurers to exercise good risk management and its ability to prompt timely and appropriate regulatory interventions against insurers that fail to do a good job in managing their financial risk.

3. IAIS and corporate governance

Both the Organisation for Economic Cooperation and Development (OECD) and the IAIS began to develop corporate governance principles in the late 1990s.[41] In 1999, the OECD developed a set of Principles of Corporate Governance that have influenced how both OECD and non-OECD nations view corporate governance (OECD 2004). These principles serve as one of the FSB's Twelve Key Standards for a Sound Financial System. These principles also form the basis of the corporate governance component of the World Bank and International Monetary Fund (IMF) Reports on the Observance of Standards and Codes. Six basic principles form the heart of the OECD Principles of Corporate Governance. A corporate governance framework should: 1) promote transparent and efficient markets, comply with the law, and delineate responsibilities among the government actors; 2) protect shareholders' rights; 3) treat shareholders equally; 4) recognize the rights of stakeholders and encourage cooperation between corporations and stakeholders; 5) disclose all significant matters regarding the corporation; and 6) provide strategic guidance for the firm and effective monitoring of management and the board of directors (OECD 2004).

In 2007, the OECD adopted a Methodology for Assessing the Implementation of the OECD Principles of Corporate Governance (OECD 2007). This Methodology provides concrete examples of the types of practices that a reviewer should consider as providing evidence of good corporate governance in connection with each principle and sub-principle. Nevertheless, the Methodology often notes that portions of the principles

---

[41] The OECD was founded in 1961 as the successor organization of the Organization for European Economic Cooperation that had been created to run the Marshall Plan to rebuild Europe after World War II. It now has 34 members who work together to develop policies that fight poverty and promote economic growth and stability.

cannot be directly monitored and may be difficult to enforce, such as whether board members act in accordance with their duties of care and loyalty. Even when a reviewer concludes that a principle has only been partially implemented or not implemented at all, the Methodology recommends that the reviewer only make a judgment about what actions to take after assessing the relative compliance with all of the principles and engaging in a cost-benefit analysis of the proposed measures to be taken.

The IAIS's ICP 7 focuses on corporate governance by encouraging regulators or supervisors to require insurers to adopt a corporate governance framework 'which provides for sound and prudent management and oversight of the insurer's business and adequately recognizes and protects the interests of policyholders' (IAIS 2011). The IAIS Guidance for ICP 7 provides few clear goal posts that supervisors should require insurers to meet. Paralleling the OECD Principles of Corporate Governance, it encourages insurers to create a business plan and clearly define the duties and powers of the board of directors and management. IAIS's ICP 7 reiterates the standard duties of good faith, care, and loyalty that directors in most developed countries are already legally required to fulfill. Finally, the IAIS's ICP 7 states that governmental regulators or supervisors should require insurers to 'demonstrate the adequacy and effectiveness of its corporate governance framework' as part of periodic examinations (IAIS 2011).

4. Assessment of corporate governance reforms

The corporate governance principles for insurers articulated by US regulations, Solvency II principles, OECD principles, or the IAIS's ICPs generally do not provide clear sign posts for when a principle has been met, and thus, give regulators broad discretion for determining whether an insurer is engaging in sound corporate governance practices. As a result, the insurance regulator is in a position akin to that of US Supreme Court Justice Potter Stewart, who could not define pornography but claimed that 'I know it when I see it'. The insurance regulator needs to be able to identify good corporate governance without being able to refer to clearly defined standards. Thus, the effectiveness of these regulations turns on the training and abilities of the regulators implementing them. Jurisdictions unable to attract competent regulators because of poor pay or working conditions or whose regulators lack the training or skills to properly evaluate corporate governance practices seem unlikely to be able to enhance the solvency of the insurers in their care by attempting to implement these principles.

C. Group Supervision

1. Group supervision in the US

In the past, US regulators generally did not engage in group-wide supervision but focused only on those legal entities actually engaged in the business of insurance. US regulators were authorized to take action if they determined that a company or group affiliated with an insurer was likely to negatively impact the insurer's financial condition and the insurer's ability to pay claims when due. In addition, insurers had to obtain approval from the relevant state insurance commissioner for any material related party transactions.

In 2010, the NAIC issued the US Insurance Financial Solvency Regulatory Monitoring Requirements and adopted the revised Insurance Holding Company System Regulatory Act and the Insurance Holding Company System Model Regulation with Reporting Forms and Instructions. Under the requirements set forth in these documents, regulators must review the financial condition of nationally significant insurers or groups every quarter and prioritize those performing badly for more detailed reviews by NAIC groups such as the NAIC Financial Analysis Working Group (FAWG), comprised of experienced financial regulators. Nationally significant insurers or groups are those whose operations pose major issues at the regional level or affect multiple states. The FAWG can report its findings to the lead regulator but it has no authority to intervene to address any problems that it finds. However, if a domiciliary regulator would otherwise be inclined to ignore the FAWG's recommendations with respect to a particular insurer, regulators in other states in which the insurer does business can pressure the domiciliary regulatory to comply with the FAWG's recommendations.[42] In addition, insurance groups must annually submit several new reports to their lead regulators, including an ORSA for the group, an Enterprise Risk Report, and a revised Insurance Holding Company System Annual Registration Statement.

A 2013 FSB peer review of US insurance regulation sharply criticized the state regulatory regime in the area of group supervision (FSB 2013b). The FSB report noted that the IMF's Financial Sector Assessment Program (FSAP)[43] on the US had found that the state-based regulatory

---

[42] The regulators in the other states can suspend or revoke the insurer's license to do business, which typically compels the domiciliary regulators to follow the FAWG's recommendations.

[43] The IMF created the FSAP in 1999 to conduct a comprehensive and in-depth analysis of a country's financial sector. At the end of such an assessment, a report with its findings is issued and this report is called the Financial System

system 'lacked a systemic focus and the capacity to exercise group-wide oversight' (FSB 2013b; IMF 2010). Since the FSAP, the FSB report noted that the NAIC had adopted the revised model holding company act and regulation but that only 15 states had enacted these new rules, which limited their effectiveness. In addition, the report commented on the lack of progress in the area of group capital requirements and supervision. It stated that 'state regulators only have direct supervisory powers in relation to regulated insurance entities and cannot apply consolidated capital requirements and supervision to insurance groups' (FSB 2013b). Much to the consternation of the NAIC and the state insurance commissioners, the FSB recommended that the US needed to 'promote greater regulatory uniformity in the insurance sector, including by conferring additional powers and resources at the federal level where necessary' (FSB 2013b).

Prior to the financial crisis in the US, group supervision on a consolidated basis for financial conglomerates offering a range of financial services existed at the federal level. Unfortunately, one federal agency was not responsible for regulating all financial conglomerates. Whether the Federal Reserve, the OTS, or the Securities and Exchange Commission (SEC) regulated a financial conglomerate depended primarily on what, if any, depository institution was a member of the financial conglomerate. For example, the OTS regulated AIG because AIG owned subsidiaries that were thrifts, but not banks. In addition, the Federal Reserve, the OTS, and the SEC subjected the financial conglomerates under their respective supervision to substantially different capital requirements.

The Dodd-Frank Act made several modifications to how financial conglomerates are regulated in the US. First, the Federal Reserve regulates all bank holding companies (BHCs), financial holding companies (FHCs), and thrift holding companies (THCs). Second, the Dodd-Frank Act prevents certain financial conglomerates from avoiding regulation by the Federal Reserve by reorganizing their group structure. The financial conglomerates in question must meet two requirements: 1) they were classified as either FHCs or BHCs and had more than $50 billion in total consolidated assets on January 1, 2010; and 2) they received bailout funds from the federal government under the Troubled Assets Relief Program (TARP) during the financial crisis. Such conglomerates cannot escape Federal Reserve supervision simply by spinning off or changing the charter of any banking subsidiary in an attempt to cease to be classified as a BHC or FHC.

Stability Assessment. The IMF uses these reports as part of its surveillance of the international economy.

Only 24 FHCs and BHCs had more than $50 billion in total assets on January 1, 2010 and accepted TARP funds (Brown 2011). All of the hundreds of other BHCs and FHCs could escape supervision by the Federal Reserve if they spun off their banking and thrift subsidiaries or converted them into industrial loan companies, which are state-chartered depository institutions that can act like banks but are not classified as banks. MetLife did just this by selling off its bank subsidiaries and obtaining the approval from the Federal Deposit Insurance Corporation and the Federal Reserve to deregister as a bank holding company (MetLife 2013).

Third, the Dodd-Frank Act created a new interagency body, the FSOC, to promote financial stability and allowed it to designate 'nonbank financial companies' that pose risks to the financial stability of the US as SIFIs and subject to supervision by the Federal Reserve.[44] Two-thirds of FSOC's ten voting members must approve this designation.[45] The Dodd-Frank Act defines a 'nonbank financial company' as a company that 'predominately engaged in financial activities' but was not classified as a BHC, THC, or a FHC. Under the Act, a firm will be deemed to be 'predominately engaged in financial activities' if 85 percent of its gross revenues on a consolidated basis or 85 percent of its total assets on a consolidated basis are derived from 'financial activities' as that term is defined in §4(k) of the Bank Holding Company Act. On June 3, 2013, the FSOC voted to designate AIG, Prudential Financial Inc., the second largest American life insurer, and GE Capital as SIFIs subject to supervision by the Federal Reserve. AIG was already subject to Federal Reserve supervision as a THC. On September 14, 2014, the FSOC designated MetLife Inc. as a SIFI subject to Federal Reserve supervision. MetLife filed a suit on January 13, 2015, in the US District Court for the District of Columbia challenging FSOC's decision to classify MetLife as a SIFI.

---

[44] Although the Dodd-Frank Act does not use the term 'systemically important financial institutions' or 'SIFIs' when referring to these firms, it embodies the same concept. As a result, the term 'SIFIs' is frequently used as a short-hand for the actual language in the statute.

[45] FSOC's ten voting members include the Treasury Secretary, the Chairman of the Federal Reserve Board of Governors, the Comptroller of the Currency, the Director of the Federal Deposit Insurance Corporation, the Securities and Exchange Commission Chairman, the Commodity Futures Trading Commission Chairman, Director of the Consumer Financial Protection Bureau, the Director of the Federal Housing Finance Agency, the Chairman of the NCUA, and an insurance expert appointed by the president. The FSOC has five non-voting members – the Director of the Federal Insurance Office (FIO), the Director of the Office of Financial Research, and three representatives from the state financial regulators with one of these representing each of the major sectors: banking, securities, and insurance.

Fourth, the Dodd-Frank Act contains an anti-evasion provision that permits two-thirds of the voting members of the FSOC to place under the supervision of the Federal Reserve any company that has organized itself in such a way as to fall outside of the definition of a nonbank financial company, provided that the 'material distress' of the company poses a threat to the financial stability of the US. Berkshire Hathaway, one of the ten largest financial conglomerates in the world, illustrates why the anti-evasion provision is needed.

Berkshire Hathaway is not a BHC, a FHC, or a THC because it does not own a bank or a thrift, and so is not supervised by the Federal Reserve. In 2009, almost 90 percent of its total revenues came from financial activities, predominantly its insurance subsidiaries (Berkshire Hathaway Inc. 2010). In 2010, Berkshire Hathaway acquired Burlington Northern Santa Fe Corporation, a railroad company (Berkshire Hathaway Inc. 2011). In the wake of that acquisition, only about 80 percent of Berkshire Hathaway's total revenues came from financial activities for the years 2010, 2011, and 2012 (Berkshire Hathaway Inc. 2011; Berkshire Hathaway Inc. 2012; Berkshire Hathaway Inc. 2013). Going forward, it is unlikely that Berkshire Hathaway's total revenues from financial activities or total assets from financial activities will exceed the 85 percent thresholds set forth in the Dodd-Frank Act. If the anti-evasion provision did not exist, any firm that did not want to be classified as a nonbank financial company could simply follow Berkshire Hathaway's approach and acquire enough non-financial subsidiaries so that its total revenues from financial activities or total assets from financial activities fell below the thresholds set forth in the Dodd-Frank Act. The FSOC reportedly is in the preliminary stages of determining whether to consider Berkshire Hathaway as a SIFI.

The requirement that two-thirds of the FSOC voting members approve designating a firm as a SIFI may prove highly problematic. The FSOC membership is made up of ten different agencies with different regulatory views and different constituencies. These agencies do not have the best history of working together and have at times engaged in significant turf wars over who should be responsible for regulating a new product or service. In addition, financial conglomerates that are well-connected politically may be able to capture enough of the voting members of the FSOC to delay or prevent the FSOC from designating them as SIFIs.

State regulators and industry representatives are more concerned about the FSOC being over-inclusive rather than under-inclusive when deciding who to classify as SIFIs. Their fears are based on the fact that FSOC's membership is very bank-centric with five of its ten voting members coming from agencies that regulate banks in some manner. Neither the FIO nor the representative from the state insurance commissioners has a vote in the FSOC.

In addition, the FSOC is likely to be heavily influenced by the FSB when making determinations about threats to the stability of the financial system. US insurers are concerned that the FSOC will seek to designate as SIFIs any firms that the FSB has designated as G-SIIs. Like that of any organization, the FSB's views are shaped by its membership. The FSB tends to be dominated by national banking supervisors, although the IAIS is also a member of the FSB. For example, the US representatives on the FSB are the Federal Reserve, the Treasury Department, and the SEC. Neither the FIO nor any state insurance commissioner directly participates in the FSB's deliberations.

State insurance commissioners and insurance industry officials have also voiced concerns about whether the Federal Reserve is well-suited to regulating large insurance groups as SIFIs, given its lack of experience regulating insurance companies. US insurers believe that the Federal Reserve applies more stringent solvency standards to the SIFIs that it supervises, which are more appropriate for banks than insurers. When MetLife was still a FHC, it failed the Federal Reserve's stress tests in March 2012. At that time, MetLife claimed that the tests were too strict for a conglomerate that was primarily an insurance provider and that it would have passed if insurance capital adequacy standards had been applied. On the other hand, the Federal Reserve may be better positioned to supervise large financial conglomerates with insurance subsidiaries than state insurance regulators who have little to no experience supervising financial conglomerates and lack the financial resources available to the Federal Reserve to hire the most qualified personnel.

2. Group supervision in the EU

The EU has four directives that play a role in the group supervision of insurers: the Insurance Groups Directive (EC/1998/78), the Financial Conglomerates Directive (EC/2002/87), the Solvency II Directive (EC/2009/138), and the Omnibus II Directive (EU/2014/51). The Insurance Groups Directive established new processes and procedures for regulating insurance undertakings within a group. Each entity within the insurance group must meet its own individual solvency requirements. In order to prevent the use of the same capital to support more than one insurance business, the Directive requires adjustments to the test applied to determine if the insurance entity has met its solvency margin obligations.[46] In addition, it provides for the supervision of intra-group transactions and the

---

46 The solvency margin is the amount by which assets of an insurer exceed its liabilities and regulators set minimum requirements for this. It is similar to the

methods to be used for determining the solvency of the holding company for the insurance group. The EU Financial Conglomerates Directive requires supervisors and financial groups to measure, on a consolidated basis, the prudential soundness of groups with significant business in the banking, securities, and insurance sectors and that are operating within the EU. It also requires non-EU financial conglomerates operating within the EU to have their home country supervisors provide a form of consolidated supervision that is equivalent to that provided by the EU Financial Conglomerates Directive or to be supervised on a consolidated basis by a financial supervisor within one of the EU member nations. The EU has recognized the Federal Reserve as providing supervision equivalent to that provided under the EU Financial Conglomerates Directive. Solvency II would require supervisors not only to monitor insurance groups on a consolidated basis but also to monitor risk concentrations, consider the risk management of all entities belonging to the group, and to select a single group supervisor.

The EU group supervision requirements differ significantly from the US requirements. US state insurance laws do not require insurance groups to meet group capital requirements or even to report group capital levels. Additionally, the new NAIC proposed rules for group supervision still do not require state regulators to evaluate the entity level risks posed by non-insurance firms within the group, while Solvency II requires supervisors to evaluate every member of an insurance group. Finally, only nationally significant insurers or groups subject to state supervision, or the large financial conglomerates subject to supervision by the Federal Reserve, must annually report on group-wide solvency, while Solvency II requires all financial firms to report on group-wide solvency. As noted above, the US and the EU are currently discussing what is necessary for a finding that the two regimes are 'equivalent'. The NAIC, FIO, EIOPA, and the European Commission created the EU–US Dialogue Project in January 2012 to try to find some common ground regarding insurance regulatory standards. These discussions are continuing even though the EU unilaterally resolved the issue (at least temporarily) by enacting the Omnibus II Directive in 2014, as noted in section III above. Under this Directive, the European Commission and EIOPA jointly can determine that the US state regimes are provisionally equivalent to the EU's Solvency II standards for a renewable period of ten years. The US states do not need to apply to the European Commission and EIOPA for such a determination to be issued.

---

concept of capital adequacy. The EU Insurance Group Directive, however, uses the term solvency margin, not capital adequacy.

3. Group supervision and the IAIS

For over a decade, the IAIS's ICP 23 has recommended that governmental supervisors engage in both legal entity and group-wide supervision. ICP 23 requires all 'relevant entities' to be included in the group-wide supervision (IAIS 2011). 'Relevant entities' include, but are not limited to: operating and non-operating holding companies, insurers, other regulated entities like banks or securities companies, non-regulated entities such as parent companies or subsidiaries substantially controlled or managed by entities within the group, and special purpose entities (IAIS 2011). The IAIS encourages regulators to utilize supervisory colleges to coordinate the supervision of financial groups or conglomerates among a variety of regulators. Finally, supervisors need to set up a system for reviewing and reporting on an insurance group's compliance with regulatory requirements. The reviews under this system include both on-site and off-site monitoring of the group.

As noted above, IAIS's ComFrame seeks to create a framework for the supervision of IAIGs. The group supervisor for an IAIG would be the supervisor in which the headquarters for the IAIG is located, where the IAIG's insurance operations are actually controlled, and where the supervisor has the legal authority to supervise the parent or holding company of the IAIG. The supervisors involved in regulating some portion of the IAIG's operations would determine which one of them should serve as the group supervisor.

The FIO has worked with the NAIC and the state regulators to develop a coordinated US policy for the standards to be adopted by ComFrame. Coordinating US policy towards ComFrame will not be easy as many state insurance commissioners and industry representatives view the current direction of ComFrame as one that will undermine the competitiveness of US insurers and impose unnecessary costs on consumers if it is implemented in the US (Festa with Postal 2013). NAIC officials and state insurance commissioners are also increasingly concerned that the FSB is having an undue influence on the ComFrame process and that the FSB's viewpoint is skewed towards bringing insurance regulatory standards, particular capital adequacy requirements, in line with those applied to banks, which they feel are inappropriate for insurance groups.

VI. SUMMARY AND CONCLUDING REMARKS

Whither solvency regulation? The IAIS and the EU have embraced an ERM approach to capital standards within an integrated solvency framework that welcomes the use of both standard and internal models. Having committed themselves to this course, it is unlikely that they will deviate from it. NAIC and state insurance regulators seem equally wedded to their RBC standards and probably will not budge significantly absent the threat of action by the federal government to impose uniform prudential standards on them. The Dodd-Frank Act gave the US Treasury and the USTR the authority to negotiate international agreements establishing prudential insurance standards. If the EU changes its mind and refuses to declare the US state regulatory system as at least provisionally equivalent (which seems highly unlikely), then the major US insurers that operate internationally will likely begin to lobby the federal government heavily to take action to correct this problem. In addition, international bodies like the FSB may increase their pressure on the federal government to create a national insurance regulator, particularly if they feel the states are not doing enough to address systemic risks.

More likely, the EU will classify the US system as provisionally equivalent without requiring any material changes on the part of the US regulators other than those already adopted or contemplated under the NAIC's SMI. If this occurs, as is likely, then two different solvency regimes will continue to operate in the EU and the US until the next financial crisis reveals the flaws in one or both systems.

As for the rest of the world, developed nations like Japan probably will move closer to adopting a system similar to Solvency II, while developing and emerging nations continue to use traditional fixed capital requirement systems or some form of RBC standards. Developing and emerging nations lack the economic resources and the personnel to administer a system like Solvency II. While these different solvency systems generally have not proven problematic when insurance was still mostly comprised of separate, national markets, it is unclear if it will continue to work as the insurance market becomes more global and interconnected with other financial services.

REFERENCES

Association of British Insurers Research Department, 2007. ABI Response to the European Commission Inquiry into the European Business Insurance Sector: Profitability and Concentration in the UK General Insurance Market (April 10, 2007).

Barrese, James, Gene Lai, and Nicos Scordis, 2007. 'Ownership Concentration and Governance in the U.S. Insurance Industry' 30 *Journal of Insurance Issues* 1–30.

Basel Committee on Banking Supervision (Basel Committee), 2001. Consultative Document: Operational Risk (January).

Berkshire Hathaway Inc., 2010. 2009 Annual Report. (Omaha, NE: Berkshire Hathaway Inc.)

Berkshire Hathaway Inc., 2011. 2010 Annual Report. (Omaha, NE: Berkshire Hathaway Inc.)

Berkshire Hathaway Inc., 2012. 2011 Annual Report. (Omaha, NE: Berkshire Hathaway Inc.)
Berkshire Hathaway Inc., 2013. 2012 Annual Report. (Omaha, NE: Berkshire Hathaway Inc.)
Bohn, James G., and Brian Hall, 1999. 'The Moral Hazard of Insuring the Insurers' in Kenneth A. Froot, ed., *The Financing of Catastrophe Risk* (Chicago, IL: University of Chicago Press).
Brown, Elizabeth F., 2011. 'The New Laws and Regulations for Financial Conglomerates: Will They Better Manage The Risks Than the Previous Ones?' 60 *American University Law Review* 1339–415.
Butsic, Robert P., 1993. 'Report on Covariance Method for Property-Casualty Risk-Based Capital' *Casualty Actuarial Society Forum*, Summer: 173–202.
Casualty Actuarial Society, 2012. Solvency II Standard Formula and NAIC Risk-Based Capital (RBC): Report 3 of the CAS Risk-Based Capital (RBC) Research Working Parties Issued by RBC Dependencies and Calibration Working Party (DCWP), Casualty Actuarial Society *E-Forum*, Fall 2012, Vol. 2, 1–37.
ChandraShekar, P., and S.R. Warrier, 2007. 'Risk-Based Capital Management: A "Principles Based Approach" to Insurer Solvency Management', Paper presented at the 2007 Asia Pacific Risk and Insurance Association Meeting, July 22–5.
Cummins, J. David, and Richard D. Phillips, 2009. 'Capital Adequacy and Insurance Risk Based Capital Systems' 28/1 *Journal of Insurance Regulation* 25–72.
Cummins, J. David and Mary A. Weiss, 2014. 'Systemic Risk in the Insurance Industry' in Georges Dionne, ed., *Handbook of Insurance* (2nd Edition) Berlin: Springer.
Cummins, J. David, Martin F. Grace, and Richard D. Phillips, 1999. 'Regulatory Solvency Prediction in Property-Liability Insurance: Risk-Based Capital, Audit Ratios, and Cash Flow Simulation' 66/3 *Journal of Risk and Insurance* 417–58.
Cummins, J. David, Scott E. Harrington, and Robert W. Klein, 1995. 'Insolvency Experience, Risk-Based Capital, and Prompt Corrective Action in Property-Liability Insurance' 19/4 *Journal of Banking and Finance* 511–27.
Eling, Martin, Robert W. Klein, and Joan T. Schmit, 2009. 'A Comparison of Insurance Regulation in the United States and the European Union' in Lars Powell, ed., *Insurance Choices: Competition and the Future of Property and Casualty Insurance Markets* (Oakland, CA: The Independent Institute).
European Commission, 2008. Amended Proposal for a Directive of the European Parliament and of the Council on the Taking-up and Pursuit of Business of Insurance and Reinsurance (Solvency II), COM(2008) 119 final (February 26).
European Insurance and Occupational Pensions Authority (EIOPA), 2011. EIOPA Report on the fifth Quantitative Impact Study (QIS5) for Solvency II, EIOPA-TFQISS-11/001.
European Union, 2009. Directive 2009/138/EC of the European Parliament and of the Council of 25 November 2009 on the Taking-up and Pursuit of the Business of Insurance and Reinsurance (Solvency II), published in Official Journal of the European Union L335, 1 (December 17, 2009).
European Union, 2014. Directive 2014/51/EC of the European Parliament and of the Council of the European Union of 16 April 2014, published in Official Journal of the European Union L151, 1 (May 22, 2014).
Federal Insurance Office (FIO), 2013. How to Modernize and Improve the System of Insurance Regulation in the United States, Washington, DC: US Department of the Treasury.
Festa, Elizabeth, with Dave Postal, 2013. 'Neugebauer to FIO: I'm Concerned About IAIS Proposals' LifeHealthPro (March 26, 2013).
Financial Stability Board (FSB), 2013a. Global Systemically Important Insurers (G-SIIs) and the Policy Measures That Will Apply to Them (July 18).
Financial Stability Board (FSB), 2013b. Peer Review of the United States (August 27).
Grace, Martin F., 2010. 'The Insurance Industry and Systemic Risk: Evidence and Discussion' Networks Financial Institute Policy Brief 2010-PB-02, April.

Grace, Martin F., Scott E. Harrington, and Robert W. Klein, 1998a. 'Risk-Based Capital and Solvency Screening in Property-Liability Insurance,' 65/2 *Journal of Risk and Insurance* 213–243.

Grace, Martin F., Scott E. Harrington, and Robert W. Klein, 1998b. 'Identifying Troubled Life Insurers: An Analysis of the NAIC FAST System,' 16 *Journal of Insurance Regulation*: 249–290.

Grace, Martin F., Robert W. Klein, and Richard D. Phillips, 2003. 'Insurance Company Insolvencies: Why Do They Cost So Much?,' available at http://papers.ssrn.com/sol3/papers.cfm?abstract_id=463103.

Grace, Martin F., J. Tyler Leverty, Richard D. Phillips, and Prakash Shimpi, 2015. 'The Value of Investing in Enterprise Risk Management' (forthcoming in the *Journal of Risk and Insurance*).

Grey, Alistair, 2013. 'Insurers Relieved Over Solvency II Deal' *Financial Times* (November 14).

Holzmuller, Ines, 2009. 'The United States RBC Standards, Solvency II and the Swiss Solvency Test: A Comparative Assessment' 34 *Geneva Papers on Risk and Insurance – Issues and Practice* 56–77.

International Association of Insurance Supervisors (IAIS), 2005. A New Framework for Insurance Supervision: Towards a Common Structure and Common Standards for the Assessment of Insurer Insolvency (October).

International Association of Insurance Supervisors (IAIS), 2007. The IAIS Common Structure for the Assessment of Insurer Solvency (February).

International Association of Insurance Supervisors (IAIS), 2011. Insurance Core Principles, Standards, Guidance, and Assessment Methodology (October 1).

International Association of Insurance Supervisors (IAIS), 2012. Draft Common Framework of Internationally Active Insurance Groups (July 2).

International Association of Insurance Supervisors (IAIS), 2013a. Common Framework of Internationally Active Insurance Groups for Consultation (October 17).

International Association of Insurance Supervisors (IAIS), 2013b. Press Release, Public Consultation Begins on 2013 Draft ComFrame; IAIS Adopts Coordinated Implementation Framework and First Self-Assessment and Peer Review Report (October 17).

International Monetary Fund (IMF), 2010. United States: Publication of Financial Sector Assessment Program Documentation – Financial System Stability Assessment (July).

Jaffee, Dwight M., and Thomas Russell, 1998. 'The Causes and Consequences of Rate Regulation in the Auto Insurance Industry' in David Bradford, ed., *The Economics of Property-Casualty Insurance* (Cambridge, MA: National Bureau of Economic Research).

Klein, Robert W., 1995. 'Insurance Regulation in Transition' 62/3 *Journal of Risk and Insurance* 363–404.

Klein, Robert W., 2012. 'Principles for Insurance Regulation: An Evaluation of Current Practices and Potential Reforms' 37/1 *Geneva Papers on Risk and Insurance – Issues and Practice* 175–199.

Klein, Robert W., 2013. 'The Modernization of Insurance Solvency Regulation in the United States: An Economist's Perspective' 1 *Journal of Applied Risk Management and Insurance* 15–65.

Klein, Robert W., and Shaun Wang, 2007. 'Catastrophe Risk Financing in the United States and the European Union: A Comparison of Alternative Regulatory Approaches' paper presented at the SCOR-JRI Conference on Insurance, Reinsurance, And Capital Market Transformations, Paris, September.

Lam, James, 2003. *Enterprise Risk Management: From Incentives to Controls*, Hoboken, NJ: Wiley.

Meier, Kenneth J., 1985. *Regulation: Politics, Bureaucracy and Economics* (New York, NY: St. Martin's Press).

Meier, Kenneth J., 1988. *The Political Economy of Regulation: The Case of Insurance* (Albany, NY: SUNY Press).
Meier, Kenneth J., 1991. 'The Politics of Insurance Regulation' 58/4 *Journal of Risk and Insurance* 701–13.
MetLife, 2013. Press Release, MetLife Sheds Bank Holding Company Status with Approvals from the Federal Reserve and FDIC (February 14).
Munch, Patricia, and Dennis E. Smallwood, 1980. 'Solvency Regulation in the Property-Liability Insurance Industry: Empirical Evidence' 11 *Bell Journal of Economics* 261–79.
National Association of Insurance Commissioners (NAIC), 2011. NAIC Own Risk and Solvency Assessment (ORSA) Guidance Manual, November 11 (Kansas City, MO).
National Association of Insurance Commissioners (NAIC), 2012. Solvency Modernization Initiative Roadmap (Washington, DC).
Organisation for Economic Cooperation and Development (OECD), 2004. Principles of Corporate Governance. Paris, France.
Organisation for Economic Cooperation and Development (OECD), 2007. Methodology for Assessing the Implementation of the OECD Principles of Corporate Governance. Paris, France.
Peltzman, Sam, 1976. 'Toward a More General Theory of Regulation' 19 *Journal of Law and Economics*, 211–40.
Pottier, Stephen, and David Sommer, 2002. 'The Effectiveness of Public and Private Sector Summary Risk Measures in Predicting Insurer Insolvencies' 21/1 *Journal of Financial Services Research* 101–16.
Roe, Mark J., 1993. 'Foundations of Corporate Finance: The 1906 Pacification of the Insurance Industry' 93 *Columbia Law Review* 639.
Saunders, Anthony, and Marcia M. Cornett, 2003. *Financial Institutions Management: A Risk Management Approach* (Boston, MA: McGraw-Hill).
Scherer, Frederic M., and David S. Ross, 1990. *Industrial Market Structure and Economic Performance* (Boston, MA: Houghton-Mifflin).
Schwarcz, Daniel, and Steven L. Schwarcz, 2014. 'Regulating Systemic Risk in Insurance' Minnesota Legal Studies Research Paper No. 14-18. Available at http://ssrn.com/abstract=2404492.
Skipper, Harold D., and Robert W. Klein, 2000. 'Insurance Regulation in the Public Interest: The Path Towards Solvent, Competitive Markets' 25 *The Geneva Papers on Risk and Insurance – Issues and Practice* 482–504.
Spulber, Daniel F., 1989. *Regulation and Markets* (Boston, MA: MIT Press).
Stigler, George J., 1971. 'The Theory of Economic Regulation' 2 *Bell Journal of Economics and Management Science* 3–21.
Swiss Re, 2013. 'World Insurance in 2012: Progressing on the Long and Winding Road to Recovery' *Sigma* 3/2013.
Vaughan, Therese M., 2009. The Implications of Solvency II for U.S. Insurance Regulation', Networks Financial Institute Policy Brief PB-2009-03, February.
Viscusi, W. Kip, Joseph E. Harrington, and John M. Vernon, 2000. *Economics of Regulation and Antitrust* (3rd edition) (Boston, MA: MIT Press).
Wang, Shaun, Gang Ma, Eric R. Ulm, Xiangjing Wei, and George Zanjani, 2009. The Financial Crisis and Lessons for Insurers, Society of Actuaries. Available at https://www.soa.org/Research/Research-Projects/Finance-Investment/research-fin-crisis.aspx.

9. Classification risk and its regulation

Kenneth S. Abraham and Pierre-André Chiappori[1]

INTRODUCTION

In *McGann* v. *H&H Music Company* (McGann),[2] a man with group health insurance provided through his employer contracted AIDS. At the expiration of the policy period, his employer changed the terms of coverage, which previously had provided lifetime coverage of $1 million, by limiting lifetime coverage of AIDS-related claims to a maximum of $5,000. McGann sued for 'discrimination' under the Employment Retirement Income Security Act of 1974 (ERISA, § 510).[3] The court held that there had been no discrimination in the sense prohibited under ERISA, because the new lifetime maximum applied to all employees, not just to McGann himself. ERISA, said the court, does not regulate the actual terms of employee benefits, only the manner in which those terms are administered and applied.

It seems likely that, whatever personal attitudes the employer had toward AIDS, it had understandable economic reasons for making the change. The employer probably was providing health insurance to a comparatively small group of employees. After one of them incurred the need for expensive treatment, the employer's premiums would likely have increased steeply when the policy period (and therefore the insurance contract) expired, if the employer continued to provide the same coverage. So new, more limited coverage was negotiated in order to keep overall premiums manageable.

The general lesson of the case, therefore, is that if an employer wishes to limit coverage for AIDS-related treatment, or kidney dialysis, or acupuncture, or any other condition or disease, because the employer has a limited amount of money available to pay for health insurance, nothing in ERISA

---

1 We are indebted to Sarah Krutov, Ethan Post, Daniel Schwarcz, Peter Siegelman, Maxine Verne and participants to the 'Law and Economics of Insurance' conference for helpful comments.

2 *McGann* v. *H&H Music Company*, 946 F. 2d 401 (5th Cir. 1991).

3 ERISA, 42 U.S.C.

prohibits the employer from doing so. The employee, not the employer or the insurer, bears the risk that his or her health status will change and that, as a result, the terms and/or price of coverage under future policies will also change. To some extent this will change after the Affordable Care Act (ACA)[4] takes full effect – a point that will be discussed below.

John McGann's case involved the application of a particular federal statute, to a particular situation, under a particular form of insurance. But McGann's case is emblematic of a more general problem that arises in insurance. Any party not only faces the risk of suffering loss, but also the risk of being classified as at high risk of suffering a loss. Because insurance is a risk-transfer and risk-diversification mechanism, both the risks of suffering a loss and the risk of being classified by an insurer as a high risk – what we call 'classification risk' – are potentially subject to insurance. For reasons we will discuss, however, insuring classification risk – as well as regulating or even mandating the insurance of classification risk – poses specific challenges, both because of its potentially serious impact on welfare and because of the difficulties and complexities it generates. Indeed, as we will show below, the ACA's prohibitions on almost all medical underwriting and its guaranteed renewal requirement, both of which address classification risk, are important examples of both the Act's potential to increase welfare and to generate such difficulties and complexities.

These difficulties and complexities arise largely in, and because of the typical operation of, private insurance markets. Public systems of insurance, such as governmentally provided insurance on the model of certain European health insurance schemes, pose different issues. We therefore set aside the issue of classification risk as it may or may not arise in public schemes. Our subject in this chapter is classification risk in private insurance and the issues associated with regulation of that risk.

1. RISK CLASSIFICATION IN A STATIC CONTEXT: BASIC CONCEPTS

Diversification, Differentiation, and Discrimination

We begin with three basic concepts. *Diversification* refers to a statistical fact: the aggregation of a large number of small, similar risks results in a

[4] Affordable Care Act, the 'Patient Protection and Affordable Care Act,' 124 Stat. 119.

portfolio that, on a per dollar basis, is less risky than any of the individual risks covered. For instance, if the individual risks are independent and have the same variance, then the variance (per dollar covered) of the diversified portfolio is inversely proportional to the number of individual risks. In practice, individual risks are often correlated, which decreases the speed at which the per dollar variance shrinks. Still, as long as correlation is not perfect, diversification does reduce risk.

Therefore, when it comes to covering the irreducible risk of the occurrence of individual accidents over a large population, insurers are comparatively efficient risk bearers, because they are in a position to diversify risk. In practice, this means that risk is spread among all policyholders (in mutual insurance companies), plus possibly shareholders and financial markets (in stock companies). The more nearly this occurs, the more efficient is the result. Specifically, the 'mutualization principle' states that under efficient risk sharing, the welfare of any agent should only depend on aggregate factors affecting the risk sharing group, not on the agent's idiosyncratic or discrete shocks.

This principle, however, leaves open another question, namely: what price should an individual pay to obtain insurance that includes coverage of classification risk? Indeed, the need to spread the risk over a large population does not per se imply that, when purchasing an insurance contract, different individuals should pay the same premium. '*Ex ante*' – when the contract is purchased – several pricing policies are compatible with efficiency. In particular, insurance companies typically differentiate the pricing (and often even the design) of their contracts to adapt them to the specific, *ex ante* level of risk of each insured. Economists classically distinguish the notions of 'price *differentiation*' and 'price *discrimination*': the former relates to situations in which different goods or services are sold at different prices, while the latter refers to the fact that the *same* good can be sold at different prices to different people in order to exploit discrepancies in preferences (or in marginal willingness to pay). In the case of insurance, the 'commodities' sold consist of protection against a given risk, defined by a specific probability distribution; in particular, from an economist's perspective, contracts sold to individuals with different risks are different commodities, even if the losses covered are the same (for instance, an automobile insurance contract sold to a young driver or to an experienced one are viewed as two different goods). As a consequence, charging different prices to parties posing different risks is price differentiation (differences in prices reflect differences in commodities sold), whereas charging different prices to parties posing identical risks but different price elasticities is price discrimination.

Insurance law draws a related but different set of distinctions. Many states have enacted statutes that prohibit 'unfairly discriminatory' insurance premiums (Abraham 2010: 119). The general understanding of these provisions is that they usually permit what we are calling 'price differentiation' when based on actuarially supported distinctions among classes of policyholders, but may prohibit even actuarially supported distinctions – for example, based on race or gender – when they have undesirable effects or connotations. We are not aware of any situations in which an insurer or organization of insurers has proposed rates that explicitly reflect what we have just called 'price discrimination' – changes in premiums or rates based on preferences or marginal willingness to pay. We think that any such explicit or direct price discrimination would probably be legally impermissible on the ground that it was 'unfairly discriminatory' under the statutes referred to above. This does not mean that insurers do not attempt to price discriminate indirectly or informally to the extent that this is feasible. Since in this chapter our focus is mainly on price differentiation rather than price discrimination, however, this possibility does not occupy us further.

Competition Generates Differentiation

In insurance, competition among insurers tends to generate a high degree of price differentiation. Competition inevitably produces risk classification among insurers as a result of a process that is sometimes called 'cream-skimming'. The idea can be seen in a simple example. Assume that individuals belong to two distinguishable classes, say green and red, which pose different risks (say, red individuals are riskier), but company A charges the same premium to both. Then A makes more profit on green applicants than on reds (it may even lose money on reds); de facto, there exists a cross subsidy between the two contracts, whereby green individuals are relatively 'taxed' while reds are subsidized. But then a competitor, say company B, could target ('cream-skim') green applicants by offering a lower premium to them and a higher premium to the reds; note that the lower premium is feasible because B, unlike A, does not subsidize red applicants. If green people move to B, then A's profit declines (it is left with the higher risk red individuals), and A may have to increase its premium. In the end, green and red insureds will pay different premiums.

There is evidence of such effects in the literature, not only in the extreme (e.g. Harvard's health insurance plans, see Cutler and Reber 1998) but also in the routine, common form. More than a negligible portion of drivers are unable to purchase auto liability insurance in the private market because they are regarded as posing an excessively high risk of loss in light of the maximum premiums regulators permit auto insurers charge. An auto insurer that covered such drivers at artificially 'low' rates would have to compensate the expected losses by overcharging safer drivers, thus finding itself subject to the skimming phenomenon. To enable these individuals to obtain insurance, states have found it necessary either to create residual markets, by establishing and requiring insurer participation in assigned risk pools and joint underwriting associations, or to move from regulating rates to open competition (Abraham 2010: 770–3).

Clearly, there are practical limitations to the cream-skimming mechanism. One is that classification is not costless (Abraham 1986: 67–8). For example, it is costly to acquire risk related information, and may be costly to identify which risk classes policyholders occupy, depending on what distinguishes classes. Therefore, classification occurs only up to the point of optimality. Second, demand may not be perfectly elastic (see Pauly et al. 2003); small differences in prices are unlikely to generate massive customer movements (the viscosity being due to so-called 'switching costs'). Insurers actually invest in reducing their customers' price elasticities (by building up 'customer loyalty', constructing a strong brand for which parties are willing to overpay, differentiating the service offered, developing a network of local agents and brokers, etc.). For these reasons, insurance is typically a long-term relationship. Competition therefore results in subsidizing new customers and overcharging existing ones (this is quite obvious in automobile insurance, where young drivers – especially males – are typically subsidized). Lastly, the practical importance of these effects depends on the form taken by competition. For instance, the growth of the internet (and the development of 'direct' insurers) has to some extent changed pricing policies.

Still, it remains the case that a large degree of classification and price differentiation is the unavoidable consequence of competition.

Classification Risk: The Risk of Being Classified as a High Risk (and Priced Accordingly)

As we stated in the Introduction, in insurance the insured party not only faces the risk of suffering loss, but also the risk of being classified as at high risk of suffering a loss. From a theoretical perspective, one can always decompose a risk into a classification risk and a risk of loss occurrence conditional on classification. While the latter can in general be covered efficiently by a competitive insurance market, covering the former is often more problematic.

Take, for instance, the risk of developing a genetic disease. This can be decomposed into (1) the risk of carrying the gene, and (2) the conditional risk of developing the disease, given the genetic context. In monogenic diseases (e.g. Huntington's Disease), the conditional risk of disease given the absence of the gene is nil; conversely, the conditional risk given the presence of the gene is basically one, although in practice much uncertainty remains regarding the precise date of occurrence. In other words, most of the Huntington's risk is in fact a classification risk. No one not carrying the gene would buy insurance against Huntington's; for those carrying the gene, on the other hand, insurance is likely to be extremely expensive.

Obviously, this is an extreme example; most of the time, genes simply indicate a predisposition that changes (sometimes marginally) the likelihood of developing the disease. In all cases, however, the distinction between classification risk and conditional occurrence risk remains valid – although their respective importance may vary. Note also that the distinction applies to all types of tests (not only genetic – HIV being an obvious example), and more generally to pre-existing conditions, which we define broadly to include not only the health conditions to which the term normally refers, but also to any factor or characteristic that bears on the level of risk posed by a prospective purchaser of insurance.[5] The crucial issue here is that what we call the classification risk is realized *before* the issuance of the insurance contract. From the insurer's viewpoint, therefore, it is one of the risk relevant characteristics on which the underwriting process – and therefore the premium charged in a competitive context – will depend.

The foregoing analysis yields the conclusion that, in a competitive market, coverage of classification risk will be hard to obtain. If, at the beginning of the contractual relationship, different people pose different levels of risk (due to their genes, their pre-existing conditions, or any other factor), an unregulated, competitive insurance market will tend to price according to this individualized risk – which simply means that the classification risk will not be covered. In particular, whenever most of the risk corresponds to classification, the very possibility of insurance will be severely limited.

---

[5] Note also that the classification risk is almost always a *financial* risk. The problem is not in the party's inability to purchase insurance against the conditional occurrence risk, but rather the price at which this coverage would be purchased. Of course, the distinction is sometimes blurred: if the cost of purchasing insurance against a risk is close to the total cost of the risk itself (as would be the case with some monogenic diseases, for instance), it is de facto not much different from a pure inability to insure.

Moral Hazard

A caveat that should be added is that, in some cases, imposing (part of) the classification risk on agents may be welfare improving. This is typically the case under *moral hazard*. This is a situation in which the classification risk is (at least partly) *endogenous*, in the sense that it is affected by the insured party's conduct. For instance, smokers are typically charged more when purchasing life or health insurance. Since smoking status predates the contract, it is a classification risk. However, smoking is a person's decision; if bearing the additional classification risk provides sufficient incentive for the applicant to stop smoking, the applicant's risk is decreased and welfare is improved. In a similar way, and barring specific regulations, homeowners insurance is typically more expensive for houses located in a flood plain; but this location has been chosen by the owner.

In such situations, the risk ultimately depends on the *incentives* parties face. The curse of insurance is that its mere existence tends to favor an increase in the endogenous risk: by protecting an insured against the adverse consequences of her decisions, insurance weakens her incentives to reduce risk. Conversely, any mechanism allowing the risk to be taken into account in the agent's decision is likely to restore risk-reduction incentives, and ultimately result in a global reduction of the actual risk – which may be beneficial to all, including the party herself. Thus, if the social cost (in terms of higher expected losses) of building in a flood-prone location is reflected in the price of the home insurance coverage, then homeowners will have more incentives to consider the risk when choosing where to build.

Another way of restoring incentives is to leave some of the *ex post* risk to be borne by the insured. The literature has long discussed the ways in which partial insurance can be welfare enhancing through such devices as deductibles, coinsurance, coverage exclusions directed at the most egregious forms of moral hazard such as intentional wrongdoing, and the establishment of monetary ceilings on the amount of insurance provided to policyholders.[6] The general conclusion, here, is that whenever individuals have some control of the (classification) risk, the optimal insurance design must also consider the incentives generated; in many cases, full coverage of the risk at a uniform price, by biasing incentives toward excessive risk taking, may be welfare decreasing. Clearly, these concepts are equally applicable to any insurance against classification risk, to the extent that individuals can control them (at least to some degree).

---

[6] The reader is referred to the *Handbook of Insurance* (Dionne 2014) for detailed presentation.

2. CLASSIFICATION AND RECLASSIFICATION IN A DYNAMIC CONTEXT

The Hirschleifer Effect

Classification risk is defined as the part of a risk that is realized *ex ante*, i.e. *before* the contract was issued, whereas the conditional occurrence risk materializes afterwards. This timing is precisely what creates the problem. A risk that is realized before an insurance contract can be issued (or, more generally, before a risk sharing agreement can be implemented) cannot be covered by that agreement, at least not in a competitive context; in a sense, it is no longer a risk, but a certainty, and insurance markets cannot handle certainties. A somewhat paradoxical consequence of this point is that, in some cases, the mere availability of relevant information, by transforming a risk into a certainty, can be welfare decreasing, a point made by Hirschleifer (1971) in an influential paper. Consider a world in which *ex ante* identical individuals are faced with a risk. Assume, now, that some technological change takes place that improves the quality of predictions regarding the risk; for instance, a genetic test is developed that allows computing individual-specific probabilities of a loss occurring. This creates a classification risk, since *ex ante* identical individuals, who used to purchase the same insurance contract at the same price, may now be classified in different categories (and charged different premiums). If this classification risk cannot be covered, the new technology ultimately reduces risk sharing possibilities in the economy, which decreases overall welfare.

In order to protect oneself against this risk, a natural inclination would be to purchase insurance against the classification risk itself; that is, to acquire, *before* the test is performed, insurance against a negative outcome of the test – which would in that case compensate the insured for the additional costs (higher premium, etc.) stemming from this outcome. In general, however, such insurance contracts are not feasible, for reasons that will be discussed below. To the extent that this is the case, comparing welfare before and after the technological innovation, the development of the test unambiguously decreased well-being, because it destroyed the possibility of insurance against the classification risk – whereas such an insurance was initially (and implicitly) provided by the absence of price differentiation. Before the innovation, all parties were covered by the same contract; after it, different people are offered different contracts, and the risk of being charged a very high premium cannot be covered.

This is only the extreme case. Obviously, in many cases an effective test has benefits that exceed by far its insurance costs. Hemochromatosis (iron overload disease) is the most common genetic disease among Western populations (one person in ten carries the gene, which is recessive, and one in 400 develops the disease). Undiagnosed, the disease results in severe lesions of several organs, in particular the liver, and may provoke such pathologies as cirrhosis and liver cancer. However, following a positive test, a simple treatment is available, that basically eliminates these consequences. Obviously, the test is highly beneficial, since the information it provides enables the patient to suppress the risk; this benefit obviously exceeds any insurance costs. While not all examples are that rosy, one can think of multiple situations in which the information can be used in prevention. A person at risk for breast cancer can opt for a mastectomy, just as a person at risk for lung cancer may decide to stop smoking. In all these cases, the new technology leads to a decrease in the underlying risk that probably compensates (and beyond) any downside effect.

Even in the extreme situation where neither treatment nor prevention exists (Huntington's being a good example), knowledge of the actual risk may impact many important decisions regarding fertility, education, savings, living habits, etc. For instance, a recent study (Stoler 2004) compared individuals who (1) were at risk for Huntington's (one parent had developed the disease), (2) took the genetic test, and (3) had opposite outcomes. It shows that individuals who found they carried the gene were less likely to go to college or to have children, and actually more likely to smoke. In principle, the ability to make better informed decisions of this type constitutes a gain that should be taken into account – although a precise valuation is quite difficult. In that sense, a test always has some benefits. Still, Hirschleifer's contribution is to point out that more information may also entail a cost (in terms of loss of coverage against the classification risk) that should not be ignored.

Intrinsic Classification versus Reclassification

The analysis of classification risks in a dynamic context raises two types of issues. One relates to risks that, because of their very nature, are *intrinsically* classification risks – i.e., will always predate the insurance contract. Genetic predispositions belong to this category, since they are realized at (actually before) birth, even if they are not necessarily discoverable for practical purposes at that time. Note that even a contract signed before birth (say, by the parents) will only partially alleviate that risk, because parents themselves may carry a genetic risk that may be transmitted to the child. No insurer will cover the unborn child of a Huntington's patient against the risk of carrying the Huntington's gene, at least not at a reasonable cost.

The second issue concerns what we call the reclassification risk. This is the risk that a party who already has insurance will be reclassified because of newly developed or newly discovered information bearing on the level of risk the party poses. If I have a serious health problem today (say, a bypass surgery), the costs for me are twofold. One is the current cost of the surgery; this is an occurrence risk, and as such can (and typically will) be covered. The second cost – the reclassification risk – stems from the fact that the occurrence of this health problem changes my classification. Once the risk has realized, it drastically increases the probability of future problems of the same type. De facto, I have become a high-risk person, which will affect my future access to insurance (I may be charged higher premiums, or even be denied coverage altogether). In the case of John McGann, his reclassification risk materialized when he contracted AIDS.

Intrinsic Classification Risks

The first aspect – the 'intrinsic' classification risk – raises obvious ethical issues. Charging a higher premium to a party who poses a higher risk because of genetic predispositions makes perfect sense from an economic perspective; in fact, as we argued earlier, this is the natural outcome of a competitive insurance market, at least in the absence of regulation. At the same time, it may be perceived as deeply unfair. An interesting way of thinking about this issue is to invoke the Rawlsian notion of a 'veil of ignorance' (Rawls 1971: 136–42). Assume we decide the structure of society – and in particular the laws governing risk classification – behind the veil, i.e. before knowing which role we will play (or which genes we will be endowed with). Then a standard axiom of efficient risk sharing requires full coverage of these risks, at a price which corresponds to the average prevalence over the risk sharing group.

Exactly which classification risks to consider intrinsic is not always a purely economic question. Genetic predispositions and other characteristics subject to what Rawls calls the 'natural lottery' are certainly intrinsic, in the sense that they are fixed wholly by factors outside any party's control (Rawls 1971: 74). If the basis for the sharing of risk is a party's lack of control over a factor that affects risk level, however, then the very notion of control is contestable. (Abraham 1986: 89–90). There are any number of characteristics that are realized before an insurance contract is signed that are arguably outside a party's control. Some drivers have above-average reaction times that make it more difficult for them to apply the brakes in a car in time to avoid accidents. To the extent that this factor is considered outside a party's control, it could be considered intrinsic. On the other hand, driving is not necessary in the same way as is the receipt of medical care for disease. Those with slow reaction times could travel less and take public transportation, or at the very least drive slowly. Thus, an alternative way to conceive of this issue is that the extent of controllability impacts the degree of risk sharing that is efficient.

Note that the argument for efficient risk sharing, regardless of the factors to which it applies, does *not* necessarily imply that insurance companies should be regulated – the pros and cons of regulation (and especially of prohibiting price differentiation) will be discussed below. A more natural conclusion – fully compatible with a Rawlsian perspective, while perhaps also with a libertarian viewpoint – is to advocate redistribution through a tax-and-transfer system, implemented at the national level, in favor of people affected by non-controllable, intrinsic classification risk. The amount of any transfer payment should ideally be equal to the excess insurance premium required on a competitive insurance market to cover the increment of above-average risk. Note that this would be a rare example of government intervention with no disincentive effect – in that case, the risk is totally exogenous.

Occurrence, Classification and Commitment

Reclassification risk is more interesting from a purely economic perspective. Note, first, that the distinction between reclassification risk and occurrence risk is only a matter of timing. Taking the example of a heart bypass: by the time of the first surgery, the risk is entirely an occurrence risk (ignoring for the moment genetic predispositions, smoking and other choices). Until that moment, therefore, it could (hence should, from a social welfare viewpoint) be insured, or at least insurable. Upon issuance of the insurance contract, the insured would have purchased coverage against a risk that included not only the cost of the treatment of the problem itself (bypass surgery, post-operative surveillance), but also all future costs generated by her new condition, including the increase in premium due to the consequent reclassification. Efficient risk sharing would require all these costs to be covered. In other words, what later becomes a (re)classification risk was initially a pure occurrence risk; as such, it should have been totally covered, including its implications for future insurance premiums. Conversely, failure to cover some of the consequences (here, the future classification impact) should be seen as a failure to provide efficient insurance. This is not only a matter of fairness, but also (and perhaps mostly) a matter of efficiency.[7] Since risks posed by individuals and businesses change considerably over time, this is a significant phenomenon.

[7] Clearly, failing to cover reclassification risks has a cost. While no estimate of its size has been proposed (to the best of our knowledge), back-of-the-envelope

It is therefore somewhat surprising that, in a large number of situations, most reclassification risk is simply not covered or covered only during the period that the insurance policy is in effect. In fact, most insurance policies are issued only for a policy period of one year, without constraints on renewal – so that, for all practical purposes, the reclassification risk is not covered beyond one year. Only life and long-term care insurers voluntarily commit to renewing policies for specified, extended periods (often 20 or more years) as long as the policyholder pays predetermined premiums. In doing so, the policyholder shifts to the insurer the reclassification risk – the risk that his or her health status, and therefore his or her risk of dying – will change during the period of guaranteed renewability.

Outside life and long-term care insurance, and absent legal or regulatory intervention, such contracts exist in a limited way at most. Many large employers (including most private and public universities) provide health insurance coverage that does not depend on or preclude coverage of pre-existing conditions. However, absent the legal mandates of employment and health law that currently apply to these employers, they would not have to hire job applicants with pre-existing conditions. Nor are they required – as the McGann case makes clear – to maintain insurance plans that cover particular conditions. If by some quirk a sizeable number of employees of a particular employer's workforce were afflicted with the same disease, most employers would not be subject to any contractual commitment to continue providing health insurance for that disease. There is a de facto but not a de jure commitment in this situation. Whether even such de facto commitments would be stable in a competitive context in the absence of currently-applicable employment law mandates – or whether they would generate a self-defeating dynamic in which these firms attracted employees with severe pre-existing conditions, resulting in an excessive level of premium and a de facto differentiation – is unclear.

Another interesting fact is that the market for individual (as opposed to employer-provided) health insurance does not appear to have offered guaranteed renewable contracts of this type to any significant extent. There have been a few unverified suggestions in the literature that such contracts exist (Harrington and Neuhaus 2004: 351); but we have been unable to identify any actual examples. And the fact that, prior to the enactment of the ACA (which contains guaranteed issuance and renewal provisions), a substantial number of states had adopted legislation mandating certain forms of guaranteed renewability of individual health insurance (Patel and Pauly 2002:

computations suggest it may be massive, with a considerable impact on welfare (see, e.g., Chiappori 2006: 55–80).

W 286–7), is pretty strong evidence that voluntary guaranteed renewable individual health insurance contracts, if they existed at all, were rare.

In other lines of insurance, if anything the movement has been toward covering less and less classification and reclassification risk. Malpractice insurance was once dominated by 'occurrence' coverage, under which coverage is 'triggered,' or activated, by the occurrence of bodily injury or property damage during the policy period, no matter when a suit alleging liability for this injury or damage is brought. This provided coverage of 'long tail' liability. In providing such coverage, the insurer effectively undertook to cover the risk of long-term change in the incidence and magnitude of malpractice liability (Abraham 2010: 170–1). For practical purposes this was insurance against reclassification risk based on legal and economic change. But as soon as the rate of legal and economic change became less predictable in the mid-1970s, malpractice insurers heavily moved from occurrence to 'claims-made' coverage, which insures liability only for claims made during the policy period. The move to claims made thereby shifted back to policyholders most of the reclassification risk that occurrence policies had previously covered. For analogous reasons – the difficulty of predicting the magnitude and rate of change in long-tail toxic tort, products, and pollution liability – insurers attempt to do the same in Commercial General Liability (CGL) insurance in the mid-1980s (Abraham 2008: 163–5). Long-tail liability covered by CGL insurance policies now tends to be provided on a claims-made rather than on an occurrence basis, precisely so that insurers can shift the classification risk to policyholders, rather than having to absorb it themselves. Similarly, both commercial property and homeowners insurers appear to resist offering long-term policies.

The lack of coverage against reclassification risk in most lines of insurance certainly suggests that such coverage raises serious practical difficulties. For one thing, it may require a level of commitment to maintain coverage and premium contributions that is simply not available in practice. Moreover, if my health insurance contract comes with my job, my employer cannot credibly commit not to go bankrupt; if that happens, then I may lose my coverage. This example suggests two points. First, and quite obviously, the close links that de facto exist between employment and health coverage not only have little conceptual justification or justification in principle, but can be quite harmful in practice. Second, the 'bankruptcy curse' could conceivably be alleviated by a regulation imposing 'backup bankruptcy coverage'; this would cover the employer's contribution to the employee's health insurance in the event of the employer's bankruptcy, pretty much in the same way as insurance guarantee funds and reinsurance are in place to limit the effects of insurer bankruptcies on their policyholders. A more general proposal along these lines, by Cochrane, is discussed below.

A second concern is that full insurance would ideally require commitment from both parties – the insurer and the insured. However, while an insurer may (at least conceptually) commit to future premiums, the insured can hardly (credibly) commit not to leave the company. The two-party commitment problem, by itself, limits the level of coverage against reclassification that a market can offer. More precisely, full insurance against the reclassification risk would imply that the evolution of future premiums could not be related to any change in risk level occurring during the contractual relationship, whether favorable or adverse. If, however, the insured's risk level at some given moment were much better than expected – i.e., reclassification would operate in her favor – she could ask for a rebate on the contractually agreed premium level. Should the insurer decline, she can switch to a competitor, who would price the new contract according to her (lower) risk. This problem has been analyzed in an influential paper by Harris and Holmstrom (1982). They show that, under these circumstances, the optimal contract operates in an asymmetric way: the insured is protected against any premium increase due to adverse reclassification, but benefits from an improvement in her prospects via a rebate reflecting the decrease in risk. Obviously, such a contract relies on higher premiums being charged *ex ante* (at the beginning of the relationship), since the latter also include an insurance premium against the reclassification risk. But this may aggravate the commitment problem on the insurer's side, since the insured may have to pay large amounts upfront for the promise of future coverage at a maintained price, and will be reluctant to do that without being fully certain of the reliability of the insurer's commitment.

A standard objection to this asymmetric commitment solution is that it is not compatible with (*ex post*) competition. The argument goes as follows. If my current policy covers the reclassification risk, then it may be the case that, at some future point, my contractual premium falls well below its actuarially fair value, since it disregards my (now pre-existing) conditions. However, any alternative insurer would take my actual risk into account, and price according to it, which would mean much higher premiums. Therefore I cannot leave my current insurer (nor, actually, my current employer) without facing a serious loss; this results in a de facto monopoly (or monopsony) with serious welfare costs.

This problem can be addressed through legal regulation, as it was by the Health Insurance Portability and Accountability Act (HIPAA)[8] even

---

8 HIPAA. 110 Stat. 1936, codified in various sections of Titles 18, 26, 29, and 42 U.S.C.

before enactment of the ACA. Where HIPAA applied, health insurers were prohibited from imposing pre-existing conditions limitations in policies issued to insured who had been covered by other health insurance for at least 12 months. But market solutions may also be feasible, as argued by Cochrane (1995: 445–73). The idea is to organize a system of compensating transfers between insurers. When, after being reclassified as a higher risk, a party switches insurers, his premium should not increase, but the former insurance company should compensate the new one through a lump sum payment representing the difference between the insured's present value of future premiums and what this value should be if he was priced according to his actual risk. The Swiss health insurance system relies on a mechanism of this type; note that although market based, it requires a significant level of regulation.

3. REGULATING OR BANNING CLASSIFICATION

Finally, an alternative solution is to regulate and limit (or prohibit) the use of pre-existing conditions and thereby to promote or require insurance of classification and reclassification risk. This solution poses a number of issues.

Which Regulation?

We start with intrinsic classification risks. Take the example of genetic predisposition, and assume that we want to regulate the insurer's ability to use the results of genetic testing. In principle, different levels of regulation could be considered; for instance, by increasing order:

1. No regulation: insurance companies are free to collect and use information as they see fit.
2. Insurance companies may not collect information without the applicant's consent, but they may condition the underwriting of a contract on her taking a genetic test.
3. Insurance companies may not require a test, but they can ask whether the applicant took a test in the past, and if so may require disclosure of the results.
4. Insurance companies are prohibited from asking about previous tests, but applicants may voluntarily provide any information they find appropriate.
5. Insurance companies are prohibited from using any test-related information, even if voluntarily provided by the applicant.

From a medical or ethical perspective, much could be said about these alternatives. From an economic viewpoint, however, the main question is what consequences these various levels of regulation would have. The answer depends on several related questions, in particular whether the information about *who took a test* (independently of the test's results) would be confidential or would be available to third parties such as insurers. Paradoxically, the absence of confidential tests may benefit the insured population as a whole, at least from a pure classification risk perspective. If an applicant could credibly claim, at the issuance of the insurance contract, that she has never taken the test and has therefore no knowledge of any particular risk, then she would be charged the average premium for individuals in her risk class. In other words, by purchasing insurance coverage *before* taking the test, the insured could de facto cover the classification risk, which would be (first best) efficient. The problem, however, is that this situation is vulnerable to free entry of firms providing confidential tests. Indeed, each potential insured would benefit from secretly taking such a test: she could ask for a rebate if the outcome were favorable; if not, she could deny having taken the test, and therefore benefit from average pricing. Clearly, should such a confidential testing strategy become common, the whole insurance market would be jeopardized: insurers cannot afford, at least in the long run, to sell at the population's average cost if high-risk people are over represented in their applicant portfolio; ultimately, it may result in a 'death spiral' of the type described below, whereby the insurance market shrinks to covering only very high-risk people at a very high cost. Since the confidentiality of tests is difficult to avoid in practice (if only because people can be tested outside the country), the relevant assumption is probably that confidential tests do exist; equivalently, insurance protecting people against the classification risk (as discussed earlier) is not feasible.

If confidential testing is available, an economic analysis of these regulatory alternatives has clear cut implications, at least in a basic model in which the costs of testing are neglected. First, potential applicants for insurance are likely to take the test: as argued above, taking the test has no downside consequence, since, thanks to confidentiality, one can always deny having taken it if needed. Second, levels 1 to 4 produce basically equivalent effects. Those who take the test will report its outcome only if it is favorable (they are not at risk). Therefore, the insurer will consider someone not reporting a test result (or claiming not to have taken the test, an unverifiable claim) to be a high-risk person. In practice, under any of the first four levels, the company would charge the high premium (corresponding to individuals carrying the gene) for the general policy, but give discounts to those disclosing a negative test result. The result would be full differentiation. The overall conclusion is therefore clear: *only the full prohibition (level 5) will make a difference*.

Again, this states the extreme case and the conclusion should be qualified because tests, whether confidential or not, are not free, financially or psychologically (many people 'do not want to know'). The paradox is that in this context, expensive tests are typically (*ex ante*) welfare increasing (Chiappori 2006), at least from a classification risk perspective. If the cost of a test is so high that most applicants are unlikely to take one, then an applicant can credibly claim that she did not take it – and, as argued above, that may be sufficient to permit covering the classification risk. De facto, that is often the case. For instance, life insurance companies have rarely required the average applicant to take a genetic test for Huntington's (or any other rare genetic disease), even before they were legally prohibited from doing so. The prevalence of the disease is small; therefore, the rebate that could be obtained by testing negative is trivial, much less than the cost of the test – which invalidates the 'confidential testing' danger described above. For the general population, the classification risk for Huntington's is therefore de facto covered. This logic, however, does not apply to populations posing a large *ex ante* risk (e.g., people whose parent suffered from Huntington's), who will typically be unable to purchase insurance without a test. In the end, what matters are the respective magnitudes of the cost of the test, the expected cost of the risk under consideration, and its prevalence in the relevant population.

Legislation at both the state and federal levels has addressed this issue, particularly as it arises in health insurance. By the 1990s most states had enacted statutes restricting what use certain insurers (predominantly health insurers) could make of genetic information or tests (Jerry and Richmond 2012: 112–13). This went part of the way toward adopting our level 5 prohibition. At the federal level, HIPAA (enacted in 1996) regulates the use of genetic information in group health insurance plans. In 2008 Congress enacted the Genetic Information Nondiscrimination Act (GINA),[9] which prohibits the use of genetic information in health insurance and in employment. The final step in the legislative progression, the ACA, was enacted in 2010 and went into full effect on January 1, 2014, with the exception of certain requirements. The ACA mandates the purchase of health insurance by all individuals (subject to a tax penalty for failure to purchase) (ACA, § 5000A), mandates guaranteed renewal (ACA, § 2703), and prohibits varying premiums except based on age, geographic location, and tobacco use (ACA, § 2701).

---

9 GINA, 122 Stat. 881.

The unexpressed but obvious effect of these mandates and prohibitions is to insure virtually all substantial classification and reclassification risk. While this outcome is probably not the most discussed aspect of the ACA, it may well be the most important one, because of both the huge potential welfare gains of covering classification and reclassification risk (see for instance Chiappori 2006 for a back-of-the-envelope estimate) and the dangers implied in terms of adverse selection, as discussed below.

Moral Hazard

Banning differentiation may be welfare decreasing when the factors used in classification may be affected by the insured's acts or omissions. Under such moral hazard, to the extent that differential pricing fails to provide adequate (and effective) incentives, risk is spread inefficiently. As we noted earlier, in part the issue is what counts as being within the control of the insured. Whether smoking is entirely a person's decision (e.g., is there an 'addiction gene'?), and if so, whether incentives linked with insurance pricing work, are open questions.

In addition to philosophical or ethical issues such as these, political pressures may influence the decision about what to ban or regulate, with possible resulting moral hazard. The federal flood insurance program for many years underpriced the premiums it charged under its insurance program, and did not discourage rebuilding to as great an extent as private insurers probably would have done. As a consequence, from an economic standpoint there probably was overbuilding, and excessive rebuilding, in flood-prone areas (Tarlock 2012: 168). Similarly, after Hurricane Katrina in 2005, as private insurers partially withdrew from the market for homeowners insurance in hurricane prone areas of the South Atlantic and Gulf Coast states (Richmond 2006–07: 52), state-provided or state-supported insurance facilities that took their place may have underpriced the coverage they provided, with analogous effects on home-location and rebuilding decisions (Agnew 2007: 728; Bodiford 2010: 149).

Finally, the moral hazard problem is complicated by the fact that some factors that may appear to be wholly out of the insured's control are sometimes proxies for hidden, controllable factors. The result may be increased moral hazard. Gender (setting aside surgical change, which is statistically rare) is outside the insured's control. If males and females pose differential risks, banning differentiation based on gender may therefore appear to be welfare increasing. But if the reason for this differential is a factor within the control of insureds, then there may be hidden, though highly indirect, moral hazard. For example, suppose that, at the margin, the magnitude of the auto insurance premiums families pay affects the decision whether to purchase an additional family car when young family members begin to drive. Banning gender-based classification in auto insurance will then result in lower premiums for families with young male drivers, and more purchases of an additional family car than would otherwise occur. If increased opportunity to drive because of the availability of an additional family car then leads to more driving by young males, the result of banning gender-based classification will be to generate moral hazard. Possibilities such as this argue against banning particular differentiations before understanding what lies behind the data that drives them.

Full Prohibition, Adverse Selection, and Market Equilibrium

As we have argued above, the extreme case of regulating classification involves banning the use of any pre-existing information, even when voluntarily provided by the applicant. We may think of such a ban as prohibiting classification only, or as prohibiting both classification and the use of differentiation in the decision whether to insure at all – the underwriting decision. Depending on how much of this occurs, there may be a need for state-supported or state-organized residual markets to ensure the availability of insurance to those who are denied it in the private market.

Alternatively, we can think of a ban as prohibiting both classification and underwriting on the basis of pre-existing information. This is effectively a take-all-comers approach linked with guaranteed renewability, of the sort adopted by the ACA (ACA, § 2702). While such a regulation eliminates a major weakness of the previous system – the absence of global coverage against classification risks, or equivalently the absence of long-term coverage – it may create problems of its own.

The most obvious problem is the introduction of a potentially massive amount of adverse selection into the system – a problem that ERISA, as interpreted in the McGann case, avoided. Adverse selection is a contractual situation in which one party – here the insured – has information that is relevant to the contract – here the level of risk – that the other party either does not possess or cannot use. When facing the same price for an insurance contract, parties with different risk levels will react differently, and there will be a natural tendency for riskier parties to be more willing to buy (or willing to buy more) insurance. In that sense, the selection induced by information asymmetries is *adverse* (from the insurer's perspective): any given contract tends to attract preferentially the riskier applicants (on whom the insurer is more likely to suffer a loss).

Exclusivity

An important distinction, at this point, is between *exclusive* and *non-exclusive* contracts. Exclusivity means that, for the type of risks under consideration, an insured cannot purchase coverage of the same risk from more than one insurer. Under non-exclusivity, in contrast, an insured can independently purchase coverage of the same risk from different insurers, for the reasons that follow.

Exclusivity in insurance law

The sense in which insurance is exclusive or non-exclusive may vary depending on what is at issue. For legal purposes, outside of life insurance the 'principle of indemnity' precludes insurance recovery of more than the insured has lost. Application of this doctrine to preclude duplicate insurance recovery ensures that insurance protects against net loss, rather than creating the possibility of net gain (Abraham 2010: 83). Further, insurance policy provisions governing 'other insurance' or 'coordination of coverage' expressly address which insurers' obligation is primary and which secondary when more than one policy covers a loss (Abraham 2010: 730–7). Regarding the duplicate-recovery issue, therefore, even when insurance is non-exclusive because an insured may purchase more than one policy covering the same risks, this non-exclusivity has no impact on net recovery of benefits. The result is that duplicate insurance is rarely purchased because doing so would be pointless. No one deliberately purchases duplicate auto insurance; in this sense auto insurance is exclusive.

On the other hand, the principle of indemnity does not apply to life insurance or annuities, and probably does not apply to disability insurance, although that is a legally open question. Nor are there 'other insurance' or 'coordination of benefits' provisions in life insurance policies or annuity contracts. The reason is that, formally at least, these are not contracts of 'indemnity'; they do not replace particular monetary losses, but simply provide a measure of economic security upon the occurrence of an event that reduces economic security. As a consequence, and in this sense, life insurance and annuities are non-exclusive.

Life insurers do attempt to guard against the moral hazard that would be generated by 'overinsuring' – purchasing multiple policies providing more total coverage than the life insurer would think it prudent to offer a particular applicant. The law indisputably permits insurers to do this by asking questions on applications for coverage regarding the amounts of life insurance or annuity coverage that the applicant already owns. The law then supports insurers' efforts to obtain accurate information of this sort by granting insurers a right to rescind the contract (subject to a two-year incontestability period in life insurance) whenever there has been a material misrepresentation of information on the application (Abraham 2010: 18–19).

The economics of exclusivity

Legal rules directed at avoiding misrepresentation by applicants and preventing duplicate or 'excessive' recovery of insurance benefits – important though they may be in legal settings – have no bearing on the significance of the distinction between exclusive and non-exclusive insurance contracts for the issue with which we are concerned here. For purposes of our analysis, what matters is the differences in pricing structure in exclusive and non-exclusive insurance, and the impact of these differences on behavior.

From a theoretical perspective, exclusivity considerably increases the set of available contracts. A standard implication of adverse selection is that insurers may want to use *convex* price schedules, whereby the *unit* (i.e. per covered dollar) cost of coverage increases with the amount of insurance purchased; the idea, detailed below, is that riskier agents tend, other things being equal, to buy more insurance, and should be priced accordingly.[10] However, convex pricing is not feasible without exclusivity: if insurance is cheaper in small amounts than in larger ones, an agent can always 'linearize' the price schedule by buying several smaller contracts from different insurers.[11]

Given the increased threat of adverse selection when classification is regulated, it is no surprise that in practice, regulation of risk classifications is least rigorous in lines of insurance that are effectively exclusive, such as health, liability, and property insurance, and more rigorous in lines that are effectively non-exclusive, such as life insurance. For example, as noted earlier, federal restrictions on the use of genetic information in insurance under GINA apply to health insurance, where the majority of coverage is and has been employer-provided on a virtually automatic basis, but not to life insurance, the purchase of which is far more discretionary. At the state level, regulation follows the same pattern. Regulation of risk classification is more restrictive in auto liability insurance, which is effectively exclusive,

---

[10] This is generally possible only in lines of insurance where the unit cost would otherwise not vary too much with the amount of insurance purchased, such as life and property insurance. In liability insurance, because the risk decreases as the amount of liability insured increases (incurring a small liability is more likely than incurring a large one), optimal pricing is otherwise *concave* and neutralizing adverse selection with more nearly convex pricing would be more complex.

[11] Indeed, Cawley and Philipson (1999), analyzing a sample of life insurance contracts, found no evidence of convex pricing.

than in life and disability insurance (Avraham, Logue, and Schwarcz 2013: 15).

The crucial insight here is that in a non-exclusive line, even a small proportion of high-risk individuals can destabilize the market, provided that they purchase large amounts of insurance. At the beginning of the AIDS epidemic, a serious concern in the life insurance line was that although HIV-positive individuals were a small proportion of the total population, they would buy term life contracts for huge amounts, the beneficiaries being either partners and family members or even, possibly, unrelated third parties who would fund the operation. An analogous phenomenon might occur today in the viatical market if there were strong legal regulation of risk classification in life insurance. An individual with a fatal disease could purchase life insurance at a price that does not reflect her actual risk, and then (absent legal restrictions on quick assignment, which are not universal) assign the policy to a third party or viatical company for a significant multiple of the initial price. The absence of highly restrictive regulation of life insurance classification renders this possible threat a much more limited concern.

Selective Attrition and the Danger of the 'Death Spiral'

The economic literature has studied problems arising from adverse selection in detail. In general, competitive markets are vulnerable to the presence of adverse selection in several, different ways. A first problem, which may affect both exclusive and non-exclusive lines of insurance, relates to *selective attrition* from the insurance market. If the distribution of risks in the population is widely heterogeneous, banning price differentiation will result in massive cross-subsidies: low-risk individuals will pay a premium way above the actuarially fair value, whereas high-risk persons will be heavily subsidized. The danger is that the implicit taxation levied on the less risky part of the population may discourage them from buying insurance altogether. If they withdraw from the insurance market, the insurer's financial results will deteriorate, because the less risky constitute the most profitable part of the market. As a consequence, insurers will typically have to increase their premium to compensate for a higher per capita expected cost. But the increase may, in turn, discourage the safest part of the remaining insured population, and so on. The worst case scenario is a 'death spiral', whereby the market progressively shrinks to a higher risk/larger premium subpopulation – in which case high-risk persons do not gain much from the regulation, and low-risk people lose a lot by being de facto excluded from the insurance market. If fixed costs are large enough, the market may actually disappear altogether.

An interesting example is provided by the annuity market. There is clear evidence of large scale adverse selection on that market (see for instance Chiappori and Salanié 2014). Not only is the life expectancy of annuity holders much larger than average, but the choice of the contractual options is correlated with longevity risk: agents who choose more back-loaded contracts live much longer (Finkelstein and Poterba 2004). In addition, life expectancy at any age crucially depends on gender: women live longer than men on average, and are therefore charged a higher price (or, equivalently, receive lower annual payments for the same initial contribution). In this context, banning gender discrimination for annuity pricing, a measure recently introduced by the European Union,[12] may negatively impact the market. In a worst case scenario, demand for annuities would severely shrink in the male population, who would be de facto charged a much higher price than the actuarially fair level. As a result, the population of annuity holders would be mostly female, implying prices quite similar to those charged to women in the pre-reform context – and the only impact of the reform would have been the exclusion of most males from the annuity market.

Is such an outcome plausible? The answer is quite complex. From a theoretical perspective, the death spiral is by no means the only possible outcome; depending on the context, the outcome could also be a 'virtuous' equilibrium in which most of the population is insured, and the classification risk is eliminated. Which scenario will prevail depends on the shape of the risk distribution (in particular the size of its tails), but also on the distribution of risk aversion – very risk averse people are unlikely to drop insurance coverage even if the price is high. In practice, and somewhat surprisingly, not much is known about the joint distribution of risk and risk aversion in the population, and little has been done to empirically calibrate the problem, though there is some writing about it (Chiappori 2006; Cutler, Finkelstein, and McGarry 2008: 160–1).

At any rate, a standard response to the risk of a death spiral is to provide additional incentives to being insured; an extreme version being making insurance coverage compulsory. Indeed, the ACA introduces the mechanism of the individual mandate that all individuals purchase health insurance. Whether this mandate will actually eliminate selective attrition remains to be seen, since the option of paying a penalty (or violating the tax laws by failing to pay it) instead of purchasing health insurance is available under the ACA (ACA, § 5000A(b)(1)).

---

[12] Cf. *Association Belge des Consommateurs Test-Achats ASBL, Yann van Vugt, Charles Basselier* v. *Conseil des ministres*, Court of Justice of the European Union, Case C-236/09.

Screening with Contracts

Even when insurance contracts are exclusive, if insurers cannot classify based on pre-existing conditions then the form taken by competitive efforts to combat adverse selection affects welfare. The main insight of the existing literature, starting with Rothschild and Stiglitz's (from now on RS) seminal contribution, is that insurers may attempt to circumvent regulatory restrictions on classification by designing contracts (or, more precisely, menus of contracts) to induce self-sorting among policyholders (Rothschild and Stiglitz 1976). In RS's model, insurers offer several contracts entailing different combinations of premium and deductible. The crucial insight is that a given deductible is more costly for riskier applicants than for less risky ones – simply because the former are more likely to have to pay the deductible. This is what creates the possibility of inducing self-selection: faced with adequately designed menus of contracts, riskier agents will choose high-premium/low-deductible contracts, whereas safer ones will elect to pay a lower premium (and accept higher deductibles as a counterpart). Note that such contracts are perfect examples of the convex pricing strategies discussed earlier: contracts targeting high-risk people charge higher *unit* premium (i.e., premium divided by coverage) – which simply reflects the fact that applicants purchasing these contracts have higher risk. In practice, other differentiations can be (and have been) used: coverage limitations, ceilings, dynamic structure and experience rating, etc. But the basic mechanism remains largely similar: different contracts are valued differently by different applicants, which provides the basis for an auto-selection device.

The important question, obviously, regards the likely outcome of competition in an exclusive market plagued by adverse selection. Consider a context in which insurance companies compete 'in contracts', i.e. by offering contracts (or menus of contracts) targeting specific subpopulations. Note that the logic of 'cream skimming' is still present in this context: each firm will try to attract low-risk people and leave riskier ones to its competitors. Note, also, that this situation generates externalities across competitors. The expected profit generated by a given contract depends not only on the contract's characteristics, but also on the specific subpopulation of applicants it will attract – and this in turn depends on the set of contracts offered by the competitors. Not surprisingly, the mere notion of an 'equilibrium' is somewhat blurred: we are in a game-theoretic situation in which the gain generated by a strategy depends on the other players' moves, so that the notion of a 'best strategy' can only be defined as a 'best response' to a profile of moves by the opponents – who, of course, are also trying to 'best respond'.

How then should 'equilibrium' be defined? On this crucial question, it is fair to say that no general agreement has been reached so far. The first definition was proposed by Rothschild and Stiglitz in their initial paper. An RS equilibrium is defined as a set of contracts such that (1) no contract loses money, and (2) no additional contract could be profitably introduced. Its properties are by now well understood. An RS equilibrium may fail to exist; this will be the case, for instance, when the number of high-risk agents is relatively small. Even when it does exist, it may be 'second best' inefficient, in the sense that there exists another set of contracts that would improve welfare for *all* parties, but that is not robust to competition. The most interesting feature is that whenever it exists, an RS equilibrium always entails *full differentiation*. In the simplest framework (with only two risk classes), an RS equilibrium consists of two contracts, one with complete coverage but a large unit premium (equal, as a matter of fact, to what would be charged to high-risk agents in the absence of regulation), the other with a low premium but a large deductible; it generates perfect self-selection. In an RS context, high-risk parties pay a fair price not because of explicit differentiation, but because they voluntarily choose the corresponding option (the large deductible is so costly in expected terms that they are still better off – or more precisely not worse off – with full coverage, even at the high premium).

Extreme as this outcome may seem, competitive forces tend to push the equilibrium in this direction. For instance, 'pooling' (whereby all agents elect to choose the same contract, priced at the population's average, which would imply full coverage of the classification risk) can never occur in an RS world: if all existing insurers were offering similar pooling contracts, a new entrant could always find a combination of lower premium and higher deductible that would cream-skim low-risk agents without attracting riskier ones. Note that such an introduction, in turn, would jeopardize the profitability of the initial contracts, by tilting their population mix in an unfavorable way – an example of the externalities described above.

It follows that when an RS equilibrium exists, all insureds pay a fair premium; in particular, high-risk parties are not covered against the classification risk. Moreover, low-risk parties face in addition a large deductible. Therefore, the outcome is unambiguously worse, from a Pareto perspective, than in unregulated markets (that is, when insurers are not prohibited from using information about pre-existing conditions to differentiate among insureds): riskier insureds do not gain while less risky ones strictly lose.

An alternative equilibrium concept has been proposed by several authors, and is usually referred to as Spence-Miyazaki (from now on

SM) (Miyazaki 1977). The SM equilibrium concept differs from RS in two main dimensions. First, it relaxes the requirement that each contract must at least break even. In an SM world, a company may lose money on some contracts and make profits on others, the only requirement being that the company must break even (at least) in the aggregate. Second, and more importantly, the second requirement (no additional, profitable contract can be introduced) is modified in the following way: no additional contract can be introduced and make profits even after withdrawal of the contracts that this introduction made unprofitable. For instance, before destabilizing a pooling contract by cream-skimming low-risk applicants (as described above), a new entrant will consider the long-term consequences of this strategy. If it is successful in the short term, the incumbents' (initially pooling) contracts will be left with mostly high-risk insureds; they are likely to lose money and be withdrawn (or re-priced). But then even high-risk applicants may adopt the new entrant's contract (a larger deductible being better than no insurance), canceling its comparative advantage in terms of population mix, and ultimately leading to losses.

Economists have analyzed the properties of the SM model. An equilibrium always exists, is never pooling, and is always (second best) efficient. Regarding its *ex ante* properties (i.e., coverage of the classification risk), all depends on the context. For instance, if the fraction of high-risk agents in the population is small enough, then an SM equilibrium entails large cross-subsidies between contracts. This results in the classification risk being largely covered, so that the outcome is close to *ex ante* efficiency. However, with many high-risk agents SM and RS equilibria coincide, so that full differentiation obtains, and again the outcome is worse than no regulation.

Moreover, heterogeneous risk aversion complicates the picture. The model considered by RS is quite simplistic; in particular, it supposes that agents only differ by their risk. Heterogeneity in risk aversion alters the picture, because a contract with full coverage may attract not only high-risk agents, but also low-risk/high-risk aversion ones, resulting in a premium lower than the maximum (the maximum being defined as the actuarially fair premium for high-risk people). Similarly, the low-price/high-deductible contract will also be chosen by high-risk agents with low risk aversion, and will therefore be priced higher than in the RS context. All in all, we would end up with less price differentiation, which would mean (partial) coverage of the classification risk.

This conclusion, however, should be qualified for two reasons. First, theory suggests that in a context of bidimensional adverse selection (i.e. adverse selection affects both risk and risk aversion), contracts will typically be more complex and involve several dimensions (e.g., a deductible *and* a ceiling on reimbursements) – the idea is that it may be profitable in some cases (but not in all) to induce self-selection along the two dimensions. The abstract theory of bidimensional adverse selection is extremely difficult, and little is known of the exact form of the resulting equilibrium, particularly in the presence of risk aversion. Second, the properties of the equilibrium once again depend on the joint distribution of risk and risk aversion in the population, about which not much is known. In some cases (e.g. automobile insurance), most studies conclude that adverse selection on risk is of minor importance (see Chiappori and Salanié 2014 for a recent survey), so that the design of the optimal contract would be mostly driven by heterogeneity in risk aversion – in which case competition typically will result in efficient risk sharing. In other cases, however, adverse selection is a potentially massive problem. Clearly, prohibiting the use of pre-existing conditions in the underwriting of health insurance contracts belongs to the second category.

Regulating the Contracts

Finally, a frequent solution in the literature is to avoid the type of contract competition just described by also regulating the type of contract that can be offered. The idea is to prohibit any kind of contract differentiation that could be used as an auto-selection device. This includes large deductibles, limitations of coverage, exclusion of specific diseases and other similar clauses. Note that such a regulation must be accompanied by an obligation to accept all applications; otherwise insurers would only accept applicants whose expected cost is smaller than the population's average, and the system of cross-subsidies would unravel. To use our earlier terminology, what must be regulated is not only classification, but also underwriting, and even the design of the contracts offered on the market.

Some of these types of prohibitions are used in existing insurance regulation, and some are not. Large deductibles are rarely prohibited except where insurance is mandatory (e.g., in basic auto liability insurance). Some specific disease exclusions were permitted in health insurance pre-ACA, but others were prohibited by state mandated-benefits laws. This varied considerably from state to state (Abraham 2010: 401).

Prohibiting contractual options, however, is not without cost. First, agents have different risk attitudes, and contractual options may be welfare increasing by allowing agents to elect the contract that fits their preferences best. In particular, agents may be willing to accept a higher deductible (and be charged a lower premium) for reasons unrelated to their risk – in which case the regulation reduces their welfare. For example, those who are cash-constrained may prefer large deductibles, or other back-loaded policy provisions. Note, however, that the argument hardly applies to ceilings or exclusions, which are more difficult to justify.

A second problem is that deductibles can be used for purposes other than inducing self-selection. Deductibles may combat *ex ante* moral hazard generally. Moreover, in the presence of '*ex post* moral hazard' (e.g., whereby health insurance results in higher demand for medical services), deductibles and co-payment requirements are a standard response; it is crucial to make sure that such mechanisms can still be used if needed, since the alternative could be a severe increase in health expenditures.

Finally, a problem that most countries that introduced heavily regulated health insurance (such as Switzerland or the Netherlands) have faced is the distorted incentives the system creates for insurance companies. In principle, the system relies on a network of implicit cross-subsidies, whereby riskier insureds are de facto subsidized by less risky ones. While aggregate profit may still be positive in this context (the gain made on low-risk insureds compensating the loss made on high-risk ones), it is still the case that, for any insurer, getting rid of high expected cost insureds would unambiguously increase expected profits, possibly by a large amount. While under European systems insurers can neither decline to insure an applicant nor cancel a contract, they may try to discourage the insured (e.g., by introducing unnecessary administrative complexities, inflating delays, etc.). This has been a serious problem in the countries mentioned above; the solution adopted has been to introduce a government-level compensation scheme, whereby each company is compensated by a common fund for each insured whose risk significantly exceeds the average.

Analogous problems may arise under the ACA. First, large employers or their insurers may have an incentive to 'dump' their high-risk insureds by fashioning the terms of the health insurance they provide so as to limit coverage of conditions or diseases contracted by such insureds (echoing John McGann's experience under ERISA) (Schwarcz and Monahan 2011: 177). This is because the Act does little to mandate the terms of coverage to be provided to large groups, but substantially regulates the contracts that can be offered in small group and individual insurance. Second, although the Act contains provisions anticipating the establishment of risk-adjustments, designed to subsidize insurers who sell individual and small group insurance through health insurance exchanges and experience above-average losses because of the mix of people they insure (ACA, § 1343), how risk-adjustment among insurers will work in practice is unclear.

As of today, not much is known about the likely outcomes of competition on the health insurance market under the ACA. The most detailed analysis is due to Handel, Hendel, and Whinston (2013), who combine the estimated joint distribution of risk and risk preferences with a model of competitive insurance markets. Their conclusions are somewhat pessimistic. They find that market unravelling from adverse selection is substantial under the proposed pricing rules in the ACA, implying limited coverage for individuals beyond the lowest coverage (Bronze) health plan permitted. Although adverse selection can be attenuated by allowing (partial) pricing of health status, this would create a welfare loss from reclassification risk that is substantially larger than the gains from increasing within-year coverage, provided that consumers can borrow when young to smooth consumption or that age-based pricing is allowed. These conclusions obviously need to be confirmed (or qualified) by future investigation. Still, it is surprising to realize how little has been done on an obviously crucial issue, particularly in the design phase of the law.

CONCLUSION

Our analysis of the possibilities for insurance of classification risk reveals the difficulties that this kind of enterprise faces. Assuming something analogous to Rawls' veil of ignorance, it would be (first best) 'efficient' for all classification risk to be insured. However, for any insurance policy issued after the scope of a potential insured's classification risk has been revealed or can be determined, we cannot expect a competitive market to provide such insurance because, in effect, the risk (of a particular classification) has already materialized. Moreover, even if an insurance policy is issued before a classification risk is realized, covering the classification risk requires a degree of commitment from insurers (and in some cases insureds) that may not be available on the market. In practice, only in life and long-term care insurance do we observe guaranteed renewable insurance policies – an example of direct insurance of classification risk. Thus, whether a policy is issued before or after a classification risk is determinable, at least some and perhaps all classification risks will not be covered. In that sense, the McGann case discussed in the Introduction illustrates both the serious welfare costs resulting from the lack of insurance against the reclassification risk, and the complexities involved in regulating away such costs.

For regulation to improve the situation by re-establishing the possibility of covering classification risk, the regulation must be quite extensive, prohibiting any use of the relevant information, even when voluntarily provided by the insured. The main problem posed by such regulation is that, in attempting to mandate fair risk distribution, it creates a situation in which adverse selection is likely to undermine the very effort to distribute risk broadly. This is because the potential insured knows something about her risk of loss that is relevant to what the insurer would charge her for insurance, but by regulation that information is made unavailable to the insurer. The result falls short of efficiency. Thus, unless there is heavy regulation, the effort to achieve efficiency in the insurance of classification risk contains the seeds of its own imperfection.

The question, then, is whether (a) a competitive market with regulation and the resulting adverse selection is superior to (b) no regulation and a competitive market that is second best efficient but does not cover the classification risk. Our answer is: it depends. Approach (a) can be better, because it may involve an SM equilibrium with few high risks, in which there will be almost full coverage of classification risk. But approach (a) also can be unambiguously worse, because it may either involve an RS equilibrium, or an SM equilibrium with a large number of high risks. Both of the latter fail to cover classification risk and, in addition, impose a cost to low-risk insureds via the necessity for them to select a large deductible.

For policymakers, the dilemma is which choice to make when faced with two constraints. First, the choice between approaches (a) and (b) depends on the particular parameters that obtain in any given setting. Yet these parameters will often be unknown or at least incompletely quantifiable. Second, legal regulation inevitably must tend toward the general in its effort to employ bright-line rules. Yet because it may well be that the appropriate selection of (a) or (b) depends on the particular parameters in a particular market or line of insurance, regulation or no regulation at a high level of generality will be blunt. It may therefore produce only some of the benefits that could be captured, and have to tolerate some of the disadvantages that could be avoided, by more targeted regulation. The more that the economics of the future can tell regulators about these parameters, the closer to the optimal level of regulation the system will have the capacity to have.

REFERENCES

Abraham, Kenneth S. 1986. *Distributing Risk: Insurance, Legal Theory, and Public Policy*. New Haven, CT: Yale University Press.

Abraham, Kenneth S. 2008. *The Liability Century: Insurance and Tort Law from the Progressive Era to 9/11*. Cambridge, MA: Harvard University Press.

Abraham, Kenneth S. 2010. *Insurance Law & Regulation* (5th edn.). New York, NY: Foundation Press.

Agnew, Christine L. 2007. 'Come Hell and High Water: Can the Tax Code Solve the Post-Katrina Insurance Crisis?' 11 *Lewis & Clark Law Review* 701–52.

Avraham, Ronen, Kyle D. Logue, and Daniel Schwarcz. 2013. 'Explaining Variation in Insurance Anti-Discrimination Laws' available at http://ssrn.com/abstract=2316866 (August 27).

Bodiford, Bradley G. 2010. 'Florida's Unnatural Disaster: Who Will Pay for the Next Hurricane?' 21 *University of Florida Journal of Law & Public Policy* 147–80.

Cawley, J., and T. Philipson. 1999. 'An Empirical Examination of Information Barriers to Trade in Insurance' 89(4) *American Economic Review* 827–46.

Chiappori, Pierre-André. 2006. 'The Welfare Effects of Predictive Medicine' in P. A. Chiappori and C. Gollier, ed., *Insurance: Theoretical Analysis and Policy Implications*. CESifo conference volume, Boston, MA: MIT Press 55–80.

Chiappori, Pierre-André, and Bernard Salanié. 2014. 'Asymmetric Information in Insurance Markets: Predictions and Tests' in G. Dionne, ed., *Handbook of Insurance*. Boston, MA: Kluwer.

Cochrane, John H. 1995. 'Time Consistent Health Insurance' 103 *Journal of Political Economy* 445–73.

Cutler, D., and S. Reber. 1998. 'Paying for Health Insurance: The Tradeoff between Competition and Adverse Selection' 113(2) *Quarterly Journal of Economics* 433–66.

Cutler, David M., Amy Finkelstein, and Kathleen McGarry. 2008. 'Preference Heterogeneity and Insurance Markets: Explaining a Puzzle of Insurance' 98(2) *American Economic Review: Papers and Proceedings* 157–62.

Dionne, G., ed. 2014. *Handbook of Insurance*. Boston, MA: Kluwer.

Finkelstein, A., and J. Poterba. 2004. 'Adverse Selection in Insurance Markets: Policy-holder Evidence from the U.K. Annuity Market' 112 *Journal of Political Economy* 183–208.

Handel, B., I. Hendel, and M. Whinston. 2013. 'Equilibria in Health Exchanges: Adverse Selection vs. Reclassification Risk' mimeo, U.C. Berkeley.

Harrington, Scott, and Gregory Neuhaus. 2004. *Risk Management and Insurance* (2nd edn.) New York, NY: McGraw Hill Irwin.

Harris, Milton, and Bengt Holmstrom. 1982. 'A Theory of Wage Dynamics' 49(3) *The Review of Economic Studies* 315–33.

Hirschleifer, J. 1971. 'The Private and Social Value of Information and the Reward of Inventive Activity' 61 *American Economic Review* 561–74.

Jerry, Robert H. II, and Douglas R. Richmond. 2012. *Understanding Insurance Law* (5th edn.). New Providence, NJ: LexisNexis.

Miyazaki, H. 1977. 'The Rat Race and Internal Labor Markets' 8(2) *The Bell Journal of Economics* 394–418.

Patel, Vip, and Mark V. Pauly. 2002. 'Guaranteed Renewability and the Problem of Risk Variation in Individual Health Insurance Markets' *Health Affairs* W 280–9.

Pauly, Mark V., Kate H. Withers, Krupa Subramanian-Viswana, Jean Lemaire, John C. Hershey. 2003. 'Price Elasticity of Demand for Term Life Insurance and Adverse Selection' NBER Working Paper No. 9925.

Rawls, John. 1971. *A Theory of Justice*. Cambridge, MA: Harvard University Press.

Richmond, Douglas R. 2006–07. 'Insurance and Catastrophe in the Case of Katrina and Beyond' 26 *Mississippi College Law Review* 49–73.

Rothschild, Michael, and Joseph Stiglitz. 1976. 'Competitive Insurance Markets: An Essay on the Economics of Imperfect Information' 90 *Quarterly Journal of Economics* 629–49.

Schwarcz, Daniel, and Amy Monahan. 2011. 'Will Employers Undermine Health Care Reform by Dumping Sick Employees?' 97 *Virginia Law Review* 126–97.

Stoler, A. 2004. 'Economic Implication of Genetic Testing and Mortality Risk' mimeo, University of Chicago.

Tarlock, A. Dan. 2012. 'United States Flood Control Policy: The Incomplete Transition from the Illusion of Total Protection to Risk Management' 23 *Duke Environmental Law and Policy Forum* 151–83.

10. Economics of state versus federal regulation

Martin F. Grace

I. INTRODUCTION

A. Overview

This chapter examines the theory and evidence regarding the level at which the insurance industry should be regulated. Banking and insurance, two major financial service industries, have different regulatory treatment in the United States. One is now mostly federally regulated (banking) and the other is predominantly regulated by the states (insurance). The state's regulatory oversight for insurers, discussed further below, is mostly an historical artifact and begs the question where the regulation of financial services rightly goes in our federal system. The theory of the optimal administration and provision of public goods, such as insurance regulation, is based on Oates's (1972) theory of fiscal federalism. This theory posits that efficiency is maximized when the benefits and costs of a particular government activity are internalized to the level of government making the regulation. A simple example is whether all the benefits (and costs) of solvency regulation, which is currently conducted at the state level, remain solely within a particular state or extend to other states' residents?

Using this theoretical approach this chapter examines the available empirical evidence to provide some guidance on the optimal provision of insurance regulation. It would be nice to state unequivocally that insurance regulation is optimally placed at the federal or state level. However, the evidence is not so clear. Some aspects of insurance regulation (such as solvency regulation) may have external effects or economies of scale and might be efficiently regulated at the level of the federal government, while others (such as market conduct regulation or consumer protection), which are based on the dominance of local tastes and preferences, might be more properly conducted at the level of the state.

By examining the empirical evidence, one could conclude that areas of regulation that could be assigned to the federal government would include solvency regulation, 'commodity like' personal and commercial life products, and commercial property-liability insurance. Other products such as the traditional personal line products for auto and homeowners (which account for over 50 percent of the property and liability market in terms of premiums) seem to have a regulatory benefit from rules being consistent with local tastes and preferences. Thus, according to the theory of fiscal federalism many aspects of regulation of insurance should remain with the state while others might be properly placed at the level of the federal government.

The goal of the chapter is to assess the types of regulation currently conducted by the states and where the regulatory placement of insurance belongs. The first section will provide a general background on the history of insurance regulation and the rationale behind the economics of fiscal federalism as applied to insurance regulation. It shows that the current tensions between federal and state regulatory oversight have existed for some time. Section II will detail the general economic rationale for when government has a role in regulation of insurance markets. Section III will look at the specifics of insurance regulation as actually practiced by the states, linking empirical evidence from the literature to provide some guidance as to whether regulation is more properly placed at the federal or state level. A theme that will be repeated in this section is the comparison of costs and benefits of the regulation. Section IV concludes.

B. Brief History of Insurance Regulation in the United States

Benjamin Franklin founded the first American insurance company in 1752. The company received its charter from the Commonwealth of Pennsylvania and was regulated by restrictions in its corporate charter.[1] This insurer was a typical state corporation for the time, and was not contemplated to be more than a local company.[2] As the US economy evolved to be more integrated, commercial enterprises more frequently operated across state lines and people migrated between states. As a result, there were various calls for a federal regulatory approach to insurance. These calls were temporarily subdued in 1869 when the US Supreme Court heard a dispute between a New York insurance agent and the state of Virginia (*Paul* v. *Virginia*). The issue of the case was whether Virginia could regulate a policy issued by an out-of-state (or foreign) company to

---

[1] See Oviatt (1905) and website for the same company still operating today 'The Philadelphia Contributionship' a mutual insurance company, at www.contributionship.com/history/ (accessed September 24, 2013).

[2] There are many histories of the regulation of the insurance industry that are more in-depth than is presented here. See, e.g., Day (1970), Meier (1988), and Harrington (2000) for examples.

a Virginia resident. The court held that insurance was not interstate commerce, but local in nature.[3] In this context, insurance was understood as 'local' because it was a contract between two people entered into and performed within the same state. From the perspective of a well-developed economy in the twenty-first century, this notion of local commerce is rather quaint. However, the ruling in *Paul* was not long lived.

By the 1940s (and after the passage of the Sherman Antitrust Act of 1892), the issues changed, as states had begun to permit industry committees or underwriting associations to set rates for various lines of insurance. Such price setting arose from the problems of pricing insurance. For example, in the immediate post-Civil War era, fire insurance was becoming a necessary item for both urban homeowners and businesses. However, modern actuarial pricing theory had not yet been developed, and pricing fire risk was hit or miss.[4] This created a potential for a type of uninformed price competition, given that the insurer had an inability to accurately determine prices. As a result, firms could have more than adequate reserves or no reserves to pay claims. When fires were few and far between, profits were 'high' and the incentive to cut prices in response to new entrants was strong. New insurers formed because they saw the profits as a signal to enter. As a result of poor pricing and a geographically undiversified portfolio of policies, catastrophic city fires in Chicago, Boston, and New York bankrupted numerous insurers, leaving customers without any recourse.[5]

Over time, regulators recognized that incentives to cut prices increased the likelihood of insurer insolvency. Thus, regulators oversaw solvency by requiring prices to be 'adequate', defined in terms of reducing the likelihood of insolvency. By the 1940s, insurers were cartelized by industry associations and subject to strict price regulation in many states. This cartelization and industry-assisted price regulation started to unravel. Actuarial science had made some progress developing the notion of reserving for losses, and states became concerned that prices might be too high. In a landmark case, the State of Missouri sought to get the association of insurers who set the prices (as agents for the states) to lower prices. This association (the Southeastern Underwriters Association) declined to lower rates. Ultimately, the Department of Justice sued the association for price fixing under the Sherman Antitrust Act. In the resulting Supreme Court

[3] 75 U.S. 168 (1869).

[4] See D'Arcy and Garven (1990) and Kulp (1950) for a discussion of the history of actuarial pricing.

[5] See, e.g., Spectator, (1885) at 150–4 for a list of the firms bankrupted by the Great Chicago fire.

case, *US* v. *Southeastern Underwriters*,[6] the court overturned the holding of *Paul* v. *Virginia*, ruling that insurance was interstate commerce and the antitrust laws were properly applied to price fixing cartels in the insurance industry.

However, in a rare New Deal reluctance to regulate an industry, Congress returned regulation and taxation of the insurance industry to the states with the McCarran-Ferguson Act.[7] The Act included a limited antitrust exemption for activity that did not amount to boycott, coercion, or intimidation.[8]

Since the passage of the McCarran-Ferguson Act there have been a number of attempts to interest Congress in federal insurance regulation either through repeal of antitrust exemptions or more direct federal oversight. In 1958, only 13 years after the enactment of the McCarran-Ferguson Act, Kimball and Boyce (1958) suggested that if the states were not up to the task, the federal government would need to step in to regulate insurance. The general concern was that prices were essentially still being set by industry committees, and that the states really were not up to the task of setting prices properly, either through regulation or a competitive process. In 1958, the Senate also held hearings on insurance and the industry's limited antitrust exemption (see, e.g., Knowlton 1960).

The antitrust exemption, and the potential federal role in regulation, have been brought up again and again.[9] One could argue that enforcement of the antitrust laws against insurers is a form of market conduct regulation. It could be that if markets were more competitive and insurers could operate across state lines without the restrictions imposed by the states, consumers might get better products, better prices, and better service all resulting from increased competition. This exact issue was brought up in

---

[6] See *U.S.* v. *Southeastern Underwriters Ass'n*, 322 U.S. 533 (1944).

[7] The McCarran-Ferguson Act, 15 U.S.C. §§ 1011-1015 (2012) was passed in 1945 in response to *U.S.* v. *Southeastern Underwriters* (322 U.S. 533 (1944)), which held that the insurance business was subject to Congress's commerce power regulation in the form of the Sherman Antitrust Act. *Southeastern* in turn overturned an earlier case, *Paul* v. *Virginia* 75 U.S. 168 (1868) that held that insurance was local, not interstate, commerce. For a history see Meier (1988).

[8] 15 U.S.C. §§ 1012–13. This limited exemption could be thought of as one designed to help the industry thrive. For example, many small insurers may not have enough data on their policyholders to credibly set rates. Thus a contract to share data on losses (but not costs or profits) would arguably allow more insurance company competition. See also American Bar Association (2006) *Comments to the Antitrust Modernization Commission Regarding the McCarran-Ferguson Act* and *Hartford Fire Ins. Co.* v. *California*, 509 U.S. 764 (1993).

[9] See, e.g., The Insurance Competitive Pricing Act of 1994 (HR 9).

the health care debate when repeal of the insurance antitrust exemption was proposed as a way to obtain lower prices and better products for health insurance consumers.[10] Despite these proposals, there is really little evidence that repeal of the exemption would have a substantial effect as the state-action doctrine allows states to regulate in a manner that would otherwise contravene antitrust laws.[11] Further, because antitrust exemptions are not popular, courts have narrowly tailored the exemption to cover relatively few activities.[12] When faced with a question about whether a particular practice satisfied the exemption, the courts have essentially turned the problem into one easily examined under a rule of reason analysis like that used for any non-insurance antitrust case (Grace and Klein 2008). As a result, an antitrust exemption repeal is not likely to solve many problems.

Antitrust is an indirect approach to regulating insurance, because it is passive and narrow, covering combinations, contracts, and conspiracies that unreasonably restrict trade. It has had some success as a narrow regulatory tool. In recent decades, broader approaches to regulating at the federal level have emerged in response to a rash of insurer insolvencies.

In the late 1980s, as a number of large insurers went bankrupt arguably due to poor state regulatory oversight, Congressional interest in broad federal insurance regulation increased. Congressman Dingell and his House Subcommittee on Oversight and Investigations (US Congress 1990) held numerous hearings and issued a report entitled *Failed Promises*. This report was highly critical of state regulation. Only the rapid response and follow through of the National Association of Insurance Commissioners (NAIC) to increase states' ability to monitor and reduce the costs of insolvency stayed Congress from further action.[13]

Between the late 1980s and the enactment of the Gramm, Leach, Bliley

---

[10] See, e.g., Bacon (2010) 'House Votes to Strip Health Insurance Companies of Antitrust Exemption' *Washington Post*, February 24, 2010. Available at www.washingtonpost.com/wp-dyn/content/article/2010/02/24/AR2010022404324.html (accessed September 24, 2014). See also Sagers (2010).

[11] The state-action doctrine essentially permits states to regulate in a manner that might have anticompetitive effects. For example, states that permit only one water company or electric utility company in a given area are creating monopolies, which arguably have anticompetitive effects. See *Parker* v. *Brown*, 317 U.S. 341 (1943).

[12] For a full discussion of these issues in a modern context, see U.S. Senate Committee on the Judiciary (111th Cong.) S. Hrg. 11–458, October 14, 2009.

[13] See Klein (1995). At the time, Professor Klein was the Director of Research for the NAIC and wrote about the significant changes the NAIC undertook to satisfy Congress's concerns about state solvency regulation.

Act of 1999, which strongly reiterated that insurance was to be regulated by the states, there were other proposals for federal regulation. Perhaps the most common such proposal was to create an optional federal charter (like that seen in the banking industry) for insurers who wished to be regulated at the federal level. The federal charter proposals took some time to become proposed as legislation, but in 2001 a bill was submitted to establish an optional federal charter style of regulation (Webel 2007). In 2007, a version of the optional chartering bill was proposed in both the Senate and the House, as the National Insurance Act of 2007 (S. 40 and HR 3200). Both proposals mimicked the National Bank Act of 1863's approach, allowing insurers to choose between a federal or state charter. An insurer could obtain a national charter and be subject to a federal regulatory commission with powers that would pre-empt the states' authority to regulate. Alternatively, the insurer could choose to be regulated by the state. The rationale for these proposals is not based on a perceived consumer need to eliminate insurers' ability to fix prices, but on the need for large national companies to reduce regulatory compliance costs by having only one regulator rather than multiple regulators. The argument is that because the 50 state regulators and the District of Columbia each have slightly different rules, standards, and methods of analysis, insurers face higher compliance costs that are passed on to consumers without providing any real value.

At the time they were introduced, these optional federal charter proposals seemed likely to pass in some form, but the financial crises of 2008 intervened. AIG, an insurance-focused financial conglomerate, required a massive federal bailout and takeover, in large part due to the activities of one of its non-insurance affiliates. Many became concerned that there might be other insurers like AIG with serious and potentially hidden problems. Although AIG was an insurance-focused financial entity, the problems that it faced were (on the surface) not related to its insurance business and few other insurers experienced extensive trouble as a result of the financial crises.[14] This is in contrast to the banking system, which was predominantly regulated by the federal government. As a result, state insurance regulators were quick to point out that the state regulatory system performed much better than the federal regulatory

[14] Harrington (2009) describes in detail the source of AIG's systemic risks and they came from a subsidiary that undertook significant derivate risks in the credit default market. Also, Harrington points out that AIG's life insurance securities lending also contributed to AIG's downgrade. In addition, other insurers had securities lending programs which were made much more transparent after the statutory reports format was amended starting in 2008.

system.[15] However, the state regulators' argument that the reason insurers did better in the financial crises was due to the fact that states were better regulators is likely hard to prove. The fact that few insurers failed probably had little to do with the quality of regulation per se, but was more likely due to fundamental structural differences between banks and insurers.[16]

Congress again held hearings on insurance regulation during 2008 and 2009 as part of what came to be called the Dodd-Frank Act of 2010. That law put in place what many regard as the first stage of federal regulation, the Federal Insurance Office (FIO) established within the Department of the Treasury, which is supposed to provide information regarding the insurance industry for the federal government. The FIO has three major responsibilities. First, in theory the FIO has the authority to represent the United States in certain international settings and to advise Congress.[17] Second, the FIO has the authority to conduct studies on the state of insurance regulation. Finally, the FIO also has the responsibility to identify gaps in state and federal regulation that might lead to financial crises.

In late 2013, the FIO came out with its first study on insurance regulation (US Treasury 2013). It concluded that there were significant federal interests in the regulation of insurance in some areas, that there were significant state interests in others, and that a complete federal takeover of insurance regulation would not make sense. In fact, while the report mentioned some deficiencies in state regulation, it explicitly left the job of fixing most of these problems to the states, at least as an initial matter. The FIO report suggested that the federal government's role should currently be limited to international cooperation, the regulation of large multinational companies, mortgage insurance, and international reinsurance.

It is a mistake to think that there really is an 'either/or' approach to the proper level of government at which to regulate insurance. The FIO report demonstrates that even the entity charged with looking at insurance from a

---

15 A typical statement was that of Missouri's insurance regulator John Huff (2009) who said: 'As a result of robust state regulation, the insurance industry has provided a relative source of calm in an otherwise turbulent time. State oversight has kept insurance companies stable and protected policyholders from the worst of the financial meltdown, even as banks and investment firms failed under federal regulation.'

16 See Cummins and Weiss (2014) for a description of differences between banks' and insurers' financials.

17 The FIO was designed, in part, to be the agency of the Federal government to represent the US at meetings of international regulators and to assist the Secretary of the Treasury in negotiating international agreements on prudential regulation.

federal perspective does not advocate a complete federal takeover of regulation. Similarly, new requirements under Dodd-Frank will provide for multiple levels of regulation for Systemically Important Financial Institutions (SIFIs), which will be regulated by both the Federal Reserve Board and the states. Additionally, pension and benefit contracts between employers and employees, which are often managed and sold to employers by insurers, are completely regulated by the federal government under the Employee Retirement Income Security Act (ERISA). In addition, in 1986 Congress permitted the formation of a new class of insurers – so-called risk retention groups (RRGs).[18] These RRGs are permitted to operate in any state after becoming licensed in one state. Thus, there are multiple regulatory structures already in place or potentially available in the insurance industry.

The existence of multiple possible regulatory structures begs the question about how one could decide which level of government regulation is appropriate for the insurance industry. The next section provides some economic theory to help provide guidance.

C. Economic Theory of Federalism

The economic theory of federalism provides a framework to help understand which level of government should provide a governmental service. The theory considers cost efficiency (economies of scale), local concerns that differ across jurisdictions, and potential externalities due to actions benefiting one jurisdiction at the expense of others. Each of these economic considerations provides clues to the appropriate level of government for regulation.

Wallace Oates (1972) offered a pioneering analysis of federalism developed in the context of taxes and spending, but his insights translate easily into the domain of regulation. Oates defined fiscal federalism as the relationship between regulation and taxation at various levels of governments. He reasoned that if there were no cost advantages associated with federal provision of governmental services (regulation), then a decentralized set of activities, reflecting differences in tastes and preferences, will dominate from a welfare perspective over a uniform set of services provided nationally.

The idea of fiscal federalism is that the benefits and costs of state activity (in this case insurance regulation) should accrue mostly to the same set of residents. Thus, one should regulate at the state level if the costs and benefits of regulation accrue mostly to the residents of the state. If benefits or costs are borne at the national level, then federal regulations

---

[18] Liability Risk Retention Act of 1986, 15 U.S.C. § 3901.

are more appropriate. To the extent that voters have different preferences across states, we should allow them to exercise their power locally. This has an important benefit in the form of experimentation with different policies among the states. This allows good policies to be demonstrated and adopted over time. In contrast, if there were just one national rule, there would not be any cross-sectional experimentation among the states. (There might be inter-temporal experimentation, as the federal government changes regulations or legislation, but the benefits of that type of experimentation take longer to be revealed.)

One of the strongest arguments for federal regulation is the interstate nature of the business. Most of the insurance premiums written within a given state are written by foreign (out-of-state) insurers. This means that the regulator of a typical state has a large proportion of its premium volume from out-of-state (or foreign) companies. Table 10.1 shows the 2012 percentage of premiums written by these foreign companies within a given state. The average state has 83 percent of its property and casualty business (P&C) premiums written by foreign companies and 93 percent of its life insurance premiums written by foreign companies. This would suggest that, at least superficially, federal regulation would make more sense than state regulation.

A second argument for national regulation is efficiency. This can be found in economies of scale in regulation resulting from either a unified regulator or true harmonization where compliance with one state's law implies compliance with all other states' versions of the law. Economies can arise from two sources. First, there are regulatory economies of scale which arise from the fact that one level of government can undertake regulation more efficiently than multiple governments doing similar activities. Thus, combining state activities into a single regulator would reduce some of the fixed costs of regulation that every state bears. A second, efficiency based on economies of scale goes to the costs savings of complying with one rule rather than 50 plus rules regulating the same topic. A good example is the NAIC's Risk Based Capital Model Law which has been uniformly adopted.[19] This rule sets the same solvency standards across each state, so firms know if they are complying with their home state's rule they are complying with every rule in the US. This saves cost to the states too because each state uses the same rule and can assess solvency in the same way. They do not have to develop and enforce different standards.

[19] NAIC, Risk-Based Capital (RBC) for Insurers Model Act, viewed at www.naic.org/store/free/MDL-312.pdf, (accessed September 17, 2014). The end of the document shows the states which have adopted the Model Act. In this case every state has adopted it nearly verbatim.

Table 10.1 *Foreign (out-of-state) market shares by line of insurance for 2012*

State	P&C	Life	State	P&C	Life
AK	89.81%	100.00%	NC	86.02%	99.97%
AL	87.72%	97.68%	ND	90.28%	98.82%
AR	93.23%	98.19%	NE	91.67%	85.85%
AZ	90.46%	98.83%	NH	85.87%	99.78%
CA	70.17%	99.85%	NJ	74.10%	87.50%
CO	93.27%	95.85%	NM	96.02%	100.00%
CT	83.37%	35.71%	NV	97.57%	100.00%
DC	99.40%	99.98%	NY	81.52%	40.50%
DE	88.28%	99.16%	OH	65.90%	90.50%
FL	74.81%	99.82%	OK	90.34%	98.41%
GA	93.25%	99.35%	OR	84.17%	93.45%
HI	70.99%	98.82%	PA	75.20%	98.64%
IA	72.61%	70.90%	RI	80.50%	99.31%
ID	85.01%	99.44%	SC	95.89%	99.44%
IL	57.74%	93.82%	SD	95.34%	99.89%
IN	81.86%	88.53%	TN	85.70%	97.07%
KS	91.54%	88.90%	TX	55.43%	90.40%
KY	81.38%	99.40%	UT	91.33%	95.61%
LA	83.63%	98.31%	VA	96.23%	97.81%
MA	58.83%	83.31%	VT	72.22%	98.22%
MD	86.27%	98.43%	WA	87.67%	94.50%
ME	82.34%	96.92%	WI	57.64%	92.35%
MI	56.16%	85.80%	WV	89.32%	100.00%
MN	89.82%	88.80%	WY	91.80%	100.00%
MO	86.57%	97.48%	Average	83.40%	93.48%
MS	89.02%	96.19%	Min	55.43%	35.71%
MT	97.94%	100.00%	Max	99.40%	100.00%

Note: Foreign market share is total premiums written by out-of-state companies in a given state.

Source: NAIC Annual Statements, 2012. Author's calculations.

Another example is that the NAIC is currently trying to modernize solvency regulation and increase the speed with which they review insurers' rate and form applications.[20] This harmonized regulation also reduces

[20] The NAIC's model laws are available at www.naic.org/store_model_laws.htm (accessed September 24, 2013). For each law there is a state table that describes

costs to the regulated firms. Similarly, Congress has contemplated facilitating national regulation in the form of a non-profit clearinghouse for agent licensing to lower the costs of multistate licensing for agents and brokers.[21] This benefits both states in terms of lower regulatory costs and firms in terms of lower compliance costs.

A third rationale for regulating at national level is the potential for costs and benefits from one state's actions to spill over to other states. For example, the proposed legislation for national agent licensing would reduce such an interstate externality that may occur when one state disciplines an agent for some type of irregularity, but other states where the agent holds a license are not aware of the problem. In this case the agent can still undertake the same bad behavior in other states. Thus, economies of scale in regulation (costs savings resulting from elimination of duplication of costly activities) and the possible existence of externalities due to regulation provide rationales for national regulation over state regulation.

On the other side, the argument against national regulation is the existence of state-specific contract rules, market conduct rules, and liability rules based upon local voters' tastes and preferences. The NAIC publishes a set of tables documenting differences in state laws.[22] Many of these laws are on subjects based on, or tailored to, local tastes and preferences. So, unlike the Model Risk Based Capital law, which has been passed by every state, many state laws can vary significantly. For example, Illinois does not have auto insurance price regulation. California, in contrast, does have significant price regulation for auto insurance. New Hampshire does not have mandatory auto insurance and allows for the use of a performance bond, while almost every other state has mandatory auto insurance with minimum coverage requirements. These regulatory differences among the states are, in part, due to differences in regulatory preferences. Even when there are model laws on a particular topic, states are free to pick and choose which parts they will enact.

Variations in Property/Casualty State Guaranty Funds also illustrate how state regulation can be tailored to local preferences that vary among

---

which state has adopted the Model Law and if it has a similar provision in its statutes.

[21] See National Association of Registered Agents and Brokers Reform Act of 2013 (H.R. 1115) found at http://1.usa.gov/1bUdYv4 (accessed September 24, 2013).

[22] Table 10.2 comes from the Table of Contents of the NAIC's *Compendium of State Laws on Insurance Topics*. The Compendium provides citations to each state's laws, allowing one to look at major differences among the state laws on a given topic.

states. These funds protect policyholders who have insurance claims pending when an insurer becomes insolvent. The state funds differ in a number of ways. First, the funds differ in the types of insurance covered. For example, most cover auto, home, and workers' compensation. Other state funds might include malpractice and others include some commercial types of insurers. Another difference is the level of claim the guaranty actually covers. For example, if a homeowner's insurance company fails, a resident of Alabama will have fund coverage up to $150,000, but a resident of New York will have a claim limit of $1,000,000.[23] In contrast, the Federal Deposit Insurance Corporation (FDIC) has a nationwide rule of $250,000 for deposit insurance. The point is that there are many proper subjects for state regulation as well as many possible opportunities for the states to differ in their approach to regulation. These differences could matter from a social welfare perspective.

To support the notion that local tastes and preferences regarding insurance regulation differ, we can look at a simple table of descriptive statistics of differences in the minimum auto insurance coverage required for each state, as shown in Table 10.2. The three columns are minimum coverage required per person, per accident, and coverage for property. Thus, in California the minimum required contract would cover up to $15,000 per person in an accident, with up to $30,000 per accident and up to $5,000 in coverage for property claims. What is especially telling are the differences among the states as measured by the standard deviation and the difference between the minimum and maximum coverage requirements.[24] For the per person minimum accident coverage, the standard deviation is 7.11. This means, approximately 45 of the states fall within the range from $10,000 to $21,000 in minimum required coverage. The top five states have higher limits. For the per accident coverage, 45 of the states are in the range from $18,000 to $75,000, and for the property coverage, 45 of the states are in the range from $20,000 to $34,000. These ranges show a great deal of heterogeneity among the states and that certain states have very high (relative to the mean) minimum coverages. These differences presumably reflect the fact that states have made different policy choices. From the perspective of fiscal federalism, these different policy choices deserve to be credited, even if they are influenced by states' political processes.

---

[23] The National Conference of Insurance Guaranty Funds publishes datasheets each year describing the differences among the state funds. One can view the recent year's sheets at www.ncigf.org/datasheets (accessed September 24, 2014).

[24] I make use of this particular law because the data were easy to collect. This is just one law and should not be used to say that all states differ significantly. This is just an example.

Table 10.2 Variation in state laws: Minimum personal auto coverage (in $1,000s), 2012

	Per person	Per accident	Property
California	15.00	30.00	5.00
US minimum	10.00	20.00	5.00
US median	25.00	50.00	15.00
US maximum	23.21	46.73	16.17
US standard deviation	50.00	100.00	55.00
	7.11	14.43	8.96

Source: www.cars.com/go/advice/Story.jsp?sectionh = ink&subject = ins_req&story = state-insurance-requirements (website dated June 26, 2013 and data attributed to the PIAA).

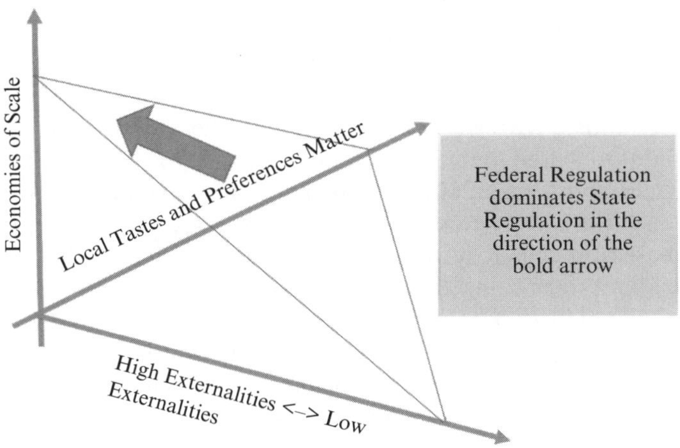

Figure 10.1 Idealized factors influencing optimality of federal versus state regulation

Figure 10.1 shows the interaction of the three factors: economies of scale in regulation; the welfare benefit of letting states set rules to comport with local tastes and preferences; and the presence of interstate externalities that require a higher level of government to reconcile benefits and costs of regulation. For example, as state preferences become more important, all things equal, regulation is better placed at the level of the state according to the model of fiscal federalism. However, when economies of scale become more important, all other things being equal, the federal (or uniform national approach) is preferred. Finally, if the presence of large interstate externalities exist, all other things being equal, then national regulation dominates state level regulation. As a result of the interaction of these three factors, it is likely that some regulation might be more properly placed at the level of the state, and some more properly placed at the level of the federal government.

II. ECONOMIC JUSTIFICATION FOR INSURANCE REGULATION

Before we assess whether state or federal regulation is appropriate for insurance regulation, we must understand the potential rationales for such regulation. Generally, economists believe regulation is beneficial to prevent or correct a market failure. Evidence of market failure and, potentially government failure, abounds in the history of insurance regulation. In addition to concerns about pricing in the 1880s to 1940s, there were major conflicts over corporate governance and control in the life insurance industry (Meier 1988; Roe 1993). There were issues involving discrimination based on race (Squires 2003; Harrington and Niehaus 1998; Klein and Grace 2001; McGlamery 2008; Avraham, Logue, and Schwarcz 2014a). More recently, concerns have been raised over discrimination based on genetic information (Chambers 1999), and now there is concern about rates being based upon individuals' ability to handle credit (see, e.g., Lee et al. 2005). Further, there are concerns about solvency that never really go away and were most recently seen during the financial crisis of 2008. Over the last two centuries, heterogeneous state responses to these concerns have led to a diverse set of state policies in almost every category of insurance regulation.

Economists generally believe that competitive markets do not need regulation.[25] A competitive market is one where there are many buyers and sellers, the product is homogeneous, there is perfect information about prices, quantity and quality, and there are no barriers to entry or exit. This is the ideal market, against which all markets are judged. No market meets this standard perfectly, but many are competitive enough so that the government need not intervene at all. In fact, there are often private market responses that mitigate potential market failures. These include third party certifiers and *ex ante* underwriting techniques.

---

[25] For a more thorough treatment of the economic rationale behind regulation, see Klein (2009).

In contrast, economists do believe that regulation may be appropriate when there is a market failure, and the regulation addresses this failure. Ideally, the government's role would be to minimize the social costs of market failure. In insurance, these potential market failures fall into three main categories. The first is informational asymmetries, including adverse selection (when one party knows more about its own riskiness than its transactional partner does) and moral hazard (when one party depends upon the actions of another party, but cannot observe these actions).

A second major rationale for intervention in insurance markets has to do with market power or unequal bargaining power between the consumer and the insurer. The government essentially becomes a referee, either by mandating prices, mandating contract terms, or mandating performance.

A third major market failure is generated by externalities. Historically, the major externality in financial regulation has been contagion (Diamond and Dybvig 1983). For example, one bank's failure can lead to concerns about other possibly healthy banks and cause risk averse depositors to remove funds from their banks, which then places these formerly healthy banks in financial jeopardy. In insurance markets, potential externalities are likely very different and are driven by the interstate nature of the business. For example, the action of one state's regulators may affect out-of-state policyholders to their detriment. This could be due to poor regulatory oversight of agents, poor regulatory oversight of the solvency of a domestic insurer with interstate sales, or an extraterritorial application of a law. These types of externalities as they arise in insurance will be discussed further below.

Given the three major rationales for intervention in the insurance market, the next step is to examine how they apply in practice. Please note that as Table 10.2 shows that there are many individual aspects of insurance regulation and this chapter cannot do justice to all of them. Instead, it provides a general model for how to think about the three major rationales as currently applied.

III. INSURANCE REGULATION IN THE STATES

This section looks at the three major rationales for government intervention in insurance markets and makes a first attempt at categorizing the proper placement of this regulation in either the state or federal government's domain. The subsections examine specific policies based upon the literature to reach conclusions about whether they should be regulated at the state or federal level.

Table 10.3 organizes most of the types of government intervention

Table 10.3 Comparison of theoretical rationales for government regulation with actual state regulation

1	2	3	4	5	6	7
Potential market failure	Effect on market		Prototypical case	Private market response	Regulatory response	Comparative advantage federal versus state?
Theoretical and insurance specific	Low	High				
Information						
Adverse selection	Higher prices/ demand reduction	Market fails	Genetics/ AIDS/hidden information	*Ex ante* underwriting	*Ex ante* underwriting regs/bad faith laws	State-local tastes and preferences
Price variability due to hard to compare contracts/search costs	Demand reduction	Larger demand reduction	Personal lines	Independent agents/ consumer reports/ advertising	Mandated forms, regulated prices, uniform contracts	State-local tastes and preferences/ economies of scale
Moral hazard	Demand reduction	Market fails due to lack of trust	Insurer manager misfeasance	Reputation building/ rating agencies etc.	Solvency regulation	Federal if externalities exist
Consumer fraud	Prices are higher to honest customers	Market fails due to lack of trust	Automobile fraud activities	Background investigations/ underwriting	Criminal sanctions	Federal if externalities
Agent/company fraud	Prices are higher to customers	Market fails due to lack of trust	Life insurance marketing practices in 1990s	Self-regulating organizations	Licensing requirements/ criminal sanctions	Federal if externalities

Market power						
Economies of scale	Demand increase due to lower costs as many companies have economies of scale	Single producer, high prices	None in insurance	Increase output	Price setting in the limit, information sharing/antitrust	Non discernible
Barriers to entry	Low prices/ more competition	High prices/less competition	None	Innovate around barriers	Regulation caused barrier/lower capital requirements	Federal due to economies of scale in overall regulation. State?
Unequal bargaining power/monopoly	Lower demand due to higher prices	Larger demand reduction and consumer choice restrictions	Mandatory insurance or position consumer faces after a claim	Creation of non-market substitutes/go naked and purchase no insurance	Contract regulation/ bad faith/mandate coverage	
Unfair market practices	Lower demand	Lower demand	Claims settlement/ misleading information about policies, financial condition etc.	Avoidance of product	Market conduct examinations	Federal
Unfair prices	Lower demand	Lower demand	Automobile, workers' compensation	Leave market if regulation is severe	Price regulation	?

Table 10.3 (continued)

1	2	3	4	5	6	7
Potential market failure	Effect on market		Prototypical case	Private market response	Regulatory response	Comparative advantage federal versus state?
Theoretical and insurance specific	Low	High				
Externalities						
Accidents (uncompensated)	Low – but some people bear large costs	Higher – more people bear high costs	Uninsured motorist	Purchase of extra coverage for uninsured motorist/ tortfeasor	Insurance mandate	State
Extra territorial Regulation	Little	Higher prices	New York life insurance regulations	Avoid NY	?	?
Contagion from other markets	Little effect	Potential large availability effect on insurance and other financial products markets	AIG	Bankruptcy, raise prices	Capital regulation for especially important companies	Federal

Contagion due to insurance insolvencies	Multi-state insolvencies – > slightly higher prices	Litigation, state regulatory moral hazard due to slack regulation	Large multistate insolvency – Mutual Benefit Life, Executive Life	No real escape/ options	NAIC accreditation	Federal
Contagion due to large loss/ uncertainty on pricing	N/A	Potentially large	Flood, terror, crop, nuclear	Leave market	Public provision	Federal
Judicial rulings or judicially/ legislatively created uncertainty	Little effect	Increased demand/ decreased supply	Concurrent causation	New contracts developed (occurrence/claims based)	Price and contract scrutiny	State?

under the three main categories, but also categorizes the interventions in a number of ways. Column 1 describes the possible market failure in insurance. Because not every market experiences full market failure problems, an attempt is made to characterize the magnitude of the problem (columns 2 and 3). Column 2 describes the effect on the market if the market failure is relatively small and has a 'low impact' on the market. Column 3 describes the effect on the market if the market failure is significant and has a 'high impact' on the market. Column 4 describes a typical case in insurance regulation that is related to the market failure. The case described here is merely an example to provide some feel for how this particular problem is handled in insurance regulation. In column 5, a possible private market response is described and in column 6 a typical regulatory response to the particular market failure is listed. Finally, column 7 is a conclusion about which level of government might have a comparative advantage. I propose these conclusions as a possible starting point for future debate about the relative advantage of state versus federal regulation. Column 7 suggests that sometimes the federal government has a comparative advantage and sometimes the state has an advantage based upon an initial assessment of the strength of economies of scale and externalities versus the value of local tastes and preferences. This is not entirely objective as there is no specific evidence for each of the types of regulation described in the table.

Before starting with the specific market failure responses shown in Table 10.3 it should be pointed out that, on the margin, there may not be a strong reason for having a regulation enforced or overseen at the state level or the federal level. This is because both levels of government may have the ability to regulate efficiently, and either national regulation or uniform state regulation at the national level might be appropriate. Further, it may be that market failures are small relative to the costs of government (state or federal) intervention, and the market could provide a simpler solution. In the case of a tie between uniform state regulation and federal regulation, it probably makes sense to presume the tie goes to the federal government. This is because uniform state regulation is almost impossible to maintain as states' interpretation of regulation will evolve differently over time without some central mechanism like a federal regulator or an interstate compact to make final decisions binding on all states. This is especially important for those types of rules for which uniformity provides significant cost savings to insurers and/or consumers.

The hidden cost of uniformity, however, is that if the uniform rule is socially costly, it could produce market failure across the entire country. Recall the fiscal federalism principle that if there is no cost advantage associated with federal provision of governmental services (regulation), then a decentralized set of activities reflecting differences in tastes and preferences, will dominate from a welfare perspective over a uniform set of services provided nationally.

For example, suppose the federal government had jurisdiction over underwriting standards and decided that life insurers could not use any information at all, including medical or demographic information, in underwriting or pricing insurance. The result would be a market that could fail or provide only relatively high-cost/low-value policies, such as the currently available 'no underwriting' policies.[26] This would likely make it difficult for consumers like a relatively young head of household to purchase affordable life insurance to protect against the chance of premature death, resulting in consumers (and insurers) being worse off. Under a federal system, states can make policy choices like this without affecting all US consumers. States can also learn from policy mistakes other states make. Of course, this is one of the benefits of federalism but it shouldn't be overlooked *merely* because the federal regulator can provide a larger degree of efficiency in terms of economies of scale in regulation. One must also understand that the costs of a uniform rule can be large enough that they negate any benefits from economies of scale.

A. Information

Normally economists speak of informational market failures in insurance markets using two terms. These are adverse selection and moral hazard.

---

[26] Here is the marketing information from an internet quote provider (netQuote) regarding the 'no medical exam' policy:

> **Guaranteed Issue Life Insurance No Medical Exam** – A guaranteed issue policy is exactly what it sounds like: you will not be turned down for coverage regardless of your health status, age, or other factors. There is a catch, however. First of all, these policies are the most expensive in the business since there is almost no underwriting involved. Second, providers who specialize in guaranteed issue life insurance deal almost exclusively in short term policies with low face values. Industry leader Globe Life Insurance, for example, only offers policies in the amounts of $5,000, $10,000, $20,000, $30,000, and $50,000 to their clients. Those amounts might seem inconsequential in an industry where $1,000,000 policies are commonplace, but they make sense when you look more closely at what those payouts are used for. Guaranteed issue policies are almost universally purchased to settle debts, pay off accrued medical expenses, and/or pay for funeral and cemetery costs when the insured passes away.

NetQuote www.netquote.com/life-insurance/understand/no-medical-life-insurance.aspx (accessed September 28, 2014).

For many these are the most important reasons for governmental intervention into insurance markets.

1. Adverse selection

Adverse selection is a classic problem in insurance markets that occurs when one party to a contract (typically the policyholder) has more information about a material fact than the other party. When the likelihood of adverse selection is relatively low, markets can function, but the lower risks pay a higher price and the higher risks pay a lower price than if risks were perfectly disclosed. In more extreme cases, insurers who could not tell the difference between a high and low risk consumer might not want to sell to anyone at all, because they might believe that all those trying to buy insurance were of the high risk type. A concern arose in the 1980s about AIDS and life insurance. If there was no way to determine who had AIDS, then life insurers would be reluctant to sell insurance in general, fearing that applicants would disproportionately be infected with the virus (Clifford and Iuculano 1987). Correspondingly, if the insurer priced everyone (those with AIDS and those without AIDS) as if they were a high risk (with AIDS), then low risks (without AIDS) would not want to purchase the policy because it would be too expensive given their risk type.

An inability to correctly classify risks could lead to a serious market failure.[27] Insurers now use various tests to help classify, or underwrite, individuals based upon the indicators of diseases. This makes it more difficult for persons with private information about their high risk status to obtain insurance priced for low risk individuals. States, however, do not grant insurers complete discretion in choosing which variables to use in underwriting or pricing (See, e.g., Avraham, Logue and Schwarcz 2014a; Avraham, Logue and Schwarcz 2014b). Every state has laws that generally permit discrimination only if the characteristic used to discriminate between a 'high' and a 'low' risk is statistically related to the actual risk. In some cases (such as race), even characteristics that may be related risk cannot be used by insurers to discriminate. However, for risks not in suspect classes, regulators will generally approve risk classifications based upon valid statistical relationships between the risk and the rating classifier.[28] Credit scoring for insurance is a recent example. Some argue

---

[27] For more details about this problem, see Abraham and Chiappori, Chapter 9 in this volume.

[28] Avraham, Logue, and Schwarcz examine the wide variety of rating law across the US and conclude that three factors are likely influential in determining whether a risk classification system is upheld. The first is the characteristics predictive ability in classifying risk, the second is the size of the adverse selection

that the use of credit information in insurance underwriting and pricing is unfair because it has nothing to do (at least on the surface) with whether one has an accident. However, statistical models do show a relationship between low credit scores and accident frequency (See, e.g., Wu and Guszcza 2003; Lee et al. 2005; Brockett and Golden 2007). This permits low risk consumers to obtain lower prices (which is often overlooked in these types of discussions) and potentially incentivizes high risk individuals to change their behavior to lower their risk and thus their insurance premiums. This second incentive is the type of dynamic efficiency that risk classification can provide to insurance markets.

One of the important responses to adverse selection is the insurer's ability to underwrite risks; there is a great deal of evidence that the auto insurance market has developed powerful ways of assessing risk so that it can eliminate some adverse selection (Chiaporri and Salanie 2000; Cohen 2005). However, what voters think is fair and proper for underwriting may differ across states (See Avraham, Logue, and Schwarcz 2014b). Thus, some states have limited the use of credit scoring, for example. To the extent that this reflects local tastes and preferences, this would imply that in the absence of economies of scale, the local rule is welfare enhancing. Other fairness related characteristics, including sex, pre-existing conditions and age, are also restricted to some extent among the states for various reasons related to what states think is fair (Abraham 1985; Avraham, Logue, and Schwarcz 2014b).[29]

2. Price variability, search and switching costs

There are other types of information problems in insurance markets as well. For example, price variability in conjunction with high consumer switching costs can create problems. High search and switching costs reduce the number of times a person searches for new prices or products, and allow incumbent firms greater leeway to raise prices over time without consumers switching to a new company. Thus the higher the search costs, the easier it is for firms to set prices above the competitive level. This

---

that would exist if the rating classification is not permitted, and finally whether the classification is socially suspect.

[29] A nice natural experiment is occurring in the EU as the European Court of Justice has ruled that insurance rating based on sex is discriminatory and is incompatible with the EU's Charter of Fundamental Rights. See Press Release, *Sex Discrimination in Insurance Contracts: Statement by European Commission Vice-President Viviane Reding, the EU's Justice Commissioner, on the European Court of Justice's ruling in the Test-Achats case* at http://europa.eu/rapid/press-release_MEMO-11-123_en.htm?locale=en (accessed September 25, 2014).

problem typically arises in personal lines, where consumers tend to stay with their insurers for long periods of time. This market power can be abated in the private market by increased competition among agents or insurers, by direct public provision of information to consumers, and by the internet (Brown and Goolsbee 2002).

State regulatory policy in this area has focused on areas such as mandated forms, standardized policies, regulated prices, readable contracts that help consumers see differences among contracts, and publically disclosed average or typical prices for various types of customers (Schwarcz 2011). These state policies are likely to be the result of local taste and preferences. However, varying state rules increase the cost of compliance for providers. One of the strong arguments for the optional federal charter approach is essentially based on the argument that one form is better than 50-plus different forms. Pottier (2007; 2011) and Schwarcz (2014) assert that only an organization like the Consumer Financial Protection Bureau can effectively undertake the proper and effective design of transparent products that the states would be hard pressed to match.

3. Moral hazard by the insurer and the consumer

Insurer-side moral hazard could be an especially important problem in life insurance regulation, where it might also be termed an agency cost. For example, suppose someone purchases a 30 year life policy. Once the customer purchases the product, the insurer is no longer subject to the customer's control: she cannot discipline the insurer's management because she is not an owner; nor can she easily exit the relationship by selling her product to a third party. Thus, the insurer is free to engage in activities that have some chance of a high payoff but that reduce the likelihood that the promised insurance will be available at some date in the future. Solvency regulation can help reduce the social costs of this insurer-side moral hazard by monitoring the company's financial status.

Does the insurer-side moral hazard problem require governmental regulation? Good firms can exert effort to build reputations for financial strength, and there are third party rating agencies that will help in choosing an insurer. But reputations and ratings can change over time. Thus, most economists agree that there is a legitimate governmental role in regulating for solvency, typically implemented via required annual reports, quarterly updates, and inspections to verify these disclosures. This makes sense from a social welfare perspective, since the government can do this at a lower cost than the private market and the customer.

There is some evidence that solvency regulation and resolution is likely to be undertaken more efficiently at a national level. Schacht and Gallanis (1993) proposed an interstate receiver compact so that interstate insolvencies could be resolved more efficiently. Grace and Phillips (2007) show that there are economies of scale in solvency regulation and that costs could be reduced by aggregating the solvency oversight at higher levels of government. For example, solvency regulation generates a relatively high fixed costs. One needs expert actuaries, accountants, and financial experts to understand complex insurers. In addition, states often share resources when conducting large exams of multisite companies because it is efficient to do so through so-called Zone Exams. These economies of scale can be attributed to larger states having lower per unit costs per financial inspection, per resolution of insolvency, or for regulation of agents, as the regulatory fixed costs get spread over more 'units of regulatory activity'. Further, for resolution of failed companies, non-expert state judges often oversee the insolvency under state insurance bankruptcy law (Grace, Klein, and Phillips 2003). Thus, if a state has few insurance bankruptcies over long periods of time due to the small number of firms within the state, there is no learning or economies of specialization that might accrue to a centralized solvency resolution system.

Customer-side moral hazard is also potentially a problem in insurance markets because the purchase of insurance simultaneously protects the consumer and reduces her incentive to avoid a loss (Arrow 1963). The private market solution to this type of moral hazard problem is via deductibles or co-insurance that leave the insured with some 'skin in the game', reducing her incentives to reduce the amount of care (Winter 2000). In extreme cases, this moral hazard can induce people to purposefully increase losses such as burning one's property to obtain insurance payments. Criminal laws against arson or fraud are typical state responses to this type of extreme moral hazard, as are exclusions for intentionally caused losses and limitations on over-insurance ('the indemnification principle').

Many information problems in insurance markets do have private market responses either in terms of consumers having to purchase information or undertaking costly research about the quality of insurance (from rating agencies or advisors), or having to bear the costs of partial insurance in the case of consumer moral hazard. These private market solutions are second best compared to the full information equilibrium. Government regulation can reduce these information costs and it makes sense for the government to do so if it can provide the information less expensively than the market. The current regulatory environment has both the government and private market providing services to the insurance consumer. This suggests that they are doing something complementary rather than perfectly substitutable. However, if the government were to operate on an interstate scale, it might be able to provide informational services more efficiently and thus reduce costs. This could also potentially be accomplished by uniform state regulation.

4. Consumer and producer fraud

Fraud is an informational problem in which one party to the transaction misrepresents a material fact in the process of entering into an agreement or determining the implications of an agreement. Both of these happen in insurance markets, and if the problem is sufficiently severe, it leads to a reduction in the demand for coverage because price increases as insurers pass-on the cost of fraudulent claims or mispriced policies. Fraud can also reduce supply, as insurers no longer desire to write in areas where fraud is problematic (see, e.g., Derrig 2002; Crocker and Tennyson 2002). Fraud by insurers or their agents is also possible. For instance, in the early 1990s agents and brokers seeking higher commissions replaced suitable low risk policies (given the consumer's risk tolerance) for unsuitable high risk and high return policies while misrepresenting the costs and benefits of these transactions (Grace and Klein 2006). One private market response to these types of fraud problems is the development of a self-regulatory organization, the Insurance Marketplace Standards Association, which developed state of the art internal audit/compliance standards for life insurance marketing. But regulations for agents and requirements for their specific training are also important in reducing these agency costs.

The appropriate level of government for regulation in this area depends upon the three items in the model of scale federalism. Is there an externality, are there economies of scale, and do local preferences matter. The proper approach for fraud is somewhat nuanced as there are elements of all three aspects of the fiscal federalism model. First, economies of scale exist for fraud regulation. Here economies of scale would be found in the development of a single data repository for agents, a single approval authority for products, and a common set of rules for enforcement. The states are attempting to obtain these economies through the National Insurance Producer Registry (NIPR)[30] (for agency licensing) and the Interstate Insurance Product Regulation Commission (IIPRC)[31] for product licensing. Of course, the federal government could do this too,

[30] See the organization's website for details about its coverage at www.nipr.com/general/about-nipr.htm (accessed September 30, 2014). The National Insurance Producer Registry is a non-profit affiliate of the NAIC.

[31] The interstate compact has 44 member states. Overall it amounts to coverage of 70 % of premiums in the US (www.insurancecompact.org/about.htm, accessed September 29, 2014). Two notable non-member states are California and Connecticut. New York has legislation pending and Florida has enacted what the

with the additional potential benefit that all states would participate, and all states, consumers, agents, and firms would be subject to the same set of rules. Note that this argument is different from a potential interstate externality imposed by agents from their fraudulent behavior.

A second potential rationale for federal regulation involves agents (and companies) and their potential for interstate malfeasance. Agents may operate in numerous states, but in the absence of an effective clearinghouse for agent conduct reports or complaints, misbehavior by an agent in one state will escape notice by consumers or regulators in other jurisdictions. As mentioned above, the NAIC has developed the NIPR to help share data among the states. To the extent that this registry is truly national and covers all agents, it would deter agent fraud and reduce the ability of agents to move from state to state to avoid regulatory sanctions. Multistate agents create the possibility of externalities, which suggests that agents should be regulated at the national level (at least to the extent that state insurance policies and practices are similar). For certain lines of coverage, it may be that state-specific policies may require more training or licensure to be consistent with states' particular tastes and preferences.

Local preferences are not as important here because the definition of fraud is likely more common among the states than, say, appropriate underwriting standards. This is an empirical question to say the least, but as Avraham, Logue, and Schwarcz (2014b) point out there is wide variety of underwriting standards in the states. There is also likely to be a wide variety of consumer fraud statutes among the states too. To the extent that fraud is undertaken on an interstate basis, however, the economies of scale in federal regulation (as well as jurisdictional scope) make the argument for federal regulation a bit cleaner.

A final item to note is that while there is some evidence of a negative externality caused by fraud in interstate markets from behavior of firms and agents, it is not necessarily true that this suggests the presence of such an externality for consumer fraud. Empirical research on consumer fraud tends to focus on local markets like that of Massachusetts. The typical fraud involves building up auto personal injury damages with a ring of attorneys, plaintiffs (auto injury victims), and medical professionals (Derrig, Weisberg and Chen 1994; Derrig and Weisberg 2004). To the extent consumer based insurance fraud is really a local concern, it would make sense to allocate this type of regulation or enforcement locally to the state.

IIPRC has called 'non-standard compact' legislation (see www.insurancecompact.org/, accessed September 29, 2014).

5. Conclusion: Proper placement for information market failure regulation

Table 10.3 column 7 shows the possible placement of regulation for each of the types of information market failures for information. Many of the regulations could be conducted at the level of the federal government if externalities exist (solvency regulation, consumer fraud, and agency licensing) and to the extent that there are economies of scale. In contrast, state and local preferences are likely to dominate in the regulation of adverse selection as there are no strong arguments for economies of scale or externalities here. For the case of price variability there are likely to be strong local tastes and preferences and economies of scale in product design oversight and regulation to reduce consumer search costs.

B. Market Power

There are several sources of market power (including economies of scale, barriers to entry, and unequal bargaining power) that can translate into unfair or inefficient market practices. Each of these factors reduces the demand for insurance, and with the exception of economies of scale, each results in inefficiencies from higher prices and restrictions on consumer choice.

1. Economies of scale

Economies of scale are the rationale for public utility style regulation, in which a single firm is granted a monopoly in a market in exchange for set prices: since costs fall with size, a single large firm is the cheapest way to provide the good or service in question. This is sometimes termed a 'natural monopoly', since no rival can match the cost advantage accruing to the largest firm. However, such scale economies are not a rationale for insurance market power regulation. If we look at the evidence regarding economies of scale in the insurance industry, it is apparent that the largest companies have constant (rather than *increasing*) returns to scale: for these firms, average cost does not fall with output. These firms are arguably the most efficient, having scaled-up operations at the lowest average costs. We see this in both the life insurance industry and the property-casualty insurance industry (Cummins and Weiss 2000). Because the largest companies operate at constant returns to scale, there is really no reason to regulate prices under a public utility rationale.

Where returns to scale become important is for small companies. These firms – it is sometimes alleged – do not have the ability to use their own resources to construct accurate prices. Thus, information sharing regarding losses is common in the industry and is immune from antitrust scrutiny due to the 'business of insurance' exception in the McCarran-Ferguson Act.[32]

The bottom line is that, with respect to economies of scale, the choice of whether to regulate at the state or federal level is easy: since there are essentially no companies that have economies of scale over the entire range of output in the market, regulation is unnecessary at *either* level. In practice, most, natural monopolies outside of insurance are regulated locally. The major exception is when electric transmission lines or pipelines cross state lines. In this case the interstate nature of the business arguably reduces the transactions costs of regulation and raises the incentive for regulators of state A to shift costs to residents of state B. Arguably this does not occur in competitive insurance markets.

2. Barriers to entry

Barriers to entry result in higher prices because firms cannot enter the market to drive down prices to the competitive level. If we look at the US insurance market, there are approximately 2,000 property-casualty companies and 1,000 life insurers (SNL Financial Database at www.snl.com). While they operate in groups, there are still hundreds of groups in unrelated single companies across the states in the various lines. Concentration evidence shows the insurance industry to be relatively un-concentrated in both the life and property-casualty businesses (Klein 2009). This is consistent with low barriers to entry.

Even if there were barriers to entry, there is an incentive to innovate around the barriers. For example, if state licensing is a requirement for operating in a state, it is still possible for consumers to find insurance products on the internet that may not be licensed in their state. While insurers cannot market to people in jurisdictions where the insurance is not licensed, consumers can still contract for coverage from a firm located outside their state of residence.

Barriers to entry in the insurance industry come from four sources. The first is the financial capital necessary to support the risks written by the company. This is generally not a significant problem, since the minimum capital level required by regulation is often quite low (say,

[32] See, e.g., American Bar Association (2006). Not all companies share data especially since the antitrust litigation involving an industry advisory group, the Insurance Services Office (ISO), in the early 1990s. In these cases, the industry relied on the ISO to develop prices based upon shared data. These prices could be used for collusion, but as a result of the litigation, the ISO now only collects information about lost costs and does not estimate what the proper price should be.

$1,000,000).[33] The second is having the requisite talent to manage a profitable company. The market for talented people is not limitless and insurance is a very technical business that requires some degree of managerial, financial, and actuarial acumen to ensure long run survival of a firm. This barrier to entry does not make insurance different from any other type of industry, but it is a barrier to entry nonetheless.

Perhaps the most significant entry deterrent is the requirement that insurers have a license from each state in which they operate. These licenses are expensive (Pottier 2011), and some have argued that they have the effect of reducing the incentive to operate in more than one state or line of business. Each state will have licensing fees and seasoning requirements that reduce the ability of entrants to branch to new states quickly as regulators in other states will want to see evidence of a functional insurer before issuing a license. License fees must be paid every year to every state where a company operates. In addition, all agents need to be licensed in each state where they write business. Finally, each company needs to pay for its regular market conduct and solvency examinations. Minimum capital requirements and other solvency restrictions set by the states can also be characterized as a barrier to entry. However, these requirements, although barriers in the classic sense, reduce the social costs of insurer failures, and are possibly valuable to customers.

A fourth barrier to entry is a complement to the third. This barrier to entry is a regulatory barrier to exit. Regulators may allow companies to enter a market, but they may also reserve the right to restrict exit from a market. This was evident when Aetna left the Massachusetts' auto market in the early 1990s (Yelen 1993). Aetna felt it could not earn a competitive return on its auto policies, and wanted to end that part of its business. Massachusetts told Aetna that if it stopped selling auto insurance, it would have to exit the entire market. It did so, but at the cost of having to leave all lines of business. Denying permission to exit may increase supply in the short run. But as Yelen pointed out, it will deter companies who have not yet entered from doing so. Florida saw the same thing after its hurricane crises, when firms desired to raise prices to offset future hurricane risks. The state refused to allow companies rate increases, and some companies left the state or reduced the number of policies sold. Further, the state tried to prevent companies from leaving immediately by requiring a slow reduction in policies

[33] The NAIC publishes a table each year. See, e.g., www.naic.org/documents/industry_ucaa_chart_min_capital_surplus.pdf (accessed September 26, 2013).

written to preserve the market from an immediate disruption. (See, e.g., Grace et al. 2003.)

Ultimately, barriers to entry in insurance are not caused by the 'production technology' or competitive environment of the industry, but are largely induced as part of the regulatory process. The barriers to entry are likely to be similar whether there is a federal solvency regulator or a state one. Perhaps a national solvency regulator might be more efficient from the point of view of the insurer as there will only be one regulator. There are some possible elements of local tastes and preferences in the licensing of insurers, but they are not likely offset by the economies of scale in federal regulation of insurer entry.

3. Unequal bargaining power

Unequal bargaining power can arise from a number of sources. It can be due to informational differences between buyers and sellers or it can be due to monopoly power. Although regulation does not prohibit market power, it does sometimes restrict a firm's ability to exercise its market power or to take advantage of a consumer's lack of information. An example of unequal bargaining power in the insurance context is when an insurer can dictate terms or prices to its customers. The resulting 'unfairness' is most serious in settings where consumers have little choice about whether to buy insurance, and from whom. If insurance is mandatory (as in auto or workers' compensation), the insured's position relative the insurer is at its weakest, and the problems may be compounded after an insurance claim is made and the insured is at the mercy of the insurer's decision to pay the claim. The private market's response here might be for consumers to find other ways of insuring or to go without coverage.

The regulatory response to market power is multidimensional. States impose good faith claims laws on insurers, they regulate contract language, and, when insurance is mandatory, prices may be regulated (Asmat and Tennyson, Chapter 12 in this volume). Courts also attempt to equalize the power difference between insurer and insureds by interpreting insurance contracts against the interest of the insurer when multiple reasonable interpretations exist, the so-called *contra proferentem* doctrine (Abraham 1996; Baker and Logue, Chapter 11 in this volume).

Each state regulates insurers' claims handling, marketing, training of agents, and the like. To the extent that consumers believe insurers engage in unfair practices, there will be lower demand for insurance. Consumers will avoid a product if they think it is not worth the cost or if the post-claim costs prove to be transparently high. Regulators attempt to mitigate these problems by regular market conduct examinations. These are essentially an audit of an insurer's marketing documents, claims process, and agent training.[34]

Market conduct exams may implicate local tastes and preferences, but this type of regulation can most efficiently be performed with a national standard because of economies of scale. The costs of duplication to insurers are so high that they dwarf the states' combined regulatory budgets (Pottier 2007; 2011).

The question of whether the state or federal government will be more efficient in regulating the effects of unequal bargaining power or of insurer market conduct probably leans towards the states. This is, in part, because of the many policy decisions involved in mandating insurance coverage terms or determining what actually constitutes bad faith. These decisions seem to implicate local tastes and preferences that vary across the country. However, this is an area where there is no strong evidence one way or the other to support federal regulation over state.

4. Unfair prices

Historically, states regulated insurance prices to keep them from being too low and thus impairing the ability of an insurer to pay claims (see Joskow 1973). After the *Southeastern Underwriters* decision regulators principally regulated prices to keep them from being too high (see, e.g., Hunter 2008). Harrington (2002) points out that compared with unregulated states, states with price regulation had higher prices some years and lower prices other years, but that over time prices were not statistically different. If one removed price regulation from the powers of insurance regulators, Harrington suggests everyone would be better off since on average prices are the same over time and price regulation is socially costly. Under fiscal federalism, local state preferences should matter because it is the local voters' decision to have price regulation or not. There are probably no economies of scale here as each state has a different set of characteristics (weather, population density, commute times, fire risk, income) that relate to the types of property owned (Lincoln versus Ford sedans) and their physical risk of loss (hurricane versus fire). Thus, it arguably makes sense to have locally determined prices based on locally determined risks of loss and tastes for price regulation.

---

[34] California posts its reports on-line. Here is an example, www20.insurance.ca.gov/epubacc/REPORT/135630.htm (accessed September 24, 2013).

5. Conclusion: Proper placement for market power regulation

Regulation in insurance cannot be justified on the basis of economies of scale in the provision of insurance. Thus, this consideration does not inform the debate for federal or state regulation. The primary barriers to entry in insurance are the regulatory minimums needed to operate an insurer. Here too, the level of the government that oversees the insurance industry will not likely have a large effect on these barriers to entry, as both federal and state regulators would have similar types of regulatory requirements. To the extent there are economies of scale in the production of this type of regulation (as opposed to the production of insurance itself), it is arguably more efficient to set this at the level of the federal government. Similarly, economies of scale in the regulation of unfair market practices might lean towards placing this regulation at the level of the federal government.

In contrast, state regulation will likely be paramount based on the supremacy of local tastes and preferences in terms of regulating unfair prices (as there is little evidence of economies of scale and no presence of externalities). Similarly, unequal bargaining power for mandated coverages (which are based on local tastes and preferences) are also likely to be optimal at the level of the state.

C. Externalities

An externality is a cost (or benefit) of an activity that is borne by people unconnected to the activity. A good example is particulate air pollution. Such pollution occurs when one party burns materials whose harmful residues are spread throughout an area, imposing harms on those who breathe them. The true cost of electricity generation, for example, includes not just the costs of inputs and generation (which are borne by the electricity-generating firm) but also the cost of the resulting air pollution, which are borne by society at large. In insurance markets, we see externalities in uncompensated accidents, potentially large catastrophic losses, and contagion from other markets or companies, legislative or judicial enactments that create uncertainty, and liability rules that are pro-consumer or pro-business rather than being neutral between parties.

1. Uncompensated accidents

In the case of two-party accidents in which the injurer is at fault, there can be an externality if the injurer is judgment proof. While the injurer would ordinarily be forced to pay for the harm he does (via liability to the victim), an injurer with no resources cannot be made to pay, leaving the victim to bear the entire cost of the accident (Shavell 1986). An important example is the case of an uninsured motorist with no wealth, who will never have to pay for any of the costs he imposes on his victim. The costs of this problem are greater the more drivers there are without insurance coverage, all other things held constant. Thus, a valid regulatory response might be to make auto insurance coverage mandatory. In fact, almost every state mandates personal responsibility or minimum coverage (Insurance Information Institute 2014). In addition, the private market provides uninsured motorist coverage to allow a driver who is not at fault to be covered if an uninsured at-fault driver causes harm to him or his property.

States differ in their mandatory minimum coverage requirements (see Table 10.2 above), which may reflect variations in local tastes and preferences. A uniform national rule here would increase prices for minimum coverage in some states and lower the minimum requirements (and prices) for consumers in other states. States are likely to be better than the federal government at deciding the proper policy response in this case. This is because state income distributions, state infrastructure (road quality), weather, liability laws, and driving rules all differ in subtle ways across states. If one believes that the states' preferences matter for decisions about road quality and liability laws, then the minimum coverage requirements should matter too. One can argue that there are no economies of scale argument that would override the states' decisions to have differing rules here because of the significant physical and demographic differences among the states.

2. Extraterritorial regulation

Extraterritorial regulation is a second potential type of externality to discuss. One state's laws might affect other states by imposing costs (or benefits) on out-of-state consumers. For example, New York has an investment law that requires life insurers operating in New York to follow the New York investment rules, no matter where the company is chartered and where else it does business. The so-called 'Appleton Rule' dates to 1906.[35] Many commentators (see Pottier and Sommer 1998) suggest that New York has the most stringent regulation, and that this rule makes New York insurers (and therefore insureds) safer. However, this rule requiring more conservative investments may result in lower investment returns, and may therefore cause insurers to charge higher

---

[35] The current version is at N.Y. INS. LAW § 1413 (2013) which says 'The superintendent may refuse a new or renewal license to any foreign insurer, if he finds that its investments do not comply in substance with the investment requirements and limitations imposed by this chapter upon like domestic insurers.'

prices to provide proper reserves. As a result, it may impose higher prices on consumers outside of New York without the input of the out-of-state consumers and voters. If the gains from increased safety are exactly offset by higher prices to insureds, then the Appleton Rule may not create externalities. However, to the extent that New York's rule is not optimal, out-of-state consumers could bear a higher cost for their policies without a sufficiently offsetting safety benefit. Of course the opposite could be true and the New York Regulation may provide a benefit to out-of-state consumers. Both are externalities. Even supposing that New York was able to choose the optimal insurance investment law for New York, there still may be externalities on other states. Pottier (2011) concludes that many insurers do not sell in New York to avoid its extraterritorial restrictions. Further, companies often set up New York-only subsidiaries to reduce the effect of this extraterritorial regulation. This imposes costs on shareholders in terms of corporate governance and on regulators in other states (extra companies to oversee merely because of a regulation in one state). This is inefficient. Federal regulation would prevent this type of extraterritorial regulation as there would be a uniform rule without the ability to opt out.

Another example of extraterritorial regulation arose in the case of *Avery* v. *State Farm*.[36] State Farm required cheaper non-original equipment parts to be used in repairs to some covered vehicles, and this apparently violated an Illinois consumer protection law that was unrelated to insurance. Some other states had policies permitting the use of these parts and State Farm argued that a nationwide class was not appropriate. Nevertheless, an Illinois trial court certified a nationwide class action against State Farm, and at trial, State Farm was found liable for over $1 billion in damages for the harm that its breach of Illinois law caused to the nationwide class. The trial court's determination was eventually overturned by the Illinois Supreme Court, but one could see that Illinois' interpretation of insurance contracts which was binding on State Farm nationally would distribute costs and benefits across the states without the approval (or disapproval) of those affected by the decision (Schwartz and Lorber 2000). One can argue that there is no externality here as out-of-state consumers would get the benefit of having original parts. However, if states considered the relative prices of parts when making their determination about allowing secondary market parts to be used to repair cars, then this nationwide application of Illinois' law is an usurpation of state sovereignty which, some may argue, is a significant external cost. This type of externality would be eliminated if there were national regulation.

---

[36] 835 NE2d 801, Ill. Supreme Court (2005).

3. Contagion to the financial system

Since the financial crisis of 2008, several papers have examined the effects of the crisis on the insurance industry (see, e.g., Grace 2010; Chen et al. 2013). Two major concepts emerge from this literature: contagion and interconnectedness. Contagion has a number of definitions, but Kaufman (2000) provides three definitions that make sense in the insurance context.

First, contagion can occur with a high correlation of insurer returns and an observational clustering of insurer failures in time. For example, a large hurricane striking Florida would lower all companies' reserves (impacting their returns) and it may be associated with a corresponding set of insurer failures.

Second, contagion can occur when one firm causes the failure of other firms due to economic linkages. The difference between the first two definitions is merely the difference between correlation and causation. An example of the second type of contagion might be if a reinsurer failed and was not able to make its payment to a primary insurer, causing the primary insurer to fail.

Third, contagion can be due to uncertainty about similarly situated firms. For example, a court may hold that an insurance policy should be interpreted in such a way as to substantially increase liability to policyholders. This, in turn, may result in the entire set of companies writing such policies being suspect from an insolvency point of view.[37] Thus, a shock creates uncertainty about the quality of numerous firms.[38] This type of contagion is not often seen in insurance markets.

The first two types of contagion – widespread contagion in the insurance industry due to correlated bad returns, and contagion due to one solvency leading to other insolvencies – present the biggest risks to insurance markets. Both of these potential externalities might be solved by federal regulation.

Widespread contagion with the result of many failed insurers may lead to availability problems if there are no new insurers to cover risks. In such instances, it is important to have a credible insurer of last resort that can step in to assure the public that it will provide liquidity or reinsurance to all solvent insurers. Such an assurance may be an important way to prevent the failure of one insurance company from toppling other companies.

---

[37] For example, the 9/11 terrorist attacks created uncertainty about the effect of the actual 9/11 attacks on other firms (Doherty, Lamm-Tennant, and Starks 2003).

[38] For example, the 9/11 terrorist attacks lead to uncertainty about the frequency and severity of future terrorist events, affecting the whole insurance industry (Cummins and Lewis 2003).

A recent example of the potential for contagion stems from the failure of AIG, one of the world's largest insurance companies. AIG had numerous insurance operations throughout the world. It also had financing and lending operations as well as leasing operations. A subsidiary of AIG called AIG Financial Products (which was not an insurer) sold financial instruments that operated much like bond insurance. If the value of the insured financial instruments fell, AIG would have to pay to make the owner whole. As debt during the lead up to the financial crises was declining in market value, the amount AIG had to hold in reserve increased dramatically. In September of 2008, AIG had to have an infusion of cash from the United States in order to avoid bankruptcy. Essentially, the Financial Products Division engaged in behavior that put the entire company in the hands of the US Government.[39]

Because of AIG's size, its failure would have had an effect on the entire financial market, affecting all banks and their major counterparties: Goldman Sachs, Merrill Lynch, Bank of America, Wachovia, Citigroup, Société Generale, Deutsche Bank, Barclays, and UBS (Harrington 2009). AIG and a small number of other insurers qualified to obtain a 'bailout' from the Federal Reserve and later from the US government under the Troubled Asset Recovery Program (TARP).[40] In addition to AIG, Lincoln National and the Hartford Insurance Group received TARP funds.[41] Most insurers did not suffer a contagion effect caused by AIG's problem, and AIG's performance was like that of other TARP recipients rather than other insurance companies (Grace 2010). The major exceptions were companies that sold highly hedged (and thus highly correlated with the market downturn) guaranteed minimum withdrawal benefit annuities. These companies also experienced significant capital pressures. Thus, while AIG was affected during the financial crises and its counterparties were also affected, there was little spillover to the insurance industry.

The US government's response to the failure of AIG and other financial institutions was to provide liquidity to financial markets generally. This included bailouts to banks and to a small number of insurers. At the time of TARP there was a great deal of misunderstanding about the role of the insurance industry as an instigator of the crises. In retrospect, it was a credit problem affecting mostly the credit markets, but Congress

---

[39] Harrington (2009) describes the activities of the Financial Product Division that bankrupted the company in detail.

[40] TARP was a program enacted under the Emergency Economic Stabilization Act of 2008, Pub. L. No. 110-343, Div. A, 122 Stat. 3765 (2008), codified, as amended, at 12 U.S.C. §§ 5201 et seq.

[41] See, e.g., Propublica (2014).

was investigating the role AIG played in the crisis and it was difficult to see that AIG, while an insurer, was not in financial distress because of its insurance activities, but due to its financial market activities.[42]

Supplying liquidity to distressed insurers is something a state government would be hard pressed to do, simply because most states lack the fiscal resources needed for the job, and only the Federal Reserve has the authority to supply unlimited liquidity via its power to print money. Thus, liquidity interventions to stem a financial crisis are something that can be accomplished only at the federal level. This power to provide liquidity solves an externality problem between companies that can only be accomplished at the federal level. As a result of the Dodd-Frank Act enacted in 2010, certain insurers have been designated SIFIs because the Federal Solvency Oversight Committee (FSOC) believes that the collapse of these particular financial institutions would pose a serious risk to the economy. Currently, AIG, Prudential, and Metropolitan Life Insurance Company have a SIFI designation. In turn, the international community is in the process of specifying Globally Systemically Important Insurers (G-SIIs) and those three US insurers have also been named as G-SIIs (Dewenter and Riddick 2015).[43] The purpose of the SIFI designation is to provide a sophisticated regulator to oversee systemically important companies that could cause the impairment of the entire financial system.

4. Contagion to other insurers

While systemic risk is an important consideration, it is essentially the effect of an inter-sector externality. There is also the problem of one insurer's failure 'causing' another insurer's failure. However, insurers are more siloed than banks, and it is difficult to have a 'run' on an insurer that translates to uncertainty about other insurers. If a bank is thought to be in trouble, depositors can withdraw their savings putting the bank at risk. If a customer is worried about the stability of a bank, it might be that all banks are suffering from the same underlying risk, and all depositors then decide to withdraw their funds causing a run on otherwise healthy banks.

Even after the financial crises, there is not much risk of contagion caused by weak insurers causing harm to other insurers.[44] This is due to

[42] The large concern was that there were more insurance companies like AIG that had all of these interconnected relationships (rather than shared liabilities).

[43] See Financial Stability Board, *List of Globally Systemically Important Insurers*, at www.financialstabilityboard.org/publications/r_130718.htm (accessed September 24, 2014).

[44] The lack of academic literature with the phrase 'run on the insurer' is telling. If one tests Google Scholar for this phrase from 1900–2007 there are

the fact that for property insurance, consumers have relatively short term contracts (six months to a year for personal lines products) that are prepaid or pay-as-you-go. For life insurance there is often little ability to get a return of premiums prior to the contract's termination.[45]

Prior to the recent financial crisis, the insolvency of one insurer was not generally believed to threaten the solvency of others. This was not always true, however. In the 1920s when homeownership became more common, many insurers sold mortgage insurance along with other insurance products. When housing prices collapsed during the Great Depression, numbers of insurers were forced into insolvency. The regulatory response was to place mortgage and title insurance into separate companies called 'monolines' which could only hold one risk (Jaffee 2006). This compartmentalization largely served to isolate all other insurers from adverse developments in the real estate market. While several mortgage insurers failed during the recent financial crisis, these failures did not jeopardize the rest of the insurance market.

Further, while we did not see widespread insurance company failures during the recent financial crises, there have been sufficient failures over the last 30 years to give some sense of the efficiency of state regulation. Grace and Phillips (2007) estimate an economic cost function model of state regulation and find that there are economies of scale of state regulation – especially solvency regulation. This method estimates a cost of regulation for each state using as inputs the wages of state regulators in different categories: actuaries, managers, and lawyers. It used as regulatory outputs solvency and market conduct exams, rule making, enforcement actions, agent oversight, model law and rule development, price regulation, and

---

11 resulting hits. From 2008 to the present there are only five results as of September 29, 2014. In contrast, if one tests for the phrase 'run on the bank,' there were 1,850 results prior to the financial crises (1900–2007) and 1,910 results after the financial crises as of September 29, 2014. Printouts of citations are available from the author.

[45] Life insurance policies with cash values often have options for loans. One could withdraw any cash built up in a policy through a loan, but one would not be able to withdraw costlessly as there are interest payments and tax considerations. However, we observed times where it paid for consumers to remove cash for reasons unrelated to an insurer's solvency. During the high inflation period of the 1970s and 1980s life insurers saw customers withdrawing cash value (at a 4% loan rate) and putting those same funds into high yield CDs, which paid 15–18 percent in some cases. These CDs were insured by the FDIC and provided inflation protection to the customer at the expense of the potential solvency of the life insurer. Most life insurers rewrote contracts to reduce this incentive for disintermediation by making the loan rate tied to the prevailing market interest rates (Black and Skipper 2000: 1111).

consumer services (mediation, hotlines). The authors found that for all but the very biggest states, there were increasing returns to scale in regulation. This means that it would be more efficient to combine states (or move to a higher level of government) to oversee the insurance industry.

Correspondingly, if the state was the most efficient level of regulation, then the state should exhibit constant returns to scale because it has reached the minimum of the average cost curve. However, the authors found that economies of scale exist, so that it would be cheaper to combine states rather than regulate as separate entities. As it is, the evidence suggests that regulation at a higher level of government would be more cost effective. In addition, Grace and Phillips (2007) found evidence that smaller states reduced their regulatory expenditures, implicitly relying on the bigger states to regulate for them. While one might think that it is optimal for a small state like Rhode Island to let New York do its regulating for them, Rhode Island is increasing the costs of regulation to New York taxpayers and consumers, without doing its fair share. Rhode Island consumers get the benefit of New York's regulatory apparatus without paying for it. This interstate externality can be remedied by federal solvency regulation that would eliminate the externalities created by multistate insolvencies and the possible contagion or interconnection effects of other financial industry failures.

5. Externalities due to large losses or uncertainties about future pricing

After large losses due to Hurricane Andrew in 1992, firms decided to reduce their market share in Florida. This exogenous shock had an effect on all the companies in the state, and they reacted in a similar way by raising prices and reducing market exposure (dropping customers). The reason this happened was either the realization of a rationally unforeseen extreme loss event or pricing that was too low for the real risk. If it was a rationally unforeseen loss, then some insurers could believe that this was a type of risk that did not fit the insurer's strategic plan because it exposed the company to too much risk. After Andrew, pricing flexibility was reduced by state regulators and in an environment where a hurricane like Andrew could occur again in the future, many insurers believed that the state would not permit insurers to use prices that would allow them to earn a profit consistent with the risk (Grace and Klein 2009).

This type of externality is not likely to be handled better at the federal as opposed to the state level. The state of Florida for political reasons seems unlikely to allow insurers to sell policies that are properly priced. But federal programs such as the Flood Insurance Program, are also improperly priced, even after Congress enacted the Biggert-Waters Flood

Insurance Reform Act in 2012,[46] which required actuarially fair prices for everyone. Political pressure undid that requirement in 2014, further reducing the ability to remove the externality caused by a subsidy to flood insurance.[47]

No private market responses have developed to reduce the costs of this type of uncertainty. Thus, this is a perfect case for government intervention. As most commentators have noted, Florida's state government has not really helped here. In addition to a market failure, we have had a government failure in Florida, which instead of correcting the problem has concentrated the risk of catastrophic losses on the state's taxpayer-supported property insurance company (Citizens Property Insurance Corporation) and on its Florida Hurricane Cat fund. Although the latter was designed to help Florida insurers by providing lower cost reinsurance, it caused insurers to purchase more of the cheaper state provided reinsurance and less of the more expensive market based reinsurance to the point where total reinsurance costs did not fall.

6. Judicial and legislative rulings favoring insurers or consumers

Suppose a state passes a new law that mandates additional coverage for insureds in the state. Insurers might be indifferent to the inclusion of the new benefit as long as they are allowed to increase prices to cover their higher costs. However, the new benefits might increase the price of the overall insurance package to the point where the demand for insurance declines. A good example of this would be the case of *Mierzwa* v. *Florida Windstorm Underwriting Assn.*[48] A Florida court held that damage caused by flood was covered under a 'wind-only' policy because the wind and the flood occurred concurrently. The homeowner's policy tried to exclude damages from flood in every possible way, as flood coverage is expensive, and mostly provided by the National Flood Insurance Program, not private market insurers. Despite such disclaimers, however, the Florida court said floods often happen simultaneously with wind losses, making it difficult to determine how much of the overall damage was attributable to flood and how much to wind. The court decided that if a consumer did not have flood insurance, then wind coverage should cover the loss, as long as the loss was 'concurrently caused'. However, the wind-only policy was originally priced on the assumption that flood losses were completely

---

[46] H.R. 4348, PL 112–141 (112th Congress).

[47] Homeowner Flood Insurance Affordability Act of 2014, H.R. 3370, PL 113–89 (113th Congress).

[48] 877 So. 2d 774 (Fla. 4th DCA 2004).

excluded, irrespective of concurrent causation. This judicial extension of benefits transferred wealth from insurers to policyholders, who were rewarded with a benefit for which they had never paid. The result could lead to higher demand for wind insurance and less demand for flood insurance. However, this extension of benefits also hurt insurers and led to fewer insurers willing to sell insurance in the state. Thus, the externality here is that a court could rewrite a contract and impose costs on those who wrote similar contracts.

Judicial and legislative rulings favoring insurers or consumers are potentially truly local in cost and benefit. Concurrent causation for wind versus water might not be an issue in other states, and even if it were, there is no requirement that courts in other states follow Florida's interpretation of the insurance contract. The expansion of coverage in the case of Florida was generated by local conditions and is not likely to provide aggregate net benefits to residents of other states.

An exception to this might be the case of product liability reform. While not technically an insurance regulation, this issue is related to insurance because of its effect on liability insurance markets. One can argue that products liability, directors and officer's liability insurance, and maybe certain other kinds of liability coverage, are really bought and sold in a national market rather than a state market. For example, a worldwide manufacturer of automobiles does not necessarily know exactly where its products are going to be sold and used. This requires some strategic thinking about the liability environment in which the automobile may be sold. One can imagine that a company might design and price the product to comport with the strictest liability rule in place. Thus, a state with a relatively large market and a very strict liability rule essentially makes the rule for the entire country (or world). The benefits of this rule are available to everyone in the country (in the sense of a lower probability of harm) and the costs of the rule (in the sense of higher prices) are borne by everyone in the country. Yet everyone in the country did not have the ability to influence or design the liability rule. Voters in the large market did. Thus, because the benefits and costs of this type of 'liability regulation' are national, it might more beneficially be placed at the federal level where national decision makers can determine the safety/cost trade off rather than the voters of a particular state.

7. Conclusion: Proper placement for externality regulation

Most of the externality concerns can be solved by federal regulation as these externalities concern all insurers in a similar manner. An important exception exists, however, for the law and regulation of uncompensated accidents. This is truly a local concern. Whether drivers should have coverage and how much they should have are based on individual state preferences. One might argue that individual states get these issues wrong, but because local state preferences dominate any evidence of economies of scale or any evidence of the existence of cross-state externalities for mandated coverage and uninsured motorists or workers' compensation, this arguably remains a local concern. The other externalities generally focus on contagion from financial risk. Solvency regulation is likely more effective at a national level as economies of scale in such regulation are evident, and there exists a possible negative externality from small states free-riding on the regulatory activities of larger states. Additionally, large losses that might be uninsurable in some markets (flood, terror, nuclear) may have such social benefit that the government should act as a backstop or upper level reinsurer. Finally, two types of externalities (extraterritorial effect of state law) and judicial or legislated rules exist that create uncertainty. This type of uncertainty could happen at either the state or federal level. Thus, neither state nor federal regulation has a comparative advantage save for the fact that if a state makes a law which increases uncertainty the effects of such a law arguably tend to stay in the state.

IV. CONCLUSION: WHERE DOES INSURANCE REGULATION BELONG?

The previous two sections covered the economic justification for regulation and what the states regulate currently. Further, an initial assessment was made of where each form of insurance regulation should be located based upon Oates's theory of fiscal federalism. This theory suggests that in the absence of cross-state externalities or compelling costs savings from combining regulatory authority at a higher governmental level, social welfare is enhanced by permitting states to regulate based upon local tastes and preferences. This suggests that not all market failures are necessarily better solved by federal regulation.

While there are market failures that generate some discussion of whether federal or state regulation might be more efficient, this next section proposes to carve out more specific categories of activities or products that are candidates for federal or state regulation. Specifically, solvency as a regulatory function should be regulated at the federal level. Commodity products or commercial products might also best be regulated at the national level rather than the state. In contrast, there are certain activities that are arguably best regulated by the states based on the absence of significant economies of scale or externalities.

A. Candidate Activities or Products for Federal Regulation

1. Solvency and resolution activities

Insurance is an interstate business and firms operate quite freely across states lines. This is supported by the data in Table 10.1 above. Economies of scale in the production of solvency regulation have been found by Grace and Phillips (2007). That is, they show that there are cost savings from providing solvency regulation at a higher level of government. In addition, they provide evidence of regulatory shirking by smaller states, which free-ride off the larger states. Thus, federal solvency regulation would appear to be consistent with the Oates model as there are economies of scale and cross-state externalities resulting from our current system.

Further, a number of authors have found that insurer insolvencies are expensive to resolve (Willenborg 2000; Grace, Klein, and Phillips 2003), and that states may therefore delay resolution of insolvent insurers for political reasons (Leverty and Grace 2012). Unlike other kinds of companies, insurance bankruptcy is handled under state law, and there are in fact three different resolution mechanisms in use.[49] Moreover, there are no specialist insurance bankruptcy judges (as there are in the federal system), since there are too few insurance insolvencies to justify a specialized judiciary at the state level. Grace, Klein, and Phillips (2003) point to this as a potential economy of scale that would allow more efficient resolution of insurer insolvencies if there were a single bankruptcy resolution entity like the FDIC for insurers. Surprisingly, multistate insolvencies tend to be resolved more quickly because multiple regulators oversee the insolvency. Insolvencies are observable by multiple regulators, and it is possible that the home state regulator does a better job because shirking responsibility, or managing an insolvency poorly, is observable by peers (Willenborg 2000).

2. Candidate products for federal regulation

Further, it may be desirable to exempt certain products from state regulation and turn them over to a federal regulator or an interstate compact for product regulation. This would be possible if the economies of scale in product design regulation were greater than the benefits due to local

---

[49] There are two different model laws in use by the states (one proposed by the NAIC and the other by the National Conference of Commissioners of Uniform State Laws). In addition, there is a proposed model law that Illinois is currently using. See Grace, Klein, and Phillips (2003) for a discussion of the frameworks in more detail.

tastes and preferences. These conditions are most likely to hold for commodity products or products purchased by sophisticated insurance customers.

'Commodity' products Term life insurance is a relatively uniform product. A 30-year term policy in Michigan is largely identical to a 30-year term policy in Kansas, all other things equal (age, sex, health, and smoking status). For such commodity products, differences in state laws for, say, contestability are probably not as important as price and solvency oversight. The significant economies of scale in product design regulation for true commodity products could outweigh the benefit of deferring to individual states' preferences and tastes. States would not have the authority to rewrite the contract or engage in a costly approval process.

We do have some data for life insurers that provides some evidence of the cost savings for reducing duplicative regulation. Pottier (2007; 2011) undertakes an efficiency analysis of life insurers regulated at the state level and finds that there are significant costs to obtaining an additional state license. For the life insurance industry, the extra costs amounted to about $5 billion per year in 2005 (Pottier 2007), a sum that is ultimately passed on to policyholders. While there may be some benefit to having more than one state regulator conducting a market conduct exam that looks at each life insurer's marketing documents and agent training, it is probably excessive to repeat this exercise in 40 or more jurisdictions. The evidence suggests that this duplication creates significant compliance costs without a corresponding consumer benefit. These costs are passed on to both consumers and shareholders of insurers, much like a tax.[50]

Commercial insurance Commercial insurance does not suffer from the same types of market conduct problems that personal insurance might, as both parties to the contract are sophisticated. Thus, there is less likely to be overreaching or unequal bargaining power between the two contracting parties. Like the commodity products, the states' oversight of contracts between more sophisticated parties does not add much value.

There is a type of insurer that operates nationally without multiple states' oversight. RRGs are insurers formed to provide commercial liability coverage for firms, making them different than a typical personal lines company.

---

[50] There is a bit more to this issue as it is relatively large companies (nationwide in scope) that are most interested in federal regulation. Small companies and agents are less interested. See Harrington (2006).

An RRG is incorporated in a particular state and is not subject to oversight in other states as it essentially has a nationwide license. The customers of an RRG are typically more sophisticated than the average consumer.

This regulatory structure provides one way to measure the potential benefits of federal regulation (or a single regulatory authority). It is possible to compare the effects of a single regulator for RRGs versus a traditional multistate regulatory scheme governing commercial liability companies. Leverty (2012) undertakes such a comparison and finds that for *single-state* companies, there are no differences in compliance costs or prices between RRGs and similar liability insurers. However, multistate liability insurers charge prices that are roughly 30 percent higher than similarly situated RRGs selling the same kinds of policies. Leverty suggests that this is largely due to the costs of duplicative regulation faced by traditional multistate liability insurers. Thus, a single federal regulator for commercial policies would reduce costs.

The purchasers of commercial insurance are businesses that – almost by definition – are more sophisticated than the individuals who purchase personal lines such as home or auto policies. Sophisticated buyers need less regulatory protection (at any level of government), simply because they are in a better position to look out for their own interests. Indeed, many states have deregulated commercial lines by relaxing rules for rate and form approval (Klein 2006). And because large liability insurers are likely to be operating across many state markets, there does not seem to be a need for each state to assess their market conduct.

3. Other considerations

In addition to solvency regulation and the regulation of certain products, there are other potential issues that might require a federal role in the regulation of insurers. International concerns, as well as the potential for socially beneficial insurance for risks that appear uninsurable, might also create a role for the federal government.

International issues The business of insurance has become increasingly international, and so, of necessity, has its regulation (Brown 2007; Cooke and Skipper 2009). The presence of 50 separate regulatory entities within the US has at times raised significant barriers to the negotiation of international agreements governing insurance. For example, when the US was negotiating the General Agreement on Trade in Services, the US government was not able to speak with a single voice, since state regulators had to weigh in on insurance trade related issues. This precipitated concerns that our style of regulatory federalism posed a barrier to trade in international insurance markets, since a foreign insurer would need to obtain 50 licenses to operate nationally, while a US insurer would only need one to operate in the EU. In response, the Dodd-Frank Act attempted to provide the FIO with the ability to coordinate the US government's response to international requirements for prudential regulation.

Public finance issues for 'uninsurable' losses Large catastrophes such as floods, hurricanes, terrorism, or a nuclear power accident, may be uninsurable, and as a result may require a federal role in the supply of insurance. On the other hand, Congress is reluctant to give away the store by socializing these risks if they can be handled in private markets. Thus, while hurricane insurance is expensive in coastal areas, Congress has not volunteered to use federal resources to provide reinsurance. Bills were proposed to do this, but never went far.[51] Congress has provided for federal insurance programs in nuclear power in the Price Anderson Act, which provides excess of loss coverage for a nuclear power accident.[52] The federal government directly provides insurance for flood and crop failure because the risks are considered uninsurable in the private market (Michel-Kerjan and Kousky 2010). Arguments of this type have also been made for terrorism risks, and Congress authorized the Treasury to be a backstop for losses above a company deductible with the total amount to be limited to $100 billion a year under the Terrorism Risk Insurance Act (TRIA) (Brown, Kroszner, and Jenn 2002; Dixon et al. 2014).

These large losses are a potential externality, or public good, that arguably only the government can provide (see Jaffee and Russell (1997) for a fuller discussion of the issues). While not everyone agrees that all of these losses are uninsurable, it is important to note the concern that large catastrophic losses might be uninsurable and that it may make sense for the federal government to be involved in the provision of such coverage if the social benefits outweigh the costs.

B. Candidates for State Regulation

If we look at the regulatory activities with little potential for economies of scale or cross-state externalities, then using the theory of fiscal federalism, state regulation will tend to dominate from a welfare perspective over national regulation because it will tend to reflect differences in tastes and preferences. So what types of activities or products fit this bill?

---

[51] See, e.g., the National Disaster Projection Partnership Act of 1994, H.R. 2873 (103rd Congress).

[52] 42 U.S.C. section 2210.

1. Contract term requirements

State laws vary widely on whether specific contract terms are required on topics such as wind or earthquake, types of insurance (no-fault), amounts of required minimum coverage, and mandated benefits. Such differences are presumably based on local risks, local weather, local liability law, income and the like. These differences are chosen by the state and in the absence of economies of scale or cross-state externalities, the presumption is that local regulation will provide a welfare dominating approach.

Similarly, personal lines products are not commodities like term life products – especially for liability coverages where liability is based upon state law. Product form regulation in every state increases compliance costs and creates delays in bringing new products to the market. Even so, state voters may value the scrutiny that regulation places on these contracts because it is presumably adapted to local conditions. This is, in part, due to differences in local risks that might cause policies to be drafted differently to provide for more or less coverage. For example, California earthquake policies might look quite different from those sold in other states with lower earthquake risks. The fact that risk is based on demographics, demand, and location all weigh heavily in the determination that personal liability lines are likely to be more efficiently regulated by the states.

2. Claims settlement practices

As mentioned above, states will differ in the way they regulate the payment of claims. For example, some states adopt a permissive attitude towards lawsuits alleging bad faith by the insurer, while others are much less tolerant (Asmat and Tennyson 2014). Bad faith law could be set at the federal level with a uniform rule, but states' tort law is within their traditional preserve and is presumably valued under fiscal federalism because there is little evidence of economies of scale or cross-state externalities. An interesting counter example, however, is that claim settlement problems may transcend states because they are the result of policies/procedures by national companies. Placing sole authority for regulating this at the state level can thus result in regulators missing larger trends and problems.[53] This is an example of a cross-state externality; however, it has to overcome the strong state interest in bad faith enforcement and the resulting insurer liability, which differs from state to state.

---

[53] This example is from Daniel Schwarcz in a comment on this chapter.

3. Pricing

Price regulation also varies greatly among the states (Harrington 2002). Some states have no price regulation (Illinois) while others have prior approval regulation (North Carolina). There is a range of practices in between with various levels of scrutiny. While the evidence is that over time prices are not lower in price-regulated states than in relatively unregulated states, this is still something that state voters arguably care about. This is especially apparent when one looks at the failure of price regulation to accomplish its goals of keeping prices lower than would otherwise occur. Further, while price regulation itself is expensive to undertake, many states still choose to undertake this style of regulation.

C. Final Assessment

Discussion of federal versus state regulation often presumes an 'either/or situation'. However, the evidence does not strongly support lodging insurance regulation solely at the federal or state level. In addition, the US already has a great deal of variation in the sources of insurance regulation. Some regulation is created through an interstate compact (Interstate Insurance Product Regulation Compact), some by federal law (employee benefits, such as annuities, retirement products, and life and health insurance, through the Employee Retirement and Income Security Act overseen by the Department of Labor), and some by one state (RRGs). Further, there is a great deal of cooperation among the states in the form of the NAIC activities, including the promulgation of model laws and regulations.

Perhaps the strongest case for federal insurance regulation can be made for solvency regulation, where there is evidence of economies of scale and cross-state externalities. A strong case can also be made for federal regulation in the case of certain commodity and commercial insurance products, where there is evidence of significant economies of scale from costs savings to insurers and to states by aggregating the level of regulation to the federal level.

At the same time, certain forms of insurance regulation are sensibly lodged at the state level. Oates would say that we should allow the states to offer a decentralized set of regulatory services in the absence of economies of scale or cross-state externalities. Neither of these are strongly present in areas such as regulation of contract terms and coverage. Products that are strongly tied to a state's negligence law are also more than likely to be provided by the state more efficiently because of fiscal federalism's assumption that states' tastes and preference are important welfare concerns. It is likely that as the markets become more integrated and firms become more national and international, there will be more evidence of economies of scale and cross-state externalities that will shift some of the weight for state regulation towards the federal provision of insurance regulation.

REFERENCES

Abraham, Kenneth S. 1985. Efficiency and Fairness in Insurance Risk Classification. 71(3) *Va. L. Rev*. 403–51.

Abraham, Kenneth S. 1996. A Theory of Insurance Policy Interpretation. 95 *University of Michigan Law Review* 531–69.

American Bar Association. 2006. Section of Antitrust Law, *Comments to the Antitrust Modernization Commission Regarding the McCarran-Ferguson Act*. Chicago, IL: American Bar Association.

Arrow, Kenneth J. 1963. Uncertainty and the Welfare Economics of Medical Care. 53(3) *The American Economic Review* 941–73.

Asmat, D. P., and S. Tennyson. 2014. Does the Threat of Insurer Liability for Bad Faith Affect Insurance Settlements? 81(1) *Journal of Risk and Insurance* 1–26.

Avraham, Ronen, Kyle D. Logue, and Daniel Schwarcz. 2014a. The Anatomy of Insurance Anti-Discrimination Laws. 87(1) *University of Southern California Law Review* 195–274.

Avraham, Ronen, Kyle D. Logue, and Daniel Schwarcz. 2014b. Explaining Variation in Insurance Anti-Discrimination Laws. 21(1) *Connecticut Insurance Law Journal* 1–52.

Black, Kenneth Jr., and Harold J. Skipper. 2000. *Life and Health Insurance* (13th edition). New Jersey: Prentice-Hall Inc.

Brockett, P. L., and L. L. Golden. 2007. Biological and Psychobehavioral Correlates of Credit Scores and Automobile Insurance Losses: Toward An Explication of Why Credit Scoring Works. 74(1) *Journal of Risk and Insurance* 23–63.

Brown, Elizabeth F. 2007. Tyranny of the Multitude Is a Multiplied Tyranny: Is the United States Financial Regulatory Structure Undermining US Competitiveness? 2 *Brook. J. Corp. Fin. and Com. L*. 369–420.

Brown, Jeffrey Robert, and Austan Goolsbee. 2002. Does the Internet Make Markets More Competitive? Evidence from the Life Insurance Industry. 110(3) *Journal of Political Economy* 481–507.

Brown, Jeffrey Robert., R. S. Kroszner, and B. H. Jenn. 2002. *Federal Terrorism Risk Insurance* (No. w9271). National Bureau of Economic Research.

Chambers, Donald C. 1999. The Future of Risk Classification in the Age of Predictive DNA-Based Testing. 3(1) *North American Actuarial Journal* 31–3.

Chen, Hua, J. David Cummins, Krupa S. Viswanathan, and Mary A Weiss. 2013. Systemic Risk and the Interconnectedness between Banks and Insurers: An Econometric Analysis. 81(3) *Journal of Risk and Insurance* 623–52.

Chiappori, P. A., and B. Salanie. 2000. Testing for Asymmetric Information in Insurance Markets. 108(1) *Journal of Political Economy* 56–78.

Cohen, Alma. 2005. Asymmetric Information and Learning: Evidence from the Automobile Insurance Market. 87(2) *Review of Economics and Statistics* 197–207.

Cooke, J. A., and H. D. Skipper. 2009. US Insurance Regulation in a Competitive World Insurance Market: An Evaluation, in Martin Grace and Robert Klein (eds.), *The Future of Insurance Regulation*. Washington, DC: Brookings Institution Press.

Clifford, Karen A., and Russell Iuculano. 1987. Aids and Insurance: The Rationale for Aids-Related Testing. 100(3) *Harvard Law Review* 1806–25.

Crocker, K. J., and S. Tennyson. 2002. Insurance Fraud and Optimal Claims Settlement Strategies. 45(2) *Journal of Law & Economics* 469–508.

Cummins, J. D., and C. M. Lewis. 2003. Catastrophic Events, Parameter Uncertainty and the Breakdown of Implicit Long-Term Contracting: The Case of Terrorism Insurance. 26(2/3) *Journal of Risk and Uncertainty* 153–78.

Cummins, J. David, and Mary A. Weiss. 2000. Analyzing Firm Performance in the Insurance Industry Using Frontier Efficiency and Productivity Methods, in D. Cummins and G. Dionne (eds.), *Handbook of Insurance* (1st edition). Berlin: Springer. 767–829.

Cummins, J. D., and Mary A. Weiss. 2014. Systemic Risk and the US Insurance Sector. 81(3) *Journal of Risk and Insurance* 489–528.

D'Arcy, S. P., and J. R. Garven. 1990. Property-liability Insurance Pricing Models: An Empirical Evaluation. 57(3) *Journal of Risk and Insurance* 391–430.

Day, John G. 1970. *Economic Regulation of Insurance in the United States*. US Government Printing Office.

Derrig, Richard A. 2002. Insurance Fraud. 69(3) *Journal of Risk and Insurance* 271–87.

Derrig, Richard A., and H. I. Weisberg. 2004. Determinants of Total Compensation for Auto Bodily Injury Liability under No-Fault: Investigation, Negotiation and the Suspicion of Fraud. 71(4) *Insurance and Risk Management* 633–62.

Derrig, Richard A., H. I. Weisberg, and X. Chen. 1994. Behavioral Factors and Lotteries Under No-Fault With a Monetary Threshold: A Study of Massachusetts Automobile Insurance Claims. 61(2) *Journal of Risk and Insurance* 245–75.

Dewenter, Kathryn L., and Leigh A. Riddick. 2015. What's the Value of a TBTF Guaranty? Evidence from the G-SII Designation for Insurance Companies (January 9). Available at SSRN: http://ssrn.com/abstract=2547723 (accessed September 25, 2015).

Diamond, D. W., and P. H. Dybvig. 1983. Bank Runs, Deposit Insurance, and Liquidity. 91(3) *Journal of Political Economy* 401–19.

Dixon, L., M. Dworsky, B. M. Jenkins, T. LaTourrette, and H. H. Willis. 2014. *The Future of the Terrorism Risk Insurance Act*. Santa Monica, CA: Rand.

Doherty, Neil A., Joan Lamm-Tennant, and Laura T. Starks. 2003. Insuring September 11th: Market Recovery and Transparency. 26(2–3) *Journal of Risk and Uncertainty* 179–99.

Grace, Martin. 2010. The Insurance Industry and Systemic Risk: Evidence and Discussion. *Networks Financial Institute Policy Brief*, (2010-PB-02). Available at SSRN: http://ssrn.com/abstract=1593645.

Grace, Martin F. and Robert W. Klein. 2006. The Economic Consequences of Voluntary Quality Certification Programs: The Case of the Insurance Marketplace Standards Association. Working Paper, Center for RMI Research. Available at researchgate.net.

Grace, Martin F., and Robert W. Klein. 2008. The Past and Future of Insurance Regulation: The McCarran-Ferguson Act and Beyond, *Searle Center Research Symposium on Insurance Markets and Regulation*, Northwestern University.

Grace, Martin F., and Robert W. Klein. 2009. The Perfect Storm: Hurricanes, Insurance, and Regulation. 12(1) *Risk Management and Insurance Review* 81–124.

Grace, Martin F., and Richard D. Phillips. 2007. The Allocation of Governmental Regulatory Authority: Federalism and the Case of Insurance Regulation. 74(1) *Journal of Risk and Insurance* 207–38.

Grace, Martin, Robert Klein, and Richard D. Phillips. 2003. Insurance Company Failures: Why Do They Cost So Much? *Georgia State University Center for Risk Management and Insurance Research Working Paper* (03-1).

Grace, Martin F., Robert W. Klein, Paul R. Kleindorfer, and Michael R. Murray (eds.). 2003. *Catastrophe Insurance*. Springer US.

Harrington, Scott. 2000. An Historical Overview of Federal Involvement in Insurance Regulation, in P. Wallison (ed.), *Optional Federal Chartering and Regulation of Insurance Companies*. Washington, DC: AEI Press, 79–131.

Harrington, Scott. 2002. Effects of Prior Approval Rate Regulation of Auto Insurance, in J. D. Cummins (ed.), *Deregulating Property-Liability Insurance: Restoring Competition and Increasing Market Efficiency*. Washington, DC: AEI-Brookings Joint Center for Regulatory Studies. 285–314.

Harrington, Scott. 2006. Federal Chartering of Insurance Companies: Options and Alternatives for Transforming Insurance Regulation. *Networks Financial Institute Policy*

Brief. (2006-PB). Available at http://indstate.edu/business/nfi/leadership/briefs/2006-pb-02_Harrington.pdf (accessed October 4, 2014).

Harrington, Scott. 2009. The Financial Crisis, Systemic Risk, and the Future of Insurance Regulation. 76(4) *Journal of Risk and Insurance* 785–819.

Harrington, Scott, and Greg Niehaus. 1998. Race, Redlining, and Automobile Insurance Prices. 71(3) *Journal of Business* 439–69.

Huff, John. 2009. Missouri Department of Insurance Press Release, *Insurance Industry Remains Healthy; State Regulation Is the Reason*. Available at https://insurance.mo.gov/news/2009/Insurance_industry_remains_healthy_state_regulation_is_the_reason_op_ed_column_ (accessed January 21, 2014).

Hunter, Robert. 2008. *State Automobile Insurance Regulation: A National Quality Assessment and In-Depth Review of California's Uniquely Effective Regulatory System*, Consumer Federation of America. Available at www.consumerfed.org/elements/www.consumerfed.org/file/finance/state_auto_insurance_report.pdf (accessed October 21, 2014).

Insurance Information Institute. 2014. (III) Compulsory Auto/Uninsured Motorists (August 2014). Available at www.iii.org/issue-update/compulsory-auto-uninsured-motorists/ (accessed September 29, 2014).

Jaffee, Dwight. 2006. Monoline Restrictions, With Applications to Mortgage Insurance and Title Insurance. 28(2) *Review of Industrial Organization* 83–108.

Jaffee, Dwight M., and Thomas Russell. 1997. Catastrophe Insurance, Capital Markets, and Uninsurable Risks. 64(2) *Journal of Risk and Insurance* 205–30.

Joskow, Paul L. 1973. Cartels, Competition and Regulation in the Property-Liability Insurance Industry. *The Bell Journal of Economics and Management Science* 375–427.

Kaufman, George G. 2000. Banking and Currency Crisis and Systemic Risk: A Taxonomy and Review. 9(2) *Financial Markets, Institutions and Instruments* 69–131.

Kimball, Spencer L., and Ronald N. Boyce. 1958. The Adequacy of State Insurance Rate Regulation: The McCarran-Ferguson Act in Historical Perspective. 56(4) *Michigan Law Review* 545–78.

Klein, Robert. 1995. Insurance Regulation in Transition. 62(3) *Journal of Risk and Insurance* 363–404.

Klein, Robert. 2006. Deregulation of Commercial Insurance, in Jozef Teugels and Bjørn Sundt (eds.), *Encyclopedia of Actuarial Science*. Hoboken, NJ: John Wiley and Sons, Ltd.

Klein, Robert W. 2009. An Overview of the Insurance Industry and Its Regulation, in Martin Grace and Robert Klein (eds.), *The Future of Insurance Regulation*. Washington, DC: Brookings Institution Press.

Klein, Robert W., and Martin F. Grace. 2001. Urban Homeowners Insurance Markets in Texas: A Search for Redlining. 68(4) *Journal of Risk and Insurance* 581–613.

Knowlton, Donald. 1960. Regulation of Insurance by the Antitrust Subcommittee of the United States Senate. *Ins. L.J.* 641–53.

Kulp, C. A. 1950. The Rate-Making Process in Property and Casualty Insurance: Goals, Technics, and Limits. 15(4) *Law and Contemporary Problems* 493–522.

Lee, Diana, Sam Sorich, Michael J. Miller, and Rob Schneider. 2005. Give Us Some Credit: The Use of Credit Information in Insurance Underwriting and Rating. 8(1) *Risk Management and Insurance Review* 31–41.

Leverty, J. Tyler. 2012. The Cost of Duplicative Regulation: Evidence from Risk Retention Groups. 79(1) *Journal of Risk and Insurance* 105–28.

Leverty, J. T., and M. F. Grace. 2012. Dupes or Incompetents? An Examination of Management's Impact on Firm Distress. 79(3) *Journal of Risk and Insurance* 751–83.

McGlamery, J. Gabriel. 2009. Race Based Underwriting and the Death of Burial Insurance. 15 *Conn. Ins. L.J.* 531–70.

Meier, Kenneth J. 1988. *The Political Economy of Regulation: The Case of Insurance*. Albany, NY: State University of New York Press.

Michel-Kerjan, E. O., and C. Kousky. 2010. Come Rain or Shine: Evidence on Flood Insurance Purchases in Florida. 77(2) *Journal of Risk and Insurance* 369–97.

Oates, Wallace. 1972. *Fiscal Federalism*. New York, NY: Harcourt Brace Jovanovich.

Oviatt, F. C. 1905. Historical Study of Fire Insurance in the United States. 26 *Annals of the American Academy of Political and Social Science* 155–78.
Pottier, Steven W. 2007. *State Regulation of Life Insurers: Implications for Economic Efficiency and Financial Strength*, prepared for the American Council of Life Insurers.
Pottier, Steven W. 2011. Life Insurer Efficiency and State Regulation: Evidence of Optimal Firm Behavior. 39(2) *Journal of Regulatory Economics* 169–93.
Pottier, Steven W., and David W Sommer. 1998. Regulatory Stringency and New York Licensed Life Insurers. 65(3) *Journal of Risk and Insurance* 485–502.
Propublica. 2014. *Bailout Recipients*. Available at http://projects.propublica.org/bailout/list (accessed September 29, 2014).
Roe, Mark J. 1993. Foundations of Corporate Finance: The 1906 Pacification of the Insurance Industry. 93(3) *Columbia Law Review* 639–84.
Sagers, Chris. 2010. Much Ado about Possibly Pretty Little: McCarran-Ferguson Repeal in the Health Care Reform Effort. 28(2) *Yale Law and Policy Review* 325–52.
Schacht, James W., and Peter G. Gallanis. 1993. The Interstate Compact as an Effective Mechanism for Insurance Receivership Reform. 12(18) *Journal of Insurance Regulation* 8–220.
Schwarcz, Daniel. 2011. Reevaluating Standardized Insurance Policies. 78 *University of Chicago Law Review* 1263–348.
Schwarcz, Daniel. 2014. Transparently Opaque: Understanding the Lack of Transparency in Insurance Consumer Protection. 61(2) *UCLA Law Review* 394–463.
Schwartz, Victor E., and Leah Lorber. 2000. State Farm v. Avery: State Court Regulation through Litigation Has Gone Too Far. 33(4) *Conn. Law Review* 1215–38.
Shavell, S. 1986. The Judgment Proof Problem. 6(1) *International Review of Law and Economics* 45–58.
Spectator Company. 1885. *The Spectator Insurance Yearbook*. New York, NY: The Spectator.
Squires, Gregory D. 2003. Racial Profiling, Insurance Style: Insurance Redlining and the Uneven Development of Metropolitan Areas. 25(4) *Journal of Urban Affairs* 391–410.
US Congress. 1990. Committee on Energy and Commerce, Subcommittee and on Oversight and Investigations. Failed Promises: Insurance Company Insolvencies. Washington, DC: US Government Printing Office.
US Treasury, Federal Office of Insurance. 2013. *How to Modernize and Improve the System of Insurance Regulation in the United States*. Available at http://1.usa.gov/1cqMfgO (accessed January 21, 2014).
Webel, Baird. 2007. Insurance Regulation: Optional Federal Charter Legislation. *CRS Report for Congress RL34286*. Washington, DC: Congressional Research Service (December 14).
Willenborg, M. 2000. Regulatory separation as a Mechanism to Curb Capture: A Study of the Decision to Act against Distressed Insurers. 67(4) *Journal of Risk and Insurance* 593–616.
Winter, Ralph A. 2000. Optimal Insurance under Moral Hazard, in George Dionne (ed.), *Handbook of Insurance*. New York, NY: Springer Science.
Wu, Cheng-Sheng Peter, and James Guszcza. 2003. Does Credit Score Really Explain Insurance Losses? Multivariate Analysis from a Data Mining Point of View. *Casualty Actuarial Society Forum* 113–38.
Yelen, Suzanne. 1993. Withdrawal Restrictions in the Automobile Insurance Market. 102(6) *Yale Law Journal* 1431–55.

PART IV

COURTS AND INSURANCE

11. Mandatory rules and default rules in insurance contracts

Tom Baker and Kyle D. Logue

I. INTRODUCTION

In the economic analysis of contracts, the rules of contract law divide into two general classes: default rules, which parties can alter by contract, and mandatory or immutable rules, which parties cannot alter (Ayres and Gertner 1989; Barnett 1992; Craswell 1999; Cohen 1999; Ayres 2012). According to this way of organizing the field, the essential normative issues similarly divide into two general questions: what substantive contract law rules are most efficient, and should those rules be mandatory or merely defaults? Insurance law raises these same questions. Although numerous scholars have examined the efficiency or inefficiency of particular substantive doctrines of insurance law, few scholars, and even fewer courts and policymakers, have considered whether and under what circumstances rules of insurance law should be default or mandatory and, if default, how they may be altered. Nor have they seriously examined how state administrative regulation of insurance forms might affect the answers to these questions. This chapter begins to fill these gaps in the literature.

Section II provides a brief summary of the law and economics of contract, with special emphasis on the theoretical justifications for making some rules of contract law, or some terms in contracts, mandatory. This section articulates a straightforward, efficiency-based approach to drawing the line between which rules or terms should be mandatory and which can be altered by agreement of the parties: namely, the line should be drawn in a way that is consistent with the market failure rationale that justifies the rule in the first place. For example, rules of contract law and implied terms in contracts that are designed to respond to informational asymmetries or cognitive biases, or that respond to externalities that the contract imposes on third parties, should generally be made mandatory, since those same asymmetries, biases, and externalities may lead the parties to alter the default rule in an inefficient manner. By contrast, in situations in which the contract produces no substantial externalities and the parties are commercially sophisticated (and hence less likely to be either ill-informed or subject to substantial and persistent cognitive biases), contract law rules and implied terms should generally be treated merely as default rules.

Section III describes how insurance law currently draws the line between mandatory rules and default rules. Section IV evaluates whether those boundaries are consistent with the applicable market failure rationales. We find that there are indeed some areas of insurance law in which the mandatory/default-rule boundary seems to be drawn in a manner that is consistent with our theory. For example, some insurance law doctrines that are based largely on externality concerns – such as the requirement of an insurable interest in life insurance – are treated as mandatory, or non-alterable, by the contracting parties. However, the most pervasive finding of our review of the law in this area is that courts often do not address explicitly whether the legal rule they are applying is mandatory or alterable by contract. Indeed, this is why one of the primary contributions of the American Law Institute's Principles of the Law of Liability Insurance (PLLI), for which we are the Reporters, has been to address the mandatory/default-rule issue explicitly and comprehensively in the liability insurance context. Section V takes into account the unique role that state insurance regulators can play in helping courts decide which rules of insurance law, or terms in insurance contracts, are mandatory and which are defaults. Section VI explains how the rules/standards distinction must be considered in the design of the optimal mandatory/default-rule boundary.

Relatively little has been written on the mandatory/default-rule boundary in the insurance law context. A number of articles have, in the context of evaluating particular insurance law doctrines, addressed whether the individual rule should be mandatory or alterable by agreement of the parties. For example, Seth Chandler (1993) and Richard Squire (Chapter 14 in this volume) have discussed whether the duty to settle should be mandatory or alterable. Similarly, Erik Knutsen (2010) argued in favor of a particular mandatory rule to address the problem of concurrent causation and Michelle Boardman (2013) explored the mandatory/default-rule question in connection with *contra proferentem*. Kenneth Abraham (2001) also pointed out a small number of judicially created mandatory insurance law rules, including the insurable interest requirement and the treatment of conflicting 'other insurance' clauses, which we discuss below. None of these articles, however, addressed the general normative question of when insurance law doctrines (or terms in insurance law contracts) should be mandatory and when they should be default, nor did they address how default rules can be altered. Again, one general thesis of this chapter is that the choice of whether to make a rule of insurance law (or judicially implied term in an insurance contract) mandatory or whether to make it alterable by the parties should be consistent with, and informed by, the rationale that justifies the rule itself, whether that rationale is paternalism or externalities or whatever. This general thesis is consistent with Ayres (2012), which sets out in some detail considerations that should be taken into account in deciding both whether rules should be mandatory or default and, if default, how – by what 'altering rules' – parties should be permitted to contract around such default rules.

II. THE ECONOMIC ANALYSIS OF CONTRACT LAW AND THE MANDATORY/DEFAULT-RULE BOUNDARY

The economic analysis of law holds that the normative objective of contract law is to maximize efficiency (R. Posner 1986; Craswell 1999; E. Posner 2002; Shavell 2004). On this view, society allows contracting parties to use the judicial system to enforce their contractual promises precisely because doing so maximizes the joint utility of the contracting parties and thus of society generally (Goetz and Scott 1983). Thus, contract law enables individuals and firms to bind themselves to an allocation of rights and responsibilities that makes both parties better off – or that at least makes one party better off without making the other worse off, which is the definition of Pareto efficiency. Assuming that the conditions of a competitive market are present (that is, the parties are reasonably well informed and suffer from no substantial cognitive biases, and there are no externalities), it follows almost tautologically that courts will maximize social utility if they enforce the explicit terms of the written agreement.[1]

Written contracts, of course, whether by design or by accident, do not always fully specify the parties' intentions. Indeed, there is a sense in which contracts never cover *every* conceivable contingency; all contracts, in other words, are on some level incomplete, which is where default rules come in. Default rules 'fill the gaps in incomplete contracts; they govern unless the parties contract around them' (Ayres and Gertner 1989; Craswell 1999; Cohen 1999). As a result, a primary role for courts when construing contracts, for legislatures when enacting laws governing contractual relationships, as well as for scholars when writing about contract law, is to identify the best default rules for various contractual situations and how parties

[1] The same conclusion is likely even when insurers have market power, because even a monopolist has an incentive to deliver the terms that buyers want, albeit at a monopoly price. Moreover, because of the problem of adverse selection, there may be conditions in which a monopolist can outperform a competitive market because a monopolist need not fear cream-skimming by competitors.

may alter them (Ayres 2012). These default rules will be the gap-filling rules that will apply where the parties fail to specify what they regard as the value-maximizing outcome.

Identifying the most efficient contractual default rules in various settings has been the objective of a fair amount of economic contracts scholarship. One insight from this literature is that contractual default rules come in two general flavors. First, there are default rules designed to approximate what most parties would have agreed to, with respect to a particular contingency, under conditions of perfect information and zero transaction costs. Such 'market-mimicking' or 'majoritarian' default rules have the advantage of minimizing the need for contracting parties to incur the costs necessary to 'contract around' the default rule. That is, majoritarian default rules can simply be used 'off the shelf' and left in place by a majority of contracting parties. Since they will need to be contracted around by only a minority of contracting parties, their use minimizes transaction costs. Some default rules, however, are not designed to minimize transaction costs, but instead they actually are designed to induce parties to take action. Such rules, sometimes referred to as 'information-forcing' or (the less appealing term) 'penalty' defaults, are designed to disfavor the party with superior information in an attempt to induce that party either to negotiate for a more efficient allocation of rights and obligations or to change their primary conduct in some way (cf. Ayres 2006).

An example of such a rule would be the damages rule set forth in *Hadley* v. *Baxendale*, 9 Ex. 341 (1854). The *Hadley* rule says that the only damages typically recoverable in a contract case are those within the reasonable contemplation of the parties at the time they entered into the contract. Under the *Hadley* rule, if one party knows that it will suffer extraordinary damages in the event of a breach but the other party does not, the damages would be unrecoverable. This, in turn, gives the informed party an incentive to reveal that information, bringing those damages within the contemplation of the previously uninformed party and, thus, within the scope of the contract. Importantly, Ayres and Gertner show, the *Hadley* rule could be efficient even if most parties would prefer a default that made the shipper responsible for all damages. By encouraging parties who may experience high damages as a result of breach to reveal this fact, penalty default rules can encourage the uninformed party to take appropriate precautions.

As insurance law scholars have pointed out in prior work (e.g., Abraham 1996; Abraham 2001; Ayres 2006; Boardman 2013), another contract doctrine that has penalty or information-forcing qualities is the interpretive doctrine of *contra proferentem*, which says that ambiguities in contractual language will be construed against the party who provided the language.

This rule confronts contract drafters with the choice either to redraft the language of the contract to be clearer or to leave the language as it is and have the term construed against them. Of course, contracting parties may elect not to contract around the court's tie-breaking interpretation of the contract term in question – for example, because redrafting the term may produce further ambiguity (Boardman 2006). But it is at least possible.[2]

Information-forcing default rules are designed to be altered by the parties in at least some circumstances. By contrast, a mandatory rule cannot be altered.[3] From an economic perspective, a reasonable question to ask is why any rule of contract law would ever be compulsory? Why not always permit the parties to agree to terms that best suit their individual needs and preferences and thus maximize their own utility?

In the efficiency-oriented contracts literature, justifications for mandatory rules rely on claims of market failure. In particular, making a rule of contract law mandatory can make sense if one of the parties lacks ready access to important information or is subject to cognitive biases that cause them to misprocess certain types of information, and employing an information-forcing default rule cannot be expected to correct this problem. Similarly, if the contract produces external costs or benefits (costs or benefits experienced by parties who are not involved in the contract and thus not able to represent their interests in the negotiations), the contracting process can produce inefficient outcomes. Finally, if one of the parties to the contract is in the position of a monopolist, and the other party has relatively few choices, it is sometimes argued that the terms of the contract can be inefficient, although economists often respond that even a monopolist will want to include all efficient contract terms (so as to produce more value to extort in the bargaining process). For a survey of these standard arguments, see Trebilcock (1993).

A number of existing mandatory contract law doctrines can be explained in terms of these market failures. One prominent example involves product liability law. During the last century, the law of product accidents has shifted from a regime in which responsibility for product-related personal injuries was governed purely by the terms of the contract between buyer and seller (a regime in which waivers of liability for personal injuries were enforced) to a regime in which responsibility for product-related injuries

---

[2] It is worth noting that, although the doctrine of *contra proferentem* operates to create penalty default interpretations of insurance policies, the doctrine itself is best understood as a mandatory rule, as discussed in sections III and IV below.

[3] Of course, after a dispute has arisen between the parties, even a so-called mandatory term in the contract can be contracted around through a settlement of the parties' dispute (Ware 1999).

is governed by mandatory, non-waivable principles of tort law. The key point to recognize about this well-known and frequently discussed shift in products liability law is that it entailed both a change in the underlying liability rule (the rule assigning responsibility for product-related injuries)[4] and, more importantly for present purposes, a change in the *nature* of the rule, from a default rule to a mandatory rule, as attempts to contract around it were deemed unconscionable.[5]

Both changes – the change in the liability rule and the change in the nature of the rule from default to mandatory – have been justified on a number of different theoretical grounds. One of the most persuasive is a story of information asymmetry. Because product consumers as a group tend to be poorly informed relative to product sellers about the risks posed by most consumer products, and because individual consumers tend systematically to underestimate the risks of product accidents (again, relative to product sellers), the market for consumer products cannot be expected, by itself, to produce optimally safe products and optimal consumer product warranties. That is, because of this information problem we cannot expect consumer product contracts, including the warnings and disclosures made to consumers, to strike the optimal balance between product safety and product price. Consumers, being poorly informed and systematically underestimating risks of catastrophic losses that have very low probabilities, will be, contrary to their own best interests, unwilling to pay the cost for optimally safe products and for products that come with product-risk insurance (Latin 1994; Arlen 2010).

This story can be used not only to explain why it makes sense on efficiency grounds for legislatures or courts to adopt a liability rule that shifts product-injury costs to product sellers (who are, to use Calabresi's language, the cheapest cost avoiders), but also to justify making the strict liability rule mandatory, or non-waivable, by the parties to the contract. If the rule of strict products liability could be altered simply by the insertion of a product warranty waiver, such waivers would inefficiently proliferate, eliminating the effect of the rule. Consumer products that did not include the waiver, that left the strict liability rule in place, would be more expensive than the consumer products that waived the rule; and, because consumers are unaware of or underestimate the risks of product-related

---

4 *Escola* v. *Coca Cola Bottling Co.*, 24 Cal. 2d 453 (1944); *Greenman* v. *Yuba Power Products, Inc.*, 59 Cal. 2d 57 (1963); Restatement (Second) of Torts § 402A (1965).

5 *Henningsen* v. *Bloomfield Motors, Inc.*, 161 A. 2d 69 (N.J. 1960); U.C.C. §§ 2-715, 2-719 (2013).

injuries, they would not be willing to pay the additional cost, which their better informed or less cognitively biased selves would be willing to pay.

Thus, in the product liability example, *both* the choice of the particular liability rule *and* the choice to make the rule non-alterable can be, and should be, grounded on the same market failure rationale – here the problem of information asymmetry (Croley and Hanson 1993). This point applies to all rules in contract law: whatever the theoretical justification for the choice of the rule, the choice whether to treat the rule as mandatory or default in a particular case should be consistent with that theoretical justification. As a corollary to this principle, the nature of the market failure that justifies the underlying rule also bears on whether a rule should be mandatory or default for all parties and in all circumstances, or only some. Thus, insofar as the mandatory nature of modern products liability law is based on the presumption that consumers tend to underestimate product risks, the rules of products liability law should be mandatory only in circumstances in which this information problem exists.

The rules regarding the products liability mandatory/default boundary in most states are roughly consistent with this approach. For example, the Uniform Commercial Code (U.C.C.) permits disclaimers for consequential damages, but only if they are not unconscionable; and the doctrine of unconscionability itself is likely to take into account the information asymmetry problem that exists between product consumers and product sellers. Moreover, the U.C.C. rebuttably presumes that such a disclaimer is unconscionable in the case of personal injuries involving 'consumer goods' (U.C.C. § 2-719(3)).

Note that the same basic point could be made if the market failure rationale for the liability rule is something other than information asymmetry. Thus, if the argument in favor of the underlying legal rule is based on some sort of externality story or a bargaining-power asymmetry, then the choice of the mandatory/default-rule boundary should track that story as well.

III. MAPPING THE MANDATORY/DEFAULT-RULE BOUNDARY IN INSURANCE LAW

As with contract law generally, the overwhelming majority of the law that governs the actions of parties to an insurance contract is found in the language of the contracts themselves. Although the vast majority of insurance policies are standard form contracts, which policyholders (rationally) never bother to read until a loss occurs, there are good reasons why the rights and responsibilities of insurers and insureds are governed primarily by the plain language of the policies (ALI 2014). There are, however, ways in which the parties to insurance contracts are not free to choose whatever terms they wish. The common law of insurance or a particular state's insurance code (or the regulations promulgated by the insurance regulatory authority under the authority of that state's insurance code) may impose limitations on what terms may be inserted into an insurance policy, how those terms will be interpreted by courts, or what background duties will be imposed on insurers and insureds.

Such mandatory rules generally fall into three categories: (1) insurance policy terms that are expressly required by state legislatures or by state insurance regulators to be included into certain types of insurance policies; (2) common law contract and insurance law duties; and (3) the rules of contract interpretation and enforcement (including rules that expressly forbid certain terms in insurance contracts). Later in this chapter we will revisit these mandatory rules in light of the role of state administrative agencies in deciding whether to approve standard form insurance policies drafted by or on behalf of insurance companies. This approval process means that a rule that is a default rule under the common law of insurance may become an immutable rule when the state insurance department refuses to approve any insurance policy that attempts to contract around that rule. Prior literature has largely ignored this possibility and the additional options it opens up for the common law of insurance. We will do so for the moment as well.

1. Insurance Policy Terms Expressly Required by Statute or Regulation

It is well known that insurance contracts are regulated in a way that most other contracts are not. State regulation of the insurance industry traces back to the 1940s, when the McCarran-Ferguson Act, among other changes, created what might be called the reverse preemption presumption: the rule that, unless Congress clearly says otherwise, no federal law will be construed to preempt state regulation of insurance, including the regulation of insurance contracts. Since that time, all 51 jurisdictions in the US have adopted comprehensive insurance regulatory regimes. Although the primary focus of state insurance regulation has historically been the solvency of insurance companies, states also sometimes mandate that particular terms be included in certain types of insurance policies. When such laws or regulations exist, the required terms are by definition mandatory rules.

Perhaps the most famous example of mandated insurance is the Affordable Care Act's (ACA's) requirement that all individuals purchase health insurance – the so-called individual mandate. For the purposes of our analysis, however, the important part of the mandate is not the requirement that coverage be purchased, but the mandatory terms in the policies *themselves*. With respect to individual and small-group policies sold after the 2010 grandfather date, the ACA requires certain 'essential health benefits', which include ambulatory patient services, emergency services, hospitalization, maternity and newborn care, mental health and substance use disorder services, and prescription drugs (42 U.S.C. § 18022(b)).[6] Similar mandatory terms in health insurance policies have existed for years in some states (Monahan 2009). Perhaps the more pervasive state-level insurance mandates, however, appear in the area of auto insurance. Every jurisdiction in the country requires the purchase of some amount of auto liability insurance coverage. Here again, the important part of this mandate for current purposes is not that drivers must buy a policy, but that some terms of the policy are controlled by statute – namely, the minimum liability coverage limits. Many states also statutorily limit auto insurers' ability to cancel or rescind policies to situations in which premiums have not been paid or the insured's driver's license has been suspended or revoked (see, e.g., Miss. Code Ann. § 83-11-3). Similarly, with respect to uninsured and underinsured motorist coverage, state statutes forbid insurers from using policy terms that are less favorable to insureds than the statutorily prescribed coverage (see, e.g., *Steffen* v. *Progressive Northern Ins. Co.*, 276 Neb. 378 (2008) (construing the uninsured motorist law to forbid the insurer from defining an exclusion more broadly than contemplated by the statute)).

Over the years, states have begun to require specific terms in many different policies. For example, some states now require insurers to insert in *all* of their policies a term explicitly excluding coverage for losses caused 'willfully' or 'intentionally' by the insured (see, e.g., Cal. Ins. Code § 533). A somewhat controversial example of a mandatory insurance contract term involves the issue of multiple concurrent causes (Knutsen 2010). Insurance companies sometimes wish to exclude from coverage particular causes of a loss, either for moral hazard reasons (as with the intentional harm exclusion already mentioned), for market segmentation reasons (a particular risk is better insured through a different type of policy), or for other reasons (perhaps the risk in question is entirely uninsurable). The interesting question is what should be done when a given loss has more than one cause, one that is covered and one that is specifically excluded. Some insurers have drafted and redrafted their policies to make clear that

6 The minimum essential group benefits that large employers must provide under the ACA are less clear.

coverage is not owed if an excluded cause – earth movement or flood, for example – has any causal connection whatsoever to the loss, no matter how remote. The courts have tended to apply such language literally, which tends to favor insurers. In some states, however, legislatures have been unwilling to permit insurers to draft such exclusions and have instead enacted laws requiring that causal exclusions apply only if the excluded cause was the 'dominant' or 'primary' or 'efficient proximate' cause of the loss in question. Examples of this include California (Cal. Ins. Code § 530) and North Dakota (N.D. Cent. Code §§ 26.1-32-01). (Washington State has reached the same result through judicial decision, illustrating the potential overlap between legislative and common law making. *Safeco Ins. Co. of America* v. *Hirschmann*, 773 P. 2d 413 (Washington 1989).) In those states, the dominant cause requirement has in effect been made a mandatory term in every insurance policy. In other states, the efficient proximate cause rule is merely a default rule, which insurers have successfully contracted around (*Assurance Co. of Am., Inc.* v. *Jay-Mar, Inc.*, 38 F. Supp. 2d 349, 353–4 (D. N.J. 1999)).

There are many other examples of statutorily mandated insurance contract terms. In the context of occupational disability coverage, for example, California (which has more than its share of mandatory rules) has defined 'total disability' to be the insured's inability to perform the substantial and material duties of her own occupation, even if the policy contains language expressly conditioning such coverage on not being 'engaged in *any other* gainful occupation' (*Hangartner* v. *Provident Life and Acc. Ins. Co.*, 373 F. 3d 998, 1006–7 (9th Cir. 2004)).

2. Common Law Duties

Certain duties developed in the common law of contracts can also be understood as mandatory terms in every insurance policy. For example, it is hornbook law that every contract, including every insurance contract, contains an implied duty on the part of all parties to the contract to act in good faith, or to refrain from acting in bad faith, when enforcing their contractual rights or carrying out their contractual obligations or both (see, e.g., U.C.C. § 1-102(3) (stating that the obligation of contracting parties to act in good faith may not be disclaimed by agreement of the parties)). This general duty has a number of special applications in the insurance context. One example involves the insurer's duty to pay benefits owed. In most if not all jurisdictions, an insurer who relies on a patently unreasonable interpretation of the language in the policy to refuse payment to a deserving insured may later be found by a court to have breached the duty of good faith and fair dealing (Barker and Kent 2014). Such a breach can expose the insurer to not only compensatory consequential damages but also punitive damages. This duty to act in good faith is mandatory. Every insurance policy contains this implicit, non-alterable contractual term.[7]

The duty to defend and the duty to settle in liability insurance policies are examples of what might be called 'quasi-mandatory' or 'sticky' implied contract terms. The concepts of 'quasi-mandatory default rules' and 'sticky defaults' have been discussed in the law and economics contracts literature (e.g., Ayres 2012). The basic idea is that there is a continuum between regular default rules, which are relatively easy for contracting parties to alter, and mandatory rules, which by definition are impossible to contract around. Quasi-mandatory rules fall somewhere in between. Thus, quasi-mandatory rules provide courts and policymakers with another policy instrument, beyond normal default rules and mandatory rules, for responding to information asymmetry and externality concerns in contract settings.

The duty to defend and the duty to settle are 'quasi' rather than fully mandatory rules because, although insurers can eliminate the duties contractually, they can do so only by redrafting their policies in ways that substantially alter the allocation of rights and responsibilities between the insurer and insured.

Take the duty to defend. If a liability insurance policy includes a term giving the insurer the right, and imposing on the insurer the obligation, to 'defend the insured against any suit seeking damages' (as most liability insurance policies do), the meaning of that duty will necessarily be shaped by the judicial doctrine that has developed interpreting that language. Thus, for example, courts have generally interpreted the duty to defend to be broader than the duty to indemnify. This means, among other things, that if a complaint filed against an insured contains even a single allegation that if proven would be covered, the insurer must provide the insured with a defense, even if that allegation later turns out to be false or fraudulent. This 'complaint-allegation rule' is the prevailing law in most jurisdictions (ALI 2014; Silver, Chapter 13 in this volume).

What is more, it seems likely that such a rule would be applied to any liability policy that imposes on the insurer the obligation to defend the

---

7 Although no court would enforce, and in all likelihood no insurer would want to include, a term that broadly waived the implied duty of good faith and fair dealing, some insurers might want to include terms in their policies specifically permitting them to engage in particular conduct that some courts might regard as bad faith. Whether such terms would be enforced would obviously depend on a number of factors, including the nature of the term, the circumstances in the case, and the jurisdiction.

claim (and by defend the claim we mean actually provide the defense – choose the lawyer, supervise the litigation, etc., and not merely indemnify the insured's defense costs), even if the insurer attempted to contract around it. Put differently, while a liability insurer can contract out of the complaint-allegation rule by eliminating the duty to provide a defense,[8] if the insurance contract contains a term stating that the insurer will provide the defense, that term will necessarily be interpreted in light of the judicial doctrine that has developed in this area. Reflecting the prevailing common law treatment, the American Law Institute's PLLI treats these rules as mandatory for all so-called 'duty to defend' policies – that is, policies that impose on the insurer the obligation actually to handle the defense of the case, and not merely to reimburse defense costs (ALI 2014). These rules are also mandatory for 'defense cost indemnification policies' under the PLLI, if these policies obligate the insurer to pay the costs of defense as they are incurred and the policy is not issued to a large commercial policyholder. The PLLI does not impose these rules on policies that merely obligate the insurer to reimburse the costs of defense *after* the claim has been resolved, but of course that kind of insurance does not provide a policyholder with the means to contest a claim.

The duty to settle is a similarly quasi-mandatory rule. Most liability insurance policies contain a provision giving the insurer the discretion to settle any claim brought against the insured. This allocation of authority makes sense, given that the insurer, which is defending the suit, will have better access to information necessary to make a reasonable settlement decision and given that, in many cases, it is mostly the insurer's money that is on the hook. However, when there is a possibility of a judgment in excess of the policy limits, the insurer will sometimes have an incentive to reject reasonable settlement demands in favor of litigating the case, because it will be risking not only its own money but also the insured's money. Given this conflict of interest, courts have imposed a duty on the part of liability insurers that sell such policies to make reasonable settlement decisions – defined as decisions that a reasonable party facing the entire liability would make (ALI 2014). This duty greatly increases the exposure of the insurer, because breach of the duty makes the insurer responsible for a verdict in excess of the policy limits (Syverud 1990; Sykes 1993; Squire, Chapter 14 in this volume).

Although insurers could attempt to eliminate that duty – and the exposure to excess judgments – by redrafting their policies to disclaim it, we

---

[8] One way to do this would be to make it clear that it only pays for indemnification costs after liability has been resolved, and not for ongoing defense costs.

are not aware of any insurer having attempted to do so; moreover, in our judgment, a court would be unlikely to enforce such a disclaimer. This conclusion is supported by the fact that the duty to settle developed out of the duty of good faith, which, as we have already noted, is generally not waivable. An insurer that wants to avoid the potential exposure to a verdict in excess of the limit can do so by selling an insurance policy that gives it no discretion with regard to settlement, for example by selling a policy that reimburses the policyholder for reasonable settlements (thereby giving the policyholder the discretion to settle and deferring until after the fact the need for the insurer to determine whether a settlement is reasonable). But an insurer cannot keep discretion over settlement and contract around the potential exposure to an excess verdict.

The distinction between the sort of quasi-mandatory rules represented by the duties to settle and defend and ordinary default rules can be illustrated by way of an analogy – to a tuna sandwich. When you order a tuna sandwich in a deli-type restaurant, what you typically get is actually a *tuna salad* sandwich: canned tuna mixed with mayonnaise and some other ingredients, plus the bread, tomato, and lettuce. The lettuce and the tomato are fully optional, or 'ordinary default' ingredients. That is, they are ordinarily included, but easy to have removed. But the 'salad' components of the tuna salad are not so easily removed. And everyone knows that. If you do not want a tuna salad sandwich, do not ask for a sandwich with tuna in it. Get a BLT or burger or Reuben sandwich. Tuna sandwiches are tuna salad sandwiches. That is, the salad components of tuna salad are akin to a quasi-mandatory rule or a sticky default. This is not to say that you could not get the cook at some restaurants to open a can of tuna for you, but most restaurants would find this odd and would impose additional costs, formal or informal, on the purchaser. And those additional costs also make the default sticky, and the rule quasi-mandatory. Other product-sales metaphors make the same point. Think of how new automobiles are typically sold with various 'packages' of options. Further, it is usually not possible to purchase a car that does not have one of the standard packages, without incurring additional cost (in the form of extra money or extra waiting time). Our point here is that the duty to defend and the duty to settle are similar to tuna salad or automobile option packages, in the sense that courts likely will (and should) impose costs for making changes.

3. Rules of Contract Interpretation and Enforcement

The basic rules of interpretation developed in the common law of contract are generally considered mandatory, and this is true in the insurance context as well (Rappaport 1995; Boardman 2013). For example, the doctrine of *contra proferentem*, under which ambiguous terms are construed against the party who supplied the term, is routinely applied in insurance cases (typically to the benefit of insureds against insurers), irrespective of whether there is language in the policy seeking to eliminate that rule. However, it is difficult to find examples of cases in the US in which this proposition has ever been tested in an insurance case. While there are a few reported cases of policies with provisions seeking to eliminate *contra proferentem*, in none of those cases is the provision tested because the insurance policy term at issue was in fact jointly drafted by the parties (see, e.g., *Ins Co. of. N. Am., Inc.* v. *A.I.U. Ins. Co.*, 896 A. 2d 880, 885-5 (Del. Super. Ct. 2006)). Insurance policies in the US rarely contain such provisions. Indeed, we have not been able to find a single example of a standard form insurance policy issued in the US that contains a term seeking to eliminate or otherwise alter the traditional *contra proferentem* rule, either because insurance regulators will not permit such terms or because the parties believe such terms will be held unenforceable in court (or perhaps because the parties are happy with the existing rules of interpretation). There are, however, insurance policies written in other countries, between insurers and very sophisticated commercial policyholders that include provisions purporting to eliminate or alter *contra proferentem*. For example, the 'Bermuda Form', developed for use in the large commercial liability insurance market, contains an arbitration clause as well as a clause that specifically contracts around the *contra proferentem* rule (Jacobs, Masters and Stanley 2004).

Some common law decisions refusing to enforce provisions in insurance policies can also be understood as creating a kind of mandatory rule. The refusal to enforce a term in an insurance policy substitutes silence for that term, potentially making the inverse of that term a mandatory rule. In some jurisdictions, for example, courts have held that insurance for intentionally caused losses is against public policy, on the theory that permitting such insurance would increase incentives for insureds to cause losses intentionally, the classic moral hazard concern (e.g., *K2 Investment Group, LLC* v. *American Guarantee & Liability Ins. Co.*, 2013 WL 2475869 (NY Ct. Ap. 2013)). In such jurisdictions, therefore, insurance policies contain an implied, mandatory exclusion for intentionally caused losses. Likewise, the insurable interest requirement says that, if (or to the extent that) an insured has no insurable interest in the thing being insured against (that is, she stands to lose nothing if the insured event happens), the insurance policy in question will typically be found unenforceable, again on moral hazard/public policy grounds. In such jurisdictions all insurance policies can be understood to contain a mandatory insurable interest requirement.

Not all of the results of common law decisions refusing to enforce an insurance policy term signal the presence of a mandatory term, however. In some cases, a court's refusal to enforce a term may signal only that the particular exclusion or the particular coverage provision was over-broad. For example, some courts have refused to allow the application of the 'absolute pollution exclusion' to lead paint claims and carbon monoxide poisoning claims, despite the fact that the exclusion, read literally, would clearly apply (*Century Surety Co.* v. *Casino West, Inc.*, 60622, 2014 WL 2396085 (Nev. 2014)). Our judgment is that these same courts *would* enforce a specific exclusion for lead paint or carbon monoxide claims, just not through the application of an over-broad pollution exclusion. Similarly, courts in jurisdictions with rules against insurance for intentionally caused injury regularly enforce insurance policy provisions granting coverage for defamation, sexual harassment, and civil rights violations, among other reasons, on the grounds that refusing to enforce such provisions would make insurance policies specifically written to cover such liabilities illusory (French 2012).

The same can be said of insurance policy terms rendered unenforceable on grounds of unconscionability or the related, and sometimes indistinguishable, insurance law doctrine of reasonable expectations. If there is a term in a standard form insurance policy that results in the insured losing coverage and that seems patently unfair (that is, it is difficult to imagine that an informed party with any sort of bargaining options would have knowingly agreed to the term in question), or if the term is wildly out of sync with what a reasonable person would expect to find in such a contract, some courts have been known to treat such terms as unenforceable, though the number of such cases is small (see, e.g., *C&J Fertilizer* v. *Allied Mutual Ins. Co.*, 227 N.W.2d 169 (Iowa 1975)). Presumably even these courts would enforce the provisions in question, however, if the insurer was able to show that it had undertaken adequate efforts to inform the policyholder of the coverage.

Courts have also used the doctrine of 'disproportionate forfeiture' to avoid enforcing policy terms that would, if read literally, cause an insured to lose coverage for what seems like a minor breach of a technical requirement in the policy. For example, in situations in which a policyholder fails to satisfy a clearly written notice requirement in an insurance policy, most courts will nevertheless hold in favor of the insured, because the insurer failed to show 'substantial prejudice' from the delay (e.g., *Aetna Cas. & Sur. Co.* v. *Murphy*, 538 A. 2d 219 (Conn. 1988), overruled in part by *Arrowood Indem. Co.* v. *King*, 39 A. 3d 712 (Conn. 2012) (placing burden of proof on insurer to show absence of prejudice)). Whether such rules can be altered, and how, is a matter of controversy in insurance law.

For example, many courts that require the insurer to show substantial prejudice in order to avoid paying a claim because of late notice under a traditional 'accident' or 'occurrence' based liability insurance policy, do not require the insurer to prove prejudice when the notice requirement is put into the insuring agreement of a claims made policy (Works 1998–99).

4. Potential Loophole to Mandatory Rules

All three of the above-listed categories of mandatory insurance law rules are subject to one potentially large loophole, especially in the context of commercial insurance policies: the mandatory binding arbitration clause. If an insurance policy contains a mandatory arbitration provision, and if there is no state statute or insurance agency regulation that specifically says mandatory arbitration clauses are unenforceable, such a clause may well be enforced by the courts. Once an insurance dispute is in arbitration, there is no guarantee that the arbitrators will apply the rules of insurance law that are traditionally considered mandatory by the courts. Arbitration clauses often contain choice-of-law provisions, which can be used by the parties to apply the laws of a jurisdiction that has fewer mandates. For example, Bermuda Form policies, which generally contain arbitration clauses, often provide that the insurance laws of New York will apply, but that interpretive rules such as *contra proferentem* will not (Abraham and Montgomery 2003).

Whether mandatory arbitration clauses in standard form contracts are enforceable even in situations in which they run afoul of some state law contract doctrine (such as prohibitions on unconscionable terms) has become a matter of some controversy. The trend in the federal courts, especially the Supreme Court, has been to enforce arbitration clauses in such contexts, based on an expansive and thus state law preempting interpretation of the Federal Arbitration Act (FAA). The most prominent case is *AT&T Mobility* v. *Concepcion*, decided in 2011. That case involved a standard form mobile phone contract eliminating the right of customers to use any form of aggregated procedure within the arbitral setting. The Supreme Court held that applying the state's unconscionability law to strike down the mandatory arbitration provision in that contract would violate the FAA.

There is an important difference, however, between the context of standard form consumer contracts generally (including standard form mobile phone contracts) and the context of insurance contracts. As mentioned above, the insurance industry in general is much more heavily regulated than most industries, and standard form insurance contracts in particular are much more heavily regulated than most standard form contracts. One example of this difference is the regulation of mandatory arbitration clauses, which have been banned from insurance contracts in a number of states. More specifically, as of 2010, there were at least 16 states with statutes expressly forbidding arbitration clauses in insurance contracts and another three states with regulations restricting the use of arbitration terms in particular types of insurance policies (*Public Citizen* 2010). In addition there are likely to be even more state insurance departments that would refuse to approve insurance policy forms that contained an arbitration clause. (This latter possibility grows out of the same regulatory authority that we will consider below.)

It should also be noted that insurance markets are different from cell phone markets in a way that helps to explain insurance regulators' hostility to arbitration clauses. In insurance markets, arbitration clauses might be used by insurance companies as a way of skimming good risks from the pool of potential insureds. Here is how it would work: an insurance policy that contains a mandatory arbitration clause would be especially unattractive to relatively high-risk insureds, those insureds mostly likely to bring a dispute against the insurer, because the mandatory arbitration term might reduce the expected value of their future claims, since binding arbitration would remove, or at least reduce, the possibility of getting a disputed claim before a jury. If this is right, the presence of mandatory arbitration terms would be relatively attractive to low-risk insureds – the ones not expecting to have a dispute with the insurer. Such skimming of the relatively good risks by insurers can undermine the ability of relatively high-risk insureds to get coverage of any kind, a result that insurance regulators may object to. It is also a result that is much less likely in cell phone markets, where skimming through the use of arbitration clauses seems less likely.[9] Of course, even in insurance markets, insofar as insureds (rationally) do not read their policies and therefore are unaware even that their policies contain arbitration clauses, the skimming problem is eliminated. Nevertheless, the other concerns with arbitration clauses, mentioned above, would remain.

In any event, many states prohibit or restrict arbitration clauses in insurance contracts. The next question, then, is whether such state law prohibitions on arbitration clauses in insurance contracts would be enforced, despite the recently expanded interpretations of the FAA. Although the Supreme Court has not ruled on the subject, it seems likely that the McCarran-Ferguson Act, and the reverse preemption presumption

---

[9] Thanks to Peter Siegelman for bringing this difference between insurance markets and cell phone markets to our attention.

discussed above, will be found to trump the FAA, since the FAA nowhere specifically states that it was meant to preempt state insurance law or apply to the 'business of insurance' (Randall 2005). Indeed, some lower courts have so held.[10]

IV. EVALUATING THE MANDATORY/DEFAULT-RULE BOUNDARY IN INSURANCE LAW

There are two steps in the normative economic analysis of a rule of contract law. First, what rule efficiently allocates rights and responsibilities as between the contracting parties? Second, should that rule be a mandatory rule or a default rule or something in between? We have emphasized that the two questions are closely connected with each other; the same arguments that justify the choice of the efficient rule of contract law also have implications for the decision regarding *whether and to what extent* the rule should be mandatory. Thus, for example, if a rule of contract law is justified at least in part on the grounds that it is necessary to protect contracting parties who are poorly informed or unable adequately to process the relevant information, then ideally that rule should be mandatory (because poorly informed parties are not likely to alter the rule in ways that would be considered efficient), but mandatory only insofar as it applies to situations involving poorly informed parties. When the parties are not poorly informed, the rule should be merely a default. By contrast, if the rule is not a response to concerns about lack of information or cognitive biases but rather is designed, for example, to protect third parties who may be harmed by the transaction, the mandatory/default boundary should track that rationale: where the externality exists, the rule should be mandatory; where the externality does not exist, the rule should be a default.

Some aspects of the mandatory/default boundary in insurance law are consistent with this efficiency story; others are not. The doctrines of unconscionability and reasonable expectations are all typically justified on information or bargaining-power rationales. A contract term will be held unconscionable and therefore unenforceable only when there is likely to be information and/or bargaining-power asymmetries – situations involving

---

[10] See, e.g., *State of Wash. Dep't of Transp.* v. *James River Ins. Co.*, 176 Wash. 2d 390 (2013) (en banc) (holding that the FAA does not preempt state laws forbidding arbitration provisions in insurance policies because of McCarran-Ferguson and because prohibitions on arbitration clauses constitutes regulation of the business of insurance); *Mutual Reinsurance Bureau* v. *Great Plains Mutual Ins. Co.*, 969 F. 2d 931, 934 (10th Cir. 1992) (same).

standard form boilerplate terms in policies sold to consumers. And those (few) courts that apply the strong form of the doctrine of reasonable expectations have done so only in situations which the contracts are standard form personal or small business policies, which correlates with unsophisticated policyholders (Stempel 1993; Beh 2004). Given that each of these doctrines rests on information or bargaining-power rationales, it is consistent with our framework that they are all typically understood as mandatory rather than default rules.

Mandatory auto insurance presents an especially interesting case. State auto insurance statutes typically require only that the auto owner maintain a certain level of liability insurance. The primary justification given for these requirements is the desire to protect innocent third-party victims of auto accidents. Such laws were first enacted at a time when auto-related injuries and deaths were on the rise and when first-party health and disability insurance markets were not well developed. In addition, state auto liability insurance requirements responded to the problem of judgment proof drivers: drivers who have insufficient assets to cover the losses their driving might cause to others. In the absence of such mandates, judgment proof auto owners have an incentive to carry insufficient insurance to cover the losses their driving might cause. Therefore, compulsory auto insurance is primarily a response to an externality problem. This is presumably why, in some states, car owners can get out of the requirement of buying an auto insurance policy if they can prove that they otherwise are 'financially responsible' – that is, have sufficient assets to pay for any harms their driving causes. However, car owners are not permitted to avoid the auto liability insurance requirement simply by demonstrating that they are highly sophisticated or well informed about the risks. Again, this difference demonstrates the basic point: the line between mandatory and non-mandatory insurance law rules should be defined in ways that are consistent with the market failure rationales that justify the rules in the first place.

Not all auto insurance mandates are necessarily a response to externality concerns. For example, the mandatory health insurance coverage part of most auto policies is meant to protect insureds themselves from the possibility of certain types of health care expenses. But why should such terms be mandatory? Shouldn't consumers be permitted to decide for themselves whether such coverage is worth the price? The argument to the contrary must be that individual consumers do not fully understand the risks of debilitating auto injuries, and thus will underestimate the value of such coverage in the market. It is also possible, however, to make externality-type adverse selection arguments: in the absence of the mandate, relatively low-risk individuals will tend to opt out of the insurance regime, causing premiums to rise for everyone else (Smith and Wright 1992). Alternatively, this coverage may be aimed at the externalities resulting from expensive and unreimbursed emergency room visits arising out of automobile accidents.[11]

The externality argument – and the accompanying need for a mandatory, rather than default, contract term – is clearest for rules that prohibit contract terms that threaten harm to third parties. One interesting and difficult to categorize insurance law doctrine is the insurable interest requirement. Under the insurable interest doctrine, which is a mandatory rule in all jurisdictions, an insurance policy is valid only insofar as the insured has an insurable interest in the person or property that is the focus of the insurance – that is, only insofar as the insured has some economic stake in the continued existence or safety of the person or property in question. The standard rationale given for the requirement is that it helps to mitigate the problem of moral hazard. For example, if a person can take out an insurance policy on a building in which they have no financial stake (no ownership or leasehold interest, say), the existence of that policy creates an incentive for the insured to destroy the building and recover the insurance proceeds. A similar, even grimmer version of the same story could be told about life insurance.

At first blush, this explanation for the doctrine sounds like an externality justification: that is, the insurable interest doctrine is needed to protect third parties from the risk of intentional harm that can arise if people are permitted to place a bet on something bad happening to something or someone else. On this view, the mandatory nature of the rule makes sense. The externality story, however, is an oversimplification. In fact, the externality is largely internalized by insurance companies, since insurers ultimately have to pay the claims in situations such as those described above. Indeed, this is why insurers, even without the insurable interest requirement, would not be willing to write policies in situations in which extreme moral hazard is a realistic possibility.

For example, if there were no insurable interest requirement, no rational insurance company would be willing to sell you a $1 million property policy on an old abandoned warehouse in a remote location (because of moral hazard concerns), but perhaps they would be willing to sell you a life insurance policy on the Queen of England, despite your lack of an

---

[11] Note that there is a possibility that this coverage actually reduces the cost of automobile insurance coverage by reducing the number of liability claims (since the emergency room visits are covered by the victim's policy) and by reducing the cost of the remaining claims (since the victim gets prompt treatment and also there is an immediate record of the injuries, reducing the extent of fraud).

insurable interest, because the risk of moral hazard there is close to zero. If insurers are internalizing this externality already, why have the insurable interest requirement? Perhaps the answer is that insurers are willing to tolerate more moral hazard than society is. If the chance of insurance induced arson or murder are relatively low in a given case, an insurer might still sell the policy and just charge a higher premium. But society may prefer not to take such chances, even small chances. And the mandatory insurable interest requirement is the result. This solution comes at some cost, of course, as the insurable interest requirement may be invoked to deny a claim in situations in which moral hazard was not a serious issue. But that may be the price society is willing to pay.[12]

Similar arguments could apply to the public policy doctrine that forbids insurance against intentional harms, at least in the liability insurance context, where there are in fact competing externalities. On the one hand, there is an obvious moral hazard concern: if liability insurance were available for intentionally harming others, parties with such coverage would be more likely to cause such harm. That example provides an externality justification for making the lack of coverage for intentional wrongdoing mandatory. On the other hand, there is a more subtle externality that cuts in the other direction. Parties who intentionally cause harm to third parties are often judgment proof. Therefore, if their liability insurance policies (mandatorily) contain an exclusion for intentionally caused harms, those costs will be externalized either to the victims, to their first-party insurers (and their insureds), or to taxpayers through various forms of social insurance. A way of addressing these conflicting externalities would be to address the moral hazard concern, not by making the intentional harm exclusion a mandatory rule, but by permitting the insurer to cover intentional harm claims brought by third-party victims but then to be subrogated against the intentional harm-causing insured. Alternatively, the conflict could be addressed by allowing coverage for intentional wrongdoing but reducing the amount of the coverage in cases in which insureds have the capacity to pay – perhaps reducing the coverage by the amount of assets owned by the insured and available to satisfy a liability claim.

In any event, the mandatory nature of externality-based rules should, and apparently does, extend to all insureds and not just those that are poorly informed, as all insureds (if well informed) would be subject to the

[12] The other primary rationale for the insurable interest requirement is the desire to discourage gambling through insurance policies. Given the prevalence of different forms of legalized gambling, this rationale seems to be more about channeling gambling into particular accepted forms rather than about stopping gambling altogether (Baker 1996).

externalities caused by moral hazard. Here we should emphasize the difference between two types of mandatory insurance law terms: those that tend to favor a finding of coverage (such as insurers' implied duties to defend and to settle) and those terms that tend to favor a finding of no coverage (such as the public policy doctrine as applied to intentional harms). The pro-coverage mandatory terms will obviously tend to produce higher premiums, assuming the additional coverage is non-trivial in magnitude. These mandatory terms are analogous to the mandatory product-risk insurance implied by the modern products liability, as discussed above (which also results in higher product prices). The anti-coverage mandatory terms, by contrast, tend to lower premiums overall, compared with insurance policies that do not have the terms. The mandatory nature of both these types of terms, however, makes sense from an efficiency perspective: that is, in both situations, the contracts that would be produced by the market, if these terms were alterable by agreement of the parties, would likely be inefficient.

One especially interesting set of (mostly) mandatory rules in insurance law are such basic contract doctrines as *contra proferentem*, disproportionate forfeiture, waiver and estoppel, misrepresentation, and the general duty of good faith and fair dealing. As mentioned previously, American contract law seems to treat these rules as being largely mandatory, except insofar as state regulators permit insurance contracts to include mandatory arbitration clauses (and even then, it is not clear to what extent arbitration does away with such doctrines). Although articulating the full efficiency justification for each of these doctrines is far beyond the scope of this chapter, such a justification is not difficult to imagine. Indeed, such justifications have become a part of the standard economic analysis of contract law (R. Posner 1986).[13]

As an efficiency matter, should parties to insurance contracts be permitted to contract around these rules? In our view, the answer to that question is highly dependent on the particular doctrine at issue and on

---

[13] For example, Judge Posner, in an early edition of his classic book, *The Economic Analysis of Law*, explained the economic explanation of *contra proferentem* as follows: 'Take the principle that insurance contracts are to be construed against the insurer. This may seem paternalistic or sentimental, but there is an economic argument for it. One's insurance coverage will turn out to be less extensive than it appeared to be, if ambiguities in the insurance policy are resolved against the insured. The insurance company is the superior bearer of this risk, too. Of course, if all interpretive doubts are resolved against the insurance company, its costs, and hence premium rates, will be higher. But all this means is that the insured is buying some additional insurance. R. Posner (1986).

the specific facts on the ground. For example, we doubt that it makes sense to permit standard form insurance policies to include terms that waive entirely any form of the doctrine of *contra proferentem* (and we doubt that most insurance regulators would permit such a term or even that most insurers would want such a waiver), because the beneficial incentive and risk-allocative effects of the doctrine would seem to be useful for all types of insureds, sophisticated or not, and for all types of policies. Indeed, if a contract contains a term that truly cannot be given a single reasonable meaning, what rule could be more efficient than imposing the cost on the party responsible for supplying the term?[14] The same may not be true, however, with other basic contract doctrines, especially the ones whose function is to protect only the least sophisticated insureds. With such doctrines, it might make sense to permit the *most* sophisticated insurance purchasers, who do not need the protection of a rule, to opt out of it. We talk further about this possibility in section VI below.

Does the quasi-mandatory nature of the duty to defend and the duty to settle make sense from an efficiency perspective? Should liability insurers, for example, be able to alter the standard defense obligation to provide that defense costs paid by the insurer must be reimbursed by the insured if the claim being litigated is ultimately determined not to be covered under the policy – a provision which is not permitted under the standard duty to defend? Certainly in the context of policies sold to unsophisticated parties, when individuals purchase insurance that purports to cover defense costs as well as damage and settlement payments within the policy limits, it seems likely that their expectation is that the duty to defend will be broader than the duty to indemnify (Ayres (2012) makes a similar proposal with regard to quasi-mandatory default rules, arguing that altering rules should be tailored to treat diverse groups of contractors differently, so as to make certain quasi-mandatory defaults 'stickier' for groups of contractors who are of particular concern, such as the unsophisticated insurance purchaser). Being required, after the fact, to reimburse their insurer for the costs of their defense would come as a shock. Thus, just as warranty disclaimers for personal injuries in product liability cases are

[14] An argument can be made that the broadest, most aggressive versions of the doctrine of *contra proferentem* are inefficient (Rappaport 1995). However, as a 'tie-breaker,' when, even with the use of extrinsic evidence, it is not possible to identify a single most reasonable interpretation of a term, it is difficult to deny the efficiency of the traditional rule of construing the term against the drafter. This is the version of the *contra proferentem* that has been adopted by the American Law Institute (PLLI).

not enforced, perhaps the same argument would justify a mandatory no reimbursement rule for duty to defend policies.

But on this argument, why then would we permit liability policies that do not provide for coverage of defense costs at all? Would not individual insureds expect to be receiving a defense with their liability policy, even if the policy clearly provides otherwise, given that such coverage has historically been provided with liability insurance? We think that extending the mandate to require that liability insurers provide defense cost coverage to all policyholders would be going too far, and we are content to let the combination of the market and oversight by insurance regulators decide when to depart from the practice of providing defense coverage. It is our view that even unsophisticated consumers would be able to understand the distinction between liability policies that cover defense costs and those that do not, in part because such a distinction would correlate with substantial differences in premiums, whereas fine-tuning the defense mandate would easily go unnoticed, or not fully understood, given the relatively minimal effect on premiums.[15] A similar story could be told with respect to the duty to settle.

We are not suggesting that there is no level of disclosure that would be sufficient to inform unsophisticated insureds of subtle differences in the duty to settle or duty to defend. Indeed, this point can be made about information-based rationales for mandatory rules in general: to the extent an insurance law rule exists because of concerns about lack of information on the part of insureds (or because of cognitive biases in the way in which insureds process information), the rule should be mandatory rather than merely a default, unless the insurer is able adequately to inform (or de-bias) the insureds through some process of education – e.g., detailed explanations by agents. Likewise, if the insured is considered commercially sophisticated in matters such as understanding the terms in insurance contracts, the information-based rationale for making insurance law rules mandatory diminishes considerably. How best to determine if an insured is commercially sophisticated is discussed below.

Given the importance of the mandatory/default-rule issue, it is interesting that courts deciding insurance law cases so rarely, in fact almost never, address the question explicitly. This probably has to do with the fact that some insurance policy terms are simply required by law (see examples above) and it may also relate to the fact that insurance policies generally

[15] Whether it would make sense for the insurer to offer to consumers or small businesses a liability insurance policy without defense coverage is a different question – one that insurance law leaves to the insurance market to work out.

must be approved by a regulatory agency before they are used by insurers (see the next section); therefore, courts in insurance cases may feel especially inhibited from ruling on the mandatory/default-rule issue. Another reason that courts do not address the mandatory/default-rule question directly is that the issue is so rarely presented. Most implied-in-law insurance contract terms are true gap fillers, in the sense that courts create the terms in circumstances in which the insurance contract is silent or ambiguous with regard to some issue that is critical to the question of coverage in the particular case. In that context, there is just no need for the court to address the counter-factual question whether an unambiguous term to the contrary would be enforceable.

A final reason that courts rarely address directly the mandatory/default-rule question in insurance law may be that the judges realize that they probably are not in the best position to make the decision in most cases. Consider the amount of information a court would need to have to make such a ruling, if it were going to do so in a way that is consistent with the efficiency framework outlined here. Again, the question whether the rule should be mandatory or default turns on not only whether there is a market failure present but also what the nature and extent of the market failure is. This is not a type of analysis for which a court is ideally suited (Posner 2002). This may explain why most mandatory terms in insurance contracts result from legislation or regulatory intervention, rather than judicial decision.

Whereas courts are considered the best fact finders with respect to what happened in a particular case, legislatures and administrative agencies are generally thought to be better fact finders with respect to questions of general market failures and determining when and what sort of government intervention is called for. Such 'polycentric' inquiries are inherently legislative or regulatory in nature. This is, of course, not to say that courts should never take on a regulatory role. Recall the example of products liability law, where it was the courts that pioneered certain interventions in consumer product markets, including both the adoption of the strict products liability rule and the decision to make that rule mandatory and non-waivable by contract. Such judicial interventions can be appropriate and useful. But they are and should be relatively rare, and they should be carefully tailored, especially in areas in which the legislature and the regulatory authority are active, as exemplified by the number of Supreme Court preemption cases addressing the appropriate role of products liability law in the regulation of pharmaceutical products given the presence of Congressional and administrative agency regulation of that market. The following section addresses more specifically the role of state insurance regulators in drawing the mandatory/default-rule boundary.

V. CONSIDERING ADMINISTRATIVE REVIEW OF INSURANCE FORMS

The analysis of standard form contracts in the insurance setting is different from the analysis of standard form contracts in other settings in at least one important way: the terms used in insurance contracts are subject to the approval of a public regulator, the state department of insurance. This fact, which has gone largely ignored in the insurance contract law literature, has important implications for insurance law. Given that the insurance regulator should be in the best position to determine whether and to what extent a market failure exists with respect to a particular type of insurance or in a particular insurance market, it should matter to the mandatory/default-rule question whether the regulator has approved or declined to approve a particular term. But just how should it matter? This section addresses that question.

The regulation of insurance forms is one of the core functions of state insurance departments throughout the United States. State regulation of forms differs along such dimensions as: (1) whether an insurer must obtain active approval of the department before using a form or whether the insurer may use the form as long as the department does not refuse to approve the form within a certain period (recognizing that, as applied, this could be a distinction without a difference); (2) whether there are exemptions from the approval/non-disapproval requirement, for example for the very large commercial market; and (3) the amount of staff time and other resources devoted to the substantive review of insurance policy forms. Regardless of these differences, insurance departments in many, if not most, states have at least the formal legal authority to refuse to approve an insurance policy form on the grounds that, in the judgment of the insurance department, the form is not in the public interest. In those jurisdictions, insurance departments' formal legal discretion in this regard is very broad, making the department's decision the last word on whether a form may be used in the state or not.[16]

---

[16] See, e.g., Annotation, *Validity, Construction, and Effect of Approval or Disapproval by Insurance Commissioner (or Similar Official) of Form of Policy*, 119 A.L.R. 877 (1939 & Supp. 2014) (citing Mich. Comp. Laws Ann. § 500.2236 (West 2003)); *Rory* v. *Cont'l Ins. Co.*, 703 N.W. 2d 23 (Mich. 2005) ('The decision to approve, disapprove, or withdraw an insurance policy form is within the sound discretion of the Insurance Commissioner.').

1. When the Insurance Regulator Rejects a Particular Policy Term

Taking this regulatory oversight of insurance contract terms into account, consider the effect on the mandatory/default-rule boundary when an insurance regulator refuses to approve a policy term. Imagine, in particular, the case of an insurer that wants to alter a recent pro-coverage judicial interpretation of an existing term in the insurer's insurance policy. With that in mind, the insurer submits a revised version of the policy for approval by the regulator, a version that contains new language that makes explicit that there should be no coverage in the situation in which the court said that there was coverage. In such a case, if the regulator says no, then the old term – as well as the pro-coverage judicial interpretation of that term – is now clearly mandatory. It may have been mandatory before; but the regulator has removed any doubt about the question.

How likely is this to happen? The insurance contract law literature typically assumes that insurers can get whatever forms they want through the state administrative agency. Yet, insurance companies frequently complain that state insurance departments will not approve their forms. Moreover, there is circumstantial evidence that insurance departments do exercise their authority to refuse to approve insurance policy forms that would contract around implied-in-law terms. The evidence comes in three forms. First, insurance regulators in many jurisdictions have in fact issued decisions forbidding or otherwise restricting the use of particular terms. For example, as discussed above, many states limit or forbid the use of binding arbitration provisions in personal lines of insurance, and these limitations are sometimes accomplished through the issuance of regulatory decisions.[17]

The second piece of evidence is the surprising dearth of authority regarding the mandatory (or not) nature of a variety of insurance law rules that are widely disliked within the insurance industry, such as *contra proferentem*, the use of extrinsic evidence to interpret insurance policy terms, and the complaint-allegation rule approach to determining when a liability insurer has the duty to defend a claim. If insurers could get insurance departments to approve whatever terms they wanted, some would presumably have obtained approval of forms that tried to contract around these rules at least in some limited way, and those forms and the judicial reaction to them would have left traces among the hundreds of thousands

---

17 For example, the Commissioner of Insurance in Utah has issued regulations limiting the use of compulsory arbitration terms in insurance policies (Utah Admin. Code r. 590-122. (2014)).

of recorded insurance decisions. Moreover, at least some insurers do try to contract around these rules in other jurisdictions, as demonstrated by the Bermuda liability insurance form, which contains an interpretation provision that declares both *contra proferentem* and extrinsic evidence out of bounds (Jacobs, Masters and Stanley 2004).

The third piece of evidence that insurance regulators do not always accept whatever policy change insurers request is the otherwise surprising rarity of state-specific variations in insurance policy forms that attempt to contract around the results of pro-policyholder court decisions regarding insurance law issues on which state law is split.[18] For example, perhaps the relative dearth of instances in which insurers attempt to contract around *contra proferentem* holdings that go against them and in favor of coverage are the result either of regulators refusing to approve of policy revisions that would alter the outcomes of those decisions or of insurers deciding not even to attempt such policy revisions on the belief that such policyholder-unfriendly changes would be rejected by the regulators. The other reasons that insurers do not attempt more often to contract around *contra proferentem* rulings have been emphasized in Michelle Boardman's work on the persistence of ambiguous boilerplate in insurance policies (Boardman 2006). Boardman argues that insurers may choose not to redraft their forms, even though the court would permit them to do so, because they have decided that they can live with the court's implied-in-law term and, perhaps, because they can take advantage of the ambiguity in their dealings with insureds. We think the regulatory oversight (or fear of regulatory oversight) explanation is likely to be just as important in understanding why there are not more cases asking courts to consider whether their earlier implied-in-law creations are mandatory.

Another example relates to liability insurers' right to recoup their defense and settlement costs when they defend and settle a claim for which they subsequently prove that they had no duty to defend. The court decisions that refuse to permit insurers to recoup those costs point to the fact that the insurance policy does not contain a term authorizing such recoupment. Some decisions even state that they would reach a different result if there were such a provision in the policy. Yet, neither commercial general liability insurance policies nor the liability coverage part of personal liability policies explicitly permit recoupment. While there are state-specific endorsements to these forms, such endorsements appear generally to consist of terms that are mandated by state legislation or regulation,

---

[18] One exception is provisions drafting around narrow interpretations of the 'expected or intended' injury exclusion (Schwarcz 2011).

not terms that contract around state-specific default rules, such as the no-recoupment default.

At this point, we have no way of estimating how frequently insurance departments (or insurers acting strategically in relation to insurance departments) turn a default, gap-filling implied-in-law term into a mandatory insurance contract term. But our sense is that the frequency is well above *de minimis*, especially if we include in that category decisions by insurers not to redraft that are based on the judgment that there is a risk that the redrafted form will not be approved. If we are right, the regulation of policy forms by state insurance regulators may not be the rubber stamp that the insurance contract law literature assumes it to be.

2. When the Insurance Regulator Approves a Particular Policy Term

While it seems clear that the explicit regulatory disapproval of a change to a policy term (or of a change in the interpretation of the policy term), in effect, makes that term (or interpretation of the term) mandatory, the effect of a regulator's approval of a particular policy term proposed by an insurer is less clear. As courts have pointed out before, regulatory approval of a policy term does not resolve the question of interpretation; thus, even if a term has been approved for use in a policy, whether the term is ambiguous is a question that only the courts can resolve, as they are the ones who actually apply the term in question to particular situations.

The more interesting question, and one that has been largely ignored in the literature, is whether a court is obligated to enforce a term in a standard form policy that is indisputably unambiguous and that was approved by the regulator for use in the policy. Many hold the view that any indisputably unambiguous contract term should be enforced, irrespective of whether the term appears in a standard form contract. Many others, however, are of the view that, in standard form contracts (especially ones like insurance policies that are long and complicated and that reasonably go unread by almost all policyholders) even an indisputably unambiguous term should not be enforced if it is inconsistent with the reasonable expectations of the policyholder or is unconscionable. The question we pose here, directed towards those who hold the second position, is whether an indisputably unambiguous term, which is arguably contrary to reasonable expectations or unconscionable, ought nevertheless to be enforced by the courts *if* the regulator is: (a) acting within its statutorily granted authority; and (b) demonstrably carrying out its role as protector of policyholder interests. Although a full articulation of this argument is beyond the scope of this chapter, to the extent that it is persuasive, there would be an important corollary that is relevant to the current discussion: regulatory approval of a standard form term would trump any otherwise mandatory judicial doctrine or implied-in-law term that contradicts it.

The anti-concurrent causation language found in many modern property insurance policies provides an example. The vast majority of courts have been willing to enforce this language when an exclusion unambiguously results in a denial of coverage in a particular concurrent-cause situation, even when those jurisdictions had an implied-in-law rule that goes the other way (dominant or proximate cause). Thus, the implied-in-law term was a default rule. This outcome is, in our view, justifiable at least in part because a regulator approved the exclusion. If there were no such regulatory approval, as in most non-insurance contractual settings, the court would be required to do its own independent enforceability analysis, deploying such doctrines as unconscionability and reasonable expectations.[19]

On the most extreme version of this view, if a term is approved by the regulator, the court should not have the authority to find the term unenforceable, unless the court can make the case that the agency has somehow exceeded or failed to exercise its oversight authority or, perhaps, that a particular application of the term raises public policy concerns that were not considered by the agency. (A narrower formulation of the latter exception would limit it to public policy concerns that a reasonable agency would not have foreseen.) Unless one of these exceptions applied, a court should have to enforce the term even if it thought that the term was ill-conceived or the product of some sort of market failure.

The reason for such a rule has to do with comparative institutional advantage. As discussed above, insurance regulators are usually in a better position than courts to make determinations about the presence or absence of failures in insurance markets and the implications of those failures for whether terms should be mandatory or default. More generally, insurance regulators should be in a better position than courts to determine what is in the best interests of insurance purchasers – what an average insurance buyer expects to get when he or she buys coverage and how much he or she expects to pay for it. If it is true that state insurance regulators have a comparative advantage over courts (because of their information-gathering abilities and their expertise in insurance markets), then a decision by a regulator that the overall social benefits of a particular policy term outweigh the costs should not be overridden by a court.

---

[19] The decision by the Washington courts not to enforce the clear anti-concurrent-cause exclusions is an exception that proves the rule (*Safeco Ins. Co. of America* v. *Hirschmann*, 773 P. 2d 413 (Wash. 1989)).

That conclusion assumes, of course, that the insurance regulator is not exceeding its authority granted by the legislature and that the regulator is in fact doing its job. Informed decisions by active, engaged state insurance departments have much to commend them. And insurance regulators, as mentioned, are not always the rubber stamps that some scholars suggest. But they are almost certainly not always a model of regulatory efficiency and thoroughness either. Whether, when, and how much courts should defer to a state insurance department's approval of a form are big questions, too big for this chapter. But we can at least outline a few factors that a court might take into account in deciding how much to defer and under what circumstances.

Obvious factors to consider would include the need for insurance-specific expertise and agency-style fact-finding authority to make a good decision about the enforceability of an insurance policy term, the presence of the relevant expertise and fact-finding authority in the particular insurance department that approved the term at issue, and the quality of the insurance policy review process that was in place for the term being litigated. Courts that seriously consider these factors and give strong deference when appropriate, and little or no deference when not, could help improve the efficiency of the insurance market by encouraging insurance departments to invest additional resources in the policy review process. The argument here is analogous to one sometimes made in connection with judicial deference to federal agency decision making. That is, some commentators have suggested that the decision by courts to defer to federal agency interpretations of statutes should depend to some extent on whether the agency is applying special expertise in a genuine effort to carry out Congressional purposes (Eskridge and Baer 2008).

A related factor that a court might take into account is the extent to which the insurance regulator is independent of the insurance industry. We have already discussed the evidence suggesting that insurance regulators are at least not a rubber stamp for the industry when it comes to approving policy language. But that does not mean that concerns about industry capture of the insurance regulatory decision making process are entirely absent (Cummins and Tennyson 2001; Jaffee and Russell 1998). Given that fact, perhaps a court reviewing the significance of regulatory approval in making the mandatory-vs-default determination with respect to a particular provision could also take into account the extent to which there is evidence of undue industry political influence, either on the particular term at issue or more generally.

Two kinds of rules for which insurance regulators have less expertise than courts and, thus, for which significantly less deference by courts may be due are: (a) rules that are merely the insurance-specific instantiation of ordinary contract law rules, such as interpretation, waiver and estoppel, misrepresentation, the duty of good faith, and remedies; and (b) rules that relate to the involvement of insurance in the civil justice system. Courts, judges in particular, have substantial relevant expertise regarding both sets of rules, especially the first. With regard to the second, courts are most likely to have insurance-specific expertise in the context of liability actions, and they are more likely than insurance departments to prioritize access to civil justice. Thus, to the extent insurance law rules should take into account such civil justice externalities as victim compensation and civil recourse, courts have greater institutional competence, since courts decide not only insurance contract cases but also tort cases. This obviously is a concern only with respect to insurance law doctrines as they are applied to liability insurance, where there are injured victims who: (a) are not a party to the insurance contract, and thus will not necessarily be well protected by the terms of the agreement between insurer and insured; and (b) are not an active and engaged constituency of the insurance regulator, and thus will not necessarily be well protected by the decisions of the agency.

VI. RULES VERSUS STANDARDS IN THE DRAWING THE MANDATORY/DEFAULT-RULE BOUNDARY

The distinction between rules and standards in law is familiar, and the economic analysis of this distinction is well known. Rules require the lawmaker to have a great deal of information *ex ante*, before the regulated event takes place. Standards are relatively vague and open-ended by comparison, and their efficiency depends on the ability of the legal decision maker, often a court, to provide those standards with content in the application to particular cases after the regulated event takes place. For example, whereas choosing the optimal speed limit (the quintessential rule) can be difficult and in some ways arbitrary, applying that rule to particular cases is relatively simple. One is either speeding or not. By contrast, a standard that prohibits 'reckless driving' must be given content by the courts applying the standard to particular cases. The economic analysis of rules and standards reaches an unsurprising conclusion: sometimes rules are more efficient; sometimes standards are; and sometimes it is efficient to have both.

How does the rule/standard distinction apply to the mandatory/default-rule question in contract law and insurance law? As it turns out, there is an approach to drawing the mandatory/default-rule boundary that is more standards-based and there is an approach that is more rules-based.

Which approach is more efficient will depend on the situation. To see this basic point, consider an example of a rules-based approach adopted in the recently approved first chapter of the American Law Institute's PLLI. The PLLI recommends a new rule designed to protect a particular class of insureds who are likely to be relatively unsophisticated in commercial matters. The rule itself has to do with the insurer's defense of misrepresentation. The traditional rule is that an insurer may defend against a claim for payment under a policy, and may retroactively rescind that policy, if it can show that the insured made a material misrepresentation on which it (the insurer) reasonably relied. And the rule, as stated in the hornbooks and as applied in most jurisdictions, has something of a strict liability flavor to it. That is, the insurer is not required to show any sort of fault on the part of the insured. This rule has proven to be disastrous for insureds who make innocent misstatements on their insurance applications that turn out to be material. The new PLLI rule provides protection for innocent insureds by limiting insurers' rescission remedies to situations in which they can demonstrate that the misrepresentation by the insured was either intentional or reckless. The rule is meant to protect the relatively unsophisticated insured. However, the relevant question for current purposes is whether this new rule should be mandatory or waivable by contract.

In answering this question one could imagine either a standards-based approach or a rules-based approach. A standards-based approach might permit insurance contracts to waive this new protection for the insured if and only if the court enforcing the contract were to determine that the insured in the case was sufficiently commercially sophisticated to be able to protect itself in the negotiation process. Under such an approach, courts hearing insurance contract disputes would be called on to assess the relative sophistication of the insureds. The benefit of this approach would be its flexibility: only the parties in need of protection would receive it, at least insofar as the courts do a good job of drawing the distinction between commercially sophisticated and commercially unsophisticated parties. The downside of such a standards-based approach, however, is apparent: not only would it be difficult for courts to determine commercial sophistication in particular cases, the fact that such a determination would have to be made in each case would itself create uncertainty for insurers. They would have to guess what rules would apply to their contracts – whether particular waivers of the new misrepresentation protection would be enforced – in deciding what premiums to charge.

The rules-based approach, a version of which the PLLI adopted, is much simpler and entails less uncertainty. Under such an approach, the class of parties who would be entitled to contract around the new misrepresentation protection would be defined *ex ante* (as with the speed limit). Thus, the PLLI provides specifically that the new protection for unintentional and non-reckless misrepresentations should be merely a default rule for 'large commercial policyholders' but should be mandatory for everyone else. Further, the PLLI defines a large commercial policyholder in a very specific way, tying the definition to a particular net-asset threshold that is used in federal securities laws (which is presently $10 million). The idea behind this particular way of drawing the mandatory/default-rule boundary is that: (a) consumer insureds will be mandatorily protected; (b) small business insureds will also be mandatorily protected; but (c) larger business insureds would be able to contract out of the new remedy if they so choose. The obvious downside of the rule is that it is both over-inclusive and under-inclusive. On the over-inclusive side, some consumer and small business insureds are in fact commercially sophisticated and can probably take care of themselves; if they choose to waive the new misrepresentation protection, then it is probably the efficient outcome. But the PLLI's rule-based approach does not permit them to do that. On the under-inclusive side, some business insureds with more than $10 million in net assets may well be relatively unsophisticated when it comes to purchasing insurance, but they are not protected by the PLLI's rule; if their policies contain a waiver of the new protection, the PLLI say that such a waiver should be enforced. Our view is that the costs of this rule-based approach are exceeded by the benefits, which is to say that they are exceeded by the costs of the alternative, standards-based approach, described above.

VII. CONCLUSION

Designing an efficient regime of insurance law, as with contract law generally, requires not only efficient default rules and mandatory rules, but also a sensible way of determining when a rule will be one or the other. Most insurance policies are standard form agreements whose language is crafted by insurance companies and their representatives. Most of the terms of those policies can be altered by the drafters, within the limits of what state regulators will allow. Although most of insurance law, therefore, is determined by the agreement of the parties, some terms in policies are made mandatory by legislation or by regulatory fiat; and some insurance law doctrines impose mandatory obligations on the parties. This chapter has provided a typology of mandatory insurance law rules and argued that those rules should be made mandatory only when there is a market failure rationale for doing so. In addition, the chapter explains the appropriate role of the insurance regulator in determining whether a particular rule of insurance law is mandatory or merely a default. For example, some terms are probably included in insurance policies by insurers, and some terms are probably excluded, because of the belief that the regulator would otherwise not permit the policy to be sold. This is a form of implicit regulatory mandate for those terms. Finally, the chapter explains how the rules/standard distinction can play a role in the optimal mandatory/default-rule boundary.

REFERENCES

Abraham, Kenneth S. 1996. 'A Theory of Insurance Policy Interpretation' 95 *Michigan Law Review* 531–69.

Abraham, Kenneth S. 2001. 'Peril and Fortuity in Property and Liability Insurance' 36 *Tort & Insurance Law Journal* 777–802.

Abraham, Kenneth S., and J. W. Montgomery, III. 2003. 'The Lawlessness of Arbitration' 9 *Connecticut Insurance Law Journal* 355–69.

American Law Institute (ALI). 2014. *Principles of the Law of Liability Insurance.*

Arlen, Jennifer. 2010. 'Contracting over Malpractice Liability' 158 *University of Pennsylvania Law Review* 957–1023.

Ayres, Ian. 2006. 'Ya-HUH: There Are and Should Be Penalty Defaults' 33 *Florida State University Law Review* 589.

Ayres, Ian. 2012. 'Regulating Opt-Out: An Economic Theory of Altering Rules' 121 *Yale Law Journal* 2032.

Ayres, Ian, and Robert Gertner. 1989. 'Filling Gaps in Incomplete Contracts: An Economic Theory of Default Rules' 99 *Yale Law Journal* 87–130.

Baker, Tom. 1996. 'On the Genealogy of Moral Hazard' 75 *Texas Law Review* 237.

Barker, William T., and Ronald D. Kent. 2014. *New Appleman Insurance Bad Faith Litigation* (2nd edn: Lexis Nexis).

Barnett, Randy E. 1992. 'The Sound of Silence: Default Rules and Contractual Consent' 78 *Virginia Law Review* 821–911.

Beh, Hazel Glenn. 2004. 'Reassessing the Sophisticated Insured Exception' 39 *Tort Trial & Insurance Practice Law Journal* 85–120.

Boardman, Michelle E. 2006. 'Contra Proferentem: The Allure of Ambiguous Boilerplate' 104 *Michigan Law Review* 1105–28.

Boardman, Michelle E. 2013. 'Penalty Default Rules in Insurance Law' 40 *Florida State University Law Review* 305–48.

Chandler, Seth J. 1993. 'Reconsidering the Duty to Settle' 42 *Drake Law Review* 741–806.

Cohen, George M. 1999. 'Implied Terms and Interpretation in Contract Law' in Boudewijn Bouckaert and Gerrit De Geest (eds.), *Encyclopedia of Law and Economics, Volume III: The Regulation of Contracts* (Cheltenham, UK, and Northampton, MA: Edward Elgar).

Craswell, Richard. 1999. 'Contract Law: General Theories,' in Boudewijn Bouckaert and Gerrit De Geest (eds.), *Encyclopedia of Law and Economics, Volume III: The Regulation of Contracts* (Cheltenham, UK, and Northampton, MA: Edward Elgar).

Croley, Steven P., and Jon D. Hanson. 1993. 'Rescuing the Revolution: The Revived Case for Enterprise Liability' 91 *Michigan Law Review* 683–797.

Cummins, David, and Sharon Tennyson. 2001. 'Regulation, Political Influence and the Price of Automobile Insurance' 20 *Journal of Insurance Regulation* 9–50.

Eskridge, William N. Jr., and Lauren E. Baer. 2008. 'The Continuum of Deference: Supreme Court Treatment of Agency Statutory Interpretations from Chevron to Hamdan' 96 *Georgetown Law Review* 1083–226.

French, Christopher C. 2012. 'Debunking the Myth that Insurance Coverage is not Available for Intentional Torts or Damages' 8 *Hastings Bus. L. J.* 65.

Goetz, Charles J., and Robert E. Scott. 1983. 'The Mitigation Principle: Toward a General Theory of Contractual Obligation' 69 *Virginia Law Review* 967–1024.
Jacobs, Richard, Lorelie S. Masters, and Paul Stanley. 2004. *Liability Insurance in International Arbitration: The Bermuda Form* (Oxford, UK, and Portland, OR: Hart Publishing).
Jaffee, Dwight, and Thomas Russell. 1998. 'The Causes and Consequences of Rate Regulation in the Auto Insurance Industry' in David F. Bradford (ed.), *The Economics of Property-Casualty Insurance* (Chicago, IL: University of Chicago Press) 81–112.
Knutsen, Erik S. 2010. 'Confusion about Causation in Insurance: Solutions for Catastrophic' 61 *Alabama Law Review* 957–1023.
Latin, Howard. 1994. '"Good" Warnings, Bad Products, and Cognitive Limitations' 41 *UCLA Law Review* 1193–295.
Monahan, Amy. 2009. 'Value-Based Mandated Health Benefits' 80 *University of Colorado Law Review* 127–200.
Posner, Eric. 2002. 'Economic Analysis of Contract Law after Three Decades: Success or Failure?' 112 *Yale Law Journal* 829–80.
Posner, Richard. 1986. *Economic Analysis of Law* (3rd edn., Boston, MA, and Toronto: Little Brown).
Public Citizen. 2010. 'State Laws Regulating Arbitration in Insurance Contracts' available online at www.citizen.org/congress/article_redirect.cfm?ID=6560.
Randall, Susan. 2005. 'Mandatory Arbitration in Insurance Disputes: Inverse Preemption of the Federal Arbitration Act' 11 *Conn. Ins. L.J.* 253, 264–92.
Rappaport, Michael B. 1995. 'The Ambiguity Rule and Insurance Law: Why Insurance Contracts Should Not Be Construed Against the Drafter' 30 *Georgia Law Review* 171–257.
Schwarcz, Daniel. 2011. 'Reevaluating Standardized Insurance Policies' 78 *University of Chicago Law Review* 1263.
Shavell, Steven. 2004. *Foundations of Economic Analysis of Law* (Cambridge, MA and London, UK: Harvard University Press).
Smith, Eric, and Randall Wright.1992. 'Why is Automobile Insurance in Philadelphia so Damn Expensive' 82 *American Economic Review* 756.
Stempel, Jeffrey W. 1993. 'Reassessing the "Sophisticated Policyholder" Defense in Insurance Coverage Litigation' 42 *Drake Law Review* 807–58.
Sykes, Alan O. 1993. 'Judicial Limitations on the Discretion of Liability Insurers to Settle or Litigate: An Economic Critique' 72 *Texas Law Review* 1345.
Syverud, Kent D. 1990. 'The Duty to Settle' 76 *Virginia Law Review* 1113.
Trebilcock, Michael J. 1993. *The Limits of Freedom of Contract* (Cambridge, MA and London, UK: Harvard University Press).
Ware, Stephen J. 1999. 'Default Rules from Mandatory Rules: Privatizing Law through Arbitration' 83 *Minnesota Law Review* 703–54.
Works, Bob. 1998–99. 'Excusing Nonoccurrence of Insurance Policy Conditions to Avoid Disproportionate Forfeiture: Claims Made Formats as a Test Case' 5 *Conn. Ins. L. J.* 505.

12. The law and economics of insurance bad faith liability

Danial Asmat and Sharon Tennyson

INTRODUCTION

In the US and many other countries, the law of contracts holds that parties have a *general duty* of good faith in the performance of contracts. Performance in good faith is notoriously difficult to define, but according to one broad definition constitutes 'honesty in fact and the observance of reasonable commercial standards of fair dealing' (Uniform Commercial Code (UCC) 1-201). The law's recognition of this general duty is often viewed as filling gaps in incomplete contractual language, and is aimed at preventing a contracting party from gaining unfair advantage through overly-strict interpretation of this language (see, e.g., Dubroff 2006; Cooter and Ulen 2008).

In insurance contracting, under US law the duty of good faith explicitly extends for the duration of the insurance contract and includes an insurer's actions in settling claims. The idea is that the insurer implicitly undertook a duty to promptly investigate claims and fully pay those claims that are covered under the terms of the policy, even if no specific contractual language defines exactly what those duties consist of in practice. In its Unfair Trade Practices Model Act (2008) the National Association of Insurance Commissioners (NAIC) considers insurer actions such as 'failing to acknowledge promptly a communication from a policyholder relating to a claim, failing to adopt and implement reasonable standards for the prompt investigation and settlement of claims, and not attempting in good faith to effectuate prompt, fair, and equitable settlement of submitted claims for which it is reasonably clear a payment is owed' to breach the duty of good faith in claims settlement.

While the good faith standard implies that the policyholder and insurer each have a mutual duty of honest dealings, traditional contract law effectively placed a higher burden on the policyholder than on the insurer. For example, breach of a disclosure duty by an insurance buyer may lead to nullification of the insurance contract, thereby voiding all coverage. Breach of a disclosure duty by an insurance seller also permits the policyholder to nullify the contract, but that would leave the policyholder without any insurance coverage. Alternatively, the policyholder could demand nullification of only the violating section of the policy, but this merely expands coverage to the level originally expected by the policyholder. Thus, contract nullifications provide an insurance buyer little effective recourse for a seller's breach of a disclosure duty. In disputes between policyholders and insurers regarding claims, the expectation damage principle of contract law provides that the policyholder may recover damages only up to the amount that would put him in the position he would have been in had the insurer handled the claim as implicitly promised. Under ordinary contract law principles the policyholder would typically not be allowed to recover emotional distress damages or attorneys' fees.[1] Given the costs and delays involved in legal disputes, seeking damages for mishandling of a claim provides little effective recourse for the policyholder. This significantly disadvantages policyholders in claim disputes with their insurers.

To address this disparity, state courts and legislatures in the US have expanded the remedies available to policyholders when insurers violate their good faith duty in settling claims. This area of law has become known as the law of *first-party insurance bad faith* and permits wronged policyholders to collect compensation in excess of the amount owed under the original terms of insurance. In many states the awarding of additional damages is facilitated by adjudicating first-party insurance bad faith cases under tort law. Compared with other remedies, tort liability greatly increases the potential damages faced by a liable defendant. Unlike contract law, tort law allows for the recovery for all harm or injuries sustained (including legal expenses, economic loss, and mental distress), and permits punitive damages awards.

This chapter summarizes the state of the literature on the economic analysis of first-party insurance bad faith law. After reviewing the various legal regimes in place for adjudicating first-party insurer bad faith, the predicted benefits, costs, and incentive effects on insurance claims and claim settlements are discussed. The likely effects of bad faith liability on legal disputes and dispute resolution costs are also considered. While many predicted effects are unambiguous, a central theme which emerges is that expanded liability for insurer bad faith engenders trade-offs that make the resulting net social welfare gains uncertain. Moreover, the net social benefits of the law depend crucially on its implementation by courts and

---

[1] See Sykes (1996). Contract law permits recovery of emotional distress damages in cases where they are particularly likely to result from the breach. Based on this idea, some courts have allowed for recovery of these damages in cases of an insurer's breach (Baker 1994).

legislatures. Evidence from a growing empirical literature on the impact of bad faith law on insurance claims, settlements and disputes is reviewed to provide insights into the importance of these trade-offs and the effectiveness of the law in achieving its intended objectives. Results suggest that bad faith liability has had a measurable impact on insurance claim settlements – increasing settlement amounts and reducing underpayment of claims – but has failed to reduce costly claims litigation.

LEGAL REGIMES

Regulatory standards for insurer behaviors are imposed in jurisdictions around the globe, many with the aim of preventing insurer opportunism in claim settlement (Midlige, Re, and Hoffman 2011). In the US, for example, each state has an Unfair Trade Practices Act based on the NAIC Model Act described above, which is enforceable by the state insurance department and Attorney General. All state insurance departments also accept and aid in the resolution of individual consumer complaints, although they have no legal power to force a resolution unless the complaint involves a regulatory violation by the insurer (Schwarcz 2009). However, in many other countries, including both Canada and the UK, a financial services ombudsman office is empowered with enforcement authority to resolve consumers' disputes with insurers.[2] Schwarcz (2009) analyzes dispute handling by the UK's Financial Services Ombudsman and concludes that its system of integrating complaint handling and arbitration provides effective protections for insurance consumers.

In the absence of a binding system of mediation, insurance claim disputes in the US may be decided in the courts. In such disputes a policyholder may seek the court's assistance in obtaining what he perceives as rightful payment of the claim, and may allege in addition that the insurer violated standards of good faith in the claim negotiation process. Thus, the charge of insurer bad faith is a secondary issue that may be added to a policyholder's lawsuit over a disputed claim. In deciding the case, the courts must rule on the disputed claim and on the separate question of whether the insurer's behavior warrants a finding of bad faith. The denial

---

[2] In Canada the ombudsman offices operate at the province level. The European Union and individual member states have alternative dispute resolution mechanisms in place for financial services, most of which include insurance. Australia, New Zealand, India and many other countries also resolve insurance disputes through an ombudsman office, and many Asian countries are strengthening alternative dispute resolution mechanisms for insurance disputes.

of a claim may constitute a breach of contract, but it does not necessarily constitute bad faith. The determining issues are whether the insurer undertook a proper investigation, and whether the results of the investigation were subjected to a reasonable evaluation and review. Most US states permit extra-contractual damages to be awarded to a policyholder in the event of an insurer's bad faith; in cases of egregious behaviors by an insurer, many states permit punitive damages to be awarded.

This system of liability for bad faith in contracting applies specifically to insurance. Liability has been expanded in the insurance context because insurance policies are 'peace of mind' contracts – i.e. entered into by the policyholder not for financial gain but due to the insurer's pledge to provide peace of mind (Kent and Ip 2012). Over time, the special nature of insurance contracts combined with the general duty of good faith in contracting has led to recognition of a policyholder's right to seek damages for an insurer's bad faith in settling a claim. This is, however, exclusively a North American legal doctrine. While other countries impose a general duty of good faith in contracts, the view of insurance as exceptional in this regard has not followed. In many countries, including the UK, no compensation beyond the insurance payment and interest due may be awarded in cases of wrongful denial or late payment of a claim (Law Commission 2010).

Insurance Bad Faith Liability

The law of first-party insurer bad faith liability developed over the past century in the US, and has expanded into Canada in recent years.[3] Until the late 1950s US courts did not recognize insurer bad faith as a separate cause of action, applying standard contract law principles in such cases (Kornblum 1988; Stempel 2006). The 1958 California Supreme Court case *Comunale* v. *Traders & General Insurance Co*. was the first to identify insurer bad faith as a tort, albeit in the liability insurance setting rather than in first-party insurance. The *Comunale* case established liability insurers' now well-established 'duty to settle' on behalf of the insured policyholder. Because in *Comunale* the insurer 'rejected a reasonable offer of settlement' and 'wrongfully refused to defend' the insured, the court held the insurer liable for amounts in excess of the policy limits.[4]

---

[3] This discussion of bad faith legal regimes in the US relies heavily on Tennyson and Warfel (2010) and Richman and Tennyson (2013). For further analysis of the duty to settle see Squire, Chapter 14 in this volume.

[4] 50 Cal. 2d 654 (1958).

The extension of the tort of bad faith to first-party insurance followed reasonably soon thereafter but has been much more controversial (e.g. Jerry 1986). Some argue that breach of contract should be the exclusive cause of action for first-party insurance bad faith actions, because the relationship between insurer and policyholder differs from that in liability insurance. The relationship between insurer and policyholder in the liability insurance context is fiduciary: an unrelated third-party is the insurance claimant and the insurer accepts or rejects settlements on behalf of the policyholder. If the insurer fails to accept a reasonable settlement and the case proceeds to court, the policyholder may be financially liable for judgments in excess of the policy limits. In contrast, in the first-party insurance context the policyholder is the insurance claimant, and is therefore the insurer's opponent in the adversarial claim settlement process. First-party insurer bad faith is thus a unique application of tort law, applying to disputes over the terms of a contract between two contracting parties.

While an insurer's failure to pay a reasonable settlement demand in first-party insurance does not leave the policyholder open to future liability judgments, it does leave the policyholder with uncompensated financial losses. Thus, the California Supreme Court found the reasoning from *Comunale* extended to the first-party insurance case, first in the 1967 case *Crisci* v. *Security Insurance Co*[5] and again in *Gruenberg* v. *Aetna Insurance Company* in 1973.[6] In the latter case the court articulated that the first-party insurer's 'duty not to withhold unreasonably payments due under a policy' is simply another aspect of the third-party insurer's 'duty to accept reasonable settlements'.[7] In both cases the court ruled that an insurer's failure to reasonably settle an insurance claim may permit a tort action for breach of the implied covenant of good faith and fair dealing.

More than 40 years after these precedent-setting cases, a majority of states now provide remedies for insurer bad faith which permit damage awards greater than the insured loss amount (Browne, Pryor, and Puelz 2004). Tennyson and Warfel (2010) catalog the different approaches used by the states, based on the case evidence and classifications reported in Stempel (2006) and GenRe (2008). The authors conclude that 26 states permit private tort actions; nine states have rejected the application of tort law but permit private actions against insurers for bad faith under contract law; and at least 25 states recognize (additionally or alternatively)

5 66 Cal. 2d 425, 430 (1967).
6 510 P. 2d 1032 (Cal. 1973).
7 Ibid., at 1037.

a statute-based, private right of action alleging bad faith by a first-party insurer.

Cause of action under tort law

In states that recognize tort actions for a first-party insurer's breach of the duty of good faith in settling a claim, aggrieved policyholders are not required to allege an independent tort in order to recover under the tort laws. The general rule of damages in tort is that the injured party may recover for all harm or injuries sustained, including emotional distress damages, regardless of whether these damages could have been anticipated. Assuming that the conduct giving rise to liability was particularly egregious, punitive damages may be awarded.

States differ in the standards of behavior required to demonstrate insurer bad faith, and the various regimes are often categorized into those that use a 'negligence' standard and those that use an 'intentional tort' standard. The standard first applied in *Gruenberg*, referencing an insurer's duty to behave reasonably, is akin to a negligence standard. This standard holds an insurer liable for failure to take the appropriate standard of care in considering a claim, which the courts have interpreted as requiring equal weighing of the insured's interest and its own.[8] The standard more closely resembling that for an intentional tort was first adopted in *Anderson* v. *Continental Insurance Company* in Wisconsin in 1978.[9] For a finding of bad faith, this standard requires that an insurer acted with full knowledge of or in reckless disregard of the lack of a reasonable basis for denying an insurance claim. And, in the opinion of the Wisconsin court, punitive damages are warranted only in cases of extreme misconduct: '[An insurer] must not only intentionally have breached [its] duty of good faith, but in addition must have been guilty of oppression, fraud, or malice.'[10]

Stempel (2006: 10–87) interprets the law of each state, but cautions that '[t]o appreciate the differences across the states concerning insurer bad faith, one must pay attention to the nuances of precedent and doctrine, which tend to be glossed over in any classification'. While bearing this caution in mind, Tennyson and Warfel (2010) categorize the state tort regimes and conclude that a small majority of those states require a demonstration of insurer behaviors that amount to an 'intentional tort'.[11]

---

8 Ibid.

9 85 Wis. 2d 675, 691, 271 N.W. 2d 368 (1978).

10 Ibid.

11 One state, Arkansas, has imposed a yet more stringent standard that Tennyson and Warfel (2010) characterize as a 'quasi-criminal' standard. See Stempel (2006) for in-depth discussion of varying state standards.

They conclude that among the 26 states permitting tort claims for insurer bad faith, around 11 apply a 'negligence' standard.

Cause of action under contract law

A few states have continued to reject the application of tort law in first-party insurance bad faith cases, but permit private actions alleging insurer bad faith under contract law. The rationale for a contract law treatment is exemplified in the Utah case of *Beck* v. *Farmers Insurance Exchange*,[12] in which the court reasoned that 'the practical end of providing a strong incentive for insurers to fulfill their contractual obligations can be accomplished . . . through a contract cause of action, without the analytical straining necessitated by the tort approach and with far less potential for unforeseen consequences to the law of contracts'.[13]

As noted above, damages are ordinarily limited under contract law, with reimbursement for attorney fees routinely denied. An independent tort such as fraud or intentional infliction of emotional distress must be alleged in order to make a claim for punitive damages. Consequential damages for economic losses caused by a contract breach are restricted to losses that were reasonably foreseeable at the time the contract was made (Garner 1999). This means that insurers could escape liability on the grounds that the losses experienced were beyond their contemplation at the time of contract formation (Sykes 1996).

However, as documented by Stempel (2006) and discussed in Baker (1994), in many states that adjudicate insurer bad faith cases under contract law, courts often allow a broader definition of damages, including prejudgment interest, attorney fees, and emotional distress. Baker further notes that such exceptions are also common in other contracts for which emotional distress should be a reasonably foreseeable consequence of a contract breach (Baker 1994: 1427). Thus, the most important distinction between contract and tort law for cases of insurer bad faith may be the potential for punitive damages under tort law.

Cause of action under statute

In states where the courts have failed to recognize a common law cause of action for first-party insurance bad faith, state legislatures have often responded by enacting a statute that permits such a cause of action. In other states, legislatures seek to modify the court-made law through statute. Typically, statutes identify the standard of conduct, the burden

12 701 P. 2d 795, 801–2 (Utah 1985).

13 Ibid., at 799.

of proof, and the damages that can be recovered in a first-party bad faith action. Depending on the state, awardable damages may include prejudgment interest and legal expenses, damages for economic loss and mental distress and, in some instances, punitive damages. Nonetheless, allowable damages in statute are generally more specifically defined and are generally lower than those which could be awarded under tort law (Browne, Pryor, and Puelz 2004; GenRe 2008).

Recent Developments

Much of the revolution in the US law of first-party insurer bad faith liability occurred several decades ago, and Abraham (1994) opined that the legal doctrine of bad faith was stable and relatively known after over three decades of development. Nonetheless, the law is still evolving and recent years have seen more activity than in previous decades. Tennyson and Warfel (2010) note that the statutory basis for first-party insurance bad faith continues to develop, and discuss legislation enacted in a number of states since 2004.[14] Conversely, Feinman (2012) identifies recent trends in court decisions that suggest a narrowing of bad faith liability. Abraham (2012) contends that the nature of bad faith claims is changing, with cases alleging institutional bad faith becoming more prevalent, and likens this to the shift from manufacturing defects cases to design defects cases in products liability law.

Change is in the air in other countries as well. As noted above, the doctrine of insurance bad faith liability has recently spread to Canada. Courts in both New Brunswick and Saskatchewan have ruled that insurance bad faith is a tort, and these rulings have been upheld by the Supreme Court of Canada.[15] Proposed revisions to insurance contract law put forward by the Law Commissions of England and Scotland would make insurers liable to pay damages for any foreseeable loss resulting from such actions (Hertzell and Burgoyne 2013). If adopted this may change the insurance bad faith landscape in Europe, although based on principles that remain consistent with contract law as the frame of reference.

---

[14] The Property Casualty Insurance Association of America (PCIAA) reports that seven states have enacted insurance bad faith statutes in the past ten years.

[15] The Supreme Court did, however, impose a cap on punitive damages amounts and a high threshold for the awarding of punitive damages (Kent and Ip 2012).

BAD FAITH LIABILITY IN THEORY

Economic Reasoning

From an economic perspective, applying tort law to cases of first-party insurance bad faith represents a classic remedy designed to eliminate incentives for opportunistic behaviors: a levy of damages on the offender greater than the value of potential gains. Large parts of the American legal system utilize such damages remedies to prevent consumers from experiencing harms from sellers, from antitrust law to product liability and medical malpractice. An extensive literature in law and economics has considered the basis and operation of this legal approach, and we draw on this to provide insights into the economic rationale and role of tort liability for insurer bad faith.

In a perfectly competitive insurance market, competition among insurers and information flows between consumers would constrain insurers from bad faith behavior in settling claims, since such actions would negatively impact consumers' demand for their products. But under incomplete or costly information flows, market forces may not be sufficient to prevent bad faith behaviors, since negative reputation effects may not spread to all consumers or may take a long time to materialize. Thus, potential gains to an insurer from underpaying or denying a claim may outweigh the costs of any subsequent declines in demand (Sykes 1996). The notorious case of Unum/Provident, which brought to light this insurer's deliberate and systematic denial of vast numbers of valid disability claims for nearly a decade, illustrates the imperfect nature of market discipline in deterring insurer bad faith.[16]

In addition, although market forces may reduce an unscrupulous insurer's future demand, they fail to provide compensation to policyholders whose claims were unfairly denied. Regulated solutions often have similar limitations. Regulatory standards often primarily address systematic or 'institutional' bad faith actions by an insurer, i.e. actions that are expressly part of the insurer's claim processing system (Richmond 2010). Compensatory payments are not widely available to individuals in single cases of insurer bad faith. An aggrieved policyholder may file a complaint with the insurance regulator or (in some countries) with the insurance

---

16 See Langbein (2007) for an account of the Unum/Provident scandal and development of the view that insufficient penalties for bad faith denial of benefits under the Employment Retirement Income Security Act (ERISA) were an enabling factor in the insurer's bad faith.

ombudsman and obtain an arbitrated settlement, but generally without hope of monetary damages. Thus, regulatory prohibitions may not be sufficient to protect an individual policyholder from insurer opportunism in claim settlement.[17]

Economic theory suggests that when an actor's decisions are driven solely by expected monetary returns (as may be presumed in the case of a firm, for example), and when the harm caused another is equal to the gains received from committing the harm (as may be presumed in the case of insurance claim disputes), appropriately sized damages can be an effective deterrent even if the perpetrators of harms are not always punished. Becker's (1968) path-breaking theory of crime and punishment first demonstrated that when the probability of punishment is less than one, damages *must be* set higher than the value of harms in order to deter the harmful behaviors.[18] Damages that are optimally set will force a violator to completely internalize all social costs of the harm; in turn, anticipating such a penalty will lead potential violators to reduce their harmful activities to the socially optimal level.[19]

Applying this reasoning, tort liability for bad faith actions may supplement market forces because profit-maximizing insurers consider expected benefits and costs when determining their actions. One cost associated with a claim settlement strategy is the expected costs of disputed claims. The insurer's costs of disputed claims depend on the likelihood that a policyholder actively disputes the settlement, the transactions costs associated with the dispute, and the potential damages if the dispute is resolved in the policyholder's favor. By permitting extra-contractual damages, tort liability increases the insurer's expected costs of a disputed

---

[17] A public mediation process through an insurance ombudsman office is one means of imposing monetary and reputational costs on an insurer for bad faith actions (Schwarcz 2009). In countries (such as the UK) where consumer complaints and ombudsman mediation decisions are made public, information from the ombudsman office will enhance and speed the process of private information sharing, supplementing the forces of market discipline. This will increase the reputational costs of bad faith to insurers, and may provide a deterrent to insurer opportunism.

[18] The optimal damages amount (D) equals the value of harm (H) divided by the probability that the harm is detected and punished (p), i.e. $D=H/p$. If the probability of punishment is less than one, the optimal damage amount exceeds the value of the harms caused; as the probability of detection falls, the optimal damage amount increases proportionally.

[19] The socially optimal level of the harmful activities will be zero as long as reducing the activities can be done at zero cost, and there are no attendant social benefits from the activities.

claim. Moreover, allowing recovery of damages greater than the original insurance claim value provides policyholders with a financial incentive to incur the costs of pursuing an action against the insurer. These effects will reduce the expected value to the insurer of denying, delaying, or underpaying a claim (Sykes 1996; Crocker and Tennyson 2002). Thus, the economic role of extra-contractual damages in bad faith cases is twofold: it reassures consumers that seeking redress for harms is feasible, and reduces the likelihood of harms occurring.

Additionally, super-compensatory damages may enhance the functioning of insurance markets. In the absence of enforceable legal sanctions, the insurance contract is merely a promise to pay (legitimate) claims, and it is difficult for insurers to provide credible and binding commitments that such claims will be paid. The possibility of extra-contractual or punitive damages for reckless or negligent denial of claims helps to commit insurers to avoid engaging in bad faith actions by imposing a financial penalty for doing so (Sykes 1996). This will increase the value of insurers' promises and promote trade in insurance markets (Abraham 1986).

Predicted Effects on Insurance Settlements

As emphasized above, greater expected financial penalties in the event of a bad faith ruling by the courts increases the expected costs to an insurer of disputed claims determined by trial outcomes. This reduces insurers' incentives to deny 'reasonably disputable' claims (Abraham 1986), and should lead to a reduction in the fraction of claims denied. The increase in insurers' expected costs of a disputed claim will also alter negotiations over claim payment amounts. Bargaining theory predicts that the costs each negotiating party faces in the event of no agreement will affect the negotiation outcome.[20] This is because each party will agree to a negotiated outcome only if the net gain from the outcome exceeds the expected net gain in the event of no agreement. If a party's no-agreement alternative or 'outside option' (what they expect to obtain should the dispute be decided in court) is low, their power to achieve a high pay-off in negotiations is reduced.

Under traditional contract law, in which a policyholder may sue to obtain those payments due from an insurer but cannot receive compensatory damages or reimbursement of legal fees, a policyholder's outside

---

[20] Cooter and Rubinfeld (1989) and Spier (2007) provide comprehensive reviews of the theoretical law and economics literature on litigation and dispute resolution.

option is unfavorable: the most that could be received in the absence of an agreement is the claim amount owed less legal fees. Tort liability for insurer bad faith raises policyholders' potential payouts in successfully disputed claims, improving their outside options. Simultaneously (and symmetrically), tort liability increases insurers' costs of claims that are successfully disputed by a policyholder. This difference in the litigation environment for disputed claims will increase the bargaining power of policyholders in insurance settlement negotiations. This should lead to higher insurance settlement amounts on average (Browne, Pryor, and Puelz 2004; Asmat and Tennyson 2014).

In addition to higher settlement amounts on average, theory also predicts that substantial underpayments of claimed amounts will be less likely. A policyholder who receives a settlement offer that is far less than the full amount of loss will have a greater potential financial gain from disputing the claim. This means that there is a larger likelihood of a claim dispute, which may be accompanied by an allegation of insurer bad faith. This implies that insurers in a tort liability regime for bad faith will be less likely to severely underpay claims that are settled with some positive payment.

Predicted Effects on Insurance Claim Fraud

The increased pressure on insurers to pay claims and to offer more generous settlements may affect not just policyholders' bargaining stance, but also their insurance claiming behavior. In the law generally, a key concern about larger damages awards is their potential to induce plaintiff opportunism. A form of plaintiff opportunism specific to the insurance context is fraudulent insurance claiming. Claim fraud is recognized in both theory and practice as an intrinsic business risk for insurers (Baker 1994; Picard 2013), and a variety of empirical evidence suggests it is an important problem in insurance markets (Weisberg and Derrig 1998; Carroll and Abrahamse 2001).

Legal scholars have noted the potential for insurance bad faith liability to increase fraud by reducing insurers' willingness to investigate for fraud (Abraham 1986; Sykes 1996). The logic is that suspected fraud may require costly investigations that result in settlement delays or claim denials, actions which may lead to allegations of insurer bad faith if the claim is in fact legitimate. Insurers will balance the benefits of reduced fraud with the expected costs of investigation and disputed claims, and may decide simply to pay claims suspected of fraud under tort liability regimes for bad faith. The courts have also recognized this potential. In its 1978 decision in *Anderson* v. *Continental Insurance Company*, the Wisconsin Supreme

Court cautioned that punitive damages should rarely be awarded and that the tort of bad faith should be confined to extreme cases of misconduct, to avoid inappropriately deterring insurers from questioning false, suspicious, or inflated claims.

It is also important to understand that insurers may not only use investigations to combat fraud, but may also strategically use claim denials or underpayment for this purpose. A considerable body of theoretical work demonstrates the value to an insurer of this strategy (Crocker and Morgan 1998; Crocker and Tennyson 2002; Sykes 1996), and empirical research finds insurance settlement patterns consistent with the theory (Crocker and Tennyson 2002; Loughran 2005). The theoretical framework assumes that investigating is not an effective means of determining whether a claim is legitimate, and that it is more costly for a policyholder to construct a fraudulent or over-stated claim. Crocker and Tennyson (2002) show that in such cases, underpayment of claim categories that are the least costly for policyholders to falsify can be an optimal strategy to deter over-claiming. Sykes (1996) demonstrates that a policyholder with a fraudulent claim will be less likely to persist in the face of a claim denial than a claimant with a valid claim. The constraint on insurers' use of this approach is the potential for litigation due to wrongful denial or underpayment of a claim. Thus, by increasing the expected costs of disputed claims, the tort of bad faith reduces the expected benefits of these strategies to limit fraud (Sykes 1996; Crocker and Tennyson 2002).[21]

Reductions in insurers' fraud fighting efforts will raise the pay-off to a policyholder from engaging in fraud or exaggeration. Over time, this could induce an increase in the filing of fraudulent or exaggerated claims. This will lead to additional increases in fraud, compounding the effects from the reductions in insurers' efforts. Another way to state this is that reductions in insurers' auditing of claims for fraud will reduce not just fraud *detection* but also fraud *deterrence*. This is important because a key insight

---

[21] The efficiency consequences of reducing insurers' fraud-fighting via higher damages for insurer bad faith may nonetheless be positive. As noted by Crocker and Tennyson (2002), an insurer balancing the costs and benefits of claims monitoring actions will not take into account the costs experienced by policyholders with legitimate claims. These claimants may face aggressive auditing, delayed payment, and other inconveniences associated with the monitoring process. This will mean that, all else equal, insurers may engage in excessive monitoring for fraud. The presence of potentially large damages for violations of good faith standards will provide the insurer with incentives to consider the costs experienced by claimants with legitimate claims when designing a fraud-monitoring strategy. This internalizes the externality because the insurer realizes both the benefits and the costs of the claims settlement strategy.

from the economics literature on optimal auditing for fraud (reviewed in Picard 2013), is that the largest savings from such audits may accrue from their deterrent effect on the filing of fraudulent claims rather than from detecting and denying the fraudulent claims which are filed.[22] If insurer bad faith liability leads to both a reduction in fraud investigations and an increase in fraudulent claiming, costs associated with insurance fraud could substantially increase.

Predicted Effects on Legal Disputes

We have thus far discussed how expanded liability for bad faith changes incentives of both insurer and policyholder in the insurance claims settlement process. These consequences occur in the 'shadow' of the law: a changed legal regime alters behavior that takes place outside the legal system. But a changed legal regime also affects the legal system directly through its influence on the number and type of claims that require legal resolution. When an insurance claim fails to settle routinely and the policyholder files suit, transaction costs start building for both parties: attorney's fees, the opportunity cost of additional months or years to claims resolution, and possibly a jury trial with significant damages awarded. In considering the costs and benefits of first-party insurance bad faith liability, it is therefore critical to consider its effect on legal disputes. As Coase (1960) argued in his famous theorem: because transaction costs are positive and vary with the organizational form chosen, organizational form or property rights should be allocated to minimize transaction costs so that the efficient solution can be negotiated with minimum waste. If the bad faith liability remedy imposes significant transaction costs, it may reason to consider other remedies instead.

The theoretical literature in law and economics shows that increases in judgment amounts will affect lawsuits, settlements, and the legal effort put forth by both parties (e.g. Landes 1971; Gould 1973; Shavell 1982; Salop and White 1986; Cooter and Rubinfeld 1989). Permitting tort suits for bad faith liability may therefore have the unintended consequence of increasing the number of disputed claims and the number of disputes proceeding to lawsuits and/or trial. It may also increase incentives for 'nuisance

[22] In fact, the theory shows that if insurers could perfectly pre-commit to the optimal auditing strategy (for all time) then all claims fraud would be eliminated and audits would serve only to deter fraud. More realistically, when precommitment is not possible, for example because insurers will make new decisions about auditing each year based on currently observed fraud rates, auditing serves partially to detect fraud and partially to deter fraud (Khalil 1997).

suits' – policyholders engaging in litigation against insurers for bad faith handling of a claim, even though the policyholder knows that the claim is invalid (Abraham 1986; Regan and Rettinger 1998).

This is an important fundamental question about the impact of tort liability for insurer bad faith that has received little attention in the literature: does tort liability for insurer bad faith lead to an increase or a decrease in the incidence of claims that are disputed through the legal system? Asmat and Tennyson (2015) consider this question, and note that an increase in damages available to a policyholder in a bad faith suit creates two competing effects: the potential injurer commits fewer violations, but the policyholder has a higher incentive to sue. Based on this reasoning, they show that tort liability can lead to an increase or a decrease in bad faith lawsuits depending on which effect dominates. Similar predictions can be derived regarding the likelihood that a lawsuit will settle or go to trial.

Examining the effects of expanded damages requires measuring the difference in outcomes between states that recognize bad faith under contract or statute law and states that recognize bad faith as a tort violation. Because the two sets of states adjudicate the primary insurance claim dispute in a similar manner but differ in their treatment of the bad faith claim, the effects of the different legal regimes may be analyzed by abstracting from the primary insurance dispute to focus on the bad faith claim. This case is developed below, borrowing the theoretical framework of Salop and White (1986) and assuming risk-aversion of both the insurer and the policyholder.[23]

Specifically, define:

H = Present value of the harm (damages) suffered by policyholder;
B = Present value of the benefits of an illegal practice to insurer;
m = Damages multiple to which a victorious policyholder is entitled;
$c[p]$ = Policyholder's cost of bringing a suit;
$c[d]$ = Insurer's cost of defending a suit.

If the policyholder considers himself to be the victim of a violation or believes he can convince a court of this fact, he will sue if the Von-Neumann Morgenstern expected utility gains from the suit exceed his expected utility costs. Plaintiffs who win the trial are entitled to additional punitive damages. Thus, he will sue if:

---

[23] Asmat and Tennyson (2015) consider the case of risk-neutral litigants and develop additional results.

$$\pi[p](mH - c[p]) > (1 - \pi[p])c[p] \tag{12.1}$$

where $\pi[p]$ is the policyholder's subjective probability of winning a suit. By rearranging condition (11.1), the minimum perceived probability $\pi[p]$ of prevailing required for the policyholder to bring the suit is given by:

$$\pi^*[p] = c[p] \,/\, (mH) \tag{12.2}$$

Likewise, any insurer must decide whether to engage in the violation. It will do so if the expected utility of gains, including the probability of not being sued and the probability of prevailing if sued, exceed the expected utility of costs. Costs include multiple damages and typical expenses in defending a suit. Thus the insurer's objective function is:

$$(1 - s)B + s(1 - \pi[d])(B - c[d]) + s\,\pi[d](b - c[d]) > sc[d] + s\,\pi[d]\,(mH) \tag{12.3}$$

where s is the insurer's perception of the probability of being sued if committing a violation, $\pi[d]$ is the perception of the probability that the *policyholder* will prevail at trial, and b is the value of the benefits to the insurer up to the time of judgment. The weak inequality constrains utility to be greater than 0. Rearranging the constrained objective function (12.3) to obtain $\pi^*[d]$, the maximum perceived probability (by the insurer) that the plaintiff wins such that the insurer would still be willing to violate (and would always violate):

$$\pi^*[d] = B \,/\, [s(B + mH - b)] \tag{12.4}$$

We can allow s to be endogenous without affecting the results:

$$s = s(H, m, c[p]) \tag{12.5}$$

with s increasing in H, and m and decreasing in $c[p]$. Further, the insurer may perceive a positive relationship between B on the one hand and H and R on the other. Violations occur only when the $\pi[d]$ for a given practice is smaller than $\pi^*[d]$; suits occur when there is a violation *and* the $\pi[p]$ for that practice is greater than $\pi^*[p]$. The volume of suits, then, will be a function of the distance between $\pi^*[p]$ and $\pi^*[d]$ and the percentage of business practices that fall into that range.

The effects of permitting damages multipliers in bad faith suits are now readily seen. Inspection of equations (12.2) and (12.4) indicates that an increase in m causes both $\pi^*[p]$ and $\pi^*[d]$ to decline. The latter result causes violations to unequivocally decline, but the former means that policyholders have become more inclined to sue. The actual number of suits is a function of the distance between $\pi^*[p]$ and $\pi^*[d]$ and the density of business practices that fall into this interval; the density is in general (as an examination of $d(\pi^*[d] - \pi^*[p]) / dm$ shows) ambiguous for a given change in m. Accordingly, although an increase in the damages multiple will bring fewer violations, it is unclear whether lawsuit filings will increase or decrease because the incentive to sue has simultaneously increased.

Similarly, we can derive comparative-statics results for increases in the damages multiple on pre-trial settlement rates. The effect of a higher damages multiple on the likelihood of settlement before trial is ambiguous: it depends on the relative optimism of the parties. The intuition is that a higher m raises both the insurer's maximum offer and the policyholder's minimum acceptance. More specifically, the effect of higher m depends on the differences in the two parties' subjective probabilities of both policyholder success and harm suffered by the policyholder. If the policyholder has higher values of both, then increasing the damages multiple actually reduces the incidence of settlement. If the policyholder has lower values of both, increasing the damages multiple increases the incidence of settlement. Finally, if the relative values differ across the two subjective measures (e.g. the policyholder has a higher subjective probability of success but the insurer has a higher subjective valuation of the harm, or vice versa), then increasing the damages multiple has an ambiguous effect on the likelihood of settlement before trial.

These results demonstrate that, in general, an increase in the damages multiple can result in either greater or fewer lawsuits being filed and greater or fewer pre-trial settlements if a lawsuit is filed. This translates into a highly uncertain prediction – even under theoretically precise conditions – regarding the impact on legal disputes of adjudicating insurance bad faith cases under a tort standard.

BAD FAITH LIABILITY IN PRACTICE

Judicial Application

Based on theory, there are clear economic rationales for awarding damages greater than the claim amount to penalize and deter insurer bad faith, and there is a uniquely optimal amount by which to penalize a bad faith action. However, the impact of the tort of bad faith on insurance outcomes is less clear, even in theory. As shown above, while theory explains that tort liability could level the playing field by reducing claim denials and claim underpayments, it also shows that it could raise the incidence of fraudulent insurance claims and the incidence of legal disputes over claims.

Application of the theoretical principles in practice is also less clear, due to a variety of problems that arise from the environment of imperfect and asymmetric information in which the insurance claim is processed. As made clear in numerous court decisions and discussed in Baker (1994) and Sykes (1996), the insurer's *intent* is key in determining a finding of insurer bad faith under tort law. Given the complexity of insurance contracts, the business necessity for insurers of verifying and validating claims prior to payment, and the differing information available to the policyholder and insurer, disputes over claims will arise. Even in cases where the insurer delays, denies, or underpays a claim and the policyholder feels badly treated in the process, it may be difficult for the courts to determine the intent of the insurer in so doing.

Factoring in uncertainty in court standards creates additional sources of ambiguity in the predicted effects of bad faith liability (Salop and White 1986). Imprecise application of bad faith standards or damages amounts due to informational constraints and measurement difficulties will lead to potential differences in the actual incentive effects of bad faith law from those intended in theory. If the standard for a finding of insurer bad faith is unclear, changing, or prone to error, this can lead insurers to overinvest in avoidance of bad faith allegations (Shavell 1987; Craswell and Calfee 1986). Alternatively, because an allegation of insurer bad faith is only secondary to an insurance claim dispute, it is possible that the bad faith has little effect on insurers' behavior (Browne, Pryor, and Puelz 2004). Finally, the impact of bad faith liability may change over time. When a law is first implemented, insurers and policyholders face a highly uncertain trial verdict in the final stage of any bargaining game that they play. As disputes proceed through the legal system a clearer precedent takes shape and parties gain confidence in their legal forecasts. For all of these reasons – ambiguous theoretical predictions, imprecise judicial application, and changing legal standards – rigorous empirical study is needed to assess the effects of bad faith liability. Such empirical studies are relatively scarce, with the first study (Browne, Pryor, and Puelz 2004) published in 2004, but a literature is developing. Although a comprehensive cost-benefit calculation of bad faith tort law remains yet to be done, the results of the nascent empirical literature demonstrate consistency with theoretical predictions and quantify specific intended and unintended consequences of the law. We review here the main findings of this literature.

Impact on Insurance Settlements

Browne, Pryor, and Puelz (2004) provide the first empirical analysis of the effect of bad faith liability on insurance contracting, and focus on the effects of claim settlement amounts. Their study uses data on individual claims settled under uninsured motorist (UM) automobile policies from 38 states in 1992, and tests the hypothesis that settlement amounts are larger in states permitting tort actions for insurer bad faith. UM is first-party insurance that provides compensation for injury to a policyholder in accidents in which another driver is at fault but does not carry liability insurance to pay for the injury costs. Because UM provides payment for losses that should have been compensated through the liability insurance of the at-fault driver, both economic and non-economic damages may be awarded.

The authors estimate regression models of the settlement amount, controlling for characteristics of the claimant, accident, injury and state legal environment in addition to the state's bad faith regime. Results show that settlements are significantly larger in states that permit tort actions, and that the larger settlement amounts occur for both economic and non-economic damages. Interestingly, the impact of bad faith liability in increasing the settlement amount was found to be larger and more statistically significant for claimants not represented by an attorney. Whether this reflects endogenous selection into attorney representation based on loss amount or other claim characteristics, or differential treatment of unrepresented claimants by insurers, could not be discerned in the study.

Asmat and Tennyson (2014) provide the most recent study establishing that the tort of first-party insurance bad faith induces changes in insurance claims settlements. The authors provide difference-in-differences estimates using the same source of data as Browne, Pryor, and Puelz (2004) on individual UM auto insurance claims, but examine claims closed over three decades (1977, 1987, and 1997). Results show that insurers in states subject to the tort of bad faith pay out significantly more on equivalent claims than do insurers in non-tort states. After controlling for the amount of losses claimed, the estimated impact of bad faith liability on settlements remains positive and marginally statistically significant (10 percent confidence level, two-sided test), with an estimated magnitude 11 to 12 percent. Additional estimates also show that bad faith liability reduces the probability that a claim is substantially underpaid, and the magnitude of the estimated impact is a reduction of 7 percent. These findings are consistent with the hypothesis that expanded liability for insurer bad faith increases policyholder bargaining power.

Impact on Insurance Fraud

Because of the often noted concern that larger damages awards and heightened insurer liability may increase the prevalence of fraudulent insurance claims, and based on earlier findings that insurance fraud is more often manifested as claim build-up (exaggeration) than as falsified accidents (Weisberg and Derrig 1991), Asmat and Tennyson (2014) also test for an effect of bad faith tort liability on the claimed amounts for losses in their dataset. The estimates show that claimed losses are an average of 15 to 16 percent higher under tort bad faith regimes, even after controlling for a variety of claimant, accident, and injury characteristics. However, this effect is very imprecisely estimated (results are not statistically significant) and the analysis provides no direct indicators of fraud or exaggeration.

Tennyson and Warfel (2010) use data on UM auto insurance claims settled in 1997 to examine the hypothesis that expanded bad faith liability increases pressure on insurers to pay fraudulent or exaggerated claims. The authors compare univariate statistics on selected characteristics of claims settled in states with more expansive bad faith regimes to those settled in other states. They hypothesize that claims will be more likely to exhibit characteristics consistent with (possible) fraud, and that insurers will be less likely to aggressively monitor for fraud, in states with more expansive bad faith regimes. To identify possible fraud, they rely on several claim characteristics that insurance adjustors or medical professionals view as fraud suspicion indicators or 'red flags' (Dionne and St-Michel 1991; Weisberg and Derrig 1991). These include lack of a police report, lack of visible injury at the scene of the accident, only (or primarily) a sprain or strain injury, and large treatment costs from chiropractors. Insurer investigations are measured using indicators of whether the insurer conducted an audit of medical treatments and costs (in-house or externally), and whether the insurer requested an independent medical examination of the claimant using a medical practitioner of the insurer's choosing.

Comparisons are made across states that permit tort actions, actions under contract law or statute, and states that do not permit bad faith actions. The tort states that require different standards of proof for punitive damages ('negligence' versus 'intentional tort') are also compared. Robustness checks include adjusting for claim severity – by comparing claims that fall only within the same quarter of the claim distribution. Comparisons are also made after omitting states with no-fault auto insurance from the sample, and after omitting California (which accounts for nearly one-quarter of claims in the database) from the sample.

Results vary somewhat depending on the specific indicator, the difference measure (distribution means or quartiles), and the states included in the sample, but generally show that greater potential liability for bad faith is associated with more fraud 'red flags' among paid claims. Specifically, claims settled in states that recognize insurer bad faith as a tort are significantly less likely to include a police report from the scene of the accident, significantly more likely to involve claims for injuries that were not visible at the scene of the accident, and significantly more likely to involve only sprain or strain injuries. There are no significant differences in numbers of chiropractor visits. These significant differences remain in comparisons of two subsamples of claims – those in the quarter just below the median claim amount and those in the quarter just above the median claim amount. However, differences in the prevalence of police reports from the accident scene appear to be driven by patterns in California: when California is omitted from the sample, police reports are no less prevalent in bad faith tort states than in other states.

More consistent results are found for the use of investigations by insurers, especially independent medical exams (IMEs). An IME is an examination of the injured policyholder by a medical professional chosen by the insurance company; it is costly and detailed, and necessitates the cooperation and involvement of the policyholder (Weisberg and Derrig 1991). Results using the full sample of claims found that insurers requested an IME for only 6.6 percent of claims in states that permit bad faith tort claims; in 12.0 percent of claims in states that recognize bad faith suits under contract law or statute; and in 26.3 percent of claims in states that do not permit any private actions for insurer bad faith. This pattern remains in the analysis of subsamples of the data, including when only claims of similar size are compared, and when California is omitted from the sample. Without California, insurers request IMEs in 4.8 percent of claims in states with the tort of bad faith, but in 14.8 percent of claims in states that do not. This suggests that insurers are more willing to investigate the possibility of fraud in states without a tort bad faith regime.

Several weaknesses of the study – including the use of cross-sectional data and simple statistical comparisons, and availability of only a few fraud 'red flags' in the database – prohibit strong conclusions from the results. Nonetheless, the largest effects were found in states that treat insurer bad faith as a tort, and effects were larger in tort states that use a 'negligence' standard than in tort states that use an 'intentional tort' standard. Moreover, the differences between tort states and states that do not recognize bad faith actions are larger than those between tort states and states that allow actions under contract law or statute. These patterns advocate for interpreting the findings as indicative of effects of bad faith regimes on insurers' claim settlement strategies.

Impact on Legal Disputes

Asmat and Tennyson (2015) examine the impact of the bad faith tort law on equilibrium rates of filed lawsuits and pre-trial settlements using the same sample of individual UM claims data (for 1977, 1987, and 1997) as Asmat and Tennyson (2014). Legal disputes are an important component of the total cost-benefit calculation of bad faith tort regimes because they impose large transaction costs from attorney and administrative fees and raise the possibility of bargaining breakdowns. As discussed, law and economics theory is unable to predict the direction of the effect of extra-contractual damages on lawsuits and pre-trial settlements.

Using difference-in-differences estimates, the authors find that the change in lawsuit rates attributable to punitive damages is weakly positive or indistinguishable from zero for the duration of the sample period, but that rates increased by up to 7 percent early in the sample period and among the earliest states that recognize the tort of bad faith. They also find that pre-trial settlement rates decrease in the tort states by an average of 2 to 4 percent over the sample period, and that the change is driven by the earliest states to switch to tort law. These results imply that bad faith liability induces real and significant changes in legal strategies, in directions which suggest an increase in legal disputes and associated transaction costs.

CONCLUSION

The state-by-state introduction of a private right of action for bad faith liability over the last several decades has illustrated the inherent difficulty of employing legal remedies to generate an equal bargaining position between policyholders and insurers. Empirical research exploiting the state- and time-varying nature of law changes in the US has highlighted the singular role of punitive damages among distinctions in the burden of proof and standards of conduct for a finding of insurer bad faith.

Empirical results provide strong evidence that tort liability for bad faith induces insurers to pay higher settlement amounts on otherwise-equivalent insurance claims. However, results also provide some (weaker) evidence that tort liability leads to lower rates of fraud investigations by insurers. While consistent with law and economics theory, in the absence of a definitive measure of the socially optimal levels of insurance settlements and fraud investigations, it is not possible to say whether these are beneficial or harmful effects of tort-based bad faith regimes. The story most consistent with theory is that – in the absence of the tort of bad faith – first-party insurers will have a propensity to underpay claims and to investigate for fraud too actively. Under these assumptions, tort liability for insurer bad faith appears to reduce the associated harms. Even in this case, however, it cannot be concluded that the observed increases in claim payments and decreases in fraud investigations are of an appropriate magnitude; excessive judgments or legal uncertainty may have led to over-avoidance by insurers.

Empirical research also shows that the higher damages associated with tort liability raise the probability that policyholders will file lawsuits and will take a higher proportion of them to trial, at least in the early years of the legal regime. These effects diminish over time, but do not reverse, suggesting that bad faith liability fails in its objective to reduce transaction costs of claim disputes. Whether this is due to insufficient deterrence of bad faith actions by insurers, or to excessive encouragement of legal actions by policyholders, cannot be determined from the available evidence. Nonetheless, the fact that bad faith liability has not reduced the burden of disputes on the legal system is an unambiguous failing of the law from a social welfare perspective.

This suggests that whether an insurer's breach of the duty of good faith in settling a claim should be viewed by the courts as a tort should remain an open question. As has been argued by Baker (1994) and others, treating unfair claim settlement behavior by an insurer as a tort is not necessary to award extra-contractual damages to aggrieved insureds. Damages under contract law may be expanded and regulatory or legislative solutions could be created. Schwarcz (2009) argues for an alternative approach entirely, through a public mediation process for disputed insurance claims as a means of supplementing market discipline. Additional empirical study of insurance bad faith liability regimes and their alternatives is needed to further these debates.

REFERENCES

Abraham, Kenneth S. 1986. *Distributing Risk: Insurance Legal Theory, and Public Policy*. New Haven, CT: Yale University Press.

Abraham, Kenneth S. 1994. The Natural History of the Insurer's Liability for Bad Faith. 72 *Texas Law Review* 1295.

Abraham, Kenneth S. 2012. Liability for Bad Faith and the Principle without a Name (Yet). 10 *Connecticut Insurance Law Journal* 1–12.

Asmat, Danial and Sharon Tennyson. 2014. Does the Threat of Insurer Liability for 'Bad Faith' Affect Insurance Settlements? 81 *Journal of Risk and Insurance* 1–23.

Asmat, Danial and Sharon Tennyson. 2015. Punitive Damages. Litigation and Settlement Evidence from the Auto Industry. Working Paper, 2015, on file with authors.

Baker, Tom. 1994. Constructing the Insurance Relationship: Sales Stories, Claims Stories, and Insurance Contract Damages. 72 *Texas Law Review* 1395–433.
Becker, Gary. 1968. Crime and Punishment: An Economic Approach. 76 *The Journal of Political Economy* 169–217.
Browne, Mark, Ellen Sue Pryor, and Bob Puelz. 2004. The Effect of Bad-Faith Laws on First-Party Insurance Claims Decisions. 33 *The Journal of Legal Studies* 355.
Carroll, Steven and Allan Abrahamse. 2001. The Frequency of Excess Auto Personal Injury Claims. 3 *American Law and Economics Review* 228–50.
Coase, Ronald H. 1960. The Problem of Social Cost. 3 *Journal of Law and Economics* 1.
Cooter, Robert D. and Daniel L. Rubinfeld. 1989. Economic Analysis of Legal Disputes and Their Resolution. 27 *Journal of Economic Literature* 1067–97.
Cooter, Robert D. and Thomas Ulen. 2008. *Law and Economics*, 5th edition. Boston, MA: Pearson Addison-Wesley.
Craswell, Richard and John E. Calfee. 1986. Deterrence and Uncertain Legal Standards. 2 *Journal of Law, Economics and Organization* 279.
Crocker, Keith J. and John Morgan. 1998. Is Honesty the Best Policy? Curtailing Insurance Fraud through Optimal Incentive Contracts. 106 *Journal of Political Economy* 355–75.
Crocker, Keith J. and Sharon Tennyson. 2002. Insurance Fraud and Optimal Claims Settlement Strategies: An Empirical Investigation of Liability Insurance Settlements. 45 *The Journal of Law and Economics* 469–508.
Dionne, Georges and Pierre St-Michel. 1991. Workers' Compensation and Moral Hazard. 73 *The Review of Economics and Statistics* 236–44.
Dubroff, Harold. 2006. The Implied Covenant of Good Faith in Contract Interpretation and Gap-Filling: Reviling a Revered Relic. 80 *St. John's Law Review* 559.
Feinman, Jay M. 2012. The Law of Insurance Claim Practices: Beyond Bad Faith. 47 *Tort Trial & Insurance Practice Law Journal* 693–740.
Garner, B. A. (ed.). 1999. *Black's Law Dictionary*. St. Paul, MN: West Group.
GenRe and Edwards Angell Palmer & Dodge LLP. 2008. *Bad Faith Laws for Property/Casualty Claims*.
Gould, John P. 1973. The Economics of Legal Conflicts. 2 *The Journal of Legal Studies* 179–300.
Hertzell, David and Louis Burgoyne. 2013. The Law Commissions and Insurance Contract Law Reform: An Update. 19 *The Journal of International Maritime Law* 105–23.
Jerry, Robert H. 1986. Remedying Insurers' Bad Faith Contractual Performance: A Reassessment. 18 *Connecticut Law Review* 271.
Kent, Nigel P. and Samantha Ip. 2012. Bad Faith Litigation in Canada: Much Ado About Nothing? Fall/Winter *US Law*.
Khalil, Fahad A. 1997. Auditing Without Commitment. 28 *Rand Journal of Economics* 629–40.
Kornblum, Guy O. 1988. The Current State of Bad Faith and Punitive Damage Litigation in the U.S. 23 *Tort and Insurance Law Journal* 812–48.
Landes, William M. 1971. An Economic Analysis of the Courts. 14 *The Journal of Law and Economics* 61–107.
Langbein, John H. 2007. Trust Law as Regulatory Law: The UNUM/Provident Scandal and Judicial Review of Benefit Denials under ERISA. 101 *Northwestern University Law Review* 1315–42.
Law Commission and the Scottish Law Commission. 2010. *Damages for Late Payment and the Insurer's Duty of Good Faith*. Joint Review of Insurance Contract Law, Issues Paper 6. Available at http://lawcommission.justice.gov.uk/areas/insurance-contract-law.htm.
Loughran, David S. 2005. Deterring Fraud: The Role of General Damage Awards in Auto Insurance Settlements. 72 *Journal of Risk and Insurance* 551–75.
Midlige, Suzanne, Robert Re, and William Hoffman. 2011. Claims: An Overview of the US Tort of 'Bad Faith' – A Common Law Approach to Regulating Insurer Claims Handling and Settlements. In Julian M. Burling and Kevin Lazarus (eds.), *Research Handbook on*

International Insurance Law and Regulation. Cheltenham, UK and Northampton, MA, USA: Edward Elgar Publishing 120–46.
Picard, Pierre. 2013. Economic Analysis of Insurance Fraud. In G. Dionne (ed.), *Handbook of Insurance*. New York, NY: Springer-Verlag 349–95.
Regan, Laureen and Paul M. Rettinger. 1998. Private Rights of Action under State Unfair Claims Settlement Practices Acts: A Review. 16 *Journal of Insurance Regulation* 291–312.
Richman, Brian and Sharon Tennyson. 2013. The Impact of Expanding Insurers' Duty to Settle: Evidence from the *Royal Globe* Doctrine. Working Paper, January. SRN_ID2585106_code74301.pdf.
Richmond, Douglas R. 2010. Defining and Confining Institutional Bad Faith in Insurance. 46 *Tort Trial & Insurance Practice Law Journal* 1–32.
Salop, Steven C. and Lawrence J. White. 1986. Economic Analysis of Private Antitrust Litigation. 74 *Georgetown Law Journal* 1001–64.
Schwarcz, Daniel. 2009. Redesigning Consumer Dispute Resolution: A Case Study of the British and American Approaches to Insurance Claims Conflict. 83 *Tulane Law Review* 735–812.
Shavell, Steven. 1982. Suit, Settlement and Trial: The Theoretical Analysis Under Alternative Methods for the Allocation of Legal Costs. 11 *The Journal of Legal Studies* 55–81.
Shavell, Steven. 1987. *Economic Analysis of Accident Law*. Cambridge, MA: Harvard University Press, 1987.
Spier, Katherine. 2007. Litigation. In A. Mitchell Polinsky and Steven Shavell (eds.), *The Handbook of Law & Economics*. North-Holland.
Stempel, Jeffrey W. 2006. *Stempel on Insurance Contracts*. New York, NY: Aspen Publishers.
Sykes, Alan O. 1996. 'Bad Faith' Breach of Contract by First-Party Insurers. 25 *Journal of Legal Studies* 405.
Tennyson, Sharon and William J. Warfel. 2010. The Law and Economics of First-Party Insurance Bad Faith Liability. 15 *Connecticut Insurance Law Journal* 203–42.
Weisberg, Herbert I. and Richard A. Derrig. 1991. Fraud and Automobile Insurance: A Report on the Baseline Study of Bodily Injury Claims in Massachusetts. 9 *Journal of Insurance Regulation* 497–541.
Weisberg, Herbert I. and Richard A. Derrig. 1998. Quantitative Methods for Detecting Fraudulent Automobile Bodily Injury Claims. 35 *Risques* 75–101.

13. Basic economics of the defense of covered claims

Charles Silver

I. INTRODUCTION

Liability insurance arrangements generate wealth by transferring risks from policyholders to insurers, who can bear them more cheaply. One such risk attends the defense of covered claims. The cost of defending claims has considerable potential to vary, and the manner of conducting the defense can affect the amount paid to a claimant. It is therefore important to deploy resources efficiently when defending claims. The standard law and economics approach to contracting suggests that suitable arrangements will evolve when liability coverage is sold in competitive markets, because carriers and policyholders should prefer arrangements that maximize their joint wealth.

This chapter describes the basic economics of the defense of covered claims. It also discusses contractual arrangements and other devices that insurers and policyholders use to defend liability claims. Although these working arrangements are imperfect, they have obvious and strong efficiency justifications.

II. BACKGROUND ON THE DUTY TO INDEMNIFY, THE DUTY TO DEFEND, AND THE RIGHT TO DEFEND

Most liability insurance policies contain three distinct features: a duty to shoulder identified payments to claimants; a duty to bear the cost of defending claims falling within the coverage provisions; and a right to control the defense of covered claims. In this chapter, these components are referred to as the duty to indemnify, the duty to defend, and the right to defend, respectively.[1] These features serve different functions. The two

[1] Although this terminology is fairly standard, not all insurance policies employ it and some contain different provisions. For example, one D&O policy saddles the insureds with the duty to defend but also imposes an obligation on the

duties, both of which are often but not always borne by insurers, transfer risks that arise in connection with liability suits. The lone right equips its holder, again usually but not always an insurer, to manage the costs liability risks entail.

The duty to indemnify and the duty to defend appear together in policies of many types, including standard personal and commercial lines. But because they cover distinct risks, they can be sold separately and sometimes are. Many insurers offer straight indemnity policies, and many excess insurance policies cover liabilities but expressly negate the duty to defend. Some insurers also sell stand-alone coverage for defense costs. '[Defense-only] coverage is most commonly (although not exclusively) used to cover defense costs associated with employment practices liability . . . claims, in which defense payments represent the majority of claim-related costs' (International Risk Management Institute 2014). Defense-only policies are also sold to professionals who may face allegations of illegal conduct, such as the securities fraud claims brought against the directors and officers of public companies or False Claims Act allegations lodged against doctors who bill governmental payers.[2] Policies that contain only the duty to indemnify or only the duty to defend raise interesting moral hazard problems, which are discussed below.

Because the right to defend is a loss-management technique, not a means of transferring risks from policyholders to insurers, there is no such thing as 'right-to-defend insurance'. Certainly, one can imagine situations in which a defendant would find it advantageous to transfer control of litigation to a third-party and in which the third-party would willingly accept the responsibility, whether in exchange for a payment or other reasons.[3] But in these situations the transfer of control from the named defendant to the third-party would not be an insurance transaction, because no risks would change hands. It would merely be a contractual exchange by means of which an actual or potential defendant would hire a superior litigation manager.

In theory, the right to defend may be paired with the duty to indemnify or the duty to defend; it may also be omitted. In practice, many combinations are observed, though not all. Most modern commercial liability policies contain all three provisions – the duty to indemnify, the duty to

---

carrier to advance money for defense costs upon request. Scottsdale Indemnity Company (Undatedb).

[2] For a description of the policy, see Trentini 2011.

[3] For example, Manufacturer A might want to defend a product defect claim against Manufacturer B if the two companies' products are similar and a loss by B in pending litigation might unleash a flood of similar claims against A.

defend, and the right to defend – but insurers formerly sold indemnity-only policies, which gave them the right to defend but not the duty. Some indemnity policies still use language that confers 'the right, but not the duty to defend'.[4]

Carriers also sell defense-only policies that come without the right to defend. The policy mentioned above that covers defense costs incurred by doctors in False Claims Act (FCA) proceedings is an example. It entitles the physician to choose defense counsel and control the defense. The insurer operates mainly as a banker. The moral hazard problem associated with this simple third-party payment is obvious. The doctor, who controls the defense and benefits from it, has an incentive to overspend. An insurer may want to guard against this problem, for example, by auditing defense counsel's bills or refusing to renew policies when defense spending is excessive. But making an unlimited budget available may also be a strength. Normally, the government enjoys an enormous budgetary advantage when suing under the FCA. When the defendant also has substantial resources, the playing field is more nearly level and the government may be more likely to drop the suit or settle.

For reasons that are not clear, insurers appear not to offer policies that pair defense-only coverage with the right to defend. However, a general liability policy resembles such a policy under certain conditions. For example, suppose that a suit seeking both compensatory and punitive damages is filed against an insured in a state that forbids coverage of punitive damages. The law requires the insurer to defend the entire suit, even though it may not indemnify the policyholder against any punitive award. Insofar as the punitive damages portion of the case is concerned, then, the insurer has the duty to defend and the right to defend, but not the duty to indemnify.

Table 13.1 summarizes the types of insurance policies that are available, using the three components identified in this discussion.

Under standard liability insurance policies, a carrier's duty to provide a defense is activated by a lawsuit seeking covered damages. An insuring provision found in a commercial general liability policy might obligate the insurer to 'pay on behalf of the insured all sums which the insured shall become legally obligated to pay as damages because of [specified types of injuries] to which this insurance applies', and give the insurer 'the right and

---

[4] See, e.g., AIG/Chartis (Undated): Coverage Section Six, 2(f) ('The Insurer has the right, but not the duty, to defend any Regulatory Action.'). For a discussion, see Bernstein 2005.

Table 13.1 Types of insurance policies with identified features

	Duty to indemnify?	Duty to defend?	Right to defend?	Insurance policies*
1	Yes	Yes	Yes	Personal auto, commercial general liability, medical professional liability
2	Yes	Yes	No	D&O insurance, lawyers professional liability coverage
3	Yes	No	Yes	Financial institutions risk protector
4	Yes	No	No	Indemnity, D&O insurance, excess coverage
5	No	Yes	Yes	Not available
6	No	Yes	No	Legal defense cost coverage

Note: *When a policy type is listed, it means that some policies of the identified type have the identified characteristics. Policies of the same general type can have different structures, however, in which event the same policy type would warrant placement in more than one row.

duty to defend any suit against the insured seeking damages on account of such injury'.

The duty to defend does not depend on whether the allegations in the complaint have merit. Again quoting standard policy language, it arises 'even if the allegations of the suit are groundless, false or fraudulent'. The duty to defend thus provides comprehensive protections against litigation costs likely to be incurred when defending lawsuits alleging covered claims, even when the defendant owes the plaintiff nothing. For this reason, the duty to defend is best thought of as a form of first-party insurance that is normally packaged with third-party liability coverage. Third-party insurance protects one from losses suffered by others for which one is legally responsible. First-party coverage protects one from losses incurred directly. Defense cost coverage is first-party insurance because it is not conditioned on liability and because it protects policyholders from costs they would normally incur directly. '[T]he insured's right to a defense is a type of first-party benefit, no different in principle from the right to reimbursement of medical expenses.'[5]

The connection between the duty to defend and the liability policy is important, however, because the latter defines the first-party risk that is transferred. Speaking generally and setting aside cases in which complaints

[5] Shernoff, Gage, and Levine 2014: Sec. 3.08[3]. See also Pryor 2000.

allege both covered and uncovered claims, the duty to defend protects the policyholder only from costs incurred in the course of responding to lawsuits seeking damages that the liability policy covers. To the cost of defending other lawsuits, the policyholder remains exposed.

A host of common law rules govern the application of the duty to defend in concrete contexts. For example, the so-called 'complaint allegation rule' establishes that an insurer may consider only the facts alleged in a complaint when deciding whether a suit triggers its duty to defend. But some jurisdictions allow carriers to take account of unpleaded facts of which they are aware in some situations. Still other common law rules govern the liability of insurers for wrongfully failing to defend and the damages they must pay as a result.

Both the contractual structure of the duty to defend and the related common law rules affect litigation practices (Silver and Syverud 1995). For example, the complaint allegation rule has fostered a practice known as 'pleading into coverage'.[6] By pleading a claim that falls within the scope of the defendant's liability policy, a plaintiff's attorney can trigger the duty to defend and force an insurer to bear litigation costs. Rather than pay these expenses, an insurer may find it advisable to offer something to settle the claim. Because liability carriers often contribute the only dollars that change hands when lawsuits settle, an important part of a plaintiffs' attorney's job is to identify all potentially applicable insurance policies and trigger them. This may mean suing many defendants or asserting many types of claims, including claims that are weaker than others (negligent rather than intentional misconduct) or that seem unsupported by facts.[7]

---

[6] For an example of pleading into coverage, see *Boyles* v. *Kerr* 855 S.W. 2d 593 (Texas 1993), where the complaint asserted both negligent and intentional infliction of emotional distress. When the defendant moved for a directed verdict on the negligence claim – no evidence of anything other than intentional misconduct having been offered during the trial – the plaintiff's attorney stated candidly that he would have dropped his client into the grease if the motion were granted, there being no insurance coverage for the claim of intentional wrongdoing.

[7] Because the need to keep insurers involved is so great, plaintiffs' attorneys need to know which losses liability insurance policies cover. Consequently, many plaintiffs' attorneys are coverage experts or work in teams with lawyers who specialize in coverage.

III. BASIC ECONOMICS OF THE DEFENSE OF COVERED CLAIMS

A defendant with unlimited means who bears 100 percent of the expected loss on a claim at trial – the so-called 'judgment risk' – has reason to expend the privately optimal level of resources on the defense. Assuming decreasing marginal returns to effort and increasing marginal costs, a sole holder of unlimited liability will find it economically rational to invest in the defense until the last dollar spent reduces the expected trial loss by $1. This level of spending minimizes the total private cost of responding to a claim, including defense costs and liability payments.[8]

When defendants are judgment-proof, that is, when their attachable assets are less than the expected legal value of the injuries for which they are sued, the privately optimal level of defensive outlays will reflect their value of their assets, rather than the expected judgment, because they will care about only the portion of the expected judgment they will actually pay.[9] In the limit, a defendant with no attachable assets may find it economically irrational to spend any money defending a claim (Sykes 1994). Knowing that there is nothing for the claimant to collect, an insolvent defendant might rather incur a worthless default judgment than bear positive defense costs. A judgment-proof defendant who happens to be insured may even find it desirable to waive his or her coverage, thereby also avoiding the secondary costs of responding to claims.[10] Although insurance normally protects policyholders with assets from the consequences of engaging in risky activities, it can make attractive litigation targets out of insolvent policyholders who would not otherwise be sued (Syverud 1994).

For defendants that are not judgment proof, liability insurance alters the private cost-benefit calculation regarding how much to invest in litigation defense by dividing responsibility for losses. When a third-party insurer bears part of the liability exposure, a solvent defendant recoups only a fraction of the returns on defensive outlays. The size of the fraction depends on the size of the claim and the details of the insurance arrangement. For example, when a liability carrier shoulders the responsibility for losses above a self-insured retention (SIR), the policyholder's incentive is diminished when all or part of a loss is expected to exceed the SIR and fall into the overlying coverage layer. The extent of the diminution depends

---

[8] This analysis ignores agency costs of all kinds and assumes away other interests defendants may have, such as reputational interests in vindication.

[9] This is the application to defense spending of the effect being judgment proof has on potential tortfeasors' willingness to take care. See Shavell 1986.

[10] For examples, see Giles 2013.

upon the portion of the expected loss the policyholder expects the carrier to bear.

In the limit, when an insurer bears all of the judgment risk, the policyholder may have no incentive to reduce the expected trial loss. The defendant may even have reasons to increase it. For example, the policyholder may want to see the claimant compensated or may view a lavish settlement payment as a way to avoid bad publicity or the inconvenience of testifying. Even when some interest in avoiding the judgment risk remains, because, for example, the policyholder has a stake in protecting its reputation, the incentive to bear defense costs may not relate directly to the judgment risk.

It bears emphasis that liability insurance transfers responsibility for the judgment risk and the cost of defending against covered claims, not for collateral matters that may interest a policyholder. A policyholder may want to protect its reputation, keep its customers happy, see that adequate compensation flows to family members or employees who are injured in accidents for which the policyholder is responsible, or avoid having to testify under oath. Standard liability policies do not protect collateral interests like these.

Insurers' defense-related incentives may also be deficient when responsibility for the judgment risk is shared. The basic problem, as before, is that the party funding the defense bears 100 percent of the cost but garners only a fraction of the returns. As a result, the payer's private cost may exceed the payer's share of the expected gain, even when the total expected gain measured from the perspective of all participants in the insurance arrangement is greater. As Cooter (1985) notes, 'the incentives of private individuals are socially efficient when costs and benefits are fully internalized, whereas incentives are inefficient when some costs and benefits are externalized'. In the language of economics (though not of the common law courts), insurers and policyholders are agents for each other. After coverage is extended, each can influence the level of risk the other bears (Stiglitz 2008). A central problem of liability insurance design is therefore to encourage the contracting parties to act in ways that are welfare-maximizing. Dividing financial responsibility for the judgment risk and defense costs complicates the matter by creating opportunities for each contracting party to externalize costs onto the other. For example, an insurer may save money by mounting an inadequate defense when the bulk of the financial exposure on a claim falls above the policy limits, and a policyholder may save money by failing to assist the defense when the primary limits are sufficient to cover the entire expected loss.

Fortunately, at the time of contracting, all participants in insurance arrangements have an interest in encouraging behaviors that are jointly rational. For example, optimal defensive outlays minimize expected liability losses and are therefore jointly wealth-maximizing from the perspective of all contracting parties *ex ante*. In other words, loss-minimizing contracts should cost less than other contracts, so both policyholders and insurers should prefer them. They should want first-best insurance contracts, which would require them to always act for the joint good of all.

Because contracting costs are positive, however, insurance contracts sold in competitive markets are unlikely to contain provisions that motivate all participants to act for the common good in all situations. Real insurance contracts may enable participants to gain by acting opportunistically, that is, by pursuing their private advantage instead of the common good. Real insurance contracts are 'constrained efficient'. They reduce the frequency and severity of conflicts to efficient levels, given positive contracting costs and informational constraints, but they do not fully harmonize the interests of all in all situations (Schwartz and Scott 2003).

The defense-related provisions found in standard insurance contracts, billions of which are in force at any given time, are exceedingly simple. Many personal lines policies say only that the insurer has the right and duty to defend lawsuits seeking covered damages. Nothing is said about the resources an insurer must devote to the task, the level of care it must exercise when defending the policyholder, or any other matter that might be of interest. The standard settlement clause is also brief. It merely gives the carrier discretion to settle claims at its own expense. Standard policy language neither requires an insurer to use its discretion reasonably nor sheds any light on what reasonable settlement behavior might be.

The brevity of the defense and settlement provisions has at least three possible explanations. First, although it may seem easy for parties to subject the conduct of the defense and settlement of liability claims to contractual standards, it is actually difficult because the parties are contracting over the use of knowledge. In the typical case, where the insurer controls both the defense and settlement of claims, the joint hope *ex ante* is that the insurer will make judgments requiring the application of special expertise and private information for the benefit of all. But, '[w]hen one party hires the other's knowledge and expertise, there is not much they can write down' (Easterbrook and Fischel 1993). The difficulty of elaborating contractual standards to govern the conduct of sophisticated agents is well known.

Second, good incentives often reduce the need for more detailed contractual language. Although insurance contracts divide responsibility for liability risks between policyholders and insurers, fragmentation may often be of greater theoretical than practical interest. Consider excess exposure, which arises when policyholders risk incurring losses above the primary insurance policy limits. In theory, excess exposure is a common problem because many lawsuits generate a positive, if small, probability of a high jury verdict. In practice, however, excess exposure ripens into uninsured liability infrequently. Cases in which policyholders use personal or business assets to resolve liability claims are rare. As a practical matter, insurers often carry all of the liability exposure even when, in theory, that exposure is shared. Consequently, insurers have incentives to put their control of defense and settlement decisions to good use.

Third, the simplicity of defense and settlement provisions may reflect the efficiency of common law elaborations to these provisions. Common law doctrines supplement vague insurance contracts in diverse, fact-sensitive ways as disputes arise over the rights and obligations of policyholders and insurers (Baker and Logue, Chapter 11 in this volume). Judges thus enhance the value of insurance contracts by fixing their meaning (Boardman 2006). Their interpretations can be inefficient, however, in which event insurers must adjust their prices or modify their contracts, a process that entails its own costs and risks. In the case of core policy provisions that have been used for over a century in policies of diverse types, of which the duty to indemnify, the duty to defend, and the right to defend are all examples, the advantage of retaining language that courts have generally interpreted in efficiency-enhancing ways is obvious.

The case law establishes that the simple right to defend language found in many primary insurance policies endows its possessor with plenary and exclusive control of the defense, meaning that the insurer makes all decisions normally made by a defendant in litigation (Barker and Silver 2013: § 2.05). If this blanket rule were inefficient, the parties could qualify it by providing for shared control. In fact, they often do. Many excess insurance policies and Directors' and Officers' (D&O) policies provide that the carrier is entitled to associate in the defense of claims, but not to exercise exclusive control.[11] The express provision for shared control in some contexts strengthens the impression that placing control in the hands of a single decision maker is the efficient arrangement in contexts where the standard right-to-defend language is used.

The common law has also supplied a standard to which an insurer must conform when defending a lawsuit in which a policyholder is a named defendant: reasonable care. A defending insurer is 'liable for its own

[11] Standard excess policy language provides that 'the company shall not be called upon to assume charge of the settlement or defense of any claim made or proceeding instituted against the insured; but the company shall have the right and opportunity to associate with the insured in the defense and control of any claim or proceeding reasonably likely to involve the company. In such event the insured and the company shall cooperate fully.' Epstein 2009.

negligence or misconduct in selecting counsel or managing the defense' (Barker 2013: § 6.07). Again, parties could deviate from this standard when contracting for insurance, but seem not to have done so with any frequency, suggesting that the common law gloss is efficient.

In a few instances, courts have imposed immutable requirements on insurers, some of which appear in insurance law (Baker and Logue, Chapter 11 in this volume) and some of which appear elsewhere. An example of the latter exists in states whose rules governing lawyers prevent insurers from becoming co-clients of the lawyers they engage to defend lawsuits against policyholders (Barker and Silver 2013: § 4.06). Regardless of where they appear, immutable rules that prevent insurers from using efficient working arrangements will raise insurance costs. Whether immutable rules serve the contracting parties' interest in maximizing their joint wealth depends on the facts, including the possible existence of bargaining impediments or other obstacles that may prevent parties from adopting efficient rules on their own.

IV. UNDERSTANDING COMMON INSURANCE DEFENSE ARRANGEMENTS

Defense costs can vary greatly. At one extreme, they can be zero and often are. Insurers can avoid even the minimal cost of retaining lawyers to file answers to complaints by settling with claimants or, less commonly, by allowing default judgments to be taken and paying them in full. Defense costs are often positive, too, and the range of defensive outlays is enormous.

Using a large database containing Texas claims that closed with positive payouts and that were covered by one of five lines of commercial insurance, researchers found that the frequency of incurring defense costs varied from a low of 76 percent in commercial auto cases to a high of 96 percent in cases alleging medical malpractice (Black et al. 2008). Mean (median) defense costs per claim also varied greatly, from a low of $12,000 ($4,000) in commercial auto cases to a high of $38,000 ($25,000) in medical liability cases. Finally, across lines of coverage the ratio of mean (median) defense cost to payout per claim ranged from a low of 15 percent (5 percent) in commercial auto cases to a high of 45 percent (22 percent) for medical liability.

Because defense costs can vary, both in absolute terms and as compared to payouts, across claims that fall within coverage lines, these costs must be managed with an eye to minimizing total losses. Otherwise, losses will be excessive and insurance arrangements will be inefficient. Managing defense costs does not necessarily mean reducing them, however. Good cost management means directing resources efficiently, so that dollars are spent, when appropriate, to reduce total losses, including payments to claimants. Defense dollars that generate more than offsetting reductions in payouts on claims are well spent.

The observation just made might lead one to infer that defense spending can never efficiently exceed the amount at issue in a given case. How could it be economically advantageous to spend more than $500,000 defending a $500,000 claim? It would be cheaper to pay the claimant and settle the case. In fact, insurers sometimes spend more defending claims than the claims are worth, as do other defendants. Their behavior is not necessarily irrational, however. By developing reputations as aggressive litigants, insurers may discourage plaintiffs' attorneys from filing many cases and may also gain bargaining leverage in settlement negotiations. Because liability insurers are repeat players in litigation, their interests are larger than the amount in controversy in any particular case, and the rationality of their defense outlays cannot properly be gauged by means of that measure.

Because under-spending on the defense can cause total losses to rise above the level that maximizes the parties' joint wealth, it would be senseless to assign the duty to defend to a party who lacked the wherewithal to underwrite an optimal defense. This is one reason why personal lines policies never assign the duty to policyholders. Few have the sophistication or the resources to efficiently make defense-related decisions. Some commercial policyholders do shoulder the duty to defend, however. This is true of businesses that maintain SIRs.

Of course, even a contracting party wealthy and sophisticated enough to mount an optimal defense may or may not have an incentive to provide one. To address this problem, an insurance arrangement must give the purse-strings to a party with a strong desire to minimize the loss. Normally, the controlling party has such an interest because it also bears a significant fraction of the variable judgment risk.

Consider a commercial policyholder with a SIR that must be exhausted before an insurer's overlying layer can be tapped. Standard arrangements give the policyholder control initially and transfer it to the insurer when responsibility for losses changes hands. For example, SIRs typically require policyholders to bear defense costs and pay the first dollars toward the settlement of claims, up to the limit of the SIR. Once settlements exhaust the SIR and the overlying layer is tapper, the insurer assumes control of the defense, bears its cost, and takes control of and bears financial responsibility for settlements as well. Often, exhaustion of a SIR occurs over the course of multiple claims, so that these responsibilities may move from the policyholder to the insurer while claims are pending.

Sometimes, a pending claim may implicate both the policyholder's SIR and the carrier's overlying coverage layer. When the exposure to loss is shared, the parties often share control of the defense as well. A typical arrangement would give the policyholder the final say, but entitle the carrier to participate in the litigation, obtain information, and seek to influence decisions by deploying monitoring counsel to work alongside the policyholder's defense lawyer. Excess insurers use similar working arrangements.

One way to ensure that the party controlling the defense bears a significant fraction of the variable judgment risk is simply to transfer essentially all of that risk to the defending insurer. This occurs in most personal lines policies and in many commercial policies as well. In litigation brought on claims covered by these policies, out-of-pocket payments by policyholders above the insurance limits are rare, meaning that the carrier is essentially a sole holder of the liability exposure (Baker 2001). A study of closed medical malpractice claims found that primary carriers contributed over 99 percent of the dollars paid to claimants (Zeiler et al. 2007). Physicians contributed to resolutions in a tiny fraction of the cases. Insurers even paid the majority of the dollars *over* the policy limits that changed hands, probably because they agreed to hold physicians harmless when requesting their permission to reject within-limits settlement demands.

In a subsequent article, the same researchers expanded their focus to all five lines of commercial insurance in the Texas closed claim dataset (Hyman, Black, and Silver 2011). They found that payments above the primary policy limits were more common in medical malpractice cases than in lawsuits covered by other insurance lines. They also found that in all coverage lines, payment frequency spiked at the policy limits, meaning that claimants rarely recovered more. The likely inference is that physicians' exposure above the policy limits is minuscule, and that commercial policyholders' uninsured exposure is even smaller in other lines of coverage.

Saddling the insurer with all the judgment risk does not guarantee that any defensive outlays will be made, however. The carrier's privately optimal level of expenditures may be $0. This will be true when the expected judgment at trial will plainly exceed the policy limits no matter how a case is defended. Rather than bear defense costs, the carrier will rationally prefer to exhaust its limits by settling with the claimant.[12] Settling at the coverage limits might be the preferred strategy, for example,

---

[12] An insurer may also allow a default judgment to be entered against a policyholder, if it is willing to pay the judgment in full.

when a policyholder with the minimum amount of liability coverage required by law causes an automobile accident in which several people are severely injured or killed.[13]

An analogous situation may arise when a policyholder has an excess layer of coverage above a primary layer. Ordinarily, an excess insurer has neither a right to control the defense nor a duty to bear defense costs.[14] The primary carrier has both. However, under many policies, courts have required excess carriers to 'drop down' and assume defensive responsibilities when primary carriers' limits are exhausted, when primary carriers refuse to defend, or when primary carriers become insolvent (Barker 2013: § 7.08[3][a]). The obvious reason for transferring control and financial responsibility in these situations is that the primary carrier cannot be relied upon to mount an adequate defense to the claim. The law governing the obligation to 'drop down' is not uniform, however, and gaps exist in which the party that is legally responsible for the defense has limited incentives. The reported cases suggest that, in these situations, a good deal of inefficient jockeying occurs as the policyholder and the insurer(s) with indemnity exposure seek to force defense costs onto each other. The cause of the failure to address these gaps through *ex ante* contracts is not clear.

Not all policies saddle excess carriers with defensive responsibilities. Some require policyholders to assume them when primary carriers' limits are exhausted. These arrangements are puzzling because the excess insurers seem to have the strongest interest in an efficient defense. One suspects that policies of this type are sold only to commercial insureds that possess sufficient assets to shoulder the burden and that face significant exposures to litigation losses.[15]

Typically, then, insurance arrangements assign both the right to defend and the duty to defend to the same party, and that party is also responsible for paying all or a substantial part of future variable losses. Still, as shown, the right to defend can be separated from the duty to defend and

---

13 On the assumption that the policyholder is judgment-proof, which follows naturally from the characterization of the insurer as the bearer of the entire judgment risk, exhaustion while spending nothing on the defense is also the optimal approach for the insured and insurer as a group.

14 See Epstein 2009 (quoting policy form language providing that '[i]f underlying insurance is exhausted by any occurrence, [the Excess Insurer] shall be obligated to assume charge of the settlement or defense of any claim or proceedings against the insured resulting from the same occurrence, but only where this policy applies immediately in excess of such underlying insurance without the intervention of excess insurance of another carrier').

15 For an example, see *Ford Motor Co.* v. *Northbrook Ins. Co.*, 838 F. 2d 829 (6th Cir. Mich. 1988).

sometimes is. In this situation, the party with the duty to defend is a mere litigation funder and the party exercising control usually has a strong interest in reducing the variable portion of the judgment risk. Insurance policies that protect directors and officers of public companies from suits by shareholders have this structure.[16]

When one contracting party funds litigation that is managed by another, a standard third-party payer problem arises. The controlling party may want to wage an excessively lavish defense, its dollars not being at risk. The party with the duty to fund will therefore protect itself in various ways. For example, the following language appears in a D&O liability policy that obligates the carrier to fund a defense controlled by the insureds.

> The Insured Persons, and not the Company, have the duty to defend any Claim made against the Insured Persons. The Insured Persons shall not . . . incur any Defense Costs without the prior written consent of the Company, such consent not to be unreasonably withheld. The Company shall have the right to effectively associate with the Insured Persons in the defense of any Claim that involves or appears reasonably likely to involve the Company, including negotiating a settlement. The Insured Persons shall give the Company full cooperation and such information as it may reasonably require (Scottsdale Indemnity Company (Undateda)).

The rights granted by this provision help the funding insurer guard against excessive expenditures by monitoring the conduct of the defense, reviewing proposed outlays, and, at least in theory, rejecting proposed expenditures that are excessive.

Insofar as policyholders and carriers are concerned, the tendency of third-party payer arrangements to encourage profligacy may not be entirely bad.[17] Knowing that the directors and officers of public companies will spend lavishly on the defense because their insurers are bearing the freight, plaintiffs' attorneys may be less inclined to sue them and may file only the strongest cases that come across their desks. Whether the preference for defense cost policies reflects this advantage is unclear, however. Agency costs provide an alternative explanation. The managers of public companies, who have enormous reputational interests at stake in

---

16 See Baker and Swedloff 2013 (explaining that 'D&O insurance policies are "defense cost payment" policies, rather than "duty to defend" policies, so that someone insured by a D&O policy gets to choose their own defense lawyer and direct their own defense'). Some professional liability policies for attorneys also leave lawyers in charge. For an example, see LawPro 2013.

17 On spending by directors and officers in securities lawsuits, see Baker and Griffith 2010; Squire 2012.

securities fraud suits, may prefer defense cost policies, which are relatively expensive, because they can use corporate assets to cover the cost. One third-party payer problem may beget another.

A different risk of overspending may be thought to flow from the language of the standard defense clause, which obligates a carrier to bear defense costs seemingly without limit. All policies contain indemnity limits that cap the amounts insurers must pay to claimants on behalf of insureds. Some also limit defense costs by providing that defense outlays erode the indemnity limits. Under these policies, the duty to defend ends when the policy limits are consumed by settlements, defense costs, or both in combination. But many policies, especially those in the personal lines area, do not cap the duty to bear defense costs in any obvious way. They require the insurer to defend suits seeking covered damages, and they do not count defensive outlays against the policy limits. Because only payments to claimants can exhaust these policies, insurers are, in theory, responsible for defense costs without limit.

Even under policies that impose an unlimited duty to defend, the risk of overspending is small. Excessive outlays are especially unlikely when the right to defend, the duty to defend, and the duty to indemnify all rest in the same hands, because the party funding and controlling the defense would harm itself by spending too much. Pairing the duty to defend with the duty to indemnify also reduces the risk, because the duty to defend normally disappears when payments on claims exhaust the policy limits. Rather than bear unlimited defense costs going forward, a rational insurer would seek to exhaust its limits by settling with a claimant.[18] A carrier might even pay a claimant more than the policy limits to avoid this fate.[19] Because recoveries from policyholders' personal assets are rare, a decision to offer the policy limits usually maximizes the claimant's recovery and has a good chance of being accepted.

The unlimited duty to defend creates a serious prospect of excessive spending mainly when a carrier is prevented from settling a claim. For example, some professional liability policies contain consent-to-settle clauses that permit insurers to resolve claims only when policyholders agree. These clauses enable policyholders to protect themselves from

[18] This assumes away all interests a carrier might have in spending more than the policy limits to defend a claim, such as the desire to establish a reputation for defending aggressively regardless of case size. The logic of exhausting the limits rather than bearing additional defense costs also applies to policyholders with SIRs.

[19] Although the policy limits cap the carrier's legal responsibility, insurers remain free to pay more and sometimes do. Zeiler et al. 2007.

the collateral effects of settlements, such as loss of reputation or mandatory license reviews. By opposing a settlement, a policyholder with such a policy can force a carrier to incur defense costs it would rather avoid. This is why consent-to-settle policies cost more than standard policies; they expose carriers to greater risks by limiting their ability to manage costs.[20] Settlements may also be impeded when many insurers have partial coverage of the same claim. This may be true when a policyholder has a tower of coverages sold by several insurers or a lawsuit implicates policies issued by different carriers in different years (Squire 2012; Chapter 14 in this volume).

Finally, when, as often is true, a policyholder bears neither defense costs nor substantial exposure on a liability claim, the incentive to participate in the defense is weakened and may even disappear. For this reason, insurance policies typically contain clauses that require policyholders to assist carriers' defensive efforts in various ways. Policyholders must give carriers prompt notice of accidents and lawsuits, and must also cooperate in the investigation, settlement, and defense of claims. The duty to cooperate may require a policyholder to help identify and locate witnesses, answer interrogatories, give deposition testimony, and appear at trial (Barker 2013: § 23.07).

V. LIABILITY INSURERS AS LITIGATION MANAGERS

The right to control the defense is a tool for managing defense costs. Because the party in charge of the defense decides how litigation dollars are deployed, that person can take advantage of opportunities to save money. In the period, now longer than a century in the United States, during which liability insurance arrangements have allocated control of the defense of liability suits, many cost-reducing devices have evolved. The most important innovations are: co-client status of the defending insurer; staff counsel operations; specialized panel counsel; litigation management guidelines and audits; and value-based fee arrangements. Each will be briefly discussed.

---

[20] A consent-to-settle clause creates an obvious risk that a policyholder will reject a reasonable, i.e., loss minimizing, settlement demand. Insurance policies therefore contain other clauses to help manage this risk. See Syverud 1990. Insurers also use the threat of nonrenewal to discourage policyholders from rejecting settlement demands for bad reasons.

A. Status of the Defending Insurer

When asked to defend a lawsuit against a policyholder, an insurer will often hire a lawyer to defend the case. At the hiring stage, a question will arise: Will the lawyer represent the policyholder only, the insurer only, or both the policyholder and the insurer? In most jurisdictions, all three options are available when the interests of carriers and policyholders are harmonious. The answer therefore depends on the understanding reached between the insurer and the defense lawyer when the lawyer is engaged. A minority of American states provide as a matter of law that a defense lawyer represents only a policyholder. The minority view is misguided because, in all jurisdictions, client status is determined by agreement under agency law. Still, in these states, defending insurers have no option but to act as non-client, third-party payers (Barker and Silver 2013: § 4.04 et seq.).

The choice of working arrangements matters to insurers, suggesting that it has efficiency implications. Speaking generally, they prefer to be co-clients with policyholders. The reason for this is simple: clients can demand more from lawyers than non-clients can because clients have more rights. They can require lawyers to protect their interests, follow their instructions, keep their secrets, and give them information. Clients can also hire lawyers, fire them, and sue them for poor performance. By all these means, clients can encourage lawyers to serve them well.

Jurisdictions that deny insurers the option of becoming co-clients have had to come to grips with the practical need of insurers to control the defense and manage costs. They have done so in various ways, most commonly by expanding the ability of third-party payers to influence the conduct of litigation. The *Restatement (Third) of the Law Governing Lawyers* reflects this tendency in § 134(2), which allows a non-client payer to direct a lawyer's conduct if, among other things, 'the direction is reasonable in scope and character, such as by reflecting obligations borne by the person directing the lawyer' (American Law Institute 2000–13).

Insurers are especially well positioned to manage defense lawyers and defense costs. They are wealthy, highly sophisticated, and experienced purchasers of legal services, and they participate in long-term relationships with the lawyers they employ. As a result, they can obtain legal services on attractive terms. They can also minimize agency costs by monitoring the quality of defense lawyers' performance.

A policyholder's presence as a co-client rarely impedes an insurer's ability to manage litigation effectively. Under most standard insurance contracts, the policyholder is required to remain passive when the carrier controls the defense. It must provide assistance of various sorts, but it may not interfere. Most policyholders are also happy to let insurers call the shots. They are fully covered against losses, and they have better things to do than devote time and energy to litigation.

B. Staff Counsel Operations

Many insurers find it beneficial to produce legal services internally instead of purchasing them in the market. They use in-house legal departments, commonly known as staff counsel offices, to defend suits against policyholders. Historically, this option was attractive mainly in coverage lines like personal automobile insurance that generate claims in volume year after year. Insurers used lawyers employed at independent law firms, known as 'panel counsel,' to defend cases of other types. In recent years, however, insurers have kept a larger variety of cases in-house.

Whether to obtain legal services from staff counsel or panel counsel is a 'make or buy' decision. Running a law firm is expensive and risky, whether the firm operates inside a larger business or independently. But it can be advantageous to produce legal services internally, as the existence of general counsel operations within companies of many kinds suggests. In-house legal departments can provide services of comparable or superior quality at less cost. They can be monitored more effectively too.

Liability insurers are especially well positioned to evaluate the performance of in-house attorneys. They collect enormous amounts of data on claims, such as injury type, time-to-close, settlement costs, defense costs, and jury verdicts, which they can use to compare the performance of staff attorneys and panel counsel over blocks of cases. With the results in hand, they can assign cases going forward in a manner calculated to minimize their losses. In fact, insurers have closed some staff counsel offices and expanded others, suggesting that they make real efforts to identify efficient working arrangements (Silver 1998).

C. Specialized Panel Counsel

When using panel counsel, insurance carriers take advantage of scale economies and expertise by concentrating cases of particular types in identified firms.[21] For example, an automobile insurer operating in a metropolitan area may send hundreds of accident cases to a single outside defense firm. This enables the law firm to develop great expertise and to reduce operating costs by reusing materials, such as legal memoranda,

---

21 On the operation of panel counsel defense firms, see Kritzer 2006.

motions, and briefs. The firm may also learn how particular plaintiffs' firms operate, enabling it to make better recommendations on defensive strategies and settlements.

The use of specialized panel counsel is also important, perhaps especially so, in areas like medical malpractice that generate fewer cases. In these areas, several insurers may 'share' an outside defense firm, increasing the number of cases it sees. This helps the firm deepen its expertise and lower its costs.

D. Litigation Management Guidelines and Audits

By reducing their defense costs, insurers can charge less for coverage and compete more successfully for business. In recent decades, insurers (and other businesses) have sought to minimize defense costs while maintaining the quality of legal services by requiring lawyers to adhere to litigation management guidelines and auditing lawyers' compliance. Typical guidelines for outside defense counsel identify the lawyers who will handle a matter, set the rates they will charge, and require periodic communication about diverse matters, such as litigation budgets, time expended, costs incurred, and expected trial outcomes.[22] Guidelines also require lawyers to obtain carriers' permission before incurring expenses for travel, discovery, or expert witnesses. Audits enable insurers to monitor lawyers' adherence to and also discourage billing fraud, a notorious problem when lawyers are paid by the hour, as defense lawyers often are.

Insurers' use of litigation management guidelines and external auditors initially provoked heated controversy. Wanting to preserve their independence and, one suspects, to protect their fees, outside defense lawyers sought opinions from state bar associations and courts on the permissibility of guidelines and audits. On the whole, guidelines survived these challenges but third-party audits did not. Insurers may still audit defense lawyers' bills and performance using in-house personnel, however. Consequently, the likely net effect of the many ethics opinions that prohibit defense lawyers from sharing information without third-party auditors is that insurers must manufacture auditing services in-house instead of buying them on the market, at some modest loss efficiency.[23]

---

[22] See, e.g., Zurich (Undated). On outside counsel guidelines used by companies of diverse types, see Whelan and Ziv 2012.

[23] On the controversies surrounding litigation management guidelines and third-party fee audits, see Silver 2002.

E. Value-Based Fee Arrangements

Although liability carriers continue to pay most defense lawyers by the hour, they have experimented with value-based arrangements designed to incentivize lawyers to produce better results or operate at less cost. For example, insurers have experimented with various types of flat fee arrangements. These piecework arrangements have in common that lawyers are paid a fixed amount for an identified task, which may be a case or a portion of a case, regardless of the amount of time consumed. Piecework compensation transfers the risk that a task will require an unexpectedly large amount of effort from the insurer to the lawyer, whose fee is fixed. It also encourages lawyers to complete tasks quickly, so as to maximize their effective hourly rates.

Because fast work is not necessarily good work, insurers that use flat fee arrangements must worry about the quality of the services defense lawyers supply. Carriers have used monitoring and supplemental incentives to address this concern. Because they pay judgments and settlements themselves, they can learn whether lawyers working for flat fees are underperforming. Because they control large flows of legal work, they can also punish lawyers whose results are sub-par by moving cases to other law firms. Insurers have used carrots to motivate superior performance too. When sending law firms large blocks of cases, all of which are subject to flat fee arrangements, insurers have agreed to pay bonuses tied to the cost of resolving the claims. For example, a law firm that closed a block of cases for $1 million less than the predicted cost based on the insurer's historical results might receive a $500,000 bonus.

Like litigation management guidelines and bill audits, flat fee arrangements were once controversial. Speaking generally, they survived review by state bar ethics committees and courts, meaning that insurers are free to use them.

An example from outside the insurance sector shows how innovative fee arrangements can work (Zahorsky 2012). In 2004, Tyco International, which had relationships with over 160 outside law firms, issued a request for proposals in the hope of engaging a single firm to handle its work. To facilitate bidding by law firms that were interested in competing for its business, it distributed historical information on its litigation docket, which contained more than 500 cases. Eventually, Tyco hired Shook Hardy & Bacon LLP as its sole outside provider under an arrangement that predicts future defense costs and allows the firm to retain a portion of any amount saved as a bonus. If expenses exceed the estimate, the law firm is responsible for a portion of the overage. The mechanics of the working arrangement also include a centralized knowledge management system that captures case updates, deposition summaries, and other valuable developments, and a cost-tracking system that enables the law firm and Tyco to study expenses. The law firm also hired several non-partner, mid-level lawyers with eight to ten years of experience to handle the bulk of Tyco's work.

VI. CONCLUSION

The economics of the defense of insured claims are reasonably straightforward. At the highest level, they reflect the parties' object of maximizing their joint gains which, in this context, is accomplished by minimizing the losses that are expected to be associated with liability claims. Just as insurers can more readily bear liability risks than policyholders, they can more easily carry the risk of incurring defense costs as well. Putting the indemnity and defense risks in the same hands also ameliorates a principal-agent problem that arises when the two are separated, because the party responsible for funding the defense then enjoys the benefits an efficient defense provides. The alignment of interests is not perfect, however. Because insurers' exposure to liability risks is capped, some defensive services may benefit only insureds and carriers may lack incentives to purchase them. Empirical studies of policyholders' contributions to settlements suggest that this problem is manageable.

Standard policies also give insurers control of the defense, not just the obligation to provide funding. Control enables them to manage defense costs and to use resources efficiently. Because insurers deal with claims in volume, they possess a good deal of private information about litigation. They can also manage attorneys well by using long-term relationships, litigation guidelines, and audits to obtain good performance at reasonable cost.

Given how well the duty to indemnify, the duty to defend, and the right to control the defense work together when held by the same party, the question is why insurance contracts sometimes place them in different hands. Separation makes sense in the contexts where it occurs for factual reasons, such as the insured's ability to fund a large SIR or to manage an effective defense.

REFERENCES

AIG/Chartis. Undated. *Financial Institutions Risk Protector*. Available at www.chartisinsurance.com/do-eo_295_392358.html (accessed March 9, 2015).

American Law Institute. 2000–13. *Restatement (Third) of the Law Governing Lawyers*.
Baker, Tom. 2001. 'Blood Money, New Money, and the Moral Economy of Tort Law in Action' 35 *Law & Society Review* 275–319.
Baker, Tom, and Sean J. Griffith. 2010. *Ensuring Corporate Misconduct: How Liability Insurance Undermines Shareholder Litigation*. Chicago: IL: University of Chicago Press 134–5.
Baker, Tom, and Rick Swedloff. 2013. 'Regulation by Liability Insurance: From Auto to Lawyers Professional Liability' Research Paper No. 13-412, Institute for Law and Economics, University of Pennsylvania School of Law. Available at http://ssrn.com/abstract=2202314 (accessed March 9, 2015).
Barker, William T. 2013. *New Appleman Law of Liability Insurance*. Mathew Bender & Company, Inc.
Barker, William T., and Charles Silver. 2013. *Professional Responsibilities of Insurance Defense Counsel*. Mathew Bender & Company, Inc.
Bernstein, Wayne. 2005. 'Duty to or Non-Duty to Defend: What is the Best Defense Provision?' *Insurance Journal*. Available at www.insurancejournal.com/magazines/features/2005/12/19/64090.htm (accessed March 9, 2015).
Black, Bernard S., David A. Hyman, Charles Silver, and William M. Sage. 2008. 'Defense Costs and Insurer Reserves in Medical Malpractice and Other Personal Injury Cases: Evidence from Texas, 1988–2004' 10 *American Law & Economics Review* 185–245.
Boardman, Michelle E. 2006. 'Contra Proferentem: The Allure of Ambiguous Boilerplate' 104 *Michigan Law Review* 1105–28.
Cooter, Robert. 1985. 'Unity in Tort, Contract, and Property: The Model of Precaution' 73 *California Law Review* 1–51.
Easterbrook, Frank H., and Daniel R. Fischel. 1993. 'Contract and Fiduciary Duty' 36 *Journal of Law & Economics* 425–46.
Epstein, Lee M. 2009. 'On the Defensive: Excess Insurers and the Duty to Defend' *Coverage Law*. Available at http://coveragelaw.blogspot.com/2009/02/on-defensive-excess-insurers-and-duty.html (accessed March 9, 2015).
Giles, Nicholas J. 2013. 'Rethinking the Cooperation Clause in Standard Liability Insurance Contracts' 161 *University of Pennsylvania Law Review* 585–621.
Hyman, David A., Bernard S. Black, and Charles Silver. 2011. 'The Impact of the Duty to Settle on Settlement: Evidence From Texas' 8 *Journal of Empirical Legal Studies* 48–84.
International Risk Management Institute, Inc. 2014. Glossary, Defense-only coverage. Available at www.irmi.com/online/insurance-glossary/terms/d/defense-only-coverage.aspx (accessed March 9, 2015).
Kritzer, Herbert M. 2006. 'The Commodification of Insurance Defense Practice' 59 *Vanderbilt Law Review* 2053–94.
LawPro. 2013. *2013 Professional Liability Insurance for Lawyers*. Available at www.lawpro.ca/insurance/pdf/LAWPRO_Policy2013.pdf (accessed March 18, 2015).
Pryor, Ellen S. 2000. 'Mapping the Changing Boundaries of the Duty to Defend in Texas' 31 *Texas Tech Law Review* 869–930.
Schwartz, Alan, and Robert E. Scott. 2003. 'Contract Theory and the Limits of Contract Law' 113 *Yale Law Journal* 541–619.
Scottsdale Indemnity Company. Undateda. *Directors, Officers and Entity Liability Insurance Policy*. Available at http://freedomspecialtyins.com/fs/forms/policy_forms/00064292.pdf (accessed March 9, 2015).
Scottsdale Indemnity Company. Undatedb. *A-Side Directors and Officers Liability Insurance Policy*. Available at http://freedomspecialtyins.com/fs/forms/policy_forms/00064300.pdf (accessed March 9, 2015).
Shavell, S. 1986. 'The Judgment Proof Problem' 6 *International Review of Law and Economics* 45–58.
Shernoff, William M., Sanford M. Gage, and Harvey R. Levine. 2014. *New Appleman Insurance Bad Faith Litigation*. 2nd edition. Mathew Bender & Company, Inc.
Silver, Charles. 1998. 'Flat Fees and Staff Attorneys: Unnecessary Casualties in the Battle

over the Law Governing Insurance Defense Lawyers' 4 *Connecticut Insurance Law Journal* 205–57.
Silver, Charles. 2002. 'When Should Government Regulate Lawyer-Client Relationships? The Campaign to Prevent Insurers from Managing Defense Costs' 44 *Arizona Law Review* 787–824.
Silver, Charles, and Kent D. Syverud. 1995. 'The Professional Responsibilities of Insurance Defense Lawyers' 45 *Duke Law Journal* 255–363.
Squire, Richard. 2012. 'How Collective Settlements Camouflage the Costs of Shareholder Lawsuits' 62 *Duke Law Journal* 1–77.
Stiglitz, Joseph E. 2008. 'Principal and Agent (ii)' in Steven N. Durlauf and Lawrence E. Blume (eds.), *The New Palgrave Dictionary of Economics*. 2nd edition. Palgrave Macmillan.
Sykes, A. O. 1994. 'Judicial Limitations on the Discretion of Liability Insurers to Settle or Litigate: An Economic Critique' 72 *Texas Law Review* 1345–74.
Syverud, Kent D. 1990. 'The Duty to Settle' 76 *Virginia Law Review* 1113–209.
Syverud, Kent D. 1994. 'On the Demand for Liability Insurance' 72 *Texas Law Review* 1629–54.
Trentini, Linda J. 2011. 'Legal Defense Cost Coverage' *Medical Liability Mutual Insurance Company Underwriting Update* (on file with authors).
Whelan, Christopher J., and Neta Ziv. 2012. 'Privatizing Professionalism: Client Control of Lawyers' Ethics' 80 *Fordham Law Review* 2577–609.
Zahorsky, Rachel M. 2012. 'Facing the Alternative: How Does a Flat Fee System Really Work?' *ABA Journal*. Available at www.abajournal.com/magazine/article/facing_the_alternative_how_does_a_flat_fee_system_really_work/ (accessed March 9, 2015).
Zeiler, Kathryn, Bernard S. Black, Charles Silver, David A. Hyman, and William Sage. 2007. 'Physicians' Insurance Limits and Malpractice Payments: Evidence from Texas Closed Claims 1990–2003' 36 *Journal of Legal Studies* S9–S45.
Zurich. Undated. *Litigation Management: Guidelines for Defence Counsel*. Available at www.zurich.com/NR/rdonlyres/E4145DF3-23EF-48CC-93A6-07D10F1B791F/0/LMG.pdf (accessed March 9, 2015).

14. The artificial collective-action problem in lawsuits against insured defendants

*Richard Squire**

I. INTRODUCTION

Liability insurance complicates efforts to settle lawsuits. It introduces a conflict of interests whenever the trial outcome is uncertain and the potential damages exceed the limit of the defendant's liability policy. When such a case settles before trial, the insurer typically pays more, and the policyholder less, than each expected to pay had the case reached a verdict. This shift in liability from policyholder to insurer predisposes the policyholder toward settling, and the insurer toward trial. Therefore, if the insurer has the authority to settle on behalf of the policyholder, there is an *undersettlement hazard*. The insurer will sometimes choose trial even when settling would minimize the expected value of the total defense costs, which consist of payments to the plaintiff plus the defense's litigation expenses. But giving settlement authority instead to the policyholder introduces an *overpayment hazard*: the policyholder will sometimes choose to settle even when the plaintiff's settlement demand exceeds the expected costs to the defense of a trial.

Liability insurers and policyholders would be better off if they could prevent this conflict of interests. When they enter into a liability policy, the insurer and the policyholder share an interest in minimizing total defense costs in lawsuits that the policy will cover. Minimizing such costs maximizes the joint surplus from the contract, which the insurer and policyholder divide between themselves when they set the price for coverage (the premium). The conflict of interests in settlement negotiations, however, drives up total defense costs: the undersettlement hazard increases litigation expenses, while the overpayment hazard increases payments to plaintiffs. In this way, settlement conflict among defense-side parties (defendants and their liability insurers) produces a collective-action problem: it causes them to act individually during settlement negotiations in ways that are contrary to their common interests.

* I am very grateful to Daniel Schwarcz and Peter Siegelman for thoughtful suggestions on an earlier draft of this chapter.

To mitigate this collective-action problem, courts – sometimes with contractual prompting – hold that liability insurers have a duty to accept 'reasonable' settlement offers in covered lawsuits when the offered settlement would require the insurer to pay no more than its policy amount. Breach of this duty renders the insurer liable for the full amount of any damages awarded in the suit, including any amount in excess of its policy limit. This 'disregard-the-limits' rule seeks to mediate between the insurer's disinclination to settle and the policyholder's over-eagerness to do so. But the rule generates its own costs. Enforcing it requires additional litigation, and insurers who anticipate being sued by their policyholders will expend resources documenting the 'reasonableness' of their settlement decisions. In addition, courts can make mistakes that, depending on their direction, cause either the undersettlement hazard or the overpayment hazard to persist.

Several scholars have argued that courts could dispense with the reasonableness standard when enforcing insurer settlement duties. Courts could, they argue, encourage optimal settlement decisions by holding an insurer strictly liable for the full damages award in a covered lawsuit if the insurer could have settled the suit without paying more than its policy amount. Such a strict-liability rule would purportedly minimize total defense costs by inducing insurers to settle if, and only if, the plaintiff's settlement demand is less than the expected costs to the defense of a trial.

This chapter makes two arguments about the collective-action problem in negotiations to settle covered lawsuits. First, the strict-liability rule that some scholars advocate would neutralize the undersettlement hazard but not the overpayment hazard. It therefore solves the collective-action problem only in cases in which the policyholder has no say in the settlement decision. Second, the collective-action problem is artificial, as there is no compelling legal reason for settlements of covered lawsuits to be collective. The current practice is for plaintiffs, policyholders and insurers to negotiate toward a single, collectively binding settlement amount. But they instead could follow a 'segmented' approach, under which each defense-side party would negotiate separately with the plaintiff for a release of the plaintiff's right to collect any damages which, if awarded at trial, would be that defense-side party's responsibility. Under this alternative approach, policy limits do not introduce a conflict of interests into settlement negotiations. The approach would therefore render insurer settlement duties – whether or not tempered by a reasonableness standard – obsolete. Why parties have not adopted this seemingly more efficient method for settling covered lawsuits is an open question in the scholarship on liability insurance.

To understand this chapter's first argument – that a strict-liability rule solves the undersettlement problem but not the overpayment problem – it is

Table 14.1 The four settlement-duty scenarios

	Post-judgment context	Post-settlement context
Within-limit demand (duty to settle)	Scenario A	Scenario B
Above-limit demand (duty to contribute)	Scenario C	Scenario D

useful to divide covered lawsuits into several categories. We can divide the lawsuits initially based on the type of settlement demand that the plaintiff makes. The plaintiff might offer to settle within the insurer's policy limit, triggering the insurer's *duty to settle* as it is traditionally defined. Or, the plaintiff might demand to settle for more than the policy limit and the policyholder (or an excess insurer) offers to pay the above-limit portion. This fact pattern implicates the insurer's *duty to contribute*. Each of these two types of case – duty-to-settle cases and duty-to-contribute cases – can then be subdivided based on how, assuming the insurer rejects the settlement demand, the case is then resolved. One possibility is that the case proceeds to a trial that produces an above-limit damages award. When that happens, the subsequent suit against the insurer for breach of its settlement duties occurs in the *post-judgment* context. The other possibility is that the policyholder (or an excess insurer) agrees to pay the plaintiff's full settlement demand. In that situation, the policyholder (or excess insurer) then sues the insurer for reimbursement in the *post-settlement* context. The result of these divisions is the four scenarios identified in Table 14.1.

This chapter will show that strict insurer liability for failure to settle would minimize total defense costs only in Table 14.1's Scenario A: the within-limit demand, post-judgment scenario. This is the 'classic' duty-to-settle case that most scholars focus on when analyzing insurer settlement duties. It is a misleading scenario from which to generalize because it uniquely presents no overpayment hazard. In Scenario A, the insurer retains sole settlement authority throughout the lawsuit. In the other three scenarios, the policyholder exercises shared or exclusive settlement authority, and therefore a rule of strict insurer liability would lead to settlements that overcompensate plaintiffs. For these scenarios, another rule is needed. This chapter will explain why, if we assume a strict-liability rule for Scenario A, the best rule for Scenario B (within-limit demand, post-settlement context) is that the insurer have *no* settlement duty. As for Scenarios C and D (involving an above-limit settlement demand), this chapter will show that a duty to contribute is needed to avoid the undersettlement hazard, but that the duty must be subject to a reasonableness standard to police the overpayment hazard. The implication is that the reasonableness standard is indispensable in at least some cases, despite the costs it generates through additional litigation, compliance efforts, and the risk of legal error.

This chapter's second argument is that the need for *any* insurer settlement duty – whether or not tempered by a reasonableness standard – arises *only* when parties settle covered lawsuits collectively. Under the collective approach, the parties negotiate toward a single settlement amount that binds the plaintiff and all defense-side parties. Other scholars have presupposed the collective approach, as does the analysis summarized in Table 14.1. But there is no principle of positive law that requires settlements of covered lawsuits to be collective. As an alternative, each defense-side party could settle separately with the plaintiff, paying him to release his right to collect any damages which, if awarded at trial, would be that defense-side party's responsibility. If settlements were segmented in this way, the conflict of interests attributed to policy limits would disappear from *all four* scenarios in Table 14.1, and all settlement duties – whether governed by reasonableness or strict liability – would be unnecessary.

The segmented approach solves the collective-action problem because it avoids the liability shift that is inherent in the collective approach. Under the segmented approach, the primary insurer would pay to settle only its segment of the range of potential damages. The primary insurer would therefore no longer have to assume additional liability by also paying the plaintiff to release his right to collect damages that exceed the primary policy limit – damages which, if awarded at trial, would be the contractual responsibility of the policyholder or an excess insurer. The primary insurer would therefore no longer have an incentive to underspend on settlement. And because the policyholder would only enter into a settlement that covered the above-limit damages, she could no longer shift liability to her insurers by agreeing to a settlement payment that would be partly or wholly their responsibility. She therefore would no longer have an incentive to overspend on settlement. Once the segmented approach were adopted, defense-side parties would adjust policy limits to preserve the same effective level of coverage that policyholders enjoy now. But that coverage would be cheaper because the costs of settlement conflict, including the costs of enforcing settlement duties designed to resolve that conflict, would no longer drive up premiums.

When the defendant in a covered lawsuit is an individual, there are typically just two defense-side parties: the insurer and the policyholder. Cases against corporate defendants, by contrast, often involve numerous defense-side parties, as corporations typically have a primary insurer plus several excess insurers, forming an insurance 'tower'. These additional insurers complicate settlement negotiations but do not alter the essential conflict of interests. When settlements are collective, the primary insurer is biased toward trial, the policyholder is biased toward settlement, and the excess insurers divide in their biases depending on where the potential and expected damages fall within the tower. As is true when the policyholder has only one insurer, these conflicting biases entail costly settlement duties that could be eliminated if settlements were segmented.

Given that the collective-action problem in settlements of covered lawsuits is avoidable, why do parties continue to follow the collective approach? In covered lawsuits against individuals (as opposed to corporations), reluctance among plaintiffs' attorneys to seize personal assets, and technicalities related to who would pay for the defense attorney after the insurer settled separately, may explain why parties have not adopted the segmented approach by contract. These considerations cannot, however, explain why parties continue to follow the collective approach in covered lawsuits against corporate defendants. In that context, the explanation may be that corporate managers prefer the collective approach because it increases the likelihood of an insurer-paid settlement, thereby smoothing out the corporation's reported earnings. Notably, this consequence of collective settlements seems to be socially inefficient, advancing managers' private interests at the expense of shareholder interests.

II. THE TERMS OF LIABILITY INSURANCE

The observation that policy limits introduce a collective-action problem in covered lawsuits raises the question of why policies have coverage limits in the first place. The main reason for limits is that they make policies more affordable by reducing the insurer's exposure and hence the premium it can charge. How much a policyholder is willing to spend on liability insurance depends on her risk aversion, her probability of being sued, her wealth, and factors such as whether the law requires her to buy insurance. Her wealth matters because it increases her willingness to pay for goods generally and for wealth protection specifically (Sykes 1994a).

A second function of policy limits is to protect insurers against large losses that might threaten their solvency (Syverud 1990). This is not a concern with auto liability insurance and professional malpractice insurance, which cover losses that are small relative to the typical insurer's net worth. But it matters with directors-and-officers (D&O) insurance and other commercial liability coverage, and it helps explain why corporations often buy several excess policies in addition to a primary policy. The implication is that many corporations wish to buy more liability coverage than any one insurer is willing to provide.

Besides policy limits, two other features of liability insurance influence settlement negotiations in covered lawsuits: coverage for litigation expenses (which consist mostly of attorneys' fees), and assignment of control over the settlement decision. Liability policies typically cover litigation expenses along with legal liability (payments to plaintiffs in settlements or judgments), and they usually give the insurer both the right and the duty to settle covered suits. Because the insurer is responsible for liability to the plaintiff, giving it control over the defense prevents underspending on defense attorneys, while making it responsible for litigation expenses discourages it from overspending. When the insurer controls the defense, the policy usually allows it to settle the case without the policyholder's permission. Medical malpractice policies are an exception: because policyholders fear that a settlement could stigmatize them, these policies typically require the insurer to obtain the policyholder's consent in order to settle. Conversely, D&O policies give the policyholder the right to control the defense, and it is the insurer's permission that must be sought before settling. D&O policies are unusual for a second reason: their coverage for litigation expenses is not unlimited; rather, expense coverage and legal-liability coverage count cumulatively toward the policy limit (Baker and Griffith 2010).

D&O coverage illustrates another feature of liability insurance that shapes settlement negotiations. When corporations buy D&O coverage and other general liability insurance, they often acquire not just one policy but a stack of them, forming an insurance tower. The bottom floor holds the primary insurer, responsible for initial liability in a lawsuit up to the primary policy limit. Each upper floor holds an excess insurer whose coverage begins at the limit of the policy immediately below it in the tower. In this way, the tower provides continuous coverage as liability in a lawsuit mounts, exhausting the policies in succession. The policyholder stands on the roof, responsible for any remaining liability beyond the limit of the last excess policy (Baker and Griffith 2010).[1]

The image of a tower is useful for visualizing settlement conflict. When settlements are collective and the trial outcome is uncertain, settling rather than going to trial shifts liability downward – onto the primary insurer, and perhaps some lower-level excess insurers. This downward liability compression inclines occupants of lower floors toward trial and occupants of upper floors – as well as the policyholder – toward settling.

---

[1] The policyholder will also co-occupy the tower's ground floor if the primary policy provides for a 'retention' – that is, a deductible.

III. SCENARIO A: WITHIN-LIMIT DEMAND, POST-JUDGMENT CONTEXT

Most commentators on liability-insurer settlement duties focus on Scenario A, in which the policyholder is sued, her liability insurer rejects a within-limit settlement demand, and then trial produces a damages award that exceeds the policy limit. Surely the insurer is liable up to the policy limit, but must it also pay for the excess?

As an illustration of settlement conflict in this scenario,[2] imagine the following lawsuit. Insurer has sold Policyholder a liability policy with no deductible and a $1M limit. Plaintiff sues Policyholder for $1.5M for a tort covered by the policy. Plaintiff has a 50 percent chance of winning $1.5M in damages at trial and a 50 percent chance of losing (receiving $0). Therefore, the lawsuit's actuarially fair value – defined here as the expected damages, ignoring the time value of money – is $0.75M. We will assume that all parties know the particulars of the lawsuit specified here. Suppose that, before trial, Plaintiff makes a non-negotiable settlement demand for his suit's actuarially fair value. Should Insurer and Policyholder accept?

If we consider the defense-side parties' *combined* interests, the answer is yes. The settlement demand of $0.75M equals the expected damages award at trial, but trial would also force the defense to incur litigation expenses that settlement would avoid. Therefore, accepting Plaintiff's settlement demand would minimize the expected value of the total defense costs: liability to the plaintiff (in a settlement payment or damages award) plus the defense's litigation expenses. When they entered into their insurance contract, Policyholder and Insurer had a common interest in establishing settlement rules that would minimize expected total defense costs. Doing so would have increased the joint surplus created by the contract, which they divided between themselves when they set the premium.

Now however, that the policy has been issued and a covered lawsuit is underway, are Insurer and Policyholder *each* still better off accepting Plaintiff's settlement demand? As Table 14.2 indicates, the answer is no. Because of the policy limit, Insurer's expected trial liability (excluding expenses) is $0.5M, reflecting a 50 percent chance of a $1.5M verdict, Insurer's share of which would be $1M. But if the case settles for the expected damages of $0.75M, the liability burden will fall entirely on Insurer because that amount is within the policy limit. Insurer thus

---

2 Although defense-side conflict can be modeled formally (Spier 2007; Squire 2012), the essence of the conflict can be demonstrated through simple, numerical examples of hypothetical lawsuits.

Table 14.2 Legal liability distribution, within-limit demand

	Expected trial liability	Liability in a settlement for the expected damages	Benefit (cost) of settling
Insurer ($1M limit)	$0.50M	$0.75M	($0.25M)
Policyholder/excess insurer	$0.25M	$0	$0.25M
Total	$0.75M	$0.75M	–

increases its expected liability to Plaintiff by $0.25M by settling rather than going to trial. Meanwhile, the converse is true for Policyholder: settling shifts her full liability exposure to Insurer. In this way, the $1M policy limit, combined with the possibility of an above-limit damages award, has driven a wedge between the distribution of the expected trial liability and the distribution of the settlement burden. The result is that Policyholder is biased toward settlement and Insurer toward trial. The same conflict of interests would be present if Policyholder had purchased an excess policy whose coverage began at Insurer's policy limit. Settlement would then shift liability from the excess insurer to the primary insurer, inclining the former toward settling, and the latter against it.

Settlement shifts liability onto primary insurers because it requires them to compensate plaintiffs for releases of their right to collect damages that, if awarded at trial, would exceed the policy limit and therefore be another defense-side party's responsibility. Note that the expected damages in Table 14.2 can be split into two components: $0.5M in expected within-limit damages, and $0.25M in expected above-limit damages. The first piece is Insurer's expected trial liability, and the second is Policyholder's; settlement requires Insurer to compensate Plaintiff for both.

Because settlement shifts the liability burden, whether the parties reach a settlement may depend on who controls the settlement decision on behalf of the defense. If Insurer controls, it might reject Plaintiff's $0.75M settlement demand, forcing trial, the costlier outcome. Therefore, if the policy assigns control to Insurer, the undersettlement hazard arises. The policy could obviate this hazard by instead assigning settlement authority to Policyholder: she surely would accept Plaintiff's $0.75M demand, the cost-minimizing result. But then the opposite hazard would arise. Plaintiff would be irrational to demand just $0.75M if Policyholder controlled the settlement decision, as Policyholder would have no reason to reject any demand under $1M, the full policy amount. Unless the defense's projected trial expenses exceed $0.25, settling for $1M would contravene

Policyholder's and Insurer's joint interest in minimizing total defense costs. Therefore, transferring settlement authority from Insurer to Policyholder would trade the undersettlement hazard for the overpayment hazard.

Most liability policies attempt to counteract the undersettlement hazard not by assigning settlement authority to the policyholder, but rather by making the insurer liable for the defense's litigation expenses. As an example, assume in our hypothetical lawsuit that the policy assigns Insurer both settlement authority and responsibility for expenses. If the defense's projected trial expenses exceed $0.25M, Insurer will accept Plaintiff's $0.75M settlement demand despite the $0.25 liability shift that settlement causes. Coverage for litigation expenses is, however, only a partial corrective. If the defense's trial expenses are instead projected to be less than $0.25M, then Insurer is still better off rejecting Plaintiff's actuarially fair settlement demand.

To further deter undersettlement, courts in most jurisdictions have held that liability insurers are subject to settlement duties. Under the traditional articulation of the 'duty to settle', a liability insurer forfeits its policy limit in a covered suit, making it liable for the full damages awarded at trial, if it acted negligently by rejecting a 'reasonable' within-limit settlement demand. As an alternative route to the same result, courts in some jurisdictions have held that an insurer in such a case acts in bad faith and thus breaches the implied covenant of good faith and fair dealing. The courts of all but two US states have recognized a duty to settle along such lines (Stempel 2006). California combines the standards, with 'good faith' defined to require acceptance of reasonable settlement demands. *PPG Industries* v. *Transamerica Ins. Co.*, 975 P. 2d 652, 659 (Cal. 1999).

Several scholars have argued that courts should dispense with the reasonableness standard when enforcing the duty to settle. They argue that courts should instead apply a strict-liability rule, under which the insurer would automatically become liable for excess damages in a covered suit whenever it rejected a within-limit settlement demand (Keeton 1954; Peterson 1966; Schwartz 1975).[3] Such a rule would fully correct the undersettlement problem: once the plaintiff made a within-limit demand, strict liability would shift all defense costs to the insurer, thereby merging the

---

[3] Scholars who discuss the duty to settle often assume that the private goal of minimizing total defense costs advances the social goal of maximizing total wealth. An exception is Meurer (1992), who observed that insurers not bound by a duty to settle might have an advantage in settlement negotiations that benefits their policyholders but that, though lower total settlement amounts, could lead to underdeterrence of torts. Meurer's analysis assumes that policyholders cannot be drawn into settlement discussions, an assumption that Sykes (1994b) questioned.

insurer's individual interest in minimizing its liability with the insurer's and policyholder's joint interest in minimizing total defense costs. Therefore, a strict-liability version of the duty to settle would induce insurers to accept settlement demands that are less than the expected total defense costs of trial. In the lawsuit summarized in Table 14.2, a strict-liability rule would induce Insurer to accept Plaintiff's \$0.75M demand, which would be the cost-minimizing result.

Besides neutralizing the undersettlement hazard, a strict-liability duty to settle also avoids the overpayment hazard, provided that the insurer retains exclusive control over the settlement decision. Even when subject to strict liability, a profit-maximizing insurer will reject settlement demands that exceed the expected total defense costs of trial. For example, if Plaintiff in our hypothetical lawsuit demands \$0.9M, and the defense's projected trial expenses are \$0.1M, then Insurer will reject the demand because the expected total defense costs of trial are only \$0.85M.

In theory, courts could achieve the same harmony of interests through a well-designed reasonableness standard that required insurers to accept only those settlement demands which are less than the expected total costs to the defense of a trial. Properly enforced, such a standard would similarly induce insurers to minimize total defense costs. But such a standard is unnecessary because strict liability achieves the same result without judicial second-guessing of rejected settlement demands. In this way, a strict-liability version of the duty to settle would be self-regulating. Besides being superfluous, the reasonableness standard is costly: it encourages follow-up lawsuits against insurers, and it introduces the risk of legal error. A judge or jury could underestimate the expected trial costs and thereby fail to hold the insurer liable for the above-limit damages. Anticipating this possibility, insurers will reject some settlement opportunities that would have minimized total defense costs, and the undersettlement hazard will persist. In addition, insurers will expend resources documenting the 'reasonableness' of their settlement decisions. All of these costs of enforcing a reasonableness (or good faith) standard ultimately drive up the cost of liability insurance.

An important exception to the conclusion that strict liability induces insurers to minimize total defense costs occurs when the above-limit potential damages exceed the policyholder's recoverable personal assets.[4] To see why, imagine in our hypothetical lawsuit that Policyholder has

[4] State statutes place some personal property out of the reach of creditors, and these refuges are respected by the federal Bankruptcy Code (11 U.S.C. § 522; Baker 2001).

\$0.2M in recoverable personal wealth in addition to her \$1M liability policy. The expected *recoverable* damages if the case goes to trial are now only 50 percent x \$1.2M = \$0.6M, even though the expected damages *award* remains \$0.75M. Therefore, Insurer would minimize expected total defense costs by rejecting the settlement demand of \$0.75M, assuming that the defense's projected trial expenses are less than \$0.15M. Yet a strict-liability rule would induce Insurer to accept the \$0.75M demand. Because this result would not minimize total defense costs, its possibility would drive up insurance premiums, causing some would-be tortfeasors to buy less coverage (Logue 1994). Anticipating this concern, Schwartz (1975) proposed to modify the strict-liability rule to cap the plaintiff's above-limit recovery, payable by the insurer if it rejected a within-limit settlement demand, at the value of the policyholder's recoverable assets. In 1990, the Michigan Supreme Court adopted a version of Schwartz's proposal in the case *Frankenmuth Mutual Insurance Co.* v. *Keeley*, 461 N.W. 2d 666, 667 (Mich. 1990). To date, courts in most other states have not done the same, making the 'Michigan Rule' the minority approach (Logue 1994).[5]

As modified by the Michigan Rule, the strict-liability version of the duty to settle has much to recommend it. When a plaintiff offers to settle within the policy limit, the rule resolves the defense-side conflict of interests with a minimum of enforcement costs. Despite this self-regulating virtue, parties do not write the rule into liability policies. Why not? One answer offered by Syverud (1990) is that strict liability could lead plaintiffs, immediately upon filing a lawsuit, to offer to settle at the policy limit, thereby triggering the insurer's above-limit liability. Such a strategy would, however, be risky for plaintiffs in many cases. If the expected damages exceed the policy limit (and hence the settlement demand) and the policyholder has recoverable personal assets, the strategy will backfire: the insurer will accept the demand, leaving the plaintiff with less than its expected trial recovery. And if the expected damages are less than the policy limit (and hence the settlement demand), the insurer will reject the demand, forcing the plaintiff to make a more reasonable offer that would also have triggered strict liability if made initially. The outcome might be different if the plaintiff makes his demand so quickly that the insurer lacks time to appraise the lawsuit. But that possibility could be accommodated by modifying the rule so that a

---

[5] By reducing payouts to some tort victims, the Michigan Rule could reduce tort deterrence. As, however, Logue (1994) observed, the Michigan Rule also makes insurance cheaper per dollar of coverage, inducing some would-be tortfeasors to buy more coverage than they would otherwise.

within-limit demand triggers strict liability only if the insurer has sufficient time to investigate the case before responding.

In liability policies sold to individuals (as opposed to corporations), there is a second possible reason for parties' failure to adopt a strict-liability rule by contract. Baker (2001) observed that most plaintiffs and their lawyers are loath to collect damages not covered by insurance. Colloquially, damages that the defendant must pay out of her own pocket are 'blood money', suggesting that plaintiffs who seek them desire not just compensation but also vengeance. Accordingly, most plaintiffs' attorneys try to seize a defendant's personal assets only if the defendant committed an egregious tort or deliberately underinsured.

Given this 'blood money' taboo, individual policyholders might derive little benefit from a strict-liability version of the duty to settle. That rule would reduce the likelihood that defendants rather than their insurers are legally responsible for above-limit damages. But if plaintiffs rarely force defendants to pay above-limit damages anyway, a strict-liability rule would raise costs for liability insurers without providing a commensurate benefit to policyholders. The rule would thus increase total defense costs, and parties would reasonably choose not to adopt it by contract. This explanation for the status quo applies only to insurance sold to individuals, as there is no indication that plaintiffs' attorneys are squeamish about extracting 'blood money' from corporate defendants.

A final possible reason that parties have not adopted strict liability by contract is that courts, despite speaking of 'reasonableness' and 'good faith', in fact rarely rule for the insurer in classic duty-to-settle cases. In other words, making strict liability explicit may be unnecessary because insurers already face strict liability de facto. Evidence for this explanation comes from interviews with trial attorneys, who report that courts almost always hold the insurer liable for the full damages award if the insurer previously rejected a within-limit settlement demand (Baker 2001). Hindsight bias might be at work here: after the plaintiff has won an above-limit damages award, the insurer could find it difficult to convince a judge or jury that its earlier rejection of a within-limit settlement demand was reasonable. Indeed, the California Supreme Court has explicitly endorsed hindsight bias, holding that the fact of an above-limit damages award supports an inference that accepting a within-limit demand would have been 'the most reasonable method of dealing with the claim' (*Crisci* v. *Sec. Ins. Co.*, 426 P. 2d 652, 173, 177 (Cal. 1967)).

De facto strict insurer liability for excess damages may be a good rule in Scenario A given the absence of an overpayment hazard. The risk, however, is that courts will adopt a similar anti-insurer bias in the other three scenarios analyzed in this chapter, in which strict liability would lead to overcompensation because, in those scenarios, policyholders and excess insurers have a say in settlement negotiations. Exacerbating this risk is the failure of most courts and commentators to distinguish clearly among the different situations in which settlement conflict arises.

IV. SCENARIO B: WITHIN-LIMIT DEMAND, POST-SETTLEMENT CONTEXT

A second scenario in which insurers face liability under the duty to settle is when the insurer rejects a within-limit settlement demand in a covered suit but then, instead of proceeding to a verdict, the case settles because the policyholder steps in and pays the demand herself. She then sues the insurer for reimbursement. What should the insurer's liability be in that case, if anything?

As we saw in the previous section, authorizing a policyholder (or excess insurer) to settle a covered lawsuit replaces the undersettlement hazard with the overpayment hazard. In the suit summarized in Table 14.2, Policyholder would rationally accept any settlement demand up to \$1M as long as she can shift the cost to Insurer via the duty to settle. Unless, however, the defense's projected trial expenses are at least \$0.25M, a \$1M settlement would exceed the expected total defense costs of a trial.

This example illustrates how the self-regulating virtue that strict liability exhibits in Scenario A disappears in Scenario B. Holding the insurer strictly liable for within-limit settlement demands paid by the policyholder would encourage plaintiff overcompensation because the party accepting the plaintiff's demand (the policyholder) would not bear the cost. Accordingly, liability policies that give the insurer a duty to defend typically prohibit the policyholder from settling, except at her own expense. Enforcing such provisions as written seems to have much to commend it. If courts instead insisted upon a bright-line rule of strict insurer liability for within-limit settlements, they would not only contravene defense-side parties' common interest in minimizing total defense costs, but they would also impose costs on third parties. Strict insurer liability in Scenario-B cases would encourage settlements that overcompensate plaintiffs relative to expected damages, thereby encouraging more tort suits than are necessary to deter undesirable conduct.

Moreover, if the duty to settle were governed by a strict-liability rule in Scenario A (the post-judgment context), then the rationale for *any* settlement duty in Scenario B (the post-settlement context) would disappear. Strict insurer liability in the post-judgment context would ensure the policyholder's immunity whenever the plaintiff made a within-limit demand.

The policyholder would therefore have no justification for entering into her own within-limit settlement and then sending the bill to the insurer. In this way, a rule of *no liability* for Scenario B is a natural corollary of a rule of *strict liability* for Scenario A.

Under current law, however, the policyholder's position in Scenario B is not so secure. When her insurer rejects a within-limit demand, she faces the risk of above-limit liability because a judge or jury might find that the insurer acted reasonably (or in good faith). Hindsight bias shrinks this risk but might not eliminate it. An especially risk-averse policyholder might therefore decide that, to protect herself, she should pay the plaintiff's settlement demand out of her own pocket. Should she then be allowed to force the insurer to reimburse her? Policy provisions that give insurers exclusive settlement authority imply that the answer is no. But some judges might nonetheless conclude that the parties did not really intend to force the policyholder to choose between two unattractive options: meeting a within-limit settlement demand at her own expense; or running the risk of an above-limit damages ward at trial, after which she would have to sue her insurer in order to learn whether she is liable for the excess damages. Given that courts have not formally adopted a strict liability rule for Scenario A, some judges might reason that the parties contemplated suits for reimbursement – subject to a reasonableness standard (to counteract the overpayment hazard) – in Scenario B.

The contractual (though not economic) analysis changes when the policyholder retains the right to defend the lawsuit, as is typical in D&O policies. While such policies allow the policyholder to negotiate settlements of covered lawsuits, they require the policyholder to obtain the insurer's consent to any settlement amount. The insurer's veto power is restricted, however, because policies also provide that the insurer's consent will not be 'unreasonably withheld' (Baker and Griffith 2010). At least some courts have interpreted such policies to contemplate policyholder lawsuits for reimbursement of settlements that the insurer rejected, subject to review under the reasonableness standard to police the overpayment hazard. But courts might not apply the standard evenhandedly: pro-settlement bias among judges, and anti-insurer sentiment among juries, could tip the scales toward policyholders, leading to settlements that overcompensate plaintiffs.

The Second Circuit's decision in *Schwartz* v. *Liberty Mutual Insurance Co.*, 539 F. 3d 135 (2d Cir. 2008), illustrates how courts seem to be unaware of the overpayment hazard when they enforce the duty to settle in the post-settlement context. A securities class action was brought against a corporate CEO protected by a D&O insurance tower that provided $50 million in total coverage. The insurers and plaintiffs failed to reach a settlement agreement before trial. On the day before he was scheduled to testify, the CEO paid the plaintiffs' $20 million settlement demand by personal check. He then sued the first four insurers in the tower for reimbursement, arguing that their failure to meet the settlement demand themselves reflected bad faith. The case presented a large overpayment hazard because the settlement demand was well within the tower's overall coverage limit, leaving the CEO little incentive to negotiate for a lower figure. But in its opinion affirming a jury verdict for the CEO, the Second Circuit made no mention of the overpayment hazard. Instead, the court treated the case as no different from a classic duty-to-settle case, and it cited opinions from post-judgment cases describing how policy limits can discourage insurers from settling. In other words, the court seemed unaware that post-settlement cases (Scenario B) raise a hazard not present in post-judgment cases (Scenario A). If the judges who approve jury instructions are not cognizant of the overpayment hazard, there is little chance that juries will heed the hazard when deciding whether insurers must reimburse policyholders for within-limit settlements.

V. SCENARIO C: ABOVE-LIMIT DEMAND, POST-JUDGMENT CONTEXT

In the two scenarios considered so far, the plaintiff makes a within-limit settlement demand, implicating the traditional duty to settle. Settlement dynamics under that duty are relatively straightforward, suggesting a pair of bright-line rules to govern it: strict insurer liability for excess damages in the post-judgment context; no insurer liability in the post-settlement context. When, however, the plaintiff's settlement demand exceeds the primary policy limit, settlement dynamics change. Following a previous article (Squire 2012), this chapter will use the term 'duty to contribute' to refer to insurer settlement duties in these scenarios. The duty to contribute is implicated when the plaintiff makes an above-limit settlement demand, the policyholder (or excess insurer) offers to pay the above-limit portion, but the insurer refuses to participate. The case could then go to trial and produce an above-limit damages award. The insurer is then clearly liability up to its policy limit, but should it have to pay the excess?

To see each party's settlement incentives in this context, it will be useful to consider again the hypothetical lawsuit involving Insurer, Policyholder, and Plaintiff, but now to assume that the potential damages are $3M rather than $1.5M. We will continue to assume that Plaintiff has a 50 percent chance of a favorable verdict and that the policy limit is $1M. The distribution of expected liability is presented in Table 14.3.

Table 14.3 Liability distribution, above-limit demand

	Expected trial liability	Liability in a settlement for the expected damages	Benefit (cost) of settling
Insurer ($1M limit)	$0.5M	$1.0M	($0.5M)
Policyholder/excess insurer	$1.0M	$0.5M	$0.5M
Total	$1.5M	$1.5M	–

Pre-trial settlement for the lawsuit's actuarially fair value ($1.5M) would once again increase liability for Insurer relative to its expected trial liability: Insurer would have to pay $1M (its policy amount) toward the settlement, whereas its expected trial liability is only $0.5M (plus trial expenses). This hypothetical lawsuit shows that a primary insurer is undermotivated to settle when the trial outcome is uncertain and the potential damages exceed its policy limit, regardless of whether the expected damages – and hence the plaintiff's likely settlement demand – are above or below the limit. As was true in Scenario A, a no-liability rule for Insurer in Scenario C would be untenable. Some mechanism is needed to deter Insurer from rejecting settlement opportunities that would minimize expected total defense costs.

Recognizing this problem, Schwartz (1975), who first proposed what came to be known as the Michigan Rule, also proposed a strict-liability rule for cases implicating the duty to contribute (although he did not use that term). He argued that an insurer should be held strictly liable for the full damages award in a covered lawsuit if it rejected an above-limit settlement demand when the policyholder was willing to pay the above-limit portion. In the lawsuit summarized in Table 14.3, Schwartz's proposal would make Insurer strictly liable for the full $3M in potential damages if Plaintiff demanded $1.5M, and Policyholder offered to contribute the above-limit portion of $0.5M, but Insurer rejected the demand, sending the case to trial.

If, however, we assume a savvier plaintiff, we see that such a strict-liability rule for Scenario C would, like a no-liability rule, be untenable. Assume now that Plaintiff demands $1.9M, well more than the expected damages. If Insurer were subject to strict liability as per Schwartz's proposal, Policyholder would accept that demand because her settlement liability would then be $0.9M, as contrasted with her $1M expected trial liability. Moreover, once Policyholder indicated her willingness to settle, a strict-liability version of the duty to contribute would induce Insurer to contribute its $1M policy limit as well. Insurer would do this to avoid its expected trial liability, which under the strict-liability rule would be the full expected damages of \$1.5M plus trial expenses. Yet a \$1.9M settlement fails to minimize expected total defense costs if the defense's projected trial expenses are less than \$0.4M. Strict liability would therefore replace the undersettlement hazard with the overpayment hazard, generating excessive settlement amounts and driving up insurance premiums (Squire 2012).

A possible objection to this critique of a strict-liability rule for Scenario C is that Plaintiff's \$1.9M demand is not credible given the expected damages of only \$1.5M. Policyholder should be able to negotiate Plaintiff down to that amount, saving herself \$0.4M. (Indeed, Plaintiff should be willing to settle for even less to avoid his own trial expenses.) By the same token, however, Policyholder's rejection of the \$1.9M demand is not credible; that demand would require her to pay \$0.9M, while her expected trial liability is \$1.0M. Plaintiff therefore should be able to negotiate her *up* to a \$2.0M total settlement. In fact, any settlement between \$1.5M and \$2.0M would make both Plaintiff and Policyholder better off relative to trial. The range is \$0.5M wide because that is the liability that the parties are able to shift to Insurer, relative to Insurer's expected trial liability, by settling. Looked at another way, Plaintiff can save Policyholder up to \$0.5M by agreeing with her to settle pre-verdict, as long as she can shift \$1M in settlement liability to Insurer. Plaintiff and Policyholder therefore will negotiate to split between themselves this \$0.5M value transfer, with the division depending on their relative bargaining power. Only at the bottom of the range – where Policyholder captures the full transfer for herself – is Plaintiff not overpaid relative to the expected damages.

We see that neither a strict-liability rule nor a no-liability rule avails in Scenario C. A duty to contribute is needed to correct the undersettlement hazard, but liability must be conditioned on judicial review of the settlement demand to police the overpayment hazard. Therefore, follow-up lawsuits to enforce a reasonableness standard, which appear unnecessary in duty-to-settle cases, seem unavoidable in duty-to-contribute cases, at least in the post-judgment context.

Although the volume of case law addressing Scenario C is thin, the few relevant judicial opinions suggest that courts are unaware of the overpayment hazard. An example is *Ranger Insurance Co.* v. *Travelers Indemnity Co.*, 389 So. 2d. 272 (Fla. Ct. App. 1980), which involved coverage for injuries caused by one of the policyholder's employees. The policyholder had a \$100,000 primary policy and an excess policy. The primary insurer rejected a \$125,000 settlement demand even though the excess insurer was willing to pay the portion above the primary limit. After a jury verdict for

$170,000, the excess insurer sued the primary insurer for bad faith refusal to settle, seeking reimbursement for the $70,000 in excess liability. The trial judge dismissed the complaint. On appeal, the court held first that the primary insurer's duty of good faith, normally owed to the policyholder, could be enforced by the excess insurer through equitable subrogation. The court then held that the case could proceed to trial even though the plaintiff had not offered to settle within the primary policy: the primary insurer could be held liable merely for failing to participate in a settlement in which its own liability would not have exceeded its policy amount. Notably, the *Ranger* court did not mention the overpayment hazard lurking in the case before it. But without understanding that hazard, a court cannot frame a standard of review (regardless of whether labeled as 'good faith' or 'reasonableness') that encourages socially optimal results.

Ranger is a typical duty-to-contribute case in that it was brought by an excess insurer rather than a policyholder. But it is unusual in that it occurred in the post-judgment context. Most suits seeking to enforce the duty to contribute arise in the post-settlement context, discussed next.

VI. SCENARIO D: ABOVE-LIMIT DEMAND, POST-SETTLEMENT CONTEXT

Scenario D, like Scenario C, begins with the primary insurer's rejection of an above-limit settlement demand in a covered lawsuit. Instead, however, of proceeding to a judgment at trial, this time the suit settles because the excess insurer (or, less often, the policyholder) pays the plaintiff's demand itself. Which liability rule for the primary insurer minimizes expected total defense costs: strict liability, liability subject to a reasonableness standard, or no liability?

We will consider strict liability first because it is the easiest to analyze. As shown in the previous section, a strict-liability version of the duty to contribute encourages settlements that overcompensate plaintiffs. In the case summarized in Table 14.3, if Policyholder can use the duty to force Insurer to contribute $1M (Insurer's policy amount), then she could accept a settlement demand of $1.9M and still reduce her expected liability relative to trial. But $1.9M exceeds the expected total defense costs of trial whenever the defense's projected trial expenses are less than $0.4M. Therefore, strict liability leads to plaintiff overcompensation in Scenario D, just as it does in Scenario C.

Consistent with this conclusion is the fact that courts in most Scenario-D cases have held that insurers have a duty to contribute subject to a reasonableness or good-faith standard. When the policyholder retains the right to defend, as is true in most D&O policies, the policy's 'reasonable consent' provision implies that the parties contemplated post-settlement lawsuits to enforce the duty to contribute. When, however, the policy assigns the insurer a duty to defend, the contractual basis for a duty to contribute is murkier, as such policies do not require the insurer to pay for settlements (reasonable or not) to which it did not consent. Yet most courts in Scenario-D cases have subjected the insurer to liability even without an express contractual foundation. An example is *Continental Casualty Co.* v. *Reserve Insurance Co.*, 238 N.W. 2d 862 (Minn. 1976), which followed from a lawsuit against a liquor-store owner under a dram-shop law. The store owner had a $50,000 primary liability policy and an excess policy. After the primary insurer declined the excess insurer's invitation to contribute to a settlement, the excess insurer settled the case for $200,000 and sued the primary insurer for the primary policy amount. The Supreme Court of Minnesota held that the excess insurer could, through its right of subrogation, sue the primary insurer for breaching its duty to the policyholder to evaluate settlement demands in good faith. And the court further held that the primary insurer could be liable even though there was no verdict against the policyholder in the covered lawsuit. Once again, the court did not mention the overpayment hazard. Most other courts in Scenario-D cases have agreed that the primary insurer is liable if it acted unreasonably or in bad faith. See, e.g., *Westerhol* v. *20th Century Ins. Co.*, 130 Cal. Rptr. 164, 165 (Ct. App. 1976); *Fireman's Fund Ins. Co.* v. *Sec. Ins. Co. of Hartford*, 367 A. 2d 864, 869 (N.J. 1976); *Evans* v. *Cont'l Cas. Co.*, 245 P. 2d 470, 479 (Wash. 1952).

Although courts have not explicitly recognized the overpayment hazard in duty-to-contribute cases, their general preference for some kind of insurer settlement duty in those cases, subject to a reasonableness standard, has much to recommend it. As we saw in the discussion of Scenario C, the underpayment hazard is present when the plaintiff's settlement demand exceeds the coverage limit, just as is true when the offer is within the limit. Thus, liability insurers should be subject to a settlement duty of some kind, but the duty should be tempered by a reasonableness standard to police the overpayment hazard.

A Virginia appeals court reached the contrary conclusion in *Sentry Ins.* v. *U.S. Fidelity & Guaranty Co.*, No. LF-2387-4, 2000 WL 288467 (Va. Cir. Ct. Mar. 15, 2000). The court categorically rejected insurer liability in the post-settlement context, holding that liability under any settlement duty requires an above-limit damages award in the covered lawsuit. The holding raises the question whether the threat of liability in Scenario C suffices to overcome insurers' reluctance to settle, making suits against insurers in Scenario D unnecessary.

There is good reason to think that a no-liability rule is not optimal for Scenario D, even though it might be the right rule for Scenario B, the other post-settlement scenario. The argument for a no-liability rule in Scenario B is strongest if a strict liability rule governs Scenario A. As, however, we saw in the last section, a strict-liability rule in Scenario C would result in plaintiff overcompensation. For this reason, Scenario D and Scenario B are not exactly parallel. In addition, we might expect judicial assessments of the reasonableness of settlement demands to be more accurate in the post-settlement context because, unlike in the post-judgment context, there is no danger of hindsight bias caused by an above-limit damages award. For these reasons, the rule provided by *Sentry* may be contrary to the common interests of defense-side parties.

Table 14.4 Defense-cost-minimizing insurer settlement duties (collective settlements)

	Post-judgment context	Post-settlement context
Within-limit demand (duty to settle)	Strict excess liability (capped for limited policyholder wealth)	No liability
Above-limit demand (duty to contribute)	Excess liability under reasonableness standard	Within-limit liability under reasonableness standard

Table 14.4 summarizes this chapter's conclusions so far. It indicates that the right rule for resolving the conflict of interests in collective settlements of covered lawsuits depends on two distinctions: whether the total settlement demand was within the policy limit; and whether the lawsuit produced an above-limit damages award or instead settled pre-verdict. But judicial opinions do not apply these distinctions when defining insurer settlement duties. Instead, courts typically invoke a generic 'duty to settle' that extends to all four scenarios.

Why do liability policies not define the insurer's settlement duties in context-specific terms like those in Table 14.4? Given that most scholarly literature on settlement conflict also does not distinguish among Table 14.4's scenarios, nor recognize how strict liability is appropriate for only one of them, one possibility is that most insurance buyers do not understand how the defense-side conflict of interests changes across the scenarios, making it difficult for insurers to charge premiums that capture the benefits of duty differentiation.

As the header for Table 14.4 indicates, the analysis summarized there presupposes the collective approach to settlements. We reach different conclusions about the need for insurer settlement duties if we allow each defense-side party to settle with the plaintiff separately, as discussed next.

VII. ELIMINATING THE COLLECTIVE-ACTION PROBLEM THROUGH SEGMENTED SETTLEMENTS

When the settlement of a covered lawsuit is collective, the primary insurer's settlement payment to the plaintiff often includes compensation for a release of the plaintiff's right to collect damages which, if awarded at trial, would be the responsibility of an excess insurer or the policyholder. In essence, the primary insurer assumes at least some of these parties' liability burden by settling. It is this shift in liability that introduces the conflict of interests which settlement duties target. But settlements would not shift liability to the primary insurer if each defense-side party settled separately with the plaintiff. Under a 'segmented' approach, each defense-side party would bargain for a release of the plaintiff's right to collect any damages which would be that defense-side party's responsibility if awarded at trial. Were parties to settle in that way, each defense-side party's settlement liability would match its expected liability to the plaintiff at trial. Settlement negotiations would be burdened by neither an undersettlement hazard nor an overpayment hazard, and settlement duties could be scrapped (Squire 2012).

As an illustration, consider again the lawsuit summarized in Table 14.2, in which Policyholder owns a $1M policy (with no deductible), Plaintiff has a 50 percent chance of winning at trial, and the potential damages are $1.5M. Under the collective approach, an actuarially fair settlement of $0.75M shifts $0.25M in expected liability from Policyholder to Insurer, introducing the conflict of interests that calls for a duty to settle. But if settlements were segmented, no conflict would arise. In negotiating with Plaintiff, Insurer and Policyholder would seek to settle only their respective segments of the range of potential damages. Neither would have the power to bind the other in settlement, nor would either require the other's consent to settle. Plaintiff would therefore submit separate settlement demands to each. Upon settling with Insurer, Plaintiff would release his right to collect the first $1M of any damages award, this being Insurer's liability segment. And in settling with Policyholder, Plaintiff would waive his right to collect any damages *above* the first $1M, which constitute

Policyholder's slice of the potential damages range.[6] Trial would occur unless both defense-side parties settled. If Plaintiff made actuarially fair settlement demands of $0.5M and $0.25M to Insurer and Policyholder, respectively, each presumably would settle to avoid trial expenses (the allocation of which is discussed below). Because the settlement demand submitted to each defense-side party equals that party's expected liability to Plaintiff at trial, there is no conflict of interests resulting from the $1M policy limit and hence no need to subject Insurer to a duty to settle.

A similar analysis applies to Table 14.3's lawsuit, which is like Table 14.2's except that the potential damages are $3M rather than $1.5M. Assuming equal bargaining power, Plaintiff would enter into two separate pre-trial settlements with Insurer and Policyholder, with Insurer paying its expected trial liability of $0.5M (excluding expenses) and Policyholder paying her expected trial liability of $1.0M. Plaintiff would therefore collect his case's actuarially fair value of $1.5M. Because there would be neither an undersettlement hazard nor an underpayment hazard, there would be no need for a duty to contribute and hence no need for expensive and error-prone lawsuits over the reasonableness of rejected settlement demands.

At first glance, the segmented approach seems to increase Policyholder's settlement liability, undermining insurance's risk-spreading function. This perception arises from the inability under the segmented approach for a policyholder or excess insurer to use settlement duties to shift liability to the primary insurer. But the perception is misleading because parties would adjust policy limits upon adopting the segmented approach. Since settlements would no longer shift liability to primary insurers, primary policies would be cheaper per dollar of coverage. (Note how, in the last hypothetical lawsuit, Insurer pays $1.0M under the collective approach but only $0.5M under the segmented approach.) Policyholders could therefore buy primary policies with higher limits without having to pay

---

[6] French (2013) criticized the segmented approach by arguing that, after a policyholder settled her segment separately, the lawsuit against her would lack a defendant and thus be tried against an 'empty chair'. Technically, however, the policyholder would still be the defendant; she simply would have no liability for above-limit damages. Practically, then, the situation would be the same as a case in which the potential damages are within the policy limit. In either case, the policyholder still has an incentive to aid the insurer in mounting a defense, as otherwise she could forfeit coverage through breach of the cooperation clause that all liability policies contain (Plitt, Maldanado, and Rogers 2011). Liability policies would continue to include cooperation clauses if settlements were segmented, as otherwise insurance would be costlier and hence potentially unaffordable, just as is true if the clauses were omitted now.

higher premiums. Once policy limits adjusted upward, overall policyholder exposure would be the same.

Indeed, the segmented approach's efficiencies would enable policyholders to buy *more* coverage per dollar in premiums than they can now. Under the collective approach, the parties to insurance contracts ultimately bear the various costs of enforcing settlement duties, reducing the joint surplus. Liability insurers could provide coverage more cheaply if they did not have to litigate over settlement duties or document the reasonableness of their settlement decisions. Lower costs would translate into lower premiums, allowing for more coverage per dollar spent by policyholders.

How would parties allocate responsibility for the defense's litigation expenses if settlements were segmented? We can predict that liability policies would be written to incorporate two principles: first, that the insurer's coverage for expenses does not count toward the policy limit; second, that the insurer has no further responsibility for litigation expenses after it settles separately. These principles would preserve the insurer's incentive to settle in order to avoid trial expenses. Within that framework, parties could allocate responsibility for expenses in various ways. For example, policies might provide that the insurers in a tower who have yet to settle will bear litigation expenses pro rata (or by some other formula). Alternatively, the rule might be that the primary insurer must cover expenses until it settles, at which point responsibility shifts to the lowest-level defense-side party who remains in the case. Under either approach, each defense-side party would both impose a burden and confer a benefit on the others by settling separately. The burden would be increased potential responsibility for expenses. But this increased responsibility would be salutary because it would force parties to internalize the costs of their choice not to settle. The benefit conferred by settling would be a reduction in the plaintiff's potential trial recovery, which would make the plaintiff more eager to settle the remaining segments in order to avoid his own trial expenses (Squire 2012).

Why, despite its advantages, have parties not adopted the segmented approach by contract? There is little reason to think that courts would refuse to enforce the approach if written into liability policies, at least as long as the policyholder were given clear notice that the insurer had the right to settle separately.[7] Indeed, one court – in an admittedly old

[7] Courts have recently interpreted language in excess policies to permit liability for the excess insurer only when the underlying insurers have paid their full policy amounts. See, e.g., *Comerica Inc.* v. *Zurich Am. Ins. Co.*, 498 F.Supp. 2d 1019, 1034 (E.D. Mich. 2007). This interpretation is incompatible with segmented settlements, which require that each defense-side party be able to settle without affecting the

case – opined that a contract provision which *prohibited* the policyholder from settling separately in exchange for a release of above-limit liability would be void as against public policy. *General Accident, Fire & Life Assurance Corp., Ltd.* v. *Louisville Home Telephone Co.*, 193 S.W. 1031, 1034 (Ky. Ct. App. 1917).

With respect to liability insurance sold to individuals rather than corporations, one possible explanation for the persistence of the collective approach is a lack of sophistication among insurance buyers. Since, however, policies that adopted the approach would carry lower premiums per dollar of coverage, the approach's efficiency would be 'explained' to buyers directly through the price mechanism, making it unlikely that such policies would be entirely unmarketable.

Another possible concern, which again applies only to liability insurance sold to individuals, relates to the question of who would pay for the continuing litigation expenses when the insurer has settled out of the case but the policyholder has not. Policies could specify that the insurer must then continue to pay for the defense attorney, a solution consistent with the insurer's standard duty to defend. But this solution would blunt the insurer's salutary incentive to settle separately as a way of avoiding litigation expenses. To address this problem, the policyholder could buy a separate policy that covered her continuing litigation expenses after her liability insurer had settled. Such coverage would, however, introduce a moral hazard by encouraging the policyholder to overspend on her defense. The expenses-only insurer could temper this hazard by capping coverage at a fixed amount or percentage, but this solution would attenuate insurance's risk-spreading benefit. The possibility – however small – that the policyholder might have to pay some portion of her attorneys' fees might make the segmented approach unattractive to some individual insurance buyers, notwithstanding the approach's countervailing efficiencies.

Such concerns cannot, however, explain the persistence of the collective approach in lawsuits against corporate policyholders. Liability policies sold to corporations already risk overspending on attorneys by giving the policyholder control of the defense.[8] And, because such policies cap

---

other parties' liability to the plaintiff. The question is, however, purely contractual, and excess policies could be rewritten to permit the segmented approach.

[8] D&O policies try to deter overspending by requiring the insurer's consent to the policyholder's choice of lawyer and by counting expense coverage cumulatively with liability coverage toward the policy limit (Baker and Griffith, 2010). The first of these correctives could be preserved under the segmented approach, and the second could be conformed to it by having separate policy limits for liability and expenses.

coverage for litigation expenses, they also already countenance the possibility that the policyholder will have to pay some of its attorneys' fees.

With respect to D&O insurance in particular, principal-agent conflict between managers and shareholders in public corporations could explain why settlements remain collective. Corporate managers prefer that shareholder lawsuits settle before reaching trial. Unflattering information can come to light at trial, and the judge or jury could find that the managers acted in bad faith in the transaction that is the subject of the lawsuit, disqualifying them from indemnification by the corporation for their personal liability. And, in addition to preferring to avoid trial, managers would rather that the insurer, instead of the corporation, pay for any settlement. A settlement paid by the corporation could dent reported earnings and reduce the managers' performance-based pay (Squire 2012).

Even, however, when the corporation has D&O coverage, its insurers will resist settling if they think the plaintiff is demanding more than his case is worth, or that a verdict could trigger a policy exclusion. The managers will then be stuck between two bad options: allow the case to reach trial, or agree to a settlement that reduces reported earnings. The duty to contribute can rescue managers from that tight spot. Because it transfers liability to the primary insurer, the duty increases excess insurers' willingness to settle.[9] In some cases, the liability shift could be large enough to induce an excess insurer to accept a settlement demand even though it thinks the plaintiff has overvalued his case or that a trial could excuse it from coverage altogether. If, however, settlements were segmented, the conflict of interest that justifies the duty to contribute would disappear. This analysis suggests a reason why managers of public corporations might prefer the status quo (Squire 2012).

A final possibility, of course, is that the segmented approach has drawbacks that those who study insurance law have yet to identify.

VIII. CONCLUSION

The collective-action problem in negotiations to settle lawsuits against defendants with liability insurance is both hard and easy to solve. It is

---

[9] French (2013) noted that excess insurers are often reluctant to settle or to pay their full policy amounts, an observation that supports the hypothesis that managers would rather preserve the duty to contribute – and hence collective settlements – as a device for overcoming such resistance.

hard to solve under the current practice whereby all defense-side parties (defendants and their liability insurers) negotiate toward a single, collectively binding settlement amount. When a settlement is collective, the primary insurer often pays the plaintiff to release the right to recover damages that, if awarded at trial, would be the responsibility of an excess insurer or the policyholder. As a result, the primary insurer's settlement liability often exceeds its expected trial liability, making it reluctant to settle. For the same reason, the policyholder is overeager to settle. The excess insurers, if any, align with either the primary insurer or the policyholder, depending on where the potential and expected damages fall within the insurance tower.

To overcome primary insurers' disinclination to settle, courts could hold that a liability insurer automatically forfeits its policy limit if it declined an opportunity to settle for no more than its policy amount. But this strict-liability rule would correct the collective-action problem only in cases in which the insurer first rejected a within-limit settlement demand and then the plaintiff won an above-limit damages award at trial. In other cases – when the plaintiff's total settlement demand exceeds the policy limit, or when the policyholder settles without the insurer's consent – strict liability would encourage settlements that overcompensate plaintiffs. To prevent plaintiff overcompensation in such cases, the insurer's settlement duty needs to be tempered by a reasonableness standard. But that standard generates costs of its own, including additional litigation, insurer documentation efforts, and the risk of judicial error.

The collective-action problem in covered lawsuits is *easy* to solve in the sense that it is artificial, a byproduct of the choice to settle lawsuits collectively. No statute or other principle of positive law requires that settlements of covered lawsuits be collective. As an alternative, each defense-side party could bargain separately with the plaintiff for a release of the plaintiff's right to collect any damages that, if awarded at trial, would be that defense-side party's responsibility. This 'segmented' approach avoids the liability shift that makes some defense-side parties reluctant, and others overeager, to settle. Each defense-side party would settle if, and only if, doing so would reduce expected total defense costs. Settlement duties could be discarded because there would be no conflict of interests for them to resolve. This chapter has offered several potential explanations for why, despite this seemingly more efficient option, defendants and their liability insurers persist in an approach to settlements that produces an avoidable collective-action problem.

REFERENCES

Baker, T. 2001. 'Blood Money, New Money, and the Moral Economy of Tort Law in Action' 36 *Law & Society Review* 275–320.

Baker, T., and S. Griffith. 2010. *Ensuring Corporate Conduct: How Liability Insurance Undermines Shareholder Litigation*. Chicago, IL: University of Chicago Press 53, 140, 144.

French, C. C. 2013. 'Segmented Settlements are Not the Answer: A Response to Professor Squire's Article, *How Collective Settlements Camouflage the Costs of Shareholder Lawsuits*' 7 *Virginia Law & Business Review* 589–618.

Keeton, R. E. 1954. 'Liability Insurance and Responsibility for Settlement' 67 *Harvard Law Review* 1136–86.

Logue, K. D. 1994. 'Solving the Judgment-Proof Problem' 72 *Texas Law Review* 1375–94.

Meurer, M. J. 1992. 'The Gains from Faith in an Unfaithful Agent: Settlement Conflicts between Defendants and Liability Insurers' 8 *Journal of Law, Economics & Organization* 502–22.

Peterson, R. W. 1966. 'Excess Liability: Reconsideration of California's Bad Faith Negligence Rule' 18 *Stanford Law Review* 475–85.

Plitt, S., D. Maldanado and J. D. Rogers. 2011. 14 *Couch on Insurance* 3rd edition. § 200:1, Thomson Reuters (3d ed.).

Schwartz, V. E. 1975. 'Statutory Strict Liability for an Insurer's Failure to Settle: A Balanced Plan for an Unresolved Problem' 1975 *Duke Law Journal* 901–19.

Spier, K. E. 2007. 'Litigation' in A. M. Polinsky and S. Shavell (eds.), *Handbook of Law and Economics*. Vol. I, Amsterdam: Elsevier B.V. 330–31.

Squire, R. 2012. 'How Collective Settlements Camouflage the Costs of Shareholder Lawsuits' 62 *Duke Law Journal* 1–78.

Stempel, J. W. 2006. *Stempel on Insurance Contracts*. 3rd edition. 9–146 and note 363, Aspen Publishers, New York, N.Y. (3d ed.).

Sykes, A. O. 1994a. 'Judicial Limitations on the Discretion of Liability Insurers to Settle or Litigate: An Economic Critique' 72 *Texas Law Review* 1345–74.

Sykes, A. O. 1994b. '"Bad Faith" Refusal to Settle by Liability Insurers: Some Implications of the Judgment-Proof Problem' 23 *Journal of Legal Studies* 77–110.

Syverud, K. D. 1990. 'The Duty to Settle' 76 *Virginia Law Review* 1113–209.

15. The law and economics of liability insurance: A theoretical and empirical review

*Tom Baker and Peter Siegelman**

I. INTRODUCTION

Tort cases are typically denominated in terms of a victim suing an injurer. But injurers do *not* typically pay the damages (if any) for which they are held liable, insurers do.[1] The presence of insurance shapes who is sued, and for what; it shapes litigation strategy and settlement negotiations; and, in some cases, it even affects the underlying liability itself (Baker 2006). Indeed, echoing the great biologist Theodosius Dobzhansky, we suggest that little or nothing in tort law makes sense except in the light of liability insurance.[2] In similar fashion, Kenneth Abraham (2008) describes the relationship between tort law and liability insurance using the metaphor of a binary star: separate bodies that form a common gravitational field.

Tort's deterrence function requires that injurers internalize the social costs of the injuries they cause when they fail to take due care. Liability insurance would seem to sever the link between injurers' behavior and its financial consequences, since the insured risk takers would seem to have little reason to pay for a loss for which others are liable. This is the well-known problem of moral hazard.[3] Economic theory reveals, however, that

* This chapter originally appeared in Jennifer Arlen, ed., RESEARCH HANDBOOK ON THE ECONOMICS OF TORTS (Cheltenham, UK and Northampton, MA, USA: Edward Elgar (2013)). We thank Jennifer Arlen, Kenneth Abraham, Sachin Pandya, Adam Scales, Daniel Schwarcz, Steven Shavell, and an anonymous referee for helpful comments and suggestions.

1 As a result, empirical legal researchers conventionally use liability insurance premiums as a reasonably good proxy for those damages (Baker 2012).

2 *Nothing in Biology Makes Sense Except in the Light of Evolution*, 35 AMER. BIO. TEACHER 125 (1973).

3 Somewhat loosely speaking, moral hazard is the tendency of insurance to diminish an insured's incentives to take care that would reduce the risk being insured against. It arises because of a classic externality: the *costs* of taking care fall on the insured, but the *benefits* of care accrue to the party who will pay for any losses, namely the insurer. For example, suppose an injurer is fully insured against

insurance nevertheless can be compatible with robust deterrence, because insurers have various ways of reducing risk taking by insureds – thereby remedying the moral hazard problem. As we explain in detail below, insurance contracts contain numerous structural features designed to limit moral hazard. These features seem to work reasonably well. (On the other hand, although empirical evidence is scanty, there do appear to be some types of moral hazard that are not so well controlled.)

Tort law is also centrally concerned with problems of compensation for victims. In this context, first-party insurance may work as an alternative to tort; society need worry less about making injurers pay victims if the latter can collect from their own insurers instead. The significance of these other compensation systems to tort law can be seen in the attention paid to them by the global reinsurance companies that reinsure liability risks (Lahnstein 2011). Countries with more first-party insurance, especially social insurance, have less need for tort law compensation. The relationship between workers' compensation and tort law is similar. For example, one explanation for the size of asbestos liability losses in the US as compared to other highly industrialized countries is the willingness of workers' compensation and other social insurance arrangements to compensate asbestos bodily injury losses in countries such as France and Japan (Lahnstein 2011).

After a short review of the history of liability insurance, this chapter briefly reviews the standard economic model of tort law, and then goes on to discuss how the introduction of risk aversion and insurance influence the model's conclusions.

II. HISTORY

Although now widely accepted in the US, insurance against tort (and tort-like) liability was controversial when introduced in the US in the late nineteenth century (McNeely 1941; Abraham 2008; Pandya 2011).

---

liability for any accident he causes. He could eliminate any risk of a \$100 accident by spending \$2 on care, but without the care, the accident risk is 50 percent. If uninsured, the injurer would obviously prefer to spend \$2 on care and save himself \$50 (= $1/2 \times 100$) in expected liability. But with full insurance, the \$2 eliminates a risk that the insured would not be responsible for, since liability is borne by his insurer. Now, the \$2 is a complete waste from the insured's perspective, even though it is in society's interest to have him make this investment. Note that moral hazard can only occur if the insured's level of care is unobservable to the insurer: if that were not the case, the insurer could simply specify the required level of care as part of the insurance contract, and then refuse to pay if the insured tried to slack-off by taking less than the specified level of care.

The experience in Europe was similar: some opposition in the early years, followed by acceptance and then encouragement of liability insurance in order to promote the financial responsibility of tortfeasors (Tunc 1983: 50–5). Under Soviet law, liability insurance was prohibited until recent years (ibid.). The key issue, then as now, was moral hazard (Baker 1996): many believed that allowing liability insurance would lead potential tortfeasors to be less careful to prevent injuries, since they could shift the cost of any liability to their insurer.

There was often a moral or policy objection as well, founded on the belief that tort sanctions were meant to punish wrongdoers, a purpose that liability insurance would frustrate. The early debates were undertaken without benefit of any real empirical evidence or theoretical framework. What may ultimately have carried the day in favor of liability insurance was the absence of any organized interest with a stake in opposing it (Pandya 2011). Echoes of these earlier controversies can be heard today in more modest debates over insurance coverage for punitive damages (Sharkey 2005), for liability arising under various employment laws (Employment Practices Liability Insurance or EPLI; e.g., Gabel, Mansfield and Jones 2006; Mootz 1997; Gallagher 1994), and for tort liabilities that are also crimes (Baker 2009). (See also Baker and Griffith 2010 on early objections to directors' and officers' liability insurance.) The reach of liability insurance has largely expanded to include these areas.

III. JUSTIFICATIONS FOR THE PURCHASE OF LIABILITY INSURANCE

A. Individuals

In the standard model, individuals and large corporations purchase insurance against tort liability for different reasons. Individuals are risk averse, meaning that they have a declining marginal utility of money. Insurance against liability risks, like other kinds of insurance, allows individuals to shift money from states of the world where there is no loss to states of the world where the loss occurs and the marginal utility of wealth is high. The cost of the accident is then shifted to the insurer. As long as the insurer is risk neutral or bears a large number of independent risks, welfare increases. The interested reader can refer to the Appendix for a summary of the standard analysis of the demand for, and welfare effects of, insurance.

Because of the law of large numbers, insurance is superior to precautionary savings for this purpose, as long as the liability risks of individuals in the pool are not too strongly correlated. In addition, individuals are sometimes required to purchase liability insurance (e.g., auto), or find it bundled with other insurance they are required to buy (e.g., homeowners insurance, which is required by lenders and which covers some liability risks).

B. Corporations

Publicly traded corporations are understood to be owned for investment purposes by individuals with diversified portfolios, and thus do not need insurance for risk distribution purposes. One intuition is that a fully diversified individual would own shares in both the tortfeasor and the supplier of liability insurance. Indeed, because of the downside protection from limited liability, diversified investors may actually want corporations to be risk preferring. Yet the available evidence suggests that corporations widely purchase insurance (Baker and Griffith 2010).

Several explanations – with varying welfare consequences – have been offered for why publicly held corporations nevertheless purchase liability insurance. One reason is agency costs. Managers may be risk averse if they earn rents as a result of their investment in firm-specific human capital, which ties their earnings to the profits of their employer (Arlen 1992: 419–20). Although shareholders can fully diversify with respect to losses of the firm, its managers cannot: if the share price plummets or the firm goes bankrupt, its managers stand to lose their rents. Indeed, managers' contractual compensation ostensibly *requires* them to bear some risks in order to motivate them to avoid shirking. Managers thus may cause the firm to purchase insurance to reduce the variability of corporate profits, and hence of their own remuneration, even though this is not in shareholders' interests (Baker and Griffith 2010 provide qualitative evidence in support of this explanation).

Other explanations for corporate liability insurance are more benign. Mayers and Smith identify institutional reasons for why a publicly traded corporation may benefit from shifting money from no loss to loss states of the world: increasing marginal income tax rates, bankruptcy costs, and what they called the 'underinvestment' problem (which relates to different incentives for equity and debt investors in certain situations) (Mayers and Smith 1982; 1987; MacMinn and Garven 2000). Froot, Scharfstein, and Stein (1993) suggest that the higher costs of external capital (as compared to internal capital) constitute an additional institutional justification for corporate insurance and other forms of hedging. In addition, corporations may purchase insurance because it is bundled with other services that they value, such as loss prevention and claims management (Mayers and Smith

1982; Skogh 1989). Having the same firm sell loss control advice and insurance makes loss control recommendations more credible, because the entity making the recommendation is also responsible for paying any losses that might occur. Insurance companies can thus more fully 'bond' their loss prevention and claims management services than can separate loss control service providers (Cohen 1997–98). Of course, corporations might also demand insurance because regulators or counterparties require it (Goldberg 2009).

Finally, privately held corporations and non-profit corporations have similar reasons to purchase insurance (except that non-profits are not taxed and private firms may not face the same agency costs). In addition, privately held corporations would seem more likely to have non-diversified owners, and non-profits, by definition, are not owned for investment purposes and, thus, are unlikely to be risk neutral (Arlen 1992: 419).

IV. THE CLASSIC MODEL OF LIABILITY AND INSURANCE

The canonical formal analysis of the moral hazard effects of liability insurance is due to Shavell (1982; 2004); Calabresi (1970) earlier offered significant insights. Shavell begins with the fact that insurance is socially valuable to the extent that parties are risk averse, because bearing risk is costly. On the other hand, liability insurance may reduce social welfare to the extent that insurance enables risk imposers to avoid bearing the expected costs of their risky activities: this is the familiar tension between the risk spreading benefits of insurance and its potential risk-creating consequences (via moral hazard). Shavell's contribution is to show that this tradeoff is significantly more complicated than had been previously realized, and under certain conditions, may not exist at all; even if it does, the presence of liability insurance can still be shown to be welfare improving relative to no insurance, at least in many instances of the canonical tort model.

A. The Canonical Model without Insurance (Risk Neutrality)

Shavell (1982) situates insurance in the canonical model of negligence and strict liability (Brown 1973; Shavell 1980).[4] To set up our later analysis of liability in the presence of insurance, we briefly review that model here,

---

[4] The application of this model to accidents involving customers is discussed in Daughety and Reinganum (2013) and Arlen (2013).

under the standard initial assumption that both injurers and victims are risk neutral, and thus do not demand insurance. Both injurers and victims are assumed to be able to take care to prevent an accident. Care is costly to the party taking it, and thus, absent liability, injurers will not take care, since doing so only benefits victims. Without insurance or liability, victims *will* take the optimal amount of care, however, because they bear both the cost and obtain the expected benefit of care (reduction in harm to themselves). Introducing pure strict liability (and assuming that litigation is costless and that damages are set equal to the actual harm suffered by victims) reverses these results (Shavell 1980). Now, injurers take optimal care, because they bear the total expected costs of accidents and their prevention. But victims take too little care because they are essentially fully insured by the injurer for their harms.

A key insight of the Shavell model is that injurers have more than one way of reducing accident risks: they can incur costs of precaution – 'care' (such as driving more slowly) – and they can undertake the activity less often (e.g., by driving less frequently). Under a strict liability regime, injurers will be led to consider *all* possible ways of reducing accident risks, because injurers will always be liable for any harms that materialize. Thus, strict liability leads injurers to optimize on both the activity level (frequency) margin and the care/precaution margin in managing liability risk (Shavell 1980). By contrast, negligence does not optimally regulate injurers' activity levels, since the law defines 'due care' with respect to precaution costs and not activity levels. Injurers subject to optimal negligence liability will take due care in order to avoid liability for the harms they cause when they do so.[5] Accordingly, assuming that injurers know when they are taking due care and have full control over how much care they take, they will never be negligent – so long as courts set due care equal to optimal care (Shavell 1980), damages are set at optimal levels (Cooter 1984), and courts do not err in determining whether injurers and victims are negligent.[6] Accordingly, in a perfect world, negligence liability in effect

---

[5] This result depends on the additional assumption that injurers can always comply because they always know when they are negligent and have full control over whether they take care. For a discussion of optimal accident law when injurers are organizations, and thus have less than perfect control of their actions, see Kraakman (2013).

[6] More refined versions of the model do predict injurer negligence under some circumstances. For example, if the standard of care is set very high, injurers may find it cheaper to take the cost-minimizing level of care – even though that is below the standard – and pay for those accidents that result. Injurers may also be negligent because of errors they make in estimating the standard of care (Arlen and

translates into a rule of *no* liability for the injurer in equilibrium, since he will never be at fault. Injurers thus will take due care but will have no reason to limit their activity levels. Victims, in turn, will take due care with respect to their own safety, for the same reason they do under a regime of no liability. Victims also have optimal incentives to control their activity levels (Shavell 1980). The key intuition here is that victims know that if they are ever injured, it will be by a non-negligent, and thus non-liable injurer. It follows that victims themselves will always bear the full costs of any injuries that do occur.

B. The Canonical Model with Insurance

The analysis changes if injurers and victims are risk averse, and hence have a demand for full insurance that is fairly priced, as shown in Table 15.1 (Shavell 1982).[7] Risk aversion complicates the social welfare analysis. On the one hand, we want to spread or allocate risks optimally, ideally shifting them away from risk averse parties who find bearing them costly. Yet we also want to provide both injurers and victims with incentives to take optimal care, and engage optimally in risky activities.[8]

1. Strict liability

Consider first a rule of strict liability, as shown in column 2 of Table 15.1.[9] Under this regime, victims are already in effect fully insured by injurers (who are obliged to pay for whatever accidents occur), and hence have

---

MacLeod 2005), or mistakes by courts in applying the standard to injurer behavior, among many other reasons (Cooter 1984; Calfee and Craswell 1984).

[7] As discussed above, corporations may demand insurance for many reasons other than risk aversion. The benign conclusions of the Shavell analysis would presumably change if the corporate demand for insurance derives from, for example, managerial exploitation of agency costs – at shareholders' expense – rather than risk aversion. We know of no systematic theoretical inquiry into this issue, however.

[8] The analysis here focuses exclusively on injuries that involve replaceable commodities – i.e., things that can be translated into monetary values and thus represent pure losses to wealth. Injuries to irreplaceable commodities or entitlements (Cook and Graham 1977) may affect both the location of the utility function and the marginal utility of wealth (holding wealth constant). When the injury is to a normal good, victims do not want to fully insure. Insurance demand thus looks different for losses such as death or serious permanent injury; see section V.C below (discussing tort coverage of pain and suffering losses).

[9] When insurers can observe care and activity levels, there is no informational asymmetry, and the first-best solution – to require the efficient level of care and provide full insurance – is achievable by contract.

*Table 15.1 Shavell's analysis of the effects of liability insurance**

Actor	Liability regime		
	Strict liability	Negligence	
Victim			
Insurance purchase? (1st Party)	None, already fully-insured by SL	Yes, because injurer will be non-negligent, regardless of liability insurance, so victim will bear all losses	
Risk bearing?	None	Some, because of incomplete coverage	
Care incentive?	None	Some, because of incomplete coverage	
Activity incentive?	None	Some, because of incomplete coverage	
Injurer		(a) No errors in negligence rule	(b) Possible errors in negligence rule
Insurance purchase?	Probably partial, even when insurers are willing to provide full insurance	None	Yes, designed to cover their own lapses or judicial error**
Risk bearing?	Sub-optimal, injurer retains some risk	None: injurer will take standard of care, thus never liable	None
Care incentive?	Sub-optimal, injurer takes insufficient precaution	Injurer will take standard of care	Injurers will take the standard of care; insurance might be helpful in reducing *excessive* care taken because of uncertain legal std
Activity incentive?	Sub-optimal, injurer engages in activity too frequently	None	Policy may require some control over activity
Overall assessment	Insurance improves **injurer** welfare by risk spreading, leaves **victims** indifferent, and covers its cost to **insurers** *via* fair premium. Hence, it is an unambiguous improvement over no insurance, although still not first best	Insurance is irrelevant to injurer, because she has already 'purchased' full immunity from liability by taking standard of care. Victims will purchase partial insurance, which	Insurance helps injurers avoid liability for own lapses and/or judicial error; will be designed and priced to maintain injurers' incentives to take standard of care. Injurors gain from risk spreading, without increase in moral hazard

Table 15.1 (continued)

Actor	Liability regime		
	Strict liability	Negligence	
Overall assessment		reduces risk, but dilutes incentives to take care, with overall net gains to victims and no effect on injurers or insurers	Insurance may *raise* welfare by mitigating over-compliance or controlling activity level. Victims are indifferent

Notes:
* Assumptions (based on Shavell 1982): All parties are risk averse. Insurer cannot observe amount of care or activity level. The regimes are pure strict liability or negligence, with no contributory or comparative elements. Premiums are actuarially fair. Losses are purely pecuniary. Injurers can always pay for any harm they may cause.
** Policy will not be attractively priced for an injurer wishing to be deliberately negligent.

no demand for insurance. In the extreme case, victims bear no risk and take no precautions, so the presence of insurance does not alter their behavior at all. On the injurer's side, strict liability causes injurers to bear the full-expected cost of accidents. Risk averse injurers thus will want to insure against liability risk. Initially, it might seem that this insurance would fully undermine the incentive effects of the tort system because fully insured injurers have no incentive to invest in avoiding accidents. Yet this generally is not the case for two reasons.

First, insured injurers will retain an incentive to invest in care if liability insurers can observe their care and activity levels and price insurance accordingly. In addition, injurers will retain strong incentives to invest in care if liability insurance is 'experience-rated', in that premiums are based on the injurers' past claims history.

Even when insurers cannot observe care or activity levels, insured injurers will also retain some incentive to invest in care (albeit weakened) to the extent they purchase insurance with a significant deductible. Partial insurance is cheaper than full insurance, because partial insurance preserves some incentive for the insured to take care, and thus generates lower premiums per dollar covered. This means that, even allowing for risk aversion, injurers will likely prefer only partial coverage.[10] Partial coverage

[10] This result might not hold if care is very unproductive and injurers are very risk averse.

does diminish injurers' incentives to take care, however, so there is some moral hazard effect. Shavell (1982) nicely demonstrates that the introduction of liability insurance in this context will nevertheless raise welfare (as opposed to a world of no insurance), even though the equilibrium is only second-best optimal. The reason is that injurers obviously value the reduction in risk from partial coverage by more than the cost of such coverage (since they bought the insurance). Victims are fully insured by strict liability, regardless of whether the injurer has insurance or pays for losses itself, so victim welfare is unaffected by the introduction of insurance; and insurers are willing to sell fairly priced insurance to injurers. Thus, no one is made worse off by the introduction of insurance, and injurers gain from bearing less risk.

2. Negligence

Now consider the operation of a negligence rule, and assume for the moment that neither courts nor injurers make any errors in assessing or applying the standard of care[11] (column 3 of Table 15.1). In this situation it will (almost) always be cheapest for injurers to comply with the standard of care, since this affords them complete immunity from liability. That in turn implies that compliant injurers face no liability risk, and thus demand no insurance.

In this context, liability insurance does not decrease incentives to take care because injurers will not buy insurance in order to reduce their care levels below the standard of care. In this simple model, injurers face no risk of liability if they take due care, and thus insurers know that any injurer who seeks liability insurance plans to be negligent. Insurers will thus rationally price insurance assuming that those who buy it take no care whatsoever. The premium for such insurance would be very high – higher than the cost to the injurer of taking optimal (due) care.[12] Indeed, since complying with the standard care is cheaper for injurers than not (because injurers will be liable for the resulting accidents), injurers will find

---

[11] In other words, the standard is applied perfectly, both by injurers in deciding how much care to take *ex ante*, and by courts in comparing injurer conduct to the standard of care *ex post*.

[12] If due care equals optimal care, then we know that due care minimizes the total expected cost of taking care plus expected accident costs. Given this, we know that it is cheaper to take due care and pay the expected cost of accidents than to take zero care and pay a premium equal to the expected costs of accidents when injurers take zero care. Accordingly, injurers certainly are better off taking due care and not paying any accident costs than taking no care and purchasing correctly priced insurance.

it cheaper to comply with the standard of care than to buy insurance and slack off on care.

Knowing all this, victims will predict that they will bear the cost of any injuries they suffer, since these will be caused by a non-negligent injurer. Victims will thus demand (first-party) insurance to cover the accident risks they expect to bear.[13] Full insurance would lead victims to take no care at all, and will thus be priced disadvantageously relative to partial insurance. There is thus some moral hazard that takes place on the part of victims, but despite this, victims can be shown to gain more from risk spreading than society loses due to moral hazard, so the introduction of insurance is welfare enhancing (Shavell 1982). Shavell's model also encompasses settings where the negligence standard is not applied flawlessly, either because injurers misperceive the standard of care or because courts misapply it, either of which can lead injurers to be held negligent. In this situation, compliance with the standard of care does not immunize an injurer from liability, so injurers *will* demand insurance to cover this risk. The insurance will optimally be designed to protect against liability for negligence due to errors or lapses,[14] so injurers will still find it cost effective to take the standard of care and avoid expensive policies that would permit them to take no care. In this context, insurance improves welfare by risk spreading, without creating moral hazard; it may also be welfare enhancing because its presence can mitigate *over*-compliance that would otherwise result (in some models) from uncertainty over the standard of care (Calfee and Craswell 1984).

Injurers might also be negligent because they cannot perfectly control their own behavior. Such imperfections can occur because exercising due care sometimes requires ongoing attention by the injurer (as opposed to 'durable' precautions such as fire extinguishers that need only be installed once), and people's attention sometimes wanders (Grady 1988; Cooter 1991). Injurers can also be negligent because they do not have sufficient information to know what course of conduct satisfies the due care standard (as in medical malpractice) (Arlen and MacLeod 2005). Lapses in control can also occur because of agency costs, for example when a firm is unable to perfectly monitor the behavior of employees who otherwise

---

[13] Injurers taking the standard of care are not liable, so their victims cannot expect compensation from them or their insurers. Victims' risk of being injured by a non-negligent injurer creates the demand for first-party insurance on the part of victims.

[14] An example might be the restriction of pollution liability coverage to 'sudden or accidental' events, which was drafted for inclusion in standard Commercial General Liability policies in the early 1970s (Abraham 1988).

face insufficient incentives to invest in care (Kornhauser 1982; Arlen and MacLeod 2005). Under these circumstances, injurers will sometimes be negligent, even when they strive (optimally) not to be, providing further reason to conclude that there are risk spreading benefits from liability insurance.

An important lacuna in the Shavell model is the assumption that all victims sue, and are fully compensated for their injuries. If this is not the case, and liability insurances creates some moral hazard, it is possible that victims might be worse off, since there will be more uncompensated injuries. We discuss this problem further in the next section.

V. MORAL HAZARD IN LIABILITY INSURANCE

A. Contract Design

As the preceding discussion implies, moral hazard has been perhaps the most significant theoretical concern animating law and economic research on liability insurance. The canonical model both relies on, and makes predictions about, the design of insurance contracts for liability risk that mitigate the potential moral hazard of liability insurance. Shavell (1982; 2004), for example, concludes that even when care levels cannot be observed directly, moral hazard can be significantly controlled through the design and implementation of insurance contracts. In large part, Shavell's model either assumes or predicts that liability insurers will control moral hazard sufficiently so that liability insurance will be welfare enhancing. Whether and when this assumption/prediction is borne out in practice is a very important and not yet adequately answered empirical question.

In theory, the list of moral hazard control devices in liability insurance is large, and many are not unique to liability insurance. Empirical studies of their efficacy are much more limited, however, in part because data on insurance policy design and insured behavior are often proprietary or difficult to obtain. Institutional research on moral hazard control in insurance dates to Heimer (1985), though of course insurance companies have engaged in applied research for centuries (Baker 1996). Table 15.2 lists some of the leading studies on the ability of liability insurance contracting to limit moral hazard, organized according to the moral hazard control technique investigated. We distinguish between *ex ante* moral hazard (reduction in care that would prevent liability), *ex post* moral hazard (reduction in care that would manage the extent of an asserted liability), and insurer moral hazard (shirking in contractual responsibilities). These last two categories are absent from the canonical tort/insurance model,

Table 15.2 Controlling moral hazard in liability insurance

Technique	Effect	Literature
Underwriting: screen in advance for 'good character' or other evidence of good loss control	Reduce *ex ante* moral hazard, possibly reduce *ex post*	Heimer (1985); Glenn (2000); Baker and Griffith (2010)
Experience rating (and non-renewal). Charge more for (or drop) those with poorer claims histories	Reduce *ex ante* and *ex post* moral hazard	Cohen (2006); Derrig and Tennyson (2011); Israel (2004); Robinson and Zheng (2010)
Coverage design: A) Exclusions and sub-limits that scale coverage to reflect injurers' control B) Bundling defense and indemnity C) Cost-sharing and partial coverage, including deductibles	A) Reduce *ex ante* moral hazard B) Reduce *ex post* moral hazard and reduce insurer moral hazard C) Reduce *ex ante* and *ex post* moral hazard	A) Heimer (1985); Baker (2008) B) Danzon (1985); Sykes (1994); Baker (1998) C) Heimer (1985); Baker and Griffith (2010); Wang, Chung and Tzeng (2008)
Loss control: loss prevention advice/ control (distinguish from liability prevention)	Reduce *ex ante* and *ex post* moral hazard	Skogh (1989); Simon (1994); Cohen (1997–98); Van der Veer (2005–06); Abraham (2005); Baker and Griffith (2010)
Ex post auditing to enforce the techniques above	Reduce *ex ante* and *ex post* moral hazard	Dionne (2000); Picard (2000); Ericson and Doyle (2004); Tennyson (2008); Derrig and Tennyson (2011); Weisberg and Derrig (1991)
Reliance on other regulators A) Moral or professional values B) Government agency C) Legal rules, e.g.: • duty to settle • damages for bad faith breach • waiver of coverage defense upon breach of duty to defend • prejudice rule for breach of conditions • anti-fraud laws D) Organizational form	Reduce *ex ante*, *ex post*, and insurer moral hazard	A) Cummins and Tennyson (1996); Cohen (1997–98); Tennyson (2002); Baker (2001) B) Kneuper and Yandle (1994) C) Sykes (1994); Hawken, Carroll and Abrahamse (2001); Hoyt, Mustard and Powell (2006); Asmat and Tennyson (2010); Syverud (1990). D) Choi and Liang (2007)

but nevertheless play a significant role in defining the relationship between tort and insurance. Insurers employ a variety of different mechanisms to reduce moral hazard by both the insured and the insurer. These can be divided into six categories.

1. Underwriting

Underwriting is the process of selecting among insurance applicants and assigning them to risk categories according to, inter alia, their propensity to engage in loss prevention behavior and honesty in relation to claims practices. Underwriting has the potential to reduce both *ex ante* and *ex post* moral hazard.

2. Experience-rating

Experience-rating and non-renewal is the process of adjusting the premium at renewal based on the prior claims experience and refusing to renew policyholders with the worst claims experience. Experience-rating has the potential to reduce both *ex ante* and *ex post* moral hazard (Robinson and Zheng 2010).

3. Coverage design

Insurers can design insurance coverage to reduce moral hazard by both the insured and the insurer. First, insurers can use exclusions and sub-limits to eliminate or reduce the coverage available for liability losses that pose a high degree of moral hazard, most commonly because of the more substantial control that the policyholder has over the occurrence of the loss. These contract features have the potential to decrease *ex ante* moral hazard. They may limit *ex post* moral hazard as well, via provisions that require insureds to cooperate with the insurer in any lawsuit. Second, insurers can also reduce the insured's moral hazard by requiring the insured to bear some of the cost of the accident through cost sharing and partial coverage, which can be accomplished through deductibles, coinsurance, and limits on coverage that are less than the total potential liability exposure. All of these features keep insureds' 'skin in the game', and thus have the potential to reduce both *ex ante* and *ex post* moral hazard (Wang, Chung and Tzeng 2008). While 'aggregate deductibles' (which apply to all losses over the life of the policy) are optimal in theory (Arrow 1963), they are rarely observed in practice, for reasons explained in Cohen (2006). Finally, insurers can reduce insurer moral hazard through the common practice of bundling defense coverage (paying the defense lawyer) with indemnity coverage (paying for settlements and judgments) and giving the insurer control (greater or lesser depending on the type of policy and circumstances) over both.

4. Loss control

Insurers can also reduce insureds' moral hazard by bundling loss control services with insurance. These loss control services can involve mandatory conditions or simply loss prevention advice, which should be reliable because it is bonded by the insurer's promise to pay for any claims that result (Cohen 1997–98). Conventionally, the term 'loss control' is used for activities that reduce loss or moral hazard *ex ante*, rather than manage the extent of the loss, *ex post*, but it is possible to understand defense and settlement control provisions in insurance policies as *ex post* loss or moral hazard control arrangements.[15]

5. *Ex post* auditing

Insurers can enhance the effectiveness of the moral hazard control measures falling into categories 1–4 by employing *ex post* auditing techniques to enforce policyholders' representations or responsibilities under their contracts.

6. External control measures

Finally, insurers can benefit from some extra-contractual institutions that operate to reduce moral hazard. Here we distinguish among the following three types of external regulation: (1) moral or professional norms, which have the potential to reduce all three forms of moral hazard (Arrow 1968); (2) administrative regulation, which may also reduce all three forms of moral hazard; (3) legal rules promoting the enforcement of insurance contracts, which are largely directed at reducing insurer moral hazard.

The studies listed in Table 15.2 generally conclude that moral hazard

---

[15] From the perspective of the insurance contract, 'loss control' means anything that reduces liability. But controls that prevent losses *ex ante* have very different welfare implications from those that merely avoid injurer *liability* for those losses *ex post*. For example, EPLI insurers often insist on sexual harassment training for employees as a condition of coverage. Most such training probably has little or no effect on actual behavior – that is, on losses due to the occurrence of sexual harassment. (Grossman (2003: 3) concludes that 'sexual harassment policies and procedures do not seem to have any reliably negative effect on the incidence of sexual harassment'.) But after the Supreme Court decided that employers were not vicariously liable for harassment by managers if the company had taken steps to prevent and promptly correct the problem (*Faragher* v. *City of Boca Raton*, 524 U.S. 775 (1998)), sexual harassment training became a kind of 'bureaucratic vaccine against lawsuits for harassment' (Dobbin and Kelly 2007: 1234). From a welfare perspective, there is a substantial difference between loss controls that actually reduce the incidence of harassment *ex ante* and those that simply shift the costs of harassment onto victims by forestalling injurer liability *ex post*.

is present, but that institutional devices for controlling it work reasonably well (with the caveat that differences among liability and insurance institutions can make it difficult to extend the findings beyond the specific context investigated). The exception is Baker and Griffith (2010), who conclude, based on qualitative research, that the moral hazard created by directors' and officers' (D&O) liability insurance may undercut the deterrence function of shareholder litigation by reducing the incentive of corporate boards to demand accurate financial reporting. Even they conclude that this type of moral hazard could be managed, however. If corporations disclosed the details of D&O insurance contract terms (including pricing), securities analysts could incorporate that information into a more refined measure of corporate liability risk.

Moral hazard is difficult to measure, even with access to the necessary proprietary data, because of the need to distinguish between causal and selection effects (Abbring et al. 2003). Changes in insurance contract design or other techniques that are understood to control or exacerbate moral hazard produce changes in claims data through selection effects (i.e., through the mix of people who are insured) in addition to, or perhaps rather than, moral hazard (ibid.; see also Cohen and Siegelman (2010) and sources cited therein for discussion of attempts to distinguish adverse selection from moral hazard). In recent work, Abbring, Chiappori and Zavadil (2008) review the prior literature and use advanced econometric techniques and Dutch automobile insurance data to separate these effects. They find both *ex ante* and *ex post* moral hazard effects from the unique experience-rating system in Dutch automobile insurance, which contains features that facilitate the econometric separation of these effects.

None of the econometric studies listed in Table 15.2 employs techniques comparable to Abbring, Chiappori and Zavadil, and thus, judged from the perspective of the state of the art in econometric analysis, even the findings from the other econometric studies must be regarded as provisional, at least in detail. For that reason among others, the conceptual line between 'generalizable' econometric findings and 'non-generalizable' qualitative findings is less hard and fast than commonly believed. Theoretically and institutionally informed qualitative research also produces useful empirical insights, especially but not only when the data needed to conduct econometric research are proprietary. Among other benefits, qualitative research may identify questions for subsequent econometric analysis. For example, Baker's (2001) qualitative research describing the legal rules and professional norms that limit plaintiffs' ability to collect 'blood money' from defendants – thereby reducing the deterrence effect, if any, of liability – prompted efforts to test this hypothesis using a unique public dataset of liability claims information (Zeiler et al. 2007; Hyman, Paik and Black (2013): both studies support the hypothesis).

B. *Ex post* Moral Hazard

The standard tort/insurance model assumes that moral hazard only occurs when insured injurers or victims take less care to prevent losses because of the presence of insurance. Insurance may lead not only to reduced care *ex ante*, however. It may also lead to increased claiming *ex post*. That might be a good thing from an efficiency perspective, if there would be too few meritorious claims in the absence of insurance (see, e.g., Andrews et al. 1997 (finding that only 7 percent of all patients injured during their stay at a Chicago hospital made a claim based on their injury)). But insurance could also generate an increase in non-meritorious claims. In the most extreme case, this might amount to outright fraud on an organized scale (e.g., *In Re: Silica Products Liability Litigation* (398 F. Supp. 2d 563 (S.D. Tex. 2005)) (finding systematic fraud involving 10,000 plaintiffs and sanctioning the lawyers who brought the suits in the amount of $825,000)), but more ambiguous motivations are also possible.[16]

Estimates of the amount of fraud in liability insurance are difficult to come by for at least three reasons. First, detecting fraud is difficult, and conclusively proving it even more so. Relatedly, one wants to know not just the amount of detected fraud, but also the total volume of fraud, including those cases that are not detected, which requires making difficult inferences. Finally, insurers, who control the data, may have an interest in overstating the amount of fraud. Carron and Dionne's (1997) careful study suggests a best-guess estimate of 9.5 percent of all auto claims in Quebec involve fraud, although with a wide range of uncertainty. These authors also deploy a clever methodology that allows them to estimate undetected fraud, and which suggests that insurers are not especially good at catching fraud. Tennyson (2008) summarizes the conventional wisdom that roughly 10 percent of claims involve fraud of some kind (including overstated damages), but goes on to suggest that 'this statistic appears to be more folk wisdom than fact' (ibid.: 1184; see also Weisberg and Derrig 1991).

What is missing from the literature is a rigorous attempt to integrate estimates of the extent and cost of fraudulent claims with the risk spreading benefits of insurance to arrive at a net estimate of the welfare gains from insurance. A few authors (notably D'Arcy 1994; Syverud 1994) have

---

16 For an economic analysis of frivolous litigation see Wickelgren (2013).

Table 15.3 Hypothetical effects of introducing liability insurance on volume and composition of litigation, when not all victims sue, and some non-victims also sue

	No insurance	Insurance	Increase	Description of effect
Number injured	100	110	10	*Ex ante* moral hazard
Total lawsuits	25	33	8	*Ex post* moral hazard
Litigation rate	25%	30%		
'Valid' lawsuits	24	30	6	'Good' *ex post* moral hazard
'Non-valid' lawsuits	1	3	2	'Bad' *ex post* moral hazard

suggested that there might be a downside to liability insurance that is not visible in the standard model, but without rigorously developing the *ex post* moral hazard argument. For example, Syverud suggests that liability insurance in effect creates its own demand, by encouraging litigation that would not be worthwhile in the absence of the deep-pockets insurance provides.

Table 15.3 provides a hypothetical example of the complex welfare calculations that might arise in the presence of *ex ante* and *ex post* moral hazard, given that there are victims who do not sue and non-victims who do. Suppose that there is initially no insurance for injurers, and that there are 100 actual injuries, 25 lawsuits are filed, of which 24 are 'legitimate' or valid and one is by a non-injured party, merely seeking to extract a settlement from some defendant. Introducing liability insurance results in a relatively modest amount of (*ex ante*) moral hazard on the part of injurers. The reduction in care leads to ten additional injuries, and eight additional lawsuits, of which six are valid and two are not. Sorting out the welfare implications of all this is extraordinarily complicated. First, two additional victims do not receive compensation, while six additional victims who would not otherwise have sued now do so. On net, therefore, the presence of insurance has beneficially raised the litigation rate and led to greater compensation and more deterrence, although some victims and injurers are worse off than before. It is thus important to distinguish between 'good' and 'bad' *ex post* moral hazard. The presence of insurance triples the number of 'invalid' lawsuits (from one to three). If the social cost of these invalid suits is sufficiently high (or of course if the increase is larger than in our example), the welfare costs could outweigh the benefits described above.

C. Moral Hazard in Workers' Compensation Insurance

Historically, workers' compensation (WC) represented the first large-scale attempt to substitute insurance for tort liability. WC has generated an extensive literature that is too large to discuss here in depth. The same problems of moral hazard that are central in other liability insurance relationships also appear in WC, but greater availability of data has led to a larger volume of studies. Fortin and Lanoie (2000) survey the empirical literature on incentive effects of WC, and conclude that the number (and also the duration) of WC claims responds positively to the generosity of benefits (with an elasticity of about 0.6) across a wide variety of studies (438). They point out, however, that the studies do not allow one to distinguish between 'legitimate changes in injury rates following increases in WC coverage (the reporting effect), and changes that could reflect an abusive use of the system' (439), leaving the question of moral hazard open. Their bottom line conclusion is that the long-term rise in US WC costs as a percentage of payroll, accompanied by a steady fall in the rate of workplace fatalities (which are 'presumably a good proxy for job safety', 453) is 'worrying,' because it suggests an increase in unjustified claiming or *ex post* moral hazard. Yet, the aggregate costs of the health care component of WC now exceed those of the income replacement component. Moreover, there is some evidence that medical care providers have shifted costs to the WC system through changes in diagnosis patterns that respond to more generous reimbursements by WC insurance providers than managed care organizations (Butler, Hartwig and Gardner 1997). Thus, the WC moral hazard story is a complicated one that involves much more than worker claiming patterns (Baker 1996). Confirming this conclusion, Guo and Burton (2010) find that 'much of the substantial decline in actual benefits in the 1990s was due to changes in state compensability rules and administrative stringency' (340), rather than to worker behavior.[17]

[17] The apparent contradiction between Fortin and Lanoie's report of a long-term rise in WC costs as a percentage of payroll and Guo and Burton's report of a decline in actual benefits in the 1990s results from differences in the data to which they had access. Guo and Burton had ten more years of data, which showed that the long-term increase in WC costs reported by Fortin and Lanoie stopped in the 1990s.

VI. ADDITIONAL ECONOMIC INSIGHTS ON LIABILITY AND INSURANCE

Insurance has been the site of much productive economic theorizing (e.g., Arrow 1963; Rothschild and Stiglitz 1976). Much of that work relates to insurance generally, not specifically to liability insurance or to the relationship between liability and insurance and, thus, will not be further addressed in this review. The literature specifically related to liability and insurance has focused on the following issues.

A. Judgment Proof Problems

It has long been recognized that injurers can cause harm that substantially exceeds their wealth or ability to pay (Sinn 1982; Shavell 1986; Gilles 2006; Harrington and Danzon 2000). Absent insurance, in this circumstance, victims will be inadequately compensated by any tort judgment, since injurers are unable to pay for the full extent of the harms they cause. There are efficiency consequences as well. Judgment proof injurers will tend to make riskier decisions: Since there is effectively no liability for harms that exceed an injurers' ability to pay, such losses are externalized to victims. As stressed by Sinn (1982), the existence of a minimum threshold for utility (e.g., *via* shielding of some assets in bankruptcy or through a social welfare system that provides a basic guarantee for all citizens) also reduces the demand for liability insurance by introducing non-concavities into the injurer's utility function. (Intuitively, the judgment proof insured may have higher expected utility from going uninsured than from buying insurance because fairly priced insurance would have to cover and charge for losses that the insured would never have to pay if uninsured.)

Smith and Wright (1992) apply these ideas to the auto insurance market, in which liability insurance is sold as a package with uninsured motorist coverage (insurance that covers first-party losses in circumstances in which an at-fault driver is uninsured). They suggest that poor and/or judgment proof drivers will have little or no demand for liability insurance. Thus, in local markets where there are large numbers of such drivers, those who *do* wish to purchase insurance have to pay very high premiums to cover the costs of harms imposed on them by the uninsured. This in turn makes insurance even less attractive to the non-judgment proof, and can lead to multiple equilibria, in some of which insurance is very expensive and relatively few drivers are insured. Smith and Wright's empirical evidence on insurance costs and poverty rates across US cities supports this conclusion.

Shavell (1986) discusses the menu of options for dealing with the judgment proof problem, one of which is to mandate insurance purchase. Paradoxically, another option is to ban coverage altogether (Shavell 2004: 278); this can be superior to mandating coverage if insurers cannot observe care levels, because injurers might be motivated to take more care than they would with insurance (even though they would take less care than would be socially optimal). Most states have some modest insurance requirements for automobile use, although these are frequently under-enforced and typically set at much lower levels of coverage than the maximum liability a driver can cause (for details, see Baker 2008). In the Smith and Wright (1992) model, mandating insurance (or enforcing existing mandates) can lower premiums and raise welfare. Another (complimentary) alternative is simply to regulate the conduct of the risky activity directly (e.g., nuclear power).

B. The Problem of Correlated (Socio-Legal) Risk

Harrington and Danzon (2000) point out that liability insurance will often entail non-independent risks. This dependence occurs because changes in legal precedents, institutions, or norms can influence many claims simultaneously and in the same direction. For example, a single Supreme Court decision about eligibility of asbestos victims for medical monitoring expenses (*Metro North Commuter Railroad* v. *Buckley*, 521 US 424 (1997)) would presumably control insurers' liability in every one of the thousands of pending asbestos cases. Similarly, a single state Supreme Court decision clarifying how liability insurance contracts apply to asbestos cases could also affect how insurers' share liability for those cases (e.g., *Owens-Illinois, Inc.* v. *United Ins. Co.*, 650 A.2d 974 (N.J. 1994)). While the lack of independence among risks does not make insurance impossible (Jaffee and Russell 1997), it does make liability insurance more difficult to price and, at least in theory, more expensive as result, reducing the net benefits from the risk distribution (Baker 2004).

C. Tort Liability and Insurance versus First-Party Insurance

Law and economic analysis has helped clarify the relationship between first-party insurance (such as health insurance) and liability insurance (commonly referred to as third-party insurance in this context). Where some early and mid twentieth century tort theorists saw tort law and liability insurance as important victim compensation mechanisms, economic theorists identified the very high transaction costs of tort and liability insurance as compared to first-party insurance. (e.g., Calabresi 1970; see Abraham and Liebman (1993) for a useful effort to estimate the relative roles of tort and first-party insurance as compensation for injuries). As a result, economic analysis does not consider victim compensation to be the primary function of tort law and liability insurance. Victims are efficient beneficiaries of tort law remedies (and therefore receive compensation through tort law) because their injuries are a good measure of the harm that could have been avoided by compliance with the standard of care, and because they have good access to information about those injuries, and generally the best incentives to bring claims against injurers. Of course, what matters for deterrence is that injurers pay, not that victims are compensated, so payments from injurers need not necessarily go to victims in order to achieve deterrence.

Calfee and Rubin (1992) review and extend the argument that, because tort law functions as a form of mandatory victim compensation insurance, the compensation that tort law provides ought to be limited to the kind of coverage victims would want from first-party insurance that they bought to cover their own injuries (see also Epstein 1985). This tends to suggest that since first-party insurance does not ordinarily provide compensation for pain and suffering, the tort system should not either. At best, this argument would apply to tort claims between contracting parties, such as in medical malpractice. Even in that context, however, voluntary limitations on tort damages are likely to reduce care. As Arlen (2010) explains, contract-based limits on damages present a collective action problem in which rational individual consumers may tend to choose a (socially inefficient) low level of tort protection. The reason for the inefficiency is that the existence of the warranty provides a signal of the manufacturer's information that the goods sold are of high quality. But if a consumer can simply observe the presence of an optional warranty, without actually buying it, he can make the inference of high quality and avoid the cost of the warranty. Of course, if every consumer reasons similarly, the manufacturer will have no reason to offer the warranty.[18]

---

[18] Steven Shavell points out (personal communication) that this argument depends on the waivability of warranties. There would be no collective action problem if a seller sold a good with an *unwaivable* warranty. In that case, every consumer would know that if he bought a widget from the seller, he and all other consumers would receive payments if the product turns out to be defective, so the seller would have an incentive to take care in its manufacture. While the Uniform Commercial Code restricts *sellers*' ability to waive warranties (see, e.g., §§2-314 through 2–316), it does so to 'protect a buyer from unexpected and unbargained language of disclaimer' (§2-316, Comment 1). The Code does not appear to prohibit sellers from making unwaivable warranties. Arlen (2010) suggests that in the medical malpractice context, at least, the only realistic way to achieve an unwaivable warranty would be through a standard form contract (because of the

Further undermining the case for limited damages, Wickelgren (2006) and Arlen and MacLeod (2005) explain that patients who undervalue the insurance provided by liability (whether because they underestimate the risk of liability or because the transaction costs of tort increase the price of insurance through liability) will bargain out of liability. Finally, some experimental evidence (Avraham 2005) suggests that people *do* actually demand coverage for pain and suffering, and Hanson and Croley (1995) point out that insureds may fail to buy first-party insurance for certain kinds of losses not because they do not want such coverage, but because insurers will not supply it for fear of adverse selection or moral hazard.

Like moral hazard, adverse selection (Rothschild and Stiglitz 1976) requires an informational asymmetry. Here, however, what is unobservable (to the insurer) is not the insured's level of care, but rather the insured's exogenously given level of riskiness. The theory of adverse selection predicts that when insureds know their own riskiness better than insurers do, the best risks will tend to select out of the insurance pool, since they find insurance that is priced for the average risk to be unattractive to them. The worst risks will be delighted to buy insurance priced for the average person. As a result, insurers will end up selling policies priced for the average risk to only the worst risks, which is obviously adverse to their interests. Cohen and Siegelman (2010) provide an empirical/methodological survey of adverse selection in insurance markets.

Interestingly, the problem of adverse selection in liability insurance has attracted much less scholarly attention than that of moral hazard, although both are widely understood to plague insurance markets in general.[19] It may be that insureds do not have superior information vis-à-vis insurers with respect to liability risk. Alternatively, perhaps the methods for controlling selection are sufficient to prevent the worst risks from

---

problem of duress in individual negotiations), which would present an adverse selection problem. The products liability context also presents a risk of adverse selection, provided that the risk of injury is a function of both product safety and victim behavior. Arlen points out (personal communication) that whether this undermines the case for contract would turn on whether consumers are better off under a pooling equilibrium with cross-subsidization from low risk to high risk, or under a separating equilibrium with low risks signaling their status by waiving liability (and getting low cost, but less safe products than they want) and high risks purchasing the warranty.

[19] Recent work by Arlen (2010) and Choi and Spier (2010) takes up the problem of adverse selection in medical malpractice and products liability contexts. Both papers suggest that adverse selection may justify mandatory (non-waivable) liability; both papers conclude that allowing waivers may lead to inefficient un-pooling of heterogeneous customers.

pooling with better ones. An influential article by Priest (1987) blamed an adverse selection-like mechanism for the liability insurance crisis in the mid-1980s, suggesting that a variety of pro-plaintiff decisions caused unraveling in several sub-markets for liability insurance. Even if the law moved in the way Priest suggested, however, it is difficult to see how new legal rules could create asymmetric information favoring insureds (Ayres and Siegelman 1989). (Absent such informational asymmetry, insurers would simply charge more for additional liability risks, and insureds would agree to pay more for coverage, with no unraveling of the market.) In sum, the scholarly literature does not seem to consider adverse selection to be a serious problem in liability insurance markets.

As compared to first-party insurance, tort law and liability insurance present less risk of adverse selection (because tort law applies to everyone, and in that sense is mandatory) and less risk of *ex post* moral hazard (because it is harder to fake a tort than an insurance claim[20]). In any event, because compensation is not the primary economic function of tort law, the debate over what level of tort 'insurance' consumers are or should be willing to pay for is beside the point. Thus, for example, whether consumers do or do not purchase first-party insurance for pain and suffering losses should not be relevant to the law and economic analysis of tort damages.[21] From an economic perspective, the appropriate measure of damages is that which will induce compliance with the standard of care (Geistfeld 1995).[22]

---

20 A tort claim is harder to fabricate than a first-party insurance claim because there is – in most cases – a third party, in addition to the insurance company, with a significant interest in verifying the accuracy of the claim: the defendant. In some cases, of course, defendants and plaintiffs may have a sufficiently close relationship that the defendant may be willing to 'admit' to a liability that did not exist. For that reason, liability insurance contracts often contain provisions that exclude coverage for claims brought by people with too close a relationship with the insured party. Examples include the family member exclusion in personal liability insurance policies and the insured versus insured exclusion in directors' and officers' insurance policies.

21 It is worth noting that some first-party insurance for pain and suffering damages is widely purchased: uninsured and underinsured motorists coverage. While a certain level of coverage typically is mandated, many people voluntarily purchase much higher levels of coverage. Moreover, because tort-based compensation poses less adverse selection and moral hazard (at least for victims) than first-party insurance, tort-based compensation can be more complete than voluntary first-party insurance.

22 Note that Arlen and MacLeod (2005) would modify this in situations in which injurers face a significant risk of accidental negligence (such as medical malpractice) because it is costly for them to obtain the information needed to

D. The Liability Insurance Underwriting Cycle

The liability insurance crisis of the mid 1980s prompted extensive research that acquainted law and economics scholars with the insurance underwriting cycle, an insurance industry business cycle characterized by relatively long periods of stable nominal (declining in real) insurance prices and periodic short periods of rapidly increasing insurance prices and contractions in supply (Harrington 2004). In a prominent and widely cited early contribution, Priest (1987) asserted that the crisis was caused by the shift to strict products liability, with resulting adverse selection consequences attributable to manufacturers' private information regarding the safety of their products. Schwartz (1992) subsequently concluded that product liability law did not change so fundamentally during the years leading up to the crisis and, as Harrington and Danzon (2000) report, no systematic empirical evidence has been produced to support Priest's adverse selection hypothesis. The academic literature has settled on the view that the mid-1980s liability insurance crisis was an extreme dip in the longstanding underwriting cycle in property casualty insurance (e.g., Winter 1988), perhaps exacerbated by a mid-1980s change in taxation rules governing the reserves held by property casualty insurance companies (Logue 1996).

The liability insurance crisis of the early 2000s prompted another round of research (Harrington, Danzon and Epstein 2008; Baker 2005). This research supported the emerging consensus that (a) competition leads to excessive price cutting in liability insurance markets (perhaps because of weak incentives for solvency), which (b) gradually eliminates insurance capital until (c) a tipping point is reached (perhaps because of an external shock), at which point (d) insurers sharply raise prices and loss expectations, creating an extreme short-term capital shortage, which allows insurers to earn large profits, prompting, with a delay, (e) external capital to flow into the insurance market (Gron 1994; Gron and Winton 2001), which, with another delay, leads back to (a) another round of excessive price cutting, and so forth (Harrington, Danzon and Epstein 2008; see Fitzpatrick (2004) for a behavioral explanation from an insurance industry insider). So understood, the large increase in expected losses that accompany the crisis stage of the cycle is an *effect* of the crisis, not a cause (Baker 2005). A very recent comparison of US liability and property

know what action satisfies the standard of care, and in which optimal investment in this information still leaves them with a positive probability of error. In this case, tort damages must both induce informed injurers to comply with the standard of care as well as ensure that injurers will want to invest optimally in information.

insurance premiums from 1958 to 2008 shows that aggregate real premiums for both kinds of insurance have grown at approximately the same rate over this period as real growth in US GDP (Baker 2011). The pattern of growth differs, however, with liability insurance premiums exhibiting much greater growth during the peaks of the insurance underwriting cycle, when media coverage of liability insurance also peaks, suggesting that the popular perception that liability costs are growing much more rapidly than the economy may be the result of generalizations from a biased set of observations (ibid.).

E. Liability Insurance Data as a Window on Tort Claiming and Litigation

Empirical law and economics researchers have made widespread use of liability insurance data to study the operation of the tort system. Relying on Texas Department of Insurance medical malpractice data, one productive research team has documented that plaintiffs rarely receive the amount that juries award, settlements rarely exceed liability insurance policy limits, and the dollar value of medical malpractice claiming has declined in real terms since the late 1990s (e.g., Black et al. 2005; Hyman et al. 2007; Zeiler et al. 2007; see also Viscusi, Hersch and O'Connell 2007 for similar research using Florida data). Carroll and Abrahamse (2005) used automobile insurance data from the Insurance Research Council to measure the impact of different tort law rules on the rate of claims arising out of soft tissue injuries, finding strong evidence of the 'bad' kind of *ex post* moral hazard discussed above. Hersch and Viscusi (2007) used the Texas Department of Insurance commercial liability insurance settlement database to provide useful descriptive statistics about commercial litigation, which has not received the same attention in the empirical literature as personal injury litigation. Born and Viscusi have used the aggregate liability insurance data filed by insurance companies with state insurance regulators to document that caps on tort damages reduce aggregate insurance losses (e.g., Born, Viscusi and Baker 2009).

Yoon has used data from individual insurance companies to measure the impact of limits on punitive damages and changes in rules regarding offers of judgment, finding that both sets of legal reforms achieve their intended results (Yoon 2001; Yoon and Baker 2006). In addition, a variety of researchers have used insurance companies' closed claim files to conduct audits on the performance of tort litigation, largely concluding that the tort claim process 'works' in the sense that payments are strongly and appropriately correlated with evidence of injury and negligence (e.g., Studdert et al. 2006).

VII. CONCLUSIONS

The canonical model of the interaction between insurance and tort liability is too stark and simple to be a satisfactory description of the real world, but it nevertheless offers some important insights. It suggests that the interaction of insurance with the legal rules for liability may not cause much moral hazard after all; and even when it does, it is still likely to be welfare enhancing, because the risk spreading gains are typically larger than the losses due to reduced investments in care or precautions. Thus, the existence of some moral hazard is not necessarily a system failure in a second-best world (where care is unobservable). The model also makes predictions about the kind of insurance contracts that we should observe: moral hazard will tend to be limited by pricing and contractual design, so as to discourage substantial deviation from the standard of care (a standard with which uninsured injurers operating under a negligence regime would arguably wish to comply in the absence of insurance). The standard model also directs attention to the failures of ordinary tort law: when injurers can evade liability because they are judgment proof, or because causation can be difficult to prove, efficiency may require regulation of liability insurance coverage – either mandating it or banning it. The range of potential contract designs is vast, however. Greater knowledge of institutional detail and much more empirical investigation is needed to identify and understand which designs are employed in which context and why. Ideally, the results of this empirical research will be fed back into the modeling through an iterative process that improves our understanding of the dynamics behind the real world of liability and insurance.

REFERENCES

Abbring, Jaap H., Pierre-André Chiappori, and Tibor Zavadil (2008), *Better Safe than Sorry? Ex Ante and Ex Post Moral Hazard in Dynamic Insurance Data*, Tinbergen Institute Discussion Paper No. 08-075/3; CentER Discussion Paper No. 2008-77, available at SSRN: http://ssrn.com/abstract=1260168.

Abbring, Jaap H., Pierre-André Chiappori, James Heckman, and J. Pinquet (2003), *Adverse Selection and Moral Hazard in Insurance: Can Dynamic Data Help to Distinguish?*, J. Euro. Econ. Assn: Papers and Proceedings, 1, 512–21.

Abraham, Kenneth S. (1988), *Environmental Liability and the Limits of Insurance*, Columbia Law Review, 88, 942–88.

Abraham, Kenneth S. (2005), *Liability Insurance and Accident Prevention: Evolution of an Idea*, Maryland Law Review, 64, 573–612.

Abraham, Kenneth S. (2008), The Liability Century: Insurance and Tort Law from the Progressive Era to 9/11 (Cambridge, MA: Harvard University Press).

Abraham, Kenneth S., and Lance Liebman (1993). *Private Insurance, Social Insurance, and*

Tort Reform: Toward a New Vision of Compensation for Illness and Injury, COLUMBIA LAW REVIEW, 93, 75–88.

Andrews, Lori B., C. Stocking, T. Krizek, L. Gottlieb, C. Krizek, T. Vargish, and M. Siegler (1997), *An Alternative Strategy for Studying Adverse Events in Medical Care*, LANCET, 1997, 309–13.

Arlen, Jennifer (1992), *Should Defendants' Wealth Matter*, JOURNAL OF LEGAL STUDIES, 21, 413–29.

Arlen, Jennifer (2010), *Contracting over Malpractice Liability*, UNIVERSITY OF PENNSYLVANIA LAW REVIEW, 158, 957–1023.

Arlen, Jennifer (2013), *Economic Analysis of Medical Malpractice Liability and its Reform*, in Jennifer Arlen, ed., RESEARCH HANDBOOK ON THE ECONOMICS OF TORTS (Cheltenham, UK and Northampton, MA, USA: Edward Elgar).

Arlen, Jennifer, and W. Bentley MacLeod (2005), *Torts, Expertise, and Authority: Liability of Physicians and Managed Care Organizations*, RAND JOURNAL OF ECONOMICS, 36, 494–519.

Arrow, Kenneth J. (1963), *Uncertainty and the Welfare Economics of Medical Care*, 53 AMERICAN ECONOMIC REVIEW, 53, 941–73.

Arrow, Kenneth J. (1968), *The Economics of Moral Hazard: Further Comment*, AMERICAN ECONOMIC REVIEW, 58, 537–9.

Asmat, Daniel P., and Sharon L. Tennyson (2010), *Bargaining in the Shadow of the Law: How do 'Bad Faith' Laws Affect Insurance Settlements?* (2010), Working Paper, available at www.researchgate.net/publication/228141885_Bargaining_in_the_Shadow_of_the_Law_How_do_%27Bad_Faith%27_Laws_Affect_Insurance_Settlements.

Avraham, Ronen (2005), *Should Pain-And-Suffering Damages Be Abolished From Tort Law? More Experimental Evidence*, TORONTO LAW JOURNAL, 55, 941–79.

Ayres, Ian, and Peter Siegelman (1989), *The Economics of the Insurance Anti-Trust Suits: Toward an Exclusionary Theory*, TULANE LAW REVIEW, 63, 971–95.

Baker, Tom (1996), *On the Genealogy of Moral Hazard*, TEXAS LAW REVIEW, 75, 237–92.

Baker, Tom (1998), *Liability Insurance Conflicts and Defense Lawyers: From Triangles to Tetrahedrons*, CONNECTICUT INSURANCE LAW JOURNAL, 4, 101–50.

Baker, Tom (2001), *Blood Money, New Money and the Moral Economy of Tort Law in Action*, LAW AND SOCIETY REVIEW, 35, 275–319.

Baker, Tom (2004), *Insuring Liability Risks*, GENEVA PAPERS ON RISK & INSURANCE, 29, 128–49.

Baker, Tom (2005), *Medical Malpractice and the Insurance Underwriting Cycle*, DEPAUL LAW REVIEW, 54, 393–438.

Baker, Tom (2006), *Insurance as Tort Regulation: Six Ways that Liability Insurance Shapes Tort Law*, in Gerhard Wagner, ed., LIABILITY IN TORT AND LIABILITY INSURANCE, (European Centre for Tort and Insurance Law).

Baker, Tom (2008), *Liability Insurance, Moral Luck, and Auto Accidents*, THEORETICAL INQUIRIES IN LAW, 9, 165–84.

Baker, Tom (2009), *Liability Insurance at the Tort-Crime Boundary*, in David M. Engel and Michael McCann, eds., FAULT LINES: TORT LAW AS CULTURAL PRACTICE, (Stanford, CA: Stanford University Press).

Baker, Tom (2011), *The Shifting Terrain of Risk and Uncertainty on the Liability Insurance Field*, DEPAUL LAW REVIEW, 60, 521–38.

Baker, Tom (2012), *Transparency through Insurance: Mandates Dominate Discretion*, in Joseph Doherty and Robert T. Reville, eds., TRANSPARENCY IN THE UNITED STATES CIVIL JUSTICE SYSTEM: AN EMPIRICAL ANALYSIS WITH PRESCRIPTIONS FOR REFORM (Oxford: Oxford University Press).

Baker, Tom, and Sean Griffith (2010), ENSURING CORPORATE MISCONDUCT: HOW LIABILITY INSURANCE UNDERMINES SHAREHOLDER LITIGATION (Chicago, IL: University of Chicago Press).

Black, Bernard S., Charles M. Silver, David A. Hyman, and William M. Sage, (2005), *Stability, Not Crisis: Medical Malpractice Claim Outcomes in Texas, 1988–2002*, JOURNAL OF EMPIRICAL LEGAL STUDIES, 2, 207–59.

Born, Patricia, Kip Viscusi, and Tom Baker (2009), *The Effects of Tort Reform on Medical Malpractice Insurers' Ultimate Losses*, JOURNAL OF RISK & INSURANCE, 76, 197–219.
Brown, John Prather (1973), *Toward an Economic Theory of Liability*, THE JOURNAL OF LEGAL STUDIES, 2, 323–49.
Butler, Richard J., Robert P. Hartwig, and Harold Gardner (1997), *HMOs, Moral Hazard and Cost Shifting in Workers Compensation*, JOURNAL OF HEALTH ECONOMICS, 16, 191–206.
Calabresi, Guido (1970), THE COST OF ACCIDENTS: A LEGAL AND ECONOMIC ANALYSIS, (New Haven, CT: Yale University Press).
Calfee, John E., and Richard Craswell (1984), *Some Effects of Uncertainty on Compliance With Legal Standards*, VIRGINIA LAW REVIEW, 70, 965–1003.
Calfee, John E., and Paul H. Rubin (1992), *Some Implications of Damage Payments for Nonpecuniary Losses*, JOURNAL OF LEGAL STUDIES, 21, 371–411.
Carroll, Stephen, and Allan Abrahamse (2005), *The Frequency of Excess Auto Personal Injury Claims*, AMERICAN LAW & ECONOMICS REVIEW, 3, 228–50.
Carron, Louis, and Georges Dionne (1997), *Insurance Fraud Estimation: More Evidence from the Quebec Automobile Insurance Industry*, ASSURANCES, 64, 567–78.
Choi, Albert, and Kathryn Spier (2010), *Should Consumers be Permitted to Waive Products Liability? Product Safety, Private Contracts, and Adverse Selection*, Harvard Law and Economics Discussion Paper No. 680.
Choi, William, and Lan Liang (2007), *Reverse Moral Hazard of Liability Insurers: Evidence From Medical Malpractice Claims*, APPLIED ECONOMICS, 39, 2331–40.
Cohen, Alma (2006), *Disadvantages of Aggregate Deductibles*, B.E. JOURNALS IN ECONOMIC ANALYSIS & POLICY, Vol. 6, No. 1.
Cohen, Alma, and Peter Siegelman (2010), *Testing for Adverse Selection in Insurance Markets*, JOURNAL OF RISK & INSURANCE, 77, 39–84.
Cohen, George M. (1997–98), *Legal Malpractice Insurance and Loss Prevention: A Comparative Analysis of Economic Institutions*, CONNECTICUT INSURANCE LAW JOURNAL, 4, 305–51.
Cook, Philip J., and Daniel A. Graham (1977), *The Demand for Insurance and Protection: The Case of Irreplaceable Commodities*, QUARTERLY JOURNAL OF ECONOMICS, 91, 143–56.
Cooter, Robert D. (1984), *Prices and Sanctions*, COLUMBIA LAW REVIEW, 84, 1523–60.
Cooter, Robert D. (1991), *Lapses, Conflict and Akrasia in Torts and Crimes: Towards an Economic Theory of the Will*, INTERNATIONAL REVIEW OF LAW & ECONOMICS, 11, 149–64.
Cummins J. David, and Sharon Tennyson (1996), *Moral Hazard in Insurance Claiming: Evidence from Automobile Insurance*, JOURNAL OF RISK & UNCERTAINTY, 12, 29–50.
D'Arcy, Stephen P. (1994), *The Dark Side of Insurance*, in Sandra G. Gustavson and Scott E. Harrington, eds., INSURANCE, RISK MANAGEMENT, AND PUBLIC POLICY: ESSAYS IN MEMORY OF ROBERT E. MEHR (Boston, MA: Kluwer Academic Publishers).
Danzon, Patricia M. (1985), *Liability and Liability Insurance for Medical Malpractice*, JOURNAL OF HEALTH ECONOMICS, 4(4), 309–31.
Daughety, Andrew, and Jennifer Reinganum (2013), *Economic Analysis of Products Liability: Theory*, in Jennifer Arlen, ed., RESEARCH HANDBOOK ON THE ECONOMICS OF TORTS (Cheltenham, UK and Northampton, MA, USA: Edward Elgar).
Derrig, Richard, and Sharon Tennyson (2011), *The Impact of Rate Regulation on Claims: Evidence from Massachusetts Automobile Insurance*, RISK MANAGEMENT AND INSURANCE REVIEW, 14(2). Fall 2011, 173–200.
Dionne, G. (2000), *The Empirical Measure of Information Problems with Emphasis on Insurance Fraud*, in G. Dionne, ed., HANDBOOK OF INSURANCE (Boston, MA: Kluwer Academic Publishers), 395–419.
Dobbin, Frank, and Erin Kelly (2007), *How to Stop Harassment: The Professional Construction of Legal Compliance in Organizations*, AMERICAN JOURNAL OF SOCIOLOGY, 112, 1203–43.
Epstein, Richard A. (1985), *Products Liability as an Insurance Market*, JOURNAL OF LEGAL STUDIES, 14, 645–69.

Ericson, Richard, and Aaron Doyle (2004), UNCERTAIN BUSINESS: RISK, INSURANCE AND THE LIMITS OF KNOWLEDGE (Toronto: University of Toronto Press).
Fitzpatrick, Sean (2004), *Fear is the Key: a Behavioral Guide to Insurance Underwriting Cycles*, CONNECTICUT INSURANCE LAW JOURNAL, 10, 255–75.
Fortin, Bernard, and Paul Lanoie (2000), *Incentive Effects of Workers Compensation: A Survey*, in G. Dionne, ed., HANDBOOK OF INSURANCE (Boston, MA: Kluwer Academic Press).
Froot, Kenneth, David S. Scharfstein, and Jeremy C. Stein (1993), *Risk Management: Coordinating Corporate Investment and Financing Policies*, JOURNAL OF FINANCE, 48, 1629–58.
Gabel, Joan T.A., Nancy R. Mansfield, and Gregory T. Jones (2006), *The Peculiar Moral Hazard of Employment Practices Liability Insurance: Realignment of the Incentive to Transfer Risk with the Incentive to Prevent Discrimination*, NOTRE DAME JOURNAL OF LAW, ETHICS, & PUBLIC POLICY, 20, 639–54.
Gallagher, Sean W. (1994), *Note: The Public Policy Exclusion and Insurance for Intentional Employment Discrimination*, MICHIGAN LAW REVIEW, 92, 1256–326.
Geistfeld, Mark (1995), *Placing a Price on Pain and Suffering: A Method for Helping Juries Determine Tort Damages for Nonmonetary Injuries*, CALIFORNIA LAW REVIEW, 85, 773–852.
Gilles, Stephen (2006), *The Judgment Proof Society*, WASHINGTON & LEE LAW REVIEW, 63, 603–715.
Glenn, Brian (2000), *The Shifting Rhetoric of Insurance Denial*, LAW & SOCIETY REVIEW, 34, 779–808.
Goldberg, Victor P. (2009), *The Devil Made Me Do It: The Corporate Purchase of Insurance*, REVIEW OF LAW & ECONOMICS, 5, Article 22, available at http://www.bepress.com/rle/vol5/iss1/art22.
Grady, Mark F. (1988), *Why Are People Negligent? Technology, Nondurable Precautions and the Medical Malpractice Explosion*, NORTHWESTERN UNIVERSITY LAW REVIEW, 82, 293–334.
Gron, Anne (1994), *Evidence of Capacity Constraints in Insurance Markets*, JOURNAL OF LAW & ECONOMICS, 37, 349–69.
Gron, Anne, and Andrew Winton (2001), *Risk Overhang and Market Behavior*, 74 JOURNAL OF BUSINESS, 74, 591–612.
Grossman, Joanna L. (2003), *The Culture of Compliance: The Final Triumph of Form over Substance in Sexual Harassment Law*, HARVARD WOMEN'S LAW JOURNAL, 26, 3–75.
Guo, Xuguang, and John F. Burton, Jr. (2010), *Workers' Compensation: Recent Developments in Moral Hazard and Benefit Payments*, INDUSTRIAL & LABOR RELATIONS REVIEW, 63, 340–55.
Hanson, Jon, and Steven Croley (1995), *The Nonpecuniary Costs of Accidents: Pain-and-Suffering Damages in Tort Law*, HARVARD LAW REVIEW, 108, 1785–917.
Harrington, Scott (2004), *Tort Liability, Insurance Rates, and the Insurance Cycle*, in R. Litan and R. Herring, eds., BROOKINGS-WHARTON PAPERS ON FINANCIAL SERVICES: 2004, (Washington, DC: Brookings Institution Press).
Harrington, Scott, and Patricia Danzon (2000), *The Economics of Liability Insurance*, in G. Dionne, ed., THE HANDBOOK OF INSURANCE (Boston, MA: Kluwer Academic Press).
Harrington, Scott E., Patricia M. Danzon, and Andrew J. Epstein (2008), *'Crises' in Medical Malpractice Insurance: Evidence of Excessive Price-cutting in the Preceding Soft Market*, JOURNAL OF BANKING & FINANCE, 32, 157–70.
Hawken, Angela, Stephen J. Carroll, and Allan F. Abrahamse (2001), THE EFFECTS OF THIRD-PARTY BAD FAITH DOCTRINE ON AUTOMOBILE INSURANCE COSTS AND COMPENSATION (Santa Monica, CA: RAND Corporation).
Heimer, Carol (1985), REACTIVE RISK AND RATIONAL ACTION: MANAGING MORAL HAZARD IN INSURANCE CONTRACTS (Berkeley, CA: University of California Press).
Hersch, Joni, and Kip Viscusi (2007), *Tort Liability Costs for Commercial Claims*, AMERICAN LAW & ECONOMICS REVIEW, 9, 330–69.
Hoyt, Robert E., David B. Mustard, and Lawrence S. Powell (2006), *The Effectiveness*

of State Legislation in Mitigating Moral Hazard: Evidence from Automobile Insurance, JOURNAL OF LAW & ECONOMICS, 49, 427–50.
Hyman, David A., Bernard S. Black, Kathryn Zeiler, Charles M. Silver, and William M. Sage (2007), *Do Defendants Pay What Juries Award? Post-verdict Haircuts in Texas Medical Malpractice Cases, 1988–2003*, JOURNAL OF EMPIRICAL LEGAL STUDIES, 4, 3–68.
Hyman, David A., Myungho Paik, and Bernard S. Black (2013), *The Receding Tide of Medical Malpractice Litigation*, Working Paper available at SSRN: http://papers.ssrn.com/sol3/papers.cfm?abstract_id=2109679.
Israel, Mark (2004), *Do We Drive More Safely When Accidents are More Expensive? Identifying Moral Hazard from Experience Rating Schemes*, Mimeo, Northwestern University, available at http://www.wcas.northwestern.edu/csio/Papers/2004/CSIO-WP-0043.pdf.
Jaffee, Dwight M., and Thomas Russell (1997), *Catastrophe Insurance, Capital Markets and Uninsurable Risk*, JOURNAL OF RISK & INSURANCE, 64, 205–30.
Kneuper, Robert, and Bruce Yandle (1994), *Auto Insurers and the Air Bag*, JOURNAL OF RISK & INSURANCE, 61, 107–16.
Kornhauser, Lewis A. (1982), *An Economic Analysis of the Choice between Enterprise and Personal Liability for Accidents*, CALIFORNIA LAW REVIEW, 70, 1345–92.
Kraakman, Reinier (2013), *Economic Policy and the Vicarious Liability of Firms*, in Jennifer Arlen, ed., RESEARCH HANDBOOK ON THE ECONOMICS OF TORTS (Cheltenham, UK and Northampton, MA, USA: Edward Elgar).
Lahnstein, Christian (2011), *Employers' Liability: Creating Transparency*, 1/2001 TOPICS MAGAZINE (published by Munich Re).
Logue, Kyle D. (1996), *Toward a Tax-based Explanation of the Liability Insurance Crisis*, VIRGINIA LAW REVIEW, 82, 895–959.
MacMinn, Richard, and James Garven (2000), *On Corporate Insurance*, in G. Dionne, ed., THE HANDBOOK OF INSURANCE (Boston, MA: Kluwer Academic Press).
Mayers, David, and Clifford W. Smith (1982), *On the Corporate Demand for Insurance*, JOURNAL OF BUSINESS, 55, 281–96.
Mayers, David, and Clifford W. Smith (1987), *Corporate Insurance and the Underinvestment Problem*, JOURNAL OF RISK & INSURANCE, 54, 45–54.
McNeely, Mary Coate (1941), *Illegality as a Factor in Liability Insurance*, COLUMBIA LAW REVIEW, 41, 26–60.
Mootz, Francis J. III (1997), *Insurance Coverage of Employment Discrimination Claims*, UNIVERSITY OF MIAMI LAW REVIEW, 52, 1–78.
Pandya, Sachin (2011), *From Goods to Bodies: The Legal Reaction to Liability Insurance for Personal Injury Accidents in America, 1886–1910* (mimeo).
Picard, Pierre (2000), *Economic Analysis of Insurance Fraud*, in G. Dionne, ed., THE HANDBOOK OF INSURANCE (Boston, MA: Kluwer Academic Press).
Priest, George (1987), *The Current Insurance Crisis and Modern Tort Law*, YALE LAW JOURNAL, 96, 1521–90.
Robinson, Chris M., and Bingyong Zheng (2010), *Moral Hazard, Insurance Claims, and Repeated Insurance Contracts*, CANADIAN JOURNAL OF ECONOMICS, 43, 967–93.
Rothschild, Michael, and Joseph Stiglitz (1976), *Equilibrium in Competitive Insurance Markets*, QUARTERLY JOURNAL OF ECONOMICS, 90, 629–49.
Schwartz, Gary (1992), *The Beginning and the Possible End of the Rise of Modern American Tort Law*, GEORGIA LAW REVIEW, 26, 601–702.
Sharkey, Catherine (2005), *Revisiting the Noninsurable Costs of Accidents*, MARYLAND LAW REVIEW, 64, 409–56.
Shavell, Steven (1980), *Strict Liability versus Negligence*, JOURNAL OF LEGAL STUDIES, 9, 1–25.
Shavell, Steven (1982), *On Liability and Insurance*, BELL JOURNAL OF ECONOMICS, 13, 120–32.
Shavell, Steven (1986), *The Judgment Proof Problem*, INTERNATIONAL REVIEW OF LAW & ECONOMICS, 6, 45–58.
Shavell, Steven (2004), FOUNDATIONS OF ECONOMIC ANALYSIS OF LAW (Cambridge, MA: Belknap Press).

Simon, Jonathan (1994), *In the Place of the Parent: Risk Management and the Government of Campus Life*, SOCIAL & LEGAL STUDIES, 3, 15–45.

Sinn, Hans-Werner (1982), *Kinked Utility and the Demand for Human Wealth and Liability Insurance*, EUROPEAN ECONOMIC REVIEW, 17, 149–62.

Skogh, Goran (1989), *The Transactions Cost Theory of Insurance: Contracting Impediments and Costs*, JOURNAL OF RISK & INSURANCE, 56, 726–32.

Smith, Eric, and Randall Wright (1992), *Why is Automobile Insurance in Philadelphia so Damn Expensive?*, AMERICAN ECONOMIC REVIEW, 82, 756–72.

Studdert, David M., Michelle M. Mello, Atul A. Gawande, Tejal K. Gandhi, Allen Dachalia, Catherine Yoon, Ann Louise Puopolo, and Troyen A. Brennan (2006), *Claims, Errors, and Compensation Payments in Medical Malpractice Litigation*, NEW ENGLAND JOURNAL OF MEDICINE, 354, 2024–33.

Sykes, Alan O. (1994), *Judicial Limitations on the Discretion of Liability Insurers to Settle or Litigate: An Economic Critique*, TEXAS LAW REVIEW, 72, 1345–74.

Syverud, Kent (1990), *The Duty to Settle*, VIRGINIA LAW REVIEW, 76, 1113–209.

Syverud, Kent (1994), *On the Demand for Liability Insurance*, TEXAS LAW REVIEW, 72, 1629–54.

Tennyson, Sharon (2002), *Insurance Experience and Consumers' Attitudes Toward Insurance Fraud*, 21 JOURNAL OF INSURANCE REGULATION, 21, 35–55.

Tennyson, Sharon (2008), *Moral, Social, and Economic Dimensions of Insurance Claims Fraud*, SOCIAL RESEARCH, 75, 1181–204.

Tunc, Andre (1983), *An Historical and Geographical Survey of the Law of Tort*, in 11 INTERNATIONAL ENCYCLOPEDIA OF COMPARATIVE LAW.

Van der Veer, Nancy H. (2005–2006), *Employment Practices Liability Insurance: Are EPLI Policies a License to Discriminate? Or Are They a Necessary Reality Check for Employers*, CONNECTICUT INSURANCE LAW JOURNAL, 12, 173–206.

Viscusi, Kip, Joni Hersch, and Jeffrey O'Connell (2007), *An Empirical Assessment of Early Offer Reform for Medical Malpractice*, JOURNAL OF LEGAL STUDIES, 36, 231–59.

Wang, J. L., C. F. Chung, and L. Y. Tzeng (2008), *An Empirical Analysis of the Effects of Increasing Deductibles on Moral Hazard*, JOURNAL OF RISK & INSURANCE, 75, 551–66.

Weisberg, H. I., and R. A. Derrig (1991), *Fraud and Automobile Insurance: A Report on the Baseline Study of Bodily Injury Claims in Massachusetts*, JOURNAL OF INSURANCE REGULATION, 9, 427–541.

Wickelgren, Abraham L. (2006), *The Inefficiency of Contractually-Based Liability with Rational Consumers*, JOURNAL OF LAW, ECONOMICS, & ORGANIZATION, 22, 168–83.

Wickelgren, Abraham L. (2013), *Law and Economics of Settlement*, in Jennifer Arlen, ed., RESEARCH HANDBOOK ON THE ECONOMICS OF TORTS (Cheltenham, UK and Northampton, MA, USA: Edward Elgar).

Winter, Ralph A. (1988), *The Liability Crisis and the Dynamics of Competitive Insurance Markets*, YALE JOURNAL ON REGULATION, 5, 455–99.

Yoon, Albert (2001), *Damage Caps and Civil Litigation: An Empirical Study of Medical Malpractice Litigation in the South*, AMERICAN LAW & ECONOMICS REVIEW, 3, 199–227.

Yoon, Albert, and Tom Baker (2006), *A Market Solution to Civil Litigation?: An Empirical Study of Offer-of-Judgment Rules*, VANDERBILT LAW REVIEW, 59, 155–96.

Zeiler, Kathryn, Charles Silver, Bernard Black, David Hyman, and William Sage (2007), *Physicians' Insurance Limits and Malpractice Payment: Evidence from Texas Closed Claims 1990–2003*, JOURNAL OF LEGAL STUDIES, 36, S9–S45.

APPENDIX: RISK AVERSION AND THE DEMAND FOR INSURANCE

The demand for insurance arises from risk aversion on the part of insureds. Risk-aversion is a term of art. It means only that someone has a decreasing marginal utility of wealth – as their wealth increases, the gain from adding another dollar to their wealth (the slope of the utility function) gets smaller and smaller. This concept is depicted in Figure 15A.1.

Risk averse individuals experience equal-sized monetary gains and losses asymmetrically in utility terms: they suffer a larger change in utility from a loss of $X than from a gain of $X. Consider Jane, who has initial wealth W, as in Figure 15A.2. If she were to experience a gain in wealth of 100 percent, she would move to wealth level W'. But notice that because of the curvature of her utility function, this 100 percent gain in *dollar* terms translates into a much smaller percentage gain in utility (well-being), as measured by the small rise in utility from U(W) to U(W') on the vertical axis. Her wealth gets converted into utility at a less- and less-favorable rate as wealth increases. The converse is also true. A *drop* in wealth hurts much more in utility terms than its cost in dollars, because each dollar lost is worth more and more (in terms of utility) as Jane has fewer of them.

Now suppose that Jane starts with wealth W' (=2W). Assume she

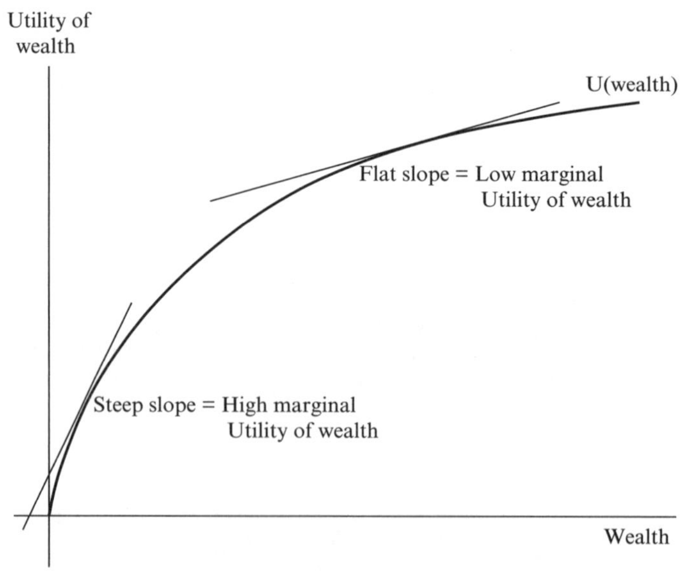

Figure 15A.1 Decreasing marginal utility of wealth

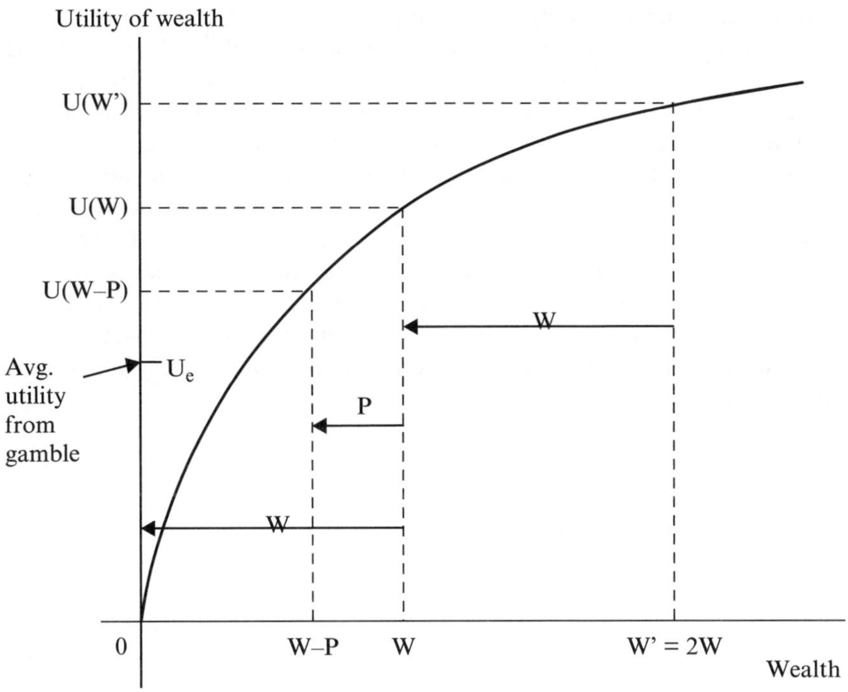

Figure 15A.2 Demand for insurance

faces a 50 percent probability that she will be liable for injuring someone, and that the liability would equal her entire wealth. Thus, she faces two possibilities: wealth of 0, or wealth unchanged at W'. Her average or expected wealth is equals $\frac{1}{2} \times 0 + \frac{1}{2} \times W' = W$, which lies midway between 0 and W'. But Jane's average (or expected) *utility* is given by $\frac{1}{2} \times U(0) + \frac{1}{2} \times U(W')$, which is depicted in the Figure as U_e, and is half-way between 0 and U(W'). Notice that this is considerably *less* than the utility she would get from having wealth W with certainty, which is given by U(W).

This forms the basis for insurance. A risk neutral insurance company[23] would be willing to take on this risk if it could charge a premium equal to its average payout. The payout is either 0 (if the loss does not occur), or 2W (if it does not), each with 50 percent probability. In other words, the average payout is just W.

---

[23] For these purposes, we assume that there are no costs to running the insurance company; this is obviously incorrect, but it makes the exposition simpler without fundamentally changing the analysis.

Were the insurance company to charge her W to assume the risk, Jane would then have a guaranteed wealth of W (= W' − W, and a guaranteed utility of U(W)).[24] Since this is higher than the *expected* utility from bearing the risk herself (U_e), she would be better off with insurance than without it. In fact, she would be willing to pay somewhat more than W to be free of the risk. Consider starting at wealth W' and paying an amount (W+P) to eliminate the risk altogether: that leaves Jane with certain wealth (W − P), which nevertheless has a utility level that is higher than that associated with the gamble (U_e). Put differently, insurance is a way to move wealth from states of the world where it is relatively plentiful (and hence, where an extra dollar is worth little in utility terms) to states of the world where wealth is scarce (and where an extra dollar is very valuable in utility terms).

[24] Jane would pay her insurer W. If the risk materialized (which happens with probability ½), Jane would receive 2W, leaving her with wealth of 2W−W = W. If the risk did not materialize (also with probability of ½), Jane would receive nothing, leaving her with wealth of 2W−W = W. So her wealth is W regardless of whether the risk occurs or not.

Index